HISTORY
OF
THE CALIPHS

BY

JALALUDDIN A'S SUYUTI,

TRANSLATED FROM THE ORIGINAL ARABIC

BY

MAJOR H.S. JARRETT,

Secretary and Member, Board of Examiners, Fort William,
Fellow of the Calcutta University

KITAB BHAVAN
NEW DELHI-110002

KITAB BHAVAN

Publishers, Distributors, Exporters & Importers
1784, Kalan Mahal, Darya Ganj,
New Delhi - 1100 02 (India)

Phones : (91-11) 23277392 / 93, 23274686
Fax : (91-11) 23263383

Online Store: www.kitabbavan.net

Email : info@kitabbhavan.net
: nasri@vsnl.com

2nd Edition : 2017

ISBN : 81-7151-383-2
Book Code No. : H00077

Printed & Published in India by :
Nusrat Ali Nasri for KITAB BHAVAN
Moonis Ali Nasri for KITAB BHAVAN
1784, Kalan Mahal, Darya Ganj,
New Delhi - 1100 02 [India]

INTRODUCTION

Extensive as is the reputation of the Suyuti as a distinguished author and scholar, and unsurpassed for the number and range of the works which in every branch of literature known to his age, his unwearied pen never ceased to produce, we are indebted to the malice or envy of but one of his contemporaries and to his own testimony, for the few details of his life and studies that we possess. Reference to one or other of his multitudinous volumes is made by writers of his own and succeeding times where the kindred subject of which they treat naturally calls for it, but only one contemporary biographical notice of him besides his own, is extant. To these I shall presently refer.

Háji Khalífah, at the close of his Lexicon, gives a detailed list of as Suyúti's works, prefaced by a column of laudatory epithets which have less the ring of sincere admiration than of conventional panegyric, yet his wonder or his envy might well offer the incense of adulation to the astonishing author of five hundred and four volumes. Qurãnic exegesis, Tradition and its cognate subjects, jurisprudence, philology, rhetoric, prose and poetical composition, the phenomena of nature, curiosities of literature, discourses on social questions, criticism, history, biography, all these were fields not too vast for his discursive intelligence and none too minute for his indefatigable industry. Some of his compositions are indeed, nothing more than pamphlets of smaller compass than many an article of a modern Review, but a considerable number, to judge from some of those, about one-fifth of the whole, that have come down to us, must have been of goodly bulk. It would doubtless have been better for his reputation as it would assuredly have been more profitable to the generality of his readers, had he confined his labours to the production of a few works of universal interest and written for posterity rather than for his day. By far the greater part of his writings were on subjects which have no interest to a European Student. Two hundred and six works on Tradition and ninety-one on Jurisprudence would, it might be supposed, have been thoroughly exhaustive had not another line been previously written regarding them, yet this was the contribution of but one author to the store of countless volumes that had already preceded his labours and had been forgotten, to be followed by others as countless and as unremembered.

However much we may regret this misapplied diligence, the age in which as Suyuti lived, naturally moulded his literary tastes and influenced his course of study, and he but reflected its spirit in seeking pre-eminence among the scholarly and erudite of his nation after the manner in which they had attained it. Legal studies, inseparably connected as they are with the religion of the Muslims, were of the utmost consequence from the very infancy of Islam, and at a time when the Crescent waved from the pillars of Hercules to the steppes of Tartary, they formed a necessary part of the education of all cultured minds. Every Muslims author or nearly every one with whom we are acquainted, was either a recognized doctor of jurisprudence or had studied it under some one of its famous masters. No college was founded but we read that its first chairs were those of Tradition and Law. Other branches of knowledge were indeed, far from neglected. Grammar, Medicine and the complicated problems of Inheritance were cultivated with assiduity and success, but with the exception of the first mentioned of this Eastern Trivium, which is rather an instrument of knowledge than an end in itself, they occupied, the second place. In the great Mustansiriyah College built on the eastern bank of the Tigris at Baghdad by the Caliph al Mustansir and endowed by his splendid munificence, provision was first made, as Suyuti tells us, for Chairs of the four great Schools of Muhammadan Law. The next was that of Tradition, the third of Grammer, followed by professorships of Medicine and the Law of Inheritance. De Slane in his Introduction to Ibn Khallikan's Biographical Dictionary has described the system of education pursued during the times of which we write. The young student, he says, commenced his labours by learning the Qurãn by heart, and as many of the traditions as he was able to acquire at his native place : to this he joined a slight acquaintance with grammar and some knowledge of poetry. On attaining the age of fourteen or sixteen, he began his travels and visited the great cities where he learnt traditions and received certificates of licence to relate them, from eminent traditionists. He then followed the courses of lectures held in the mosques or colleges, and generally attached himself to one of the professors. He there learnt by heart the most approved works on the dogmas of religion, and studied their commentaries under the tuition of his master. He acquired a knowledge of the different readings of the Qurãn and of its orthodox interpretation, whilst he pursued the study of ancient poetry and philology, grammar and rhetoric. The secondary points of jurisprudence, forming the doctrines of the school of which he belonged, next became the object of his study and an acqaintance with logic and dialectics completed his education. Having obtained form his professors, certificates of capacity and license to teach the works he had mastered, he was eligible for the posts of preacher, Kadhi, Mufti, Imam or Professor.

Under a system so universal in its adoption and so rigidly upheld by learned opinion as the sole method of orthodox mental discipline, profitable as a means of worldly advancement as well as the most salutary for the soul. it is not surprising that the literary efforts of as Suyuti should bear principally upon those studies to which such an exagggerated importance was attached by his age. Besides the treatises on Jurisprudence and Tradition already mentioned, his commentaries and writings on the Qurãn number thirty-five. Philology, Grammar and Rhetoric claim sixty-three of his volumes. Seventy-six were his contribution to general literature, and thirty-three were devoted to history and biography. For this classified list of his writings, we are indebted to his own autobiography in his well-known work entitled Husn al Muhadhirah fi Akhbar i'l Misr Wa'l Kahirah (*agreeable Colloquy on Misr and Cairo)*. This autobiography has been published with a Latin version by Albert Meursinge in the Prolegomena to his edition of as Suyuti's Tabakat u'l Mufassirin (*Classes of the Interpreters of the* Qurãn). But as it is a work not easily accessible and no English translation of the original has as yet appeared I cannot more fitly introduced the author to those interested in his life, than in his own words.

"The author of this work," he writes, "is Abu'l Fadhl Abdur

Rahman b-ul Kamal Abu Bakr b. Nasiriddin Muhammad b. Sabikiddin Abi Bakr b. Fakhr Othman b. Nasiriddin Muhammad b. Sayfiddin Khidhr b. Najmiddin Abi's Salab Ayyub b Nasiriddin Muhammad bis Shaykh Humamiddin al Khudhyri al Usuyuti.[1]

In recording the narrative of my life in this book, I have but followed the example of recent, writers, for it is rarely that any of them has published a history without introducing therein his own biography[2] Regarding my ancestor Humamuddin, I have to observe that he was one of the masters of the spiritual life and of the doctors of the mystics. Mention of him will follow in the section treating on the Sufis. The others who came after him were men of position and authority. Of these, one exercised judicial functions in his own city, another held the office of inspector of markets, another accompanied the Amir Shaykhu[3] and founded and endowed a college at Suyut;[4] another was a wealthy merchant, but I know of none who altogether devoted himself to the acquisition of learning except my father, a notice of whom will occur in the section treating of the Shafiite jurisconsults.

As regards our connection with the name of Khudhayri, I do not know to what it can refer save the Khudhayri quarter of Baghdad, and in fact, a person whom I can implicitly trust, told me that he heard my father-may God have mercy on him-say, that his ancestor was a Persian or from the East. The connection therefore is apparently with the quarter above mentioned.

I was born after sunset on Saturday night the 1st Rajab, 819 (3rd *October,* 1445), and I was carried, my father being then living, to the Nafisi[5] tomb, who gave me his blessing. I grew up an orphan

1 The name is written Usuyuti or Suyuti indifferently.

2 I here omit a list of authors and their works, as irrelevant to the main subject of the writers life.

3 See page 685. Further particulars of him are furnished by Weil. Gesch Abb. Cal. Eg. pp. 475, 477, seq.

4 In Upper Egypt on the western bank of the Nile about 27° lat. Yakut speaks of it as having contained 75 Christian churches and a large Christian population.

5 See Note 3 page 659.

and I learnt the Qurãn before I was eight years of age. I next got by-heart the Umdah, the Minhajul Fikh Wal Usul and the Alfiyah of Ibn Malik. From the beginning of year 641 began to devote myself to learning. I studied jurisprudence and grammar under a number of doctors and read the law of inheritance with the learned and most distinguished professor of his age in that science, the Shaykh Shihabuddin as Sharimsahi who used to say that he had arrived at a great age and had passed a hundred by many years. God knows best. I read with him his commentary on the Majmuu,[1] and received a certificate of licence to teach the Arabic language in the beginning of the year 66. In this year I became an author. The first work I composed was an exposition of the formula اعوذ بلله[2] and بسم الله which I submitted to my master the Shaykh ul Islam Alamuddin al Bulkini[3] who wrote to me in praise of it. I continued to study jurisprudence with him till his death. I also read with him from the beginning the Tadrib,[4] by his father, up to the chapter on Procuration. I heard his lectures on the Hawi as Saghir[5] from the beginning, to thc chapter de Statibus Mulieris ; and on the Minhaj from the beginning, to the chapter on the Poor-rate; and on the Tanbih[6] from its commencement nearly up to the chapter on the Poor-rate; likewise a portion of ar Raudhah[7] from the chapter on the Judicial office: a portion of the supplement to the commentary on the Minhaj by az Zarkashi;[8] and from the chapter on the Cultivation of Waste lands,

1 Al Majmun Fiilmil Faraidh, by Abdullah Shamsuddin Muhammad b. Sharaf al Killai as Shafii : died 777 (1375). II. K.

2 My MS, has استفاذه and omits the second word. The work referred to will be found in his list under the first heading.

3 Abul Baka Salih b. Omar b. Raslan Alamuddin al Bulkini was born 791 (1388) and died 868 (1463). Mcurs. He was named Bulkini after Bulkinah in Egypt in the district of Hanf.

4 تدريب في الفروع (Exercitatus de partibus Juris specialibus) auctore Sirajuddin Omar b. Raslan Bolkeini Shafiits, anno 805 (1463) mortuo. H.K.

5 See p. 665.

6 There are many works of this name as well as that of Minhaj in H.K.

7 الروضه في الفروع cc II. K.

8 See D'Herb. art Zorkoshi.

to the chapter on Testaments or thereabouts. In the year 67 he granted me a license to teach *jurisprudence* and to decide on cases *proposed to me* and was present at my inauguration.[1]

When he died in the year 68, I resorted to the Shaykhul Islam Sharafuddin al Munawi.[2] and read with him a portion of the Minhaj. I heard his Exposition on Partition except a few lectures which I missed and I attended his readings from the commentary al Bahjah,[3] and its marginal notes by him, and from the commentary on the Qurãn by al Baydhawi. For traditions and the Arabic language, I read with out Shaykh the learned Imam Takiuddin as Shumunni the Hanafite and continued with him for four years. He wrote to me in praise of two of my compositions, a commentary on the Alfiyah of Ibn Malik and the Jamaul Jawami[4] on the Arabic language, and he gave verbal and written testimony of my proficiency in the sciences on more than one occasion. He once acquiesced in my bare statement regarding a tradition, for verily he adduced in his marginal gloss on as Shifa,[5] the tradition of Abul Hamra on Captives and alleged its citation by Ibn Majah. I had occasion to quote it with its ascriptions and I therefore searched Ibn Majah in the place where it was supposed to be, but I did not find it. Then I went through the whole book but did not light upon it. Suspecting an oversight, I read it through a second time and again found it not. I returned to it a third time but did not discover it. I saw it, however, in the Catalogue of the companions by Ibn Kani', upon which I went to the Shaykh and informed him. On hearing this from me, he at once took up and

---

1 Reference is made to this in the list of his works under the heading "Commentaries and works on the Qurãn."

2 Abu Zakariya Yahya b. Muhammad Sharafuddin al Munawi, died 871 (1466), Meurs.

3 Al Bahjah al Wardiyah a commentary on the Hawius Saghir by Zaynuddin Omar b. Mudhaffar bil Wardi : died 749 (1348). H.K.

4 جمع الجوامع في اصول الفقه by Tajuddin Abdul Wahab as Subki : died 771 (1369). H.K.

5 الشافي تعريف حقوق المصطفى by the Imam Hafidh Abul Fadhl Iyadh b. Musa Yahsabi : died 544 (1149). H.K. notes on this book at some length and mentions the gloss of as Shumunni.

wrote Ibn Kani in the margin. I was distressed at this and dismayed, on account of the great veneration in which I held the Shaykh, and the contemptuous opinion I had of myself and I said "will you notwait a little, perhaps you may consult the work yourself?" He replied : "No. I relied for Ibn Majah on the authority of Burhan al Halabi." I did not quit the Shaykh until his death, when I attended our Shaykh the learned and most eminent master al Kafiaji[1] for fourteen years. I studied under him various branches of knowledge such as Qurãnic exegesis, the fundamentals of doctrine, the Arabic language, rhetoric and others and he gave me a high diploma. I next attended many lectures of the Shaykh Sayfuddin Hanafi[2] on the Kashshaf,[3] on the Taudhih with his gloss thereon, the Talkhi'sul Maftah and the Adhud, and I began to write works in the year 66. My writings up to this time numbered 300 works exclusive of those I obliterated and left unfinished, and they penetrated, praise be to God, the countries of Syria, Hijaz, Yaman, India, Mauritania and Takrur.[4] When I made the pilgrimage, I drank of the water of the well Zemzem with various intentions: among others that I should arrive in Jurisprudence to the eminence of Shaykh Sirajuddin al Bulkini, and in Tradition to the distinction of the Hafidh Ibn Hajr. From the beginning of the year 71. I gave decisions on points of law and I employed myself in writing traditions from the beginning of the year 72. I acquired a profound knowledge of the seven sciences of Exegesis, Tradition, Jurisprudence, Grammar and the three branches of Rhetoric after the manner of the Arabs and the rhetoricians, and not after the

---

1 Se Meurs, points the name بالكافياجي محمد بن سليمان المحيوى الرومي الحنفي و يعرف born 790, died 879. According to the Lubbul Lubab his name refers

الي كافية بن الخا (الحاجب ـ ١) لكثرة قراته و اقرائه لها

2 Muhammad b. Muhammad b. Omar b. Ketlu Bogha al Yektamri, died in 881. as Suyuti wrote an elegy on him recorded in the Husn al Muhadh. Meurs.

3 The famous commentary of Zamakhshari. The Talkhis is a work on rhetoric by Kazwini, H.K. mentions several Taudhih. The Abhud is a work on grammar by Abu Ali al Farisi composed for Adhudud Dawlah. H.K.

4 In the extreme south of al Maghrab, according to Yakut, probably in the Saudan.

fashion of the Persians and Philosophers. What I am consicious of is this, that the proficiency I attained in these six sciences (save jurisprudence) and the writings thereon which I perused, none of my Shaykhs ever reached therein nor were therewith acquainted, still less those inferior to them. I do not say the same, by Allah, of jurisprudence, for my Shaykh has a deeper insight and a larger grasp of the subjects. After these seven branches of knowledge comes in a lower degree my acquaintance with the fundamentals of jurisprudence, with dialectics and grammatical inflexions. Below this, composition and epistolary style and the law of inheritance. Below this, the various readings of the Qurãn which I did not study under any Shaykh[1] and next Medicine, but Arithmetic I found the most difficult to me and the most remote from my inclination, and when I apply myself to a question appertaining thereto, it is as though I strove to support a mountain.

I have now completely acquired, praise be to the Most High, the means of diligently investigating and determining cases referred to me. I say this in acknowledgment of the favour of God and not in vain-glory, for wha is the world that one should strive to gain it in glorying, now that the time of departure from it is approaching, and hoariness hath begun, and the best part of life bath passed. And now if I wished to write on every question, a dissertation with its statements and proofs, whether cited or reasoned from analogy, the perceptions of it by the mind, its refutations and vindications, and a comparison between the contrary opinions held regarding it, I should be able to do so by the grace of the Most High, and through Him, not of my own strength and ability, for there is no power or virtue but in God. Whatever God willeth, there is no power *to accomplish it* save in God Himself.

At the commencement of my studies, I read somewhat of the science of logic, but subsequently the Lord put a dislike of it into my heart, and haring that Ibnus Salah[2] had decided a reference to him

---

1 ولم اخذ هاعن شيخ these words are in Meursinge, but not in my MS.

2 See page 557.

on the subject to interdicting it, I abandoned it for that reason, and the Lord supplied its place to me with the science of tradition which is the noblest of all studies. As for my Shakhs in the relation of traditions whom I heard, or from whom I received certificates of licence, they were numerous. I have adduced them in my Catalogue[1] to the number of about 150. I did not however, devote myself much to the hearing of traditions as I was employed on what was of more *importance, viz,* the study of their critical examination."

With these words concludes the autobiography which is followed by a catalogue of the author's works. I have now to notice the only other memoir of him which we possess, and to which I have already alluded. This is furnished to us by his contemporary Muhammad b. Abdir Rahman b. Muhammad Shamsuddin as Sakhawi, and is given by Meursinge in his Prolegomena and translated by him into Latin. This fragments, he states, is taken from the Leyden Codex 518. (*Catal No* 1876) entitled البدر الطالع من الضؤ اللامع *(Luna Oriens ex lumine micante)* by Ahmad b. Abdi's Salam Kadhi of Manuf. It contains an except of the principal work of as Sakhawi called الضؤ اللامع الاهل قرن القاسع (*l u m e n micans hominibus saculi noni*) and gives amongst the celebrities of that age, the following notice of as Suyuti:

"He was born on the first night of the month of Rajab 849, his mother being a Turkish slave, and he was reared an orphan. He learnt by-heart the Qurãn, the Umdah, the Minhaj both the section on the derivative and part of the fundamental principles, and the Alfiyah on grammar. Having proved his capacity in the year 64, he studied grammar under shamsuddin Muhammad b. Musa al Hanafi Imam of the Shaykhuniyah College, and under al Fakhr Othman al Maksi,[2] as Shams al Bami,[3] Ibn ul Falati,[4] Ibn Yusuf one of the most

---

1 There are two of these, called the Greater and the Lesser Muajam which are given in his list of works.

2 Othman b. Abdillah b. Othman al Fakhr Abu Amr al Maksi born 818 (1415), died 877 (1472). Maks is a village on the Nile adjacent to Cairo.

3 Muhammad b. Ahmad as Shams al Bami, born 820 (1417) died 885 (1480). Meurs.

4 Muhammad b. Ali al Kusi as Shafii, born 824, died 870, Ibid.

eminent doctors of the Shaykhuniyah, al Burhan al Ajluni, and according to some, under an Nuamani, with some of them, jurisprudence, with some, grammar. He progressed until he read some works on jurisprudence under al Alam al Bulkini. He then read with al Munawi for a very short time who gave him a lesson in good manners when, pained at his taking a seat at the head of the assembly, he said, "when we were young, we never sat save behind the circle of distinguished personages such as these." On this he broke off[1] from him and read altogether with as Sayfuddin, as Shumunni and al Kafiyaji the Hanafites, somewhat of the sciences, and also, as he asserts, with as Shihab as Sharimsahi a part of his commentary on the Majmuu of al Kallai : Likewise under al Izz al Mikati[2] his treatise on the Mikat, and under Muhammad b. Ibrahim as Sharwani or Rumi[3] the Physician at Cairo, two abridgments on medicine by Ibnul Jamaah,[4] and under al Izz al Hanbali some studies in the fundamental principles of jurisprudence from the Jama ul Jawami.

Here ends what he asserts to have done. He attached himself to me for some time and wrote to me in a long prose epistle *the following words,* "and verily we presented ourselves uninvited to the feast of his comprehensive bounty, and we made camel of our affliction knell in the spacious courtyard of his affluence."[5] Moreover

---

1 I do not follow Meursinge in his translation of انقطع "tum vero tetom se scientiis vovit." This form of the verb bears the meaning of devoting one's self to a thing, but the object is not mentioned and the ordinary signification of the word is here most applicable. The preceding passage is also misunderstood. The speaker is al Munawri not as Suyuti.

2 The Mikat is an appointed place of rendezvous for pilgrims proceeding to Mecca where they first enter into the state of Ibram or prohibition from lawful acts which are at that period unlawful. These stations will be found mentioned in the Jami Rumuz by Shamsuddin Muhammad al Kohistani. Meursinge's translation of Mikat "horologia" is quite untenable

3 Born 778 (1376), died 873 (1468). Meurs.

4 Izzuddin Muhammad b. Sharafuddin Abi Bakr, born 759 (1358), died 819 (1416). Ibid.

5 As Suyuti means to say that he owed much of solace in his toil to the bounty of as Sakhawi.

he praised me on other occasions in verse and prose as I have elsewhere shown. In the same way, for a very short period he frequented the lectures of az Zayn Kasim al Hanafi and al Bikai'i. He also practised himself in poetry under as Shihab al Mansuri,[1] and he heard traditions from the compilers of tradition then living such as al Kammasi, al Hijazi, as Shawi, al Muktumi Nashwan and Hajir, and some doctors of Aleppo gave him certificates of licence to relate traditions, among them Ibn Mukbil. The last who gave him a certificate was as Salah b. Abi Omar, but nevertheless he had made no profound study of all that I have alluded to. He then travelled to Fayyum, Damietta, al Mahallah and other places and took down in writing what he had heard from those who professed versification, as al Muhyiddin b. Sakiyah and al Alabul Janadi al Hanafi. Thence to Mecca by sea in Rabii' II, 69 and studied a little under al Muhyiddin Addul Kadir al Maliki and profited by the assistance of our friend Ibn Fadhl[2] among others, and more than one granted him a licence to teach and instruct. Al Alam al Bulkini granted him his encouragement until he obtained the chair of jurisprudence in the Shaykhuniyah mosque which had come down to him from his father and was present with him at some conferences therein.

Then he held himself aloof[3] and affected the airs of a Shaykh and applied himself to the sciences suitable to that profession. Moreover at the time when he used constantly to visit me, he carried off many of my compositions such as الاسما البنسوية الخصال المرحيه للضلال موت الابنا ـ الصلاه علي النبى and other I need not enumerate. Nay he took from the books of the Mahmudiyah College and elsewhere, many ancient compositions which were unknown to many of his contemporaries, on various sciences, altered them slightly, transposed them and gave them cut as his own, and prefaced them with pretentious introductions from which the unlearned reader might

---

1 Ahmad b. Muhammad, born 798, died 887, Meurs.

2 The Hafidh, author of a work entitled Durrar as Sunniyah wa Bahiyah, a treatise on Muhammadan law, composed 855. A.H. D'Herb.

3 Meursinge does not find the 7th form this verb انجمع and translates it omnes collegit vires suas." Lane gives the form and example انجمع عن الناس 'he withdrew himself from men.'

expect much, but not a part of which was fulfilled. The first he produced was a paper on the interdiction of the science of logic which he had extracted from a work of Ibn Taymiyah and in the greater part of it he was indebted to may assistance. Upon this many emiment scholars opposed him and even al Alam al Bulkini rejected him and took from him what he had dictated to him in his lectures on this questions, and had it not been for my good offices with a number of these, such as al Anbasi,[1] Ibnul Falati and Ibn Kasim,[2] the result would have been disastrous.

He also lectured to a number of the common people in the mosque of Ahmad b. Tulun; moreover he acquired a predominance[3] over some who were themselves good for nothing, so that this was the means of his being favoured by his executor Shihabuddin but Tabbakh who provided for his being brought up under Barsabai[4] Comptroller of the Household. After this he attached himself to Inal al Ashkar,[5] president of the order of prefects[6] until that personage appointed him professor of tradition in the Shakhuniyah College after the death of the Shaykh Othman al Maksi, **notwithstanding he had left a son. He was also appointed to the post of lecturer *on the Sahihayn of al Bukhari and Muslim* although he was unable to fulfil the condition attached to those**

---

1 **Abdur Rahim b. Ibrahim b. Hajjaj Zaynuddin al Anbasi, as Shafii, born 829, died 891. M.**

2 Muhammad b. Kasim b. Ali Shamsuddin al Maksi as Shafii, born 817, **died 893.**

3 **I differ** from M. in the translation of this passage. He would omit the second علي in صارعلي على بعضهم I would retain it and read the first علي or perhaps اعلى his rendering of وصي as "Pupillus" is, I think, inadmissible.

4 Probably Barsabai al Bajashi. See Weil. Gesch. Abb. Cal. Eg.II, p. 313.

5 Inalal Ashkar az Azhiri, Mention of his is made by Weil first in the reign of Sultan Khush Kadam in 867 (1462) when he was Atabek of Aleppo. **In the** reign of al Malik al Ashraf Kaitbai, he was transferred from the government of Malatiyah to that of **Aleppo, pp. 307. 333.**

6 **See Carlyles edit. Of the Maured allatafat (*Cantabrig* 1792) for this title. Note 7, p. 41.**

offices by the endower,[1] and to lecture on Mysticism at the Mausoleum of Barkuk[2] governor of Syria, which is by the gate of al Karafah *at Cairo,* through the favour of his townsman Abu Tayyib as Suyuti, and to other posts. All this, though he was not fitted for those nor nearly so, and for this reason it was said proverbially, that he undertook what he was not qualified to perform. He then gave a loose to his tongue and his pen against his Shaykhs who were his superiors, even to saying of Kadhi Adhud that he was not of as much consequence as a prick in the foot of Ibnus Salah, and for this he was reproved by one of the Hanabalite vice-presidents in the presence of their Kadhi. He also disparaged as Sayyid[3] and ar Radhi on a point of grammar without sufficient foundation, so that he withdrew his statement to a stranger who, when he met him, said, "verily thou assertest that the Sayyid al Jurjani maintains that a letter (حرف)[4] intrinsically hath no meaning either inherent in it or otherwise, but this statement of the Sayyid's testifieth to the falsehood of what thou dost allege." He replied, "verily I have seen no statement of his to that effect, but when I was at Mecca, I conversed with a distinguished person on this subject, he told me what I have asserted and I relied upon his authority." The other answered, "it is strange how any one who is an author himself could depend upon such a statement in connection with such a

1 What those conditions were is mentioned in the Husn al Muhadhirah in describing the foundation of the Amir Shaykhu. It was begun in Muharram 756 (*Jan. Feb.*1355). Chairs were appointed for the four orthodox doctrinal schools, a chair of Tradition, of Qurãn reading, lectures (اسماع) on the Sahihayn and the Shifa'. The head professor who lectured on Mysticism and the Hanafite theology, was required to be the most learned Hanafits in Egypt, and to be profoundly versed in exegesis and the fundamentals of Jurisprudence, and was not to be a Kadhi, and this condition was a general one for all the salaried College officials.

2 Consult D'Herb, art. Barkok, and Weil. Gesch. Abb. Cal. Eg. 510 *seq.*

3 Abul Hasan Ali b. Muhammad Zaynuddin al Husayni al Jurjani known as as Sayyid as Sharif, died 816. Meurs.

4 (حرف) has two senses grammatically speaking, one a letter, the other a particle, i.e., what is used to express a meaning and is not a noun or a verb. See Lane.

master." Thus far this assertion. He also said that any one who read with ar Radhi and his grammatical teaching, have never reached such a degree of proficiency as to entitle him to be called moderately acquainted with grammar.

He continued thus displaying his presumption till he declared himself profoundly versed in the seven sciences.[1]

He further maintained that if all the learned men of the time were to propound thousands of questions to him, he could answer them all by the sole exercise of his reasoning powers, and were he to set them but a tenth part of the same, they would be unable to solve them. He likewise elaborated a work to facilitate the acquisition of the degree of Mujtahid[2] in order to assert his own claim to it. And how well spoke one of the professors of arithmetic,- "that which he hath confessed[3] regarding himself in order that it might be inferred that he was impartial, is a proof of this science that it is one needing quick intelligence."

And similar to this is the saying of some one that he claimed the rank of Mujtahid to hide his own errors. And to this effect also are his own words when a certain distinguished person met him and desired to confer with him on some point, "it cannot be that my store of knowledge in scholastic theology is of small account."

The following speech was made to him by another - "inform me regarding the means of acquiring the degree of Mujtadhid. Is there any one living conversant with them?" He replied, "Yes, there are those who have some knowledge of them, but they are not

---

1 Here follows an extract from as Suyuti which has already been translated in preceding autobiography.

2 This term is employed to denote a doctor who exerts all his capacity for the purpose of forming a right opinion upon a legal question. The little was common in the first ages of Islam, but the principal points having been fixed by the great doctors, the exercise of private judgment in legal questions soon ceased to be recognized. Some later doctors like as Suyuti claimed the title and the right, but both were refused to them by public opinion. See De Slane I.K.I. p. 201.

3 Alluding to as Suyutis disinclination to that study.

collectively united in one person but dispersed *among a number.*" The other rejoined, "tell me who they are, and we will bring them together for thee, and thou shalt speak with them and if each one of them confesseth that thou hast a knowledge of his subject and noteth thee as distinguished therein, it is possible that we may allow thy claim." And he was silent and uttered not a word.

He mentions that his compositions number more than 300 volumes, but I have seen some of them consisting only of one page, and those that are less than a "kurrasah"[1] are numerous. He mentions amongst them a commentary on the Shatibiyah[2] and the Alfiyah on the readings of the Qurãn, notwithstanding his own confession, as has already gone before, that he had studied them under no Shaykh.

Among his writings, the following were fraudulently appropriated from the compositions of our Shaykh.[3]

لباب النقول في اسباب النزول- عين الاصابة في معرفة لصحابه- أ النكت البديعات علي الموضوعات- المَدَرج الي المُدرج- تذكرة الموتسي بمن حدث و نسي- تحفة النابة بقلخيص المتشابه- مارواه الواَعون في اخبار الطاون- الاساس في مناقب بني العباس جزء في اسما المدلسين- كشف النقاب عن الالقاب- نشر العبير فى تخريج احاديث الشرح الكبير-

All these are the dissertations of our Shaykh, and would that he had not altered them when he appropriated them, for if he had given them as they were, it would have been more profitable. The works belonging to other authors also, among his compositions are numerous. This would be seen were all the works named at hand, but in any case, he was given to much arrogant boasting. He came to me once and asserted that he had read the Musnad of a Shafi'i with al Kammasi, and of his own accord communicated to me what

1 A "kurrasah" according to De Slane (Vol. II, p. 98) generally contains 20 pages.

2 See Note, p. 651.

3 Meursings understands him to mean here, al Bulkini, as Sakhawi speaks of him under this title (شيخنا) in his biography.

contained a falsehood in every part of it. In the same way be related on the authority of al Kamal brother of al Jalal al Mahalli, al dream in which al Kamal proved his untruth. Al Badruddin the Hanbalite Kadhi said to me, "I never saw him reading the Jamaul Jawami with my Shaykh notwithstanding my constant zeal in attendance on him (*the Shaykh*); but indeed Khayruddin ar Rishi the Nakib studied it under him." I said, "Perhaps he used to come at the same time." He replied. "I never observed it."

He asserted that he composed the Nafhatul Miskiyah wal Tuhfatul Makikyah (*The Musky Fragrance and the Meccan gift*) in one 'kurrasah' when he was at Mecca after the manner of the U'nwanus Sharaf of Ibnul Mukri[1] in the single day, and that he wrote an Alfiyah on tradition superior to the Alfiyahul Iraki[2] and other things which it would be tedious to mention. Similar to this is his saying (which verifies the adage that forgetfulness is the undoing of falsehood) in one place that he knew by heart a part of the Minhaj on Fundamentals, and in another that he knew the whole of it, and that the course of Dictation was discontinued after the death of our Shaykh until he reinstated it. So too his assertion that the first who was appointed to the Shaykhumiyah College was al Kafiyaji, and his remarking to me several times," by Allah, if the Turkish Superintendent had not appointed him, or had I alone to do in the affair, I would not have preferred him from my knowledge of the special claim of another." Add to all this the inversions and solecisms in prounciation that fell from him and what arose from his misaprehension of meaning, through his not frequenting the lectures of the learned nor attending their evening and nightly assemblies, instead of which he worked alone, deep among codices and tomes, and relied upon what had not secured the approval of accurate scholars; moreover he was opposed by all men universally when he claimed the degree of Mujtahid. He composed the following works:

---

1 See note, 660.

2 Alfiyahul Iraki fi Usulul Hafiidh by the Hafidh Zaynuddin Abdur Rahim bil Husayn al Iraki : died 806 (1403). This and its commentaries are noticed at some length by H.K.

اللفظ الجوهري في رد خباط الجوجرى۔
الكر علي عبد البر۔ عضب الجبار علي ابن الابار۔ الصارم الصقيل في قطع الطويل۔ القول المجمل في رد علي المهمل۔

All this during his stay at Mecca, treating discourteously therein the people of Hijaz for which he richly deserved severe reproof, some of these compositions being more foul than others. Of these I have seen only the first which contains great disparagement of al Jaujari and mush arrogance which in parts shows his folly, nay his rabid rage. The fourth is in refutation of al Burhan an Nuamani[1] where he reads the words of the Kadhi Iyadh at the close of the Shifa ويخصنا بخصيصي in the dual number, after he had written him a paper containing hard and coarse language not proper to the addressed to scholars, which induced al Burhan to procure learned opinion upon it and those who wrote agreeing with his reading were al Amin al Iksirai, al Ubbadi, al Bami, as Zayn Kasim al Hanafi, al Fakhr ad Dayyimi and the writer of this memoir. Al Burhan wrote a pamphlet which he entitled al Kaul al Mufassal fi radd alal Mughaffal. (*A clear tractate in refutation of the imbecile*); moreover one of the disciples of al Jaujari wrote also in support of him but al Jaujari[2] was incensed against him who undertook this on

---

1 The Imam Hafidh Abul Fadhl Iyadh b. Musa Yahsabi, called as Sabti because he was a native of Ceuta. He was born in 470 (1077) died in 544 (1149). Among his best known works are a history of Cordova a devotional work called Azhar ur Ryadh, and the Shifa (Note 3 p.vii). See his life in D'Herb. The words at the close of the Shifa alluded to are, (*teste Mcurs* ويخصنا بخصيصي زمره نبينا و جماعته Et peculiarem nobis facers volet (*Deus*) peculiarem favorem turboe Prophets nostri ejusque agminis. خصيصى is here an inf. n. of خص like دليلي and فخيرى Burhanuddin took it as a dual number. Weijers' note on this in Meurs, is remarkable. Quo mode vero Burhanoddinus iste ibi in duali numero … legere…..equidem plane non intelligo :et magis etiam mirror partium stadium eorum eruditorum, qui nuda, ut videtur, Sojuti invidia ducti, Borhannodino illi adversus hunc adstipulati, aut certe illi non plane oblecuti sunt.

2 Muhammad b. Abdil Munim Shamsuddin al Jaujari al Kahiri as Shafii : born 822 (1419) died 889 (1489). M. He was the author against whom was directed the first treatise mentioned in the last page.

account of the praise of the person eulogized that his work contained. As Suyuti also wrote a letter to al Kamal b. Abi Sharif[1] and filled it with unworthy attacks on al Kirmani. Al Khatib al Waziri sent his son to him at Raudhah[2] to exhibit his proficiency in study, but he sent him back, alleging as an excuse that he did not fulfil his father's description[3] of him on certain points and that his letter for other reasons, likewise, was not satisfactory to him.

When a certain student once spoke of the impiety of Ibnul Arabi,[4] he replied, "verily war is announced[5] that shall come upon him from God, though the judge can find nought against him and he himself deprecates examination of his writings for points which he judges orthodox in which the believer and discerner of true doctrine cannot concur with him." Moreover he reported of him that he said, "it is forbidden to examine may words." As Suyuti was one of those who adopted this tenet *(of Ibn Arabis')* from A'bdullah Muhammad b. Omar al Maghrabi who lived near the Karakiha al Hasani College whose lectures he attended for some time. More might be said, but

---

1 Abul Hana Muhammad al Kamaluddin b. Abi Sharif as Shafii : born 822 Meurs.

2 A place, according to Meursinge where as Suyuti had an estate.

3 I must differe from Meursinge"s rendering of this, "non poses se patri ejus (in response suo) omnes quos oporteret titulos dare."

4 Muhyiddin b. Ali a most voluminous writer on Sufism, a native of Murcia: born 560 (1165), died 638 (1240). Consult Haj, Khal and the Tabakat al Mufase, of as Suyuti, edit, Meurs, also De Slane. I.K. Vol. IV, p. 351. In Suyutis notice of him it is stated that some of his expressions were not altogether orthodox and that though outwardly comfirming to the faith, he had some peculiar views on doctrine, but ad Dahabi excuses him on the ground that his writings on Sufism and his austerities, had disturbed his intellect, and he imagined things that had no existence. See also D'Herb. Art. Arabi.

5 Referring to Qur. II. فاذنوابحرب من الله و رسوله *(be apprized of war that shall come upon you from God and his apostle.)* Meaning, "you threaten him with war from God on account of his impiety, though the temporal judge can find nothing to substantiate the charge ; and he himself deprecates examination of his writings to prove him unorthodox by wresting his words from their proper sense." The Arabic of this passage is obscure and probably corrupt.

were I to discuss all that regarded him. I should transgress due limits. To be brief, he wrote hastily[1] without reflection: I never knew him to be anything but vain and overweening, even towards his own mother, so that she used constantly to complain of him, and his conduct continued to grow worse in this respect, - may the Most High inspire him with rectitude.

The Caliph favoured him and appointed him Shaykh of the Baybarsiyah College in succession to al Jalal al Bakri,[2] after which his zeal abated, nay became congealed, so that he sought retirement from the world according to what he himself says, "I gave up lecturing and resolving cases of law and turned myself to the Most High." Before this time he asserted that he had a dream in which the prophet upbraided him, and his Vicegerent as Siddik ordered him to be imprisoned for a year, that he might revert to lecturing and expounding the law when he took it upon himself to abandom them, and that he asked pardon and desisted from his purpose : so that if any one came to him with a case, though he were about to drown at the time, he would take it to write his decision thereon. It was not long after this, that he said what has gone before.

Al-Muhyiddin b-ul Mughayzil left him when he experienced from him great ill-treatment, after he had acted towards him previously with generosity and he has related instances of his extravagant pretensions which the circumstances themselves verify. As an example, he requested al Burhanuddin al Karaki to appoint him to conduct a judicial case which was under his charge. The latter complied and on his own part furnished in addition a duplicate of the original process. As Suyuti went to him accompanied by al Alamuddin Sulayman al Khalifati to take it, and he never thanked him nor uttered a word expressive of his obligation. He on one occasion related to Muhyiddin after as Sunbati's death, a circumstance showing his injustice. He said, "why hast thou told

---

1 I cannot concur in Meursinges translation "Et hoc celeriter describe potest."

2 Abdul Baka Muhammad b. Abdir Rahman ad Dahruti, known as Jalaluddin al Bakri, born 807 (1404), died 891 (1486). M. The Caliph who appointed him must have been al Mutawakkit alallah Abul Izz who died in 903.

me of this only after his death?" As Suyuti replied, "that thou mayest know the hearts of men." And this notwithstanding his great kindness to him, especially during the time of the high prices when there was a dearth of weekly as he states himself. In the same way a certain Turk left him, whom from a Hanafite he had made a Shafiite, notwithstanding that as Suyuti had begun by showing great kindness and courtesy towards him. Al Maghrabi likewise abandoned him, the same who used to assert his great sanctity, and also al Fath al Karni.[1]

An instance of his arrogance, is his saying to one of his attendants, "when I receive the office of Kadhi, I will appoint thee to such and such a thing, nay thou shalt obtain every thing."

Subsequently in the year 898, the Shaykh Abun Naja son[2] of Shaykh Khalaf opposed him and publicly exposed his deficiencies and faults, and he was humbled by him and greatly abased. The Imam al Karaki spoke highly of Abun Naja as I have fully shown in the Hawadith.[3] Previously to this as Suyuti wrote a work entitled, "the Cautery in refutation of as Sakhawi," in which he opposed what is affirmed in the Sahih,[4] although I never touched upon the subject save some time before nay my course towards it having been to speak neither in affirmation or denial. Let us praise God the Distributor of understanding."

---

1 Meursinge conceive that these were all instances of persons who were at first attached to us Suyuti but were afterwards driven from him by his violence and harshness.

2 Abun Naja b. Khalaf al Misri as Shafii, born 849. He used to hold assemblies in the mosques and other public places to which he drew large numbers even from the quarters where as Suyuti lived, and even lectured in Suyutis own college the Baybarsiyah. M. note 183, p. 43.

3 Meursinge supposes that this is the name of a book (*De rebus gestis*) by az Sakhawi but of which no mention is made by Haji Khalifah.

4 Meursinge translate في الصحيح "inter vera." I understand Sahih to signify the authentic traditions that are known under that name.

The Compiler[1] adds, "The Sultan al Aadil Tumani Bai[2] removed him from the post of professor of the Baybarsiyah on Monday the 12th Rajab 906 (*1st February* 1501) when a number of the Sufi Shaykhs of the Madrassah held a meeting against him on account of his niggardliness with them and his hostility to them by depriving many of them of their stipends and appointing others thereto. He received many humiliations such as judicial mandates, annoyances, interdictions : and other similar things occured. In the professorship after him was appointed Laishin al Bilbisi, known as Ibnul Ballan, on Monday the 26th of the said month, although there were others superior to him in desert, but fortune prevails over merit. Yet he was in no way at ease, fearful lest Jalaluddin (*as Suyuti*) should disturb him by asserting that al Aadil had forced him publicly to forego his right. And indeed this move of al Jalaluddin actually took place though not persisted in, and thus the position of al Bilbisi was insecure. After this Jalaluddin's affairs became tranquil and he turned aisde from this office and that of professor of tradition in the Shykhuniyah with a view to a life of withdrawal from worldly affairs, and he broke off all connection with society by residing at Raudhah, and I have heard that a number of the principal nobles used to visit him whom he did not rise to greet.

The professorship of the Baybarsiyah was offered to him on the death of al Bilbisi on Saturday the 25th of Dul Hijjah 909, but he declined it and al Kamaluddin at Tawil assumed it on Monday the 27th of the said month after he had expended largely, it is said, on that account, Jalaluddin continued in retirement till he died on Thursday the 18th Jumada 1,911 *(17th October 1505)*. May the Lord have mercy upon him and upon us."

Having now given as Sakhawis strictures on as Suyuti, I cannot in justice refrain from presenting to the reader the latter's opinion of his critic, and for this I am indebted to Meursinge who has

---

1 The word قلت here indicates the termination of as Sakhawis narrative and that what follows is by the author who has extracted it.

2 One of the Circassian Mamelukes who reigned three years and a half, 906-9 (1501-3). M.

extracted the following notice from a work of the historian's, entitled اعيان الاعبان و ابذاء زمان*(the choicest of the great and sons of the Age)*, Cod. 416,th P. 94.

"Muhammad b. Abdir Rahman b. Muhammad Abi Bark b. Othman b. Muhammad as Sakhawi Shamsuddin, the traditionist, the historian, the ealumniator, was born in 831 (1427-8) and attended while he was yet young, the dictations of the Hafith Ibn Hajr who fostered in him a love of the science of tradition. He frequented his classes and wrote out many of his compositions with his own hand. He studied under very many collectors of traditions in Egypt, Syria and Hijaz and he selected and extracted them for himself and for others, notwithstanding his misreading of them and his being destitute of all knowledge, so that he was good for nothing but in the mere science of tradition. Then he fell upon history and dissipated his life therein and devoted all his efforts to it, and lacerated therein the reputations of men and filled it with their misdeeds, and all that had been imputed to them whether true or false, and asserted that he was thus doing a necessary duty, *viz,* apportioning blame or praise, whereas this is manifest folly and error and blasphemy against God.

Moreover he was guilty of a fragrant violation of right and was under the burden of many sins, as I have shown in the preface to this book. I mention this only that no one may be seduced by him or trust to any thing that is in his historical writings defamatory of men, especially the learned, or pay heed thereunto. He died in Shaaban 902." *(April 1497).*

The Leyden copy of the work from which this is taken, Meursinge believes to be the only one existing in Europe, and he proposed to himself to treat further of it on some future occasion as it contains momoirs more or less full, of the distinguished men of a Suyuti's age. Whether he ever fulfilled his intentions I do not know, and am therefore unable to give further particulars regarding the irregularities alluded to at the close of the above extract. This is, however, of little importance. The recriminations of authors are little to their credit, and are read with indifference when the passions and jealousies which evoked them are hushed and forgotten. The supplement to as Sakhawi's narrative bears unwilling evidence of the reverence in which as Suyuti was held at a time when, retired from the world, he still received the unsolicited visits of the great. His petulant notice of the historian's just criticism, of Burhanuddin's reading of the Shifa of Kadhi Iyadh, and the evident jealousy which induced the learned reference to side with Burhan, his hints of the dis-approval with which Bulkini and Munawi regarded our author who never theless speaks of them in his Husn al Muhadhirah in terms of unqualified esteem, sufficiently prove the unfairness and suggest the untruthfulness of the writer. His rancour against the historian was probably caused by as Suyuti's criticism of his work the Dhu'l Lami, in his pamphlet entitled the Cautery, and the name out indistinctly hints that the iron was applied red hot. Possibly previous differences may have made his duty a grateful one, and a critique undertaken in this spirit, would not be altogether just. The angry retort of his patient, however, inflicted as keen a wound as he received and the passing satisfaction of an incisive and now forgotten criticism, was more than avenged by the immortality of his victim's reply.

The length to which these hitherto little known particulars of as Suyuti's life have unavoidably led me, precludes any extended notice of the work which is here presented to the public. The sources whence the author derived the materials for his history are indicated by him as its close, and if their treatment does not discover any evidence of originality of design, it has at least the merit of condensing into a readable compass, not only the principal events which occurred during the reign of each Caliph, but the personal details and sketches of court life and manners which are often wanting in Abul Fida but which lend their chief interest to the lively narrative of Masaudi. To the dignity of a history according to the European acceptation of the term, it has indeed no pretensions. To investigate the relations of cause and effect, to trace the growth and development of communities and assign the reasons of their arrestation or decline, to discuss the social, political and religious questions which disturb the tranquillity or affect the fortunes of states, to analyze the characters of public men and the influences which bear on their conduct; to paint vivid descriptions of battle-scenes and pageantries of state; to survey the arts, manufactures, trades and products of a country and all that constitutes and adorns its national life, this ideal epic of poetry and philosophy, no Eastern historian has ever attempted. Historical science in its infancy among the Moslems as De Slane has shown, began with oral traditions transmitted from one Hafidh to another, together with the series of authorities for each independent fact, till their accumulated store became too burdensome for retention by memory. They were then committed to writing in the form of a collection of statements supported by lines of ascription reaching to the original narrators who were in most cases eye-witnesses of what they related. A subsequent writer suppressed the ascriptions to a large extent, marshalled the facts and blended the disconnected traditions into one continuous but bulky history. Such were Ibnul Athir and at Tabari. Then came the abridger who condensed the work of his predecessor into a simpler and smaller volume while the greater work was consigned to veneration and decay in some public library. Such were Abul Fida and as Suyuti. De Slane has, I think, unfairly censure these last-mentioned writers. He considers them to have done nearly as much injury to their predecessors as Justin and Florus have done to Livy and Tacitus. I do not admit the justness of the parallel nor perceive its relevancy. Justin's history, is a compilation of extracts rather than an abridgment of the lost books of Trogus Pompeius whose guides were exclusively Greek, and who treated in the main but with voluminous digressions, of the rise, decline and fall of the Macedonian monarch. Though Justin has been censured for omitting much from his original that was worthy or record, yet that original was professedly not Tacitus, whose Histories and Annals are concerned with the period between the second consulship of Galba and the death of Domitian, and from the death of August to the death of Nero. It is true that the Editio Princeps of Florus published about 1471, bore the title, "Titi Livii Epithoma," but it is not regarded by modern scholars as an abridgment of Livy, but a compilation from various authorities epitomizing the leading events from the building of the city to the rise of the Empire. The Epitomes of the books of Livy have been ascribed to Florus, and with equal probability to Livy himself. There is no internal testimony in favour of either conclusion, and external evidence is altogether wanting.[1] It is difficult, therefore to perceive in what way the assumed injury has been affected. The parallel applied to the Easterns fails in a similar manner. Their merit would perhaps be slight, were it confined to their condensation, however judicious, of a single work, but this is far from being the case. Abul Fida cites no less than fourteen authors, and as Suyuti, twelve to whose voluminous pages they are indebted for their materials. The greater number of the work which they mention have perished, and it is to their labours we owe the preservation of much that would otherwise have been irretrievably lost. Reiske's eloquent commendation of Abul Fida is a just and sufficient testimony to his eminence, and his concluding words will suffice me for any penegyric of as Suyuti,-ipse usus eum commendabit, quare laudibus ejus celebrandis parcam.

The MSS. from which the text of this work was edited, which is but one among the many services of the accomplished Orientalist Colonel Nassau Lees to the world of letters, were the following:-

Calcutta Madrassah : this copy is now missing.

"The property of Maulvie Abdus Shukur of Jounpore. Likewise missing.

"in the possession of the Asiatic Society, Calcutta. This latter is the only one with which I have been able to collate the text.

Another MS. is mentioned by Weil in his history of the Abbaside Caliphs in Egypt (note, p. 122, Vol. II,) and numbered Cod.

Goth. No 321, which I have not seen.

The System of transliteration of Arabic proper names adopted by me, is the same now in general use throughout India. The following letters alone present any difficulty, and are thus represented. :

---

1 Consult. Ramsay's art, on Livy in William Smith. CI. D.

	is written	
ح	"	h
ذ	"	d
ص	"	s
ض	"	dh
ط	"	t
ظ	"	dh
ع	"	with a comma over the vowel.

Some proper names of persons, such as Omar and Othman, and those of certain towns and countries, the corrupt spelling of which has been consecrated and fixed by custom, are left unaltered.

In concluding, I have to acknowledge my indebtebness to Maulvie Kabiruddin Ahmad whose wide range of reading and intelligent acquaintance with the historical, philosophical and doctrinal literature of the Arabs have been of great service to me. In what pertains to the accuracy of the translation and the manner of it, I must leave to the Criticism of the learned, the correction and removal of defects in both, of which I am only too conscious, but which with the best endeavours, I have failed to amend.

H.S.J.

HISTORY OF THE CALIPHS

BY

JALALUDDIN A'S SUYUTI.

After the praises of God, of Him who promises and performs, and who threatens and forgives,—and blessings and peace upon our Chief, Muhammad, Prince of the nobly born, progenitor of the Caliphs-and upon his family companions, the possessors of magnanimity and good faith, I proceed to give in this slight historical sketch, a biographical account of the Caliphs, the Princes of the Faithful, who have stood in authority over the people from the age of Abu Bakr the Witness to the Truth-may God approve him-up to this my time, according to the order of their reigns one after another. And I have mentioned in the lives of all them, the remarkable occurrences which happened during the reign of each, and the chief doctors of the faith, and the illustrious personages who lived during their time.

Many circumstances instigated the composition of this work: among them, that a collection of the biographies of the chiefs of the faith, and those endowed with virtue, was desirable and would be welcome, and in truth, there are those who have compiled histories in which they have introduced these distinguished men, but unsytematically, and without giving a full account of them, and their completion would entail prolixity and weariness. For this reason I was desirous of separately detailing each class of men in a work *apart,* which would be more advantageous for those who wished for particulars of any one class, and easier to consult. Thus I have set apart one book for the prophets-upon whom be the benediction and peace of God,-and another for the Companions of the Prophet; abridged from the "Isaba" of the Shaykhul Islam Ibn Hajr;-and another comprising the various commentators of the Qurãn; and an abridged work on the lives of the Huffadh,[1] epitomized from the Tabakat of ad Dahabi; and a voluminous work on the grammarians and Philologists, and similar to which had not been before composed; and a book on those learned in the fundamentals of the faith,-and a voluminous work on those famed for sanctity; and another on the doctors of the law of Inheritance; and another on Rhetoricians; and another on Writers, that is, authors of prose composition; and another on those celebrated for calligraphy;[2] and another on the Arab poets whose works are authorities in the language, and these comprehend the greater number of eminent men of the nation.

I rest satisfied, regarding doctors of Law, with what other men have written on that subject, on account of its abundance, and independence of *any further information* thereon,-and I have likewise contented myself with what the Tabakat of ad Dahabi[3] contains on the Readers of the Qurãn. The Kadhis are included

---

1 A Hafidh or one who remembers what he has heard or read, is of the 3rd grade of the Traditionists,. Of these there are five. The Hafidh must know 300,000 traditions by heart, and be able to name the lines of authorities of each. Consult Ibn-Salah on tradition.

2 The Khattul Mansub is a species of handwriting, the invention of which is attributed by Ibn Khall (see life of al-Bawwab) to Abu Abdullah al-Hasan brother of Ibn Muklah, while ad Dahabi (Tarikhul Islam) gives the credit of it to the latter. See De Slane's notes on this handwriting. Art. Ibn al Aamidi the Kadhi.

3 Abu Abdullah Muhammad a doctor of the Shafii school, surnamed the 'sun of religion' born at Damascus A.H. 673, (1276) but his ancestors were Turkoman. He was the chief Hafidh and Qurãn reader of Syria. His works are very numerous. The Tabakat there mentioned is a biography of the Readers of the Qurãn. See Ibn Khall.

among the preceding, and therefore, among personages of distinction, *the history* of the Caliphs alone remains *unwritten,* notwithstanding the eagerness of men for accounts of them. I have therefore set apart this book for them but have not included in it, any who disputed the Caliphate by force of arms, and did not succeed to power, such as many of the descendants of Ali and a few of the House of Abbas : neither have I made mention of any of the Caliphs, the descendants of Ubaydullah,[1] because their authority was illegal for many reasons-among them-this, that they were not of the tribe of the Kuraysh, and although the ignorant vulgar have named them Fatimites, nevertheless their ancestor was a worshipper of fire. Kadhi Abdul Jabbar of Basrah says that the name of the ancestor of the Egyptain Caliphs was said and his father was a Jew blacksmith of Salamiyah.[2]

The Kadhi Abu Bakr al Bakilani[3] says that al Kaddah the grandfather of Ubaydullah, called al Mahdi, was a fire-worshipper, and Ubaydullah went to Africa and asserted that he was a descendant of Ali; none of the genealogist recognised him as such, but ignorant people called them Fatimites.

Ibn Khallakan remarks that most of the learned did not hold as valid, the pedigree of Ubaydullah al Mahdi, the ancestor of the Egyptian Caliphs, insomuch that when al Aziz billah son of al Muizz

---

1 The founder of this house was Ubaydullah al Mahdi who assumed the Caliphate in 296 A.H. (A.D. 908). At the same period Abdullah was Caliph in Spain, and al Muktadir at Baghdad : "In the 10th century" says Gibbon "the chair of Mahomed was disputed by three Caliphs who reigned at Baghdad, Cairoan and Cordova, excommunicated each other and agreed in a principle of discord that a sectary is more odious and criminal than an unbeliever."

2 The printed edition has نشابة an arrow-maker-the MS. Has of سليميه Sulaymiah-the latter is probably a copyist's error for سلميه sa small town in the district of Enessa where according to Ibn Khallakan al Mahdi was born-I have preferred the latter reading.

3 Called Bakilani or vendor of beans. He was of Basrah but long resident in Baghdad and celebrated as a doctor of Scholastic theology a voluminous author, died A.H. 403 (1013 A.D.) Ibn Khall.

in the beginning of his reign, ascended the pulpit on a Friday, he found there a piece of paper, and in it these lines-

"We have heard a false pedigree
Road from the pulpit in the mosque.
If thou art truly what thou assertest,
Then name *thy* ancestor up to the fifth[1] generation.
And if thou mean to verify what thous sayest
Then give us thy pedigree like that of at Taia.[2]
If not then leave thy pedigree in obscurity
And enter with us into a common ancestry
For the genealogies of the sons of Hashim
To them aspires not the desire of the ambitious.

Al Aziz wrote to the Umayyad,[3] then ruler of Spain, a letter in which he reviled and satirized him, whereupon the Umayyad replied, saying, "After the usual greetings, verily thou knewest me, therefore hast thou satirized me, and surely if I knew thee, I would answer thee:" and this came sorely upon al Aziz and silenced him from reply, for it meant that he was an impostor and his family unknown.

Ad Dahabi says that authorities are agreed upon this, that Ubaydullah al Mahdi was not a descendant of Ali; and how wellspoke his grandson al Muizz, the ruler of Cairo, when Ibn Tabataba,[4] the descendant of Ali questioned him regarding their

---

1 The text and MS. Have سابع instead of رابع it is clear from Ibn Khallakan that the former is incorrect as al Aziz was fifth in descent from al Mahdi.

2 A contemporary of al Aziz. At Taialillah reigned as Caliph at Baghdad in A.H. 363 (A.D. 913) A lineal descendant from Hashim great-grandfather of Muhammad.

3 This must have been either Hakam or Hisham called al Mustansir. Hakam died one year after the accession of al Aziz and was succeeded by Hisham al Muayyad.

4 Abu Muhammad Abdullah 9th in descent from Ali, a native of Hijaz but an inhabitant of Egypt. He was a Sharif noted for the nobility of his character, his vast possessions and the style in which he lived, born A.H. 286 (A.H. 899) and died 4th Rajab at Cairo A.H, 348 (September A.D. 959). Ibn Khall.

origin! He half drew his sword from the scabbard and said "This is my pdigree," and scattering gold among the nobles and those who were present, said "here *are the proofs of my* nobility."

And among *the reasons aforesaid is this,* that the greater number of them were Magians beyond the pale of Islam; and there were of them, some who reviled the prophets, and among them some who held the use of the best of them were heretics, unclean and base, who directed the execration of the Companions *of the prophet*-may God approve them-and to such as these, homage is not binding and their headship is illegal. And Abu Bakr al Bakilani says that Ubaydullah al Mahdi, was a vile Batini,[1] eager for the subversion of the orthodox faith. He perseeuted learned men and doctors of law, that he might be able to seduce the people, and his descendants followed his ways. They gave a license to wine and fornication and promulgated heresy. Ad Dahabi says that al Kaim the son of al Mahdi, was more wicked than his father, an accursed Magian, who openly reviled the prophets, and he adds that the House of Ubaydullah was more malevolent towards the Orthodox faith than the Tartars.

Abul Hasan al Kabasi[2] says that Ubayullah and his deseendants put on death four thousand of the learned and pious, seeking to turn them from acknowledging the Companions *of the prophet,* but they preferred death-then, well indeed, had he been only a heretic but he was a Magian. (Zindik).[3]

---

1 This is the same sect as the Assassins so often mentioned in the history of the Crusades, founded by Hasan Saba, known as the Old Man of the Mountain. The word signifies possessing inward light and knowledge. See Von Hammer-Gesech-dor Assassinen.

2 A doctor of the Maliki school. A great traditionist-died A.H. 403, (A.D. 1012). Ibn Khall.

3 This term primarily implies an assertor of the doctrine of Dualism, but it is also used to signify an atheist or one who denies the world to come and maintains the eternityof the present. Consult, Lane, art زندق De Sac, Chresth, Ar. 2nd Ed, II. P 274.

The Kadhi Iyadh tells *us* that[1] Abut Muhammad al Kayruwani, al Kizani, one of the doctors of the Maliki school was asked as to the case of one compelled by the house of Ubayd, namely the Caliphs of Egypt-to acknowledge their claims or die. He replied "he must choose death and no one can be excused in such an instance: their assumption of authority at first took place before their pretensions were understood, but afterwards flight was imperative and no one through fear *of death* could excuse his *voluntary* abiding, forasmuch as residence in a place, the people of which are required to abandon the religious precepts of *Islam* is not permissible; nevertheless some few doctors of law did remain exceptionally for them, lost *a knowledge of* their religious ordinances might be wanting to the Muslims and *the rulers* seduce them from their faith."

And Yusuf ur Ruayni says that the learned of Kayruwan were agreed that the House of Ubayd were in the condition of apostates and Magians, for they declared openly against the law. Ibn Khallakan remarks *as follows*: "Verily they laid claim to the knowledge of hidden things, and accounts of them regarding this are well-known, for when al Aziz one day, ascended the pulpit, he observed a piece of paper in which was written—

Verily we are patient under tyranny and oppression
But not under infidelity and folly;
If thou art gifted with the knowledge of what is hidden
Reveal to us the writer of this letter.

A woman, also, *once* addressed to him a petition in which was written: "By Him who hath exalted the Jews through Misha[2] and the Christians through Ibn Nastur, and hath disgraced the true believers in thee, see that thou look into my case," and Misha the

---

1 Abdul Fadhl Iyadh a traditionist-the greatest authority of his age on Arabic history and litereature. He was educated at Cordova and died in Morocco-A.H. 544 (A.D. 1150). Ibn Khall.

2 The readings of the MS. Vary in both places where this name occurs.

Jew was intendant of the finances in Syria and Ibn Nastur in Egypt.

Among other *reasons* is this, that their assumption of the *Caliphate,* occurred at a time when an Abbasi Imam was already in possession with priority of allegiance; it was therefore illegal, for a covenant of fealty to two Imams at the same time cannot be justified, and the first is the rightful one. And again thee is a tradition to this effect, that this authority when it shall come into the possession of the children of Abbas, shall not depart from them until hey themselves shall resign it unto Jesus the Son of Mary, or al Mahdi.[1] It is therefore ascertained that whosoever assumes the Caliphate during their incumbency is a schismatic *and* a rebel.

For these reasons therefore, I have made no mention of any of the House of Ubayd, nor of other schismatics but only of the Caliphs who unite orthodoxy of headship and a covenant of allegiance.

I have prefaced the beginning of the book with a few chapters, *containing* observations of importance and what I have introduced of strange and remarkable occurrences, is taken from the history of the Hafidh ad Dahabi, and the responsibility for his own work is upon him, and the Lord is my helper.

In explanation of how the Prophet left no successor and the mystery of this.[2]

Al-Bazzar[3] in his Musnad (collection of traditions) state on the authority of Hudayfah[1] that *the Companions of the Prophet* said:

1 The last of the Imams who it is believed, will appear before the Day of Judgement, to overthrow Dajjal-the Man of Sin that is to come.

2 As the mention of the lines of authorities for each tradition is of no profit to the general reader, they will be omitted, the first and last alone being given.

3 Abu Bakr Muhammad Ibn Abdul Baki, surnamed the Kadhi of the infirmary, a great tradtionist-flourished about A.D. 1123. The MS. has al Bazzaz of whom I can find no notice as traditionist but only as a teacher of Qurãn reading. Another al Bazzar is Abu Bakr Muhammad Abdullah b. Ibrahim-a Shafiite doctor author of the Ghilaniyat, died A.H. 354.

O ! Apostle of God, wilt thou not appoint a successor unto us?" He replied, "Verily did I appoint a successor over you, and were you to rebel against the successor appointed by me, punishment would come upon you."

The two Shaykhs[2] have recorded regarding Omar that he said when he was stabbed. "Were I to name a successor, then, verily, he named a successor, who was greater than I," (meaning Abu Bakr,), "and were I to leave you *without one*, then, verily, he also hath left you so, who was greater than I," (meaning the Apostle of God).

Ahmad and al Bayhaki[3] in their Proofs of Prophecy, have related on good authority from Amar b. Sufiyan, that when Ali was victorious on the day of the Camel,[4] he said, "O! men, verily the Apostle of God hath committed nothing unto us in regard to this authority, in order that we might of our own judgment approve and appoint Abu Bakr, who ruled and so continued until he went his way; then Abu Bakr thought fit to nominate Omar who ruled and so continued until the right became established.[5] Then the people sought worldly advantages sand events occurred regarding, which may the Lord determine." Al Hakim[6] in his Mustadrak has recorded, and al Bayhaki has confirmed it in his "Proofs" on the testimony of Abu Wail, that it was asked of Ali. "Wilt thou not appoint a successor

---

1 Abu Abdullah bul Yaman, one of the companions died. A.D. 656 *Ibn Hajar*

2 Al Bukhari and Muslim, the two greatest of the six highest authorities on tradition-the other are at Tirmidhi, Abu Dauud, an Nasai and Ibn Maja.

3 Abu Bakr bal Husayn called al Bayhaki from his birthplace near Naysabur an eminent traditionist born 384 (994) died 458 (1066). Ibn Khall.

4 The battle so called from the camel ridden by Aysha when defeated and taken prisoner by Ali under the walls of Basrah A.H. 66. See Gibbon, Vol. VI. P 275.

5 Fortnis curious meaning of ضرب بجرانه see Lane art.جرن .

6 Abu Abdullah Muhammad born at Naysabur 321 A.H. (933) and held the office of KAdhi under the Samani rule, and died their A.H. 405 (A.D. 1014). He was the most eminent traditionist of his time. The Mustadrak alas Sahihayn (Supplement to the two Sahihs of al Bukhari and Muslim) is the work alluded to. He compesed numerous others, on the sciences connected with tradition. Consult, Ibn Khall.

unto us?" He replied, "The Apostle of God appointed none, shall I therefore do so? but if God desireth the good of the people. He will unite them after me upon the best of themselves, as He united them after their prophet upon the best among them.

Ad Dahabi remarks that among the heretics there are some idle traditions that *the Prophet* bequeathed *the Caliphate* to Ali, and verily Huzayl b. Shurahbil[1] says, "Did Abu Bakr obey Ali, the legatee of the apostle of God? Abu Bakr would have been glad to have received the bequest from the apostle of God, for then he would have forced Ali to submit."

Ibn Saad[2] has recorded on the authority of Hasan that Ali said, "When the apostle of God died, he deliberated upon our mode of government, and we found that the Prophet had made Abu Bakr take the lead in public prayers. We approved, therefore, for our temporal affairs one whom the apostle of God approved for our spiritual concerns. We thus gave precedence to Abu Bakr." Al Bukhari says in his history that it is related on the authority of Safinah[3] that the Prophet said of Abu Bakr, Omar, and Othman- "these shall be the Caliphs after me," but this is not to be followed, says al Bukhari because Omar Ali, and Othman have asserted that the Prophet did not appoint a successor.

Ibn-Haban[4] has recorded the above tradition and relates on the authority of Safinah that when the apostle of God built the mosque *at Medina,* he laid a stone on the foundation and said to

---

1 Of the tribe Aud. He was what is called a Tabi or one next in time to the Companions. An Nawawi.

2 Abdullah Muhammad, b. Saad of Basrah called Katib i. Wakidi from having transcribed and completed the works of that historian. Also author of the Tabukati Kabir, died 846. A.D. Ibn Khall.

3 Abu Abdur Rahman Mihran surnamed Safinah by Muhammad whose freedman he was, on account of his having carried across a stroam some of the Companions with whom Muhammad was one day walking, Safina signifiying a boat. An Nawawi.

4 Abu Abdullah Muhammad b. Yahya b. Haban, died at Medina A.D. 739, at the age of 74 An. Naw.

Abu Bakr, "Lay thy stone by the side of my stone;" then he said to Omar "Lay thy stone by the side of the stone of Abu Bakr;" then he said to Othman, "lay thy stone by the side of the stone of Omar." Then he said "These shall be the Caliphs after me."

Abu Zarah says that his authorities are not unreliable, and indeed al Hakim has recorded it in his Mustadark and al-Bayhaki has confirmed it in his "Proofs" and others besides these two. I remark that there is no contradiction between it and the saying of Omar and Ali that *the Prophet* did not name a successor, for the meaning of these two is that at the time of his death, he did not lay down an authoritative injunction for the succession of any *particular* one, and this other refers to what occurred at a period antecedent, for it is similar to a saying of the Prophet in another tradition, "Obey my law, and the law of the Caliphs after me, the orthodox, the rightly guided," and to his saying, "Follow those after me Abu Bakr and Omar" and others from among the traditions referring to the Caliphate.

On the Imams being of the Kuraysh, and the Caliphate being the prerogative of these.

Abu Dauud at Tayalisi[1] in his collection of traditions has recorded from Abu Barzah[2] that the Prophet said- "The Imams *shall be* of the Kuraysh, as long as they shall rule and do justice and promise and fulfil and pardon is implored of them and they are compassionate." And at Tirmidi[3] from Abu Hurayrah[4] that the

1 Abu Dauud Sulayman a Persian by birth resident at Basrah, died A.D. 818. Ibn Khall.

2 Abu Barzah Nazlah b. Ubayd one of the Companions who fought by Muhammads he in seven engagements, died during the campaign in Khurasan 684. Ibn Hajr.

3 Abu Isa Muhammad called after his birthplace Tirmid on the banks of the Oxus. He is one of the six great traditionists, died A.D. 892.

4 A well-known Companion of Muhammad, his real name is a subject of dispute Ibn Hajr places his death in A.H. 59.

apostle of God said; "the sovereignty shall rest in the Kuraysh and Judicial authority with the Auxiliaries, and calling to prayers with the Abyssinians." And Imam Ahmad in his Musnad from Utbah b. Abdan that the Prophet said: "The Caliphate *shall rest* in the Kuraysh and judicial authority with the Auxiliaries and the office of calling to prayer with the Abyssinians." His authorities are trustworthy. Al Bazzar has recorded from Ali Ibn Abi Talib that the apostle of God said: "The princes *shall be* of the Kuraysh; the just among them rulers of the just, and the wicked, rulers of the wicked."

The Imam Ahmad[1] has related on the authority of Safinah that he heard the Apostle of God say: "The Caliphate *shall last* for thirty years and after it, shall follow a monarch." The learned say that in these thirty years are included only the four Caliphs and the reign of al Hasan. And al Bazzar from Abu Ubaydah b-ul[2] Jarrah that the Prophet said "Your religion began with the prophetic mission and in clemency : it shall continue with the Caliphate and in clemency; then shall follow monarchy and despotism." A reliable tradition. Abdullah b. Ahmad records on the authority of Jabir b. Samurah from the Prophet that he said; "This rule shall continue in honour, *its holders* overcoming all that oppose them therein, up to twelve Caliphs, all of them of the Kuraysh." The two Shaykhs and others have recorded this and there are other lines of ascription and readings of it; among them-"this rule shall continue secure," and "this rule shall remain in force"- and, according to Muslim, "the rule over the people shall continue in force until twelve men shall have ruled them;" and also according to him "this authority shall not come to an end until twelve Caliphs shall have passed away in it from among the people,"- and "Islam shall continue

1 The Imam Abu Abdullah Ahmad as Shaybani al Marwazi (native of Marw) was the son of Muhammad b. Hanbal, born at Baghdad A.H. 164 (A.D. 780), a traditionist of the first class. It is said he knew by heart a million of these traditions, al Bukhari and Muslim were his disciples. His persistence in refusing to declare the Qurãn created is well-known. He died at Baghdad A.H. 241 (855).

2 Abu Ubaydah commonly called the son of al Jarrah-but incorrectly according to Ibn Hajr and an Nawawi who maintain that his father was Abdullah and his grandfather al Jarrab.

revered and unassailable until *there shall have been* twelve Caliphs;" and according to al Bazzar, "the sway of my people shall continue to abide until twelve Caliphs, all of them of the Kuraysh shall have passed away"- and according to Abu Dauud there is an addition; "and when he returned to his house, there came to him the Kuraysh and they said, "then what will follow?" He replied, "there will follow sedition." And also according to him, "This faith shall continue to abide until twelve Caliphs shall have been over you, upon all of whom the people shall be gathered together:" and according to Ahmad and al Bazzar from Ibn Masaud who was asked, "How many of the Caliphs shall rule this people?" He replied: "We asked the Apostle of God concerned them, and he answered "Twelve, like unto the number of the chiefs of the children of Israel." Kadhi Iyadh says that the meaning of the twelve Caliphs in this tradition and in those resembling it, is perhaps this, that they would flourish during the period of the glory of the Caliphate and the vigour of Islam, and the integrity of its government, and the gathering of the people around him who assumed the vicegerency, and these *conditions* were found in those round whom the people gathered until the away of the children of Umayyah was troubled and discord fell among them in the reign of Walid b. Yazid, and thus it continued among them until arose the Abbaside power and they overthrew their sovereignty."

The Shaykhul Islam Ibn Hajr in the "Commentary on al Bukhari says;"-the words of the Kadhi Iyadh are the best that have been uttered on this tradition, and the most important, on account of their confirmation of his remark on some of the lines of ascription of the authentic tradition, "upon all of whom the people shall be gathered together:" and the elucidation of this is, that the meaning of gathering together, is their submission to do him homage, and this very thing came to pass, for the people gathered round Abu Bakr, then Omar, then Othman, then Ali until occurred the affair of the "two

Arbitrators" at Siffin,[1] and Muawiyah assumed the Caliphate from that day.

Then the people gathered round Muawiyah at the time of the treaty with al Hasan: then they united upon his son Yazid and the authority of all Husayn was never established-nay-he was killed before its accomplishment. Then when Yazid died, discord fell among them until they gathered round Abdul Malik b. Marwan, after the death of Ibn us Zubayr. Then they gathered round his four sons, al Walid, and Sulayman, and Yazid and Hisham; and between Sulayman and Yazid, there intervened Omar b. Abdil Aziz. These, therefore, are seven, after the orthodox Caliphs, and the twelfth is Walid b. Yazid b. Abdil Malik, round whom the people gathered when Hisham, his father's brother died. He reigned about four years. The they rose up against him and slew him and dissension prevailed and things were changed from that day, and it never happened after that, that the people gathered round any Caliph, for the reign of Yazid b. Walid, the same who rose against his cousin al Walid b. Yazid was not long : for there marched against him before he died, the son of his father's uncle, Marwan b. Muhammad b. Marwan. When Yazid died, his brother Ibrahim reigned but Marwan slew him; thereupon the sons of Abbas made war upon Marwan until he was slain. Then the first of the Caliphs of the children of Abbas was a Saffah, but his reign was not protracted by reason of the multitude of those who went out against him. Then his brother al Mansur held sway, and his reign was long but the remote west passed away from them through the conquest of Spain by the deseendants of Marwan, and it continued in their hands predominant over it, until they afterwards assumed the Caliphate-and things came to such a pass that nothing remained of the Caliphate in the provinces but the name, after it had been that in the time of the children of Abdul Malik b. Marwan, the Khutbah was read in the name of the Caliphs in all the regions of the earth, the east and the

1 Abu Musa Ashari on the part of Ali and Amr bul Aas on the part of Muawiyah. The plain of Siffin, says Gibbon, which extends along the western bank of the Euphrates, is determind by D'Anville (I' Euphrate et le Tigre, p.29) to be the Campus Barbarius of Procopius.

west, the right hand and the left, wherever the true believer had been victorious, and none in any one of all the provinces, was appointed to hold a single office, except by order of the Caliph.

Regarding the immoderate lengths to which things went, verily in the fifth century in Spain alone, there were six persons who assumed the title of Caliph and together with them, a descendant of Ubaydullah ruler in Egypt and an Abbasi in Baghdad, exclusive of those who claimed the Caliphate in the regions of the earth, of the descendants of Ali and the schismatics." He adds, "perhaps this interpretation is the meaning of the *Prophets* words "thee will follow sedition," that is, slaughter arising from sedition openly occurring and continuous, and such actually occurred. And it has been also said that the meaning of it is, the appearance of the twelve Caliphs during the whole duration of Islam until the day of judgement, acting according to the truth, although their reigns may not follow in succession one after another; and this confirms what has been recorded by Musaddad in his Musnad-i-Kabir from Abul Khuld who says, "This people shall not perish until there shall have been from among them, twelve Caliphs, all of them labouring in the way of salvation and the true faith, and among them, two shall be of the family of Muhammad." According to this, therefore, the meaning of his words "there will follow sedition" is, the troubles foretelling the resurrection by the coming of Dajjal and the issue thereof - (here he ends)." I observe that according to this, of the twelve Caliphs, are accounted for the four and al Hasan and Muawiyah and Omar Ibn Abdil Aziz : these are eight and it is probable that there may be added to them, al Muhtadi of the House of Abbas, for he is among them what Omar b. Abdil Aziz is, among the children of Umayyah, and in the same way, ad Dhahir,[1] on account of what was vouchsafed unto him of rectitude of conduct, and there remain two who are to be awaited, one among them al Mahdi, for he is of the family of Mahammad, upon whom be the blessing and peace of God.

1 Ad Dhahir biamrillah.

On the traditions premonitory of Caliphate of the children of Umayyah.

At Tirmidi relates on the authority of Yusuf b. Saad that a man stood up before al Hasan the son of Ali, after he had sworn allegiance to Muawiyah, and said, "Thou hast blackened the faces of the true believers," and he replied "Reproach me not, may the Lord have mercy on them, for the Prophet saw the children of Umayyah on his pulpit, and it troubled him: then was revealed to him "Verily we have given thee al Kauthar"[1] and there was *also* revealed to him" we sent down *the Qurãn* on a night of power and what shall make thee understand *how excellent* the night of power *is:* the night of power is greater than a thousand months"[2] "in which the children of Umayyah shall possess the Caliphate, O Muhammad." Al Kasim says, "I have computed and lo ! it is a thousand months, no more and no less." At Tirmidi says "this but once recorded tradition, I know only from the tradition of al Kasim who is reliable but his master is unknown." Al Hakim has given this tradition in his Mustadrak *(Supplement)* and Ibn Jarir in his Commentary-but the Hafidh Abul Hajjaj and Ibn Kathir say that it is unreliable.

Ibn Jarir[3] in his Commentary has related on the authority of the grandfather of Abu Sahl that he said, "the Apostle of God saw the children of al Hakam b. Abil Aas leap upon his pulpit with the leap of apes, and that troubled him and the never brought himself to smile until his death, and God revealed to him concerning it, "We have appointed the vision which we showed thee only for an occasion of dispute unto men."[4] The authorities are weak, but there

---

1 Qur. VIII-Al Kauthar is a stream in Paradise-the word signifies "abundance of good." Hence the gift of wisdom. See Sale.

2 Qur. XVIII-the concluding sentence is not in the Qurãn.

3 Abu Jaafar Muhammad b. Jarir at Tabari is the author of a great Commentary on the Qurãn and a famous history. He was a master of the highest authority (Imam) on various branches of knowledge, such as tradition, jurisprudence and the like-born A.H. 224 (838-9) at Amul in Tabaristan and died at Baghdad A.H. 310 (A.D. 923) Ibn Khall.

4 Qur. XVII. This verse is generally supposed to refer to the prophet's journey of heaven, which was the occasion of much dispute amongst his followers until confirmed by the testimony of Abu Bakr. See Sale.

are concurring testimonies from the traditions of Abdullah b. Omar, and Yala b. Murrah, Husayn b. Ali and others. I have quoted it with its authorities in the Commentary and Musnad, and alluded to it in my work, the "Reasons of Revelation.

On the traditions annunciatory of the Caliphate of the children of Abbas.

Al Bazzar has related from Abu Hurayrah that the Apostle of God said to Abbas- "in ye shall rest prophecy and sovereignty :" and at Tirmidi from Ibn Abbas, that the Apostle of god said to Abbas, "when it shall be the morning of the second day, come to me, thou and thy son, that I may invoke upon *thy descendants* a blessing by which, may God profit thee and thy son;" and he went at dawn and I went with him and he clothed us with a mantle ; then he said, "O Lord! vouchsafe unto Abbas and unto his son, an outward and inward mercy ; leave them not in sin ; O Lord, preserve him in his son." Thus has at Tirmidi quoted it in his "Jami," and Razin[1] al Abdari has added to the end of it, "and make the Caliphate abiding in his posterity." I observe that this tradition, and that which precedes it, are the best that have come down on this subject.

At Tabarani[2] records that the Apostle of God said, "I saw *in vision* the children of Marwan taking possession of my pulpit, one

---

1 Abul Hasan Razin b. Muawiyah b. Ammar a member of the tribe of Abdud Dar, a native of Saragossa in Spain, was Imam to the Maliki school at Mecca. His work is generally desiguated Kitab I Razin, in which he assembled and classed all the traditions contained in the Sahih of al Bukhari, and Muslim, the Muwatta of Malik, the Jami of at Tirmidi and the Sunan of Abu Dauud, died at Mecca A.H. 525 (A.D. 1130). Ibn Khall. De Slane.

2 Abul Kasim Sulayman b. Ahmad of the tribe of Lakhm, the chief Hafidh of his time-born at Tabariya in Syria and having settled at Ispahan continued there till his death on Saturday 28th of Dul Kaadah A.H. 360 (September A.D. 971) at the age of about one hundred. His Dictionary (Mujam) of the traditionists is the best known of his works, the large (kabir), small (saghir) and medium (ausat) editions of which are frequently alluded to. Ibn Khall.

after another, which troubled me, and I saw the children of Abbas taking possession of my pulpit one after another and that gladdened me:" and Abu Nuaym[1] in his Huliyah, from Abu Hurayrah, that the Apostle of God came forth, and there met him Abbas and he said, "Shall I not give thee good tidings, O father of excellence?" who replied 'Yes, O Apostle of God," and he said. "Verily God hath begun this authority with me and will fulfil it in thy posterity." (The ascription is unreliable.) There has also come down a tradition of Ali's on authorities still weaker than this, quoted by Ibn Asakir[2] from the ascription of Muhammad b. Yunas al Karimi (and he was a fabricator of traditions) up to Ali, that the Apostle of God, said to Abbas. "Verily God hath begun this authority with me and will fulfil it in thy posterity." And the same has been handed down in the tradition of Ibn Abbas quoted by al Khatib[3] in his history, and the reading of *as follows*: "With ye shall begin this authority and in ye shall it be fulfilled," and this will appear with its ascription in the life of al Muhtadi billah. It has also come down in the tradition of Ammar b. Yasir, quoted by al Khatib, and Abu Nuaym records in the Huliyah on the authority of Jabir b. Abdullah, that the Apostle of God said; "there shall be kings of the posterity of Abbas, who shall be the rulers of my people; my God glorify the faith through them." Also in his "Proofs" from Ummul Fadhl[4] who said "I was passing by the Prophet when he exclaimed - "verily thou art pregnant of a boy and

---

1 Hafidh Abu Nuaym Ahmad b. Abdullah author of the حليه الاولياء or ornament of the Saints "containing the lives of the principal Muslim Saints, born in Rajab 386 (A.D. 948 and died at Ispahan in Safar 430 (A.D. 1038). Ibn Khall.

2 Abul Kasim Ali, surnamed Thikatuddin, a native of Damascus and chief traditionist of Syria who acquired a superiority in that science that no other hand over attained, born A.H. 499. (1105) died at Damascus A.H. 571 (A.D. 1176). Ibn Khall.

3 Hafidh Abu Bakr Ahmad b. Ali known as Alkhatib or the preacher a native of Baghdad who composed a history of the city and is the author of nearly one hundred works. Though a doctor of law, he made tradition his principal study, born A.H. 392 (A.D. 1002) and died A.H. 463 (A.D. 1071). Ibn Khall.

4 The "Mother of Excellence," the name of the wife of Abbas and also of his daughter, the former is here meant.

when thou givest him birth, then bring him to me," and when I gave birth to him, I went to the Prophet and he called out the Adan in his right ear, and the[1] Ikamah in his left, and he made him drink of his spittle and named him Abdullah and said *to me* "depart with the Father of the Caliphs." I made this known to Abbas and he spoke of it to the Apostle who said, "he is what she told you; he is the Father of the Caliphs among who, shall be as Saffah and among whom shall be al Mahdi, and among whom shall be one who shall pray together with Jesus the Son of Mary, upon Him to peace."

Ad Daylami[2] in his Musnadul Firdaus has related from Aysha a tradition ascribed to the Prophet- "It shall come to pass that the children of Abbas shall posses a standard, and it shall not depart from their hands as long as they shall uphold righteousness." And Darakutni[3] in his "Afrad" from Ibn Abbas that the Prophet said to Abbas, "When thy posterity shall inhabit the Sawwad[4] and clothe themselves in black and their follower shall be the people of Khurasan, dominion shall not cease to abide with them until they resign it unto Jesus, the Son of Mary." Ahmad b. Ibrahim is a worthless authority and his master is unknown and the tradition is so little reliable that Ibnul Jauzi[5] has mentioned it in his "Fabrications"-but there is evidence for it in a tradition ascribed to

---

1 The Ikamah is a sentence which is said after the conclusion of the Adan or call to prayer and which announces that prayers have begun. This ceremons is still occasionally performed at the birth of a child –but is not obligatory.

2 Abu Shujaa Shiruyiah b. Shahrdar b. Shiruyiah b. Fanna Khusran of Hamadan ad Daylami. He was the Author of a history of Hamadan and the "Musnadul Firdaus." Hafidh Yahya b. Mandah says of him that though fairly well read, his knowledge of traditions was imperfect, and he could not distinguish between goes and untrust-worthy ones and therefore his Firdaus is full of idle tales, died .A.H. 509 Bustanul Muhaddithin,

3 Abul Hasan Ali b. Omar. A Hafidh of great learning and a Shafii doctor, was a native of Baghdad-the name Darakutni means belonging to Darul Kutn (Cotton house) a quarter of Baghdad, born A.H. 306 (A.D. 919) and died A.H. 385 (A.D. 995).

4 The towns and villages of Babylonian Iraq.

5 Abul Faraj Ibnul Jauzi a celebrated preacher and doctor of the Hanbalites. His compositions are so numerous that it is said (cont)

the Prophet, quoted by at Tabarani in the "Kabir"- "the Caliphate shall abide among the children of my paternal uncle, and of the race of my father, until they deliver it unto the Messiah." (Ad Daylami has quoted it from Ummi Salimah[1] with a different ascription).

Al Ukayli[2] records in his book of "Invalid authorities," a tradition ascribed to the Propeht "the children of Abbas shall reign two days for every day in which the children of Umayyah shall reign, and two months for every month." Ibnul Jauzi has quoted this in his 'Fabrications' and has invalidated it on account of the *untrustworthiness of* Bakkar,[3] but it is not as he has said, for verily, Bakkar should not be accused of falsehood nor fabrication; moreover Ibn Adi says of him, that he is among the doubtful authorities whose traditions are recorded, and has added 'I hope there is no harm in *accepting* him *as an authority ;"* and on my life, the purport of this tradition is not far *from the truth,* for the Abbaside rule, at the time of its splendour, and the extension of its authority throughout the countries of the earth, towards the rising and the setting sun, besides the remote west, may be placed between the year one hundred and thirty and odd and the year 290 when al Muktadir reigned, and in his time, its organisation was broken up, and the whole west seceded from its sway : then followed dissension

---

(cont- 18) (with some exaggeration) that he wrote 180 pages a day; and the parings of his pens were gathered up into a heap and in pursuance of his last orders, were employed to heat the water with which his corpse was washed. Born about A.H. 508 (1114-5), died at Baghdad A.H. 597 (A.D. 1281). His "Fabricated Traditions" –is in 4 Vols. Ibn Khall. Saadi of Shiraz mentions him in the Gulistan as having counseled him to forego profane music, the neglect of which advice was avenged on the sensitive ears of the poet, at a convivial meeting as therein related.

1 One of the Prophets wives.

2 De Slane so writes the name, but in a note (Vol. IV, p. 199), he remarks that according to Ibn Duraid, عقيل should be pronounced Akil. This is so in respect of the son of Abu Talib and Akil b. Mukarrin the Companion, but Ukayl was the eponymous ancestor of a branch of the Hawazin who were of the tribe of Kays. See the Muntahal Arab.

3 One of the authorities in the line of ascription.

and trouble in his government and after him, as will appear. Thus the period of the glory of their sovereignty and their dominion was about 160 years, and that is double the reign of the illustrious children of Umayyah for that lasted 92 years, from which *must be deducted* nine years, during which, the authority was vested in Ibnuz Zubayr: thus there remains 83 years and a fraction and that is a thousand months exactly and so I have afforded confirmation of the tradition.

Az Zubayr b. Bakkar[1] records in his 'Muwaffakiyat, from Ibn Abbas, that he said to Muawiyah "ye shall not reign a day, but we shall reign two, and not a month but we shall reign two months, and not a year but we shall reign two years:" and, "the black standards shall be for us, the people of the *Prophetical* House," and, "their overhrow shall not come save from the side of the west." Ibn Asakir relates in his history of Damascus from Ibn Abbas[2] that the Apostle of God said to him "O God, defend Abbas and the son of Abbas," and he said this three times : then he exclaimed, "O uncle, dost thou not know, that al Mahdi shall be of thy descendants, - prospered of God, happy, and approved. "(al Karimi[3] is a fabricator). Ibn Saad records in his Tabakat (classes) from Ibn Abbas, that al Abbas the son of Abdul Muttalib, sent to the children of Abdul Muttalib, and he gathered them together about him and Ali held a place in his estimation which no other possessed, and al Abbas said- "O son of my brother, verily I have formed an opinion and I do not wish to determine anything regarding it until I have sought counsel of thee ;" then Ali said- "What is it?" He replied. "Go to

---

1 Abu Abdullah az Zubayr, a member of the tribe of Kuraysh. He was Kadhi of Mecca and composed the genealogies of the Kuraysh, a standard authority on the subject. He also taught traditions and died at Mecca. A.H. 256 (A.D. 870) aged 84. Ibn Khall. He named the book mentioned in the text after his son al Muwaffak to whom he dedicated it. Masudi Tome VII. p. 91.

2 Abul Abbas Abdullah son of Abbas uncle of Muhammad, born three years before the Hijrah. He was considered the ablest interpreter of the Qurãn of his day and the most learned in the traditions, the legal decisions of the first three Caliphs, the law, and the sciences of poetry and arithmetic. Appointed governor of Basrah by the Caliph Ali, died at Taif A.H. 68 (A.D. 687) aged 70. Ibn Khall. De Slane.

3 Al Karimi is one of the authorities in the line of ascription.

the Prophet and ask of him, in whom shall rest this authority after him and if it rest in us, we shall not resign it, by Allah, while there remaineth of us a chief upon the earth, and if it rest in other than us, we shall never seek it." Ali said, "O uncle, in whom shall abide this authority save in thee, and will any contend with you regarding this authority ?"

Ad Daylami in his Musnadul Firdaus, records a tradition ascribed to the Prophet "When God Willeth to form any one for the Caliphate, he toucheth his forehead with his right hand."

On the dignity of the Prophetic mantle which the Caliphs wore in succession to the very last.

As Silafi,[1] in his Tuyuriyat, has quoted, with its ascription to al Asmai,[2] on the authority of Ibn Amr bil Ala, that when Kaab b-uz Zubayr read out beforc the Prophet his poem *beginning* Banat Suad,[3] he threw to him the mantle that was upon him ; and when Muawiyah reigned, he wrote to Kaab *saying*, "sell me the mantle

---

1 Abul Tahir Ahmad, called as Silafi after his grandfather, from the Persian (Sehlabi three lips-he received this name as one of his lips was split and appeared double. He was a Hafidh an taugh traditions and was appointed President of the College called after him, founded in A.H. 546. (1151) by al Aadil as Sallar at Alexandria : born at Ispahan 472 A.H. (1079) and died A.H. 576 (1180). Ibn Khall. The printed edition has Turyat for Tuyuriyat.

2 Abu Said Abdul Malik the celebrated philologer, a native of Basrah, but removed to Baghdad in the reign of Harunur Rashid. He was a complete master of the Arabic language and was consulted by al Mamun on all doubtful points of literature; for his numerous treatises, consult Ibn Khall, born A.H. 122 (740). Died at Basrah 216 (813).

3 This well-known poem was recite before Muhammad on the poets embracing Islam. He had written some satirical verses on the Prophet, who in consequence ordered his followers to put him to death if thy caught him. Kaab not caring to indulge his wit at the expense of his life, made his submission. The poem begins with the praise of his mistress Suad and ends with an entreaty of pardon.

of the Apostle of God for ten thousand dirhams," but he refused and when Kaab died, Muawiyah sent to his children *an offer* of twenty thousand dirhams, and he received from them the mantle the same which was in the possession of the Caliphs of the House of Abbas, and this has been related by others. But ad Dahabi says in his history ; "regarding the mantle in the possession of the Caliphs of the House of Abbas, verily Yunas-b. Bukary relates from the account of the expedition of Tabuk of Ibn Ishak, that the Prophet gave a mantle to the people of Aylah,[1] with his letter, the same that he wrote to them granting them immunity and Abul Abbas as Saffah purchased it for 300 dinars." I remark that which Muawiyah bought was lost in the decline of the House of Umayyah. The Imam Ahmad b. Hambal records in his "Zuhd" from Urwah bus Zubayr[2] that the garment in which the Apostle of God went out to meet deputations was a mantle from Hadhramaut, its length four cubits, and its breadth two cubits and a span, which was in the possession of the Caliphs and it became thread bare, and they lined it with stuffs *and* it used to be worn on the festivals of Adha and Fitr. Verily this mantle was in the possession of the Caliphs, and they inherited it in succession and wore it upon their shoulders, on state occasions, *whether* in assembly or mounted cavalcade, and it was upon al Muktadir when he was slain, and was stained with his blood, and I think it was lost during the irruption of the Tartars-'for we belong to God and unto him shall we return." (Qur II).

---

1 On the Red Sea, the Elana of Ptolemy.

2 Abu Abdullah, one of the seven great jurisconsults of Medina. His father a Zubyr b. Awwam was one of the ten Companions to whom Muhammad promised Paradise. His mother was Asma-d. of Abu Bakr-born A.H. 2 (642-3), died A.H. 93 (711-2). Ibn Khall.

On some observations which occur scattered throughout these biographies, but the mention of which here in one place is most suitable and advantageous.

Ibnul Jauzi narrates that according to as Suli,[1] it is said that every sixth *Caliph* who ruled over the people was deposed, and adds "I reflected on this and observed it with wonder. The supreme authority was vested in our Prophet ; then there arose Abu Bakr, and Omar and Othman and Ali and al Hasan-and he was deposed. Then Muawiyah and Yazid b. Muawiyah and Muawiyah b. Yazid and Marwan, and Abdul Malik b. Marwan and Ibnuz Zubayr and he was deposed. Then al Walid and Sulayman and Omar b. Abdil Aziz and Yazid and Hisham and al Walid and he was deposed. After this the dominion of the House of Umayyah ceased, and as Saffah reigned, and al Mansur and al Mahdi and al Hadi and ar Rashid and al Amim and he was deposed. Then al Mamun and al Muatasim and al Wathik and al Mutawakkil and al Muntasir and al Mustain and he was deposed. Then al Muatazz and al Muhtadi, and al Mautamid and al Muatadhid and al Muktafi and al Muktadir and he was deposed, and again a second time and then put to death. Then al Kahir and ar Radhi and al Muttaki and al Mustakfi and al Mutii and at Taii and he was deposed. The al Kadir and al Kaim and al Muktadi and al Mustadhir and al Mustarshid and ar Rashid and he was deposed." This is the end of the narration of Ibul Jauzi Ad Dahabi says that what al Jauzi has mentioned is defective in several points. One of them is his statement, that Abdul Malik was succeeded by Ibnuz Zubayr, but this was not the case, for Ibnuz Zubayr was fifth and after him came Abdul Malik. Either both of them most be fifth, or one was the true Caliph and the other a rebel, for unto Ibnuz Zubayr was sworn a prior allegiance, and therefore the Caliphate of Abdul Malik was legally established only from the time whom Ibnuz Zubayr was killed. The second point is,

---

1 Abu Bakr as Suli known as the chess-player. He was an accomplished scholar and traditionist. He became one of the Caliph ar Radhis boon Companions and was intimate with al Muktafi and al Muktadir. He composed numerous works ; the chief science he cultivated was biography, died at Basrah A.H. 335 (A.D. 986-7). Ibn Khall.

his omitting to count Yazid An Nakis and his brother Ibrahim who was deposed and Marwan; for thus computing them, al Amin would be the ninth. I remark that it has already been said, that Marwan falls out of the account, because he was a rebel, and also Muawiyah b Yazid, for allegiance was sworn to Ibnuz Zubayr after the death of Yazid, and Muawiyah opposed him in Syria : these two are therefore one, and the authority of Ibrahim, he who succeed Yazid An Nakis was not completely established, for some acknowledged him as Caliph, and others did not so acknowledge him ; and there were some who claimed for him the supreme power, but not the Caliphate, and he ruled but for forty or seventy days. Therefore according to this computation, Marwan the Ass,[1] was the sixth, for he was the twelfth from Muawiyah, and al Amin after him, the sixth. Thirdly, the deposals are not confined to every sixth, for al Muatazz was deprived of office and likewise al Kahir, al Muttaki and al Mustakfi. I reply that *his statement* is not affected by this *objection* because the meaning is, that as *regards* every sixth, the deposal is undoubted, but he does not deny that there were others besides them who were deposed as well. He adds in addition to what Ibnul Jauzi has stated, that after ar Rashid, reigned al Muktafi and al Mustanjid and al Mustadhii, and an Nasir and al Dhahir and al Mustansir who was the sixth but was not deposed. Then al Mustasim, and he was the same whom the Tartars slew, and was the last of the sovereign Caliphs. The Caliphate was interrupted subsequently for three years and a half ; then al Mustansir afterwards was elected, but the did not actually assume the Caliphate, for he was acknowledged in Egypt and he marched into Iraq and encountered the Tartars and was killed likewise, and the Caliphate remained in abeyance a year. Then it was established in Egypt, and the first of the Caliphs was al hakim, then al Mustakfi,

1 "Before his accession to the throne" says Gibbon "he had deserved by his Georgian warfare, the honorable epithet of the Ass of Mesopotamia. He had been governor of Mesopotamia and the Arabic proverb praises the courage of that warlike breed of asses who never fly from an enemy. The surname of Mervan may justify the comparisen of Homer (Iliad a. 557) and both will silence the moderns who consider the ass a stupid and ignoble emblem."

then al Wathik, then al Hakim, then al Muatadhid, them al Mutawakkıl who was the sixth and was deposed. Then reigned al Muatasim but he was deposed after fifteen days and al Mutawakkil recalled. He was again deposed and al Wathik acknowledged : then al Muatasim and he was deposed, and al Mutawakkil recalled who continued to reign until his death. Next al Mustain, and al Muatadhid and al Mustakfii, then al kaim, who was the sixth from al Muatasim the first (who was also al Muatasim the second) and he was deposed. Then al Mustanjid the reigning Caliph, the fifty first of the Caliphs of the House of Abbas.

Note : It is said that the House of Abbas is *distinguished by* a beginning, a middle, and an end-The beginning was al Mansur, the middle al Mamun and the end al Muatadhid. The Caliphs of the House of Abbas, were all of them the children of concubines, except as saffah, al Mahdi and al Amin, and no Hashimite, the son of a Hashimite woman, ever ruled the Caliphate except. Ali b. Abi Talib and his son al Hasan, and al Amin (so says as Suli)-and no one whose name was Ali ever held the Caliphate except Ali the sone of Abu Talib and Ali al Muktafi (Ad Dahabi). I remark that the greater number of the names of the Caliphs occur but once, and few twice, and those most frequently recurring are Abdullah, Ahmad and Muhammad,-and all the surnames of the Caliphs occur singly up to al Mustasim, the last of the Caliphs of Iraq-Then recur the surnames of the Caliphs of Egypt-thus al Mustansir recurs, and al Mustakfi, and al Wathik, and al Hakim, and al Muatadhid, and al Mutawakkil, and al Muatasim,[1] and al Mustain, and al Kaim, and al Mustanjid, All of these recur but once, except al Mustakfi and al Muatadhid which recur once oftener, for among the Abbaside Caliphs, three are called by those two names.

Not one of the Caliphs of the House of Abbas is distinguished by a surname of the House of Ubayd, except al Kaim, al Hakim, Ad Dhahir and al Mustansir, but *as regards* al Mahdi and al Mansur, the assumption of these surnames by the House of Abbas preceded the rise of the House of Ubayd. And some writers have mentioned

---

1 The text has Mustasim incorrectly. The MS. Is accurate in the name.

that none surnamed al Kahir was prosperous, either among the Caliphs or the temporal sovereigns and I add also, al Mustakfi and al Musta'in, by which *surnames* two of the House of Abbas were distinguished, and those two were deposed and expelled but al Muatadhid is among the most glorious of surname and the most blessed for him who was called by it. No one held the Caliphate after the son of his brothers, except al Mustakfi after ar Rashid, and al Mustansir after al Muatasim. Ad Dahabi states this, and adds, that no three brothers possessed the Caliphate, except the sons of ar Rashid, *viz.*, al Amin, al Mamun, and al Muatasim, and the sons of al Mutawakkil, *viz.,* al Mustansir, al Muatazz and al Muatamid, and the sons of al Muktadir, *viz.,* ar Radhi, al Muktafi and al Mutii. He continues, that four of the sons of Abdul Malik governed the state, and that no parallel to this is to be found, except among temporal sovereigns. I remark that a parallel case to it occurs among the Caliphs after the Prophet, for four, nay five of the sons of al Mutawakkil Muhammad, held the Caliphate, *viz.,* al Mustain, and al Muatadhid, and al Mustakfi, and al Kaim and al Mustanjid the reigning Caliph. No one ruled the Caliphate during the lifetime of his father except Abu Bakr as Siddik, and Abu Bakr at Taii b-ul Mutii, whose father was struck by paralysis and who voluntarily abdicated in favour of his son.

The learned say that the first who governed the Caliphate while his father was alive, was Abu Bakr, and he was the first who appointed a successor, and the first who instituted a public treasury and the first who named the Qurãn al Mushaf. The first who was called, prince of the Faithful, was Omar b-ul Khattab, and he was the first who made use of the scourge, and the first who established the date from the Flight, and the first who ordered the prayers called at Tarawih,[1] and the first who established the public registers.

The first who interdicted pasturage from encroachment, was Othman, and he was the first who assigned lands on feudal tenure,

1 A form of payer performed at some period of the night, in the month of Ramadhan, after the ordnary prayer of nightfall consisting of twenty or more rekahs, according to different persuasicus. Lane's Lex. Art. ترويحه

that is to say, the first who did so to any extent, and the first who made the addition of the call to prayer on Fridays, and the first who sanctioned an stipend for the eriers to prayers, and the first who was confused in speech while reading the Khutoah, and the first who appointed a chief Officer of Constabulary.

The first who during his lifetime named an heir to succeed him, was Muawiyah, and he was the first who introduced eunuchs into his service. The first who ever caused the heads *of criminals* to be brought before him was Abdullah b-uz Zubayr. The first who caused his name to be struck on the coinage, was Abdul Malik b Marwan. The first who prohibited his being addressed by name was al Walid b. Abdil Malik.

The first in roduction of surnames, was by the House of Abbas. Ibn Fadhlillah says that some think that the House of Umayyah had surnames similar to those of the House of Abbas. I remark that certain writers assert the surname of Muawiyah to have been an Nasir li dinillah, and the surname of Yazid, al Mustansir, and that of Muawiyah his son, ar - Raji ilil Hakk, and that of Marwan, al Mutamin billah and that of Abdul Malik, al Muwaffak li amrillah, and that of his son al Walid, al Muntakim billah, and that of Omar b. Abdil Aziz, al Masum billah, and that of Yazid b. Abdil Malik, al Kadir bi Sana illah, and that of Yazid an Nakis, as Shakir li anu'mi'llah.

The first time that public opinion became conflicting and disunited was in the reign of as Saffah. The first Caliph who gave access to astrologers and acted according to the judgments of the stars was al Mansur, and he was the first who employed slaves in offices of trust and gave them precedence over Arabs. The first who ordered the composition of polemical writings to refute the enemies *of the Faith* was al Mahdi. The first before whom men walked with swords and maces, was al Hadi. The First who played at polo in the open plain was ar Rashid. In the reign of al Amin, the caliph was first addressed by word and in writing, by his surname. Al Muatasim was the first who employed Turks in the office of the public registers. Al Mutawakkil was the first who ordered a distinguishing garb for Jews and Christians. The first whom the

Turks adjudged to death was al Mutawakkil : and from this is seen the confirmation of the Prophetical tradition as quoted by at Tabarani by a respectable line of ascription, from Ibn Masaud who stated that the Apostle of God said, "Molest not the Turks, as long as they leave ye unmolested, for verily they who shall first take from my people their kingdom and the things which the Lord hath conferred upon them, are the sons of Kantura."[1]

The first who invented large sleeves and diminished the size of the head-dress was al Mustain. Al Muatazz was the first Caliph who introduced ornaments of gold on riding animals. Al Muatamid was the first Caliph treated with severity and kept under restraint and guarded. The first who ruled the Caliphate among minors was al Muktadir. The last Caliph who kept the troops and public effects under his personal direction was ar Radhi, and he too was the last Caliph, whose poems were collected into a Diwan, and the last Caliph who uniformly read the Khutbah and prayed before the people, and the last Caliph who sat in company with boon companions, and the last Caliph whose expenses and gifts and rewards, retinue, and stipend, and treasury and meats and drinks and festal assemblies, and chamberlains, and *other* affairs *were conducted* after the manner of the early Caliphate, and he was the last Caliph who went journeying in garments like unto the Caliphs of former times.

The first time that surnames recurred was after the reign of al Mustansir, he who ruled after al Mustasim. *(This is mentioned* in the Awail of al Askari[2]). The first Caliph who reigned during his mother's lifetime, was Othman b. Affan, then al Hadi, and ar Rashid, and al Amin and al Mutawakkil, al Mustansir, al Mustain, al Mustazz

1 Banu Kantura. Turks or Nubians according to the Muntahalul Arab. Or as some say Kantura was the name of a slave of Abraham's, from whom the Turks are descended.

2 Al Hasan b. Abdillah b. Sahl. Abu Hilal al Askari, a disciple of Abu Ahmad al Askari ; author of a Commentary on the Qurãn in 5 Vols. : the Awail (Initions): a work on prose and verse, and another en Proverbs. A scholar of exemplary life. Died subsequently to the year 400 A.H. (1009). Tabakatul Mufassirin, as Suyuti Edit, Mearsinge. No. 29.

al Muatadhid and al Mutii'. No one held the Caliphate during the lifetime of his father, except Abu Bakr as Siddik, and to him may be added at Taii'.

As Suli says : "I know of no woman who gave birth to two Caliphs, except Wiladah, the mother of al Walid and as Sulayman, the two sons of Abdul Malik ; and Shahin, the mother of Yazid an Nakis and Ibrahim, the two sons of al Walid : and Khayzuran, the mother of al Hadi and ar Rashid." I remark, that there may be added, the mother of al Abbas and Hamzah, and the mother of Dauud and Sulayman, the children of the last Mutawakkil.

Those who assumed the title of Caliph, of the House of Ubayd, were fourteen : three in Africa, al Mahdi, al Kaim, and al Mansur, and eleven in Egypt, al Muizz, al Aziz, ad Dhahir, al Mustansir, al Mustali, al Amir, al Hafidh, ad Dhafir, al Faiz and al Aadhid. The beginning of their rule was in the year two hundred and ninety and odd, and its extinction in the year 567.

Ad Dahabi says that this may be called the Magian or the Jewish dynasty, but not *that* of the descendants of Ali, or the Batinite[1] not the Fatimite, and they were fourteen violaters of covenant not successors to the vicegerency, (here he ends).

Those who assumed the title of Caliph among the descendants of Umayyah in the West,[2] were in a better position than the descendants of Ubaydullah in many ways, *as regards* orthodoxy, and tradition and justice and merit, and knowledge, and battling and warring with infidels, and they were many in number, so that there

---

1 Ubaydullah, the founder of this dynasty, claimed descent from Ismail b. Jaafar the seventh Imam of the posterity of Ali, and his descendants are termed by the Oriental writers, the Ismailites of the West to distinguish them from another branch of the same race, the Ismailites of the East. These latter were the famous assassins, called also Batinis from their mystical interpretation of the Qurãn, under whose terrible daggers, the East crouched for two hundred years.

2 The Arabs termed Spain and Africa, indifferently, the West (AL Maghrab)- The word 'Afrikiya." Which they sometimes use, is not the whole but only a portion of al Maghrab. For its divisions, consult D'Herbelot.

were together at one time in Spain, six persons, each of them calling himself Caliph.

Some former writers have compiled histories of the Caliphs : among them, that by Niftawayh the Grammarian, in two volumes, up to the reign of al Kahir, and the Aurak of as Suli, in which he has mentioned the Abbasides only up to[1] -with which I am acquainted, and the history of the Caliphs by Abu'l Fadhl Ahmad b. Abi Tahir al Marwazi, al Katib one of the most excellent of poets who died in the year 280 A.H. ; and the history of the Abbaside Caliphs by Amir Abu Musa Harun b. Muhammad al Abbasi.

Al Khatib in his History, records with authorities from Muhammad b. Abbad that none of the Caliphs knew the Qurãn by heart, except Othman b Affan and al Mamun. I remark that, that restriction is not to pass unchallenged , for Abu Bakr knew it accurately also, and several *authors* have made this clear, among them an Nawami in his Tahdibul Asma ; and of Ali likewise it is handed down by one line *of tradition* that he had the whole of it by heart, after the death of the Prophet. Ibus Saai says- "I was present at the ceremony of allegiance sworn to the Caliph ad Dhahir, and he was seated at the window of a chamber in a white robe, and about him a cloak of camels hair, and upon his shoulders, the mantle of the Prophet : the wazir was standing in front of him upon a pulpit, and the Comptroller of the Household upon a step below him, and he was taking the covenant from the people : and the words of the covenant were, "I do homage to our lord and master the Imam, to whom obedience is a bounden duty upon all men, Abu Nasr Muhammad an Dhahir biamrillah according to the book of God, and the law of the Prophet and the decision of the prince of the faithful, and verily there is no Caliph but he."

---

1 The MS. has here a blank-the text inserts. الي قلت و As Suli died in A.H. 335 and as his History professes only to relate what he had himself seen (see Kashfud Dhunun), the blank might be filled up with the name of al Mutii li'llah who succeeded to the Caliphate in A.H. 334

Abu Bakr as Siddik

Abu Bakr as Siddik, the vicegerent of the apostle of God whose name is Abdullah b. Abi Kuhafah Othman, b Aamir, b Amr, b. Kaab, b. Saad, b. Taym, b. Murrah, b. Kaab, b. Luwayy, b. Ghalib, al Kurayshi, at Taymi, unites with *the genealogy* of the Apostle of God in Murrah."[1]

An Nawawi in his Tahdib says "What I have stated regarding the name of Abu Bakr being Abdullah, is correct, and well known. It is said also, that his name was Atik *(the Liberated)*, but the truth upon which all the learned are agreed, is that al Atik was his surname, not a name, and he was surnamed al Atik on account of his exemption from hell fire[2] as has come down in the tradition given by at Tirmidi : and it is also said, on account of the "Itakat" of his countenance, that is to say, its comeliness and its beauty. It is said likewise that there is nothing in his genealogy which can be found fault with. Musab b-uz Zubayr and others say, that the people concurred in naming him as Siddik *(Witness to the Truth),* because he hastened to testify to the Apostle of God, and steadfastly adhered to truth, and there never escaped from him on any one of the *many* events of *his life* any remissness or hesitation, and he held exalted

---

1 Murrah

Tamim	Kilab
Saad	Kusayy
Kaasb	Abd Manaf
Amr	Hashim
Aamir	Abdul Muttalib
Abu Kuhafa	Abdullah
Abu Bakr	Muhammad.

2 Nine others are included by Muhammad as sharing this distinction, Omar, Othman, Ali, Talhah, az Zubayr, Saad Ibn Abi Wakkas, Said, Abu Ubaydah, and Abdur Rahman b. Auf.

positions in Islam. Among those *events,* were his conduct regarding the Nocturnal journey, and his steadfastness and reply to the unbelievers regarding it, and his flight with the Apostle of God, and his forsaking his family and children, and his being with the Apostle in the cave, and throughout the whole journey : then his exhortations on the day of Badr, and the day of Hudaybiyah[1] when the delay in entering Mecca, was the occasion of grave doubts to others : then his weeping when the Apostle of God said "Verily, God hath given his servant a choice between this world and the next:" then his firmness on the day of the death of the Apostle of God, and his reading the Khutbah to the people and consoling them : then, in the contention regarding the oath of allegiance, his undertaking *the charge* for the good of the true believers : next, his diligence in despatching the army of Usamah b. Zayd to Syria, and his determination regarding it : then his rising up to oppose the apostates, and his dispute with the companions, until he overwhelmed them with arguments and God opened their hearts as He had opened his heart to *the understanding* of the truth, *viz.,* to do, battle with the apostates : then his fitting out the army for Syria for his conquests and sending it succour : lastly the conclusion of this *career* by an important action which was among the best of his good deeds, and most glorious of his titles to honour, and that was, his appointing Omar as his successor over the true believers : and what virtues, and dignities, and excellencies without number belong not to the Witness to the Truth?" (an Nawawi). I add that I am desirous of enlarging upon the biography of as Siddik to some extent, mentioning therein much of what I know of him regarding his life, and I shall arrange this in sections.

---

1 "Muhammad" says Sale "when at Hudaybiyah sent Jawwas b. Ommeyya the Khozaite to acquaint the Meccans that he was come with a peaceable intention to visit the temple, but they refusing to admit him, he sent Othman whom they imprisoned and a report ran that he was slain whereupon, Muhammad called his men about him and they took an oath to be faithful to him even to death."

Regarding his name and surname an allusion to which has already preceded.

Ibn Kathir[1] says, that all admit that his name was Abdullah b. Othman, except the narration of Ibn Saad on the authority of Ibn Sirin,[2] which *asserts* his name *to have been* Atik whereas the truth is that it was his surname. Then there is some disagreement as to the time of his being so surnamed, and the reason of it : for some say that it was on account of the "itakat" of his countenance that is, its beauty—but Abu Nuaym al Fadhl b. Dukayn says, that it was on account of his priority[3] in merit-and also it is said, on account of the nobility of his pedigree, that is its purity, as there is nothing in his lineage that can be accounted a stain, and it is said too that he was first so named and afterwards called Abdullah. At Tabarani relates from al Kasim b. Muhammad[4] that he questioned Ayesha as to the name of Abu Bakr, and she replied, "Abdullah:" then he said that the people called him Atik : she answered that Abu Kuhafah had three sons whom hc named Atik, answered that Abu Kuhafah had three sons whom he named Muatak, and Muaytak.

Ibn Mandah[5] and Ibn Asakir record on the authority of Musa b. Talhah that he said, "I asked my father Talhah, why Abu Bakr

---

1 The Hafidh Imaduddin Ismail b. Abdullah ad Damashki died in 774 A.H. The name of his well known history is the "Bidayah Wal Nihayah fit Tarikh"—the beginning and the end of history." Consult, Haj, Khal.

2 Abu Bakr Muhammad a native of Basrah. He was born A.H. 33. (A.D. 653-4) two years before the death of the Caliph Othman and died at Basrah. A.H. 110 (A.D. 729). He was a draper by profession, delivered traditions on the authority of Abu Hurayra and others and was skilled in the interpretation of dreams. Ibn Khall

3 Atik signifying also ancient, noble.

4 Grandson of Abu Bakr one of the most eminent of the Tabiis and of the seven great jurisconsults of Medina. Ibn Khall.

5 Abu Abdullah Mandah a celebrated traditionist and a Hafidh of high authority, author of a history of Ispahan, died A.H. 301, (A.D. 913-4). Ibn Khall.

was called Atik;" he replied, "his mother had no son surviving and when she gave him birth, she took him to the temple and exclaimed, 'O God! if this one is granted immunity from death, then bestow him upon me.'" At Tabarani records from Ibn Abbas, that he was called Atik, from the beauty of his countenances, and Ibn Asakir from Ayesha that she said "the name of Abu Bakr, that by which his family called him, was Abdullah, but the name of Atik superseded it"- and in one reading, "but the Prophet name him Atik."

Abu Yala[1] records in his Musnad (Likewise Ibn Saa'd and al Hakim) and confirms it on the testimony of Ayesha, that she said. "By Allah verily I was in my house on a certain day and the Apostle of God and his Companions were in the courtyard, and a curtain between me and them, and lo! Abu Bakr came up, and the Prophet said, "he who would rejoice in looking upon one exempted from hell fire, let him behold Abu Bakr," and verily his name, that by which his family called him was Abbullah but the name of Atik superseded it." And at Tirmidi and al Hakim from Ayesha, that Abu Bakr went to the Apostle of God and he said. "O ! Abu Bakr, thou art exempted by the Lord from hell fire," and from that day, he was called Atik. al Bazzar and at Tabarani record on good authority from Abdullah b-uz Zubayr, that the name of Abu Bakr was Abdullah, and the Apostle of God said to him "thou art exempted by the Lord from hell fire;" thus he received the name of Atik.

As regards as Siddik, it is said that he was so called in the time of ignorance, because he was distinguished for his *love of* truth. (Ibn Mandah[2]) ; and also because he hastened to certify to the truth of the Prophet with regard to what he announced.

---

1 Hafidh Abu Yala Ahmad author of a well know collection of traditions and of work on ascetic devotion and other subjects, born at Mosal A.H. 210 (826) died A.H. 307, (919-20). De Slane, I.K.

2 So the MS.; the text has Ibn Masada who was one of al Mamun's vizns, an elegant writer but not stated by Ibn Khallakan to be a traditionist.

Ibn Ishak[1] records on the authority of Hasan al Basri[2] and Katadah,[3] that the first time he was known by it was the morning after the "Nocturnal Journey." Al Hakim relates in his Mustadrark (Supplement) on the authority of Ayesha, that the idolaters went to Abu Bakr and said "What dost thou think of thy companion, who pretends that he was borns by night to Jerusalem?" He replied, "and did he say that?" They answered "Yes;" then he said "Verily he hath spoken the truth, and indeed I would testify to him in more than that, even to the announcement of *his journey to* Heaven, going in the morning and returing in the evening," and for this he was called the Witness to the Truth. (The authorities are good).

Said b Mansur narrates in his "Traditions" from Ibn Wahab, the freedman of Abu Hurayrah that when the Apostle of God returned on the night of his Nocturnal journey, he arrived at Du Tua[4] and said. "O! Gabriel, verily my people will not believe me.: He replied "Abu Bakr will testify to thee, for he is a Witness to the Truth."

Al Hakim in his Mustadrak, (Supplement) records on the authority of Nazal b. Sabrah that he tells us, "I said unto 'Ali, O

---

1 Muhammad b. Ishak b. Yasar the freedman of Kays b. Makhramah. Yasar was one of the prisoners taken al Aynut Tamr, sent by Khalid b. Walid to Abu Bakr at Medina. He is held by the majority of the learned to be a sure authority on tradition and his work the "Maghazi was Siyar (conquests and expeditions) bears a high character. He went to the Caliph Abu Jaafar al Mansur at Hira and put the Maghazi in writing for his use and the learned of Kufa heard him read and explain that work; ; died at Baghdad A.H. 151, (768). Ibn Khall.

2 Abu Said al Hasan of Basrah one of the most eminent of the Tabiis his mother was a slave of Umm Salimah one of the Prophet's wives. He was born at Medina two years before the death of the Caliph Omar and died al Basrah A.H. 110 (1128). Ibn Khall.

4 Katadah b. Dyama as Sadusi, a native of Basrah and one of the Tabiis, blind from birth, but of the greatest learning, much consulted by the Ummyyad family on points of history, genealogy and poetry, born A.H. 60. (679-80), died at Wasit A.H. 117, (735-6). Ibid.

5 A village near Mecca, not to be confounded with the valley of Tua or Tawn, according to Sale, where Moses saw the burning bush, (Qurãn XX.) consult Yakuqt Muaj. Bul.

Prince of the Faithful tell me of Abu Bakr." He replied "The Lord named that man as Siddik by the tongue of Gabriel and by the tongue of Muhammad. He was the vicegerent of the Apostle of God in Public prayers. He approved him for our spiritual concerns, and we have acquiesced in him for our worldly government." (The authorities for this are good). And Darakutni and al Hakim from Abu Yahya.[1] "It is beyond computation how often I have heard Ali say upon the pulpit that the Lord named Abu Bakr, as Siddik upon the tongue of Gabriel ;" and at Tabarani on good unexceptionable authorities from Hakim b. Saad, "I have heard Ali declare and confirm by oath, that God undoubtedly revealed from Heaven, the name of Abu Bakr as Siddik.

In the tradition relative to the Battle of Ohud, *the Prophet said,* "Be at peace for verily unto you there is *given* a Prophet, a witness to the truth and two mart rs."

The mother of Abu Bakr was the daughter of his father's uncle. Her name was Salma, the daughter of Sakhar, b. Aamir, b. Kaab and she received the surname of the "mother of goodness" (Ummul Khayr).

On his Nativity and place of birth.

He was born two years and some months after the birth of Muhammad for he died when he was sixty-three years of age. Ibn Kathir says, that what is recorded by Khalifah b-ul Khayyat,[2] on the authority of Yazid b-ul Asamm, *viz.,* that the Prophet said to Abu Bakr "Verily am I the greater or art thou?" and he replied

1 The MS. Has abul Hayya. There are no less than eleven of this name given by Ibn Hajr as being acquainted with Muhammad.

2 Abu Amr surnamed Shabab a native of Basrah and author of the Tabakat, was a Hafidh versed in history and of great talents. Al Bukhari gives traditions on authority, died A.H. 240. (A.D. 854-9). Consult, Ibn Khall-who omits the def. article before Khayyat.

"thou art greater, but I am older in years," is a tradition of an imperfect line of ascription and cited but by one authority, for the contrary is notorious, and indeed confirmed on the authority of Ibn Abbas.

His birthplace was Mecca which he never left except to trade, and he was that possessor of great wealth in his tribe, and a man of perfect generosity courtesy, and beneficence among them ; as Ibnul Dughannah says, "Verily thou art affectionate to thy kindred and speakest the truth in what thou narratest, and acquirest what others are denied and givest help in worldly troubles, and art hospitable to the stranger." An Nawawi says that he was one of the chiefs of the Kuraysh in the time of Ignorance, and one of their councillors, and beloved among them, and the wisest in *the direction of* their affairs : and when the true faith came, he chose it above all things and entered it with the most perfect submission.

Az Zubayr b. Bakkar and Ibn Asakir record on the authority of Maruf b. Kharrabud, that Abu Bakr as Siddik was one of ten amongst the Kuraysh to whom attached pre-eminence both in the time of Ignorance, and Islam : for upon him lay the settlement of blood-money and fines, and that was because the Kuraysh had no king upon whom the direction of all affairs might devolve : moreover in each tribe there existed a general jurisdiction exercised by its several chiefs, and to the Banu Hashim pertained the right of Sikayah and Rifadah,[1] the meaning of which is, that no one might eat or drink except of their food and their drink ; and to the Banu Abdud Dar, the office of door-deeper and guardian *of the Kaabah,* and the Banner and the Council, that is to say, no one might enter the Kaabah except with their permission, and when the Kuraysh fastened on the banner of war, the Banu Abdud Dar bound it for them, and

---

1 Rifadah was a contribution which the tribe of the Kuraysh made in the time of Ignorance, for the purpose of purchasing for the pilgrims, wheat and raisins for the beverage called. نبيذ. Each gave according to his ability, and thus they collected a great sum in the days of the assembling of the pilgrims. And they continued to feed the pilgrims until the end of those days ; the "Sikayah" was the supplying this beverage and Rafadah, these provisions. Lane.

when they assembled together for any purpose either to confirm or to annul, their gathering could not take place except in the Hall of Council and nothing could take effect, save *done* therein and it appertained to the Banu Abdud Dar.

Abu Bakr was the most abstinent of men in the time of Ignorance. Ibn Asakir records with accurate authorities from Ayesha; "by Allah, Abu Bakr never recited poetry,[1] whether in the time of ignorance of Islam, and indeed he and Othman forbore from wine *even* in the time of Ignorance ;" and Abn Nuaym records from her on excellent authority, "Verily Abu Bakr denied himself wine in the time of Ignorance:" and Ibn Asakir from Abdullah b-uz Zubayr, "Abu Bakr never recited a *verse;"* and from Abu illah b-uz Zubayr, "Abu Bakr never recited a *verse;"* and from Abul Aaliyah ar Riahi, that it was asked of Abu Bakr in an assembly of the Companions of the Apostle of God "didst then ever drink wine in the time of Ignorance?" he replied "God forbid," and they said, "why not?" He answered, "I sought to preserve my reputation and retain my decorum, and verily he who drinketh wine destroyeth his reputation and his decorum." The Narrator says that when this reached the apostle of God, he said," Abu Bakr hath spoken truly Abu Bakr hath spoken truly," twice. *This tradition* is wanting in regularity of transmission and is cited but by one authority *both as regards* authorities and the text.

---

1 The Qurãn though not directly forbidding yet discredits the profession of verse making. ما علمناه الشعر و لاينبغي له ."We have not taught (Muhammad) the art of poetry nor is it expedient for him, "Qur. XXXVI. Sale remarks that this was in answer to the infidels who pretended that the Qurãn was only a poetical composition. Again الشعرا يتبعهم الغارون Qur. XXVI. "Those err who follow the steps of the poets." But the learned have determind that moral, didactic and religious poetry is permissible. There are verses imputed to the great Shafii in which he doclares that were not men of his cloth prohibited from writing poetry, he would have surpassed Labid.

On his outward description

Ibn Saa'd relates on the authority of Ayesha that a man said to her, "describe to me Abu Bakr," and she replied, "he was a man of a very fair complexion, of slender build, thin cheeked and with a stoop ; he could not keep up his lower garments from slipping over his loins ; he was lean, with eyes deep set, his forehead prominent, and the backs of his hand fleshless. Such is his description. He states also on her authority, that Abu Bakr made use of the tinctures of hinna and katam; and on the authoirty of[2] Anas, that when the apostle of God went to Medina, there was none among the companions with grizzled hair, except Abu Bakr, and he dyed it with hinna and katam.

On his embracing the faith.

At Tirmidi, and Ibn Haban in his Sahih, (an thentic traditions) record on the authority of Abu Suid[3] al Khudir, that Abu Bakr said. "Have not I the greatest claim among men to it," that is, the Caliphate: "was not I the first to embrace the faith ? was it not I who did such a thing ? was it not I who did such *another* thing ?" And Ibn Asakir on the ascription of al Harith from Ali, that he said, "the first who embraced the faith among the men was Abu Bakr";

1 Lawsonia inermis, -the Katam is a herb which mixed with eypress is used as a tincture.

2 Abu Sulayt Anas b. Abi Anas, one of the Banu Najjar, he was a companion of Muhammad and fought on his side at Badr. De Slane I.K.

3 Abu Said Saad b. Malik of the tribe of Khudra a Companion and an Ansar of the third class. At the age of 13 he accompanied his father to Ohud who fell at that battle. The son accompanied Muhammad in twelve expeditions, died at Medina A.H. 74 (693-4). De Slane I.K.

and Khaythamah[1] on accurate authorities from Zayd b. Arkam,[2] "the first man who prayed with the Prophet, was Abu Bakr as Siddik" and Ibn Saa'd on the authority of Abu Arwa ad Dausi the Companion, that the first who embraced Islam was Abu Bakr as Siddik.

At Tabarani in his Kabir, and Abdulah b. Ahmad in the "Zawaidun Zuhd," record on the authority of as Shaabi[3] that he said, "I asked Ibn Abbas what man was the first *to embrace* Islam ?" he replied, "Abu Bakr as Siddiq. Hast thou not heard the words of Hassan[4] where he says ?

> "When thou rememberest the affliction of a faithful brother.
> Then remember too thy brother Abu Bakr and what he hath done.
> The best of men, the most pious and most just of them.
> Save the Prophet and the most faithful in performing what he hath undertaken.
> The second,[5] the followers, the place of whose witnessing is extolled
> And the first among those who have borne witness to the Prophet."

---

1 Abu Khaythamah Zuhayr an eminent traditionist of Nasa who settled at Baghdad and died A.H. 234 (A.D. 849). De Slane I.K.

2 One of the Companions, accompanied Muhammad in seventeen expeditions settled at Kufah and died there A.H. 56 or as some say 68, An Nawawi.

3 Abu Amr Aamir sprang from Himyar and was accounted a member of the tribe of Hamdan of which Shaab is a branch. He held high rank among the Tabiis and was distinguished for his learning, born about A.H. 19, died A.H. 104 (722). Ibn Khall.

4 Hassan b. Thabit was one of the poets who espoused the cause of Muhammad. His son Abdur Rahman lived under Muawiyah and used to address complimentary poems to Ramla, daughter of that Caliph. De Slane I.K. For his elegy on Muhammad's death see Weil. Leben Muhammad. Vol. II, p. 356.

5 Abu Bark, is referred to in Qur. IX as الثاني اثنين اذا همافي الغار "the second of the two when they two were in the cave."

Abu Nua'ym records on the authority Furat b. Saib that he said, "I inquired of Maymun b. Mihran saying, 'is Ali the most excellent in thy opinion, or Abu Bakr, or Omar ?" He trembled so that the staff fell from his hand and them replied "I never thought that I should live to the time when *any one* should be compared to those two-to God be attributed their good deeds-they two were the chief in Islam." I said "then was Abu Bakr the first to embrace Islam or Ali ?" he answered "By Allah, verily Abu Bakr believed in the Prophet in the time of Buhayra, the monk[1] on the occasion of his meeting him." Accounts vary as to *priority in Islam* between him and Khadijah when he procured her marriage with *the Prophet,*[2] and all this was before Ali was born and verily there are many among the Companions and their immediate successors, and others who say, that he was the first to embrace Islam, indeed, some of them assert that there is universal assent to this. Again, it is said that Ali was the first to join the true faith, and some say, Khadijah, but there is a reconciliation of these accounts, in that Abu Bakr was the first to embrace the faith among, men, Ali among children and Khadijah among women and the first who pointed out this reconciliation, was Abu Hanifah from whom Nua'ym quotes it.

Ibn Abi Shaybah[3] and Ibn Asakir record on the authority of Salim b Abi Jaad that he said, "I asked of Muhammad b Hanifah,-

---

1 Muhammad was reclining under a lote tree says Ibn Hajr, while Abu Bakr was conversing with Buhayra. The latter asked him who it was, that was seated there; he replied that it was Muhammad the son of Abullah. "Then by Allah, said Buhayra, he is the Prophet for none has taken shelter under that tree since the time of Jesus the son of Mary." This impressed itself on Abu Bakr's mind and was the cause of his early conversion. I may add that Ibn Hajr discords as erroneous the opinion held by Ibn Athir (and adopted by Sprenger) that this Buhayra was the same person as the one who figures in a deputation to Muhammad from the king of Abyasinia forty years afterwards.

2 By assisting Muhammad with money on that occasion as is generally believed.

3 The Hafidh Othman a native of Kufah, died A.H. 239. (A.D. 853-4). He composed a commentary on the Qurãn and a collection of traditions ; 30,000 persons are said to have attended his lessons. De Slane I.K.

was Abu Bakr the first of the people to adopt Islam ?" He replied- "no." I said, "for what reason then is he exalted and preferred, so that no one speaks of any but Abu Bakr ?" He replied, "because he was the most excellent of them in Islam, from the time he embranced the faith until he attained to his God." And Ibn Asakir on a reliable ascription from Muhammad b. Saad b Abi Wakkas,[1] that he said to his father Saad,- "was Abu Bakr as Siddik the first of you in embracing the faith ?" He said. "No, for there were more than five in the faith before him but he was the best of us in Islam."

Ibn Kathir says, "it is clear that Muhammad's family believed before every other-his wife Khadijah, his freedman Zayd and the wife of Zayd Ummi Ayman and Ali and Warakah." Ibn Asakir records on the authority of I'sa'l Yazid that Abu Bakr said, "I was seated in the courtyard of the Kaabah where Zayd b Amr b. Nufayl was sitting, when there passed by him Umayyah b Abi Salt[2] and he said. "How art thou, thou O seeker after good ?" He answered "well." The other said "hast thou, discovered anything ?" He replied 'No :' then the other said-

"Every religion in the day of judgment : save that founded of God in truth, shall perish."

But regarding the Prophet, he that men look for, shall he be from among us or from among you ?" Abu Bakr continues, "and I, had not heard before that of a Prophet expected who was to be

---

1 Abu IshaK Saa'd b. Abi Wakkas, a descendant of Abdu Manat was by his own account the third convert to Islam, he being then 17 years of age. He fought in all the Prophet's battles ; his death occurred between A.H. 50-8. De Slane I.K.

2 He was a poet of some reputation of the tribe of Thakif. Ibn Hajr says that he was an enquirey after truth, but more for the curiosity of the discovery than with intent to fellow it. "His verses," said Muhammad "are pious enough but his heart is unbelieving." There is a doubt whether he was ever converted, but by some he is considered a Companion. His excuse for not testifying to the Prophet was, that he had once hinted to his tribe that he himself was likely to be the Prophet to come.

sent." He adus. "Then I went out to Warakah-b-Naufal[1] and he was one who constantly watched the heavens and muttered frequently to himself and I stopped him and related to him the circumstance. He said "yea-O! son of my brother, I am skilled in the scriptures and in knowledge; know, that this Prophet, he whom men await, shall be by descent of the most noble of the Arabs. I am likewise skilled in genealogy, and thy tribe is by descent, the most noble among the Arabs." I said, "O uncle, and what will the Prophet say?" he replied, "he shall speak that which hath been said to him, and known, that he shall not oppress nor be oppressed nor desire you to oppress each other." Therefore when the Apostle of God was sent, I believed in him and testified to him."

Ibn Ishak says, that he heard from Muhammad b Abdur Rahman b. Abdullah bil Hasin at Tamimi that the Apostle of God said, "I never called any one to the true faith but there arose in him an aversion to it, and an irresolution and deliberation, except Abu Bakr who delayed not from it when I spoke to him, and did not hesitate therein." Al Bayhaki says "and this was because he had been accustomed to behold the proofs of the Prophetic mission of the Apostle of God, and to hear its traditions, before his call, and when *the Prophet* summoned him, then verily thought and deliberation had passed by for him and he at once embraced Islam." He then records on the authority Abu Maysarah[2] that when the Apostle of God went forth, he used to hear one calling to him "O Muhammad," and when he heard the voice he would turn fleeing : he told this in secret to Abu Bakr who was his intimate friend in the time of Ignorance."

Abu Nua'ym and Ibn Asakir record on the authority of Ibn Abbas that the Apostle of God said, "I never spoke to any one regarding Islam but he denied me and rejected my words, save the son of Abu Kuhafa and verily I never said unto him a thing but he

---

1 A cousin of Muhammad's said to have been a convert to Christianity and to have been acquainted with the Scriptures, and to have transcribed some portions of the Gospels into Hebrew or Arabic. See Muir, Vol. II P, 51.

2 The freedman of al Abbas b. Abdil Muttablib. Ibn Hajr.

acqiesced in it and was steadfast therein."

And al Bukhari[1] Ibn Ahud Barda that the apostle of God said, "will ye not have unto me my companion? verily I said O! men, I am the apostle of God unto ye all, and ye said "thou hist." and Abu Bakr said : "thou hust spoken truly."

On his companionship with the Prophet and the expeditions which he accompanied.

The learned say that Abu Bakr accompanied the Prophet from the time he embraced Islam to his death and never separated himself from him either in journeying or residence at home, except when he had permission to depart on account of pilgrimage of war and he was present with him in all his expeditions, and accompanied him in his flight, and for-sook his family and children with cheerfulness for the sake of God and his Apostle, and he was his companion in the cave. The Lord called him. "the second of the two when they two were in the cave" when *the Prophet* said to his companion, "be not said for God is with us," and he assisted the Apostle of God on other occasions. Splendid were his services in the wars : he was steadfast on the day of Ohud and the day of Hunayn when the people fled, as will appear in the chapter on his courage.

Ibn Asakir records on the testimony of Abu Hurayrah, that the angels took part in the battle of Badr and they said "See ye not as Siddik, with the Apostle of God in a Shed ?" and Abu Yala and al Hakim and Ahmad from Ali that he said, "the Apostle of God said to me and to Abu Bakr on the day of Badr. "with one of you two is Gabriel and with the other Michael." And Ibn Asakir from Ibn Sirin, that Abdur Rahman the son of Abu Bakr on the day of Badr

---

1 One of the Companions. The particulars of this narration will be found in Bukhari's as Sahih. Vol. VI, Kitabul Manakib.

was on the side of the idolaters, and when he was converted to Islam, he said to his father," verily, thou wert exposed as a mark to me on the day of Badr, but I turned away from thee and did not slay thee." Abu Bakr said, "as to thee, hadst thou come beforeme, I should not have turned away from thee."

On his bravery, for he was the bravest of the Companions.

Al Bazzar records in his Musnad from Ali that he said: Tell me who is the bravest of men;" they said "thou art." He replied "Verily I never encountered and one but it was even with him, but tell me, who was the bravest of men ?" They said, "we know not : who is he ?" He said "Abu Bakr for verily on the day of Badr, we made for the Apostle of God a shelter from the sun, and we said, "who shall, remain with the Apostle of God lest any of the idolaters fall upon him ?" then by Allah, not one of up approached except Abu Bakr who brandished a sword over the head of the Apostle of God: no one attached him but he attached him likewise : he is therefore the bravest of men." Ali said. "I saw the Apostle of God assaulted by the Kuraysh, and one threatened him and another shook him violently and they said, "thou art he who makest of the gods, one god;" he added, and by Allah not one of us approached except Abu Bakr who struck one and threatened another and pushed aside another and said "woe unto ye—will ye lay a man who saith—my God is Allah ?" Then Ali lifted up the mantle that was on him and wept, so that his beard was wet *with tears* and he said "I conjure ye by Allah, *to say* whether was he true believer[1] of the family of Pharoah the better or Abu Bakr ?" and the people were silent, and he said, "do ye not answer me ? by Allah, a single hour of Abu

1 This person, according to tradition, was an Egyptian and Pharoh's uncle's son, but a trus believer, who finding that the king had been informed of what Moses had done, and designed to put him to death, gave him notice to provide for his safety by flight. He is mentioned in the Qurãn. Chapters XXVIII and XI,. See Sale.

Bakr is better than a thousand hours of the believer of the family of Pharoah, for the man concealed his faith and this man proclaimed it."

Al Bukhari records from Urwah b-uz Zubayr that he said, "I asked of Abdullah b Amr bil Aas,[1] what was the greatest violence that the idolaters had offered to the Apostle of God ; he replied "I saw Ukbah-b-Abi Muayt go towards the Prophet who was praying and throw his cloak about his neck, and throttle him violently, whereupon Abu Bakr came and drove him from him and said, "will ye slay a man who saith-my God is Allah ? and in truth he hath come to you with manifestations from your God!" And al Haytham b. Kulayb in his Musnad from Abu Bakr, "On the day of Ohud, all the people forsook the Apostle of God and I was the first to return to him."-the rest of the tradition with appear in the Musnad as he has related it-And Ibn Asakir from Ayesha. "When the Prophet gathered the Companions together there were thirty eight persons. Abu Bakr then entreated the Apostle of God to declare himself openly, but he said "O! Abu Bakr we are only a few ;" but Abu Bakr did not desist from importuning the Apostle of God, until he declared himself. The Muslims were seattered round about the Mosque each man among his kindred, when Abu Bakr rose before the people preaching and he was the first who summoned the people to God and to his Apostle ; then the idolaters fell upon Abu Bakr and upon the Muslims and beat them with heavy blows round about the Mosque"-the rest of the tradition will follow in the biography of Omar.

Ibn Asakir records from Ali, that when Abu Bakr was converted, he declared his faith and summoned the people to God and to his apostle.

---

1 Abu Muhammad or Abu Abdur Rahman, the Companion, An Nawawi says that the name Aas commonly so spelt, should be more properly written Aasi. He was 12 or 13 years younger than his father and was converted to Islam before him and received no less than 790 traditions from Muhammad. His devotion and learning were universally acknowledged. The date of his death is differently stated, according to some as early as 55 A.H. according to others in 73. Consult An Nawawi and Ibn Khall.

On his spending his substance on the Apostle of God for he was the most generous of the Companions.

The Lord hath said, "But he who strictly bewareth *idolatry and rebellion,* shall be removed far from the same : (hell fire)- who giveth his substance in alms" &c. to the end of the Sura. (Qur XCII). Ibnul Jauzi says that the learned are agreed, that this was reveale regarding Abu Bakr. Ahmad records on the authority of Abu Hurayrah that the Apostle of God said, "No wealth hat ever availed me, as hath availed me the wealth of Abu Bakr." and abu Bakr wept and said- "I and my wealth are they not for thee O! Apostle o God ?" Al Khatib relates a traditions imperfect in regularity of transmission, on the authority of Sai'd b-ul Musayyab,[1] and adds that the Apostle of God made use of the substance of Abu Bakr as if it were his own.-And Ibn Asakir from Ayesha with different authorities, and from Urwah b-uz Zubayr, that on the day when Abu Bakr was converted, he had forty thousand dinars— and according to another reading, forty thousand dirhams, and he spent them upon the Apostle of God.

Abu Sai'd al Aarabi records on the authority of Ibn Omar, that on the day when Abu Bakr was converted, he had in his house forty thousand dirhams, and when he set out for Madina at the time of the Flight, he had no, more than five thousand, all of which he spent upon the manumission of slaves and in aid of Islam. And Ibn Asakir on that of Ayesha, that Abu Bakr gave freedom to seven slaves all of whom had suffered persecution for the sake of God.

Ibn Shahin[2] records in his "Sunnah," and al Baghawi[3] in his

---

1 Abu Muhammad Said b-ul Musayyab, Kurayshi, one of the seven great jurisconsults of Medina. He was the chief of the first series of Tabiis-he married the daughter of Abu Hurayra and related traditions on his authority, born A.H. 15-16, (636-7). Died at Median A.H. 91, (A.H. 709-10). Ibn Khall.

2 The Hafidh Abu Hafs Omar b. Shahin of Baghdad composed works computed at 330 in number, among them a Commentary on the Qurãn and a collection of traditions, died A.H. 385. (A.D. 995). De Slane I.K.

3 Abu Muhammad al Husayn-known as al Farra al Baghawi, aShafii doctor, Traditionist and Commentator on the Qurãn, died A.H. 510 (A.D. 1117) at Marwarrud. Baghawi is the relative adjective, irregularly formed, (cont...)

commentary on the Qurãn, and Ibn Asakir from Ibn Omar,[1] that he said, "I was near the Prophet, and by him was Abu Bakr, and upon him a garment of goat's hair, and he had pinned it together on his breast with a skewer : then Gabriel came down to him and said "O! Muhammad, how is it that I see Abu Bakr *wearing* a garment of goat's hair which he hath pinned on his breast by a skewer ?" He replied "O! Gabriel, he spent his substance upon me before the conquest *of Mecca*." Gabriel said "Then the Lord sendeth him His benediction an saith, "Say unto him-art thou content with me in this thy poverty or angry ?" Abu Bakr said, "Can I be angry with my God? I am content with my God-I am content with my God-I am content with my God," (related only by one authority and its ascription is untrustworthy).

Al Khatib records also a weak ascription, through Ibn Omar to the Prophet, who said, "Gabriel, upon whom be peace, came down to me and upon him was a coarse garment fastened together with a skewer, and I said to him. "O! Gabriel what is this ?" He replied, "Verily the Lord hath commanded the angels to fasten their garments in heaven as Abu Bakr fastens his upon earth." Ibn Kathir remarks that this is excessively untrustworthy and adds that were it not that this and the preceding tradition have been handed down by so many people, the rejection of the two would be advisable.

Abu[2] Dauud and at Tirmidi relate on the authority of Omar b-ul

---

(cont. 47) derived from Bagh or Baghshur a town in Khorasan. (Ibn Khall). There is also a traditionist Abul Kasim al Baghawi, a Hafidh of great repute, died A.H. 317, (A.D. 929). De Slane I.K.

1 Abu Abdur Rahman, Abdullah b. Omaril Khattab one of the most eminent of the Companions for his piety, learning and contempt of the world. During the civil wars which raged among the followers of Islam, he remained neutral, occupied in the duties of religion. For a period of sixty years, persons came from all parts to consult him, and his generosity was so great that he would frequently distribute 30, 000 dirhams, in charity on the days in which he gave audience. Died at Mecca, A.H. 72 (692-3) aged 84. De Slane I.K.

2 Abu Dauud Sulayman b-ul Ashath of the tribe of Azd, as Sijistani, was a Hafidh in the traditions, eminent for his piety and holy life. He was one of the earliest who complied a book of traditions (Kitab us Sunan). He was born A.H. 202, (817-8) and died at Basrah A.H. 275 (889). Ibn Khall.

Khattab, that he said, "the Apostle of God commanded us to give alms and that was in proportion to the property I possessed, and I said *to myself*, "to-day I will surpass Abu Bakr if I am to surpass him on any day, and I brought half of my property." Then the Apostle of God said "what hast thou kept for thy family ?" I replied, "The like unto that;" and Abu Bakr came with all the property that he had, and *the Prophet* said, "O Abu Bakr ! what hast thou kept for thy family ?" He replied, "I have reserved for them God and his Prophet ;" then I said, "I shall never surpass him in anything." (At Tirmidi says that the tradition is good and trustworthy.)

Abu Nua'ym records in his 'Huliyal', on the authority of al Hasan al Basri that Abu Bakr brought his alms to the Prophet secretly and said, "O Apostle of God this is my alms and with God belongeth for me the world to come;" then Omar brought his offering and showed it openly and said, "O Apostle of God this is my alms, and for me belongeth with God the world to come." The Apostle of God exclaimed "there is the same difference between your offerings as between your words." (The ascription is good but interrupted in transmission.) And at Tirmidi from Abu Hurayrah, that the Apostle of God said, "I have never been under obligation to any one but I have requited him, save Abu Bakr, and verily he hath put obligations upon me, which God will requite unto him on the day of resurrection, and the wealth of none hath ever availed me, as hath availed me the wealth of Abu Bakr."

Al Bazzar records on the authority of Abu Bakr that he said, "I brought *my father* Abu Kuhafah to the Prophet who said, "why didst thou not leave the Shaykh *where he was* that I might go to him ?" I[1] said "it is his duty rather to go to thee." He answered, "I would be considerate towards him for the kindnesses of his son towards me." And Ibn Asakir from Ibn Abbas that the Apostle of God said "No one hath benefited me in greater measure than Abu Bakr, who hath aided me with his person and his substance and hath given me his daughter in marriage.

---

1 The text has قال meaning "Abu Bakr said."

On his learning, for verily he was the wisest of the Companions and the most sagacious of them.

An Nawawi says in his "Tahdib" (and I have copied it from his work). "The learned of our time have adduced in proof of his great wisdom his words in the tradition verified in the "Sahihayn,"[1] "by Allah I will oppose by force every one who maketh a difference between prayers and alms;[2] by Allah, if they withhold from me *as much as* the halter of a camel which they used to pay to the Apostle of God, I will oppose them by force for withholding it." The Shaykh Abu Ishak has brought forward this and other things in his Tabakat, (Classes) in testimony that Abu Bakr was the wisest of the Companions, for they all of them, with the exception of him, fell short of comprehending the wisdom of this course. He then explained to them in his discussion of it with them, that his judgment was the right one, and they were converted to it. It has been related to me on the authority of Ibn Omar, that he was asked who used to decide cases for the people in the time of the Apostle of God. He answered, "Abu Bakr and Omar, I know of no others besides those two." And the two Shaykhs record on the authority of Abu Sa'id al Khudri that he narrates, that the Apostle of God addressed the people and said "God, the Holy and Most High, hath given unto one o his servants a choice between this world and the things which are His, and that servant hath chosen that which is with the Lord God;" and Abu Bakr wept and said, "my ancestry male and female be thy ransom," and we wondered at his weeping because the Apostle of God had spoken regarding a servant that had been given a choice, but it was the Apostle of God himself who had been left

---

1 The two works entitled Sahih of al Bukhari and Muslim.

2 Referring to the people of Hira and Yaman who after the death of Muhammad accepted prayers to be an article of faith, but rejected alms-giving. The council having assembled to consider this recusancy, the Companions were in favor of letting it pass as a matter of little moment, but Abu Bakr strongly insisted on repressing this heresy on the spot lost the dangerous example should be followed by others to the peril of the rising faith.

to choose, and Abu Bakr was wiser than we were. Then the Apostle of God said. "Abu Bakr has been the most generous of men towards me, in his companionship and worldly goods, and were I to choose a friend besides my God, I would assuredly choose Abu Bakr, but the brotherhood of Islam and its affection[1] is sufficient for me. There shall not remain a door[2] but it shall be closed except the door of Abu Bakr." (These are the words of An Nawawi.)

Ibn Kathir says, that as Siddik was the best read, that is the most learned of the Companions in the Qurãn, inasmuch as the Prophet gave him precedence of the Companions, as Imam in public prayers by his words, "the most learned of the people in the Qurãn shall be their Imam." At Tirmidi records from Ayesha, that the Apostle of God said, "it is not expedient for a people among whom is Abu Bakr that another than he should act as Imam to them." He was withal the most skilled in the traditionary law, so that when the Companions referred to him on several occasions he came out before them, with a relation of the sayings of the Prophet, which he recollected and brought forward when there was necessity for it, and which they knew not; and how could it be otherwise for verily he was constantly in the society of the Apostle of God from the beginning of his mission till his death : and withal he was one of the most acute-minded of the servants of God and the most learned of them, and although there are but few traditions recorded, orally transmitted from him, on account of the fewness of his days and his death following quickly on that of the Prophet, yet had his life been prolonged, assuredly they would have been for greater in number, and the narrators would not have left a single tradition of his but they would have transmitted it, but these, in his day, were

---

1 This termination of this sentence is not in the printed text or MS. Which is abrupt and incomplete, but I find it supplied by al Bukhari in his Sharah an the authority of Ibn Abbas.

2 The Commentators give various interpretation of this passage ; the most probable opinion is, that the doors spoken of are those of the Mosque built by Muhammad at Medina and one of which opened on to his house, another on to that of Abu Bakr, and the like with Omar and Ali ; and the closing of all but Abu Bakr's door, was a secret allusion to his succession to the Caliphate.

the Companions, none of whom had occasion to relate on his authority, as event in which they themselves had taken part with him: they therefore related on his authority *only* what they did not themselves know.

Abul Kasim al Baghawi records on the authority of Maymum b. Mihran, that Abu Bakr, when a plaintiff came before him, used to look into the book of God, and if he found in it that which would decide between the claimants, he decided according to it, and if it *were not* in the Book, and he was aware of a tradition of the Prophet respecting such a case, he decided according to it; but if it embarrassed him, he would go forth and ask of the true believers and say, "such a one and such a one came to me ; now do ye know whether the Apostle of God passed judgment on such a case ?" Then sometimes a number of the popple would gather round him, all of them relating a decision of the Apostle of God in such a matter, and he would say, "Praise be to God who hath set amongst us those who bear in mind traditions from the Prophet." But if it embarassed him to discover a tradition of the Apostle of God concerning it he would assemble the chiefs of the people, and the chosen among them and consult them, and if their opinions concurred in one decision, he would decide accordingly. Omar used to do likewise, and when he was unable to find a decision in the Qurãn or traditional usage, he would look to see if there were a judgment by Abu Bakr in such a case, and if he discovered that Abu Bakr had adjudged such a matter, he would decide according to that judgment ; otherwise, he would summon the chiefs of the people, and when they had concurred in a decision, he acted according to it. As Siddik was also the most learned of men in the genealogy of the Arabs, more especially that of the Kuraysh.

Ibn Ishak records on the authority of Yakub b. Utbah, who had it from an Ansar Shaykh that Jubayr b. Mutim[1] was amongst the

1 Abu Muhammad or Abu Adi Jubayr b. Mutim, a Companion, of the tribe of Kuraysh; was converted before the Kbybar Expedition and some say on the day of the conquest of Mecca; died at Medina, A.H. 54 and some say 59. An Nawawi T.A.

most learned of the Kuraysh in the pedigrees of the Kuraysh and the Arabs in general, and he used to say, "verily I learnt genealogy from Abu Bakr who was one of the most learned in genealogy of the Arabs." And further, as Siddik was skilled in the science of the interpretation of dreams, and he used to interpret dreams in the time of the Prophet, and indeed Muhammad b. Sirin say (and he was by common consent, the first in this science) that Abu Bakr was, after the Prophet the best interpreter *of dreams* of this nation. (Ibn Saa'd).

Ad Daylami records in his Musnadul Firdaus, and Ibn Asakir on the authority of Samurah,[1] that the Apostle of God said "I have been commanded to cause dreams to be interpreted by Abu Bakr."

Ibn Kathir says that he was one of the most elopquent of men, and the best preacher among them. Az Zubayr-b. Bakkar says "I have heard certain of the learned declare that the most eloquent preachers, among the Companions of the Apostle of God, were Abu Bakr as Siddik and Ali b. Abi Talib ;" and the saying of Omar will appear in the tradition of Sakifah.[2]

He was likewise the most learned of men in *the knowledge* of the Lord, and he most God-fearing of them : his utterances regarding that and regarding the interpretation of dreams and his preaching will all of them follow in a future section. Among the proofs which point to his being the wises of the Companions, is the tradition on the truce of Hudaybiyah,[3] when Omar inquired of the Apostle of

---

1 Abu Said Abu Muhammad or Abu Abdullah Samurah b. Jundab the Companion-fought at Ohud and other battles, by the side of the Prophet-resident at Basreh where he acted as governor during the absence of Ziyad b. Abihi at Kufa ; died at Basrah 58 or 59. An Nawawi.

2 As Sakifah was a building in Medina belonging to the Banu Saad, where after the death of the Prophet, the rival claims of the *fugitives* of Mecca and the *auxiliaries* of Medina to elect a successor were urged with a fierceness, perilous to the common cause.

3 "According to Jallaluddin, says Sale, fourscore of the infidels came privately to Muhammad's camp with an intent to surprise some of his men, but were taken and brought before the Prophet who pardoned them and ordered them to be set at liberty, and this generous action was the occasion of the truce struck up by the Kuraysh with Muhammad."

God regarding that truce and said "why should we accept dishonour in our religion ?" and the Prophet answered him : then he went to Abu Bakr and inquired of him regarding that which he had asked of the Apostle of God, and as Saddik answered him with the same answer as the Prophet's exactly." (Al Bukhari and others).

He was withal, the most judicious of the Companions in counsel and the most perfect of them in wisdom.

Tamam ar Razi records in his "Fuwaid" and Ibn Asakir from Abdullah b. Amar bil Aas that he narrates, "I heard the Apostle of God say-Gabriel, came to me and said "verily God commands thee to take counsel of Abu Bakr." And At Tabarani and Abu Nua'ym and others, from Muad b Jabal,[1] that when the Prophet desired to send Muad to Yaman, he took counsel of some of the Companions, among them, Abu Bakr, and Omar and Othman and Talhah and Az Zubayr and Usayd b. Hudhayr, and each one of the number gave his opinion : then the Prophet said, "what dost thou think, O Muad?" (*Muad continues*) I said I approve what Abu Bakr hath spoken: the Prophet exclaimed "verily the Lord in the heavens above willeth not that Abu Bakr should err." Ibn Usamah *relates this* in his Musnad *thus,* "verily the Lord in heaven willeth not that Abu Bakr as Siddik should err upon earth;" and at Tabarani records in his Ausat from Sahl b Saad[2] as Saidi that the Apostle of God said "verily the Lord willeth not that Abu Bakr should err,' (his authorities are trustworthy).

An Nawawi says in his Tahdib, that as Siddik was one of the companions who knew the Qurãn by heart, and a number others, among them Ibn Kathir in his commentary, have stated the same.

---

1 Of the tribe of Khazraj, a native of Medina and one of the Companions, died A.H. 18 (A.D. 639) aged thirty-three (and some say, thirty-four, and thirty-eight) of the plague at Emaus. An Nawawi.

2 Abul Abbas or Yahya Sahl b. Saad one of the Companions and a native of Medina ; delivered 188 traditions, died at Medina A.H. 88. (A.H. 707). His name was Huzn and he was called Sahl by the Prophet to avoid the ill-omen of its meaning. Huzn signifying "grief," and "Sahl," "easy"- "facile." An Nawawi, T.A.

But the tradition of Anas *which says* "Four persons collected the Qurãn in the time of the Apostle of God," means, four among the auxiliaries, as he has explained in his work Al Ittkan;[1] but what Ibn Abi Dauud says, on the authority of as Shaabi, *viz.*, that Abu Bakr died and the Qurãn was not collected, is either to be rejected or interpreted to mean, its collection into a book according to the arrangement adopted by Othman.

On his being the most eminent of the Companions and the most virtuous.

The Sunnis are agreed that the most eminent of men, after the Apostle of God were, Abu Bakr, then Omar, then Othman, then Ali, then the rest of the ten,[2] then the rest of those engaged at Badr, then the rest of those engaged at Ohud : then the rest of the people of the Covenant,[3] then the rest of the Companions. Abu Mansur al Baghdadi[4] relates this as a fact upon which all are agreed.

Al Bukhari narrates on the authority of Ibn Omar that he said, "we were making a choice among men in the time of the Apostle of God, and we preferred Abu Bakr, then Omar, then Othman ;" and at Tabarani adds in the "Kabir" "and the Prophet knew of this and did not disapprove it."

---

1 كتاب الاتقان في علوم القران

2 Called عشره مبشره or the ten to whom joyful tidings are given. See note, page 25.

3 Those whom he called together al Hudaybiyah and who swore to be faithful to him till death.

4 Abu Mansur Abdul Kahir a native of Baghdad, a dogmatic theologian of the Shafii school, well acquainted with general literature and versed in a number of other sciences particularly arithmetic ; a book of his on the latter bears the name of at Takmila. He was likewise skilled in the law of inheritance and composed poetry, died at Isfarain. A.H. 429, (A.D. 1037-8) and was interred by the grave of his master Abu Ishak. Ibn Khall.

Ibn Asakir records on the authority of Ibn Omar, that he said, "we (and among us was the Apostle of God) gave the preference first to Abu Bakr, then to Omar, then to Othman, then to Ali ;" and from Abu Hurayrah, "we, a gathering of the Companions of the Apostle of God, being a considerable number together said, the most distinguished of this people after their Prophet, are Abu Bakr, then Omar then Othman-then we were silent."

At Tirmidi records from Jabir b Abdullah[1] that Omar said to Abu Bakr "O best of men after the Apostle of God," and Abu Bakr replied- nay, thou if thou speakest thus, then verily, I have heard *the Prophet* say "the sun hath never risen upon a man better than Omar." And al Bukhari from Ali b Abi Talib. "I said to may father - who among men is the best after the Apostle of God?" He replied "Abu Bakr." I said "Who after him," He replied "Omar," and I feared lest he should say Othman. I continued "then thou." He answered "I am nothing but one among the true believers." And Ahmad and others from Ali, "the best of this people after its Prophet, is Abu Bakr and then Omar." Ad Dahabi says "this hath come down in regular transmission from Ali, therefore may God curse the heretics[2] how ignorant are they!"

At Tirmidi and al Hukim record on the authority of Omar b'ul Khattab that he said, "Abu Bakr is our chief and the most excellent of us, and the most beloved among us of the Apostle of God." And Ibn Asakir from Abdur Rahman[3] b. Abi Layla, that Omar ascended the pulpit and said, "know that the most eminent of this people after its Prophet is Abu Bakr, and whosoever speaketh otherwise is a slanderer : upon him be *the retribution* that overtaketh the

---

1 Abu Abdullah Jabir b. Abdillah as Salami al Ansari, embraced Islam one year before the first pact, made with Muhammad al Akabah (Abul Feda, Tom 1, page 53) and was present at the second ; died A.H. 78 (A.D. 697-8) aged ninety-four years. De Slane, I.K.

2 The Shiahs and such as maintain the pre-eminence of Ali over his three predecessors.

3 Abu Isa Abdur Rahman one of the principal Tabiis born at Kufah where his father had settled, 6 years before Omar's death. He died A.H. 83. An Nawawi.

slanderer," and that Ali said, "let not any one prefer me in merit to Abu Bakr or Omar, or I shall scourge him according to the punishment of the law for the slanderer."

Abdur Rahman b. Hamid in his Musnad, and Abu Nua'ym and others, record with different authorities from Abud Darda, that the Apostle of God said, "The sun hath never risen and hath never gone down upon one more eminent that Abu Bakr, save he were a Prophet ;" and in another reading "upon one of the true believers, after the Prophets and Apostles, more eminent than Abu Bakr." And the same from the tradition of Jabir with the reading "The sun hath never risen upon one amongst you more eminent than he." At Tabarani and others record this and it has evidence from other sources which determine its accuracy or trustworthiness and indeed Ibn Kathir hath pointed out its absolute authenticity.

At Taharani records from Salimah b-ul Akwaa[1] that the Apostle of God said "Abu Bakr as Siddik is the most eminent of men, save it be a Prophet ;" and in his Ausat from Saad b. Zurarah, that the Apostle of God Said, "The holy spirit Gabriel announced to me,-"the best of thy people after thee is Abu Bakr."

And the two Shaykhs from Amr b-ul Aas, "I said 'O Apostle of God, who among mankind is the most beloved by thee ?" He replied "Ayesha," I said "among men ?" "Her father." I said "then who ?" he replied. "Then Omar b'ul Khattab." This tradition without the "then Omar" has come down in the narrative of Anas and Ibn Omar and Ibn Abbas.

At Tirmidi, an Nasai,[2] and al Hakim record on the authority of

---

1 Salimah b-ul Akwaa, one of the Companions. He swore allegiance to Muhammad on the day of Hudaybiyah and accompanied him in seven of his expeditions. He used to reside at Medina, but on the death of Omar, he left it for Rabadah and returned to Medina a few days before his death, A.H. 74 (6930 at the age of 80. An Nawawi.

2 The Hafidh, Abu Abdur Rahman, chief traditionist of his age and author of a Sunan or collection of traditions, was an inhabitant of old Cairo. He was a great advocate of the rights of Ali and was maltreated by the mob on that account, under the effects of which he died A.H. 303. (A.D. 916). Born at Nasa a city of Khorasan A.H. 214-5. (A.D. 829-30). He composed a work called the Al Khasais (Characteristics) on the merits of Ali. Ibn Khall.

Abudllah b. Shakik that he narrates, "I said to Ayesha-which of the companions of the Apostle of God was most beloved by him?" She answered "Abu Bakr." I said "which next ?" She replied "Then Omar" I said "which next?" She answered Abu Ubaydah b-ul Jarrah." And at Tirmidi from Anas, that the Apostle of God said of Abu Bakr and Omar, "These are the chief of the adult dwellers in paradise, of those who have been the first and of those who will be the last, save they be Prophets and Apostles."[1]

At Tabarani records in his Ausat, on the authority of Ammar b. Yasir[2] that he said, "whosoever giveth precedence to any one of the Companions of the Apostle of God over Abu Bakr and Omar, verily he putteth a slight upon the Fugitives and Auxiliaries." And Ibn Said on the authority of az Zuhri,[3] that the Apostle of God said to Hassan b. Thabit. "Hast thou said anything *in verse* of Abu Bakr ?" He answered "yes." Then he said "speak and I will listen," and he repeated this verse-

> "The second of the two in the glorious cave and verily
> The enemy went round about it when they ascended the mountain
> And Verily they knew that he was the beloved of the Apostle of God:
> Who hold no one his equal among the people."

---

1 The Muhammadan doctors place the Apostle higher in degree than the Prophets. The two words نبي مرسل "Prophet apostle," are employed only for those who bear the double character. By the latter they signify, one whose divine mission is testified to by a sacred book whereas the Prophetical office alone is not always so distinguished. The Prophet Apostle are four, Moses, David, Jesus, Muhammad.

2 One of the Companions, who fell in the battle fought (A.H. 37) between Ali and Muawiyah at Siffin. Ibn Khall.

3 Abu Bakr Muhammad Ibn Shihab of the Kuraysh, one of the most eminent of the Tabiis, jurisconsults and traditionists of Median. He saw ten of Muhammad's Companions. He was made Kadhi by Yazid b. Abdil Malik and died A.H. 124 (A.D. 742) at the age of seventy-two or three. Ibn Khall.

and the Apostle of God laughed on that his back teeth were visible, and said, "thou hast spoken truly, O Hassan, he is as thou sayest."

Ahmad and at Tirmidi record from Anas[1] b. Malik that the Apostle of God said. "The most compassionate of my people unto my people is Abu Bakr, and the most zealous of them in *upholding* the commands of God, Omar, and the most truly modest among them, Othman, and the most learned of them in things lawful and unlawful Muad b. Jabal, and the most skilled in the law of inheritance, Zayd b. Thabit,[2] and the most learned of them in the Qurãn Ubayy b. Kaab,[3] and in every people, there is one that is confided in, and the trusted one of this people is Abu Ubaydah b-ul Jarrah." Abu Yala has taken this from the tradition of Ibn Omar and added to it "and the best of them in adjudication, Ali." Ad Daylami quotes this in his Musnadul Firdaus from the tradition of Shaddad b. Aus and added "and Abu Darr,[4] the most devout of my people and the most sincere, and Abud Darda, the most pious of my people, and the

---

1 Abu Hamzah, Anas b. Malik surnamed "the servant of God's Apostle." خادم رسول الله was one of the most eminent of the Companions. At his mother's request Muhammad prayed for his spiritual and temporal prosperity, through which the riches of Anas multiplied, his date trees bore fruit twice a year and he was the father of 78 sons; he was 10 years in his master's service and on his death removed to Basrah. He died A.H. 93 (A.D. 711-2). De Slane, I.K.

2 Abu Said Zayd b. Thabit a Companion and native of Medina. He was Muhammad's Secretary and used to commit his dictation of the Qurãn to writing and carried on his master's ordinary, correspondence and afterwards acted in the same capacity under Abu Bakr and Omar. He was one of the three to whom Abu Bakr committed the task of collecting the Qurãn. He was celebrated for his knowledge of the law of inheritance among other subjects and had the charge of the public treasury in the Caliphate of Othman. He died at Median A.H. 54. An Nawawi.

3 One of the Companions, present at the second pact of al Akabah ; fought at Badr and other engagements. Muhammad recited to him the 98th Sura of the Qurãn as he said, at the express divine command, an honour which no other Companion, shared with him ; died at Medina before A.H. 30 in the Caliphate of Othman. An Nawawi, T.A.

4 Jundub b. Junadah Abu Darr ali Ghaffari, one of the Companions of an ascetic life and one of the earliest converts. There is much (Cont..)

most God-fearing and Muawiyah b. Ali Sufiyan, he most benign of my people and the most munificent." And verily my most erudite master Al Kafiji[1] was asked whether these characteristics were at variance with those before given, and he replied that there was no contradiction.

On what has been revealed in the verses of the Qurãn in his praise and his witnessing to the truth and other matters regarding him.

Know, that I have seen a work of a certain author on the names of those regarding whom there hath been a revelation in the Qurãn, but in-accurate and incomplete and, I therefore myself composed a work on that subject, comprehensive, exhaustive and accurate and I extract from it here, whatever refers to As Siddik.

The Lord said, "The second of the two when they two were in the cave : when he said unto his Companion, "be not grieved for God is with us. And God sent down his security upon him." (Qur. C. ix.) The true believers are agreed that the Companion mentioned is Abu Bakr, and there will appear a tradition from him on this subject.

Ibn Abi Hatim records from Ibn Abbas concerning the divine words "and God sent down his security upon him," that he said, "that is, upon Abu Bakr, for as to the Prophet, the security never ceased to be with him" And from Ibn Masaud,[2] that Abu Bakr

---

(Cont. 59) variance of opinion regarding his real name. He died at Rabadah a village three miles from Medina. A.H. 32. For particulars of his life consult Ibn Hajr, and an Naw.

1 This name is written Kafiaji by Moursinge. See Introduction.

2 Abdullah b. Masaud b. Ghafil. A eminent Companion and one of the Fugitives both to Abyasinia and Medina and a trusty confident of Muhammad's whom he accompanied on all his expeditions. Some say he died at Kufah, other, at Medina about A.H. 32, being a little more than sixty years of age. An Nawawi.

purchased Bilal[1] from Umayyah b. Khalaf and Ubayy b. Khalaf, for a cloak and ten pieces of money and he set him free for the sake of God: then God revealed. "By the night when it covereth" (Qur XCII) to the words "verily your endeavour is different" *that is* the endeavour of Abu Bakr and Umayyah and Ubayy.

Ibn Jarir records from Aamir B. Abdullah biz Zubayr that Abu Bakr used to give manumission in Mecca to slaves of the true faith, and thus he used to set free old women and other woman when they embraced Islam and his father said to him, "O my son, I see that thou freest weak women, but if thou wert to free strong men, they would stand by thee and protect thee, and repel *harm* from thee." He replied, "O father I desire the things which are of God." He adds "I was told by some of my family that this verse was revealed concerning him "now who is obedient and feareth God" (Qur XCII)-to the end.

Ibn Abi Hatim and at Tabarani record from Urwah that Abu Bakr freed seven *slaves,* all of whom had suffered persecution for the sake of God and regarding him was revealed, "but he who strictly bewareth *idolatry and rebellion* shall be removed, for *from the same*" to the end of the Sura (Qur. XCII). All Bazzar records from Abdullah b-uz Zubayr, that this verse, "by whom no benefit is bestowed on any that it may be recompensed," to the end, (Qur, XCII) was revealed concerning Abu Bakr : and al Bukhari records from Ayesha that Abu Bakr never violated an oath until God revealed the atonement for an oath *violated* (Qur. V).

Al Bazzar and Ibn Asakir record from Usayd-b-Safwan (who enjoyed the Companionship *of the Prophet*) that Ali said, "and he who brought the truth was Muhammad and Abu Bakr as Siddik testified to him." Ibn Asakir says, "this is the tradition regarding this reading but perhaps it is a reading of Ali's.[2]

1 Muhammad's Abyassinian caller to prayer.

2 That is with the words "bil Hakk." The word in the Qurãn is "Sidk" and not "Hakk"- الزي حاء بالصدق و صدق Qun. XXXIX.

Al Hakim records from Ibn Abbas regarding the words of God, "and consult them in the affair" (Qur. III.), that they were revealed concerning Abu Bakr and Omar. And Ibn Abi Hatim from Ibn Shaudab *that the verse* "but for him who dreadeth the tribunal of his Lord *are prepared* two gardens," (Qur. LV), was revealed regarding Abu Bakr, and there are other ascriptions' which I have mentioned in the Reasons of Revelation.

At Tabarani records in his Ausat from Ibn Omar and Ibn Abbas that the divine words "and the good man among the faithful" (Qur. LXVI) were revealed concerning Abu Bakr and Omar. And Abdullah b. Abi Hamid in his Commentary, from Mujahid,[1] that when "verily God and his angels bless the Prophet" (Qur, XXXIII) was revealed, Abu Bakr said, "O Apostle of God! God hath never revealed to thee a blessing but he hath included me in it." Then was revealed this verse "it is he who is gracious to you and his angels *intercede for you* ." (Qur. XXXIII).

Ibn Asakir records from 'Ali b-ul Husayn, that the following verse was revealed regarding Abu Bakr, Omar and Ali, "and we will remove all grudges from their breasts : *they shall be as* brethren sitting over against one another on couches" (Qur. XV); and from Ibn Abbas, that, "we have commanded man *to show* kindness to his parents" down to the words "this was revealed regarding Abu Bakr as Siddik ; and from Ibn Uaynah,[2] that God had chided all the true believers through the Apostle of God, except Abu Bakr alone who had escaped from the reproach : and he recites *the words* "if ye assist not *the Prophet,* verily God *will assist him as He* assisted him formerly when the unbelievers drove him out *of Mecca,* the second of the two when they two were in the cave." (Qur. IX).

---

1 The celebrated Imam and Tabii Abul Hajjaj Mujahid b. Jubayr, was a doctor of high authority on jurisprudence and Qurãnic interpretation. Abdullah b. Omar respected him to such a degree that he held his stirrup when he mounted on horseback, died, A.H. 101, (A.D. 719-20). De Slane I.K.

2 Abu Muhammad Sufiyan b. Uaynah, born at Kufah A.H. 107 and taken by his father to Mecca where he died. A.H. 198 (814 A.D.) He was an Imam of learning piety and of a mortified life, distinguished for the exactitude of the traditions which he handed down. Ibn Khall.

On the traditions handed down regarding his merit coupled with that of Omar over and above what has preceded.

The two Shaykhs record from Abu Hurayrah that he said, "I heard the Apostle of God say, "whilst a shepherd was in the midst of his flock, a wolf rushed upon it and carried off from it a sheep and the shepherd pursued it. The wolf turned to him and said "who *will be a protector* to it on the day of resurrection ?-the day when there will be no other shepherd than myself ;"[1] and as a man was driving an ox which he had laden, it turned to him and spake and said "verily I was not created for this but I was created for tillage" and the people cried out. "Good God, that an ox should talk.!" The Prophet said, "I believe in it and *likewise do* Abu Bakr and Omar;" and Abu Bakr and Omar were not there, that is, they were not present in the assembly, but he bore witness for them both as to their belief in it, because of his knowledge of the perfection of their faith."

At Tirmidi records from Abu Sai'd al Khudri, that the Apostle of God said, "there was never a Prophet but hc had two ministers from the dwellers in heaven, and two ministers from among the dwellers on earth, and my two ministers of the dwellers in heaven, are Gabriel and Michael, and my two minsiters of the dwellers on earth are Abu Bakr and Omar." The traditionists and others record from Said b Zayd,. "I heard the Apostle of God say, "Abu Bakr shall be in paradise and Omar shall be in paradise, and Othman shall be in paradise and Ali shall be in paradise," and he mentioned the whole of the ten;[2] and Al Tirmidi from Abu Sai'd "verily the dwellers in the lofty mansions *(of paradise)*- they that are below them shall see them as ye see the stars shining in the horizon of the

---

1 "Saba" in Yakut (Muajam ul Buldan) is a valley in Palestine in which tradition says, mankind will be assembled for the judgment. This very tradition is quoted in proof – but it also stated that there are other interpretations-what they are I cannot discover. In Kustulani's commentary on al Bukhari this tradition is noted but without explanation. See also Lane. Art, سبع

2 See page 35. Note 1.

sky, and verily Abu Bakr and Omar shall be among them ;" and from Anas, that the Apostle of God went out to his Companions, of the Fugitives and Auxiliaries, an there were seated among them Abu Bakr and Omar, but none of them raised his eyes to him except Abu Bakr and Omar, and they remained gazing upon him and he upon them, and smiling upon him and he upon them.

At Tirmidi and al Hakim record from Ibn Omar that the Apostle of God went forth one day and entered the mosque, with Abu Bakr and Omar, one of them upon his right hand and the other upon his left, and he held their hands and said, "thus shall we arise on the day of judgment :" and at Tirmidi from Ibn Omar, that the Apostle of God said, "I shall be the first from whom the earth shall be rent asunder, then Abu Bakr and then Omar ;" and he and al Hakim record, confirming it on the authority of Ibn Handhalah that the Prophet looked upon Abu Bakr and Omar and said, "These are *my* hearing and *my* sight."

Al Bazzar, and al Hakim record from Abu Arwa and Dausi,[1] that he said, "I was with the Prophet when Abu Bakr and Omar approached and he said "praise be to God who hath strengthened me with ye two." And Abu Yala from Ammar b. Yasir, that the Apostle of God said, "a little while ago, Gabriel came to me and I said "O Gabriel, recount unto me the merits of Omar b-ul Khattab," and he answered "If I were to relate to thee the merits of Omar, the narration of his merits would not be ended during the period in which Noah tarried with his people, for verily Omar is a good work amongst the good works of Abu Bakr;" and Ahmad from Abdur Rahman b. Ghanam, that the Apostle of God said to Ab Bakr and Omar "if you were agreed upon a counsel, I would not oppose you."

Ibn Saa'd relates on the authority of Ibn Omar that he was

---

1 Ibn Hajr can give no account of this person beyond the mention of one or two traditions (including this with a slightly different reading) on his authority. His name and genealogy are unknown-he is supposed to have been present with the Prophet at the affair of "Karkarat ul Kudr" and died at the close of Muawiyah's reign.

asked who used to give decisions in the time of the Apostle of God, and he replied, "Abu Bakr and Omar, and I know of no others besides those two ;" and from Abul Kasim b. Muhammad, that Abu Bakr, Omar, Othman and Ali used to decide cases in the time of the Apostle of God; and at Tabarani, from Ibn Masaud that the Apostle of God said, "every Prophet hath a chosen one among his people, and verily my elect from among my companions, are Abu Bakr and Omar ;" and Ibn Asakir from Ali that the Apostle of God said, "may God have mercy upon Abu Bakr who hath given me his daughter in marriage, and bore me to the city of refuge (Madina) and gave freedom to Bilal - may God have mercy upon Omar who ever speaketh the truth though it be bitter, for the *speaking of the* truth hath left him without a friend-may God have mercy upon Othman before whom the angels are abashed - may God have mercy upon Ali-O God encompass him with the truth whithersoever he goeth."

And at Tabarani records from Sahl that when the Prophet returned from his last pilgrimage, he ascended the pulpit and blessed God and glorified Him and said, 'O people,' verily I am content with him and with Omar and Othman and Ali and Talhah and az Zubayr and Saad and Abdur Rahman b. Auf,[1] and the First Fugitives,[2] know this of them."

Abdullah b. Ahmad records in the "Zawaid uz Zuhd" from Ibn Abi Hazim, that a man came to Ali b-ul Husayn and said, "what place did Abu Bakr and Omar hold near the Apostle of God ?" He replied "that which they hold at this moment." And Ibn Saa'd from Bistam-b. Muslim, that the Apostle of God said to Abu Bakr and Omar, "no one shall have authority over you two after me;" and

---

1 Abu Muhammad Abdur Rahman b. Auf of the Kuraysh a native of Medina, one of the ten to whom paradise was assured, died A.H. 32, aged 72. An Nawawi.

2 The first fugitives to Abyasinia who were driven by the persecution of the Kuraysh to seek shelter with the king (Najashi) of that country. There were eleven in number, and four of them were accompanied by their wives. See Muir's Life of Muhammad Vol. II p. 133.

Ibn Asakir, a tradition relating direct to the Prophet through Anas, "Love towards Abu Bakr and Omar is faith, hatred towards them is infidelity;" and from Ibn Masaud, "Love towards Abu Bakr and Omar and a knowledge of them is an injunction of the law : " and from Anas, direct from the Prophet, "verily I hope *for the same benefit* to my people, by their *profession of love* towards Abu Bakr and Omar, that I hope for them for their profession *of faith* "there is no God but God."

On the traditions handed referring exclusively to his merit, over and above what has preceded.

The two Shaykhs record on the authority of Abu Hurayrah that he said, "I heard the Apostle of God say," he who repeatedly[1] giveth of the things *that are his,* for the sake of God, shall be summoned through the gates of paradise *in these words:* "'O servant of God, this is good *for thee to enter by,"* and he who is of those who pray, shall be summoned through the Gate of Prayers, and he who is of those who have fought for the faith, shall be summoned through the Gate of Religious War, and he who is of those who give in alms, shall be summoned through the Gate of Alms, and he who is of those who fast shall be summoned through the Gate of Fasting-*that is*[2] the Gate of Satiety." Then Abu Bakr said, "it cannot be necessary that one should be summoned though these gates-shall, then, one be summoned through them all ?" And he answered, "yes, and I hope that thou wilt be among them, O Abu Bakr :" and Ibn Dauud and al Hakim from Abu Hurayrah that the Apostle of God said, "but thou, O Abu Bakr, shall be the first, of my people to enter paradise :" and the two Shaykhs from Abu

---

1 My authorities for this sense of the word زوجين are Turbushti and Tibi, see the Commentary of Kustulani on this tradition.

2 The MS. Omits "the Gate of Fasting." The printed text is correct here : the words من باب الصيام being in al Bukhari – where it is explained as I have translated it.

Sai'd that the Apostle of God said, "he who hath laid me under the greatest obligation of all men both with his person and his goods, is Abu Bakr, and if I were to take a friend other than my Lord, I would surely take Abu Bakr, but the brotherhood of the faith *is sufficient.*"

Al Bukhari records on the authority of Abud Darda that he said, "I was sitting with the Prophet when there came forward Abu Bakr, and greeted him and said, "verily a dispute arose between me and Omar and I was hasty with him, but afterwards I repented and besought him to forgive me, but he refused, wherefore I have come to thee," and he said "My God have mercy upon thee, O Abu Bakr" three times. Afterwards, verily Omar repented and went to the house of Abu Bakr, but found him not, and he hastened to the Prophet and the face of the Prophet became flushed with wrath so that Abu bakr was afraid, and he fell upon his knees and said twice. "O Apostle of God, I was more intemperate than he." The Prophet exclaimed *to the bystanders* "verily, the Lord sent me unto you as a Prophet, and you said, "thou liest," and Abu Bakr said, "thou hast spoken truly," and he comforted me with *the service of* his person and his goods ; then will ye not leave me to me my Companion ?" *this he said* twice and after that he was troubled no more." Ibn Adi records a similar *account* from the tradition of Ibn Omar in which *is the following*, "the Apostle of God said," afflict me not in my Companion, for verily the Lord sent me as a guide unto salvation and the true faith and you said, "thou hast lied," and Abu Bakr said, "thou hast spoken truly," and had it not been that the Lord had named him "Companion," verily I would have taken him as an intimate friend but the brotherhood of Islam *is sufficient.*" And Ibn Asakir from al Mikdam[1] that Akil[2] the son of Abu Talib, and

1 Al Mikdam b. Madi Karib, one of the Companions-he resided at Emessa, and related forty-seven traditions regarding his master, died in Syria A.H. 87 at the age of 91. An Nawawi.

2 Abu Yazid or Abu Isa the 2nd son of Abu Talib ; he fought unwillingly on the side of the infidels al Badr, and was taken prisoner and was converted before Hudaybiyah. He was a distinguished genealogist. He was quick in repartee says an Nawawi, and generally silence his antagonist. He died in the Caliphate of Muawiyah, having lost his sight-and was buried at al Bakii the cemetery at Medina.

Abu Bakr were reviling each other and he adds that Abu Bakr used to be a great reviler as well as a great genealogist but that he had learned courtesy of manner from his Companionship with the Prophet and he turned away from Akil and complained to the Prophet, and the Apostle of God rose up before the people and said, "will ye not leave unto me my Companion, what is your worth and his ? By Allah there is not a man among you, but darkness is upon the door of his house, save the door of Abu Bakr, and verily upon his door, there is light-and by Allah, verily ye said *to me,* "thou hast lied," and Abu Bakr said "thou hast spoken truly," and ye withheld your possession, but he gave unto me that which he had, and ye withheld your possessions, but he gave unto me that which he had, and ye reviled me, but he cherished me and followed me." And al Bukhari from Ibn Omar that the Apostle of God said, "he who traileth his garments haughtily, the Lord will not book upon him on the day of judgment," and Abu Bakr said "should either of the two sides of my garment trail loosely, must I be careful of that?" The Apostle of god replied "thou art not he who doeth that in pride." And Muslim from Abu Hurayrah, that the Apostle of God said, "who among you hath begun the day fasting ?" And Abu Bakr replied "I have ;" then he said "who among you hath fed the poor to-day ?" Abu Bakr replied "I;" then he said, "who among you, hath visited the sick to-day," and Abu Bakr replied "I;" then the Apostle of God said "these things shall not come together in a man, but he shall enter paradise." Verily this tradition hath been handed down through the narration o Anas b Malik and Abdur Rahman b. Abi Bakr, and[1] has mentioned this tradition of Anas and at the end of it "paradise shall surely be thy portion." And al Bazzar records the tradition of Abdur Rahman and its words *are these*, "the Apostle of God read the prayers in the morning : then he turned to his Companions and said "who, among you, hath begun the day fasting ?" Omar replied 'O! Apostle of God, I did not purpose to myself, during the past night, to fast, thus I have become

1 The MS. has here a blank and the printed text does not supply the omission.

this morning as one who hath broken his fast,"[1] and Abu Bakr said "but I purposed to myself during the night to fast, and thus I have risen fasting." Then *the Prophet* said "Hath any among you visited the sick to-day ?" and Omar replied, "O Apostle of God, we have not gone forth *from here,* how then can we have visited the sick ?" but Abu Bakr said "I heard that my brother[2] Abdur Rahman b. Auf was sick and I went round that way to him, to see how he was this morning." Then he said "hath any one among you fed the poor today ?" and Omar replied, "we have been praying, O Apostle of God, and have not gone forth, but Abu Bakr said, "I entered the mosque when, behold ! there came a beggar, and I found a piece of barley bread in the hand of Abdur Rahman and I took it and gave it to him," and he said, "Rejoice with the good tidings of paradise;" then he spoke a word which comforted Omar, and Omar knew that he should never purpose to do a good work but Abu Bakr would be before him in it."

Abu Yala records from Ibn Masaud, that he said "I was in the mosque praying when there entered the Apostle of God, and with him Abu Bakr and Omar and he found me praying and he said, "ask-it shall be granted unto you," then he said "whosoever wishes to read the Qurãn in a fresh and joyous manner, let him read it with the reading of the son of Umm Abd."[3] Then I returned to my house and Abu Bakr came to me and gave me the good tidings *regarding what the Prophet had said :* then came Omar and he found Abu Bakr going forth, having already been before him and he said "verily thou art the foremost in good." Ahmad records on good authority from Rabiihul Aslami,[4] that he said, "a disputation

1 The mere act a abstaining from food during the day, does not constitute a fast *religiously* speaking. The *intention* to fast, must precede the abstention to make it efficacious. During the long fast of the Ramadhan the intention is pre-supposed and need not be daily renewed.

2 The term brother is, as is well-known, applied to all of a tribe indiscriminately without reference to consanguinity.

3 The mother of Ibn Masaud.

4 Rabiih b. Kaab b. Malik al Aslami Hijazi, one of the Companions, settled at Medina and died at Harrah in A.H. 63. Ibn Hajr.

arose between me and Abu Bakr, when he said to me a word which I disliked, and he repented and said to me, "O Rabiih return it to me likewise, so that there may be retaliation." I replied "I shall not do so." He answered "Thou shalt say it or I shall call up against thee, the Apostle of God." I said, "I will not do so," and Abu Bakr departed and there came some men of the tribe of Aslam and they said to me, "may God have mercy upon Abu Bakr! for what reason hath he called up against thee *the Prophet,* he being the one that hath said to thee what he hath said?" And I replied, "Know ye not who is Abu Bakr as Siddik ? he is the "second of the two"- and he is the grey beard of the Muslims-look to yourselves that he turn not and see ye abetting me against him, lest he be angered and the Apostle of God come and be wroth on account of his anger, and the Lord, be wrathful on account of the anger of those two, and Rabiih perish ;" and Abu Bakr departed and I followed him alone until he came to the Apostle of God and he related to him the story as it occurred : then *the Prophet* lifted up his head towards me and said," O Rabiih, what hath happened between thee and as Siddik?" I replied, "O Apostle of God such and such a thing happened and he said to me a word which I disliked, then he said to me, "speak to me as I have spoken, so that there may be a retaliation," and I refused." Then the Apostle of God said good, do not return it, but say 'the Lord have mercy upon the, O Abu Bakr :'" then I said "the Lord have mercy upon thee O Abu Bakr."

Al Tirmidi records and approves a tradition on the authority of Ibn Omar, that the Apostle of God said to Abu Bakr "Thou shalt be my Companion at the Pool,[1] as thou wert my Companion in the Cave; and Abdullah b. Ahmad from Ibn Abbas,[2] that the Apostle of God said, "Abu Bakr was my Companion and my Conforter in the

---

1 Salsabil, the fountain in paradise where the Prophet is believed to give drink to the faithful who are thirsty.

2 These words "from Ibn Abbas" are omitted in the printed edition but supplied by the MS.

cave;" and al Bayhaki from Hudayfah[1] that the Apostle of God said "verily there is a bird in paradise *whose flesh tasteth* like *that of* Bactrian Camels ;" Abu Bakr said, "it is then delicate of flavour, O Apostle of God"-he replied, "he who eateth of them shall enjoy them and thou shalt be of those who shall eat of them :" and Abu Yala from Abu Hurayrah, that the Apostle of God said, "I was borne towards the heavens, and I passed no heaven but I found therein my name Muhammad the Apostle of God and Abu Bakr as Siddik as my vicegerent." Its authorities are weak, but the same has been handed down in the tradition of Ibn Abbas, Ibn Omar, Anas, Abu Sai'd and Abu d. Darda with weak ascriptions, but supporting each other reciprocally.

Abu Abi Hatim and Abu Nuaym record on the authority of Said b. Jubayr[2] that he said, "I was reading *this verse* before the Prophet- "Oh thou soul which art at rest," (Qur. LXXXIX), when Abu Bakr said "O Apostle of God surely this is a good saying." and the Apostle of God replied, "yea, verily, the angel shall say it to thee at the time of the death." And Ibn Abi Hatim from Aamir b Abdillah biz Zubayr that he said, that when *the verse,* "and if we had commanded them, *saying*, slay yourselves," (Qur. IV) was revealed, Abu Bakr said, "O Apostle of God, didst thou command me to slay myself, I would do so," and he replied "thou speakest truly." And Abul Kasim al Baghawi from Ibn Abi Mulaykah, "the Apostle of

---

1 Abu Abdullah Hudayfah b-ul Yaman. He and his father were both at the battle of Ohud when his father was accidentally killed by his own side. He was much trusted by Muhammad and employed on secret and important negotiations. He was engaged in the campaign of Nahawand and commanded the troops at the capture of Hamadan, Ray and Dinawar. Omar made him governor of Madain where he died in A.H. 36, forty days after the assassination of Omar. An Nawawi, T.A.

2 Abu Abdullah or Muhammad Said b. Jubayr b. Hisham al Asadi was a black and a client by enfranchisement to the tribe of Waliba b-ul Harith. He was an eminent Tabii and a native of Kufah. He learnt his traditions from Ibn Omar and Ibn Abbas. He was put to death by Hajjaj b. Yusuf for his revolt against Abdul Malik b. Marwan, and the last hours of Hajjaj were said to have been tormented by his victim's apparition. His death took place in A.H. 95 (A.D. 714) and was followed in the same year by that of his murderer. Ibn Khall.

God and his Companions went into a pool and he commmanded that every man should swim towards his friend ;" he adds, "and every man swam until there were left the Apostle of God and Abu Bakr, and the Apostle of God swam towards Abu Bakr and embraced him and said, "were I to choose an intimate friend until such time as I saw the Lord face to face, verily I would take Abu Bakr, But he is my Companion." Wakii[1] has followed him on the authority of Abdul Jabbar b-ul Ward, (state Ibn Asakir,) and Abdul Jabbar is trustworthy, and his master, was the Imam Ibn Abu Mulaykah but it is irregular in transmission and narrated but by one authority. I remark that at Tabarani has recorded it in the "Kabir" and Ibn Shahin in the "Sunnat" in a different manner, but in uninterrupted succession from Ibn Abbas. Ibn[2] Abid Dunya records in the "Makarimul Akhlaq," (noble qualities) and Ibn Asakir, according to the ascription of Sadakah b. Maymun al Karashi, from Sulayman b. Yasar[3] that the Apostle of God said, "virtuous qualities are three hundred and sixty *in number ;* when God desires a good servant, he creates in him one of these qualities through which, he may gain admission to paradise." Abu Bakr said "O Apostle of God is there in me one of them ?" He replied, "Yes, the sum of them all." And Ibn Asakir according to another ascription through Sadakah from some other, "virtuous qualities are three hundred and sixty ;" and Abu Bakr said "have I any of these ?" He replied, 'all of them are in thee, therefore I give thee joy, O Abu Bark." And Ibn Asakir, according to the ascription of Mujamma; b. Yaqub the Auxiliary,

---

1 Abu Sufiyan Wakii b-ul Jarrah, born at Kufah A.H. 129 an eminent jurisconsult and traditionist. He studied under Abu Hanifah and used to decide points of law. He made the pilgrimage 70 times and on returning from the last, he died at Fayd, a town midway between Mecca and Kufah A.H. 197 (A.D. 812-3). De Slane, I.K.

2 Abu Bakr Abdullah b. Muhammad b. Ubayd a member by adoption, of the Kuraysh, and surnamed Ibn Abi d Dunya, composed works on ascetic and other subjects, and was a traditionist. He was preceptor to some of the Abbaside family and one of the pupils was al Muatadhid. He received a pension of fifteen dinars a month. Died A.H. 281, (A.D. 894). De Slane, I.K.

3 A Tabii and one of the seven great jurisconsults of Medina and a traditionist of repute, lied A.H. 103. An Nawawi.

from his father, who said, "there was a circle of the people round the Apostle of God, clustered together, so that they were as walls *around him,* but the seat of Abu Bakr among them was vacant, and no one among the people sought to take it, and when Abu Bakr came, he sat down on that seat, and the Prophet turned his face towards him and directed to him his discourse, and the people listened." And from Anas that the Apostle of God said, "the love of Abu Bakr, and gratitude towards him is incumbent upon every one of my people." And he records the same from the tradition of Sahl-b-Saa'd. And from Ayesha, direct from the Prophet, "all men shall be judged excepting Abu Bakr."

On what has been handed down of the sayings of the Companions and pious early Muslims[1] regarding his merit.

Al Bukhari records on the authority of Jabir, that Omar-b'ul Khattab said, "Abu Bakr is our prince." And al Bayhaki in the "Shaabul Iman" (people of the faith) from Omar, that he said, "If the faith of Abu Bakr were weighed against the faith of mankind, it would surely out weigh them." And Ibn Abi Khaythamah and Abdullah b. Ahmad in the Zawaid uz Zuhd (Profusions of Piety) from Omar that he said, "verily Abu Bakr was every foremost and conspicuous-verily I would I were a hair on the breast of Abu Bakr" (Musaddad in his Musnad) ; and "I would wish to be in paradise that I might behold Abu Bakr" (Ibn Abid Dunya and Ibn Asakir) ; and "the fragrance of Abu Bakr is sweeter than the fragrance of musk" (Abu Nuaym).

Ibn Asakir records from Ali that he went to Abu Bakr and *found that* he was reciting the praises of God, and he said "no one

1 According to Abul Mahasin السلف is particularly applied to Ayesha, Abu Bakr, Omar, Othman Talhah, az Zubayr, Muawiyah and Amr b-ul Aas : السلف الصالح is applied to the first chief persons of the Tabiis. Lane,

shall look upon God, with the record of his deeds *in his hand,*[1] who is dearer to me than this praiser of the Lord." And from Abdur Rahman b Abi Bakr as Siddik that the Apostle of God said, "Omar, the son of al Khattab hath told me that he never *attempted to* precede Abu Bakr in a good deed, but Abut Bakr was before him in it." And at Tabarani in his Ausat, from Ali that he said, "by Him in whose hand is my life, I never sought to be foremost in any good action, but Abu Bakr anticipated me in it," and from Juhayfah, that Ali said, "the best of men after the Apostle of God, are Abu Bakr and Omar-never shall there be joined together love of me and hatred towards Abu Bakr and Omar in the heart of a true believer." And in the "Kabir" from Amir, that he said, "three among the Kuraysh are the most comely of the Kuraysh in face, the best of them in disposition, the most constant in heart ; if they converse with thee, they will not lie to thee, and if thou speakest with them, they will not give thee the lie, Abu Bakr as Siddik, Abu Ubaydah b-ul Jarrah and Othman b Affan." Ibn Saad records on the authority of Ibrahim[2] and Nakhai, that Abu Bakr was named the Compassionate on account of his benignity and clemency. And Ibn Asakir from ar Rabii b Anas, that it is written in the Primeval Record,[3] "Abu Bakr is like unto raid *which* wherever it falleth, it doeth good." Also that ar Rabii said "I looked among the Companions of the Prophet, but I found not a Prophet that had a Companion like unto Abu Bakr as Siddik." And from Az Zuhri, "among the virtues of Abu Bakr *was this,* that he never doubted concerning God a single moment ?" And from az Zubayr b. Bakkar, "I heard several of the learned say that the preachers among the Companions of the Apostle of God were abu Bakr and Ali." And from Abu Hasin, "there was never

---

1 It is the Muhammadan belief that at the last day, every man shall stand before the judgment seat holding in his hand the record of his actions inscribed in it by the "Katibayn" or the two attendant angels who are with each man during his life.

2 Abu Imran Ibrahim b. Yazid an Nakhai native of Kufah and celebrated as an Imam and doctor. He died A.H. 95 or 96 (A.D. 713-4) aged 49. Nakhai is from Nakha' a great branch of the tribe of Madhij in Yaman. Ibn Khall.

3 Called also لوح محفوظ the Guarded Tablet, existing before all time in which is inscribed everything destined to occur.

begotten of Adam among his progeny, after the Prophets and Apostle, any more eminent than Abu Bakr, and verily Abu Bakr on the day of Apostasy[1] stood up as a Prophet among the Prophets."

Ad Dinauri records in the "Mujalisat,"[2] and Ibn Asakir from as Shaabi, that he said, "the most pure, the most High God hath distinguished Abu Bakr by four qualities, by which He hath distinguished none other among men : he named him 'the Witness to the Truth,' (as Siddik) and hath named 'The Witness to the Truth' none other besides him, and he was the Companion in the Cave with the Apostle of God, and his associate in his flight, and the Apostle of God commanded him to read te Prayers, the Muslims being witnesses." And Ibn Abi Dauud[3] in the Kitabul Masabih from Abu Jaafar, that Abu Bakr used to hear the secret converse of Gabriel with the Prophet but did not see him. And al Hakim from Ibnul Musayyab,[4] that Abu Bakr stood to the Prophet in the place of a Wazir, for he used to consult him in all his affairs, and he was the second to embrace Islam, and the second in the Cave and the second in the shed on the day of Badr, and the second in his sepulcher,[5] and the Apostle of God never gave precedence of him to any one.

---

1 See not 2, page 50.

2 A work partly on tradition, partly historical, with extracts from poetical authors by Ahmad b. Mardan ad Dinauri of the Maliki school who died A.H. 113. Ittihafun Nabala by Sadik Hasan Khan of Bhopal.

3 Abu Bakr Abdullah b. Abi Dauud was a Hafidh of the first eminence at Baghdad, son of the great traditionist Abu Dauud. He died A.H. 316 (A.D. 928). Ibn Khallakan says that he composed a work called "Kitabul Masabih (the Book of Lanterns). Both the printed text and MS. Have "Kitab ul Masahif" which must be an error.

4 His father's name must be pronounced Musayyab, says Ibn Khallakan, (as being the passive participle of the verb Sayab) but it is said that Said pronounced it Musayyib (active participle) because he had said "may God reward (sayab) him who pronounces my father's name Musayyib."

5 His tomb at Medina is between the tomb of the Prophet and that of Omar.

On the tradition and the verse of the Qurãn indicative of the Caliphate of Abu Bakr and the sayings of the doctors thereon.

At Tirmidi records with approval, and al Hakim likewise, confirming it on the authority of Hudayfah that the Apostle of God said, "Follow these two after me, Abu Bakr and Omar." And Abul Kasim al Baghawi on good authority from Abdullah b. Omar, "I heard the Apostle of God say, 'there shall be twelve Caliphs succeeding me, but Abu Bakr shall tarry but a little while'" There is unanimity regarding the correctness of the first part of this tradition, handed down in several lines of ascription, and indeed the explanation of it hath already gone before in the beginning of this book. In the "Sahihayn" *it is stated* regarding the preceding tradition, that when the Prophet was preaching near upon the time of his death and said, "God hath given his servant a choice," and at the end *of the tradition*[1] "there shall not remain a door but it shall be closed save the door of Abu Bakr," and in another reading of the two authorities, "there shall not remain a wicket in the mosque, but the wicket of Abu Bakr," the learned assert that this was indicative of his Caliphate, for he used to go forth through it to prayer with the Muslims." Indeed this reading has come down in the tradition of Anas and its words *are these,* "close ye these doors leading into the mosque, except the door of Abu Bakr."

The two Shaykhs record on the authority of Jubayr b. Mutim that he said, "a woman went to the Prophet, and he commanded her to come to him another time; she said, 'suppose I come and find thee not ?" (as if she spoke of his death). He answered, 'if thou findest me not, then go to Abu Bakr.'" Al Hakim records and verifies *the tradition* on the authority of Anas that he said, 'the

1 See p. 51.

Banu Mustalik[1] sent to the Apostle of God, *saying,* 'ask him – to whom must we give our poor-rate after his death ?" and I went to him and asked him, and he said unto Abu Bakr,'" And Ibn Asakir from Ibn Abbas that he said, "a woman went to the Prophet to ask something and he said to her 'come again *another time.'* She replied 'O Apostle of God, if I come and find thee not ?' (referring to his death). He said 'if thou comest and findest me not, then go to Abu Bakr, for verily he *shall be* Caliph after me.'" And Muslim from Ayesha, "the Apostle of God said to me in his *last* illness call to me thy father and thy brother that I may write a testament, for, verily I fear lest the covetous should covet and speak, saying, "I am the most worthy,' but God and the true believers will reject *all* save Abu Bakr.'" And Ahmad and others record the same from her with other ascriptions: according to one *of them,* she said, 'the Apostle of God in his illness o which he died, said to me, 'call to me Abdul Rahman the son of Abu Bakr, that I may write a testament in favour of Abu Bakr, so that none may oppose him after me;' then he said, 'nay, leave it, God forbid that the true believers should be at strife regarding Abu Bakr.," And Muslim from Ayesha, that she was asked whom the Apostle of God would have named as a successor, if he had appointed one : she replied "Abu Bakr." It was said to her "whom next after Abu Bakr ?" she answered "Omar." They said to her "whom after Omar ?" She replied "Abu Ubaydah b-ul Jarrah." And the two Shaykhs from Abu Musa[2] al Ashari that he said, "the Prophet fell ill and his sickness increased,

---

1 The Banu Mustalik (descended from Mustalik b. Amr b. Rabii b. Kharijah) dwell in the district of Kudayd, between Mecca and Medina near the sea coast. In A.H. 5, this tribe rebelled against Muhammad, but were brought to obedience by his marching against them in person, with Omar and defeating them. Raudhat us Safa. Muhammad b. Khawand Shah. It was on his return from the expedition that Ayesha was by an accident, left asleep by the side of the road and discovered next morning by Safwan b-ul Muattal and brought to camp. To save her reputation was the object of the 24th Chapter of the Qurãn.

2 Abdullah b. Kays Abu Musa al Ashari-such is his name given by Ibn Hajr. He was the arbitrator (See page 10) at Siffin on the part of Ali. He had served as governor under Muhammad, Abu Bakr, Omar, Othman and Ali, and died in A.H. 50 (A.D. 670-1). Ibn Khall.

and he said, command Abu Bakr to rad prayers before the people.' Ayesha answered, 'O Apostle of God, verily he is a man of soft heart : when he rises up in thy place, he will be unable to pray before the people.' Then he said, 'command Abu Bakr to pray before the people,' but she only repeated what she had said. Again he exclaimed, 'command Abu Bakr to pray before the people – verily ye are the mistresses[1] of Joseph'-and the Apostle went to him himself. Thus he prayed before the people during the lifetime of the Apostle of God."[2] In one of the traditions from Ayesha, *the reading is,* "I frequently returned *to this subject* with the Apostle of God and nothing induced me to this frequent recurrence, but that it did not come into my mind that the people would ever be satisfied that any man should stand in his place after him, and that I saw that no one would stand in his place but the people would take it as an ill omen, therefore I hoped that might turn the Apostle of God from *naming* Abu Bakr." And in the tradition of Ibn Zama'a *it is recorded,* that the Apostle of God ordered them to read the prayers, and Abu Bakr was not present, but Omar came forth and prayed, then the Apostle of God cried out, "No-no-no-God and the Muslims will not suffer any but Abu Bakr to pray before the people." And according to the tradition of Ibn Omar, "Omar recited the Takbir and raised his head angrily and said 'where is the son of Abu Kuhafah ?" The learned say that in this tradition is the clearest proof that as Siddik was the most eminent of the Companions absolutely, and the most deserving of the Caliphate among them and the best of them in the office of Imam. Al Ashari says, "it is indeed undoubtedly ascertained that the Apostle of God commanded as Siddik to pray before the people in the presence of the Fugitives and the Auxiliaries, by his words, he shall stand as Imam before the people who is the best read, (of them in the Book of God.' This proves that he was the best read,) that is the most learned of them in the Qurãn : and verily the Companions thems elves were

---

2 Meaning "enticers to evil." The MS. and printed edition have انكن for انقن Lane gives the tradition with انقن .

3 Here follows a list of other authorities for this tradition which to avoid the tedious repetition of names. I have omitted. The few whom these could interest are not likely to look for them in the English translation.

convinced that he was the most deserving of the Caliphate, and among these was Omar (and the words of Omar will follow in the section on the convenant of allegiance) and among them was *also* Ali."

Ibn Asakir records on his authority that he said, "verily the Prophet commanded Abu Bakr to pray before the people and indeed I was present, and I was not absent and was suffering from no illness ;[1] and we accepted for our temporal affairs what the Prophet had approved for our spiritual concerns." The learned say that Abu Bakr was recongnised for his fitness for the Imamate during the time of the Prophet. And Ahmad and Abu Dauud and others record on the authority of Sahl b Saad, that there was a feud in the tribe of Amr b Auf and the Prophet arrived and went to them after mid-day, that he might make peace between them, and said, "O Bilal – If the time of prayers should be at hand and I come not, then command Abu Bakr to pray before the people ;" and when the time for afternoon prayers came, Bilal announced the prayers and then commanded Abu Bakr, and he prayed.

Abu Bakr as Shafii[2] records in the "Ghilaniyat" and Ibn Asakir from Hafsah[3] that she said to the Apostle of God, "when thou wert ill, thou gravest precedence to Abu Bakr :" he replied, "It was not

---

1 That is to say that he was an eye-witness in the full possession of his senses.

2 Abu Bakr Muhammad b. Abdullah-b. Ibrahim known as al Bazzar, as Shafii, died, A.H. 354. The Ghilaniyat is a collection of traditions written from the dictation of the author's Shaykhs. It received its name probably from Abu Talib Muhammad b. Muhammad b. Ibrahim b. Ghilan, who taught the traditions. He died in A.H. 404. Ittihaful Nubala.

3 The daughter of Omar-b'ul Khattab : her first husband was Hasan b. Hudafah who fought at Badr and died at Medina –she was then offered by her father to Abu Bakr and Othman successively who both declined the proposal. Omar, mentioning this circumstance to Muhammad, he replied, "One shall marry, Hafsah who is greater than Othman (meaning himself) and one shall marry Othman who is greater than Hafsah" (meaning his own daughter Umm Kulthum). Abu Bakr afterwards excused himself to Omar by saying that his knowledge of his master's predilection for Hafsah, was the cause of his declining, otherwise he would gladly marry her. Ibn Hajr.

I who preferred him, but God who preferred him." And Ibn Saad from al Hasan, that Abu Bakr said, "O Apostle of God, I never cease to see myself in vision treading in the courtyards of men :" he replied, "thou shalf be among men as a road *for them :*" he added, "and I see on my breast what are like unto two spots." He replied "*those are* two years."[1]

Ibn Asakir records on the authority of Abu Bakr that he said, "I went to Omar and there were some people engaged in eating in his presence, and he cast his eyes upon a man, the hindmost of the number, and said, 'what dost thou find *of events* before thy time in the books thou readest ?' He replied 'the vicegerent of the Apostle, will be his witness to the truth'" (Siddik). And from Muhammad b-uz Zubayr, that he said "Omar-b. Abdil Aziz sent me to al Hasan of Basrah, to ask him concerning certain things, "and I went to him and said to him, "Satify me regarding that in which people differ- did the Apostle of God name Abu Bakr his successor ?" and al Hasan who was seated, stood erect and said, "can such a thing be in doubt ! thou hast no father. Yea, by that God than whom there is no other God, verily he named him his successor, for he was undoubtedly the most learned in divine knowledge and the most devout towards Him and the most steadfast in his fear, inasmuch as he would have died for its sake, even though He had not commanded him there-unto."[2] And Ibn Adi records from Abu Bakr b Ayyash[3] that he narrates, "ar Rashid said to me, O Abu Bakr how did the people come to appoint Abu Bakr as Siddik successor ?" I said, "O prince of the faithful, God was silent and his apostle was silent, and the true believers were silent. He replied, "By Allah, thou hast but increased my anxiety." I said[4] "O prince of the faithful,

1 Signifying that they were Prophetic of the duration of his Caliphate.

2 "If we had commanded them *saying* 'Slay yourselves or depart from your houses,' they would not have done it." Qur. IV.

3 Abu Bakr Salim b. Ayyash an eminent Traditionist and native of Kufah. Eighteen days after the death of ar Rashid, Ibn Ayyash died at Kufah, A.H. 193. (809) at the age of ninety-eight. Ibn Khall.

4 The text has "he said" meaning the narrator. In similar instances in Future, the English idiom will be followed, to avoid breaks in the narrative and references to footnotes.

the Prophet fell ill during eight days and Bilal went in to him and said, 'O Apostle of God, who is to pray before the people ?" He replied, 'command Abu Bakr to pray before the people ;' and Abu Bakr prayed before the people during the eight days, and the divine inspiration continued to descend *upon Muhammad,* but the Apostle of God was silent on account of the silence of the Lord, and the Faithful were silent on account of the silence of the Apostle of God; -this pleased him and he said 'May God bless thee.'"

Some of the learned have deduced the Caliphate of as Siddik from the verses of the Qurãn. Thus al Bayhaki records from al Hasan of Basrah regarding the divine words, "O true believers, whoever of you apostatizeth from his religion, God will certainly bring *other people to supply his place* whom He will love and who will love Him" (Qur. V), that he said, "this, by Allah, *signifieth* Abu Bakr and his Companions, for when the Arabs apostatized, Abu Bakr and his Companions waged war with them, till he brought them back to Islam." And Yunas b. Bukayr, from Katadah, that he said, "when the Prophet died the Arabs apostatized," then he goes on to relate the expedition of Abu Bakr against them till he says, "and we used to declare that this verse was revealed regarding Abu Bakr and his Companions, "God will certainly bring *other* people *to supply his place,* whom He will love and who will love Him." And Ibn Abi Hatim, from Juaybar, regarding the divine words, "say unto the Arabs of the desert who were left behind, ye shall be called forth against a mighty *and* a war like nation (Qur. XLVIII), that he said, "these were the Banu Hunayfah,"[1] Ibn Abi Hatim and Ibn Kutaybah[2] say that this verse is a proof of the Caliphate of Abu Bakr as Siddik for it was he who summoned the people to fight against them. The Shaykh Abul Hasan al

1 They inhabited al Yamamah and were the followers of Musaylama Muhammad's rival. Sale, p. 415.

2 Abu Muhammad Abdullah b. Muslim b. Kutaybah, was a grammarian and philologe of eminence. He taught traditions in Baghdad. He was author of very numerous works on a variety of subjects. His father was a native of Marw ; but he himself was born at Baghdad, or as some say at Kufah, A.H. 213, (828-9), died A.H. 270 (884). Ibn Khall.

Ashari[1] relates "I heart Abul Abbas bus Shurayh say, that the Caliphate of Abu Bakr is *predicted* in this verse of the Qurãn :" he adds, "for the learned are agreed that after its revelation there were no wars to which *the people* were summoned except those wherein Abu Bakr summoned them[2] and the people, to the reduction of the apostates and those who refused tribute." He continues "this is demonstrative of the right of the succession of Abu Bakr and the duty of allegiance to him, since God has declared that he who turneth away from it "shall be punished with a grievous punishment." (Qur. XLVIII).

Ibn Kathir says, "they who interpret the word 'nation' as being the Persians and Greeks, *for them it is sufficient* that it was as Siddik who fitted out an army against them, and the final settlement of their affairs was left in the hands of Omar and Othman, for those two were but branches of as Siddik." The Most High says, "God promiseth unto such of you as believe and do good works that he will cause them to succeed *the unbelievers* in the earth" (Qur. XXIV) : this verse, says Ibn Kathir, is applicable to the Caliphate of Abu Bakr." Ibn Abi Hatim records in his Commentary on the authority of Abdur Rahman b. Abdil Hamid al Madhi, that the Jurisdiction of Abu Bakr and Omar is *to be found* in the Book of God according to the word of God, "God promiseth unto each of you as believe and do good works, that he will cause them to succeed

---

1 Abul Hasan Ali al Ashari drew his descent from Abu Musa one of the prophet's Companions. He was an able defender of the Sunnite doctrines and the founder of the sect called Asharis. Abu Bakr al Bakilani was a great supporter of his peculiar views. He was born in Basrah, A.H. 270 (883-4) and died at Baghdad between A.H. 330 and 340, (941-52). He was at first a Motazilite but made a public renunciation of his belief in freewill and the creation of the Qurãn in the mosque at Basrah and wrote in refutation of that school. His works are 55 in number. Ibn Khall.

2 That is "the Arabs who were left behind" mentioned in the above verse. These were the Tribes of Aslam, Juhaynah, Muzaynah and Ghifar who being summoned to attend Muhammad in the expedition of Hudaybiyah, stayed behind and excused themselves by saying that their families must suffer in their absence, whereas in reality, they wanted firmness in the faith and courage to face the Kuraysh. Sale, p. 414.

the unbelievers in the earth." And al Khatib from Abu Bakr b. Ayyash, that Abu Bakr as Siddik is *mentioned* in the Qurãn as the successor of the Apostle of God, for the Most High God says, "to the poor Fugitives"[1] &c., to his word "these are men of veracity." He therefore whom God calls 'truthful" cannot lie : and the Companions used to address him "O vicegerent of the Apostle of God." Al Bayhaki records on the authority of az Zafarani[2] that he relates, "I heard as Shafii say, "the people concurred in the Caliphate of Abu Bakr and that was, because men were in perplexity after the death of the Apostle of God, but they found not beneath the expanse of heaven a better than Abu Bakr, and they placed him in authority over them."

Asad-us-Sunnah in his Fadhail, (excellencies) records on the authority of Muawiyah b. Kurrah[3] that he said, "the Companions of the Apostle of God never doubted that Abu Bakr was the Vicegerent of the Apostle of God, and they never called him anything but vicegerent of the Apostle of God, and they in no case concurred in what was false or erroneous."

Al Hakim records and confirms it on the authority of Ibn Masaud that he said, "The Muslims never approved a thing to be good, but it was good in the sight of the Lord, and they never judged a thing to be pernicious, but it was pernicious in the sight of

---

1 "*A part also belongeth* to the poor Muhajerin who have been dispossessed of their houses and their substance, seeking favour from God, and his good will and assisting God and his Apostle. These are men of veracity" (Qur. LIX.) Wherefore Muhammad distributed those spoils among the Muhajerin (Fugitives) only and gave no part to the Auxiliaries, except only to three of them who were in necessitous circumstances. Sale, p. 445.

2 Abu Ali al Hasan-b. Muhammad-b. as Sabbah, az Zufarani, was one of as Shafiis disciples. He attained an eminent rank as a doctor of law and tradition died A.H. 260 (874). Zafarani is derived from az Zafaraniyah (the saffron filed) A village near Baghdad. The street of this name in the city is called after this doctor who lived in it. Ibn Khall.

3 Muawiyah b. Kurrah-b. Iyas b. Hilal. He was the father of the celebrated Kadhi Iyas, Kadhi of Basrah, to whom Hariri alludes in his 7th Makamah, as skilled in the art of physiognomy, see his life in Ibn Khallakan ; Muawiyah died A.H. 80 (699).

the Lord, and verily all the Companions concurred in appointing Abu Bakr successor." And al Hakim, records, ad Dahabi verifying it on the authority of Murrah b-ul Tayyib that he said, "Abu Sufiyan[1] b. Harb went to Ali and said, "how is it that this authority is with the least of the Kuraysh in insignificance, and the meanest of them? (that is Abu bakr) : by Allah I would like to pour *the Kuraysh* upon him, horse and foot." He adds, Ali replied "verily it is long since that thou hast been hostile to Islam, O Abu Sufiyan, but that hurts it not at all ; we find Abu Bakr worthy of the Caliphate."

On his Covenant of allegiance.

The two Shaykhs record that Omar b-ul Khattab addressed the people on his return from the pilgrimage and said in his exhortation-"It hath come to my knowledge that a certain one among you sayeth, 'were Omar to die, I would swear allegiance to such a one,'-let not any man deceive himself so as to say that fealty to Abu Bakr was hastily given,-although it was even so, yet the Lord prevented the evil *consequences* thereof ; and there is not one among ye to-day behind whom the necks of *competitors stop short,*[2] *like unto* Abu Bakr. Verily he was the best among us when the Apostle of God died. And verily Ali and az Zubayr and they that were with them, remained behind in the house of Fatimah and all the Auxiliaries tarried behind us in the porch of the Banu Saidah, and the Fugitives gathered round Abu Bakr, and I said to him, "O Abu Bakr come with us to our brethren the Auxiliaries;" and we went, betaking ourselves to them, until we met two worthy

---

1 Abu Sufiyan Sakhr-b. Harb b. Umayya of the Kuraysh, the father of the Caliph Muawiyah.

2 "Vor dem man sich mehr beugte" is Weil's translation of this passage. Leben Muham. P. 350. Abdur Rahman-b. Ali as Shaybani in the Taysirul Wusul interprets it, "before whom the necks of riding camels are cut off or stop short." And Ibnul Athir, the brother of the historian in the Kitabun Nihaya a treatise on the obscure terms of the traditions, gives it the meaning I have rendered.

men[1] who told us what the people had done and said 'whither are ye going, ye men of the Fugitives ?" I said, "we seek our brethren of the Auxiliaries." They answered, "see, that ye do not approach them, but settle your affairs *yourselves,* ye men of the Fugitives." Then I said, "by Allah, we will go to them :" and we went on till we came up to them in the porch of the Banu Saidah-and lo! they were assembled and in the middle of them was a man muffled up in his garments and I said "who is this?" And they said "Saa'd b. Ubadah"[2] - and I said "what is the matter with him ?" They answered, "He *is in* pain." And when we were seated, their preacher arose glorified God as was befitting unto Him, and said, "and now, I say that we are the Auxiliaries of the Lord and the army of Islam, while ye, O men of the Fugitive, are but a handful amongst us, and verily a party among you have sallied forth seeking that ye may uproot us and exclude us from power." And when he was silent, I sought to speak, and verily I had embellished a discourse which pleased me, which I intended to speak in presence of Abu Bakr, and verily I feared *the want* of some severity on his part,[3] for he was calmer than I and more sedate-Then Abu Bakr said. "Softly with thee," and I was loth to anger him for he was wiser than I, and, by Allah, he did not omit a word of what had so pleased me in its composition, but he spoke it himself unpremeditatedly and surpassed it, so that I was speechless. And he said, "and now, as to what ye have said of good *regarding yourselves,* indeed ye are worthy of it, and the Arabs do not recognize this authority except in this tribe of the Kuraysh-they are the noblest of the Arabs by descent and tribe, and verily I approve for ye one of these two men whichever, ye please." Then he took my hand an the hand of Abu

---

1 These two were according to Zuhri, "Oweim b. Saidah and Maan b. Adi. Weil-Leb-Muham. Vol. II, 352, Maan was one of those killed fighting at Yemamah against Musaylamah.

2 Abu Thabit Saad b. Ubadah b. Dulaym of the Banu Saidah, native of Medina. He was the standard bearer of the Auxiliaries in their expeditions. He was distinguished for his liberality. He died in Hawran A.H. 16 and was buried at Mizzah near Damascus, An Nawawi.

3 Weil ich an ihm etwas Scharfe vermisste. Weil-Leban Muham. Vol. II. p.351.

Ubaydah b-ul Jarrah. I was not displeased with what he otherwise said, but by Allah, were I brought out that thou shouldst strike off my head, though it befell me through no crime *of mine,* it would be more pleasing to me than that I should rule a people among whom was Abu Bakr. Then a speaker of the Auxiliaries said, "I am of those by means of whose counsel people seek relief[1]- *let there be* a ruler from among us and a ruler from among ye, O men of the Kuraysh." Then the confusion increased and voices rose high until I feared a tumult, and I said, "stretch out thy hand O Abu Bakr," and he stretched out his hand, and I took the oath of fealty to him, and the Fugitives swore allegiance to him, then the Auxiliaries swore allegiance to him, and by Allah, in regard to that for which we assembled, we could find nothing more fitting than to swear fealty to Abu Bakr-we feared that it we separated from the concourse and no covenant were taken, they might conclude a covenant after our departure so that we should either have to hold to a covenant with them which we did not approve, or to oppose them, whence discord would arise."

An Nasai, Abu Yala and al Hakim record, verifying it on the authority of Ibn Masaud, that when the Apostle of God died, the Auxiliaris said, "*let there be* a ruler from among us, and from among ye a ruler," whereupon Omar b-ul Khattab went to them and said- "O ye men of the Auxiliaries, know ye not that the Apostle of God commanded Abu Bakr to lead the people in prayer ? now which of ye preferreth himself to Abu Bakr ?" The Auxiliaries exclaimed "God forbid that we should take precedence of Abu Bakr." And Ibn Saad, al Hakim, and al Bayhaki from Abu Sai'd al Khudri, "the Apostle of God died, and the people assembled in the house of Saad b. Ubadah and among them were Abu Bakr and Omar, and the preachers of the Auxiliaries aorse and a man among them began to speak *saying*, "O yemen of the Fugitives, whenever the Apostle of God appointed one from among you to any authority, he joined unto him one of us; we think therefore that two men, one from

1 Literally "I am their much – rubbed little rubbing-post and their propped little palm tree loaded with fruit" *i.e.,* as mangy camels seek relief by rubbing themselves against a post, so I am such a post for ye, and I have a family that will aid and defend me. See Lane's lex art جذل

among you, and one from among us, should assume this authority;" and the preachers of the Auxiliaries followed each other after the same manner, Then Zayd b. Thabit arose and said, "do ye *not* know that the Apostle of God was of the Fugitives, and we were the Auxiliaries of the Apostle of God therefore are we the Auxiliaries of his vicegerent, as we were his Auxiliaries." Then he took Abu Bakr by the hand and said "this is your master." Then Omar and afterwards the Fugitives and the Auxiliaries swore allegiance to him, and Abu Bakr ascended the pulpit, and he looked among the chiefs of the people, but beheld not az Zubayr. He therefore summoned az Zubayr and he came and he said, "thou sayest that thou art the son of the aunt of the Apostle of God, and his disciple, dost thou wish to break the staff of the Muslims ?" Az Zubayr replied "no blame behind on thee, O vicegerent of the Apostle of God !" and he rose and swore allegiance to him. Then Abu Bakr looked among the chiefs of the people, and he saw not Ali. He therefore summoned him and he came : then he said thou callest thyself the son of the uncle of the Apostle of God, and related unto him through his daughter, dost thou wish to break the staff of the Muslims ?" He replied "no blame be laid on thee, O vicegerent of the Apostle of God !" and he swore him allegiance."

Ibn Ishak records on his "Sirat "(record) from Anas b. Malik that after Abu Bakr had received the covenant of Allegiance in the porch of the Banu Saidah, when the morrow came he seated himself at the pulpit, and Omar rose and spoke before Abu Bakr. And he praised God and magnified him and then said ;" verily the Lord hath centred your authority on the best among you, the Companion of the Apostle of God, and "the second of the two when they two were in the cave," therefore arise and swear allegiance unto him." And the people swore unto Abu Bakr a general allegiance after the allegiance of the Porch. Then Abu Bakr spoke and praised God and magnified Him, then continued, "and now, O ye people, verily I have received authority over you though I be not the best among you, yet if I do well, assist me, and if I incline to evil, direct me aright. Truth is a *sacred* trust and falsehood is a betrayal. He that is weak among you, is strong before me, inasmuch as I shall restore unto him his due, if it please God, and he that is strong among you is weak, inasmuch as I shall take that which is due from him if it please God. A people abstaineth not from warring in the cause of the Lord, but he smiteth them with ignominy, and iniquity is never made manifest among a people, but He afllicteth them with misfortune. Obey me as long as I obey the Lord and his Apostle, and when I turn aside from the Lord and his Apostle, then obedience to me shall not be obligatory upon you. Rise up to your prayers-may the Lord have mercy upon you."

Abu Musa b Ukbah in his 'Maghazi' (Battles) records, likewise al Hakim, verifying it on the authority of Abdur Rahman b. Auf that Abu Bakr preached and spoke *saying,* "by Allah, I was never covetous of this authority, neither by day nor by night, nor desirous of it, our asked it of God either in secret or openly, but I was in fear of sedition. I have no repose in this authority. Verily I am invested with a mighty office, the power and capacity for which are not in me, save by the assistance of God." Then Ali and Az Zubayr said, "we were not incensed but for this, that we were put aside from the consultation, yet we think Abu Bakr the most deserving of the *authority* among men, for he was the Companion in the Cave, and we indeed recognize his superiority and his excellence, and verily the Apostle of God while he was yet alive commanded him to pray before the people." And Ibn Saad from Ibrahim at Taymi[1] that he said "when the Apostle of God died, Omar went to Abu Ubaydah b-ul Jarrah" and said "stretch out thy hand, for verily I will swear thee allegiance for thou art the trusted one of this people according to the word of the Apostle of God." And Abu Ubaydah replied to Omar, "never before this have I seen in thee weakness of mind since thou hast embraced Islam. What ! wilt thou swear allegiance to me when there is among you as Siddik, and he the second of the two ?" And from Muhammad, that Abu Bakr said to Omar, "stretch out thy hand, verily I will swear the allegiance," but Omar said to him "thou art more meritorious than I." Abu Bakr replied, "thou art

1 Ibrahim b-ul Harith b. Khalid b. Sakhr at Taymi, of the Kuraysh. According to al Bukhari, he and his father were among the Fugitives. That he survived Muhammad is all that is known of him by Ibn Hajr.

firmer then I" and again he repeated it, but Omar said, "then verily thou hast my firmness together with thy merit," and he swore allegiance to him. And Ahmad from Hamid-b-Abdir Rahman b. Auf, "the Apostle of God died, and Abu Bakr was with some of the people of Medina, and he came and uncovered his face and kissed it and said 'May my father and my mother be a ransom for thee ? how sweet wert thou in life and art in death ! Muhammad is dead- by the Lord of the Kaabah- "and he repeated the tradition"- he adds "Abu Bakr and Omar departed leading each other along until they came to the *Auxiliaries* and Abu Bakr spake and did not omit a thing of what had been revealed regarding the Auxiliaries, nor of what the Apostle of God had said concerning them, but he mentioned it and exclaimed, 'verily ye know that the Apostle of God said, "were the people to march, in One valley, and the Auxiliaries marched in *another* valley, I would march in the valley of the Auxiliaries:" and verily thou knowest O Saad,[1] that the Apostle of God said when thou wert seated by, "the Kuraysh are the masters of this authority and the good men will follow those of them that are good, and the wicked will follow the wicked among them." Then Saad said to him –"thou hast spoken truly-we are the ministers and ye are the princes."

Ibn Asakir records on the authority of Abu Sai'd al Khudri that when homage was paid to Abu Bakr, he saw some dissatisfaction among the people and he said, "what keeps you back O man ? am not I the most deserving of this authority among you ? was not I the first to embrace Islam? was not I this and that ?" and he mentioned his qualifications. And Ahmad Rafi'[2] ul Tai that he said, "Abu Bakr told me of the allegiance sworn to him and what the

---

1 Saad b. Ubadah.

2 Rafi b. Amr b. Jabir b. Harith at Tai. In the time of ignorance he lived as a rebber and used to fill ostrich eggs with water and hide them to various places in the desert for his own use, and when he became a convert he became a guide for the Muslims in their expeditions. He had made a particular friend of Abu Bakr at the engagement of Dat Salasil, who used to allow him to sleep on his own bedding and gave him some of his own clothes to wear and acted as his spiritual director. He died at the close of the Caliphate of Omar. Ibn Hajr.

Auxiliaries and what Omar had said to him and he added "then they swore allegiance to me and I accepted it from them, for I feared lest discord should arise and apostasy follow it." And Ibn Ishak and Ibn Aaid[1] in his 'Mazhazi,' from the same, that he said to Abu Bakr, "what brought thee to take upon thyself the government of the people, when verily thou hadst forbidden me to rule over two *of Islam* ?" he replied "I found no way of avoiding it I feared dissensions among the people of Muhammad."

And Ahmad from Kays b, Abi Hazim, verily I was seated by Abu Bakr as Siddik about a month after the death of the Apostle of God and he was relating the account of it, when the summons to prayer went forth among the people, and the people assembled together and he ascended the pulpit and said, "O men, I would indeed have been glad if another had sufficed for this in my stead, and though you have taken me according to the command of your Prophet, I am not capable *of performing its duties,* for *the Prophet* was indeed preserved from the *deceits of* the evil one, and inspiration descended upon him from heaven."

Ibn Saad records on the authority of al Hasan of Basrah that when allegiance was sworn to Abu Bakr, he stood up and preached saying, "and now, verily I have been placed in this authority, though I am averse from it, and by Allah, I would have been pleased if any of you had sufficed for it in my stead, but it you charge me to act unto you as did the Apostle of God, I could not undertake it, for the Apostle of God was a servant whom the Lord honored with His inspiration and preserved him thereby *from error,* and surely I am a mortal and am not better than any one of you-therefore watch over me-and when you see that I am steadfast, then obey me, and when you see that I turn aside *from the right path,* set me aright. And know that I have a devil that seizes upon me, therefore when you see me enraged, avoid me, *for at the time,* I cannot be influenced by your counsels or your glad salutations." And Ibn

1 The text has Aabid, for Aaid. The author's real name is Abu Abdullah Muhammad b. Aaid of the tribe of Kuraysh, a native of Damascus and like Ibn Ishak the author of a Maghazi. Kashfud Dhunun.

Saad and al Khatib, according to the narration of Malik from Urwah, that when Abu Bakr assumed the supreme power, he preached to the people and he praised God and magnified Him and said, "and now, verily I have been made to rule over you though I am not the most worthy among you; but the Qurãn was revealed and the Prophet declared the law, and instructed us and we learnt *of him* : and know, O men, that piety is the most solid goodness, and the vilest of what is vile is vice, and verily the strongest among you before me is he that is weak, inasmusch as I shall take for him what is due to him and the weakest among you before me is he that is strong inasmuch as I shall take from him that which is due by him: O men, verily I am a follower and not an innovator, therefore when I do well, said me, and if I turn aside, direct me aright. I have spoken, and may God have mercy upon me and upon you." Malik says, 'no one ever becomes Imam except upon this condition.' Al Hakim records in his Mustadrak (supplement) from Abu Hurayrah that when the Apostle of God, died, Mecca was convulsed by an earthquake, and Abu Kuhafah noticed it and said "what is this." They said, "the Apostle of God is dead." He answered. "It is a momentous thing, who then hath risen up in authority after him ?" They said, "thy son." He replied, "will be Banu Abd Manaf and the Banul Mughirah consent to this ?" They answered "Yes." He exclaimed, "there is no overthrower of that which hath been exalted, and no exalter of that which hath been humbled." Al Wakidi records with ascriptions to Ayesha, Ibn Omar, Sai'd b-ul Musayyab and others, that allegiance was sworn to Abu Bakr on the day of the death of the Apostle of God, Monday[1] the 12th of Rabii-ul-Awwal, in the 11th year of the Hijrah. And at Tabarani in his Ausat from Ibn Omar, that he said, "Abu Bakr never seated himself in the place of the Apostle of God in the pulpit, until after he had passed to the Lord, and Omar never sat in the seat of Abu Bakr nor Othman in that of Omar until they had passed to the Lord."

---

1 "Enfin Mahomed mournt un samedi, second jour do la semaine chez les Musulmans dans le moi Rabie premier." I know not on what authority Boulainvilliers makes يوم اثنين ("the second day") to be Saturday. Se Vie de Mahomed, p. 400.

On what occurred during his Caliphate and the chief events that took place during his time, such as the despatch of the army of Usamah, the slaughter of the apostates and those who refused the poor rate, Musaylamah the liar and the collection of the Qurãn.

Al Ismaili[1] records on the authority of Omar that he said, "when the Apostle of God died, some of the Arabs fell from the faith and they said, 'we will perform the prayers, but we will not pay the poor rate :' I went to Abu Bakr and said, 'O vicegerent of the Apostle of God, conciliate the people and be indulgent to them for they are but on a level with brute beasts ;' and he replied, 'I hoped for thy help and thou hast come to me withholding thy aid-*thou wert* haughty in the time of ignorance *and art* meanspirited in Islam-wherefore then should I conciliate them by lying verses and deceitful eloquence ? Alas ! Alas ! the Prophet is dead and divine inspiration is withheld ! By Allah, I will do battle with them as long as I can grasp a sword in my hand, even if they deny *me the worth of* a camel's halter.'" Omar adds, "I found him in this business more energetic and determined than myself, and he governed the affairs of the people with justice-thus many of their difficulties were made easy to me when I came to rule them." And Abul Kasim al Baghawi, and Abu Bakr as Shafii in his "Fawaid," *(Useful observations)* and Ibn Asakir record from Ayesha that she said, "when the Apostle of God died, hypocrisy raised its head, and the Arabs apostatized and the Auxiliaries turned away and it what fell upon my father had fallen upon the solid mountains, if would have crushed them ; and *the Companions* never disputed a single point,

---

1 Abu Bakr Ahmad b. Ibrahim al Ismaili, a great Shafii doctor, famous for his knowledge of the law and tradition. He was the author of numerous works on tradition. He died in Rajab A.H. 371 (982) aged 94. His son Abu Saad, called also al Ismaili, studied under his father and became Shaykh of the Shafiis in Jurjan, died A.H. 396, (A.D. 1006-6) Aged 63. De Slane, Ibn Khall.

but he was prompt with its advantages and its merits. They said 'where is the Prophet to be buried ?' and we found no one who had any knowledge regarding this ; but Abu Bakr exclaimed, I heard the Apostle of God say, no Prophet died but he was buried under the bed in which he expired.'" Ayesha adds, "they disputed regarding his inheritance, and they found no one who had any information on this point ; but Abu Bakr exclaimed, 'I heard the Apostle of God say, "we, the Company of the Prophet are not inherited of –that which we leave is the portion of the poor."

Some of the learned say that this was the first disagreement that occurred among the Companions, for some of them said, "let us bury him in Mecca, the city wherein he was born," and others said, "nay, in his mosque," and others, "nay, in the cemetery of Medina," and others "nay in Jerusalem, the Sepulchre of the Prophets," until Abu Bakr informed them of what he knew. Ibn Zunjawayh says, that as Siddik, was the single authority for this tradition among the Fugitives and Auxiliaries, and they had recourse to him for it. Al Bayhaki and Ibn Asakir record on the authority of Abu Hurayrah, that he said, "by Him, than whom there is no other God, if Abu Bakr had not been appointed Caliph, God would not have been worshipped,"-this he said a second, and again a third time ; then they said to him, "how so, O Abu Hurayrah !" and he said, "verily the Apostle of God sent Usamah-b-Zayd at the head of seen hundred men to Syria and when they reached Du Khushub[1] the Prophet died, and the Arabs round about Medina apostatized, and the Companions of the Apostle of God gathered about Abu Bakr and they said, "recall these-will you send these against the Greeks while the Arabs around Medina have apostatized ?" but he said, "by Him, than whom there is no other God, were dogs to drag the wives of the Prophet by their feet, I would not recall an army dispatched by the Apostle of God, nor would I dismount a standard that he had bound." He therefore dispatched Usamah, who so acted that he never passed in his march by a tribe inclined to apostatize but they said, "were there no strength in them, such as

1 A valley about one march from Medina. Yakut M.B.

these would not have gone forth from among them, but let us leave them to encounter the Greeks :" and they encountered them and defeated them and slew them and returned in safety whereupon those others remained steadfast in Islam." And from Urwah, "the Apostle of God kept saying in his illness, dispatch the army of Usamah.' He therefore set out until he reached "Jurf,"[1] and the Prophet's wife Fatimah sent to him *saying,* "hasten not for verily the Apostle of God is grievously sick," and he did not proceed until the Apostle of God died and when he was dead, Usamah returned to Abu Bakr and said, "verily the Apostle of God sent me forth but we were under different circumstances to what you are now-verily I fear lest the Arabs apostatize and if they apostatize, they should be the first to be attacked, and if they do not apostatize I will set forth, for with me are the chiefs of the people and the most distinguished amongst them." Then Abu Bakr preached to the people and said, "by Allah, were[2] a bird *of prey* to carry me off, it would be more pleasing to me than that I should set about anything before the command of the Apostle of God : he therefore dispatched him."

Ad Dahabi says that when the death of the Apostle of God became known round about, many of the Arab tribes apostatized from Islam and refused the payment of the poor rate, and Abu Bakr as Siddik set out to attack them, but Omar and others counseled him to abstain from attacking them, but he said, "by Allah, if they deny me *so much as a* camel's halter or a kid which they used to pay to the Apostle of God, I will war against them for the refusal of it ;" then Omar said, "how canst thou war against the people, when verily the Apostle of God said, "I have been commanded to do battle against men until they confess that there is no God but God, and verily Muhammad is the Apostle of God, and whoever confesseth it his property and life are safe from me, save in the claim and account of God therein." Abu Bakr replied, "by Allah, I will surely oppose by force those who distinguish between prayers and the poor rate, for the poor rate is a due from

1 Three miles from Medina on the road to Syria.

2 Meaning were he carrion and a feast for birds of prey.

property and verily *the Prophet* said "save in the claim therein." Omar says, "then, by Allah, I saw it was nothing else than that God had disposed the heart of Abu Bakr to combat them and I knew that it was just." And on the authority of Urwah, "Abu Bakr set out with the Fugitives and Auxiliaries until they reached Naka's over against Najd, and the Arabs fled with their families and the people addressed Abu Bakr, saying, "return to Medina and to the children and women, and set a man in command of the army," and they did not desist until he returned and appointed Khalid-b'ul Walid and said to him, "when they shall have embraced the faith, and paid the poor rate, then let any among you who so wishes, return," and he went back to Medina.

Ad Darakutni records on the authority of Ibn Omar, that when Au Bakr set forth and was mounted upon his camel, Ali-b. Abi Talib took it by the bridle and said, "whither *goest thou,* O Vicegerent of the Apostle of God ? I say unto thee that which the Apostle of God said unto thee on the day of Ohud, 'sheath thy sword and make us not anxious for thy person'- and turn back to Medina, for, by Allah, if we suffer loss in thee, Islam will never be set in order." And from Handhalah b. Ali al Laythi, that Abu Bakr dispatched Khalid and commanded him to war against men for five objects ; whosoever refused any one of these, he should attack him as he would attack any who had refused all the five *viz.,* the confession of faith "verily there is no God, but God and-verily Muhammad is hi servant and his apostle-the institution of prayers-the donation of the poor rate, the fast of Ramadhan. Khalid and those who were with him, then went forth in Jumada' l Akhirah and he attacked the Banu Asad and Ghatfan and slew whom he slew, and captured whom he captured, and the rest returned to Islam ; and of the Companions who were slain in this affair were Ukashah[1]- b. Mihsan and Thabit-b. Akram.

1 One of the Companions held in much favour by Muhammad. At Badr his sword broke and Muhammad gave him a dried palm branch which became in his hand a sword with a white blade and a firm handle with which he returned to the battle. He was one of the thousand to whom Muhammad promised paradise without the judgment being held regarding them. He was 44 years old when Muhammad died. An Nawawi.

In Ramadhan of this year, died Fatimah daughter of the apostle of God, the chief of women upon earth, her age being four and twenty. Ad Dahabi says that the Apostle of God had no descendants but by her, for the posterity of his daughter Zaynab[1] became extinct (so says az Zubayr b. Bakkar) and Umm Ayman[2] died a month before her.

In the month of Shawwal died Abdullah the son of Abu Bakr-As Siddik. After this Khalid set out with his army for Yamama to attack Musaylamah the liar towards the end of the year. The armies met and the investment[3] lasted some days. At length Musaylamah the liar, God curse him, was slain-Wahshi the slayer of Hamzah killed him.

Among the Companions that fell in the *engagement* were Abu Hudayfah b. Utabah, Salim his freedman, Shujaa b. Wahab, Zayd b-ul Khattab Abdullah b. Sahl, Malik b. Amr Tufayl b. Amr Dausi, Yazid b. Kays, Aamir b. Bukayr, Abdullah b. Makhramah, Saib b. Othman b. Madhaun, Uhad b. Bashir, Maan b. Adi, Thabit b. Kays B. Shamas, Abu Dujanah Simak b. Harb, and others amounting to seventy.[4] Musaylamah on the day he was slain was a hundred and[5]

---

1 She married her aunt's son Abul Aasi bir Rabii al Abshami. Ibn Hajr.

2 His father mother Barakah, an Abyssinian slave girl who tended Muhammad on the death of his father Abdullah, and continued in the capacity of his nurse after the death of his mother Amina. She married Zayd b. Haritha. Ibn Hajr.

3 The followers of Musaylamah retired into a garden called the "Hadikatul Abdir Rahman, and afterwards 'Hadikatu' Mawt, or the garden of death, and there defended themselves to the last. According to the account of Wahshi quoted in the Raudhat us Safa he allows Ibn Amara a share in the death of Musaylamah as they both attacked him at the same time. Hamzah the uncle of Muhammad was slain at the battle of Ohud.

4 These were only the principal men among the fallen, for says Gilbon "in the first action by were repulsed with a loss of twelve hundred men : their defeat was avenged by the slaughter of 1000 infidels and Museilama himself was piereed by an Ethiopian slave with the same javelin which had mortally wounded the uncle of Mahomet." Decline and Fall.

5 This must be a great exaggeration as it was but a short time before his death that the prophetess Sajah fell in love with him for the beauty and (cont...)

fifty years old, his birth *having taken place* before that of Abdullah the father of the Prophet.

In the year 12 A. H. as Siddik sent al Ala b-ul Hadhrami to Bahrayn where they had apostatized, and the *armies* met at Jawatha, and the Muslims were victorious. Then he sent Akramah b. Abi Jahl to Amman where they had also fallen from the faith, and he dispatched al Muhajir b. Abi Umayyah, against the people of Nujayr who likewise had apostatized, and Ziyad b. Labid the Auxiliary, against *another* body of the apostates.

In this year died Abul Ausi bur Rabii the husband of Zaynab daughter of the Apostle of God, and as Saad b. Jaththamah al Laythi and Abu Marthad al Ghanawi.

In this year likewise, after the reduction of the apostates as Siddik sent Khalid b-ul Walid to the land of Basrah, who attached Ubulla and captured it and took Madain Kisra, the one in Irak, partly by treaty and partly by force. During the same, Abu Bakr undertook the Pilgrimage and dispatched Amar b.ul Aas and the army to Syria and there occurred the battle of Ajnadaya in the month of the first Jumada A.H. 13, and the Muslims were victorious and Abu bakr received the good tidings of it when he was dying. In this *battle,* there fell Akrahmah b Abi Jahl and Hisham b-ul Aasi and others. In the same year took place the engagement of Marju's Suffar,[1] where the infidels were defeated and al Fadhi b-ul Abbas and others were killed.

(cont..96) manliness of his person. After his death she resided with the Taghlabites and was converted in the Caliphate of Muawiyah. Abul Feda Annales, P. 212.

1 Close to Damascus. Several skirmishes took place before Damascus, during the siege, little to the credit of the warriors of the Cross. For a detailed account of this period, consult the interesting pages of Ockley.

The Collection of the Qurãn.

Al Bukhari records on the authority of Zayd b. Thabit that he said, "Abu Bakr sent for me at the time of the slaughter of the people at Yamama, Omar being with him and said 'verily Omar hath come to me saying, "the slaughter of the men at Yamama was great and I fear lest the loss in action of the readers of the Qurãn in the provinces become excessive, and therefore much of the Qurãn may be lost unless they collect it together, and verily I think that the Qurãn should be collected." Abu Bakr went on, "and I replied to Omar, how shall I do the thing which the Apostle of God hath not done"? Omar answered "by Allah, it is a good work," and he did not cease to persist with me in this matter until good enlightened my mind concerning it, and I have come to think as Omar thinks." Zayd adds, "Omar, was meanwhile seated by him not speaking : then Abu Bakr said, "thou art an intelligent youth and I have no doubts regarding thee, and verily thou wert he who recorded the revelations of the Apostle of God, search therefore for the Qurãn and collect it." And by Allah, had he charged me with the carrying away of a hill from among the mountains, it would not have been weightier upon me than that which he commanded me in the collection of the Qurãn, and I said, "how can you two undertake a thing which the Apostle of God hath not done ?" and Abu Bakr said, "by Allah, it is a good work," and I did not cease discussing it with him, until God enlightened my mind in that towards which he had already disposed the minds of Abu Bakr and Omar. And I searched for the Qurãn and collected it from scraps of paper and shoulder-blades[1] and leafless palm branches, and the minds of men until I found from the Sura of Repentance (IX) two verses in the possession of Khuzaymah b. Thabit which I found with no one else *viz.*, "now hath an Apostle come to you of your own nation" (Qur. IX) to the end. The pages in which the Qurãn was collected remained with Abu Bakr until the Lord took him to Himself, then

1 On comparing the passage with the Sahih of al Bukhari I find a slight difference in the reading in various places : for 'shoulder-blades' اكفاف or as I should prefer to read اكتاف al Bukhari لخاف has thin whitish stones.

with Omar until the Lord took him to Himself, and afterwards with Hafsah daughter of Omar. Abu Yala records on the authority of Ali that he said, "the greatest among men meriting reward for the volumes *of the Qurãn* is Abu Bakr, for he it was who first collected the Qurãn between two boards."

On the things in which he was foremost.

Among these are, that he was the first to embrace Islam, the first to collect the Qurãn, the first who named it 'Mushaf' (the Book) the proof of which has been advanced, and he was the first who was called caliph. Ahmad records on the authority of Abu Bakr b. Abi Mulaykah, that he said, Abu Bakr was *once* addressed "O Vicegerent of God." He replied, "I am the Vicegerent of the Apostle of God and with this I am content." He was the first who ruled the Caliphate while his father was yet alive, and the first Caliph for whom his subjects appointed a stipend. Al Bukhari records from Ayesha that she narrates, "when Abu Bakr was appointed Caliph he said, "my people know that my profession[1] is not insufficient for the provision of my family, but I am busied with the affairs of the Muslims and family of Abu Bakr will soon consume this property *of his* while he is labouring for the Muslims." And Ibn Saad from Atabus Saib[2] that he said, "after allegiance had been sworn unto Abu Bakr, next morning he arose and was going to the market place with some mantles upon his arm, when Omar said to him, "whither art thou going ?" he replied, 'to the market place :" Omar said, "dost thou do this although thou hast been given to rule over the Muslims ?" He answered, "whence, then shall my family be fed ?" Omar replied, "Come! Abut Ubaydah shall provide for thee :" and they went to Abu Ubaydah and he said "I will set apart

---

1 He was by trade a cloth-merchant.

2 Abus Saib Atabus Saib b. Malik a member of the tribe of Thakif and a native of Kufah, a traditionist of good authority, died A.H. 136 (753-4). De Slane, I.K.

for thee, the allowance for one man of the Fugitives-neither that assigned to the best, nor to the meanest among them, and a garment for winter and for summer ; when thou hast worn a thing out ; thou canst return it and take another." Then he assigned unto him every day, half a sheep and the wherewith to cover his head and his person. And from Maymun, "when Abu Bakr became Caliph, they assigned to him two thousand *dirhams,* and he said, "increase *the sum* for me for I have a family, and you have employed me on other work than my own trade"; so they gave him an increase of five hundred dirhams."

At Tabarani records in his Musnad on the authority of al Hasan b. Ali b. Abi Talib that he said, "when Abu Bakr was near unto death, he said, "O Ayesha, behold the camel, the milk of which we have drank, and the platter in which we prepared our food, and the garments we have worn ; verily we made use of them when we governed the affairs of the Muslims. When I die, give them to Omar." When therefore Abu Bajr died, she sent them to Omar, and he said, "the Lord have mercy upon thee, Abu Bakr, for verily thou hast afflicted him who cometh after thee." And Ibn Abid Dunya, from Abu Bakr b. Hafs that he said, "Abu Bakr, when he was near unto death, said to Ayesha, "daughter-we have governed the affairs of the Muslims and have not taken for ourselves either a dinar or a dirham, but we have eaten the fill of our bellies with the coarse flour of their food, and clothed our backs with their rough garments and there doth not remain with us of the booty *taken* by the Muslims, save this Nubian slave and this camel for drawing water, and this coarse garment, but when I die, send them to Omar." He was the first also, to establish a public treasury. Ibn Saad records on the authority of Sahl b Abi Khaythamah and others that Abu Bakr had the public treasury at Sunh, [1] over which no one kept guard. It was said to him "wilt thou not place over it some one to guard it ?" He replied, "there is a lock upon it" : and he used to give away what was in it till it was empty. But when he removed into

1 In one of the suburbs of Medina about a mile distant from the house of Muhammad. Yakut, M.B.

the city he transferred it and placed it in his house ; and the revenue came in to him, and he used to distribute it amongst the poor and divide it equally amongst them. He used also to purchase camels and horses and arms and give them away for the service of God ; and he used to buy garments that were brought in from the desert tracts and distribute them amongst the widows of Medina.

When Abu Bakr died and was buried, Omar summoned the trustees amongst them being Abdur Rahman b. Auf and Othman b. Affan, and entered with them into the treasury of Abu Bakr ; and they opened the treasury, but they did not find a thing in it, neither a dinar nor a dirham.

I observe that this tradition refutes the remark of al Askari in his Awayil (Bginnings) that the first who instituted a public treasury was Omar, and that neither the Prophet possessed a public treasury nor Abu Bakr. Indeed I have refuted this in the work which I composed on the Awayil. Moreover, I have observed that al Askari himself adverted to it in another part of his book, for he says that the first who superintended the public treasury was Abu Ubaydah b-ul Jarrah on the part of Abu Bakr. Al-Hakim says that the first surname in Islam, was the surname of Abu Bakr, Atik.

The two Shaykhs record on the authority of Jabir that the Apostle of God said *to him,* "when she tribute comes from Bahrayn I will give thee so much and so much,' but when the tribute from Bahrayn came in after the death o the Apostle of God, Abu Bakr said-"he who hath a claim against the apostle of God or a promise *from him,* let him come to us," and I went and informed him and he said "take," and I took and found that *the promise* was for five hundred dirhams, but he gave me two thousand five hundred.

On some examples of his gentleness and humility.

Ibn Asakir records on the authority of Anisah,[1] that she said, "Abu Bakr settled amongst us three years before he was appointed Caliph, and one year after he became so, and the girls of the tribe used to go to him with their flocks and he used to milk them for them." And Ahmad in the "Zuhd" from Maymun b. Mihran that he said, "a man went to Abu Bakr and said 'peace be to thee, O Vicegerent of the Apostle of God.'" He replied "who among these assembled is he ?" And Ibn Asakir from Abu Salih al Ghifari, that Omar b-ul Khattab was in the habit of ministering at night to an aged blind woman in one of the suburbs of the city, and he used to give her to drink and assist her, and it came to pass that he went to her and found another who was before him with her and who did what she required. He went again another time that he might not be anticipated *in attendance* on her, and lay in wait for him and behold it was Abu Bakr who was going to her, he being at that time Caliph, and Omar exclaimed "by my life, thou art the man!" And Abu Nuaym and others from Abdur Rahman al Ispahani that al Hasan the son of Ali went to Abu Bakr, who was then on the pulpit of the Apostle of God, and said "come down from the seat of my father," and he answered, "thou speakest truly for this is thy father' seat"; and he put him on his lap and wept and Ali said, "by Allah, this was not said by my command," and Abu Bakr said, "thou speakest the truth ; by Allah, I did not suspect thee."

Ibn Saad records on the authority of Ibn Omar that he said, "the Prophet appointed Abu Bakr to lead the pilgrimage in the first pilgrimage that took place in Islam ; then the Apostle of God performed it himself the following year, and when the Apostle of God died, and Abu Bakr became Caliph, he appointed Omar b-ul Khattab to lead the pilgrimage and performed it himself the year following, and when Abu Bakr died and Omar became Caliph, he appointed Abdur Rahman b. Auf over the pilgrimage. Subsequently

1 Daughter of Khubayb b. Yasaf, one of the Auxiliaries. She accompanied Muhammad in some of his pilgrimages and related traditions from him. Ibn Hajr.

Omar failed not to perform it himself each year till his death, when Othman succeeded to the Caliphate, and he appointed Abdur Rahman b. Auf over the pilgrimage."

On his illness, death and last testament and the Caliphate of Omar.

Sayf and al Hakim record on the authority of Ibn Omar that the cause of the death of Abu Bakr was through excessive grief for the death of the Apostle of God, his body continuing to waste away until he died. And Ibn Saa'd and al Hakim on good authorities from Ibn Shihab, that Abu Bakr and al Harith b. Kaladah[1] were eating broth which had been sent as a present to Abu Bakr, when al Harith said to Abu Bakr, "with draw by hand, O Vicegerent of the Apostle of God, for by Allah, there is poison, in it, *that will do its work* in a year, and I and thou shall both die on the same day." And he withdrew his hand, and these two did not fail to sicken until they died on the same day about the close of the year. And al Hakim from Shaabi that he said, "what can we expect from this vile world when even the Apostle of God was poisoned and poisoned was Abu Bakr ?"

And al Wakidi and al Hakim from Ayesha that the beginning of the sickness of Abu Bakr, was that he bathed on Monday the 7th of Jumadal Akhirah, and the day was cold and he took fever for fifteen days and did not come forth to prayers and died on Tuesday the

1 One of Muhammad's Companions-of the tribe of Thakif, and a judge of the Arabs. His wife was al Farigha daughter to Hammam b. Urwah : going into her spartment one morning he found her picking her teeth on which he sent her a sentence of divorce for said he "if you have breakfasted before your time, you are a glutton and if you have passed the night with particles of meat between your teeth, you are a slut." To this she replied that it was neither one nor the other, but that she was removing the fragment of a toothpick. She afterwards married Yusuf b. Ukayl to whom she bore the tyrant at Hajjaj. Ibn Khall.

22nd of Jamadal Akhirah in the thirteenth year of the Hijrah being sixty-three years old (23rd August, 634).

Ibn Saad and Ibn Abid Dunya record on the authority of Abu's Safar that the Companions went in unto Abu Bakr in his sickness and said, "O Vicegerent of the Apostle of God, shall we call unto thee a physician that he may look to thee ?" He replied, "verily he hath already seen me." And they answered "what did he say ?" He said, "verily I effect that which I please."[1] And al Wakidi on different authorities, that when Abu Bakr sickened, he summoned Abdur Rahman b. Auf and said, "tell me of Omar b-ul Khattab." He replied "thou canst not ask me concerning anything but thou art better acquainted with it than I." Abu Bakr said "well, even so." Abdur Rahman answered, "by Allah, he is even better than thy opinion of him." Then he summoned Othman b. Affan and said, "tell me of Omar b-ul Khattab" and he answered, "thou knowest more of him than I." Abu Bakr replied, "Be it so." The other replied, "verily, my knowledge of him is that his inward disposition is better than his outward appearance, and indeed there is not his like amongst us." Abu Bakr consulted together with those two, Said b. Zayd, and Usayd b-ul Hudhayr, and others from among the Fugitives and Auxiliaries, and Usayd said, "verily, I think him the best after thee; he approves what merits approval, and is indignant with what deserves wrath ; what he conceals is better than what he suffers to appear, and no one can sway this authority more vigorously than he." Some of the Companions went unto Abu Bakr and one of them spake to him saying, "what wilt thou say to thy Lord, when He asketh of thee regarding the appointment of Omar over us, and verily thou seest his asperity of temper" : and Abu Bakr said, "by Allah, dost thou think to terrify me ? I shall say O God I have given the best of the people to rule over them. Tell others from me what I have said." Then he summoned Othman and said, "write-In the name of God the most merciful and compassionate. This is the testament made by Abu Bakr the son of Abu Kuhafah at the close of his life in the world as he is about to leave it, and at the beginning

1 Taken with a slight alteration from the Qur. Chapters XI and LXXXV.

of his life in the next, being about to enter it, a time when the infidel believeth and the sinner gaineth certitude, and the liar speaketh the truth. I have made Caliph over you after me. Omar b-ul Khattab- therefore hear and obey him, and verily I have not been wanting in my duty to God and His Apostle and His religion and myself and you : if therefore he acteth justly, then will my opinion regarding him and my knowledge of him be *justified,* and it he doeth the contrary, then every action receiveth that which it hath earned, and I have intended what is good and know not what is hidden, 'and they who act unjustly shall know hereafter with what treatment they shall be treated' (Qur. XXVI) and peace be to you and the mercy of God and His blessing." He then ordered that they should seal the document. After this he commanded Othman who went forth with the document sealed, and the people swore allegiance and approved it. Then Au Bakr summoned Omar in private and charged him with what he charged him and Omar left him. Then Abu Bakr lifted up his hands and said, "O God I have wished in this but their good, and I feared discord amongst them, therefore have I done regarding them that which thou knowest and exerted my faculties for them to the utmost ; and I have appointed to rule over them the best among them and the most vigorous, an the most zealous of them for that which directeth them aright ; and verily what I have recollected of thy commands, I have remembered, therefore, put another in my place over them, for they are thy servants and their forelocks[1] are in thy hands. Intruct, O Lord, their rulers and make him *whom thou appointest,* to be one of the Orthodox Caliphs and render his subjects righteous towards him."

Ibn Saad and al Hakim record on the authority of Ibn Masaud that he said, "the most sagacious of mankind were three-Abu Bakr when he appointed Omar as Caliph,—the wife of Moses when she said, "Hire him for *certain*[2] wages" (Qur. XXVIII) and the minister *of Egypt*[3] when he discerned the character of Joseph from his

1 By "forelocks" may be also signified the chiefs of the nation.

2 For this story see Qurãn XXVIII and Sale's notes, p. 319.

3 His name was Kitfir or Itfir (a corruption of Potiphar) and he was man of great consideration, being superintendent of the royal treasury (al Baydawi). Sale, p. 189.

physiognomy and said to his wife "use his honorably" (Qur. XII). And Ibn Asakir from Yasar b. Hamzah that he said, "when Abu Bakr was grievously sick, he stood up over the people from a window and said 'O ye men, verily I have made a covenant, therefore consent ye to it ; and the people said, 'we consent, O Vicegerent of the Apostle of God ;' then Ali stood up and said, 'I shall not consent unless it *be for* Omar,' and Abu Bakr replied, 'verily it is *for* Omar.' And Ahmad from Ayesha that she said, 'Abu Bakr, when he was night unto death said, "what day is this ?" They answered 'Monday:'[1] he said, 'if I die to-night delay not for me *my burial* until to-morrow, for verily the dearest to me of all days and nights is that which is nearest of them to *the time of the death of* the Apostle of God.' And Malik from Ayesha, that Abu Bakr gave to her twenty camel-loads of fruit-cuttings of the palms from his property at Ghabah,[2] and when he was nigh unto death, he said, 'O daughter, by Allah, there is not one among the people whose richness in more pleasing to me than thine, and none whose poverty would be more distressing to me after my *death,* and verily I had given to thee twenty camel-loads of the fruit-cuttings of my palms – if thou hadst cut them and taken them, they would have been thine, but now they are the property of my heirs, who are verily thy two brothers and thy two sisters-then let them divide it according to the book of God.' She replied, 'O father, even had it been so *that I had cut them,* I would have left them, but surely she, *my, sister* is Asma, who then is the other sister ?' He said, 'the child that is in the womb of the daughter of Kharijah, whom I think is a girl.' Ibn Saad records this tradition and at the end of it adds, 'the child in the womb of the daughter of Kharijah,[3] verily it hath been put into my heart that it is a girl therefore take charge of her with kindness,'

---

1 According to a tradition attested by an Nawawi and others, on a Monday Muhammad was born, on a Monday he fled from Mecca, on a Monday, he arrived at Medina. His first revelation was made to him on a Monday, and on a Monday he died.

2 Twelve miles from Medina on the road to Syria.

3 Kharijah b. Zayd b Abi Zuhayr one of the Auxiliaries, of the tribe of Khazraj. Abu Bakr married his daughter whom he left pregnant at his death. Ibn Hajr.

and from her was born Umm Kulthum."

Ibn Saad records from Urwah[1] that Abu Bakr left away a fifth of his property and said, "take of my good that which God taketh of the booty of the Muslims."[2] And by a different ascription from the same, that Abu Bakr said, "that I should bequeath a fifth is preferable to me than that I should bequeath a fourth, and to bequeath a fourth is preferable to me than if I bequeathed a third, for he who bequeaths a third, leaves nothing." And Saad b. Mansur in his Sunnan (Traditions) from ad Dhahhak, [3] that Abu Bakr and Ali bequeathed a fifth of their property to such among their relations as did not legally inherit *from them.*

Abdullah b Ahmad records in the Zawaid uz Zuhd from Ayesha that she said, "by Allah, Abu Bakr did not leave a dinar nor a dirham stamped with the name of God." And Ibn Saad and others from Ayesha, "when Abu Bakr was grievously sick, I recited this verse appositely.

> By thy life, wealth is of no avail to a man :
> On the day when the death-rattle is in his throat and his breast is contracted by it."

---

1 Urwah, was the son of Ayesha's sister Asma who received from Muhammad the title of Datun Nitakayn "wearer of the two girdles," for having torn her veil in two with one half of which she tied up the wallet of provisions and the water which Muhammad and Abu Bakr took with them in their flight to Medina. She was also the mother of the Caliph Abdullah buz Zubayr. Ibn Hajr.

2 By the Muhammadan law, a testator can leave away one-third of his property to whom he chooses, the other two-thirds going to his heirs. Abu Bakr appeared to consider that the leave away the utmost the law allowed would have been ungenerous to his heirs. A fifth of the spoils taken in war by the Muslims became the property of the Caliph for the use of the State.

3 Ad Dhahhak b. Sufiyan b Kaab b. Abdillah of the Banu Kilab. He was one of the Companions and was counted for his prowess equal to a hundred horsemen. An Nawawi states that it is a glaring error to call him the son of Kays, as some authorities do. There were to generals bearing the name of Dhahhak b. Kays, mentioned by De Slane (I.K. Vol. IV, p.122). He was placed by Muhammad at the head of the Banu Salim who numbered at that time 900 men, saying to them that one who was equal to a hundred men was well able to command a thousand.

and Abu Bakr uncovered his face and said, 'it is not so, but say and the agony of death shall come in truth ; this *O man,* is what thou soughtest to avoid'. (Qur. L)-behold these my two garments-wash them and shroud me in them, for the living is more in want of new ones than the dead." And Abu Yala from Ayesha, "I went to Abu Bakr when he was at the point of death and I said

'He whose weeping ceaseth not when he is veiled :
Verily at some time it shall flow forth.'

And he said, 'do not say that, but say "And the agony of death shall come in truth ; this, O man, is what thou, soughtest to avoid,"' then he said 'on what day did the Apostle of God die,' I answered 'on a Monday' : he said, 'I hope *for death* between this and the night ;' and he died on Tuesday and was buried before the day broke." And Abdullah b. Ahmad in the Zawaiduz Zuhd on the authority of Bakr b. Abdillah al Muzani, that when Abu Bakr was night unto death, Ayesha seated herself near his head and said,

Unto every possessor of camels, do his camels return for water:
And who so spoileth, shall himself be despoiled.

And Abu Bakr understood it and said, "it is not so, O daughter, but it is as the Lord hath said 'and the agony of death shall come'" &c. And Ahmad from Ayesha, that she recited appositely this verse when Abu Bakr was dying.

"And one so unsullied in honor that the cloud draweth moisture from his face :
The protection of orphans, the defence of widows."

And Abu Bakr said "that must be the Apostle of God." And Abdullah-b. Ahmad in the Zawaid uz Zuhd from Ubadah-b. Kays, that when Abu Bakr was night unto death, he said to Ayesha, "wash me these two garments and shroud me in them, for verily thy father shall be one of two men, either robed in the best of garments or stripped by an ignoble stripping." And Ibn Abid Dunya from Abu Mulaykah, that Abu Bakr left as his last commands that his wife Asma the daughter of Umays, should bethe him, and that Abdur

Rahman b. Abi Bakr should help her. And Ibn Saad from Said b-ul Musayyab, that Omar read prayers over Abu Bakr between the tomb and the pulpit *of Muhammad* and recited the "Takbir,"[1] four times. And from Urwah and al Kasim b. Muhammad, that Abu Bakr left as his last instructions to Ayesha, that he should be buried by the side of the Apostle of God, and when he died, they dug a grave for him and laid his head on a level with the shoulder of the Apostle of God, and the niche *of his grave* touched the grave of the Apostle of God.[2] And from Ibn Omar, that Omar Talhah, Othman and Abdur Rahman the some of Abu Bakr descended into the grave of Abu Bakr. And he records likewise on several lines of ascription, that he was buried at night. And from Ibnul Musayyab that when Abu Bakr died, Mecca was convulsed by an earthquake, and Abu Kuhafah said, "what is that ?" they answered, "thy son is dead," He said, "It is a terrible calamity- who has arisen in authority after him ?" they replied "Omar ;" he exclaimed. "He was his companion," And from Mujahid that Abu Kuhafah returned what he had inherited, from Abu Bakr to the son of Abu Bakr and Abu Kuhafah survived Abu Bakr only six months and some days, dying in Muharram A.H. 14, at the age of ninety-seven. The learned say that none but Abu Bakr ruled the Caliphate during the lifetime of his father, and the father of none but of Abu Bakr inherited *from his son* as Caliph.

Al Hakim records on the authority of Ibn Omar that Abu Bakr ruled two years and seven months ; and in the history of Ibn Asakir, *it is stated* with the ascription thereof on the authority of al Asmai,

---

1 In prayers for the dead, the "takbir," that is the saying "Allahu Akbar" God is great, is followed the first time, by the recital of the praises of God, the second time by those of Muhammad, the third time by prayers for the living and the dead, and the fourth by the salutation of dismissal "peace be to you" &c.

2 Muhammad, Abu Bakr and Omar lie side by side at Medina, the graves in echelon, so that the head of Abu Bakr's grave rests on a line with the shoulder of that of Muhammad ; see a diagram of their position in Burton's Pilgrimage, Vo. II, p. 74. The لحد or niche is cut into the side of the grave and the body rests therein.

that Khufaf[1] b. Nudbah as Salami said, mourning Abu Bakr.

Tell every living thing that there is no permanence for it :
And for the whole universe, its decree is destruction.
The goods of men are but as a trust :
Borrowed on the condition of repayment :
And a man strives, but there is one who lieth in wait for him :
The eye mourneth for him and the ardour of the voice.
He groweth old, or is slain, or subdued :
Sickness that hath no remedy maketh him to lament,
Verily Abu Bakr was as the rain
What time Orion causeth not the herbage to grow with moisture.
By Allah, there shall not attain unto *the excellence of* his days:
Neither the youth that wears the Mizar, [2] nor one that wears the Rida.
He who strives to attain unto *the excellence of* his days :
Earnestly, is apart and solitary upon the earth.

---

1 Khufaf b. Umayr bal Harith, a descendant of Imral Kays generally known as Ibn Nudbah, the letter being his mother's name. She was a captive in the possession of his grandfather Harith, who gave her to his son Umayr, who had by her Khufaf. He was present at the battle of Hunayn, and at the conquest of Mecca where he carried the standard of the Banu Salim. He shared with Durayd the honor of being the two greatest poets of the Arab chivalry ; died in the Caliphate of Omar. Ibn Hajir.

2 The Mizar or drawers, covers the lower part of the body, while the Rida is a garment worn over the upper part of the body.

On the traditions related on his authority ascribed to Muhammad.

An Nawawi says in his Tahdib-"As Siddik has narrated one hundred and forty-two traditions from the Apostle of God. The reason of the small number of his narrations is that his death preceded the spreading abroad of the traditions and the solicitude of the Tabiis in listening to them, and collecting and preserving them." I observe that Omar has mentioned in the tradition regarding the oath of allegiance[1] preceding, "that Abu Bakr did not omit a thing of what had been revealed regarding the Auxiliaries nor what the Apostle of God had said concerning them, but he mentioned it": and this is the most complete proof of the extent of his memory of the traditions, and the amplitude of his knowledge of the Qurãn,[2] and I have though it expedient to inscribe here, consecutively but briefly his traditions, mentioning after cast tradition the authorities that have recorded it, and I purpose to follow them out with their ascriptions in a collected form, if it so please God.

1. *The tradition* of the Flight, (the two Shaykhs and others.)

2. *The tradition,* "The waters of the sea are a means of purifying, its dead are lawful *to eat.*" (Darakutni.)

3. *The tradition*, "The tooth-stick is a means of purifying the mouth, a cause of approbation to the Lord." (Ahmad.)

4. *The tradition* that the Apostle of God eat *from* a shoulder *of a Sheep* and then prayed without performing ablution. (Al Bazzar and Abu Yala.)

5. *The tradition*, "Let none of you perform ablution on account of food that he hath eaten, the eating of which is lawful unto him." (Al Bazar.)

---

1 See page 71-the word ما should be inserted between لا and ذكره to make it indentical with Omar's words in the tradition quoted, though neither the MS, nor printed text have it.

2 Here follows a list of those who have related traditions on his authority, which I see no profit in trans cribing.

6. *The tradition*, the Apostle of God forbade the beating of those who were at prayer. (Abu Yala and al Bazzar).

7. *The tradition*, "The last prayers the Prophet prayed, *he prayed* behind me, wearing a single garment."

8. *The tradition,* "He who is rejoiced to read the Qurãn freshly, as it was revealed, let him read it according to the reading of Ibn Umm Abd." (Ahmad.)

9. *The tradition* that he said to the Apostle of God, "teach me a prayer, which I may say in my prayers,"—he replied, "O God I have wronged my own soul with a great wronging, and none but Thou forgiveth sins, therefore pardon me in Thy clemency, and have mercy on me, for Thou art the Clement and the Merciful. (Al Bukhari and Muslim.)

10. *The tradition* "He who prayeth in the morning, is under the protection of God, therefore seek ye not to violate the promise of God, and he who slayeth him *who doth so,* God will summon him and prostrate him upon his face in hell fire." (Ibn Majah.)[1]

11. *The tradition.* "No Prophet ever died, until one among his people had stood before him as Imam in prayer." (Al Bazzar.)

12. *The tradition.* "No man committeth a sin, and then performeth his ablution so that it be valid, and then prayeth with two bowings of the head and body, and asketh pardon of God, but He forgiveth him." (Ahmad and the authors of the Four Sunans, and Ibn Haban.)

13. *The tradition.* "God hath never taken from life a Prophet

---

1 Abu Abdullah Muhammad b. Yazid b. Majah al Kazwini a celebrated Hafidh is the author of a work in tradition entitled Kitab us Sunan. He is the author of a commentary on the Qurãn and a history of Kazwin. His book on tradition is counted one of the six Sahihs (authentic collections) : born A.H. 209 (824-5) died, A.H. 273 (887). Ibn Khall.

save in the place wherein he desireth to be buried." (At Tirmidi.)

14. *The tradition.* "God curse the Jews and the Christians- take ye the sepulchers of their Prophets as mosques." (Abu Yala.)

15. *The tradition.* "Verily a dead body[1] is sprinkled with hot water by reason of the lamentations of the living." (Abu Yala.)

16. *The tradition.* "Beware of hell fire, though it be but for half a date, for verily it maketh straight the crooked, and preventeth a wicked death, and effecteth for the hungry what it doth for him who is full."

17. *The tradition.* "The obligation of alms-deeds-in full." (Al Bukhari and others.)

18. *The tradition* from Ibn Abi Mulaykah, who said-"Often times the bridle would fall from the hand of Abu Bakr and he would strike the foreleg of his camel and make it kneel down,"-they said to him "why didst thou not command us to give it *to thee.*" He replied, "my friend the Apostle of God commanded me to ask nothing of men." (Ahmad.)

19. *The tradition.* "The Apostle of God commanded Asma the daughter of Umays when she brought forth Muhammad the son of Abu Bakr, to bathe herself and invoke the name of God."

20. *The tradition.* The Apostle of God was asked "which are the most excellent actions of the pilgrimage ?" He replied, "the raising of the voice *in the 'talbiyat,'* and the shedding

---

1 That is, punished for the profitless lamentations of the living : another tradition says, "verily the dead will be punished for his family's weeping for him. ان الميت يعذب ببكاء اهله عليه The reason of which Lane thinks to be, that the Arabs used to charge their families to weep and wail for them, and the dead are obnoxious to punishment for having done this.

of the blood of the victims brought for sacrifice." (At Tirmidhi and Ibn Majah.)

21. *The tradition.*- That he kissed the Black Stone and said, "were it not that I have, seen the Apostle of God kiss thee, I would not have kissed thee (AD Darakutni).

22. *The tradition* that the Apostle of God sent to the people of Mecca an ordinance that no idolater should make the pilgrimage after that year, and that no one should make the circuit *of the Kaaba* naked, &c. (Ahmad.)

23. *The tradition.* "Between my dwelling and my pulpit is a garden of the gardens of paradise, and my pulpit is upon a fountain of the fountains of[1] paradise." (Abu Yala.)

24. *The tradition* of Muhammad's going to the house of Abu Haytham b-ul Tayyihan, in full. (Abu Yala)

25. *The tradition* "God with gold, like with like, silver with silver, like with like, but who giveth or asketh over and above shall be in hell fire." (Abu Yala and al Bazzar.)

26. *The tradition* "Cursed by he who doeth injury to a true believer or defreaudeth him." (At Tirmidi.)

27. *The tradition,* "The avaricious man shall not enter paradise, nor the deceiver, nor the betrayer, nor he who ruleth evilly, and the first that shall enter paradise is the servant who is obedient to God and obedient to his master." (Ahmad.)

28. *The tradition.* He who freeth a slave, inherits of him. (Al Dhia[2] al Mukaddasi in the Mukhtarah.)

29. *The tradition.* "We[3] are not inherited of ; that which we

---

1 The text here has نزعة for ترعة erroneously. The MS, has the correct reading. For variations of this tradition, see Burton's Pilgrimage, Vol. II, p. 66.

2 Hafidh Dhiauddin Muhammad b. Abdul Wahid al Mukaddasi al Hanbali, died 643 A.H. (1245). The Mukhtarah (chosen) is a work on tradition. Kashfud Dhunun.

3 See page 74.

leave is the portion of the poor." (Al Bukhari.)

30. *The tradition.* "Verily when the Lord assigneth a means of subsistence to a Prophet, and afterwards taketh his life, He continueth it unto him who cometh after him." (Abu Dauud.)

31. *The tradition.* "Evading family descent, though in a trifling degree, is impiety towards God." (Al Bazzar.)

32. *The tradition.* "Thou and thy goods belong to thy father." Abu Bakr said, "he meant by that only what regards necessary maintenance." (Al Bayhaki.)

33. *The tradition.* "He whose feet become dusty in the service of God, God will preserve them from hell fire." (Al Bazzar.)

34. *The tradition.* "I was commanded to war with men." (The two Shaykhs and others.)

35. *The tradition.* "An excellent servant of God and a brother to his kindred is Khalid b-ul Walid, and a Sword of the Swords of God which He hath drawn against the infidels and hypocrites." (Ahmad.)

36. *The tradition.* "The sun hath never risen upon a better man than Omar." (At Tirmidi.)

37. *The tradition.* "He who hath swayed authority over the Muslims and hath appointed over them a governor out of favour, upon him shall be the curse of God-the Lord shall not accept from him either artifice or ransom until He maketh him to enter hell, and he who giveth to any one what is reserved for the Lord, verily violateth unlawfully what is reserved to God, upon him therefore, shall be the curse of God."

38. *The tradition* – the story of Maiz[1] and his stoning. (Ahmad.)

---

1 Maizb Malik al Aslami, one of the Companions was stoned on account of adultery.

39. *The tradition.* "He doeth not amiss who asketh pardon though he return *to his fault* seventy times a day." (At Tirmidi.)

40. *The tradition* that Muhammad held a council of war. (At Tabarani.)

41. *The tradition* when there was revealed "whose doeth evil shall be requited for it" etcetera. (Qur. IV) – (At Tirmidi, Ibn Haban and others.)

42. *The tradition.* "Verily ye read this verse 'O true believers, take care of your souls'" &C., (Qur. V.) (Ahmad and the authors of the Four Sunans,[1] and Ibn Haban.)

43. *The tradition.* "What is thy opinion of two people, of whom God maketh the third ?" (The two Shaykhs.)

44. *The tradition.* "O God *let us not die* by spear – thrusts or pestilence." (Abu Yala.)

45. *The tradition.* "The Sura of Hud hath made me grey, &c. Ad Darakutni in the Ilal (Defects *impairing the validity of traditions.)*

46. *The tradition.* "Infidelity moves more stealthily among my people than the creeping of an ant," &c (Abu Yala and others.)

47. *The tradition.* "I aid , O Apostle of God, instruct me in something that I should say in the morning time and in the evening" &c. (Al Haytham b. Kulayb in his Musnad, and also at Tirmidi and others from the ascription of Abu Hurayrah.)

48. *The tradition.* "Be careful to say, 'there is no God but God,' and to ask pardon of Him, for Satan hath said 'I destroy men by sin, and they destroy me by *saying* there

---

1 The first four of the six Great Masters of Tradition, i.e., Bukhari, Muslim Abu Dauud and at Tirmidi.

is no God but God, and the asking of pardon, and when I see that, I destroy them through their passions for they think themselves to be rightly guided." (Abu Yala.)

49. *The tradition* when there was revealed ; "life not up your voices above the voice of the Prophet"[1] I said "O Apostle of God, I will not address thee save *in the voice* of one who is decrepid." (As Sirar), al Bazzar.

50. *The tradition.* "Every or.e obtains that which is created for him." (Ahmad.)

51. *The tradition.* "He who lieth towards me of set purpose or refuseth a thing that I have commanded, shall surely dwell in a chamber of hell." (Abu Yala.)

52. *The tradition.* "There is no escape from this thing" &c., is in *that of* "there is no God but God" (Ahmad and others.)

53. *The tradition.* "Go forth and call out to the people, 'He who confesseth that 'there is no God but God,' shall assuredly possess Paradise ;' and I went forth and Omar met me &c." (Abu Yala, and this is preserved from the tradition of Abu Hurayrah-recorded by only one authority from the tradition of Abu Bakr.)

54. *The tradition.* "There are two classes of my people that shall not enter paradise-the Murgians[2] and the Kadarians."

---

1 Qur. XLIX. This verse is said to have been occasioned by a dispute between Abu Bakr and Omar concerning the appointment of a governor of a certain place in which they raised their voices so high in Muhammad's presence, that it was thought necessary to forbid it for the future. Sale.

2 These teach that the judgment of every Muslim guilty of grievous sin will be deferred till the resurrection, for which reason they pass no sentence on him in this world either of absolution or condemnation. They also hold that disobedience with faith hurteth not, and obedience with infidelity profiteth not. This sect is subdivided into four species. For the origin of the name and their further doctrines, consult Sale, p. 123. Preliminary discourse. The Kadarians deny absolute predestination, the Muatazalites are by some comprehended under this denomination. See Sale, p. 115.

(Al Darakutni in the Ilal *Defects invalidating traditions.*)

55. *The tradition.* "Ask safety of God." (Ahmad, Nasai and Ibn Majah who gives many ascriptions of it.)

56. *The tradition.* When the Apostle of God desired anything, he would say, "O God, take for me, choose for me." (At Tirmidi.)

57. *The tradition.* "The prayer of submission is, 'O God *who art* the dispeller of grief'" &c. (Al Bazzar and al Hakim.)

58. *The tradition.* "Every body that is nourished with forbidden things, hell fire is its proper portion"-and in another reading "there shall not enter Paradise a body that hath been fed on what is forbidden *to it.*" (Abu Yala.)

59. *The tradition.* "There is no part of the body that complaineth not of the sharpness of the tongue." (Abu Yala.)

60. *The tradition.* "The Lord descendeth on the night in the middle of the month of Shaaban, and in it pardoneth every mortal except an infidel, and the man in whose heart is hatred." (Al Darakutni.)

61. *The tradition.* "Verily Dajjal shall come forth from the East from a land called Khurasan, and there shall follow him peoples whose faces are like two-fold shields." (At Tirmidi and Ibn Majah.)

62. *The tradition.* "I have been given seventy thousand who shall enter Paradise without judgment being taken of them," &c. (Ahmad.)

63. *The tradition* of Intercession-in full-concerning the running to and fro of people from Prophet to Prophet.[1] (Ahmad.)

---

1 The belief being that on the Day of Judgment, people will run from Prophet to prophet praying for their intercession.

64. *The tradition.* "Were the people to march in one valley and the Auxiliaries marched in *another* valley, I would march in the valley of the Auxiliaries." (Ahmad.)

65. *The tradition.* "The Kuraysh are the masters of this authority, the good among them will follow the good among them, and the wicked among them will follow the wicked among them." (Ahmad.)

66. *The tradition* that Muhammad gave a charge regarding the Auxiliaries at the time of his death, and said, "receive those of them that do good, and pardon those of them that do evil. (Al Bazzar and at Tabarani.)

67. *The tradition.* "I know a land called Uman whose shores the sea washes-in it there is a tribe of Arabs. Were my messenger to go among them, they would no assail him with arrows or with stones." (Ahmad and Abu Yala.)

68. *The tradition* that Abu Bakr passed by al Hasan who was playing with some boys and lifted him on to his neck, and said, "by my father, he hath, a likeness to the Prophet, and hath no likeness to Ali." (Al Bukhari.) Ibn Kathir says, "this come under the class of uninterrupted ascriptions, as it is a confirmation of his remark that the Apostle of God resembled al Hasan."

69. *The tradition* that the Prophet used to visit Umm Ayman. (Muslim.)

70. *The tradition.* "The thief must be put on death for the fifth *theft*"[1] (Abu Yala and ad Daylami.)

71. *The tradition,* of the narrative of Ohud (at Tayalisi and at Tabarani.)

---

1 According to the law, the chief loses his left hand for the first offence, his right foot for the second, his right hand for the third and his left foot for the fourth. The ingenuity that could contrive a fifth theft under these disadvantages would seem to deserve commendation rather than death.

72. *The tradition.* "While I was with the apostle of God, behold I saw him driving away something from himself, and I did not see *what thing it was.* I said, 'O apostle of God, what is it thou art driving away ?" He replied 'the world wearied me and I said "away with thee," and it said to me, "what ! wilt thou not have me ?" ' (Al Bazzar.)

Thus much has Ibn Kathir recorded in the ascriptions of as Siddik, of those traditions traced uninterruptedly to the Prophet, but he has omitted others which I follow up to complete the number mentioned by an Nawawi.[1]

73. *The tradition.* "Kill a tike wherever you may find it among men." (At Tabarani in the Ausat.)

74. *The tradition.* "Reflect whose are the houses ye dwell in! whose the land ye inhabit ! and in the path of whom do ye walk !" (Ad Daylami.)

75. *The tradition.* "Be frequent in your prayers over me, for the Lord hath stationed an angel above my grave, and when a man of my people prayeth, the angel sayeth to me, 'verily such a one the son of such a one hath this moment prayed for thee." (Ad Daylami.)

76. *The tradition.* The Friday prayer, is an atonement for all that occurreth until the next Friday prayer, and ablution on a Friday is an atonement, &c. (Al Ukayli in the Dhuafa (*weak authorities*).

77. *The tradition.* "verily the heat of hell to my people shall be as that of a hot bath." (At Tabarani.)

78. *The tradition.* "Beware of lying, for lying is an estrangement from the faith." (Ibn Lal in the Makarim ul Akhlak (*noble qualities*).

---

1 An Nawawi mentions one hundred and forty-two, and as Suyuti gives but one hundred and four. I am grateful for the omission.

79. *The tradition.* "To every one who hath fought at Badr, is announced the tidings of Paradise." (Ad Darakutni in the "Afrad" *Traditions recorded but by one authority.)*

80. *The tradition.* "Religion is the weighty banner of God; who is able to sustain it?" (Ad Daylami.)

81. *The tradition.* The Sura Y. S.[1] is called the "Commonalty" (the throat), &c., (Ad Daylami and al Bayhaki in the Shaa'b u'l Iman-*People of the Faith.*)

82. *The tradition.* "A monarch just and humble, is the shadow of God and His spear upon earth, and every night and day shall be placed to his account the good works of sixty just men." (Abu'l Shaykh al U'kayli in the Dhua'fa and Ibn Haban in the "Kitab u't Thawab"-*Record of recompense.)*

83. *The tradition.* "Moses said to his Lord 'What is the reward for one who consoleth the bereaved mother?' He replied 'God will cover him with his shadow.'" (Ibn Shabin in the "Targhib." (*Incentive* and ad Daylami.)

84. *The tradition.* "O God ! Strengthen Islam in Omar b-u'l Khattab." (At Tabarani in the Ausat.)

85. *The tradition.* "No game is ever pursued, nor a thorny tree lopped, nor the root of a tree cut, but by reason of *their* infrequency in praising God." (Ibn Rahwayh[2] in his Musnad.)

---

1 The meaning of these letters is unknown ; some pretend that they stand for Yainsan (O man). This chapter is said to have several other titles given to it by Muhammad himself, and particularly that of the heart of the Qurãn It is read to persons in their dying agony. Sale.

2 Abu Yakub Ishak, a native of Marw, as Shahjan was equally distinguished for his knowledge of law and tradition as for his piety. Ibn Hanbal considered him an Imam among the Muslims and an eminent jurisconsult. His Musnad is well-known. He was born A.H. 161 (A.D. 777-8) and died at Naysabur. A.H. 238 (853). 'Rawayh, says Ibn Khallakan was a name given to his father, because he was born on the road to Mecca (rah in Persian signifying road and wayh found.) This word is also pronounced Rahuya. Ibn Khallakan's philology is not always safe to follow.

86. *The tradition.* "Had I not been sent unto you, Omar would surely have been sent" &c. (Ad Daylami).

87. *The tradition.* "Were the inhabitants of Paradise to trade, they would trade in stuffs."[1]

88. *The tradition.* "He who rebelleth claiming either for himself or for another, while an Imam ruleth the people, upon him is the curse of God, and the angels and the whole people,- therefore slay him." (Ad Daylami in the history of *Hamadan?)*

89. *The tradition.* "He who recordeth on my authority a doctrine or a tradition, the reward thereof shall not cease to be placed to his account while that doctrine or tradition continueth." (Al Hakim in the History *of the doctors of Naysabur.*)

90. *The tradition.* "He who walketh barefoot in the service of God, God will not ask of him on the Day of Judgment regarding what was Obligatory upon him." (At Tabarani in the Ausat.)

91. *The tradition.* "Whoso would be glad that God should protect him from the heat of hell and bring him under His own shadow, let him not be harsh with the true believers, but merciful unto them." (Ibn Lal in the Makarim u'l Akhlak and Abu'l Shaykh and Ibn Haban in the "Thawab" *Recompense.*)

92. *The tradition.* "He who riseth in the morning purposing to worship God, God will write down to him the recompense of his day, even though he sinneth against Him." (Ad Daylami.)

93. *The tradition.* "No people hath abstained from warring in the cause of the Lord, but He hath included them in one

---

1 Abu Bakr, Othman, Talhah Abdur Rahman b. Auf were all cloth – merchants. Ibn Kutayb.

common punishment." (At Tabarani in the Ausat.)

94. *The tradition.* "A slanderer shall not enter Paradise." (Ad Daylami but without ascription.)

95. *The tradition.* "Despise not any of the Muslims, for the meanest of the Muslims is great before God." (Ad Daylami.)

96. *The tradition.* God says "if ye desire my mercy, be merciful unto my people." (Abu'l Shaykh, Ibn Haban and ad Daylami.)

97. *The tradition.* "I asked of the apostle of God regarding the nether garment, and he touched the muscle of his leg, and I said 'O apostle of God increase *The length* for me;' then he touched the lower part of the muscle, and I said 'increase *the length* for me,' he replied, it would not be good to have it lower.' I said, 'O apostle of God we are undone:' he answered, 'O Abu Bakr, be guided aright, and take the middle course, thou wilt be safe.'" (Abu Nua'ym in the Huliyah.)

98. *The tradition.* "My palm and the palm of A'li are exactly equal." (Ad Daylami and Ibn A'sakir.)

99. *The tradition.* "Neglect not to invoke God against Satan, for if ye do not regard him, he is not heedless of ye." (Ad Daylami but without ascription.)

100. *The tradition.* "He who buildeth a temple unto God, God will build for him a mansion in Paradise." (At Tabarani in the Ausat.)

101. *The tradition.* "He who hath eaten of this unclean[1] herb, let him no approach our temple." (At Tabarani in the Ausat.)

102. *The tradition.* Of the lifting up of the hands in the

---

1 Garlic. In two traditions given in the Kitab ul Iktifa, onions are included in this prohibition. These will be found in the life of Omar in that work.

One who has neither son nor father alive.

beginning of prayer, in the bowing of the head, and in prostration,[1] (All Bayhaki in the Sunan.)

103. *The tradition.* "Give a Camel to Abu Jahl."[2] (Al Isma'ili in the Mua'jam *alphabetical Dictionary of the Traditionists.*)

104. *The tradition.* "Looking upon A'li is worship." (Ibn A'sakir.)

On what hath been handed down of as Siddik in comment on the Qurãn.

Abu'l Kasim al Baghawi records on the authority of Ibn Mulaykah that Abu Bakr was asked regarding a verse of the Qurãn and he said, "what earth would sustain me and what sky would overshadow me, were I to speak that concerning the book of God which God hath not intended." And Abu U'baydah from Ibrahim at Taymi, that Abu Bakr was asked regarding the saying of the Most High, "grapes and clover" (Qur. LXXX) and he said, "what sky would overshadow me and what earth would sustain me, did I speak regarding the book of God that which I know not." And al Bayhaki and others from Abu Bakr that he was asked regarding *the meaning* of "al Kalalah,"[3] and he answered "I will presently give an opinion regarding it and if it be just, it is from God, but if it be faulty *it cometh* from me and from the Evil One. I think it to

---

1 In the beginning of prayers, lifting up the hands is the universal practice, the Shafii school alone adopting it in the bowings and prostrations.

2 The uncle of Muhammad.

3 Qur. IV. الكلالة Translated by Sale-"a distant relation." Zamakshari in his great Commentary gives it three meanings :-

1. One who has neither son nor father alive.
2. One who has neither father living nor any issue.
3. One who has no living relative in the direct paternal line, nor through his own children.

mean lacking parent and offspring;" and when Omar became Caliph, he said, "verily, I forbear from setting aside a thing that Abu Bakr hath spoken."

Abu Nua'ym records in his Huliyah from al Aswad-b-Hilal, that Abu Bakr said to the Companions, "What say ye concerning these two verses, 'As for those who say our Lord is God and who behave uprightly' (Qur. XLI)-'and they who believe and clothe their faith with injustice' (Qur.VI). They replied, 'and who behave uprightly,'-that is, who do not sin and do not clothe their faith with sin." He replied, 'Ye have placed upon it a meaning which it will not bear;" then he said, "Who say our Lord is God and who behave uprightly"-*that is,* "who do not incline to a God other Him, and who do not clothe their faith *with infidelity* by associating others with him." And Ibn Jarir from Abu Bakr as Siddik, regarding the saying of the Most High. "They who do right *shall receive*a most excellent reward and a superabundant addition" (Qur. X), that he said it signified the looking upon the face of the Lord; and regarding the words of the Most High, "Those who say our Lord is God and who behave uprightly," that he said, "Verily the people say this, but he who dieth according to this *precept,* he it is who behaveth uprightly."

On What has been handed of established traditions from as Siddik on the subject of his words, decisions, discourses and prayers.

Al Lalakai[1] records in his Sunnat on the authority of Ibn Omar that a man went to Abu Bakr and said, "dost thou think that fornication in a man is predestioned?" He answered, "Yes." Then he said, "if God hath predestined it concerning me, will He punish me for it?" he replied "Yes, thou son of an uncircumcised woman, and by Allah, were a man by me, I would command him to bring thee to reason." And Abu Dauu'd in his Sunan from Abu Abdullah

1 Abul Kasim Hibatullah b. Hasan b. Mansur ar Razi.

as Sunabihi,[1] that he *once* prayed behind Abu Bakr at evening prayers, and Abu Bakr read during the first two bowings of the head, the first chapter of the Qurãn and a Sura of the shorter sections,[2] and he read in the third bowing, "O Lord, cause not our hearts to swerve *from truth* after thou hast directed us" (Qur. III). And Ibn Abi Khaythamah and Ibn A'sakir from Ibn U'aynah, that when Abu Bakr was engaged in condoling with a man he used to say, "there is no harm in patience and no profit in lamentation : death is easier to bear than that which precedeth it, and more severe than that which cometh after it : remember the death of the apostle of God, your sorrow will be leassened and may God increase your reward." And Ibn Abi Shaybah and ad Darakutni from Salim b. Ubayad[3] who was a Companion, that he said, "Abu Bakr used to say to me, 'Stand between me and the dawn that I may eat my morning meal.'[4] And from Abu Kilabah and Abu's Safar that they said, 'Abu Bakr as Siddik used to say, "shut the door that we may eat our morning meal."' And al Bayhaki and Abu Bakr b. Ziyad of Naysabur, in the Kitab ul Ziyadat from Hudayfah[5] b Usayd, that he said, 'verily I observed Abu Bakr and

---

1 Abu Abdullah Abdur Rahman-b. Asalat as Sunabihi, the later is a branch of Banu Murad.

2 The Mufassal is that portion of the Qurãn from the XLIXth Chapter to the end, according to the most correct opinion and so called because of the many divisions between its chapters.

3 Abu Abdullah Salim b. Ubayd b. Rabiih, the freedom of Abu Hudayfah the Companion. Abu Nuaym denies this pedigree, and others assert him to be the son of Makal. He was of Persian origin, one of the most eminent of the Companions and Auxiliaries. Omar thought so highly of him, that at his death he is reported to have said that had Salim been alive, he would not have named a Council of Consultation to elect for the Caliphate. Salim fought at Badr and Ohud and the battle of the Ditch and was killed at Yamamah where the carried the standard of the Muslims embrancing it with the stumps of his arms after his hands had been hewn off. An Nawawi.

4 After the rise of the true dawn مجر الصادق the day begins, and everything by which fasting would be broken, becomes unlawful to him who fasts.

5 Hudayfah b. Usayd one of the Companions-present at Hudaybyah and was one of those who swore to be faithful to Muhammad when he was seated under the lote tree. According to Ibn Haban, he died A.H. 42. Ibn Hajr.

Omar and what they did in the early part of the forenoon, with the intention that the example of those two might be followed." And Abu Dauud from Ibn Abbas that he said, 'I testify that Abu Bakr as Siddik said, "eat of fishes those only that swim."' And as Shafi'i[1] in the Aam (universal) from Abu Bakr as Siddik, that he was averse to the sale of flesh in exchange for a live animal. And al Bukhari, that he placed the grandfather in the same degree as the father, that is, in regard to inheriting. And Ibn Abi Shaybah in his Musannaf, from Abu Bakr, that he said, 'a grandfather stands in the place of the father, if there be no father but he, and the grandson, in place of the son, if there be no other than he.' And from al Kasim, that a man was brought before Abu Bakr, who had been disowned by his father, and Abu Bakr said 'smite *him* on the head for Satan is in *his* head.' And from Ibn Abi Malik, that *once* when Abu Bakr prayed over a dead man, he said, 'O God! His people, and his goods and his kindred have forsaken this Thy servant, and his sin was grievous but Thou art merciful and compassionate.'"

Sai'd b. Mansur records in his Sunan on the authority of Omar, that Abu Bakr decided the case of A'asim,[2] the son of Omar Khattab in favour of the mother of A'asim, saying, "her breath and fragrance and kindness are better for thee (A'asim) that thine (Omar)." And al Bayhaki from Kays b. Abi Hazim, that a man went to Abu Bakr and said, "my father desireth to take my property, *saying,* that he is in need of the whole of it," and Abu Bakr said to his father, "Surely that only of his property is thine which is sufficient for they sustenance;" he answered, "O Vicegerent of the Apostle of God, did not the Apostle of God say, 'thou and they goods belong to thy father !' He replied, 'Yes, but he meant by that only necessary

---

1 Born A.H. 150 (767-8), died A.H. 204 (820) and buried in the lesser Karafah cemetery at old Cairo near Mount Mukattam. His life and teaching are well enough known to dispense with an account of them here. Consult Ibn Khallakan.

2 Aasim was then a child, and Omar having a quarrel with the mother, wished to remove they boy from her control, but Abu Bakr decided against it. The boy became the grandfather of Omar b. Abdil Aziz the Caliph.

maintenance.' And Ahmad from the grandfather of Amr b. Shuayb,[1] that Abu Bakr used not to kill a freedom in retaliation for a slave. And al Bukhari from the grandfather of Ibn Abi Mulaykah, that a man had bitten the hand of another who in *return* knocked out his teeth, and Abu Bakr suffered it to pass with impunity. And Ibn Abi Shaybah and al Bayhaki from A'krimah[2] that Abu Bakr adjudged *the loss of a ear to be repaid* by fifteen camels and said, 'the hair and turban will conceal the disgreace of it.' And al Bayhaki and others from Abu Imam al Juni, that Abu Bakr sent troops to Syria and appointed over them Yazid b Abi Sufyan and said, "I commend to thee ten precepts. Slay not a woman nor a child, nor an aged man, and cut not down a tree that beareth fruit, and lay not waste a cultivated country, and destroy not a sheep, nor a camel, save for food, and lop not a date tree nor burn it, and conceal not plunder and be not faint of heart."'

Ahmad, and Abu Dauud and an Nasai record on the authority of Abu Barzah al Aslami, that he said, "Abu Bakr was enraged with a man and his anger became violent, and I said, to him, 'O Vicegerent of the Apostle of God shall I cut off his head?' He replied, 'woe unto thee-that is not lawful for any one after the Apostle of God.' And Sayf in the Kitabul Futuh, (*Record of Conquests*) on the authority of his Shaykhs, that two female singers were brought before Muhajir Ibn Abi Umayyah who was ruler of Yamamah, one of whom had sung in contumely of the Prophet, and he cut off her hand and pulled out her teeth ; the other had sung deriding the Muslims, and he cut off her hand and pulled out her teeth; and Abu Bakr wrote to him, *saying*, 'I have heard what thou hast done to the woman who sang in contumely of the Prophet,

---

1 Abu Ibrahim Amr b. Shuayb b. Muhammad b. Abdillah of the Kuraysh, in point of time next to the Tabiis. A great many distinguished Traditionists relate on his authority and his reputation is high amongst them for accuracy. An Nawawi.

2 There are two of this name, one the son of Abu Jahl, and the other the freedom of Ibn Abbas, one of the most distinguished of the Tabiis the accuracy of whose traditions is much praised by al Bukhari, he died A.H. 104. An Nawawi.

and if thou hadst not been beforehand with me in it, I would have ordered thee to put her to death, for punishment in regard to the Prophets is not as other punishments-he among the Muslims, therefore, who doeth such a thing is an apostate, or being a tributary subject, is a treacherous enemy : but she who sang deriding the Muslims, were she among those who profess Islam then correction and deprivation of *substance* without mutilation *would have been sufficient,* but were she a tributary suibject, then by my life, if I forgave her infidelity, it would be a great mercy, and had I been beforehand with thee in the like of this, 'I would assuredly have afflicted her sorely, but rather choose thou elemency, and beware thou of mutilating men, for it is a sin and a thing to be avoided save in retaliation.'"

Malik and ad Darakutni record on the authority of Safiyah, the daughter of Abu Ubayd, that a man seduced a slave girl, a virgin, and confessed to it, and Abu Bakr passed order on him, and he was scourged and banished to Fadak.[1] And Abu Yala from Muhammad b. Hatib that a man was brought before Abu Bakr who had committed theft, and his feet and hands had been cut off and Abu Bakr said to him, "I do not find that anything *can be done* to thee save what hath been adjudged regarding thee by the Apostle of God, on the day that he commanded thy death,[2] for verily he had knowledge of thee," and he ordered him to be put to death. And Malik from al Kasim b. Muhammad, that a man of the people of Yaman, Whose hand and foot had been cut off *for theft* came and abode with Abu Bakr and complained to him that the governor of Yaman had treated him unjustly (and the man used to pray during the night), and Abu Bakr said, "by thy father, thy night is not like unto the night of a thief." After a little time they lost an ornament belonging to Asma, daughter of Umays, the wife of Abu Bakr, and the man went round with them *searching* and saying, "O God! With thee *be retribution* upon him who hath plundered by night the people of this just house." Afterwards, they found the ornament

---

1 A village in Hijaz two days Journey form Medina.

2 See page 119. note. 1

with a goldsmith who affirmed that the mutilated man had brought it to him. Then the mutilated man either confessed or it was proved against him, and Abu Bakr passed an order upon him and his left hand was amputated, and Abu bakr said, "by Allah, his imprecation upon himself was, to me, more grievous for him than his theft." And ad Darakutni from Anas that Abu Bakr ordered amputation for *the theft of* a shield, the value of which was five dirhams. And Abu Nuaym in his Huliyah, on the authority of Abu Salih that when the people of Yaman came[1] in the time of Abu Bakr and heard the Qurãn, they began to weep, and Abu Bakr said "Thus were we, and afterwards our hearts became hardened." Abu Nuaym adds- "that is, strengthened, and tranquil with the knowledge of the Most High." And al Bukhari from Ibn Omar that Abu Bakr said, "behold, Muhammad in the people of his House." And Abu Ubayd[2] in the Gharib from Abu Bakr that he said, "happy was he who died remaining in his abode," that is, in the beginning of Islam before the breaking out of sedition.

The Four *Traditionists* and Malik record on the authority of Kabisah[3] that a grandmother went to Abu Bakr as Siddik inquiring of him regarding her inheritance and he said, "nothing is due to thee according to the book of God, and I know of nothing for thee in the traditions of the Prophet of God, therefore come back *another time,* so that I may inquire of the people, and he inquired of the people and al Mughirab[1] b. Shubah said, "I was present

---

1 That is, when Abu Bakr meditated the conquest of Syria and sent letters to the chiefs of Arabian Felix summoning them with their followers.

2 Abu Ubayd al Kasim b. Sallam, was born at Heart and was Kadhi of Tarsus for eighteen years. He was conspieuous for his piety and learning in various branches of literature, and his traditions are received as authentic. He died at Mecca in A. H. 224 according to al Bukhari. The book alluded to in the text is Gharibul Hadith (*obscure* expressions occurring in the Traditions). He also wrote a work called "Gharibul Musannaf, (Original collection of rare expression) Ibn Khall.

3 Kabisah b. Duayb one of the Tabiis, born in the year of the conquest of Mecca and died in the Caliphate of Abdul Malik b. Marwan under whom he acted in the capacity of Secretary. An Nawawi.

when he gave *such as* her one sixth;" and Abu Bakr said, "was any other with thee?" whereupon Muhammad b. Maslamah arose and said the same that al Mughirah had spoken, and Abu Bakr ordered *the like* for her. And Malik and Darakutni, from al Kasim b. Muhammad, that two grandmothers went to Abu Bakr demanding their inheritance, the mother of a mother and the mother of a father and he accorded the inheritance to the mother of the mother. Thereupon Abdur Rahman-b. Sahl the Auxiliary who had fought at Badr, and was an associate of the Banu Harith said to him, "O vicegerent of the apostle of God dost thou bestow it upon her who, if she died, would not be inherited of ?"[2] so he divided it between the two. And Abdul Razzak in his Musannaf records on the authority of Ayesha, the tradition of the wife of Rufaah who was divorced from him and married afterwards Abdur Rahman b-uz Zubayr who was unable to consummate his marriage, and she desired to return to Rufaah, but the Apostle of God said, "No, not till your marriage be consummated;" this much is in the Sahih, and Abdur Razzak adds, "then she tarried some time and then went to him and informed him that he had touched her, but he forbade her to return to her first husband and said, 'verily if it were thus with her that she returned to Ruffah, her marriage would not be consummated for the second time:"[3] then she went to Abu Bakr and Omar during their Caliphate but they prohibited her. And al

---

1 Abu Abdullah b Shubah of the tribe of Thakif a native of Kufah, one of the Companions. He was present at nearly all the expeditions and actions that took place in his time. Omar gave him the government of Basrah and afterwards of Kufah wherein he was confirmed by Othman and subsequently deposed, but again re-instated by Muawiyah, and died at Kufah A.H. 59. It is said that he married three hundred women, and some say, a thousand. An Nawawi.

2 According to the Muhammadan law a grandson does not inherit from his maternal grandmother.

3 The Muhammadan law insists on the consummation of the marriage with the second husband, before the first can receive the divorced wife back.

Bayhaki from Ukbah b. Aamir[1] that Amr b-ul Aas and Shurahbil-b. Hasanah[2] sent him as a messenger to Abu bakr with the head of Bannan the Syrian general, and when he came to Abu Bakr, he expressed his disapproval, and Ukbah said to him, 'O Vicegerent of the Apostle of God, they do the same with us,' and he replied, 'do those two follow the example of the Persians and Greeks ? let no head be brought to me for verily letters and news are sufficient.' And al Bukhari from Kays Ibn Hazim,[3] that Abu Bakr went to a woman of the tribe of Ahmas called Zaynab, and he observed that she did not speak, and he said, 'why doth she not speak ?' They replied, 'she has made the pilgrimage and is under a vow of silence.' He said to her, 'speak ! for this is not lawful, this is one of the practices of the time of Ignorance :' and she spoke and said 'who art thou?' and he said 'One of the Fugitives;' she said, 'which of the Fugitives?' he replied, 'of the Kuraysh.' She asked, 'of what family of the Kuraysh?' He said, 'verily thou art very inquisitive-I am Abu Bakr.' She said, 'How long shall be our continuance in this holy rule which God hath brought since the time of Ignorance?' He replied, 'your continuance in it shall be as long as your Imams act uprightly.' She said, 'and what are the Imams?' he answered 'Are there not in thy tribe, chiefs and leaders who govern them and whom the tribe obey?' She said, 'Yes'. He replied, 'then they are those men." And from Ayesha, that Abu Bakr had a slave who used to pay him an impost on *his earnings* and, Abu Bakr used to eat of *the fruite of* this impost, and he one day brought him a thing, of which Abu Bakr eat, and the slave said to him, 'dost thon know

---

1 One of the Companions, distinguished for his manner of reading the Qurãn-he governed Egypt for Muawiyah b. Abi Sufiyan and died there in A.H. 58. He carried the news of the taking of Damascus to Omar and reached Medina in seven days and returned to Syria in two and a half through the help of his invocations at Muhammad's tomb. An Nawawi.

2 He was appointed by Abu Bakr and subsequently by Omar to the command of the army in Syria, and continued as Omar's lieutenant in that country till his death of the plague A.H. 18, at the age of sixty-seven. Ibid.

3 One of the Tabiis. He was born before the propagation of Islam and set out to pay his homage to Muhammad who, however, died before Kays arrived. He was a resident of Kufah and died A.H. 84. Ibid.

what this is?' Abu Bakr said, 'what is it?' he replied, 'I once told the fortune of a man in the time of Ignorance, and my divination was not just inasmuch as I deceived him, but he met me and gave me this, of which thou hast eater;' whereupon Abu Bakr put his hand *in his throat* and rejected everything that was in his stomach."

Ahmad records in the "Zuhd" from Ibn Sirin that he said, "I do not know any one who sought to reject the food that he had eaten except Abut Bakr," and he related the story. And an Nasai from Aslam, that Omar beheld Abu Bakr who seized hold of his own tongue and said, "this it is that hath brought me to that to which I have come." And Abu Ubayd in the "Gharib," from Abu Bakr, that he passed by Abdur Rahman b. Auf who was quarrelling with a neighbour and he said to him, "Speak not in anger with thy neighbour for that remaineth but men pass away from thee." And Ibn Asakir from Musa b. Ukbah, that Abu Bakr as Siddik was once preaching, and he said, "Praise be to God-the Lord of created things I glorify Him and implore His assistance, and ask His mercy in what cometh after death, fro my hour and yours are approaching-and I bear witness that there is no God but God above who hath no copartner and that Muhammad is His servant, and His Prophet, whom He hath sent in the Truth as a Messenger of God tidings, and an admonisher and a shining light that he may warn the living and certify the Word to the Unbelievers-and He who obeyeth God and his Prophet, verily he hath followed the right way, and he who hath sinned against those two, verily hath erred with a manifest erring: I commend unto ye devotion to God, and adherence to the commands of God which He hath laid down for ye and, give for your guidance, for verily the whole of the precepts of Islam after the profession of faith, are the hearing and obeying those whom God hath appointed to rule over ye, and verily he who obeyeth God and those who enjoin goodness and prohibit what is unlawful hath prospered and hath performed what is incumbent upon him of his obligations ; and beware ye of following vain desire, for verily he prospereth who is preserved from lust and greed and anger : and beware ye of pride, for what pride belongeth to him who is made of earth, and who afterwards returneth to earth and then *the worm* devoureth him?

for today he is alive and tomorrow he is dead; therefore act ye uprightly from day to day and from hour to hour, and fear the prayer of the oppressed, and number yourselves among the dead; and be ye patient for every work is accomplished through patience, and be ye watchful, for watchfulness is profitable. Act uprightly for a good act is acceptable to God, and refrain from the things against which the Lord hath warned ye under pain of His wrath : and vie ye with one another in hastening *to obtain* the things which the Lord hath promised ye in His mercy ; and teach ye, and yourselves comprehend, and he heedful and in fear, for verily the Lord hath declared unto ye the things for which he hath destroyed those that were before ye, and the things through which He hath delivered those whom He delivered before ye. Verily he hath manifested unto ye in His Book His commands and His prohibitions and the works, He approveth, and those he abhorreth : and verily by my soul, I will not be wanting to you-and God is He whose assistance is implored, and there is no power nor strength but in the Lord. And know ye, verily, that in your works in which ye have been sincere with God, ye them obeyed God, and preserved your portion of excellence, and attained unto your desire, and what ye have done over and above what is enjoined for your faith, keep before ye as religious merits, that ye may make satisfaction for those who have gone before ye,-and make your charitable donations even at the time of your poverty and self-need of them. Then bethink Ye-O servants of God-of your brethren and your companions those that have departed, for they have attained to the works that they sent before them, and abide by them and are settled in misery or happiness in the state that cometh after death. Verily the Lord hath no copartner, and between Him and any of His creatures there is no mediatory influence that can bestow good upon him or avert from him evil save in His worship and obedience to his commands, for verily there is no good in the good after which cometh hell-fire, and no evil in the evil after which cometh heaven. I say unto ye these words, and may God have mercy upon me and ye, and bless ye the Prophet and peace be upon him and the mercy of God and His blessing."

Al Hakim and al Bayhaki record on the authority of Abdullah

b. Ukaym that he said, "Abu Bakr as Siddik preached to us and he glorified God and praised Him as befitted Him, and them said, 'I Commend unto ye piety to God and that ye praise Him as befitteth Him, and that ye mingle desire with fear, for the Lord God praised Zachariah and the people of his house, and said, "These strove to excel in good works and called upon us with love and with fear and humbled themselves before us" (Qur XXI) Therefore know, O servants of God, that the Lord hath your lives as a pledge what is due to Him, and hath taken your compacts[1] regarding it, and hath purchased of ye a little that is perishable, in exchange for eternal abundance ; and this Book of God is among ye, whose light cannot be extinguished, nor its wonders end; therefore seek ye illumination from its light, and accept counsel from His Book and seek light from it in the day of darkness, for verily He hath created ye for His worship and hath appointed for ye *guardian angels* "honourable *in the sight of God* writing down *your actions* who know that which ye do." (Qur. LXXXII). And know, O servants of God that ye proceed and draw nigh unto an appointed time, the knowledge of which, verily, is hidden from ye, therefore if ye are able so to do, that the appointed periods be fulfilled while ye are engaged in the works of the Lord, then so act ye, but this ye cannot do save with the permission of the Lord. Vie ye with one another in *fulfilling the obligation* of your appointed times before your appointed periods are completed, lest they cast ye upon the evilest of your works ; and verily, there are some who have made over the obligations of their appointed times on others, and have taken no heed of themselves, therefore I forbid ye to be like unto them. Then haste ! haste ! flee ! flee ! for behind ye is a nimble pursuer-swift of deed.' And Ibn Abid Dunya, and Ahmad in the Zuhd' and Abu Nuaym in the 'Huhvah' from Yahya b. Abi Kathir, that Abu

---

1 "And when thy Lord drew forth thy posterity from the loins of the sons of Adam, and took them to witness against themselves, *saying,* am I not your Lord ? They answered. *Yea, we* do bear witness, *Qur. VII.* The commentators say that Go stroked Adam's back and extracted from his loins his whole posterity and assembled them in the shape of ants, and after they had, in the presence of the angels, confessed their dependence on Him, they were returned to the loins of Adam. See Sale.

Bakr used to say in his discourse, 'where are the comely, beautiful of countenace- exulting in their youth? Where are the monarchs who built cities and entrenched them round about? Where are they who gave victory on fields of battle ? verily their pillars were overthrown when Fortune betrayed them, and they went down into the darkness of the greave. Haste! Haste! flee ! flee !' And Ahmad in the Zuhd from Salman, [1] that he said, 'I went to Abu Bakr and said, "leave me an injunction," and he replied, "O Sulman, fear God, and know that there shall shortly be victories, but I know not what may be thy portion among them, of what thou may mayest put into thy belly or cast upon thy back, but, know, that he who prayeth the five appointed times of prayer, verily he is under a covenant with God, and walketh under the protection of the Most High : therefore slay not any of the people of God's covenant, lest thou betray God in His covenant and the Lord throw thee prostrate on thy face in hell fire." And from Abu Bakr that he said, "the good shall be taken away, the best, followed by the next in merit, until there remain the dregs of the people, like the husk of dates and of barley-the Lord shall not take heed of them." And Said b. Mansur in the Sunan from Muawiyah b. Kurrah that Abu Bakr as Siddik used to say in his prayers, "O Lord! Render thou the best of my life its close, and the best of my deeds the last, and the best of my days the day of Thy meeting." And Ahmad in the Zuhd from al Hasan, "I heard that Abu Bakr used to say in his prayers, "O God verily I ask to Thee that which may be the best for me in the end-O God! Vouchsafe that the last good that Thou bestowest upon me, be Thy approbation, and the loftiest places in the gardens of delight." A from Arfajah[2] that Abu Bakr said, "he who is able to weep let him weep, or if not, let him endeavour to weep." And from Abu Bakr on the authority of Arazah, "the most deadly of things are the two that are red-gold and saffron."[1] And on the authority of Muslim b.

1 There are two Companions of the name, one the freedman of Muhammad, a native of Persia by birth, and the other Salman-b. Aamir. Consult an Nawawi.

2 Arfajah b. Asad b. Safwan, one of the Companions, of the Banu Tamim.

Yasar, [2] "the true believer is rewarded in everything, even in affliction-for, in the breaking of a shoe-latchet, or some triffle in his sleeve, should he lose it, and be in fear for it, he will find it by his side." And on the authority of Maymun b. Mihran that a raven with large wings was brought to Abu Bakr, and he turned it over and said, "no game is hunted and no tree is felled save it hath neglected the praises of God." And al Bukhari in the "Adab," and Abdullah b. Ahmad in the Zawaiduz Zuhd from as Sunabihi, that he heard Abu Bakr say that the praper of a brother for his brothers in God is accepted." And Abdullah in the Zawaiduz Zuhd from Labid the poet, that he went to Abu Bakr and repeated this verse—

"Is not every thing but God unprofitable?"
He replied. "Thou hast spoken truly." And Labid continued:
"And every joy is surely fleeting."

Abu Bakr exclaimed, "thou hast spoken falsely-there is with God a joy that never passeth away,"- and when Labid had gone, he said "Sometimes a poet speaketh words of wisdom."

On his sayings which manifest the greatness of his fear of his God.

Abu Ahmad al Hakim records on the authority of Muad b. Jabal that Abu Bakr entered a garden, and, behold, there was a ringdove in the shade of a tree, and he heaved a deep sigh and said, "happy art thou, O bird, that eatest of the trees and seekest shelter beneath them, and art not called to account-would that Abu Bakr were like unto thee." And Ibn Asakir from al Asmai that when Abu

---

1 These are said to destroy women, that is the love of gold and perfumes, as flesh meat and wine called also الاحمران are said to destroy men.

2 Abu Abdullah Muslim b. Yasar of Basrah. Some say he was the freedman of Othman, others of Talhab. He was distinguished for his knowledge of jurisprudence, he died A.H. 100-1. An Nawawi.

Bakr was once praised, he said, "O Lord, Thou knowest more of me than I myself, and I know more concerning myself than they-O God, make me better that they think me, and forgive me that which they know not, and call me not to account for what they say." And Ahmad in the Zuhd from Abu Imran al Juni, that Abu Bakr as Siddik said, "I would I were a hair in the side of a servant, a true believer." And from Mujahid, that Ibn uz Zubayr when he rose to prayers was as a stock of wood in abasement, and I have been told that Abu Bakr was the same. And from al Hasan that Abu Bakr said, "by Allah, verily I would I were this tree which is eaten of an felled." And from Katadah that he said, "it has been related to me that Abu Bakr said 'I would that I were pasture that eatle might eat me.'" And from Dhamrah b. Habib that a son of Abu Bakr's was near unto death, and the youth kept looking towards a cushion, and when he was dead, they said to Abu Bakr, "we saw thy son looking towards a cushion," and they moved him from the cushion and they found underneath it five or six dinars. Then Abu Bakr struck one hand upon the other, and uttered the two professions of faith, and kept saying 'verily we belong to God and unto Him shall we return." O such a one, how greatly doth thy body desire that it should be amplified for this."[1] And from Thabit al Bunani that Abu Bakr applied this verse by way of similitude.

> Thou shalt not cease to announce the death of a friend until thou art as he is
> And verily the youth chorisheth a hope, and dieth without attaining it.

Ibn Saad recrds on the authority of Ibn Sirin, that, after the death of the Prophet, there was no one more apprehensive on account of what he knew not, than Abu Bakr, and no one after Abu

---

1 "One the *Day of Judgment, their treasures* shall be intensely heated in the fire of hell, and their forehead and their sides and backs shall be stigmatized therewith." Kur IX. As Suyuti in his Commentary (Tafsirul Jalalayn) Says on this passage, that the bodies of these reprobates will be inflated and extended in order to become capable of receiving the brand of each coin that they have treasured. The identical word اتسع is employed by him to express this meaning.

Bakr more apprehensive on account of what he knew not, than Omar, and when a case came before Abu Bakr, and he could not find its exemplar in the Book of God, nor a tradition regarding it in the Sunnat, he would say, "I will act to the best of my judgment, and if it be just, then it is from God, and if erroneous, then it is mine, and may God pardon me."

On what has been handed down of him regarding the interpretation of dreams.

Said b. Mansur records on the authority of Sai'd b- ul Musayyab that he said, "Ayesha dreamed that there came down into her house, three moons, and she related it to Abu Bakr who was one of the most learned in interpretation among men. He said, "verily thy dream hath spoken truly-there shall be buried verily in thy house, three of the best of mankind." And when the Prophet died, he said, "O Ayesha, this is the best of thy moons." And from Omar b. Shurhabil, that the apostle of God said, "I dreamed that I drove before me some black sheep, then I drove after them white sheep, so that the black could not be seen among them." And Abu Bakr said, "O apostle of God, as for the black sheep, verily they signified the Arabs who shall embrace the faith, and increase in numbers, and the white sheep are the barbarians who shall be converted until the Arabs shall not be seen among them by reason of their numbers." The apostle of God replied, "so the angel interpreted it this morning." A tradition is also ascribed to him from Ibn Abi Laylah that the apostle of God said, "I dreamed I was at a well drawing from it, and there approached me black sheep and behind them grey sheep;" and Abu Bakr said, "suffer me to interpret it" and he continued as above.

Ibn Saad records on the authority of Muhammad Ibn Sirin that he said, "the most learned in interpretation of this people after their Prophet is Abu Bakr." And from Ibn Shihab, that the apostle of God had a dream and related it to Abu Bakr and said, "I dreamed as it were that I and thou were vying with each other in mounting a ladder, and I preceded thee by two steps and a half." He replied, "O apostle of God, the Lord will take thee unto His forgiveness and mercy and I shall live after thee two years and a half." Al Bayhaki records in the Proofs on the authority of Abdullah b. Buraydah that the apostle of god sent Amr b-ul Aas at the head of a body of troops, among them being Abu Bakr and Omar, and when they arrived at the field of war, Amr commanded that they should not light fires, and Omar was wroth and purposed going to him, but Abu Bakr prevented him and explained to him *saying,* "the apostle of God hath not placed him[1] over thee, but for his knowledge of wars this therefore cometh from him." And from an ascription of Abu Mashar that the apostle of God said "verily I shall appoint a man over the people who is the best among them, who may be vigilant of eye and clear-sighted in war."

Khalifah b Khayyat and Ahmad b. Hanbal, and Ibn Asakir record on the authority of Yazid b-ul Asamm,[2] that the Prophet said to Abu Bakr "Am I the greater or thou?" He replied "thou art the greater and nobler, but I am older than thou." This treadition is interrupted in transmission and narrated but by one authority, but if it were substantiated this answer should be accounted *as a proof* of his sagacity and reverence; but this reply is commonly ascribed to Abbas. And the same in ascribed to Said b. Yarbun (recorded by at Tabarani) and its reading, that the Apostle of God said to him, "which of us is the greater?" he replied, "thou art greater and better than I, but I am the elder."

Abu Nuaym records that it was said to Abu Bakr, "O vicegerent of the apostle of God, wilt thou not employ in service those who fought at Badr?" He replied, "I know their dignity but I am loth to defile them with the world." And Ahmad in the Zuhd

1 The printed text has يستعلمة for يستعملة

2 Abu Auf Yaxid b-ul Asamm a native of Kufah and a Tabii. He dwelt at Rakkah and died there A.H. 103. He was the son of the sister of Maymuna wife of Muhammad and the traditions related by him are considered authentic. An Nawawi.

from Ismail b. Muhammad, that Abu Bakr divided *the spoil* into portions and divided it, equally among the people, and Omar said to him, "dost thou apportion it equally among the men of Badr and the rest of the people?" Abu Bakr replied, "verily the world is a sufficiency, and the best sufficiency is that which is most comprehensive, but verily the superiority of these[1] lies in their spiritual rewards."

Ahmad records in the Zuhd on the authority of Abu Bakr b. Hafa that he said, "I have heard that Abu Bakr used to fast in summer, and break his fast[2] in winter." And Ibn Saad from Hayyan the goldsmith that the impression on the signet ring of Abu Bakr was, "excellent is the omnipotent God!"- At Tabarani records on the authority of Musa b. Ukbah that he said, "I do not know four people who attained with their sons to the time of the Prophet, save these four, Abu Kuhafah and his son Abu Bakr as Siddiq,-and his son Abdur Rahman-and Abu Atik son of Abdur Rahman whose name was Muhammad." And Ibn Mandah and Ibn Asakir from Ayesha, that the parents of none among the Fugitives embraced Islam, save the parents of Abu Bakr,-Ibn Saad and al Bazzar record on good authorities from Anas that the oldest in years of the

---

1 That is, the men of Badr.

2 This would seem to imply that even when the Ramadhan fell in winter, so orthodox a believer did not comply with the indispensable duty of fasting during that month. The explanation however, though so immaterial a point scarcely deserves it, is perhaps as follows. According to Lane, the present months of the Muhammadan year, were named by Kilab b. Murrah, an ancestor of Muhammad, about two centuries before Islam. These months were lunar, and from this period, with a view of adopting their year to the solar, the Arabs added a month, which they called النسيء at the end of every three years, until they were forbidden to do so by Qurãn (Ch. IX). The abolition of the intercalation was proclaimed by Muhammad at the pilgrimage in the tenth year of the Flight. It is obvious from the derivations of the Arabic names of the months, that they were called after the seasons in which they fell. The ضمران (from رمضي signifying vehement heat) occurred between the middle of July and the middle of August : while the years were yet adapted to the solar, there would be a fixity of recurrence, or nearly so, of the month in the same seasons, and thus Abu Bakr might well have fasted in summer frequently enough to account for the tradition.

companions of the apostle of God were Abu Bakr as Siddik and Suhayl-b. Amr b. Baydha.

Note-Al Bayhaki records in the "Proofs" on the authority of Asma daughter of Abu Bakr that she said, "In the year of the conquest of Mecca, a daughter of Abu Kuhafah went forth and some horsemen met her, and upon her neek was necklace of gold pieces, and a man wrenched it from her neck. And when the apostle of God entered the mosque, Abu Bakr stood up and said "I call upon God and Islam for the necklace of my sister'-and by Allah, no one answered him. He repeated it then a second time, but no one answered him. Then he exclaimed, 'O sister reckon *upon a reward of God* for the necklace, for by Allah, there is little honesty among men now a days.'"

Note-I have seen in the handwriting of the Hafidh ad Dahabi, *the names of* those who were unequalled in their time, in their special qualifications. Abu Bakr as Siddik in genealogy, Omar b-ul Khattab in stead-fastness in the commands of God, Othman b. Affan in modesty, Ali in judicial decision, Ubayy b. Kaab in reading the Qurãn, Zayd b. Thabit, in the law of inheritance, Abu Ubaydah b-ul Jarrah in honesty, Ibn Abbas in comment on the Qurãn, Abu Darr in truthfulness of speech, Khalid but Walid in courage, al Hasan al Basri in admonition, Wahb b. Munabbah in narration, Ibn Sirin in interpretation of dreams, Nafi in reading the Qurãn, Abu Hanifah in jurisprudence, Ibn Ishak in accounts of military expeditions, Mukatil in expounding obseurities, al Kalbi in narration from the Qurãn, al Khalil in prosody, Fudhayl b. Iyadh, in devotion, Sibawayh in grammer, Malik in science, as Shafai in knowledge of tradition, Abu Ubaydah, *in interpreting* obscure words *occurring in traditions,* Ali b-ul Madini in defects *invalidating traditions,* Yahya b. Main in traditional authorities, Abu Tammam in poetry, Ahmad b. Hanbal in the Sunnah, al Bukhari in discrimination of traditions, al Junayd in mysticism, Muhammad b. Nasr al Marwazi in reconciling the contradictory meanings of traditions, al Jubbai in expounding the tenets of the Muatazalites, al Ashari in scholastic theology, Muhammad b. Zakariya ar Razi, in medicine, Abu Mashar in astrology, Ibrahim al Kirmani in interpretation of dreams, Ibn Nubatah in preaching, Abul Faraj al Isbahani in debate, Abul Kasim at Tabarani on traditions of the highest authority, Ibn Hazm in the literal interpretation of the Qurãn, Abul Hasan al Bakri in lying, al Hariri in his discourses, Ibn Mandah in extent of travel, a Mutanabbi in poetry, al Mausili in vocal music, as Suli in chess, al Khatib al Baghdadi in quickness in reading the Qurãn, Ali b. Hilal in calligraphy, Ataas Salimi[1] in fear, al Kadhi al Fadhi, in composition, al Asmai in singular aneedotes, Ashab in covetousness, Mabid in singing, Avicenna in philosophy.

OMAR-B-UL KHATTAB

Omar b-ul Khattab, b. Nufayl b. Abdul Aza, B. Riyah b. Kurt b. Razah b. Adi b. Kaab b. Luayy, the Price of the faithful, Abu Hafs, al Kurayshi, al Adwi, al Faruk, (*the Discriminator*) embraced Islam in the sixth year of the Prophetic mission being seven and twenty years of age (ad Dahabi). An Nawawi says that Omar was born thirteen years after the year of the elephant.[2] He was one of the chiefs of the Kuraysh and was charged with the duties of an envoy in the time of Ignorance; for the Kuraysh, whenever a war took place among themselves, or between themselves and others, used to send him as envoy, that is as a representative, and whenever a challenger would contend against their honor, or a boaster contest their glory, they would send him to vie and to contend *in their*

1 Ibn Khallakan gives the life of Ata b, Abi Rabah Aslam Mufti of Mecca, and a devout ascetic. The 'fear' may therefore signify 'the fear of God' if this be the individual meant. I can discover no other name bearing any resemblance with that in the text.

2 The year of the defeat of Abraha b-ul Sabah surnamed al Ashram or the slitnosed-king or viceroy of Yaman, who marched against Mecca at the head of an army, wherein were several elephants, to avenge the profanation of the Christian Church at Sanaa, by some of the tribe of Kenanah. His fate and that of his army is well-known. See the story in Sale and his comments thereon. In this year Muhammad was born.

name. He embraced the faith early-after the conversion of forty men and ten women-or as some say, after thirty-nine men, and twenty-three women-ir as some say, after thirty-nine men, and twenty-three women, and others, forty-five men and eleven women. He had no sooner embraced Islam, than he openly declared his faith at Mecca and the Muslims rejoiced at it. An Nawawi add, that he was one of the converts, and one of the ten to whom Paradise was promised, and one of the just Caliphs, and one of the fathers-in-law of the Apostle of God, and one of the most learned and most ascetic of the Companions. Five hundred and thirty-nine traditions direct from the Apostle of God are ascribed to him. Traditions are related on his authority by Othman b. Affan by Ali and Talhah and Saad, and Ibn Auf and Ibn Masaud, and Abu Darr, and Omar b. Abasah, and his son Abdullah, and Ibn Abbas, and Ibn uz Zubayr, and Anas, and Abu Hurayrah, and Amr-b-ul Aas, and Abu Musa al Ashari, and al Baraa b. Aazib, and Abu Sai'd al Khudri, and others of the Companions and some besides them. I remark, that I will here devote some chapters to the principle observation of note connected with his biography.

On the accounts which have been handed down regarding his conversion

At Tirmidi records on the authority of Ibn Omar, that the Prophet said, "O God, glorify Islam by the most endeared to Thee of these two men, Omar the son of al Khattab or Jahl the son of Hisham." And al Hakim from Ibn Abbas, that the Prophet said, "O God, glorify Islam by Omar the son of al Khattab in particular." And Ahmad from Omar that he said, "I went forth to hinder the Apostle of God, but I found that he had preceded me to the mosque, and I stood up behind him and the sought to expound the Surah 'al Hakkah.'[1] And I began to wonder at the composition of the Qurãn

1 Ch. LXIX, entitled "the Infallible" ; the original word is one of the epithets of the Day of Judgment.

and I said, 'by Allah, this is a poet, as the Kuraysh say.' Then he read, 'This is the discourse of an honorable apostle and not the discourse of a poet-how little do ye believe,' Sc., (LXIX). And the true faith entered into my heart with a full possession." And Ibn Abi Shaybah from Jabir that he said, "the beginning of the conversion of Omar was *thus as* Omar hath related, 'the pains[1] of labour seized my sister in the night, and I went forth from the house and entered the precincts of the Kaabah, and the Prophet came and entered the enclosure and upon him were two garments, and he prayed to God for, that which God willed and then departed. And I heard a thing the like of which I had not heard before, and he went forth and I followed him and he said, "who is that?" and I replied, "Omar," then he said, "O Omar wilt thou not leave me night or day?" and I feared lest he should curse me, and I said, "I testify that thee is not God but God, and that thou art the Apostle of God." He answered "keep this secret." I replied, "No, by him who sent thee in the truth, I will surely proclaim it, as I proclaimed my infidelity." And Ibn Saa'd, and Abu Yala, and al Hakim and al Bayhaki in the "Proofs" on the authority of Anas, that Omar went forth girt with his sword and a man of the Banu Zuhrah met him and said, "whither art thou going, O Omar?" and he replied, "I intend to slay Muhammad;" the other said, "how wilt thou be secure from the Banu Hashim and the Banu Zuhrah, if thou shouldst slay Muhammad?"[2] He replied, "I cannot but think that thou hast changed thy faith." He answered, "shall I not assure thee of a strange thing, that thy brother-in-law,[3] and thy sister have changed their faith and abandoned thy religion?" Then Omar departed and went to those two with whom was Khabbab,[4] and when he heard the sound of Omar *approaching* he hid himself in the house. And Omar entered and said, "what is this muttering"-(for they were

---

1 In the text the word مخاض is pointed as the objective instead of the nominative case.

2 The father of Muhammad belonged to the former tribe, is mother to the latter.

3 Said b. Zayd.

4 Abu Abdullah Khabbab b-ul Aratt was one of the earliest converts. He had been taken prisoner in the time of Ignorance and sold as a slave (Con...)

reading the T.H.)[1] -and they said, "it is nothing but a discourse we were holding among ourselves." He said, "then perhaps you two have changed your religion," and his brother-in-law replied to him, 'O, Omar suppose the truth were in another religion than thine!" whereon Omar sprang upon him and trampled him heavily under foot; his siter then came to push him aside from her husband, but he struck her a blow with his hand, and her face bled : then being angry she said, "and suppose the truth were in another religion than thine ! verily I testify that there is no God but God, and that Muhammad is His servant and His Apostle." Then Omar exclaimed, "give me the book which you have, that I may read it." His sister said, "verily thou art unclean and 'none shall touch it except those who are clean' (Qur. LVI)-therefore rise and bathe or perform ablution." And Omar rose and made his ablutions and took the book and read the T.H., until he came to "Verily I am God; there is no God besides me; wherefore worship Me and perform *thy* prayers in remembrance of Me" (Qur. XX). Then Omar said, "direct me to Muhammad;" and when Khabbab heard the words of Omar, he came forth and said, "Rejoice with good tidings,O Omar, for verily, I trust that the prayer of the Apostle of God on Wednesday night[2] may be for thee *when he said,* 'O God, glorify Islam by Omar, the son al Khattab, or Amr[3] the son of Hisham.'" The Apostle of God

---

(Cont. page 145) at Mecca. He is said to have been a freedom of Anmar daughter of Sabaa of the tribe of Khuzaah confederate of the Banu Zuhrah. He died at Kufah A.H. 37 in the Caliphate of Ali and was buried outside the city at his special request. It had been the custom in Kufah for people to be buried at the doors of their houses, but after Khabbab's death and by his example, the custom was abolished, and the dead were buried outside the city.

1 The XXth Ch. of the Qurãn is so entitled. The meaning of the letters is uncertain.

2 The day of the Arabs begins at sunset, the night of Thursday is therefore our Wednesday night.

3 This was Abu Jahl's name. An Nawawi describes him in his biography, as Abu Jahl, the enemy of God, "the Pharaoh of this people"-this latter epithet was given to him by Muhammad as he gazed upon his dead body after the battle of Badr where he fell fighting against the new faith.

was at the time in the original house[1] which stands at the foot of as Safa, and Omar went on until he reached the house, at the door of which were Hamzah and Talhah and others. And Hmzah said, "this is Omar ; if God desireth[2] his good, he will be converted, and if He desireth otherwise, his death will sit tightly upon us." The narrator adds, "the Prophet was then within, under the divine inspiration, and he came forth and went to Omar and clasped him round all his garments and his sword belt, and said 'wilt thou not cease, O Omar, until God sendeth upon thee calamity and chastisement such as He sent upon al Walid b-ul Mughirah.[3] And Omar said 'I testify that there is no God, but God and that thou art the servant of God and His Apostle.'"

Al Bazzar, and at Tabarani and Abu Nuaym in the "Huliyah," and al Bayhaki in the "Dalail" record on the authority of Aslam[4] that he narrates : "Omar said to me-I was the most violent of men against the Apostle of God, and while I was one sultry day in the noontide heat in one of the streets of Mecca, a man met me and said, 'I wonder at thee, O son of al Khattab, that thou thinkest that thou art this and that while verily an event has occurred at thy house.' I said, 'and what is that?' he replied, 'thy sister hath embraced Islam'-Then I turned back in wrath until I knocked at the door. They asked, 'who is there?" I replied, 'Omar.' Then they hastened away and hid from me, and verily, they had been reading

---

1 The house alluded to belonged to Arkam of the Banu Makhzum, one of the earliest converts to the faith, and was a favourite resort of Muhammad's. From the converts made therein, it was styled, according to al Wakidi, the house of Islam. See Muir, Vol. II, p. 118.

2 The printed edition is here in error, there should be no 'tashdid' over this verb, which is the 4th form of رود apocopated by the particle ان.

3 One of the "scoffers" alluded to in Qur. Ch. XV. Passing by some arrows, one of them hitched in his garment, and he, out of pride, not stooping to take it off, the head of it cut a vein in his heel, and he bled to death. See the tragic end of the other four in Sale, p. 214. Sale spells the name Mugheirah, but I can find no authority for it. An Nawawi is clear upon its pronunciation.

4 The freedom of Omar b-ul Khattab. According to some, he had been one of the prisoners of Yaman-others say that he was an Abyssinian. An Nawawi.

a paper before them which they had left and forgotten. Then my sister arose' and opened the door, and I said, 'O enemy of thyself, hast thou changed thy faith?' and I struck her upon the head with a thing that was in my hand and the blood flowed and she wept and said, 'O son of al Khattab1 what thou soughtest to do, do, for verily I have changed my faith.' Omar continued, and I went in and sat upon a bedstead, and I looked upon the paper and said, 'what is that? Give it to me'-she said, 'thou art not worthy of it for thou art not purified from uncleanness, and this book "none shall touch it, except those who are clean;"' but I did not desist until she gave it to me, and I opened it, and behold! There was in it 'whatever is in the heavens and the earth singeth praise unto God.' (LVII), and I was terrified, and I read unto 'Believe in God and his Apostle.' Then I exclaimed, 'I testify that there is no God but God,' and those who had fled away, came forth to me and magnified God and said, 'rejoice with good tidings, for the Apostle of God prayed on Monday and said, "O God, glorify Thy faith by the most endeared to Thee of two men, either Abu Jahl the son of Hisham or Omar!"' and they directed me to the Prophet to the house at the foot of as Safa. And I went on until I knocked at the door, and they said, 'who is it.' I replied 'the son of al Khattab,' and, verily, they knew my violence against the Apostle of God, and no one was bold enough to open the door until Muhammad said, 'open for him,' and they opened for me and two men seized my arm, until the Prophet came to me and said, 'stand off from him.' Then he caught me round my garment and drew me to him and said, 'be converted, O son of al Khattab. O God! Direct him aright.' Then I made the profession of faith. Thereupon the Muslims magnified God, with a 'takbir' that was heard in the defiles of Mecca. They had hitherto sought concealment, and I[1] never wished to see a man, beating or being beaten, but I beheld him while nothing of this could befall me. Then I went to my maternal uncle, Abu Jahl, the son of Hisham, and he

---

1 The Arabic idiom here, is so difficult to transfer with any closeness of translation, into English, that I fear I have sacrificed intelligibility to a desire to be literal. Omar means to say, that either before his conversion, or before it was made known, his position as a chief of the Kuraysh secured him from all insult.

was a man of high consideration, and I knocked at his door and he said, 'who is that?' I replied, 'the son of al Khattab, and verily I have changed my religion,' and he said, 'do it not.' Then he went within and shut the door upon me, and I said, 'this is nothing;' and I went on to a man of the chiefs of the Kuraysh, and called out to him, and he come forth to me and I addressed him in the same words as to my uncle, and he replied to me, as my uncle had replied, and he went in and shut the door upon me and I said, 'this is nothing! Shall the Muslims be beaten and I not be beaten?' Then a man said to me, 'dost thou wish that thy being converted to Islam, should be known?' and I said 'yes.' He replied, 'when the people assemble in the precincts *of the Kaabah,* go to a certain man who cannot keep a secret and say to him that which is to be between thee and him, *viz.,* verily I have changed my faith, for it is rare that he can conceal a secret.' And I went when the people had assembled in the enclosure, and I mentioned what was to be between me and him, saying, 'verily I have changed my faith.' He replied 'Hast thou really done so?" I said 'yes,' Then he cried out at the top of his voice, 'verily the son of al Khattab hath changed his faith;' then they fell upon me, and I did not cease to beat them, nor they to boat me, while the people gathered round me. Then my uncle said, 'what is this gathering?' they said to him, 'Omar hath changed his faith." Then he stood up in the enclosoure and waved his sleeve *saying,* 'verily I take under my protection the son of my sister,' and they gave way from me. But I did, not like to see one of the Muslims beating or being beaten, but I would see him and say, 'this is nothing, perchance it may befall me,' [1] and I went to my uncle and said 'thy protection is returned to thee' and I did not cease from beating and being beaten until God exalted Islam."

---

1 That is, I hope it may befall me. The MS. Has حتى for the قد of the printed edition which makes the sense clearer. This passage is similar to the one I have already noted in a preceding page with the difference, that he is now describing a state of feeling arrived at since his conversion had been made public. His zeal as a convert and his natural pugnacity would not permit him to behold a Muslim being beaten without wishing to share in the unpopularity of the new faith. His fervour would not be content with anything but hard knocks which, however, he returned as freely as he received them.

Abu Nuaym in the "Dalail," and Ibn Asakir record on the authority of Ibn abbas that he said, "I asked of Omar, 'why art thou called al Faruk? (*the discriminator*)?' and he said, 'Hamzah embraced Islam three days before me, and I went to the mosque, and Abu Jahl hastened to the Prophet and reviled him, and Hamzah was informed of it; so he took his bow and went to the mosque towards a group of the Kuraysh in which was Abu Jahl, and he leaned upon his bow over against Abu Jahl and regarded him, and Abu Jahl saw that mischief was in his countenance,' and he said, 'what is the matter with thee O! Abu Umara?'[1] and Hamzah lifted up his bow and struck him with it upon the two cupping-veins of the neck and cut them, and the blood flowed, where-upon the Kuraysh adjusted the matter amicably, fearing mischief." Then Omar continued, "the Apostle of God was at that time concealed in the house of Arkam the son of Abul Arkam al Kakhzumi, and Hamzah went away and embraced Islam. Three days afterwards, I went forth when behold ! there came a certain man of the tribe of the Banu Makhzum, and I said,' hast thou turned away from the faith of thy fathers and followed the faith of Muhammad?' and he replied, 'if I have done so, then verily, one hath done so likewise who hath a greater claim upon thee than I.' I said-'and who is that?' He answered, 'thy sister as well as thy brother-in-law.' And I departed *and reached the house,* and I heard a low whispering, and I entered and said, 'what is this?' and words did not cease to pass between us, until I took my brother in law by the head and smote him and covered him with blood, but my sister rose against me and seized my head and said, 'verily that hath been done in spite of thee. And I was ashamed when I saw the blood and I sat down and said, 'show me this writing,' but she replied, 'none shall touch it except those who are clean.' And I arose and bathed, and they brought out to me a paper in which was 'in the name of God, the most merciful and Compassionate' (and I said 'names, good *and* holy'). T.H. we have not sent down the Qurãn unto thee that

---

1 His surname : it was also that of al Bara b. Aazib-the Companion.

thou shouldst be unhappy *and I read on* to His words 'most excellent names' (Qur. XX). And there arose in my heart a great awe and I said, 'is it from this the Kuraysh have fled?' and I embraced Islam and said, 'where is the Apostle of God?" She replied 'verily he is in the house of Arkam,' and I went and knocked at the door and the people gathered together and Hamzah said to them, 'what is it with ye?' They said, it is Omar'; he replied, 'what! Omar! Open the door to him, and if he cometh to us amicably, we will receive him, and if he turneth away from us we shall slay him;' and the Apostle of God heard that, and he came forth and Omar made the profession of faith. Then the people of the house magnified God with a 'takbir' that was heard by the dwellers in Mecca. I said, 'O Apostle of God, are we not in the Truth?" he replied, 'yes'. I said, 'then wherefore this concealment?' So we came forth in two ranks, I at the head of one of them and Hamzah, of the other, until we entered the mosque, and the Kuraysh looked upon me and upon Hamzah, and a great grief fell upon them. The Apostle of God therefore, named me the Discriminator, from that day, because Islam was made manifest and truth distinguished from falsehood." Ibn Saad records from Dakwan[1] that the narrates, "I said to Ayesha, who named Omar, the Discriminator?" she replied, "the Prophet." And Ibn Majah and al Hakim from Ibn Abbas, that he said, "when Omar embraced Islam, Gabriel descended and said, 'O Muhammad, verily the dwellers in heaven announce with rejoicing the conversion of Omar.'" Al Bazzar records, and al Hakim, who verfies it on the authority of Ibn Abbas, that when Omar was converted, the Idolaters said, "verily, to-day, the sect have avenged themselves upon us," and the Lord revealed,[2] "O Prophet! God is thy support, and such of the true believers that have followed thee" (Qur. VIII). And al Bukhari from Ibn Masaud that he said, "we continued increasing in honour from the time when Omar was converted." And Ibn Saad and at Tabarani from Ibn Masaud that he said, "the conversion of

---

1 There are seven of this name mentioned by Ibn Hajr. The one referred to in the next is probably the freedman of Muhammad.

2 Some say this passage was revealed in a plain called at Beida, between Mecca and Medina during the expedition of Badr. Sale.

Omar was a conquest, his fight[1] a victory, and his Imamate a divine mercy, and verily, we said that we were unable to pray in the House of *God* until Omar as converted, we when Omar was converted, he fought with them until they left us alone and we preyed *therein."* Ibn Saad and al Hakim record from Hudayfah, that he said, "when Omar was converted, Islam was as a man advancing who doth not progress without approaching, and when Omar was slain, Islam was as a man retreating, who doth not progress without receding." And at Tabarani from Ibn Abbas, that he said, "the first who openly manifested Islam was Omar b-ul Khattab." His authorities are trustworthy and excellent. And Ibn Saad from Suhayb, "when Omar was converted, Islam was declared and the people openly invited to it, and we sat in a circle round the temple and went in procession round the temple, and avenged ourselves on those who had oppressed us, and returned back upon them somewhat of that which they had brought *upon us."* And Ibn Saad from Aslam, the freedom of Omar, "Omar was vonverted in the month of Dul Hijjah in the sixth year of the Prophetic mission, and he was then six and twenty years old."

On his Flight.

Ibn Asakir records on the authority of Ali, that he said, "I never knew any one flee unless secretly, except Omar b.ul Khattab, for he when he resolved on flight, girt on his sword and slung over him his bow and grasped in his hand its arrows, and went to the Kaabah were in its quadrangle were the chiefs of the Kuraysh, and he went round about it seven times, then prayed two rakaahs[2] at the station *of Abraham,* and went to each, one by one, in their circle and said, 'may the faces be foul of such as desire that his mother

1 Medina with the Prophet.

2 A rakaah is a single act of standing in prayer, followed by an inclination of the head, and two prostration.

be bereaved of him and his child be left an orphan and his wife a widow, *and if there be such a one,* let him meet me behing this valley'-but no one followed him." And from al Bara,[1] that he said, "the first man who came to us, of the Fugitives was Musaab b. Umayr, then Ibn Umm Maktum,[2] then Omar b-ul Khattab with twenty horsemen, and we said, 'what is the Apostle of God doing?' He replied, 'he cometh after me;' then then Apostle of God arrived and with him Abu Bakr."[3]

An Nawawi says that Omar was present with the Apostle of God in all his expeditions, and was of those who remained steadfast to him on the day of Ohud.

On the traditions handed down regarding his merit, after than what has preceded in the life of Abu Bakr.

The two Shaykhs records on the authority of Abu Hurayrah that the Apostle of God said, "While I was asleep, I saw myself in Paradise, and beheld there was a woman performing her ablutions by the side of a house ; I said, 'whose is this house?' they replied 'Omar's.' Then I recollected thy jealousy and I turned back." And Omar wept and said, "should I be jealous of thee, O Aposlte of God!" And from Ibn Omar that the Apostle of God said, "whilst I was asleep, *I dreamt that* I drank (meaning milk) so that I saw the stream issuing from my nails, and I gave it to Omar." They said,

---

1 Ibn Hajr gives six of the name-the reference in the text is probably to al Bara b. Aazib, one of the Auxiliaries of Medina.

2 Some say his name was Abdullah, others Amr b. Kays. His mother's name was Aatikah of the Banu Makhzum. He resided at Medina after Badr, being then blind, and used to officiate as Imam at public prayers when Muhammad was absent in his expeditions. A wariful Maarif of Ibn. Kutaybah.

3 Al Bara as quoted by an Nawawi, places four others between Ibn Umm Maktum and Omar, viz., Ammar b. Yasir Saad b. Abi Wakkas, Ibn Masaud and Bilal.

"how dost thou interpret it, O Apostle of God!" He answered, "*it was* knowledge." And from Abu Sa'id, al-Khudri, "I heard the Apostle of God say, 'whilst I was sleeping, I saw the people presented, to me, and upon them were garments, some of them reaching to the breast and some of them reaching below it, and Omar was presented to me and upon him a garment which he was dragging along.' They said, 'how dost thou interpret it, O Apostle of God!' He answered-'*it was* religion.'" And from Saad b. Abi Wakkas, that the Apostle of God said, "O son of a Khattab-by Him in whose hand is my life, the devil hath never met thee walking in a road, but he hath taken a road other than thy road," And al Bukhari from Ibn Hurayrah, that the Apostle of God said, "verily there have been among those who have gone before ye among the nations, men inspired, and if there be such a one among my people, it is Omar." And at Tirmidi from Ibn Omar, that the Apostle of God said, "verily God hath placed truth upon the tongue of Omar the son of al Khattab and upon his heart."

Ibn Omar says, "never did a thing come upon the people, and they said *one thing regarding it,* and Omar *another,* but the Qurãn revealed it after the manner that Omar had said." And at Tirmidi and al Hakim, who has verified it from Ukbah b. Aamir, record, that the Aposlt of God said, "if there were to be a Prophet after me, it would be Omar the son of al Khattab." And at Tirmidhi, from Ayesha, that the Apostle of God said, "verily I behold the evil spirits among Genii and men, fleeing from before Omar." And Ibn Majah and al Hakim from Ubayy b Kaab, that the Apostle of God said, "the first with whom Truth joineth hands, and the first it blesseth, and the first it taketh by the hand and entereth Paradise, is Omar." And from Abu Darr that he narrates, "I heard the Apostle of God say, 'verily the Lord hath placed truth upon the tongue of Omar, by which He speaketh.' And Ahmad and al Bazzar from Abu Hurayrah that the Apostle of God said, 'verily the Lord hath placed truth upon the tongue of Omar and upon his heart.' And Ibn Manii in his Musuad from Ali, that he said, 'we the Conpanions of Muhammad did not doubt that the divine presence spake by the tongue of Omar.'

And al Bazzar from Ibn Omar, that the Apostle of God said, 'Omar is the lamp of the dwellers in Paradise.' And from Kudamah b. Madhuun on the authority of his brother, [1] Othman b. Madhuun, that the Apostle of God said, 'this is the bolt against discord'-and her pointed with his hand to Omar-'there shall not cease to be between you and discord, a gate strongly bolted, as long as he liveth among you.'"

At Tabarani records in the Ausat from Ibn Abbas, that Gabriel came to the Prophet and said, "greet Omar with a salutation and tell him that his anger is glory and his approval, command." And Ibn Asakir from Ayesha, that the Prophet said, "verily Satan avoideth Omar." And Ahmad on the ascription of Buraydah, [2] that the Prophet said, "verily Satan avoideth thee, O Omar!" : and Ibn Asakir from Ibn Abbas that the Apostle of God said, "there is not an angel in heaven, but he revereth Omar, and not a demon on earth but he fleeth from Omar." And at Tabarani in the Ausat from Abu Hurayrah that the Apostle of God said, "verily God gloried regarding the pilgrims of Arafah[3] in general and Omar in particular." And at Tabarani and al Daylami from al Fadhl b-ul Abbas that the Apostle of God said, "the Truth after me is with Omar wherever he may be."

The two Shaykhs record on the authority of Ibn Omar and Abu Hurayrah that the Apostle of God said, "whilst I was sleeping, I was myself by a well, upon which was a bucket, and I drew up from it what God willed : then Abu Bakr took it and he drew up a bucket-full or two, and there was feebleness in his drawing and my

---

1 The text and MS. have 'uncle' which appears to be an error.

2 Abu Abdullah Buraydah b-ul Husayb, one of the Companions. He resided at Medina, afterwards at Basrah and removed subsequently to Marw where he died A.H. 62. He related 164 traditions from Muhammad. An Nawawi.

3 This is given differently by different authorities. In the Kitab ul Iktifa (كتاب الاكتفافي فضل الاربعة الخلفا) by Ibrahim b. Abdullah, al Wasabi. Al Yamani, as Shafii-God vied with his angels regarding men on the day of Arafah. Lane give another reading, "the angels vied with them." The day of Arafah is the 9th of Dul Hijjah-for its ceremonies, consult Burton.

God have mercy upon him. then came Omar and the sought to draw, and *the bucket* became changed into a large bucket, and I have not seen a chief of the people do his wonderful deeds, so that the people satisfied their thirst and abode at the water."

An Nawawi says in his Tahdib, that the learned assert that this is an indication of the Caliphate of Abu Bakr and Omar, and the numerous conquests and triumphs of Islam during the time of Omar. At Tabarani records on the authority of Sadisah, [1] that the Apostle of God said, "verily Satan hath never met Omar since his conversion but he hath fallen prostrate on his face." And from Ubayy b. Kaab that the Apostle of God said, "Gabriel said to me, 'verily Islam will weep at the death of Omar.'" And in the Ausat from Abu Sai'd al Khudri, that the Apostle of God said, "he who hateth Omar, hath hated me, and he who loveth Omar, hath love, me and verily, the Lord gloried regarding the people on the evening of the day of Arafah in general, and rejoiced over Omar in particular, and the Lord hath never sent a Prophet, but there was among his people one inspired, and if there be such a one among my people, it is Omar." They said "O Apostle of God, how inspired?" He replied, "the angels speak by his tongue." (His authorities are good.)

On the sayings of the Companions and the early Muslims regarding him.

Abu Bakr as Siddik said, "there is not upon the face of the earth a man dearer to me than Omar." (Ibn Asakir.) It was said to Abu Bakr in his illness, "what wilt thou say to thy God, now that thou hast appointed Omar to rule?" He replied, "I will say to Him 'I have appointed over them the best of them." (Ibn Saad.) Ali said, "when the righteous are mentined, then quick and mention

1 The freed woman of Hafsah, the daughter of Omar. She belonged to the Auxiliaries. Ibn Hajr.

Omar : we used to say not without reason that the divine presence speaketh by the tongue of Omar." (At Tabarani in the Ausat.) And Ibn Omar said, "I never saw any one after the Apostle of God, from the time that he died, more vehement and yet more beneficent than Omar." (Ibn Saad.) And Ibn Masaud if the wisdom of Omar were placed in the scale of a balance, and the wisdom of living things upon the earth in *the other* scale, the wisdom of Omar would outweight them, and verily people used to think that be bore away nine-tenths of wisdom." (At Tabarani in the Kabir and al Hakim.) And Hudayfah-"it is as if the wisdom of mankind lay hidden in the bosom of Omar;" and, "by Allah I know not a man whom the reproof of the censurer in what relateth to the service of God, doth not touch, but Omar," And Ayesha speaking of Omar said, "by Allah, he was active in affairs, singly undertaking their management." And al Muawiyah, "Abu Bakr sought not the worl and it sought not him, but Omar, the world sought though he sought it not, while we are plunged in it up, to the middle." (Az Zubayr b. Bakkar in the Maukifiyat.)

Jabir relates that Ali went to Omar when he was at prayers and said, "may the mercy of God be upon thee! There is *no one* with the record of whose actions it would be more pleasing to me to meet God, (after the Companionship of the Prophet) than this performer of prayers." (Al Hakim). And Masaud has said, "when the righteous are mentioned, then quick and mention Omar-verily Omar was the most learned of us in the book of God, and the most profoundly versed in the religious ordinanace of the Most High." (At Tabarani and al Hakim.) Ibn Abbas was asked regarding Abu Bakr, and he said "he was like goondness itself;" and he was asked regarding Omar, and he said, "he was like a wary bird that seeth a snare in every path, to take it;" and he was questioned about Ali, and he said, "he was full of resolution and vigilance and wisdom and dignity" (recorded in the Tuyuriyat).

At Tabarani records on the authority of Umayr b. Rabii, that

Omar said to Kaab al Ahbar,[1] "what description of me dost thou find?" "I find thy description to be a horn of iron,"[2] he said, "and what is a horn of iron?" He replied, "a resolute prince whom the reproof of the consurer in what relateth to the service of God, doth not touch." Omar said, "then what ?" He replied "there shall come after thee a Caliph whom a cruel faction shall slay." He asked, "then what?" He answered, "then shall follow calamity." And Ahmad and al Bazzar and at Tabarani from Ibn Masaud that he said, "Omar, the son of al Khattab, was distinguished above men, for four things:

1. "In the affair of the prisoners on the day of Badr,[3] whom he ordered to be put to death and God revealed, 'unless a revelation had been previously delivered from God,' &c., (Qur. VIII).

2. "In the affair of the veil[4] He commanded the wives of the Prophet that they should be veiled and Zaynab said to him, 'thou art against us, O son of al Khattab, and yet the divine inspiration descends within our house ;' then God revealed, 'and when ye ask *of the Prophet's wives,* what ye may have occasion for, &c., (Qur. V).

3. "By the prayer of the Prophet, 'O God strengthen Islam by Omar.'

4. "By his voice in favour of Abu Bakr, he being the first to swear allegiance to him."

Ibn Asakir records from Mujahid, that he narrates, "we used

---

1 A few who embraced Islam in the time of Omar and a constant companion of that Caliph. D'Herbelot gives the name to the book in which are recorded many fabulous stories of Islam. The author he adds, is unknown and his work contains many Christian traditions, among them, that of the guardian angels. According to the Muntaha 1' Arab, al Ahhar is incorrect-it should be Hibr. (حبر) Which signifies a Jewish or Christain doctor of science.

2 Kings xxii, 11.

3 For an account of this, consult Sale, p. 146.

4 Consult Sale, p. 349.

to say that the devils were chained during the rule of Omar, and were unloosed when he perished." And from Salim b. Abdillah[1] that he said, "news of Omar was long in reaching Abu Musa, and he went to a woman possessed by a devil, and he asked her about him and she said, '*stay* till my demon cometh,' and he came and she asked of him regarding Omar, and he said, 'I left him, girt round with a garment smearing with pitch the public camels, [2] and that man, no devil seeth but be falleth upon his nostrils, the angel is before his eyes, and Gabriel speaketh by his tongue.'"

Sufyan[3] al Thauri says 'whosoever thinketh that Ali had more right to the Caliphate, than Abu Bakr or Omar, hath ascribed blame to Abu Bakr, Omar, the Fugitives and the Auxiliaries, And Sharik[4] has Observed, 'no one who hath goodness in him, placeth Ali before Abu Bakr and Omar.' And Abu Usamah says 'do ye know who were Abu Bakr and Omar?-those two men were the father of

---

1 The grandson of Omar distinguished for the piety and austerity of his life, died at Medina, A.H. 105-8.

2 "The abstinence and humility of Omar," says Gibbon : "were not inferior to the virtues of Abu Bakr : his food consisted of barley-bread or dates : his drink was water : he preached in a gown that was torn or tattered in twelve places, and a Persian satrap who paid his homage to the conqueror, found him asleep among the beggars on the steps of the mosque of Median." Decline and Fall.

3 Abu Abdullah Sufiyan at Thauri b. Said b. Masruk was a native of Kufah and of the highest authority in traditions and other sciences. He was made Kadhi of Kufah by al Mahdi, but he fled and concealed himself to avoid the honour and its heavy responsibility-an amusing account of this is given by Ibn Khallikan, Sufiyan was born A.H. 95 (A.D. 713-4) and died at Basrah A.H. 161 (777-8).

4 The printed edition has Shurayk, but this is an error. There is no one of any note bearing that name, while Abu Abdullah Sharik an Nakhai was the person who was appointed Kadhi of Kufah, after Sufiyan at Thauri a flight. He was a strong upholder of Ali's merits, and his evidence is therefore adduced in proof of the superiority, universally acknowledged, of Abu Bakr and Omar. I can, however, find in Ibn Khallikan no hint of Sharik's assertion of the pre-eminence of Abu Bakr and Omar-the evidence, seems quite the other way, and I strongly suspect that as Suyuti's citation is not to be trusted.

Islam and its mother. And Jaafar as Saddiq,[1] 'I am quiet of any one who mentioneth Abu Bakr or Omar otherwise than favorably.'"

On the coincidences of the saying of Omar with the Qurãn which some of the learned compute at more than twenty

Ibn Mardawayh records on the authority of Mujahid that Omar would form a judgement and the Qurãn would reveal it. And Ibn Asakir from Ali, that he said, "verily there are in the Qurãn some judgments after the judgment of Omar;" and from Ibn Omar, an ascription reaching to the Prophet, "the people never spake regarding a thing; Omar likewise having spoken regarding it, but the Qurãn was revealed after the manner that Omar has spoken." And the two Shaykhs from Omar that he said, "I was in accordance with my Lord in three things; I said 'O Apostle of God if we were to take the station of Abraham for a place of prayer, and there was revealed, take the station of Abrahim for a place of prayers' and there was revealed, take the station of Abraham for the place of prayers' (Qur.II): and I said,' "O Apostle of God, there go unto thy women the righteous and the sinner, and did thou but command them to be voiled !'-then was revealed the verse regarding the veiling : and the wives of the Prophet assembled in indignation and I said, 'if he divorce you, his Lord can easily give him in exchange better wives than you.' (Qur. LXVI) and the like unto that was revealed." And Muslim from Omar that he said, "I was in

1 The Imam Abu Abdullah Jaafar as Sadik (The Veracious) fourth in descent from Ali b. Abi Talib, born A.H. 80 (A.D. 699), died and buried at Medina A.H. 148 (765). The same tomb contains the bodies of his father Muhammad al Bakir, his grandfather Ali Zaynul Aabidin and his grandfather's uncle, al Hasan son of Ali. "How rich a tomb," says Ibn Khallikan "in generosity and nobility!"

accordance with my Lord in three things-regarding the veiling-regarding the prisoners of Badr-and the station of Abraham." Therefore in this tradition there is a fourth instance : again according to the Tahdib of an Nawawi, the Qurãn was revealed coincidently with his judgment, regarding the prisoners of Badr-the veiling-the station of Abraham and the prohibition of wine. Thus a fifth instance is added, the tradition regarding which is in the Sunan and the Mustadrak of al Hakim, namely, that he said, 'O God, manifest unto us regarding wine, a distinct declaration;' God then revealed its prohibition.[1]

Ibn Abi Hatim records in his Commentary on the authority of Anas that Omar said, "I was in accordance with my Lord in four things-the following verse was revealed, 'we formerly created man in a finer sort of clay' &c., (Qur. XXIII) and when it was revealed, I said, wherefore, blessed be God, the most excellent Creator,' and then came down, 'Werefore blessed be God, the most excellent Creator,' and then came down, 'Wherefore blessed be God, the most excellent Creator.' [2](Qur XXIII). A sixth instance is thus added in this tradition, and for the tradition there is another line of ascription which I have adduced in the Tafsirul Musnad. Again I have seen in the work 'Fadhai ul Imamayn (*Distinguishing merits of the two* Imams), by Abu Abdullah as Shaybani, that Omar was in accordance with his Lord in one and twenty instances. He mentions these six and adds.

7th. "The story of Abdullah b. Ubayy." I observe that its tradition is in the Sahih on the authority of Omar who said, "when Abdullah b. Ubayy died, the Apostle of God was invited to read prayers over him, and he stood over him, but I arose *and advanced* until I was abreast of him and said, 'O Apostle of God! What! Over the enemy of God, the sone of Ubayy who said one day such and such a thing,-and by Allah, but a little while after there came down "Neither

1 In Chs. III and V.

2 These words are ascribed by Sale to Abdullah b. Saad, Muhammad's amanuensis. See Sale's Qur. P. 108.

3 For the Story, consult Sale, p. 159.

do thou pray over any of them who shall die" &c.,'" (Qur. IX).[3]

8th "They will ask thee concerning wine &c., (Qur. II).

9th "O true believers, come not to prayers when ye are drunk' (Qur. IV). I remark that these two with the verse from the *Sura of the* 'Table' (IV) are but one single instance, and the three are in the preceding tradition.

10th "When the Apostle of God was frequent in asking pardon for a faction, Omar said, 'It shall be equal unto them'; then God revealed 'It shall be equal unto them, whether thou ask pardon for them' (Qur. LXIII). I observe that at Tabarani has recorded this on the authority of Ibn Abbas.

11th "When Muhammad consulted the Companions regarding the advance to Badr, Omar counseled the advance, and there came down 'as the Lord brought thee forth from they house, &c., (Qur. VIII).

12th "When he consulted the Companions regarding the affair of the Falsehood,[1] Omar said, 'who gave her to thee in marriage, O Apostle of God?' He replied 'Allah'-Omar said, 'dost thou then think that thy Lord would put a deceit upon thee regarding her? God forbid ! this is a grievous calumny,' (Qur. XXIV), and the like was revealed.

13th "The account concerning him in the matter of the fast when Omar went in unto his wife after waking from sleep, and that was forbidden in the beginning of Islam; and there was revealed, 'it is lawful for you on the right of the fast, &c.' (Qur. II). I note that Ahmad has recorded this in his Musnad.

14th "The Words of the Most High 'whoever is an enemy to Gabriel, &c.,' (Qur. II). I note that Ibn uz Zubayr and others have recorded this with numerous lines of ascription and the nearest of these to coincidence *with the Qurãn* is that recorded by Ibn Abi

1 The imputations against the conduct of Ayesha when she was accidentally left behind on the return march to Medina after the expedition against the Banu Mustalik. See Sale, p. 288.

Hakim on the authority of Abdul Rahman b. Abi Laylah, viz., that a Jew met Omar and said, 'verily Gabriel, he whom your master speaketh of, is an enemy to us;' and Omar said to him, 'whosoever is an enemy to God, or his angels, or his Apostles, or to Gabriel or Michael, verily god is an enemy to the unbelievers.' (Qur. II). Thus it was revealed by the tongue of Omar.

15th "The words of the Most High. 'And by the Lord, they will not *Perfectly* believe, &c.,' (Que. IV). I observe that Ibn Abi Hatim and Ibn Mardawyh have recorded the story of this, on the authority of Abul Aswad, who said, 'two men carried their dispute for decision before the Prophet, and he judged between them, and the man against whom he had decided, said, "let us appeal to Omar the son of al Khattab," and they went to him, and the *other* man said, "the Apostle of God has judged in my favour against this man, but he exclaimed let us appeal to Omar;" and Omar said, "was it so ?" He replied "Yes," Then Omar said, "stay where ye are until I come out unto you,"' and he went out to them grasping his sword, and he smote him who had said, 'let us appeal to Omar,' and slew him and other went back and said, 'O Apostle of God! Omar hath slain my companion.' He answered 'I should not have thought that Omar would dare to slay a true believer.' Then God revealed, 'and by thy Lord they will not *perfectly* believer,' &c.Thus the blood of the man was made lawful and Omar was absolved from *the guilt of* his death. To this tradition there is alos concurrent testimony which I have adduced in the Tafsirul Musnad.

16th "The asking permission to enter, and this was because his salve went in to him, while he was sleeping, and he said, 'O God! Forbid their entrance;' and there was revealed the verse regarding the asking permissi· (Qur. XXIV.)

17th "His words concerning the Jews, 'Verily they are a people not seeing the right course.'[1]

18th "The words of the Most High, 'And there shall be many of

---

1 This refers to Qur. II. فبهت الذي كفر.

the former and many of the latter.' (Qur. XXXVI). I not that Ibn Asakir has recorded the story of this in his history, on the authority of Jabir b. Abdullah and it it in the Asbabu'n Nuzul *(Reasons of Revelation).*

19th "He adduced the citation[1] 'The man and woman of advanced years when they commit adultery,' &c.

20th "On the day of Ohud, when Abu Sufiyan called out, 'is there a certain one among the people?' his saying, 'do not answer him,' and the Apostle of God acted conformably to his counsel. I note that Ahmad has recorded this in his Musand."

As Shaybani continues, "and there should be added to this, that which Othman b. Said ad Darami in the work 'The Refutation of the Jahmiyah,'[2] has recorded from Salim b. Abdillah, that Kaab al Ahbar, said, 'woe unto the king of earth from the king of heaven;' and Omar exclaimed, 'save unto him who calleth himself to account,' and Kaab replied 'by Him in whose hand is my life, verily it is in the Pentateuch-thou haat indeed said according to it,' and Omar fell worshipping."

I have also seen in the Kamil of Ibn Adi on the authority of Ibn Omar that Bilal used to call out, when he summoned to prayers, "I testify that there is no God, but God-come ye to prayers," and Omar said to him, "say at the end of it, 'I testify that Muhammad is the Apostle of God;' and the Apostle of God said, 'say as Omar hath spoken.'"

---

1 A case of this kind was brought before Omar, and he directed them to be stoned, quoting at the same time this verse which was revealed but never written. It is not to be found in the Qurãn, but retains all the authority of the written ordinances.

2 A sect of the Kadaris who deny absolute predestination.

On his Mircles,

Al Bayhaki and Abu Nuaym have both of them recorded in the proofs of prophecy, and al Lalakai in the commentary on the Tradition, and ad Dayr[1] Aakuli in the observations, and Ibn al Aarabi[2] in the "Miracles on the saints," and al Khatib in the Traditionists of Malik, on the authority of Ibn Omar, that he said, "Omar had despateched an army at the head of which was a man called Sariyah, and while Omar was *one day* preaching he began to call out, 'O Sariyah! The hill!' three times. After this arrived a messenger from the army, and Omar questioned him and he said, 'O prince of the faithful, we were being routed, and while we were thus, lo! We heard a voice calling out, "O Sariyah! The hill," three times, so we stayed our backs against the hill, and the Lord put them to flight.' He adds-'they said to Omar, "verily thou didst call out so." This hill near to which Sariyah was, is by Nahawand in Persian Irak.'" Ibn Mardawayh records from Ibn Omar that he said, "Omar was preaching on a Friday, when he uttered vague words in his discourse saying, 'O Sariyah ! the hill! He who asketh of the wolf to keep guard, doth wrong:' and the people looked one upon the other, and Ali said to them, 'let him explain what he hath said.' And when he ceased, they asked of him, and he replied, 'we thought that he infidels had routed our brethren, who verily were passing by a hill, and if they inclined towards it, they would have to fight on one front only, and if they passed beyond it they would be destroyed; then there went forth from me what ye thought ye heard.' He adds that a messenger arrived a month afterwards, and said that they had heard the voice, of Omar on that day, and he continued, 'we inclined towards the hill and God gave us the victory.'"

---

1 Dayrul Aakul is a town situated on the Tigris fifteen parasangs distant from Baghdad. The traditionist here alluded to is probably Yahya Abdul Karim b-ul Haytham who died in A.H. 278. Yakut M.B.

2 Abu Abdullah Muhammad b. Ziyd, a genealogist and philologer of the highest reputation ; a list of his works is given by Ibn Khall. He was born A.H. 150 (767) and died at Sarraman raa A.H. 231 (846).

Abu Nuaym records in the "Proofs" from Amr b-ul Harith[1] that he said "while Omar was preaching on a Friday, lo! he abruptly checked his discourse and exclaimed-'O Sariyah! the hill!' twice or three times, and proceeded with his preaching, and some who were present exclaimed rily he raveth-surely he is mad.' Whereon Abdur Rahman b. Auf who had confidence in him, went to him and said-'thou givest them occasion to speak against thee, for whilst thou wert preaching, behold ! thou didst cry out "O Sariyah, the hill!"-what meaneth this?' He replied, 'verily, by Allah, I could not restrain it! I saw them fighting near a hill, and they were being attacked in their front and rear, and I could not help exclaiming "O, Sariyah ! the hill," that they might gain the hill.' And they tarried until the messenger of Sariyah arrived with his dispatch, *saying,* "the enemy met us upon a Friday, and we fought them until, when the hour of congregating for prayer arrived, we heard on calling out 'O Sariyah ! the hill!" twice, and we gained, the hill and we continued to prevail over our enemy until the Lord defeated them and slew them."' Then those that had reproached Omar, said, 'leave this man alone, for verily he is in collusion with him.'"

Abul Kasim b. Bishran in the Fawaid records on the authority of Ibn Omar, that Omar b-ul Khattab said to a man, "what is thy name?" He replied, "Jamrah" (*a lice coal*). He said, "The son of whom?" He answered, "the son of Shihab" (*flame*).He asked, "of what tribe?" he replied, "al Hurkah" (*heat).* He said, "where is thy dwelling?" he answered, "at al Harrah" (*Warmth).* He asked, "at which of them?" He replied "of Dat Ladha" (*blazing)*. Then Omar said, "go to thy family for verily they have been burnt." And the man returned and found that his people had been burnt to death.

Abul Shaykh records in the Kitab ul Adhamat (*Book of greatness*) on the authority of Kays b-ul Hajjaj, who had it from

---

1 Amr b-ul Harith b. Abi Dhirar, a native of Kufah and a Companion. He was the brother of Juayriyah one of Muhammad's wives and of the Banu Mustalik. An Nawawi.

one who related it to him, that when Egypt was conquered, Amr but Aas arrived on a certain day of one of the Coptic months, and the people said to him, "verily our Nile hath an observance without which it will not rise." He asked "and what is that?" They said, "when eleven nights of this month[1] have elapsed, we seek a girl, a virgin, living with her parents, and we obtain the consent of her parents, and we robe her with garments and ornaments, the best that can be had, and throw her into this Nile." And Amr said to them-"This can never be in Islam for verily Islam destroyeth what preceded it." They therefore departed, and the Nile rose neither little nor much, so that they meditated leaving their country. And when Amr saw that, he wrote to Omar but Khattab concerning it, and Omar replied to him, *saying,* "verily thou hast acted rightly in what thou hast done, for verily, Islam destroyeth what preceded it," and he sent a slip of paper within his letter, and wrote to Amr, *saying,* "verily, I have sent thee a slip of paper within my letter, which cast into the Nile." And when the letter of Omar reached Amr b-ul Aas, he took the slip of paper and opened it, and behold, there was in it, "from the servant of God, the Prnce of the Faithful, to the Nile of Egypt-Now, if thou didst rise of thy own power, then rise not, but if the Lord caused thee to rise, then I implore the Lord, the One, the Conqueror, to make thee rise !" And he cast the slip of paper into the Nile, a day before[2] *the Festival of* the Cross. And when they entered upon the next morning, verily the Lord had caused it to rise sixteen cubits in a single night : thus the Lord put an end to this custom among the people of Egypt up to this day.

Ibn Asakir records on the authority of Tarik b. Shihab[3] that he said, "if a man spoke with Omar in conversation and told him a falsehood, he would say, 'withhold this,' then as he continued the

---

1 Abul Mahasim determines this to be the Coptic month of Bunah, that is, the Syrian month of Huzayran or our June approximately. Nujum uz Zahirah.

2 Abul Mahasin has قبل يوم عيد الصليب بيوم. This date, according to the Calendars of the Eastern and Western Churches, is the 14th September.

3 Abu Abdullah Tarik b. Shihab the Companion. He was born before the rise of Islam, and fought in about thirty or forty expeditions under Abu Bakr and Omar. He was a native of Kufah and died there in A.H. 83. An Nawawi.

conversation, he would say, withhold this also,' and the man would say to him, 'all that I said to thee was the truth, except what thou didst command me to withhold.' And from al Hasan that he said, 'if there was a man who knew a falsehood when it was spoken, it was Omar-b-ul Khattab.'"

Al Bayhaki records in the Proofs on the authority of Abu Hudbah al Himsi that he said, "Omar was informed that the people of Irak had pelted with stones their governor, and he went forth in a violent anger and prayed, but was distracted in his prayers, and when he came to the salutation, he said, 'O God, verily they have put confusion upon me, therefore put thou confusion upon them, and place over them a youth of the Banu Thakif who may rule over them after the manner of the rule of the time of Ignorance, not receiving with favour the beneficent among them, and not pardoning their evildoers.'" I observe that he referred by this to al Hajjaj. Ibn Lahia'h[1] says that at that time al Hajjaj was not born.

On some particulars of his character.

Ibn Saad records on the authority of al Ahnaf b-ul Kays[2] that

---

1 Abu Abdur Rahman Abdullah b. Lahiah al Ghafiki, a native of Egypt was a narrator of traditions and historical narratives and pieces in prose and verse but of weak memory and of little repute. He was appointed Kadhi of Old Cairo by Abu Jaafar al Mansur A.H. 155 (A.D. 772) and removed from office A.H. 164. He was the first Kadhi who made it his duty to be present when watch was kept for the new moon in Ramadhan but this custom was discontinued under the Fatimite dynasty and re—established by Salahuddin. He died at Old Cairo A.H. 174 (790) or some say A.H. 170, aged eighty-one. Ibn Khall.

2 Abu Bakr ad Dahhak b. Kays (a different person from the one who fell at Marj Rahit) surnamed at Tamimi, was generally known as al Ahnaf or the Clubfoot. He was chief of his tribe and held high rank among the Tabiis and possessed a great reputation for acuteness, learning and prudence. His influence was such, that, as Muawiyah's sister said of him, if he were angered, he had one hundred thousand of the tribe of Tamim to share his anger without asking him the reason of it. He died at Kufah about A.H. 67. The notice of his life in Ibn Khall will repay perusal.

he said, "we were seated at Omar's door, when there passed by a slave girl, and they said, 'she is the concubine of the Prince of the Faithful.' And Omar exclaimed, 'she is not a concubine of the Prince of the faithful and is not lawful to him, verily she is the property of the Lords.'[1] Then we said, 'what then is lawful to him of the property of the Most High God?' he replied, 'verily, nothing is lawful to Omar of what belongeth to the Lord, but two garments, a garment for winter and a garment for summer, and what may enable him to perform the pilgrimage and the religious visitations, and my sustenance and that of my family is like unto that of a man of the Kuraysh, neither the richest nor the poorest of them. Beyond this I am but a man among the Muslims.' Khuzaymah b. Thabit[2] says, that when Omar appointed a ruler, he would write to him and make it conditional upon him, that he should not ride a palfrey, nor eat delicacies, nor clothe himself in fine garments, nor close him doors against the needy, for if he should do this, verily punishment would come upon him." Akrimah b. Khalid and others narrate, that Hafsah[3] and Abdullah and some others expost alated with Omar and said, "if thou wert to eat good food, it would confirm thee in *maintaining* the truth :" he exclaimed, "are ye all of this opinion?" They said, "yes." He replied, "I understand your counsel, but I have left my two Companions upon a road, and if I depart from their road, I shall not find them at the journey;s end." He adds, "and a dearth fell upon the people, and he eat that year, neither butter nor fat." Ibn abi Mulaykah narrates that Ukbah b. Farkad spoke to Omar about his food, and he exclaimed, "fie on thee, shall I eat of good things during my life in this world, and seek enjoyment in them." Al Hasan states that Omar went in to his son Aasim who was eating flesh meat, and he exclaimed, "what is this?" he replied, "I had a

---

1 I. e. The State Treasury, used for the benefit of all the Muslims.

2 Abu Umarah Khuzaymah b. Thabit, was one of the Auxiliaries, and a native of Medina. Surnamed also Khatmah, from his once smiting a man on the nose (خطم) He fought al Badr and other battles, and was present with Ali at the flight of the Camel, and at Siffin where he himself was killed A.H. 37. An Nawawi.

3 His daughter (wife of Muhammad) : Abdullah was his son.

great craving for it." Omar retorted, "dost thou eat everthing thou hast a craving for? It would be sufficiently immoderate in a man that he should eat all that he desired." Aslam mentions that Omar said, "a craving for fresh fish hath come upon me." He continues, "whereon Yarfa[1] mounted his camel and rode four *miles* on and four *miles* back and purchased a basketful of a miktal weight,[2] and brought it, and then betook himself to his camel and washed it down and repaired to Omar who said, 'come, that I may see the camel,' and he looked upon it and exclaimed, 'thou hast forgotten to cleanse this sweat that is under its ear. An animal hath been punished to serve the appetite of Omar-no, by Allah, Omar shall not taste of thy basket.'"

Katadah says, that Omar when he was Caliph, used to wear a garment of woolen stuff patched partly with leather, and would wander through the streets with a scourge over his shoulders with which he chastised the people, and passing by bits of rag and dates, he would gather them up and threw them into the houses of people, that they might make use of them. Anas says, "I saw between the shoulders of Omar, four patches in his shirt." And Abu Othman an Nahdi, "I saw upon Omar a nether garment patched with leather." And Abdullah b Amir b. Rabiih,[3] "I made the pilgrimage with Omar, and he erected neither a tent of goat's hair, nor one of wool-he would throw his cloak, and mat of dressed skin upon a bush and seek shelter beneath it." And Abdullah b. Isa, "upon the face of Omar were two dark furrows *worn* from weeping." And al Hasan, "Omar would come to a verse of the Qurãn of his daily recitation, and would fall down in a faint so that it would be some days before he recovered." And Anas, "I entered an enclosure and I heard Omar say-and between me and between him there was a wall"- "Omar, son of al Khattab, Prince of the Faithful! Good ! by Allah,

---

1 The freedman of Omar.

2 About 80 Ibs.

3 Descended from Anz the son of Wail and a confederate of al Khattab the father of Omar. He was born four years before Muhammad's death, and his father was a Companion of note. He died A.H. 85. An Nawawi.

thou must fear God, son of al Khattab, or He will surely punish thee!" And Abdullah b. Aamir b. Rabiih, "I saw Omar take up a straw from the ground, and he said, 'would that I were this straw ! O! would that I were nothing! Would that my mother had not borne me!'" And Ubaydullah b. Oma b. Hafs, "Omar b-ul Khattab carried upon his neck a skin of water, and people expostulated with him regarding it, and he said-'my spirit made me vain, and I wished to abase it.' And Muhammad b. Sirin, a Kinsman of Omar's went to him and besought him to make him a grant from the public treasury, but Omar reproved him and said, 'dost thou wish that I should meet God a faithless prince ?' and he bestowed upon him ten thousand dirhams from his own property." And an Nakha'i, "Omar used to carry on trade while he was Caliph." And Anas, "the stomach of Omar-used to rumble from eating olive oil in the year of destruction,[1] and verily he had forbidden himself *the use of* butter, and he tapped his stomach with his finger and said 'verily there is nothing elese for us but that, until the people have the means of living.' And Sufiyan b. Uaynah narrates that Omar said, 'the most beloved of men to me, is he who discovers to me my faults.' Aslam says, 'I saw Omar the son of al Khattab take a horse by the ear, and with the other hand holding his own ear, leap upon the back of the horse.' And Ibn Omar, 'I never saw Omar, in a passion, but he restained himself from what he sought to do when God was mentioned to him or the fear of God put into him, or a man read him a verse of the Qurãn.' Bilal said to Aslam, 'what do you think of Omar?" He replied, 'he is the best of men, but when he is angry, thou hast but to read the Qurãn to him until his anger departs.' Al Ahwas b. Hakim narrates on the authority of his father, that some flesh-meat was brought to Omar dressed with butter, but he refused to eat them and said 'they are both delicacies.' Ibn Saad gives all these details and records on the authority of al Hasan that Omar said, 'The simple way by which I govern the people is that I frequently change their rulers."

---

1 The 17th year of the Flight in which men and cattle perished in great numbers. The word comes from رماد, ashes;-being thus called, because the earth became like ashes by reason of the drought. Lane.

On his appearance.

Ibn Saad and al Hakim record on the authority of Zirr,[1] that he said, "I went forth with the people of Medina on a festival day, and I saw Omar walking barefoot; he was advanced in years, bald, of a tawny colour- a left-handed man, tall and towering over the people." Al WAkidi observes, "it was not known to us that Omar was tawny coloured, unless it was that Zirr saw him in the year of destruction, when verily, his colour might have altered while he eat olive oil." Ibn Saad states on the authority of Ibn Omar that *the latter* was describing Omar and said, "he was a man fair of complexion, a ruddy tint prevailing, tall, bald and grey." And from Ubayd b. Umayr "Omar used to overtop the people in height." And from Salimah b-ul Akwaa', "Omar was ambidexter, that is that he could used both his hande *equally well.*"

Ibn Asakir records from Abu Raja al Utaridi that he said, "Omar was a man, tall, stout, very bald, very ruddy, with scanty hair on the cheeks, his moustache large, and the ends of it raddish." In the history of Ibn Asakir, it is recorded with various ascriptions, that the mother of Omar b-ul Khattab, was Hantamah, the daughter of Hisham b-ul Mughirab, and sister of Abu Jahl b. Hisham ; thus Abu Jahl was his maternal uncle.

On his Caliphate.

He assumed the Caliphate according to the bequest of Abu
A.H.13. Bakr in Jumada'l Akhirah, the thirteenth year of the Flight. Az
A.D.634 Zuhri says that Omar was elected to the Vicegerency on the day of the death of Abu Bakr and that was on Tuesday, the 22nd of Jumadal Akhirah, (recorded by al Hakim). He directed the

1 Probably Abu Miriam Zir. Hubaysh b. Hubasa, a member of the tribe of Asad and a native of Kufah. He was a great master in the art of reading the Qurãn and celebrated as a philologer. He died at a very advanced age A.H. 82 (A.D. 701). De Slane, I.K.

government with the most complete success and victories were numerous during his time.

In the year 14 A.H. Damascus was taken, partly by convention, partly by force: Emessa and Baalbek[1] by convention, and Basrah and Ubullah, both by force. In the same year, Omar assembled the people for the prayers called at Tarawih[2] (al Askari in the Awail).

In the year 15 A.H. the whole of the country of the Jordan was subdued by force of arms, save Tiberias which was taken by convention ; and in the same, occurred the battles of Yermuk[3] and Kadisiyyah. (Ibn Jarir). During the same Saad[4] founded Kufah, and Omar established stipends for the soldiers and instituted the registers, and assigned allowances according to priority *of merit.*[5]

In the year 16 A.H. al Ahwaz was taken and al Madain, and in the latter, Saad held the Friday prayers in the hall of Khusran, and this was the first congregation assembled in Iraq, and that was in the month of Safar. In the same year was the battle of Jalula[6] in which Yezdajird grandson of Khusran was defeated and fled to Rai; Takrit was captured and Omar marched and took Jersualem, and preached at al Jabiyah[7] his famous discourse. And in the same Kinnasrim was taken by force of arms, and Aleppo and Antloch, and Manbij by treaty and Saruj by force, and kirkisiyah by treaty. In the month of Rabiiul Awwal, the Era of the Flight was adopted by the advice of Ali.

---

1 According to Yakut, the pronunciation of this is بعلبك - Balubakka.

2 See Note, p. 26.

3 Hieromax, a stream formed by the springs of Mount Hermon, which loses itself in the Jordan below the lake of Tiberias.

4 Ibn Abi Wakkas.

5 See an Nawawi. Ar. Omar.

6 A river that flows through Bakuba, and where the Persians were defeated with great slaughter, no less than a hundred thousand it is said, having fallen. The river took its name of Jalula, says Yakut, from the excessive. (جل) Number of the slain.

7 In the province of Jaydur in Palestine-Omar's discourse will be found in the Futuhu's Sham of al Azdi, p. 227.

A.H.17. A.D.638 In the year 17 A.H. Omar enlarged the mosque of the Prophet, and a famine occurred in Hijaz and it was called the year of destruction and Omar through *the merits* of Abbas prayed for rain for the people. Ibn Saad records on the authority of Niyar al Aslami, that when Omar went forth to pray for rain he appeared with the mantle of the Apostle of God upon him. And from Ibn Aunt[1] that he said, "Omar took the hand of Abbas, and lifted it up and said, 'O God! I implore Thee by the uncle of Thy Prophet, that Thou wilt cause this drought to pass away from us, and send down rain upon us;' and they did not quit the place till it rained, and the heavens poured down rain upon them for days." During the same year al Ahwaz was taken by treaty.

In the year 18 A.H. Jundaysabur was occupied by convention, and Hulwan by force, A Pestilence also occurred at Emaus ; Edessa and Sumaysat were taken by force, and Harran and Nasibin and a part of Mesopotamia by force (though some say by convention), and Mosal and its adjacent districts.

In the year 19 A.H., Caesarea[2] was overpowered. In the year 20 A.H. Egypt was conquered by force of arms, thought it is also said, that with the exception of Alexandira which was taken, the whole of Egypt *surrendered* under convention. Ali b. Rabah says that the whole of Mauritanis was won by force of arms, [3]: Tastar[4] was also taken possession of. In the same died the Roman Emperor (*Heraclius),* and Omar expelled the Jews from Khaybar and Najran and apportioned Khaybar and Wadiul Kura *among those who had been present at the expedition.*[5]

---

1 The freedman of Miswar b. Makhramah, the Companion.

2 This word in the original should be spelt with a ص instead of a س.

3 Gibbon places the complete conquest seven years later under Othman, the conduct of the invasion being entrusted to the foster-brother of the Caliph, Abdullah b. Saad, the amanuensis of Muhammad.

4 The present Shuster in Khuzistan. Yakut.

5 Wadiul Kura is between Tayma and Khaybar. The expedition directed by Muhammad took place A.H. 7. For the apportionment of the lands, my authority is Yakut.

In the year 21 A.H. Alexandira was taken by storm, and Nahawand, and after this the Persians were unable to muster an army: also Barkah and other places.

In the year 22 A.H. Adarbijan was subdued by force, others say *surrendered* under convention, and Dinaur, Masabdan, and Hamadan captured, and Tripoli in Morocco and Rai and Askar and Kumas. A.H.22. A.D.642-3

In the year 23 A.H. took place the conquest of Kirman, Sajistan, and Makran of the mountainous districts, and Ispahan and its dependencies.

Towards the close of the year occurred the death of our prince Omar, after his return from the pilgrimage, he being martyred. Sai'd b-ul Musayyab says that when Omar returned from Mina, [1] he made his camel kneel in the watercourse and throwing himself backwards, lifted up his hands to heaven, and exclaimed, "O God ! I am advanced in years and my strength has failed, and my zeal dissipated; take me therefore to thyself while as yet I have not fallen short of my duty nor exceeded due bounds ;" and the month of Dul Hijjah did not elapse before he was slain, (al Hakim) (3rd November 644).

Abu Salih as Samman[2] narrates that Kaa'b-ul Ahbar said to Omar, "I find in the Pentateuch that thou wilt be martyred." He replied, "how can martyrdom be mine, I being in the land of Arabia?" And Aslam, that Omar said, "O God, give me for my portion, martyrdom in thy cause, and grant that my death may be in the city of Thy Apostle," (al Bukhari). Maadan b. Abi Talhah narrates that Omar preached and said, "I beheld a vision as if a fowl had struck me with its beak one or two blows, and verily I see in it but my

---

1 The return from Mina to Mecca during the ceremonies of the pilgrimage, is called an Nafr or the Flight.

2 Abu Salih as Samman named also Dhakwan and surnamed az Zaiyat, was a Mawla of the tribe of Ghatfan and an eminent Traditionist, died at Medina A.H. 101 (719-20). De Slane, I.K.

A.H.23. A.D.643. approaching death. And verily there are some who enjoin me to name a successor, and indeed the Lord will not neglect[1] his faith and His Vicegerency, but if anything overtake me, then the Vicegerency is to be determined by consultation among those six with whom the Apostle of God, when he died, approved". (al Hakim). Az Zuhri states that Omar used not to suffer a captive who had reached the age of puberty, to enter Medina, but al Mughirah b. Shuubah, being in Kufah, wrote to him and mentioned to him that he had with him, a youth, a cunning workman, and asked his permission that he might enter Medina, and added that he was a master of several trades profitable to the people for he was a blacksmith, and engrave and a carpenter. Omar therefore gave him permission to send him to Medina, and al Mughirah put a tax[2] upon him of one hundred dirhams a month. He, however, went to Omar and complained of the severity of the tax, but Omar replied that the tax was not excessive; he, therefore, departed indignantly murmuring. Omar waited some days and then sent for him and said, "was not I informed that thou sayest, that if thou wouldst thou art able to make a mill that will grind by means of the wind?" He looked upon Omar sullenly and said, "verily I will make a mill for thee that men shall talk about,": when he retired, Omar said to those that were about him, "the slave hut now threatened me." After a little, Abu Luluah[3] took a double-bladed dagger, having its haft in the middle, and hid in a corner of one of the recesses of the mosque before day-break, and remained there until Omar came forth rousing the people to prayers, and when he drew near him, he stabled him with three blows. (Ibn Saad.) Amr b. Maymun the Auxiliary narrates, that Abu Luluah, the slave of al Mughirah, struck Omar with his double bladed dagger, and wounded together with him twelve men, of whom six died, and a man of Iraq threw a

---

1 Compare Qur. III و ماكان الله ليضيع ايمانكم

2 That is, that he was to pay that sum to his master from his earnings.

3 The slave's name.

garment over him, and when he was suffocating in it, he slew himself. Abu Rafi,[1] states, that Abu Luluah the slave of al Mughirah, used to make mills, and al Mughirah tasked, him daily with an impost of four dirhams, and he met Omar and said, "O Prince of the Faithful, verily al Mughirah hath been hard upon me, therefore speak to him ; " and he answered, "act well towards thy master, and it was the intention of Omar to speak to al Mughirah regarding it. But the other grew angry and said, "the justice of Omar is extended unto all the people, save unto me." He therefore purposed his death, and took a dagger and sharpened it and poisoned it, and while Omar was exclaiming, "get ye into your ranks, before the takbir is said," the slave went and stood over against Omar in the rank and smote him in the shoulder and in the side, and Omar fell, and he wounded thirteen men with him, of whom six died. Omar was carried to his family, and the sun being about to rise, Abdur Rahman b. Auf read prayers before the people from the two shortest Suras. They brought Omar date-wine, and he drank of it and it came out of his wound, but it could not be distinguished *from the blood ;* they therefore gave him milk, and it came out of his wound, and they said, "there is no harm to thee" and he answered, "If there be harm[2] in the being slain, why when I am slain." The people then began to praise him, saying, "thou wert such and such," but he said "yet, by Allah, I would that I might escape *from judgment* with these as a sufficiency,[3] nothing due by me nor to me, and that the Companionship of the Apostle of God were a security unto A.H.23. A.D.643

---

1 There are several of this name. The one referred to is probably the freedom of Muhammad. He had been given by Abbas to Muhammad who gave him his liberty on hearing of the conversion of Abbas. Some say he died before Othman's murder, others, during the Caliphate of Ali. Ibn Hajir and an Nawawi.

2 In other narrations given in the Kitabul Iktifa on the authority of Amr b. Mayyun the outflow of the milk from the wound, was decisive in regard to the wound being mortal. The physician who was called in, told him he could not live till the evening.

3 و ددت ان ذلك كان كفافا This is the reading of the same tradition on the same authority, in the Kitab ul Iktifa. The ذلك referring to the praises which were being made of him.

A.H.23. A.D.643. me." Then Ibn Abbas praised him, but he said-"if the fullness of the earth in gold were mine, assuredly I would ranson myself therewith from the terror of the day of resurrection,[1] and verily, I have made *the election to the Caliphate* to be determined in consultation by Othman, Ali, Talhah, az Zubayr, Abdur Rahman b. Auf, and Saad." And he commanded Suhayb to pray before the people, and appointed for the six a term of three days[2] wherein to deliberate (al Hakim). Ibn Abbas says that Abu Luluah was a Magian. Amr b. Maymun narrates that Omar said, "praise be to God, that he hath not caused my death by the hand of a man who professeth Islam." Then he said to his son, "O Abdullah, see what debts I owe;" and they computed and found them to be eighty-six thousand *dirhams,* or about that. And he said, "if the property of the family of Omar be sufficient, then pay it from their goods, otherwise ask of the Banu Adi, and if they goods be not sufficient, then ask of the Kuraysh. God to Ayesha, the Mother of the Faithful, and say. 'Omar asketh leave that he may be buried with his two Companions.' And Abdullah went to her and she said, 'I wished it (meaning the place) for myself, but now I shall assuredly give him the preference over myself.' And Abdullah went *back* and said, 'verily she hath given permission;' then Omar praised the Most High God. They said also to him "make a testament, O prince of the Faithful, and appoint a successor." He answered, "I do not see any one more entitled to this authority than those men with whom the Apostle of God, when he died, was content," and he named the

---

1 المطلع lit. "the place whence one will look down *on the day of resurrection,* but it may be taken as a noun of time and applied to the day of judgment, see Lane art طلع.

2 This is made clear from the Kitab ul Iktifa, in two traditions form Simak b. Harb and Anas respectively. Omar ordered the father of Talhah to take fifty men and post themselves at the door of the house where the six were to deliberate, and to suffer no one to enter, nor the third day to elapse without the election being concluded. According to the former tradition, the Ansars were directed to confine the six for three days in a house, and if by that time their deliberations were not satisfactorily conculuded, they were to enter and slay them. An effectual method of quickening the most hesitating judgment.

six. He added, "let Abdullah the son of Omar be present with them but he must have no part in the affair, and if the government fall to Saad, then let him be the man, but if not then let whichever of ye be named to rule, seek his assisatance, for verily I did not remove him either for incapacity or treachery."[1] He went on the say, "I commend to the Caliph after me, the fear of God, and I commend to him the Fugitives and the Auxiliaries, and I Commend to him the whlfare of the people of the proviness," with other similar charges. And when he died, we went forth with him at a foot-pace and Abdullah the son of Omar, saluted and said, "Omar desireth permission," and Ayesha replied "bring him in:" and he was taken in and placed there with his Companions. When his burial was over, and they had returned, those of the Council assembled, and Abdur Rahman b. Auf said, "delegate your authority unto three among you." Then az Zubayr said, "I give my authority to Ali," and Saad said, "I give my authority to Abdul Rahman," and Talhah said, "I give my authority to Othman." *The narrator* continues, "then those three went apart and Abdur Rahman said, 'I do not desire it'-now which of you two will be quit of this affair ? and we will put it to him (and God be his witness and Islam) to consider the best among the *Muslims* in his own judgment, and to strive for the welfare of the people." Then the two Shaykhs Ali and Othman were silent, whereon Abdur Rahman said, "give *the choice* unto me, and the Lord be my witness, I shall not fail ye in *choosing* the best of ye." The two agreed and he retired apart with Ali and said, "thou hast the priority in Islam and kinship with the Apostle of God as thou well knowest, the Lord be thy witness, that if I give thee the authority, thou wilt do justice, and if put another over thee, thou wilt hear and obey!" He said, "yes." Then he retired apart with the other and said the same to him, and when he received their promises, he swore allegiance to Othman, and Ali likewise swore him allegiance.

A.H.23.
A.D.643

1 The people of Kufah complained to the Caliph against Saad, on account of his injustice and oppression, and his unorthodox manner of reading prayers, and Omar removed him from his government and appointed in his place Ammar b. Yasir. Ibn Athir. Ockley ascribes the removal of Saad to Othman, in the 35th year of the Flight.

A.H.23. A.D.643. *It is recorded* in the Musnad of Ahmad on the authority of Omar that he said, "if my death overtake me, and Abu Ubaydah be yet alive, I appoint him my successor, and if my Lord enquireth of me, I shall answer that I heard the Apostle of God say, every Prophet hath one in whom he confides, and my trusted one is Abu Ubaydah the son of al Jarrah; but if my death overtake me and Abu Ubaydah be dead, I appoint as successor Muad the son of Jabal, and if my Lord enquire of me why I appointed him, I shall answer that I heard the Apostle of God say that he would be raised up on the day, of resurrection in front of the doctors of science, a little apart."[1] However they both died during his Caliphate. In the same Musnad it is stated on the authority of Abu Rafi, that Omar when dying was spoken to regarding the appointment of a successor, and he said, "verily, I have seen among my Companions an evil covetousness, and if one of two men were attainable to me, and I could make over this authority to him. I would trust him, *viz.,* Salim[2] the freedman of Abu Hudayfah, and Abu Ubaydah b-ul Jarrah."

Omar was stabbed on Wednesday the 26th of Dul Hijjah and was buried on Sunday the first of the Sacred month of Muharram being sixty-three years old-some say he was sixty-six, and some sixty-one, and others sixty, which al Wakidi prefers. Again, according to some, he was fifty nine, and to others, fifty-five or fifty-four. Suhayb prayed over him in the mosque.

According to the Tahdib of a Muzani,[3] the impression on the signet ring of Omar was "Death is a sufficient admonisher."

At Tabarani records on the authority of Tarik b. Shihab, that

---

1 According to an Nawawi the tradition makes the distance a bow shot معاذيوم القيمه رتوة بين العلماء.

2 Salim was slain at Yamamah. See, note 3 p. 126.

3 Abu Ibrahim Ismail B. Yahya al Muzani, was a disciple of the Imam as Shafii and a native of Egypt. He was of most austere life, a Mujtahid, and a profound thinker. He was the author of many works, the most celebrated being the Mukhtasarul Mukhtasar (Abridgement abridged) a treatise on the legal doctrines of the Shaflites. He died at Misr A.H. 264 (878). Muzani signifies belonging to Muzayna a well-known tribe named after Muzayna, daughter of Kalb. Ibn Khall.

Umm Ayman said on the day that Omar was slain, "Islam is to day rent." And from Abdur Rahman b. Yasar, [1] "I wintnessed the death of Omar and the sun was eclipsed on that day." (His authorities are trustworthy.) A.H.23. A.D.643

On the things in which he was formost.

Al Askari says that he was the first who was called Princes of the Faithful, and the first who adopted the Era of the Flight, and the first who established a public treasury, and the first who instituted the prayers (*at Tarawih*) of the month of Ramadhan, and the first who went the rounds at night, and the first who punished lampooning, and the first who gave eighty *stripes* for indulgence in wine, and the first who prohibited marriage limited to a term, and the first who forbade the sale of female slaves who had borns children to their masters, and the first who assembled the people to prayers over the dead with four Takbirs, and the first who instituted the public register, and the first who made conqueses, and made a survey of the Sawad,[2] and the first who brought corn from Egypt by the bay of Aylah *(Akaba)* to Medina, and the first who constituted the poor-rate in Islam to be used unalienably for the service of God, and the first who adopted the deviation by excess in *the dicision* of inheritances,[3] and the first who instituted the dedication of horses for religious services, and the first who said, "may God lengthen thy life," (he said it to Ali) : and the first who said, "may God strengthen thee," (he said it to Ali). This is the end of al Askaris narration.

An Nawawi mentions in the Tahdib, that he was the first who

---

1 The MS. has Bushar, the printed edition. "Yasar" with (Bushar) in brackets. I can find no notice of the individual alluded to, in any works to which I have access.

2 The particulars of this survey will be found in Yakut art. بسواد

3 For the explanation of the term عول I must refer the reader to the Muhammadan Law of Inheritance, as it is too lengthy to transcribe here. Consult also Lane art. عول

A.H.23. A.D.643. adopted the use of the scourge. Ibn Saad states this in his Tabakat, and adds that it used to be said afterwards "verily the scourge of Omar is more terrible than your swords." He continues, "he was the first who established Kadhis in the provinces, and the first who founded the cities of Basrah and Kufah, and *placed in a flourishing condition* Mesopotamia, Syria, Egypt and Mosal."

Ibn Asakir records on the authority of Ismail b. Ziyad, that he said, that Ali, passing by the mosques in the month of Ramadhan in which lamps were burning, exclaimed, "may the Lord illumine Omar in his grave as he hath illumined for us our mosques."

Ibn Saad says that Omar established meal-houses, and placed within them flour and parched barley-meal, and dates and currants, and what might be necessary to aid the disabled traveler, and he stored along the road between Mecca and Medina, what would relieve those unable to continue their journey. He likewise demolished the mosque of the Prophet and increased and enlarged it and floored it with pebbles. It was he who expelled the Jews from Hijaz to Syria, and transferred the people of Najran to Kufah. He also put back to praying station of Abraham, to the place where it now stands, it having before adjoined the Temple.

On some accounts of him and his decisions.

Al askari records in the Awail, and al Tabarani in the Kabir, and al Hakim on the ascription of Ibn Shihab that Omar b. Abdil Aziz inquired of Abu Bakr b. Sulayman b. Abi Hathmah, *saying,* "how was it in the time of Abu Bakr that it used to be written, 'From the Vicegerent of the Apostle of God,' and afterwards Omar used at firat to write 'From the Vicegerent of Abu Bakr?' Who then first wrote, from the prince of the Faithful?" He answered, "as Shifa who was one of the Fugitive women, told me that Abu Bakr used to write, 'From the Vicegerent of the Apostle of God,' and Omar used to write, 'From the Vicegerent of the Vicegerent of the Apostle of God,' until Omar wrote to the perfect of Iraq to send him two sturdy men, whom he might question regarding Iraq and the people thereof ; and he sent him Labid b. Rabiih and Adi b. Hatim. They arrived at Medina and entered the mosque, and found Amr b-ul Aas, and they said, 'ask permission for us to see the prince of the Faithful." Amr replied, 'by Allah, ye have hit his name.' And Amr went in to him and exclaimed, 'peace be to thee O prince of the Faithful.' He said 'how hast thou come by this name? verily thou must explain what thou hast said.' Then the other informed him of what had happened and said 'thou art the prince and we, the Faithful.' Thus the letters have continued to be so inscribed up to this day."

A.H.23.
A.D.643

An Nawawi in his Tahdib says that Adi b. Hatim, and Labid b. Rabiih, called him by that name when they went to him from Iraq, and some say, that al Mughirah b. Shuubah called him by it. Again it is asserted that Omar said to the people, "you are the faithful, and I am your prince ;" he was therefore called prince of the faithful, and before that the was addressed as Vicegerent of the Vicegerent of the Apostle of God, but they gave up that phrase on account of its length. Ibn Asakir records on the authority of Muawiyah b. Kurrah that he said, "it used to be written, 'From Abu Bakr, Vicegerent of the Apostle of God,' and when Omar b-ul Khattab ruled, they wished to address him Vicegerent of the Vicegerent of the Apostle of God, but Omar said, 'this is too long.' They answered, 'not so, but we have mad thee to rule over us and thou art our prince.' He said, 'yea-ye are the Faithful and I am your prince.' Thus it came to be written, Prince of the Faithful."

Al Bukhari records in his history on the authority of Ibnul Musayyab that the first who adopted the usage of dating was Omar b-ul Khattab two years and a half after his accession to the Caliphate, and he dated from the 16th year of the Flight, by the advice of Ali. As Silafi in the Tuyyuriyat records from Ibn Omar, that Omar wished to write a record of memorable actions, and he prayed for the blessing of God for a month, and he arose one morning determined upon it, but after a little he said, "verily I remember a

A.H.23. A.D.643. people[1] who were before ye, who used to write books, and they gave themselves up to it, and neglected the Book of God." And Ibn Saad from Shaddad, [2] that the first sentence that Omar uttered when he ascended the pulpit, was "O God, verily I am rough in temper, thereofore soften me, and verily I am weak, therefore strengthen me, and verily I am avaricious, therefore make me generous." And Ibn Saad and Said b. Mansur and others from Omar, that he said, "I place myself with regard to the property of the Lord, in the position of a guardian of an orphan's property. If I am in good circumstances, I refrain from touching it, and if I am in distress, I take of it with moderation, and when I am again in good circumstances, I repay it."

Ibn Saad records on the authority of Ibn Omar that Omar b-ul Khattab, when he was in need, would go to the superintendent of the public treasury, and ask a loan of him, and he was often in distress, and the Superintendent of the treasury would go to him to exact the debt and press him, and Omar would be evasive with him, but sometimes his stipend would be due, and he would pay *the debt.* And from Ibnul Bara b. Marur, [3] that Omar went forth one day, and complained, of a sickness, and honey was recommended to him, and *he was told* that a bottle of it was in the public treasury, and he said, "if ye permit me, I will take it, otherwise it is unlawful for me," and they gave him permission. 'And from Salim b. Abdullah, that Omar would put his hand into the saddle gall *of his camel* and say, "verily I fear lest I may be brought to account for what hath befallen thee."

---

1 He refers to the Jews and Christians.

2 Shaddad b. Aus the Companion. He belonged to the tribe of the Najjar, and was a native of Medina, but he lived much at Jorusalem and died there A.H. 58, aged 75. His tomb, says an Nawawi, "is still to be seen outside the Gate of Mercy," one of the twenty gates of the great Masjid.

3 Bishr b-ul Bara b. Marur the Companion, an Ansar of the tribe of Khazraj he was present at Akabah, Badr and Ohud and died at Khaybar from eating of the sheep of which Muhammad partook and which the Jews are said to have poisoned. Some say he died at once, others after great suffering. An Nawawi.

And from Ibn Omar, that when Omar desired to hinder the people from anything, he would go to his family and say, "verily I know not any one who hath done a thing which I have forbidden, but I doubled his punishment." A.H.23. A.D.643

It has been related to me from another source, that Omar, went forth one night wandering about Medina, as he was frequently in the habit of doing, when he passed by *the house of* one of the women of the Arabs whose door was balted upon her, and she was saying,

> This night whose stars wander in their nightly journey, is wearisome
> And keeps me sleepless, for I have none with whom I may be merry.
> And, by Allah, were there no, God whose issues were to be feared!
> But I fear a Watcher, who keepeth ward :
> Over our souls, and whose recorded never is negligent.
> The fear of the Lord and shame bindereth me :
> And my husband, too worthy of honor that his place should be taken.

He therefore wrote to his perfects in the field that no one should be detained on military service against the enemy for more than four months.

Ibn Saad records on the authority of Salman that Omar said to him, "am I a monarch or a Caliph?" and Salman answered him, "if thou tax the land of the Muslims in dirhams, less or more, and putteth them to unlawful use, thou art a monarch and not a Caliph," and Omar took warning by it. And from Suyfay b. Abil Arja, that Omar said, "by Allah, I know not whether I am a Caliph or a monarch, if I be a monarch, it is a terrible thing." A speaker said to him, "O prince of the faithful, there is a difference between the two." He said, "what is it?" He replied, "a Caliph doth not take save lawfully, nor give save where it is due, and thou, thanks be to

God, art such, but a monarch oppresseth the people, and taketh from this and giveth to that :" and Omar was silent. And from Ibn Masaud that Omar was riding a horse, and his garment fell back from his thigh, and the people of Najran saw upon his thigh a dark mole and they said, "this is he whom we find in our books that he is to turn as forth from our land." And from Saad al Jari that Kaab al Ahbar said to Omar, "I find thee verily in the Book of God, *posted* at one of the gates of hell, hindering the people from falling into it, and when thou diest, they will continues to rush headlong into it, till the day of judgement." And from Abu Maashar, that he narrates, "my Shaykhs told me that Omar said, 'this authority cannot be rightly conducted except by severity without haughtiness and leniency without weakness.'"

Ibn Abi Shaybah records in the Musannaf on the authority of Hakam b. Umayr,[1] that Omar wrote, "now, let not the Commanders of armies and divisions inflict upon any one the scourging ordained by law until he arriveth at Darb,[2] lest rage *inspired by* Satan induce him to desert to the infidels." Ibn Abi Hatim records in his Commentary on the authority of as Shaabi, that the Roman Emperor wrote to Omar saying, "verily my messengers who come to me from thee, pretend that thou hast with thee a tree, which in its nature has none of *the qualities* of a tree. It sprouteth like asses' ears, then it opnenth out like a pearl, then it becometh green like the green emerald, then it turneth ruddy and becometh like a red ruby, next it ripeneth and cometh to maturity, and turneth into the most delicious honey-cake that is eaten. Next it drieth up and becometh the preservation of the dweller in his house, and a store for the traveler ; now if my messengers have spoken truly, then I cannot think this tree to be other than one of the trees of paradise," Whereupon Omar wrote to him *saying,* "from the servant of God,

---

1 Hakam b. Umayr al Thamali. Thamalah is a branch of the tribe of Azd Ibn Hajr has little to say of him but that he was present at Badr and that his traditions are not to be relied upon.

2 The ancient Derbe near the Cilician gates, the chief mountainous pass from the direction of the countries occupied by the Arabs into the Greek Empire. Lane.

the Prince of the Faithful, to Caesar the Roman Emperor – verily thy messengers have spoken truly. This tree which we possess, is the same which the Lord caused to sprout[1] for Mary when she bore Jesus her Son. Therefore fear God and assume not Jesus to be God, besides God, for, 'verily the likeness of Jesus in the sight of God is as the likeness of Adam : He created him out of the dust,'" &c., (Qur. III). A.H.23. A.D.643

Ibn Saad records on the authority of Ibn Omar that Omar issued an order to his perfects, among them being Saad b. Abi Wakkas, and in *accordance therewith* they wrote *the amount of* the property in their possession and Omar shared their property with them, and took half and gave them half. And from as Shaabi, that Omar when he employed a perfect wrote down the amount of his property. And from Abu Imamah b. Sahl b. Hunayf[2] that he said, "Omar remained some time without supporting himself from the public treasury until poverty thus came upon him, and he sent to the Companions of the Apostle of God and took counsel of them and said, 'verily I have diligently employed myself in this authority, what therefore do I deserve from it?' And Ali said, 'morning and evening food,' and Omar accordingly took that." And from Ibn Omar, that Omar made the pilgrimage and spent during his pilgrimage sixteen dinars, and he said *to his son* "O Abdullah, I have been wasteful of this money."

Abdul Razzak[3] records in his Musannaf on the authority of Katadah and as Shaabi, that a woman went to Omar and said, "my husband rises in the night *to pray* and fasts all day," and Omar said

---

1 This was a certain palm tree which the Muhammadan tradition supposes Mary to have leaned upon for support, and though a withered trunk, it put forth leaves and fruit that she might gather and eat, Qur. XIX. The stupidity of the Roman and the effrontery of the Arab are only to be matched by the mendacity of the narrator.

2 One of the Companions belonging to the Ansars.

3 Probably Abdur Razzak as Sanani one of the most celebrated traditionist of his age. People traveled to Yaman from all parts to hear him. Died A.H. 211 (826-7). De Slane, I.K.

A.H.23. "verily thou hast praised thy husband highly." Whereon Kaab b.
A.D.643. Siwar exclaimed, "but she complains *of him !*" And Omar said, "how?" He replied, "she means that she has not her share of her husband's *society.*" He answered, "then if thou thinkest that, judge between them." He said, "O prince of the Faithful, the Lord hath permitted to him four wives, and to her of every four days, one day, and of every four nights one neight." And from Ibn Jurayh[1] that he said, "one whom I can believe, told me that while Omar was wandering *about Medina,* he heard a woman say—

'The night is wearisome and its bounds gloomy
And it hath kept me sleepless while
I have no friend with whom to be merry.
And were there no fear of God whose like there is not!"

And Omar exclaimed, 'what is the matter with thee?' She replied, 'thou hast sent my hushand on service for some months, and I pine for him.' He said, 'dost thou desire to do evil?' She replied, 'God forbid!' then he said, 'restrain thyself, for verily, a messenger *shall go* to him,' and he sent for him, and wrote that the troops should not be kept on service for more than four months." And from Jabir b. Abdillah that he went to Omar complaining to him of the treatment he had met with from his women, and Omar said "verily, I find the same, so much so that when I ask for anything I want, *my wife* says to me, 'thou goest only after the girls of a certain tribe, watching for them.' Thereupon Abdullah b. Musaud said to him, 'hast thou not heard that Abraham, upon whom be peace, complained to the Lord of the temper of Sarah and it was said to him verily she was made from a rib[2] therefore put up with

1 The MS. has Jurayj and not Jurayh as in the printed text-of Jurayh, I can find no mention. Abdul Malik b. Jurayj, according to Ibn Khallakan was celebrated for his learning ; and it is said that he was the first after the promulgation of Islam who composed books. He was a native of Mecca and a member by adoption of the Kuraysh. Born A.H. 80 (699-70), and A.H. 149 (766).

2 Meaning that she was crooked by nature and hard. 'A crooked rib' is a metaphor for a woman amongst the unpolished sons of the desert.

what she does as long as thou seest no unsoundness in her faith." A.H.23.
And from Akrimah b. Khalid, that a son of Omar's went to him, A.D.643
and he had anointed and combed his hair, and put on the garments, and Omar smote him with his scourge until he made him cry, and Hafsah said to him, 'why dost thou strike him?' He answered, 'I saw that his spirit had made him vain, and I wished to abase it within him.' And from Layth b. Abi Salim that Omar said, 'give not as names al Hakam or Abudl Hakam, for the Lord is the only ruler (Hakam), and call not a road Sikkah.'"[1]

Al Bayhaki records in the Shaabul Imam on the authority of ad Dhahhak, that Abu Bakr said, "by Allah, I would I were a tree by the wayside, that camels might pass by me and seize me and take me in their mouths and chew me and swallow me, then cast me forth as ordure, and that I were not a mortal man." And Omar said, "would that I were a ram, that my people mught fatten me as it appeared *good* to them, so that when I became as fat as could be, those whom they loved might visit them, and they might kill me for them, and make part of me roast and part of me dried flesh, and eat me, and that I were not a mortal man." And Ibn Asakir from Abul Bakhtari,[2] that Omar Ibnul Khattab was preaching from the pulpit, when al Husayn the son of Ali stood up against him and said, "come down from the pulpit of my father!" and Omar replied, "it is the pulpit of thy father, not the pulpit of my father who hath counseled thee to this?" Then Ali rose and said, "by Allah, no one counseled him to this-but (*turning to his son*) I will assuredly make thee

---

1 The only reason I can suggest for this prohibition is the tradition مادخلت السكة دار قوم لاذلوا "The ploughshare enters not the abode of a people, but they become abased "The same word signifying, "a ploughshare" and "a road." Omar might have held its use as of ill augury to his people. The real meaning of the tradition however is, that with the introduction of agriculture begins the extortion of rulers.

2 Abul Bakhtari Wahb b. Wahb of the Kuraysh and a native of Medina : he removed from Medina to Baghdad under the Caliphate of Harun ar Rashid. He was appointed Kadhi of Medina and afterwards removed. He died at Baghdad A.H. 200 (815-16) under the Caliphate of al Mamun. He was liberal with his purse, but notorious as a fabricator of traditions and Ibn Hanbal calls him a liar. Ibn Khall.

A.H.23. A.D.643. smart, O traitor;" and Omar said, "hurt not the son of my brother, for he hath said truly that it is the pulpit of his father.? (The authorities are trustworthy.) Al Khatib in his Ruwat (*narrators*) records on the authority of Abu Salamah b. Abdir Rahman and Sai'd b-ul Mussayyab, that Omar and Othman were disputing on a certain point among themselves, when a looker on exclaimed, "verily they will never agree," but they did not separate except upon the best and most admirable *agreement,* regarding it. And Ibn Saad from al Hasan, that at the first discourse that Omar preached, he praised God and glorified Him, and then said, "verily I am tried with ye and ye are tried with me, and I have followed as Vicegerent among ye after my two Companions. As to those who are with us, wer have undertaken their affairs in person, and as to those who are away from us, we have appointed over them as rulers, men of power and trust, and he who doeth well, we will give him increase of benefits, and whoso doeth evil, we will punish, and may the Lord have mercy upon me and ye." And from Jubayr b-ul Huwayrith that Omar took counsel of the Muslims regarding the establishing of registers and Ali said to him, "divide every year the revenue that is collected for thee and keep not back anything." And Othman said, "I see that there is a large revenue sufficient for the people, and if they do not keep a register so that he who hath received may be distinguished from him who hath not received, I fear that affairs will fall into confusion." Then al Walid b. Hisham b-il Mughrah said to him. "O prince of the Faithful, verily I have been to Syria, and I have seen that its princes have established registers and organized armies, therefore, establish registers and organize troops," and he took his counsel. Then he summoned Akil-b. Abi Talib and Makhramah b. Naufal and Jubary b. Muslim who were among the most skilled genealogists of the Kuraysh, and he said, "write dwon the people according to their degrees," and they wrote beginning with the Banu Hashim, then followed them up with Abu Bakr and his people, then Omar and his people, in the Caliphate, and when Omar looked into it, he said, 'begin with the kindred of the Prophet, the nearest after the nearest, until ye place Omar where God hath placed him." And from Sai' d b-ul Musayyab, that Omar established the registers in the month of Muharram the 20th year of the Flight.

And from al Hasan, that Omar wrote to Hudayfah, *saying,* "give the men their stipends and rations," and he replied, "verily I have done so and a large sum is over." Thereupon Omar wrote to him, "verily the booty which God hath given unto them, belongeth not to Omar nor to the family of Omar,- divide it among them." A.H.23. A.D.643

Ibn Saad records on the authority of Jubayr b. Mutim, that he said 'while Omar was standing upon the mount of Arafah,[1] he heard a man call out and say, "O Caliph, O Caliph." And another man heard him, (and they were taking provisions for the way) and said "what is the matter with thee-may Allah cleave thy uvula." Then I advanced towards the man and called out to him." Jubayr continues : "verily the next day I was standing with Omar at al Akabah,[2] casting stones at it when there came a stone with force, striking violently the head of Omar. Then I turned that way and heard a man from the mount say,-"dost thou know, by the Lord of the Kaabah that Omar shall never again stand in this station after this year?" Jubayr adds. "And to ! it was he who had called ot among us the day before, and the thing weighed heavily upon me." And from Ayesha that she said, "at the time of the last pilgrimage which Omar Performed with the mothers of the true believers,[3] when we returned from Arafah, passing by al Muhassab,[4] I heard a man upon his camel saying, 'where was Omar the prince of the Faithful!' and I heard another man reply, 'here was the prince of the Faithful;' then he made his camel kneel down and raised his voice, wailing, and said,-

'Upon such an Imam as thou be peace and bless
My the hand of God, that lacerated exterior.

---

1 This was on the second day of the pilgrimage called the Yaum Arafah the 9th of Dul Hijjah.

2 Jamrat ul Akabah, or as it is vulgarly termed, Shaytan al Kabir, the great devil-one of the three pillars stoned during the ceremonies of the pilgrimage. See Burton Vol. III, pp. 238-282.

3 The wives of Muhammad.

4 The name of the way between the mountains, opening upon the part called الابطح between Mecca and Mina, so called from the pebbles in it. Lane.

A.H.23. A.D.643.

Whose[1] goeth with speed or rideth upon the wings of the ostrich:

To overtake that which thou hast sent before thee yesterday, will be out-stripped.

Thou hast adjudged affairs but left behind them

Calamities in their sleeves not yet unloosed.'

And that rider moved not, nor was it known who he was, and we used to say that he was a Jinn. And Omar returned from that pilgrimage and was stabbed (*with a dagger*) and died." And on the authority of Omar that he said, "this authority shall rest with the men of Badr as long as one of them is left; then with the men of Ohud as long as one of them is left, and then with such and such, but there shall be no part in it for a liberated slave, nor for the son of a liberated slave, nor for a Muslim *become so* at the conquest *of Mecca.*" And from an Nakhai, that a man said to Omar, "wilt thou not name as successor, Abdullah b. Omar?" He said, "may Allah smite thee ! by Allah, never have I desired this of God that I should appoint as successor a man who knoweth not properly how to divorce his wife."[2] And from Kaab that he said, "there was amongst the children of Israel a king;[3] when I recall him, I think of Omar, and when I recall Omar, I think of him. And he had with him a Prophet who was inspired, and the Lord inspired the Prophet to say to him, 'make thou they convenant, and write unto me thy testament, for verily thou art a dead man in three days.'" The Prophet therefore told him this, and when it was the third day he fell down between the wall and the bed. Then he turned to his Lord and said, "O Lord! If thou knewest that I was just in government,

---

1 سعى also signifies running to and fro between as Safa and al Marwah. The meaning is probably that the merits acquired by Omar in his pilgrimage are not to be surpassed. I prefer to read يُسبق for يَسبق as otherwise the من is left 'en I' air,' without its complement.

2 Abdullah once attempted to put her away at a time when divorce was not permitted by the Muhammadan Law.

3 Ezechias, Kings iv. xx.

and, when affairs became troubled that I followed thygiodance, and was such and such then lengthen my life, that my son may grow up and my people be set in order." And the word of the Lord came to the Prophet, *saying,* "verily he hath said so and so, and indeed hath spoken truly, and verily I have added to his life fifteen years, and during that *there is time* that his son may grow up and his people be set in order." And when Omar was stabbed, Kaab said-"if but Omar were to ask of his Lord, He would surely preserve him." Omar was informed of this, and he said, "O God, take me to Thyself *while as ye I am not* enfeebled nor under reproach." And from Sulayman b. Yasar, that the Jinns mourned over Omar. A.H.23. A.D.643

Al Hakim records on the authority of Malik b. Dinar[1] that a voice was heard on the mount of Tabalah[2] when Omar was slain, saying,

> "Let him who wept, weep for Islam :
> For verily they are about to he laid prostrate, and their appointed time hath not been exceeded.
> And the world hath gone back and its good withdrawn :
> And verily he is wearied of it who was confident in the promise."

Ibn Abi'd Dunya records on the authority of Yahya b. Abi Rashid of Basrah, that Omar said to his son, "be moderate in *the expenses* of my shround, for verily if there be aught of good with God in my favour, he will give me in exchange what is better than it, and if I have been otherwise, He will strip me and be swift in my stripping. And be moderate in my grave *that ye dig for me* for verily if there by aught of good with God in my favour, he will widen it unto me as far as my eye can reach, and if I have been otherwise, he will streaighten it upon me until my ribs interlace. And let no woman go

---

1 Abu Yahya, Malik b. Dinar of Basrah, an ascetic and one of the Tabiis. He was freedom of the one of the women of the Banu Najiah. He is regarded as a trust worthy authority, died A.H. 123 or 129. An Nawawi.

2 Eight days March from Mecca and six from Taif.

A.H.23. forth with me, and praise me not for that which is not in me for the
A.D.643. Lord knoweth best what I am. Therefore when you go forth, hasten in your going, for if there be aught of good with God in my favour, you will speed me on to that which is my good, and if I have been otherwise, ye cast from your necks an evil that ye bear."

Ibn Asakir records on the authority of Ibn Abbas that al Abbas said, "I asked of the Lord a year after Omar died, that he would show him unto me in sleep,: and I saw him after a year and he was wiping the sweat from his forehead and I said to him, "with my father- mayest thou *be ransomed,* and with my mother –how is it with thee?" He replied, "it is but now that I am free *from the Judgment* and Omar would have perished,[1] had I not indeed met one *who is* Merciful and Compassionate." And from Zayd b. Aslam,[2] that Abdullah b. Omar bil Aas saw Omar in sleep and he said, "how hast thou done?" he replied, "how long is it that I left you?" He answered, "twelve years ago." He said, "verily it is even now that I am free from Judgment." Ibn Saad records on the authority of Salim b. Abdillah b. Omar that he said, "I heard a man of the Auxiliaries say, 'I prayed to God that he would show me Omar in sleep, and I saw him after ten years and he was wiping the sweat from his forehead and I said, O prince of the Faithful, what hast thou been doing?" He replied, "I have but now been freed from Judgment, and had it not been for the mercy of my God, I had perished."

Al Hakim records on the authority of as Shaabi that Aatikah the daughter of Zeyd-b Amr b. Nufayl said, mouring Omar-

"Eye ! let thy tears and weeping be abundant :
And weary not-over the noble chief.

---

1 Lit, his means of support would have been destroyed-or his dwelling would have been demolished.

2 Abu Usamah Zayd b. Aslam the freedom of Omar, a native of Median, and one of the Tabiis, distinguished for his piety and theological learning, and much sought after for his instructions and discourses. He died at Medina about A.H. 136. An Nawawi.

Death hath afflicted me in *the fall of a* horseman A.H.23.
Distinguished in the day of battle and of contumely. A.D.643
The Stay of Faith, the defence against *inclement* fortune :
And a champion unto the afflicted and oppressed.
Say unto the heopeless and the desolate, die!
Since death hath given us to drink the cup of dissolution."

Among the distinguished people who died during Omar's time were, Utbah b. Ghazwan, al Alabul Hadhrami, Kays, bus Sakan-Abu Kuhafah father of as Siddik-Saad b. Ubadah-Suhayl b. Amr-Ibn Umm Maktim the Muaddin-Ayyash b. Abi Rabih- Abdur Rahman brother of az Zubayr b. Awam-Kays b. Abi Sasaah one of those who collected the Qurãn-Naufal b-ul Harith but Muttalib-his brother Abu Sufiyan-Mariyah, mother of the Sayyid Ibrahim-Abu Ubaydah b-ul Jarah Maad b. Jabal-Yazid b. Abi Sufiyan-Shurabhil b. Hasanah-al Fadhl b-ul Abbas-Abu Jandal b. Suhayl-Abu Malik al Ashari- Safwan b-ul Muattal-Ubbay b. Kaab-Bilal the Muaddin-Usayd b-ul Hudhayr-al-Bara b. Malik the brother of Anas-Zaynab, daughter of Jahsh-Ayadh b. Ghanam Abul Haytham but Tayyihan-Khalid b-ul Walid-al Jarud, chief of the Banu Abdil Kays-an Numan b. Mukarran-Katadah b-n Numan al Akra b. Habis-Saudah, daughter of Zamah Uwaym b. Saidah-Ghilan at Thakafi-Abu Mihjan at Thakafi-and others of the Companions.

A.H.23.
A.D.643.

OTHMAN-B-AFFAN

Othman-b. Affan b. Abil Aas-b. Umayya-b. Abdi's Shams-b. Abd Manaf b. Kusayy b. Kilab b. Murrrah b. Kaab b. Luayy b. Ghalib, al Kuryshi al Umawi, Abu Amr, called also Au Abdullah and Abu Laylah, was born in the 6th year of the Elephant. He was converted early and was one of those called to Islam by as Siddiq. He took part in the two Flights, the first to Abyasinia and the second to Medina, and married Rukayyah, the daughter of the Apostle of God before the Prophetic mission, and she died at his house on one of the nights of *the fight of* Badr, and he was detained from Badr through his attendance on her. With the persmission of the Apostle of God, who assigned to him a portion *of the spoils* and compensated him. He is therefore numbered among those Present at Badr, and the messenger arrived with the news of the victory of the Muslims at Badr, on the day that they buried her at Medina. The Apostle of God then gave him in marriage after her, her sister Umm Kulthum and she died in his house in the 9th year of the Hijrah. The learned say that no one besides him is known to have married the two daughters of a Prophet, and for that, he has been named possessor of the two Luminaries. He was one of the first early converts, and the foremost of the Fugitives and one of the Ten to whom *the attainment of* Paradise was testified, and one of the Six, with whom when the Apostle of God died he was well content, and one of the Companions who collected the Qurãn. Indeed Ibn Abbad[1] says that none but he and al Mamun, among the Caliphs, collected the Qurãn. Ibn Saad says that the Apostle of God appointed him Vicegerent at

---

1 Abul Kasim Ismail b. Abil Hasan Abbad the Sahib the wonder of his age for his talents, virtues and generosity. He was Vizir to Muwayyid ud Doulah b. Rukhnud Dawlat b. Buwayh and subsequently to his brother Fakhrud Dawlah. He was the author of numerous works, the most known being the Muhit, a work on Philology, another on epistolary writing, one on Festivals, and another on the rank of Imam, stating the merits of Ali and the legitimacy of those who preceded him. Born A.H. 326 (938) at Istakhar and died at Rai A.H. 385 (995). Ibn Khall. De Slane writes the name Abbad but according to Meursinge (De interpret, Qur. p.39) Suyuti makes it Abbas and Ibbad. The Munt. Arab, gives Abbad.

Medina during his military expeditions to Dat ur Rikaa and Ghatfan. One hundred and forty-Six traditions are related by him on the authority of the Apostle of God.[1] A.H.23. A.D.643

Ibn Saad records on the testimony of Abdur Rahman b. hatib that he said, "I never saw any one of the Companions of the Apostle of God, who when he narrated a tradition, gave it more completely and excellently than Othman b. Affan, save verily he were a man who held traditions in great fear. And on the authority of Muhammad b. Sirin that the most learned of them in the ceremonials of the pilgrimage, was Othman, and after him Ibn Omar." Al Bayhaki records in his Sunan on the authority of Abdullah b. Omar b. Aban al Juafi that he narrates, "my maternal uncle Husayn al Juafi said to me 'dost thou know why Othman hath been called Possessor of the two Luminaries?' I said, 'no.' he replied, 'none hath ever been united to the two daughters of a Prophet from the time that God created Adam, *nor shall be so* till the resurrection cometh to pass, save Othman-for that reason he hath been called Possessor of the two Luminaries.'"

Abu Nuaym records on the authority of al Hasan that he said, "verily Othman was called Possessor of the two Luminaries, because we know none save him, who hath closed his door upon the two daughters of a Prophet." And Khaythamah in the Fadhail us Sihabah, (*Merits of the Companions*) and Ibn Asakir from Ali b. Abi Talib, that he was asked regarding Othman and he said, "that man is called in the court of heaven, Possessor of two Luminaries-he was the son-in-law of the Apostle of God throught his two daughters." Al Malini records on a weak ascription from Sahl b. Saad that he said, "Othman is called Possessor of the two Luminaries because he passeth over from one station to another in Paradise and there gleameth for him two streams of light, and he is called so on that account." He adds, that he received the surname of Abu Amr in the time of Ignorance, but when Islam arose, Rukayyah bore him Abdullah, and he received the surname (*Abu Abdullah*) from him.

---

1 Here follows a list of those who have narrated traditions on his authority which I have omitted.

A.H.23. His mother was Arwa, daughter of Kurayz b. Rabiih b. Habib
A.D.643. b. Abdi's Shams, and her mother was Umm Hakim al Baidha, daughter of Abdul Mutaalib b. Hashim, twin sister of the faither of the Apostle of God. Thus the mother of Othman was the daughter of the paternal aunt of the Prophet.[1]

Ibn Ishak says that he was the fist to embrace Islam after Abu Bakr, and Ali, and Zayd b. Harithah. Ibn Asakir records on various ascriptions, that Othman was of middling stature, neiter short nor tall, of a comely aspect, fair, inclined to yellow, upon his face the scars of small-pox, full bearded, large of limb, broad between the shoulders, fleshy in the thigh, long in the forearms, which were clothed with hair. He was curly-headed, bald, having the most beautiful teeth of all men, his locks falling below his ears dyed a yellowish colour, and verily he used to bind his teeth with gold *wire.* And on the authority of Abdullah b. Hazm al Mazini,[2] that he said, "I have seen Othman the son of Affan, but I have never seen man or woman more beautiful of face than he." And from Musa b. Talha, that Othman was the most comely of men. And from Usamah b. Zayd that he said, "the Apostle of God sent me to the house of Othman with a dish of meat and I entered, and lo! There was Rukayyah seated. And I began to look now upon the face of Rukayyah, and now upon the face of Othman, and when I returned, the Apostle of God enquired of me and said, "didst thou go in to them?" I said "Yes;" he continued, "hast thou ever seen a more comely pair than those two?" I said "no-o Apostle of God."

Ibn Saad records on the authority of Muhammad b. Ibrahim

1

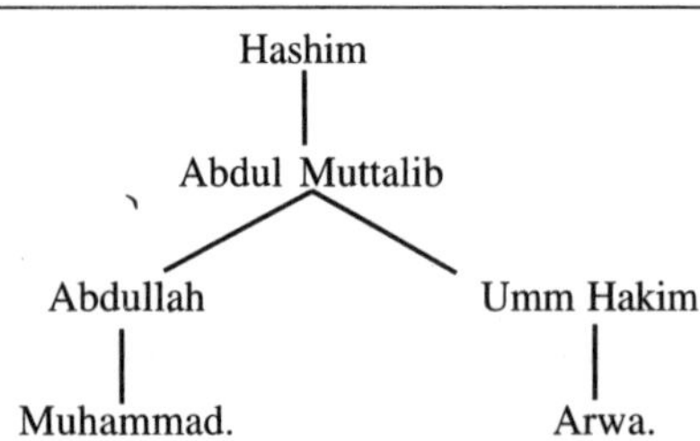

2 There are three families of the Mazins-those of the tribes of Tamim, Kays and Rabiih.

bil Harith at Taymi, that when Othman became a Muslim, his paternal uncle al Hakam b. Abil Aas b. Umayyah, took him and bound him with a cord and said, "dost thou turn from the faith of thy fathers to the religion of an innovator ? by Allah, I will never let thee go until thou abandonest what thou art about." And Othman said, "by Allah, I will never forsake it nor abandon it." And when al Hakam saw his steadfastness in his faith, he released him. A.H.23. A.D.643

Abu Yala records on the authority of Anas, that the first of the Muslims who emigrated with his family to Abyssinia was Othman b. Affan, and the Apostle of God said, "may God protect those two, for Othman was assuredly the first who emigrated with his family after Lot." And Ibn Adi from Ayesha, that when the Prophet married his daughter Umm Kulthum to Othman, he said to her, "verily thy husband resembles most, among men, thy foreafter Abraham and thy father Muhammad." And Ibn Adi and Ibn Asakir, from Ibn Omar, that the Apostle of God said, "I find a resembled in Othman to my forefather Abraham."

On the traditions handed down regarding his merits, over and above what has preceded.

The two Shaykhs record on the testimony of Ayesha, that the Prophet gathered together his garments when Othman entered, and said "shall I not be bashful before the man before whom the angels stand abashed?" And al Bukhari from Abu Abdur Rahman as Sulami,[1] that Othman when he was besieged *in his house,* stood up overlooking *the besiegers* and said, "I conjure ye, by Allah, and I call on none but the Companions of the Prophet,-do ye not know that the Apostle of God said, 'he who aideth in providing

---

1 Abu Abdur Rahman Abdullah b. Habib as Sulami al Kufi was born in the life time of Muhammad. He learned to read the Qurãn under the tuition of the Caliphs Othman and Ali and taught the same science in the mosque of Kufah, died A.H. 74 (693-4). De Slane I.K.

A.H.23. A.D.643. for the army of distress,[1] for him is Paradise'-and I fitted them out? Do ye not know that the Apostle of God said, 'he who diggeth- the well at Rumah,[2] for him is Paradise,' and I dug it?" And they testified to the truth of what he said,

At Tirmidhi records on the authority of Abdur Rahman b. Khabbab, that he said, "I saw the Apostle of God encouraging the army of distress, and Othman exclaimed, 'O Apostle of God ! I answer for one hundred camels with their housings and saddles for the sake of God:' and the Prophet continued encouraging the troops, and Othman cried out, 'O Apostle of God, I answer for two hundred camels with their housings and saddles for the sake of God.' And he went on encouraging the troops, and Othman called out, 'O Apostle of God-I answer for three hundred camels with their housings and saddles for the sake of God.' Then the Apostle of God descended from the pulpit, saying, "Othman will not be. Judged whatever he may do after this." And from Anas and al Hakim, verified on the authority of Abdur Rahman b. Samurah[3] that Othman went to the Prophet with a thousand dinars, when he was fitting out the army of distress and poured it into his lap, and the Apostle of God began turning it over, saying twice, "It shall not harm Othman, whatever he may do after this day." And from Anas that he said, "when the Apostle of God commanded the allegiance pleasing[4] *to God to be sworn to him,* Othman was the messenger of the Apostle

---

1 The army of Tabuk. This expedition against the Greeks was undertaken at a time of great head and drought, and the sufferings of the troops procured for it this name. He furnished them with 960 camels and 50 horses.

2 Between Jurf and Zighabah, near Medina ; Omar purchased it from the Jews for twenty thousand dirhams, and gave it to the Muslims. An Nawawi.

3 Abu Said, Abdur Rahman, son of Samurah the Companion. (See note 2 p. 42). He was a resident of Basrah. He fought in Khorasan in the time of Othman and overran Sigistan and Kabul. He related fourteen traditions from his master. Died at Basrah (and some say at Marv) A.H. 50 or 51. An Nawawi

4 At Hudaybiyah. The word رضوان is used, because it is employed with reference to this occasion in Qur. XLVII.

لقد رضي الله عن المومنين اذيبا يعونك تحت الشجرة

of God to the people of Mecca, and the men sware allegiance, and the Prophet said, 'verily Othman, is *employed* in the requirements of God and the needs of His Apostle,' and he struck one hand upon the other, and the hand of the Apostle of God *as a pledge* for Othman was better than their hands for themselves." And from Ibn Omar that the Apostle of God spoke of dissensions and said, *alluding* to Othman, "this one shall be wrongfully slain in them." A.H.23. A.D.643

At Tirmidi and al Hakim and Ibn Majah record on the authority of Muraah b. Kaab that he said, "I heard the apostle of God speaking of troubles that he thought to be near at hand, when a man passed by muffled up in his garment, and he said, 'this man to-day is in the path of salvation;' and I went to him and to lo! It was Othman, and I turned my face towards *the Prophet,* and said, 'this *man*?' He replied, 'yes.'" And at Tirmidi and al Hakim from Ayesha, that the Prophet said, "O Othman, perchance the Lord may clothe thee with a garment, and if the hypocrites desire to take it from thee, put it not off till thou meetest me in Paradise." And at Tirmidi from Othman that he said on the day of *the siege* of his house, "verily, the Apostle of God, hath made a covenant with me, and I am awaiting *its fulfillment."*

Al Hakim records on the authority of Abu Hurayrah that he said, "Othman purchased Paradise from the Prophet on two occasions; *viz.,* when he dug the well of Rumah, and when he fitted out the army of distress." And Ibn Asakir from Abu Hurayrah, that the Prophet said, "Othman among the Companions, most resembles me in disposition." And at Tabarani from Asamah b. Malik that he said, "when the daughter of the apostle of God died under *the roof of* Othman, the apostle of God said, "Give *your daughters* in marriage to Othman-If I had a third daughter, I would assuredly give *her* in marriage to him, and I have never wedded *any* to him save under inspiration." And Ibn Asakir from Ali, that he narrates, "I heard the apostle of God say to Othman, "if I had forty daughters, I would wed them with thee one after the other, until not one of them was left." And from Zayd b. Thabit that he narrates, "I heard the Apostle of God say, Othman passed me, and there was with me one of the angels who said, *"he shall be a*

A.H.23. A.D.643. martyr-his people shall slay him- I am abashed before him.'" Abu Yala records on the authority of Ibn Omar that the Prophet said, "verily the angels stand abashed before Othman as they stand abashed before God and his apostle." And Ibn Asakir from al Hasan that the modesty of Othman was mentioned in his hearing, and he said, "if it were that he was in the middle of his house, and the door closed upon him, and he were to put aside his clothes to pour water upon himself, modesty would forbid him to straighten his back."

On his Caliphate.

He was sworn allegiance to as Caliph three nights after Omar was buried, and it is related that the people at that time were gathered about Abdul Rahman b. Auf taking counsel with him, and speaking privily with him, and there was not a man of judgment who was in private with him who held any one equal to Othman. And when Abdur Rahman took his seat for the covenant of allegiance, he praised God and glorified him and said in his discourse, "verily I see that the people reject *all* but Othman." (Ibn Asakir from Miswar[1] b. Makhramah). But according to another account, *he said,* "and now O Ali I have regarded the people and I have not seen *any of* them equaling Othman, therefore make not a way *unto the Caliphate* for thyself" Then he took the hand of Othman and said, "I swear allegiance to thee according to the law of God, and the law of his apostle, and the law of the two Caliphs after him." And Abdur Rahman swore fealty to him, and Fugitives and the Auxiliaries swore him allegiance.

Ibn Saad records on the authority of Anas, that Omar an hour

1 Abu Abdur Rahman Miswar-b. Makhramah b. Naufal descended from Murrah. He was born at Mecca two years after the Flight and was one of the most skilled of the Companions in jurisprudence. He remained at Medina till the death of Othman and then returned to Mecca, and after the death of Muawiyah, remained with Ibn-az-Zubayr, till the siege by al Hajjaj, when he was killed by a stone from a catapult. An Nawa.

before he died sent to the father of Talhah the Auxiliary and said, "go at the head of fifty of the Auxiliaries with those men of the Council, for a I count upon it, they will aseemble together in a house. Stand thou at that door with thy Companions and suffer none to go in to them and let not the third day pass with them before they give authority to one among them." It is recorded in the Musand of Ahmad on the authority of Abu Wail[1] that he narrates, "I said to Abdur Rahman b. Auf, 'how did ye swear allegiance to Othman and pass over Ali?" he replied, 'it was not my fault. Verily I began with Ali and I said, "I will make wih thee a covenant of allegiance according to the Book of God, and the law of His Apostle, and the institutions of Abu Bakr, and Omar." And he replied "in as far as I am able;" then I offered the same to Othman and he accepted.'" A.H.23. A.D.643

And It is related that Abdur Rahman said to Othman in private, "if I make not a covenant of allegiance with thee whom doest thou counsel to me?" He replied, "Ali;" and he said to Ali, "If I made not a covenant of allegiance with thee, whom dos thou counsel to me?" he said, "Othman," Then he summoned az Zubayr and said, "if I make not a covenant of allegiance with thee, whom dost thou counsel to me?" He replied, "Ali or Othman." Then he summoned Saa'd and said, "whom dost thou counsel to me? For I and thou desire it not:" and he said, "Othman." Then Abdur Rahman took counsel with the chief men, and he said that most of them were for Othman.

Ibn Saad and al Hakim record on the authority of Ibn Masaud that he said, "when Othman was sworn allegiance to, we placed in authority the best that remained *among us,* and we were not remiss in our duty."

In this year of his Caliphate, Rai was taken for it had been taken before and lost again. In the same the people were attacked with a great issuing of blood from the nose, and it was called the

---

1 Abu Wail Shakik b. Salimah a Tabii of the tribe of Asad, native of Kufah. He was a cotemporary of Muhammad but never saw him, died A.H. 79. His authority as a traditionist is acknowledged. An Nawawi.

A.H.23. A.D.643. Year of the Haemorrhage. This Haemorrhage seized Othman, so that he was detained from the pilgrimage and deputed another *in his stead.* During the same many Grecian fortresses were taken, and Othman placed Saad b. Abi Wakkas in the government of Kufah, and removed al Mughirah.

In the year 25, Othman removed Saad from Kufah and appointed al Walid b. Ukbah b. Abi Muayt', who wa a Companion, a brother of Othman's on the mother's side, and that was the first thing with which he was reproached in that he preferred his relations to posts of authority : moreover it is related that al Walid read morning prayers to the people four rakaats, while he was intoxicated, and he looked upon them and said, "shall I go on for ye?"

In the year 26, Othman enlarged the sacred mosque and extended it and purchased the *adjoining* buildings for its augmentation. During the same Sabur[1] was taken.

In the year 27, Muawiyah led an expedition against Cyprus, and crossed the sea with his troops, and with him was Ubadah b-ul Samit[2] and his wife Umm Haram, daughter of Milhan, a woman of the Auxilaries. She fell from her mule, and died there for the faith. The Prophet had foretold to her this expedition and prayed that she might be one of them. She was buried at Cyprus.

During this year Arrajan (*Erghan*) and Darabjird were taken;[3] and in the same Othman removed Amr b-ul Aas from Egypt and appointed over it Abdullah b. Saa'd-b. Abi Sarh, who led an expedition against *Northern* Africa and overran it both plains and hills, and each man of the troops received a thousand and some say, three thousand dinars. Spain was also subsequently conquered in this year.

---

1 Shahpur probably. Near Shiraz. The MS. has Naysabur.

2 He was one of the Companions sent by Omar to Syria at the time of its conquest to teach the people the Qurãn. He died at Jerusalem and some say at Ramlah in A.H. 34, aged 72. An Nawawi.

3 An aliph is omitted in the printed edition. Darabjird is near Perscpolis : another town of the name is near Naysabur.

An anecdote *deserves mention.* Muawiyah had urged upon A.H.27. A.D.647
Omar b-ul Khattab the expedition to Cyprus and *the necessity* of reaching it by a sea voyage, and Omar wrote to Amr b-ul Aas, *sayin,* "describe to me the sea and its rider." And he wrote, saying, "Verily I saw a huge construction, upon which mounted diminutive creatures, if it is still, it rends the heart, it it moves, it terrifies the senses. With in it the faculties grow diminishing and calamities augmenting. Those inside it, are like worms in a log. If it inclines to one side, they are drowned, if it escapes, they are confounded." When Omar read the letter, he wrote to Muawiyah, *saying*, "By Allah, I will not set a true believer upon it."

Ibn Jarir says that Muawiyah proceeded against Cyprus in the time of Othman, and concluded a peace with its inhabitants on condition of tribute.

In the year 29, Persepolis was taken by force of arms an Kasa and other places. During the same, Othman enlarged the mosque of Medina and built it of carved stone, and fashioned its pillars of stones, and its roof of teakwood, and made its length one hundred and sixty cubits and its breadth one hundred and fifty cubits.

In the year 30, Jur was taken, and many towns in the land of Khursan. Naysabur was occupied by treaty, though some say, by force ; and Tus and Sarkhas both by treaty and likewise Marw and Bayhak.[1] When these extensive provinces were conquered, abundant was the tribute unto Othman, and wealth came unto him from every side, so that he established for himself treasuries and gave bountiful stipends,[2] and he would order a man a hundred thousand badras, in eah 'badrah,'[3] being four thousand ounces.

---

1 According to Yakut, Bayhak comprises the country between Naysabur, or as it is commonly written Nishapur, Kumis and Juwayn, and contains three hundred and twenty-one villages.

2 ادر might also mean that he caused provisions and the like to pour in plentifully-as in Omar's orders to the tax-gatherers ادرو القحة المسلمين: but here the context seems to refer to stipends from the treasury.

3 A badrah is a purse containing a sum of, from one thousand to ten thousand dirhams. It appears incredible that in the early days of the Caliphate such extravagance could have existed but the lavish bounty of Othman is noticed by Gibbon and it gained for him in return but ingratitude and discontent.

A.H.30.
A.D.650.

In the year 31, (Here a hiatus in the MSS. The intervening years have little to mark them). In 31, according to Abul Fida, (Annals) Yezdijird died, and a rebellion broke out in Khurasan, but was quelled by Othman. In 33 died Ibn Masaud, the Companion. In 34 and 35 occurred the seditions in Kufah against the nepotism of Othman. In the year 35 took place the assassination of Othman.

Az Zuhri says that Othman ruled the Caliphate twelve years. For six years he governed without the people having anything to reproach against him ; and he was more beloved by the Kuraysh than Omar, for Omar was stern with them, and when Othman ruled them, he treated them with leniency and was attached to them. But afterwards he became heedless of their affairs, and appointed his kinsmen and the people of his house to authority during the last six years, and bestowed upon Marwan a fifth of *the revenues of* Africa, and lavished on his kindred and family the property *of the State,* and explained it as the assistanc to kindred which the Lord had enjoined, and said, "verily Abu Bakr and Omar have neglected in that matter what was incumbent upon them, and I have taken it and divided it among my kindred;" but the people disapproved of it. (Ibn Saa'd).

Ibn Asakir records, after another account, on the authority of az Zuhri that he narrates, "I said to Sai'd b-ul-Musayyab, 'canst thou tell me the manner of the death of Othman, and how it was with the people and with him, and why the Companions of Muhammad forsook him?" and Ibnul Musayyad replied, 'Othman was slain unjustly, and he who slew him was a wrongdoer, but those who forsook him are to be excused.' I said, 'how was that?' He replied, 'when Othman assumed, the government, some of the Companions disapproved of his rule, because Othman had a great affection for his tribe. He ruled the Caliphate twelve years, and frequently appointed to office among the Banu Umayyah, those who had not enjoyed the Companionship of the Apostle of God.

Thus there were committed by his prefects those actions which A.H.35.
the Companions of Muhammad did not approve. Othman, however, A.D.655-6
favoured them and did not remove them, and during the last six years, he preferred the children of his uncle and appointed them to rule, and let none othes share with them, nor enjoined on them the fear of God. Thus he appointed Abdullah b. Saad b. Abi Sarh to govern Egypt and he remained over it some years. The people of Egypt complained and sought redress against him. And verily before this, there did occurred on the part of Othman a slight towards Abdullah b. Masaud, and Abu Darr and Ammar b. Yasir, and the Banu Hudayl and the Banu Zuhrah had in their hearts what was in them on account of Ibn Masaud, and the Banu Ghafar, and their confederates and those that were wroth concerning Abu Darr, had in their hearts what was in them, and the Banu Makhzum were wroth with Othman on account of Ammar b. Yasir. And the people of Egypt came complaining against the son of Abu Sarh, and Othman wrote to him a letter threatening him in it, but the son of Abu Sarh refused to submit to what Othman had forbidden him, and he scourged him who had come from Othman, of the people of Egypt that had gone to Othman *complaining*, and slew him. Then seven hundred of the people of Egypt went forth, and they alighted at the mosque of *Medina,* and made their complaint to the Companions at the appointed places of prayer, of what the son of Abu Sarh had done to them. Thereupon Talhah b. Ubaydillah arose and spoke harsh words to Othman, and Ayesha sent to him and said, 'the Companions of Muhammad have come to thee and asked of thee the removal of this man and thou hast refused, yet this man hath put to death a man among them. Therefore do them justice against thy governor.' And Ali b. Abi Talib went in to him and said, 'verily they demand of you one man in the place of another and have claimed for him *the revenge for* blood, therefore remove him from over them and judge between them, for a claim stands against him, therefore do them justice upon him.' He replied to them, 'choose ye a man that I may appoint him over ye in his palce.' And the people pointed out to him Muhammad the son of Abu Bakr, and said, 'place over us Muhammad the son of Abu Bakr." And he

A.H.35. A.D.655-6 wrote him his charge and appointed him. And there went forth with them a number of the Fugitives and Auxiliaries that they might see what was happening between the people of Egypt and the son of Abu Sarh, and Muhammad and those with him set forth. But when they were at the third day's stage from Medina, behold! There came up with them a black slave upon a camel striking the camel violently like to a man who pursues or is pursued, and the companions of Muhammad[1] said to him, 'what is thy adventure and thy condition? for verily thou art either fleeing or pursuing.' And he said to them, 'I am the slave of the prince of the Faithful who hath sent me to the prefect of Egypt.' And a man said to him, 'this is the prefect of Egypt.' He replied, it is not this one I want.'"

Then Muhammad the son of Abu Bakr was informed regarding him, and he sent a man in pursuit of him, who caught him and brought him before him, and he said, "slave, who art thou?" And he began saying at one time, "I am the salve of the prince of the Faithful," and at another, "I am the slave of Marwan," until a man recognized him as the slave of Othman. Then Muhammad said to him, 'Unto whom art thou sent?" He replied, "to the prefect of Egypt." He asked, "with what?" He answered, "with a letter." He said, "Is the letter with thee?" He replied, "no" whereupon they searched him, but found no letter upon him, but with him was a ewer in which was something dried up that rustled, and they shook it that it might be cast out, but it did not come out, so they broke the ever when lo! There was in it a letter from Othman to the son of Abu Sarh. Then Muhammad assembled those that were with him of the Fugitives and Auxiliaries and others, and he opened the letter in their presence, when behold! There was in it : "When Muhammad and such a one and such a one reach thee, contrive a scheme for their death, and set aside his charge, and remain in thy government until my advice reach thee, and imprison such as come to me seeking redress against thee ; verily my advice will reach thee in regard to

---

1 The usual benediction follows this name, but I am inclined to think it has been inadvertently inserted, Muhammad here referring to the son of Abu Bakr and not to the founder of Islam.

the matter, if it please God." And when they read the letter, they were terrified and confounded, and they turned back to Medina, and Muhammad sealed the letter with the seals of the people who were with him, and gave it to a man among them, and they proceeded to Medina and assembled Talhah and az Zubayr and Ali and Saad and those who were among the Companions of Muhammad. Then they reopened the letter in their presence and informed them of the story of the slave, and read to them the letter. And there was not one of the people of Medina but was wroth against Othman, and it increased the wrath and anger of those who were enraged on account of Ibn Masaud, Abu Darr, and Ammar b. Yasir. And the Companions of Muhammad went to their homes there not being one among them, but he was grieved at what they had read in the letter. And the people besieged Othman, and Muhammad the son of Abu Bakr led against him the Banu Taym and others ; and when Ali saw that, he sent to Talhah and az Zubayr and Saad and Ammar and others of the Companions, all of them being men who had fought at Badr. Then he went to Othman *taking* with him the letter, the slave and the camel, and Ali said to him, "is this slave, thy slave?" He replied, "Yes." He continued, "and this camel, thy camel?" He answered, ,"Yes," He said, "then didst thou write this letter?" he said, "no," and he swore by Allah, *saying*, "I did not write this letter, nor command it *to be written,* nor have I any knowledge of it." Ali said to him, "then is the seal thy seal?" He answered, "yes." He said, "then how could thy slave go forth with thy camel, and with a letter upon which is thy seal, thou knowing not of it?" But Othman swore by the Lord, *saying,* "I did not write this letter nor command it *to be written,* nor did I ever send this slave to Egypt."

A.H.35.
A.D.655-6

Now as to the writing, they recognized it to be the writing of Marwan, and they doubted regarding Othman, but demanded of him that he should give up to them Marwan, but he refused, Marwan being with him in the house. Then the Companions of Muhammad went forth from him much enraged, and they were in doubt regarding him for they knew that Othman would not swear falsely, save that some said, "Othman will not be absolved in our hearts,

A.H.35. A.D.655-6

unless he giveth up to us Marwan, that we may interrogate him and learn the affairs of the letter, and how he commanded the death of a man among the Companions of Muhamma without due cause, and if it be Othman that wrote it, we will depose him, and if it be Marwan that wrote it upon the suggestion of Othman, we shall consider what we shall do concerning Marwan." And they kept to their houses, but Othman refused to give Marwan up to them for he feared death for him. And the people besieged Othman and prevented him from obtaining water; he therefore looked down upon the people from above and exclaimed, "Is Ali among ye?" And they said, "no." He said, "is Saad among yet?" They replied, "no"; then he was silent. Again he exclaimed, "Will not any one inform Ali that he may give us water to drink?" Ali was then informed of this and he sent three large leathern water bottles filled with water, but it was nigh unto not reaching him, for a number of the freedom of the Banu Hashim and the Banu Umayya were wounded on account of it until the water reached him. Ali was then informed that the death of Othman was sought, and he said, "verily we desire of him Marwan, but the death of Othman-no," and he said to all Hasan and al Husayn, "go ye with your swords until ye stand over the door of Othman and suffer not any one to go in to him." And az Zubayr sent his sone and Talhah sent his son, and a number of the Companions of Muhammad sent their sons to prevent the people from going into Othman, and to demand the surrender of Marwan. And when Muhammad the son to Abu Bakr saw that, and that the people had shot arrows against Othman, until al Hasan was stained with blood at his door, and an arrow had reached Marwan who was inside the house, and Muhammad the son of Talhah was dyed *with blood* and Kanbar the freedman of Ali had his head broken, then Muhammad b. Abi Bakr feared that the Banu Hshim might be angered at the condition of al Hasan and al Husayn and provoke a tumult, so he took the hands of two men and said to them, "If the Banu Hashim arrive and see the blood upon the face of al Hasan, they will disperse the people from Othman, and what we desire will miscarry, but come with me until we climb above him upon the house, and slay him without any one's knowing it.

And Muhammad and his two Companions climbed from a house A.H.35. of a man of the Auxiliaries until they penetrated unto Othman, and A.D.655-6 not one of those who were with him knew of it, for all those that were with him were upon the tops of the house, and he was alone with his wife. Then Muhammad said to the two, "stay where ye are, for verily his wife is with him, so that I may enter before ye, and when I seize him, then come in and set upon him until ye slay him." And Muhammad entered and seized him by the beard, and Othman said to him, "by Allah, could thy father see thee, thy behaviour towards me would surely be hateful to him :" thereupon his hand relaxed its hold, but the two men went in to him and set upon him until thy slew him, and then came forth fleeing towards whence they had entered. Then his wife screamed, but her screaming was not heard by reason of the clamour in the house, and she mounted up to the people, and said, "verily the prince of the Faithful hath been slain." And the people entered and found him slain, and the news reached Ali, and Talhah and az Zubayr and Saad and those that were in Medina, and they set forth, for verily their senses left them at the news they had heard, until they went in to Othman and found him slain, and they repeated the ejaculation : "verily we belong to God and unto Him shall we return" (Qur. II). Then Ali said to his two sons, 'how was the prince of the Faithful slain and ye two at his door?" and he raised his hand and struck al Hasan, and smote the breast of al Husayn, and reviled Muhammad the son of Talhah and Abdullah the son of az Zubayr, and went forth in great anger until he reached his house. Then the people hastened to him and said, "we swear thee allegiance, wherefore stretch out thy hand, for a chief is of necessity *to us*." And Ali said, "that belongeth not to me, -verily that is with the men of Badr, for with whomsoever the men of Badr are content, he is Vicegerent."

But there was not one of the men of Badr, but went to Ali and said, "we know none more deserving of it than thee-stretch forth thy hand that we may made a covenant with thee." And they swore allegiance to him, and Marwan and his son fled, and Ali went unto the wife of Othman and said to her, "who slew Othman? "She

A.H.35. A.D.655-6 replied, "I know not : two men went in to him, whom I do not recognize and with them was Muhammad the son of Abu Bakr," and she informed Ali and the people of what Muhmmad had done. And Ali sent for Muhammad and asked him concerning what the wife of Othman had mentioned, and Muhammad said "she hath not spoken falsely-verily, by Allah, I went in to him, and I purposed to slay him, but he bid me remember my father, and I stood off from him turning in repentance to God,-by Allah, I did not slay him nor hold him ;" and the wife of Othman said, "he hath spoken truly, but he brought the two within."

Ibn Asakir records on the authority of Kananah the freedom of Safinah, and others, that it was one of the Egyptians, a man with blue eyes and ruddy complexion that slew Othman-he was called Himar. Ahmad records on the authority of al Mughirah b. Shuubah, that he went into Othman, when he was besieged and said, "thou art verily the Imam of the people, and yet there hath befallen thee what thou seest; and verily now I place before thee three courses; choose one of them. Either go forth and fight them, for surely with thee are nubers and force, and thou are in the right and they are in the wrong-or cut open for thyself a door, other than the door over which they stand, and mount thy camel and get thee to Mecca, for they will not hold it lawful *to slay* thee while thou art there,-or betake thee to Syria, for verily the people of Syria, among them is Muawiyah." But Othman said, "if I go forth and fight, I cannot be the first of those who have succeeded the Apostle of God, to shed blood-and if I set out for Mecca, then have I heard the Apostle of God say, "A man of the Kuraysh shall be buried in Mecca upon whom shall be half the chastisement of the world"-and I shall not be he-and if I betake me to Syria, then I cannot forsake the city of my Flight, and the neighbourhood of the Apostle of God."

Ibn Asakir records on the authority of Abu Thaur al Fahami that he narrates, "I went in to Othman while he was besieged and be said, "I have laid up with my Lord ten things-verily I was one of four in Islam-and the Apostle of God gave me his daughter in marriage-afterwards she died and he gave me in marriage his other daughter-and I never courted[1] nor sought *her,* nor have I applied my right hand to an unworthy use, since I made a covenant of allegiance with it, with the Apostle of God,-and never has a Friday passed over me since I became a Muslim, but I freed a slave, except when I had nothing in my possession, when I would free one afterwards,-and I have never committed fornication either in the time of Ignorance or Islam-and never have I stolen either in the time of Ignorance or Islam-and verily I collected the Qurãn in the time of the Apostle of God." A.H.35. A.D.655-6

The assassination of Othman took place in the midst of the three days next after the day of sacrifice,[2] in the year 35. It is also said that he was slain on Friday the 18th of Dul Hijjah (17th June, 656) and was buried on Friday night between sunset and night-fall in Hash Kaukab[3] in the Cemetery, and he was the first buried therein.

Others say that he was slain on Wednesday, and some, one Monday the 24th of Dul Hijjah, and on the day he was slain, he was eight-two years old. It is also said that he was eighty-one,-and eighty-four-andeighty-six-and eighty-eight or nine-and ninety. Katadah says that az Zubayr read prayers over him and buried him, Othman having charged him to do that.

Ibn Adi and Ibn Asakir record from a tradition of Anas transmitted uninterruptedly from the Prophet, "verily the Lord hath a sword sheathed in a scabbard as long as Othman liveth, and when Othman shall be slain, that sword shall be drawn, and it shall not be sheathed until the day of recurrection." Amir b. Kaid is the sole authority for this, and he is the author of traditions of

---

1 It may also mean-"I never enriched myself-nor desired *eught.*

2 I. e. the 11th, 12th and 13th of Dul Hijjah-these days were so called (ايام التشريق) because the flesh of the victims was therein cut into thin stripes and dried in the sun. Lane.

3 A piece of ground bought by Othman and attached to the cemetery at Medina, Yakut.

A.H.35. A.D.655-6 unacknowledged authority. Ibn Asakir records on the authority of Yazid b. Abi Habib that he said, "I have heard that the whole party that attached Othman were all seized with insanity." And from Hudayfah, that he said, "the beginning of seditions is the murder of Othman, and in the last times of sedition will be the coming of Dajjal, and by Him in whose hand is my life, not a man shall die having in his heart a grain's weight of the desire of Othman's murder, but he would follow Dajjal, did he attain unto his time, and if he hath not attained unto his time, he will believe in him in his grave." And from Ibn Abbas, that he said, "if the people had not sought the blood-wit of Othman, they would have been stoned from Heavan." And from al Hasan, that he said, "Othman was slain and Ali was absent on an estate belonging to him, and when he heard it, he exclaimed, "O God ! Verily I have not approved, nor abetted it."

Al Hakim has recorded and verified on the authority of Kays-b. Abbad that he narrates, "I heard Ali on the day of the Camel say, 'O God, I am guiltless before thee of the blood of Othman, and verily my mind wandered on the day of the murder of Othman, and my spirit revolted, and they came to me to swear allegiance and I exclaimed, 'verily I am ashamed to make a covenant with a people that have slain Othman, and verily I am ashamed before God that allegiance should be sworn to me while Othman is yet unburied.' Then they departed and when the people returned, they questioned me concerning the covenant of allegiance ; I replied, 'O God, I am in fear for that which hath been done against Othman.' Then they came to a determination and swore allegiance and exclaimed, 'O prince of the Faithful ;' and it was as if my heart was rent and I said, 'O God, smite me on account of Othman until thou art content.'"[1]

Ibn Asakir records on the authority of Abu Khaldah al Hanafi that he narrates, "I heard Ali say, 'verily the Banu Umayyah think

1 These reiterated asseveration of his innocence have the air of conscious guilt. Gibbon gives it as doubtful whether he was sincere in his opposition to the rebels, and adds, that it is certain that he enjoyed the benefit of their crime.

that I put Othman to death, but no !- by that God besides whom there is no other God, I did not slay nor abet, nay, verily I forbade it but they disobeyed me.' And from Samurah, that he said, 'verily Islam was in a strong fortress, and verily they have made in Islam a breach by their slaying of Othman, which will not be closed till the day of resurrection, and verily the Caliphate was with the people of Medina, but they have cast it forth and it shall not return to them.' And from Muhammad-b. Sirin, that he said, 'the piebald horses[1] were never missing in battles, and among the troops until Othman was slain, and never were there variations in the appearance of the new moons until Othman was slain, and the redness in the horizon of the sky was never seen until al Husayn was murderd." A.H.35. A.D.655-6

Abdur Razzak records in his Musannaf on the authority of Hamid b. Hilal, that Abdullah b. Salam went to the besiegers of Othman, saying, "slay him not, for by Allah, not a man among ye shall slay him but he will meet the Lord mutilated, without a hand. And verily, the sword of God hath continued sheathed, but surely by Allah, if ye slay him, the Lord will indeed draw it, and will never sheathe it from ye-never was a Prophet slain, but there were slain on account of him, seventy thousand, and never a Caliph, but there were slain on account of him, seventy thousand, and never a Caliph, but there were slain by reason of him five and thirty thousand before *the people* were again united." And Ibn Asakir from Abdur Rahman b. Mahdi, that Othman had two merits which belonged not to Abu Bakr nor to Omar *viz.,* his self-collectedness untill he was slain, and his uniting the people upon *one text* of the Qurãn. And al Hakim from as Shaabi that he says, "I have not heard among the elegies on Othman, any more beautiful than the words of Kaab b. Malik-

'He restrained his hands, and made fast his gate :
And he knew that the Lord was not heedless.

---

1 Upon which, it is feigned that the angels were mounted who fought in the Muslim ranks against the infidel.

A.H.35.
A.D.655-6

And he spake unto the people of the house, "slay ye them not
The Lord forgiveth every man that doth not contend."
Thou hast seen how the Lord hath poured out upon them
Enmity and hatred, following harmony with one another.
And thou hast seen how goodness turned fleeing afterwards
From the people, with the flight of hastening winds."

Ibn Saad records on the authority of Musa b. Talhah, that he said, "I saw Othman go forth on a Friday wearing two yellow coloured garments, and take his station at the pulpit, and the Muaddin was calling to prayers, while he was conversing, asking the people concerning their current prices and their news, and the sick among them." And from Abdullah ar Rumi, that Othman performed his ablutions at night himself, and it was said to him, "if thou didst order some of thy servants, they would suffice for thee." He replied, "no, the night is for them that they may repose therein."

Ibn Asakir records on the authority of Amr the son of Othman b. Affan, that the impression on the signet ring of Othman was, "I believe in Him who hath created and completely formed *his creatures,"* (Qur. LXXXVII). And Abu Nuaym in the "Dalail," from Ibn Omar, that Jahjah al Ghifari stood up before Othman while he was preaching, and seized his staff out of his hand, broke it across his knee, but the year did not pass by, before the Lord sent upon his foot a gangrene, of which he died.

On the things in which he was foremost.

Al Askari says in the Awail that he was the first who bestowed gifts of revenue lands, and the first who enclosed pasturage, and the first who lowered his voice in pronouncing the Takbir, and the first who embellished the mosque *at Medina,* and the first who commanded the first call to prayers on the Fridays, and the first who gave stipends to the callers to prayer. He was the first who because impeded in his speech in preaching, whereupon he exclaimed, "O ye people, the first mounting is a hard task, but after to-day, there are yet days and if I live the discourse will come to ye after its wont-for we were never preachers, but the Lord will teach us." (Ibn Saad). He was the first who made the discourse precede prayers on the Eed, and the first who committed to the discretion to the people the payment of their poor-rates, and the first who governed the Caliphate during the lifetime of his mother, and the first who established a constabulary, and the first who set apart an enclosure in the mosque, in fear lest there should befall him what befell Omar. Thus much is mentioned by al Askari. He adds, that the first occasion in which dissension fell among the people, and some accused others of error, was in his time, concerning the things for which they censured him-before that they differed in matters of jurisprudence but did not accuse each other of error. I note that there remain of the things in which he was foremost, *the following, viz.,* that he was the first of this people who emigrated with his family for the sake of God, as hath gone before, and the first who united the people upon one text in the reading *of the Qurãn*. Ibn Asakir records from Hakim b. Abbad b. Hanif that the first laxity that shewed itself in Medina when the world waxed prosperous and the fatness of men reached it height, was the flying of pigeons[1] and the shooting with[2] cross-bows. Othman appointed over this a man of the Banu Layth in the eighth year of his Caliphate, and he cut *the wings of the pigeons* and broke he bows.

A H.35.
A.D.655-6

Among the distinguished people who died during Othman's time, were, Surakah b. Malik b. Jushum-Jabbar b. Sakhr-Hatib b. Abi Baltaah-Iyadh b. Zuhayr.-Abu Usayd as Saidi-Aus bus Samit-Harith b. Naufal-Abdullah-b. Hudafah-Zayd b. Kharijah, he who spake after death-Labid the poet-al-Musayyab, the father of Sai'd-Muad b Amr bil Jamuh-Mabid b-ul Abbad-Muaykab b. Abi Fatimah ad Dausi- Abu Lababah b. Abdil Mundir, Nuaym b-ul Masaud al Ashjal and others of the Companions; and besides the Companions, Hutayah the poet, and Abu Duayb the poet, of the tribe of Hudayl.

---

1 For wagers.

2 For على in the printed edition the MS. has & both forms are allowable.

A.H.35.
A.D.655-6

ALI-B-ABI TALIB

Ali was the son of Abu Talib. The name of Abu Talib was Abd Manaf, the son of Abdul Muttalib, whose name was Shyabah, the son of Hashim. Hashim's name was Amr, son of Abd Manaf, and the latter's name al Mughirah, the son of Kusayy, whose name was Zyd b. Kilab b. Murrah-b. Kaab-b. Luayy b. Ghalib b. Fikr b. Malik b. Nadr b. Kananah. *He was called* Abul Hasan, and Abu Turah, which names the Prophet gave him as surnames. His mother was Fatimah, the daughter of Asad, the son of Hashim, and she was the first Hashimite woman giving birth to a Hashimi, that had been converted to Islam and taken part in the Flight. Ali was one of the ten to whom *the attainment of* Paradise was testified, and the brother of the Apostle of God in the Fraternal Union[1] and his son-in-law through Fatimah, the queen of womankind. He was also one of the earliest converts to Islam and one of the most learned doctors of divinity and renowned heroes and famous ascetics and most celebrated preachers. He was one of those who collected the Qurãn and read it under the tuition of the Apostle of God, and Abul Aswad ad Duali,[2] Abu Abdur Rahman as Sulami,[3] and Abdur Rahman b. Abi Laylah[4] read under his tuition.

He was the first Caliph of the Banu Hashim and the father of the two grandsons *of Muhammad.* He embrace Islam early : Indeed Ibn Abbas and Anas and Zayd b. Arkan and Salman al Farisi, and others have said that he was the first who embraced Islam, and some say that there is a consensus for this.

Abu Yala records on the authority of Ali that he said, "the

---

1 Muhammad untied the Fugitives and Auxiliaries in the brotherhood of Islam, each man taking a brother. Muhammad's choice was Ali. Hamzah took Zayd b. Harith-and Jaafar Ali's brother, took Muad b. Jabal. For the rest consult Ibn Hisham.

2 Abul Aswad Dhalim b. Amr b. Sufyan Kadhi of Basrah of which town he was a native. He was one of the Tabiis and the first who gave lectures on grammar. An Nawawi.

3 See note 1 p. 199.

4 See note 3 p. 56.

Apostle of God was sent *on his Prophetic mission on* Monday and I became a Muslim on the Tuesday." His age when he was converted was ten years and some say nine, and some eight, and others, under that." Al Hasan b. Zayd bil Hasan says, that he never worshipped idols from his infancy. (Ibn Saad.) When the Prophet fled to Medina, he commanded him to remain behind at Mecca for some days, in order to discharge for him *certain* trusts and charges and bequests which were incumbent on the Prophet, and then join him with his family, and he did so and was present with the Apostle of God at Badr and Ohud and al the expeditions except Tabuk, for verily the Prophet had appointed him his Vicegerent at Medina. Throughout all these operations, his services were conspicuous, and the Prophet gave him the standard *to carry* on many battle-fields. Sai'd b-ul Musayyab says that Ali received on the day of Ohud sixteen wounds. It is established in the Sahihayn that the Prophet gave him the standard on the day of Khaybar and told him that victory would be at his hands. The accounts of his bravery, and his services in the wars are well-known.

A.H.35.
A.D.655-6

"Ali was advanced in years, shout, bold, very hairy, of middle stature, inclining to shortness, full-bellied, with a very large beard white as cotton which filled the space between the shoulders, and very tawny-complexioned.

Jabir-b. Abdullah says that Ali on the day of Khaybar, carried the gate upon his back, so that the Muslims got upon it and took *the fort,* and indeed they dragged the gate afterwards, but it took forty men to lift it. (Ibn Asakir). Ibn Ishak has recorded in the Maghazi and Ibn Asakir, on the authority of Abu Rafi',[1] that he said, "Ali seized a gate near the fort, the fort of Khaybar, and used it as a buckler to guard himself, and it continued in his hand while he ws flighting, until the Lord gave us the victory. Then he cast it from him, and verily I know that we eight men tried to turn over the same gate, and we were not able to turn it over." Al Bukhari narrates in the Adab on the authority of Sahl b. Saa'd, that the

1 "Abu Rafe" says Gibbon with characteristic humour in relating this story, "was an eye-witness, but who shall be witness for Abu Rafe ?"

A.H.35. A.D.655-6 dearest of his own names to Ali was Abu Turab, and that he was well pleased to be called by it. It was the Prophet alone who named him Abu Turab, and that because, one day being angry with Fatimah, he went forth and lay down by the wall in the mosque, and the Prophet came up, and verily Ali's back was covered with dust. The Prophet therefore began to brush the dust from his back and to say, "sit up, O father of dust." (*Abu Turab.*) Five hundred and eighty-six traditions area scribed to him, on the direct authority of the Apostle of God, and traditions have been related on his authority by his three sons, al Hasan, al Husayn, and Muhammad b-ul Hanafiyah;-by Ibn Masaud and Ibn Omar,-Ibn Abbas-Ibn uz Zubayr-Abu Musa-Abu Sai'd-Zayd b. Arkam-Jabir b. Abdullah, Abu Imamah-Abu Hurayrah and others of the Companions and Tabi'is, upon all of whom be the approbation of God.

On the traditions transmitted regarding his merit.

The Imam Ahmad b. Hanbal says, "there hath not come down to us regarding the merits of any one of the Companions of the Apostle of God, what hath been transmitted concerning Ali." (Al Hakim). The two Shaykhs record on the authority of Saad b. Abi Wakkas, that the Apostle of God left Ali b. Abi Talib behind as his Vicegerent during the expedition of Tabuk, and Ali said, "O Apostle of God, dost thou leave me behind among the women and children?" He replied, "art thou not content to bc to me in the relation of Aaron to Moses, save that there shall be no Prophet after me?" And from Sahl b. Saad that the Apostle of God said on the day of Khaybar, "I will surely give the standard tomorrow to a man, at whose hands the Lord will give victory, *one* who loveth God and His Prophet and whom God and His Prophet love," and the people passed the night in perplexity as to the one among them to whom it would be given. And when they entered upon the dawn, they went early to the Apostle of God, *each of* all of them hoping that it would be given to him, but he said, "where is Ali the son of Abu Talib ?" They said to him, but he said, "where is Ali the son of Abu Talib?"

They said to him, "he complaineth of pain in his eyes." He replied "then send for him ;" and they brought him and the Apostle of God spat upon his eyes and prayed for him, and he was healed so that it was as if he had no pain, and he gave him the standard. Muslim records on the authority of Saad b. Abi Wakkas, that when this verse, "Let us all together, our sons and your sons," (Qur. III), was revealed, the Apostle, of God summoned Ali and Fatimah, and al Hasan and al Husayn, said, "O God, these are my family." And al Tirmidi, from the Prophet, that he said, "he whose friend I have been, Ali is *also* his friend ;" and in some *of the readings* there is this addition, "O God, befriend him who is a friend to Ali, and, be an enemy to him who is an enemy to Ali ;" and in a tradition of Ahmad from Abu Tufayl[1] *the latter* says, "Ali assembled the people in the enclosure *before the mosque,* and said, 'I ask in the name of God, of every Muslim that heard the Apostle of God speak on the day of Ghadir Khumm, [2] what he said, when he arose,' Then there stood up before him thirty of the people, and they bare witness that the Apostle of God said, 'he whose friend I have been, Ali is also his friend,-O God, befriend whomsoever is a friend to him, and be an enemy to him who is his enemy.'" And at Tirnidi and al Hakim, verified, on the authority of Buraydah, that the Apostle of God said, "verily the Lord enjoined upon me the love of four men, and declared unto me that He loved them." They said to him, "O Apostle of God, name them to us." He replied, 'Ali is among them ;" (this he said three times), "and Abu Darr and Mikdad and Salman." And at Tirmdi, an Nasai, and Ibn Majah from Hubshi b. Junadah, [3] that the Apostle of God said, "Ali is a part of me and I of Ali." And at

A.H.35.
A.D.655-6

---

1 Abu Tufayl Aamir b. Wathilah b. Abdillah one of the Companions. According to Muslim he died A.H. 109, the last of the Companions. Ibn Hajr.

2 A pool near Juhfah between Mecca and Medina ; it received the name of Khumm from a dyer so called, according to Zamakshari. The Shiias assert that it was here that Muhammad preached and constituted Ali his successor by his words that follow. Mawla may signify master as well as friend, and is their interpretation of the tradition.

3 Hubshi b. Junadah b. Nasr b. Imamah as Saluli, one of the Companions. He accompanied the Pilgrimage of Farewell and then settled at Kufah. According to al Askari he took part in some of Ali's battles. Ibn Hajr.

A.H.35. A.D.655-6 Tirmidi from Ibn Omar, that the Apostle of God united his Companions in fraternal union, and Ali approached with his eyes filled with tears, and said, "O Apostle of God, thou hast united in brotherhood thy Companions, but hast not made a brotherhood between me and between any one." And the Apostle of God replied, "thou art my brother in this world and the next."

Muslim records on the authority of Ali that he said, "by Him who hath cleft the seed and created the soul, verily the Illiterate Prophet promised me, that none but a true believer should love me, and none but a hypocrite hate me." And at Tirmidi from Abu Sai'd al Khudri that he said, "we used to distinguish the hypocrites by their hatred to Ali." And at Tirmidi and al Hakim from Ali, that the Apostle of God said, "I am the city of wisdom and Ali is its gate." This tradition is reasonably good, but not perfect, as al Hakim asserts, nor fabricated as a number of others, among them Ibn Jauzi and an Nawawi maintain : indeed, I have explained its position in the appendices to the Fabricated Traditions.

Al Hakim records and verifies on the authority of Ali, that he said, "the Apostle of God sent me to Yaman,[1] and I said, 'O Apostle of God, dost thou send me-and I a youth-to judge between them, while I know not the office of a judge ?" and he struck my breast with his hand and said, 'O God, direct him aright and confirm his tongue,' and by Him who hath cleft the seed, I never hesitated in my judgment between two parties." And Ibn Saad from Ali, that they said, to him, "How is it that thou hast the most traditions of any of the Companions of the Apostle of God?" He replied, "verily whenever I asked of him he informed me, and when I was silent he began *a discourse* with me." And from Abu Hurayrah, that Omar b- ul Khattab said, "Ali is the best of us in judicial decision." And from Ibn Masaud, that he said, "we used to declare that the

---

1 In A.H. 10, Muhammad sent Ali to Yaman to summon the people to Islam. He had already dispatched Khalid b-ul Walid, whose efforts had been unsuccessful. On Ali's arrival, he read Muhammad's letter to the people of Yaman, and the whole tribe of Hamdan were converted in a single day. The remainder shortly afterward, followed their example. Ibnul Athir. Kamil Vol. II.

best judicial authority among the people of Medina, was Ali." And from Ibn Abbas, "whenever a trustworthy person tells me a judgement[1] of Ali's, I do not deviate from it." And from Sai'd b-ul Musayyab, that Omar b-ul Khattab used to beg God to preserve him from a perplexing case which the father of al Hasan was not *present to decide* ; and, that Omar said, "none of the Companions used to say 'ask ye of me,' except Ali."

A.H.35.
A.D.655-6

Ibn Asakir records on the authority of Ibn Masa'ud that the most learned of the people of Medina in the law of inheritance and in judicial decisions was Ali. And from Ayesha, that when Ali was mentioned to her, she said, "verily he is the most learned in the Sunnah that is left." Masruk[2] says that the wisdom of the Companions culminated in Omar, Ali, Ibn Masaud and Abdullah.

Abdullah b. Ayyash b. Abi Rabiih says that Ali had an exceedingly biting tooth for knowledge, and he had pre-eminence by reason of his family connections, and priority in Islam, and his being the son-in-law of the Apostle of God, and his knowledge of the Sunnah, and intrepidity in war and liberality with his wealth. At Tabarani records in the Ausat on a weak ascription from Jabir b. Abdillah, that the Apostle of God said, "the people are of various stocks but I and Ali are of one stock." And at Tabarani and Ibn Abi Hatim from Ibn Abbas that he said, "the Lord never revealed the words[3] 'O true believers' but that Ali was *understood to be,* the lord and chief of them and verily the Lord hath reproved the Companions of the Prophet in various places, but hath never mentioned Ali save with approval." And Ibn Asakir from Ibn Abbas that there hath not been revealed in the Book of God regarding any one what hath been revealed concerning Ali, and that three hundred verses have been revealed concerning Ali.

Al Bazzar records on the authority of Saad, that the Apostle of

---

1 The MS. has بفتيا instend of الفتيا of the printed edition.

2 Abu Ayesha Masruk b-ul Ajdaa of Kufah one of the Tabiis. He is regarded as an authentic relator of traditions and was devoted to the acquisition of knowledge, died A.H. 62-3. An Nawawi.

3 Qur. XXXIII *passim.*

A.H.35. A.D.655-6 God said to Ali, "it is not lawful for any one to be in the mosque, while under the obligation of performing a total ablution except for me and for thee." And at Tabarani records and al Hakim likewise, verifying on the authority of Umm Salmah that she said, "when the Apostle of God was angered, none dared speak to him but Ali." And from Ibn Masaud that the Prophet said, "to look upon Ali is devotion." And at Tabarani in the Ausat from Ibn Abbas that he said, "Ali possessed eighteen eminent qualities which belonged to no other of this people." And Abu Yala from Abu Hurayrah that Omar b-ul Khattab said, "verily Ali hath been endowed, with three qualitites, of which had I but one, it would be more precious to me than were I given high bred camels." It was asked of him what they were; he replied, "his marriage with Fatimah, daughter *of the Prophet,* his remaining in the mosque while that is permitted to him which is not lawful for me, and *his carrying* the standard on the day of Khaydar." And Ahmad and Abu Yala according to a sound ascription from Ali that he said, "I have never had a disorder of the eyes, nor an ache of the head, since the Apostle of God, drew his hand over my face, and spat upon my eyes on the day of Khaybar when he gave me the standard." And Abu Yala and al Bazzar from Saad b. Abi Wakkas, that the Apostle of God said, "who grieveth Ali, grieveth me." And at Tabarani, according to a sound ascription from Umm Salmah, that the Apostle of God said, "he who hath loved Ali, verily he hath loved me, and who hath hated Ali, verily he hath hated me, and who hath hated me, verily he hath hated the Lord."

Ahmad records and al Hakim verifying it on the authority of Umm Salmah that she narrates, "I heard the Apostle of God say, 'he who hath reviled Ali, Verily he hath reviled me.'" And from Abu Sai'd al Khudri, that the Apostle of God said to Ali, "verily thou wilt do battle for the Qurãn, as thou hast done battle for its revelation." Al Bazzar, Abu Yala and al Hakim record from Ali, that he said, "the Apostle of God summoned me and said, 'verily there is in thee a similitude to Jesus-the Jews hated Him to that degree that they slandered His mother, and the Nazaranes so loved Him, that they gave Him a dignity that He hath not,-now verily, by reason of me two classes of men shall perish-the enthusiastic partizen that speaketh in extravagant praise of what is not in me, and the enemy whose hatred of me bringeth him to slander me.'" A.H.36. A.D.656-7

At Tabarani records in the Ausat and Saghir[1] from Umm Salmah that she narrates, "I heard the Apostle of God say, 'Ali is with the Qurãn and the Qurãn with Ali-they shall not be divided until they arrive at the fountain *of Kauthar in Paradise.*'" And Ahmad and al Hakim from Ammar b. Yasir, according to a sound ascription that the Prophet said to Ali-"the most miserable of mankind are two men-the fair man of the tribe of Thamud[2] who hamstrung the camel, and he who shall smite thee, O Ali, upon this (meaning the top of his head) until this, (meaning his beard) shall be moistened with its *blood.*" And al Hakim records, verifying it on the authority of Abu Sai'd al Khudri, that he said, 'the people complained of Ali, and the Apostle of God arose among us preaching and exclaimed, 'complain not of Ali, for by Allah, verily he is somewhat rough in respect of that which is due to God, and for the sake of God."

Ibn Saad says that allegiance was sworn to Ali as Caliph, the day after the murder of Othman, at Medina, and all those of the Companions who were there acknowledge him, and he adds that Talah and az Zubayr swore allegiance unwillingly, and not of free accord. They subsequently departed for Mecca where Ayesha was, and they took her and went forth with her to Basrah seeking *vengeance* for the blood for Othman. This reaching Ali, he set out for Iraq, and met at Basrah, Talhah, az Zubayr, and Ayesha and those that were with them. This was the battle of the camel which took place in Jumadal Akhirah in the yer 36 A.H. In it were slain Talhah and az Zubayr and others, and the slain amounted to thirteen thousand, and Ali remained at Basrah fifteen nights and then forth for Kufah. After this Muawiyah b. Abi Sufiyan and those that were with him in Syria, rose against him, and the news reached Ali and he marched forth and they met at Siffin in Safar of the year 37.

---

1 See Sale, notes f.g.h. page 124. The man's name Was Kedar.

2 See Note 2 p. 16.

A.H.36. A.D.656-7 The engagement lasted for days, and the men of Syria lifted up the Qurãn *on the points of their lances* demanding *their right* therein contained, a stratagem of Amr b-ul Aas. The people were thus loth to fight and clamoured together for a reconciliation, and they appointed two arbitrators. Ali appointed Abu Musa al Ashari, and Muawiyah, Amr b-ul Aas, and they wrote between them a document to the effect that they should meet at the beginning of the year al Adruh[1] and consider concerning the government of the nation. The people then separated and Muawiyah returned to Syria and Ali Kufah. Then there arose against him schismatics from among his companions and those that were with him, and they said, "judgment belongeth only to God," and they encamped at Harura Ali sent to them Ibn Abbas, and he contended with them and convinced them by argument, and a large body of them returned, but some remained firm and marched to an Nahrawan and obstructed the road. Ali then went out against them and overthrew them at an Nahrawan, and among them was slain Du at Thudayyah, [2] and that was in the year 35. And the people assembled at Adrub in Shaaban of that year, and Saad b. Abi Wakkas and Ibn Omar, and others of the Companions were present. Amr becunningly gave precedence of himself[3] to Abu Musa who spoke and deposed Ali ; then Amr spoke and confirmed Muawiyah and swore allegiance to him. The people separated upon this, and Ali thus became opposed to his companions, so that he bit his finger *with rage* and

1 In the district El-Belka in Syria.

2 This person, whose real name is not given by Ibn Hajr, lived in the time of Muhammad, and was noted for his exceeding devotion and piety though not a Muslim, Muhammad said that he was disbolically possessed, and Abu Bakr and Omar went into his house to kill him, but finding him in prayer, withdrew. He was found among the slain at Nahrawan, and he is said to have resembled a Nubian in appearance with one breast like that of a woman (hence his name) upon which were small hairs like that upon the tail of the Jerboa. Ibn Hajr.

3 When the two Arbitrators met, they agreed that each should deposed his master, and then proceed to adjudicate their respective claims. Amr pleading the seniority and age of Abu Musa, courteously insisted on his initiating the deposition, which having been done, Amr declared that since one of the claimants had renounced his pretensions, the best course to pursue was to confirm the other which was accordingly done.

said, "I have been rebelled against and Muawiyah is submitted to." Then there gathered together three men of the schismates, Abdur Rahman b. Muljam al Muradi, and al Burk b. Abdillah at Tamimi, and Amr B. Bukayr at Tamimi, and they met at Mecca, and entered into a covenant and bound themselves by a league that they would certainly slay those three, Ali b. Abi Talib, Muawiyah b. Abi Sufiyan, and Amrul Aas, and free the people from them ; and Ibn Muljam said, "I will take Ali for ye," and al Burk said, "I will take Muawiyah for ye," and Amr b. Bukayr said, "I will suffice for ye for Amr b-ul Aas," and they pledged themselves that it should be on the same night, the night of the 11th or the 17th of Ramadhan. Then they went each of them to the city where his man was, and Ibn Muljam arrived at Kufah, and met his companions of the schismatics, but he concealed from them what they intended *to do* on the night of Friday the 17th of Ramadahan of the year 40. And Ali awoke in the morning and said to his son al Hasan, "I saw in the night the Apostle of God, and I said, 'O Apostle of God, what have I *not* met at the hands of thy people, of oppression and contention ?' and he said to me, 'call the curse of God upon them.' And I said, 'O God, give in exchange between me and them their good to me, and take in exchange between them and me my evil, for them.' Upon this Ibnul Nabbah the Muaddin entered, and exclaimed, 'to prayers,' and Ali went forth from the door crying out, 'O people-to prayers-to prayers' and Ibn Muljam came before him, and smote him with a sword, and it struck the top of his forehead and reached his brain. Then the people rushed upon him from every side, and seized and bound him. And Ali lingered Friday and Saturday, and died on Saturday night[1] (21st January 661) and al Hasan, al Husayn and Abdullah b. Jaafar bathed him, and al Hasan read prayers over him, and he was buried in the night in the place at Kufah. The limbs of Ibn Muljam were cut off, and he was put into an osier basket and burnt in the fire." This is the whole narrative of Ibn Saad, and verily he has done well in his account of this event, and

A.H.38.
A.D.657-8

1 Well notices that though Friday the 17th of Ramadhan A.H. 40 is generally stated to be the day on which Ali was wounded, the 17th of the month actually fell on a Sunday. He thinks it probable that the day of his death was in later times confounded with that on which he was stabbed.

A.H.40. has not amplified his narrative as others have done, for it is more
A.D.661 suitable for this occasion. Muhammad has said, "when my Companions are mentioned, refrain from speaking"-and he adds, "sufficient for my Companions, *is the mention of their* death."[1]

In the Mustadrak, it is recorded on the authority of as Suddi,[2] that Abdur Rahman b. Muljam al Muradi loved a woman of the Schismatics called Katam, and he married her and assigned for her dowry three thousand dirhams and the slaying of Ali. With reference to this al Farazdak[3] has said.

"I have not seen a dowry sent by a generous man
Like unto the dowry of Katam, manifest-not obscure.
Three thousand dirhams, and a slave and a maid
And the smiting of Ali with a cleaving sword.
For there is no dowry be it ever so costly, constlier than Ali:
And no criminal violence but is less than the violence of Ibn Muljam."[4]

Abu Bakr b. Ayyash says, that the grave of Ali was kept concealed in order that the schismatics might not dig it up, and Sharik states that his son al Hasan carried him to Medina. Al

---

1 Without details regarding the manner of it. Such is the only sense I can extract from the passage. The MS. has اصحاب الفيل which is to me unintelligible.

2 The Professor Abu Muhammad Hibatullah b. Sahl b. Omar, al Bastami, generally known as Suddi. He explained the Muwatta of Malik to al Muwayyad at Tusi. Ibn Khall.

3 Abu Firas Hammam b. Ghalib b. Sasaa, a celebrated poet of the tribe of Tamim. The ancedotes told of him are very numerous ; the reader should consult Ibn Khall who has a long article on his wit and adventures, the letter not very reputable. He died at Basrah A.H. 110 (728-9) at the age of nearly a hundred. His surname Farazdak (lump of dough) was given him on account of his ugly face.

4 I do not follow M. Barbier de Reynard in his rendering of this passage : "Une ame, si energique quell soit vaut-elle I' ame d' Ibn Moldjem." Les Prairies d 'Or. Tom. IV. p. 428.

Mubarrad[1] states on the authority of Muhammad b. Habib, that the first who was transferred from one grave to another was Ali. A.H.40. A.D.661

Ibn Asakir records on the authority of Said b. Abdil Aziz, that when Ali was slain, they took him to bury him by the apostle of God, and while they were on their road one night, lo ! the camel upon which he was *borne,* fled away and it was not known whither it went, nor could they overtake it, and for this reason the people of Iraq say that he is in the clouds. Others assert that the camel came into the land of Tayy, and they took *the body* and buried it. Ali when he was slain was sixty-three years of age, and some say sixty-four, and sixty-five and fifty-seven, an fifty-eight. He had nineteen concubines.

On some of the accounts of Ali, his judicial decisions and sayings.

Ibn Asakir records on the authority of al Hasan that he said, that when Ali entered Basrah there stood up before him Ibnul Kawwa, and Kays b. Abbad, and said, "wilt thou not inform us concerning this course of thine on which thou goest, assuming authority over the people, involving them in confusion ? was it a charge of th apostle of God, that he laid upon thee ? tell us-for thou art firm and undeviating with regard to what thou hast heard." And he said, "as to there being on me a charge from the Apostle of God,

---

1 Abul Abbas Muhammad b. Yazid known as al Mubarrad, a distinguished grammarian. He resided at Baghdad and composed numerous works on literary subjects such as al Kamil, ar Roudhah and al Muktadhib. He was a contemporary of Thaalab-the author of the Fasih, and with them terminated the series of the great philologers. He was born A.H. 210 (826) and died at Baghdad A.H. 286 (899). His surname al Mubarrad was given to him from his having been concealed in the wicker case of a large water jar ; his friend who had concealed him there to avoid an importunate visitor in search of him, called out as soon as the letter had gone, al Mubarrad, al Mubarrad ! (*Who wants cool water*). Ibn Khall.

A.H.40. concerning that,-no-by Allah-surely if I was the first to maintain
A.D.661 that he spoke truth, I will not be the first to put a lie upon him, and if I had received from the Prophet a charge regarding that, I would not have suffered a brother[1] of the children of Taym the son of Murrah, nor Omar the son of al Khattab, to stand upon his pulpit, and I would surely have fought them with my own hand, even thoug I had not got but this my garment ; but the apostle of God was not slain murderously, nor did he die suddenly, but he lingered some days and nights in his illness, the Muaddin coming to him and summoning him to prayers. And he commanded Abu Bakr to pray before the people, though he knew my high consideration, and verily a woman among his wives desired to turn him from Abu Bakr, but he refused and was angered and said, "ye are the mistresses of Joseph-direct Abu Bakr to pray before the people."

And when the Lord took his Prophet, we looked into our affairs, and chose for our temporal interests, him whom he had approved for our religious affairs, for prayers were the fundamental principle of Islam and Abu Bakr was the chief of the faith and the pillar of the faith. We therefore swore allegiance unto Abu Bakr, and he was worthy of it, not two of us being at variance over him, and none of us gave testimony against another, nor denied his privilege. I therefore discharged unto Abu Bakr his due, and acknowledged obedience to him and fought on his side in his armies and I ever accepted what he bestowed upon me and fought when he sent me to war and inflicted in his presence the prescribed castigation for offences with my scourge. And when he was taken away, Omar assumed the Caliphate and governed it according to the institute of his Companion and what he knew of his polity. And we swore allegiance unto Omar, not two of us being at variance over him, and none of us gave testimony against another, nor denied his privilege I therefore discharged unto Omar his due and acknowledged obedience to him and fought on his side in his armies, and I ever accepted what he bestowed upon me, and fought when he sent me to war, and inflicted in his presence the prescribed

1 Abu Bakr.

castigation for offences with my scourge. And when he was taken away, I bethought me of my connections, and my priority in Islam, and my precedence and my merit, and I considered that Omar would not hold any one equal to me, but he feared that the Caliph after him would not commit a fault but it would attach to him in his grave, therefore the withdrew from it, himself and his son, and if there had been any partiality on his part he would surely have chosen his son for it, but he threw the responsibility of it from himself on to a party of the Kuraysh, six *in number,* I being one of them. And when the party assembled, I thought that they would not hold any one equal to me, and Abdur Rahman b. Auf took our engagements that we should hear and obey whomsoever the Lord should palce over our affairs. Then he took Othman the son of Affan by the hand, and struck his own hand upon his hand, and I regarded my own conduct, and lo! My submission had already preceded my allegiance, and behold my engagement had been taken for another. We therefore swore allegiance unto Othman, and I discharged unto him his due, and acknowledged obedience to him ; and fought on his side in his armies and I ever accepted what he bestowed upon me and fought when he sent me to war, and inflicted in his presence, the prescribed castigation for offences with my sourga. And when he was slain, I considered my own affairs, and lo! The–two Vicegerents who had assumed the government by virtue of the command of the Apostle of God unto them to read prayers, had passed away, and this one for whom the engagement had been taken, verily, was slain, therefore the people of Mecca and Medina and the men of these two cities, [1] sowre allegiance unto me-but there hath usurped the government, one who is not like unto me, and whose kinship is not as my kinship, nor his knowledge like unto my knowledge, nor his *priority in the faith* like unto my priority, and I had more claim to it than he."

A.H.40.
A.D.661

Abu Nuaym records in the Dalail, on the authority of the father of Jaafar b. Muhammad, that two men having an altercation, were brought before 'Ali who sat himself at the foot of a wall, and a man

---

1 Basrah and Kufah.

A.H.40. A.D.661 said to him, "the wall will fall down," and Ali said, "Go to-God is a sufficient protector," and he decided between them, and arose, and then the wall fell.

It is recorded in the "Tuyuriyat" with its ascription to the same authority, that a man said to Ali, "we hear thee say in thy preaching 'O God, make me righteous with that through which thou hast made righteous the orthodox Vicegerents, the rightly guided.' Who than are they ?" And his eyes filled with tears and he said, "they are my two friends Abu Bakr and Omar, the Imams of salvation, the two elders of Islam, and the two men of the Kuraysh who are followed after the Apostle of God. He who followeth those two, is preserved, and whoso goeth after their footsteps is directed aright over the Straight Bridge *above Hell,* and he who cleaveth unto those two he is of the company of the Lord." And Abdur Razzak records on the authority of Hujr al Madari, that he narrates, "Ali said to me, 'how will it go with thee when thou art ordered to curse me?" I said, 'will that come to pass?' He said, 'yes;' I answered 'then what shall I do ? He said, 'curse me, but do not renounce me.' He adds,-'and Muhammad b. Yusuf, the brother of al Hajjaj, who was governor of Yaman orderd me to curse, Ali and I said, 'the prince hath commanded me to curse Ali, therefore curse ye him with the curse of God,' and no one comprehended it but one man."

At Tabarani records in the Ausat and Abu Nuaym in the Dalail on the authority of Zadan, that Ali was relating a tradition when a man accused him of speaking falsely, and Ali said to him, "shall I curse thee if I have lied?" and he said, "curse," and Ali cursed him, and he did not quit the place till his sight left him. And from Zirr b. Hubaysh[1] that two had five loaves, and the other three loaves, and when they had placed the meal before them, a man passed an saluted them and they said, "sit down and cat," and he sat down and eat with them, and they shared equally in their meal the eight loaves, and the man arose and threw to them eight dirhams and

1 Abu Maryam Zirr-b. Hubayah, a native of Kufah one of the Tabiis. He was born in the time of Igonrance and died A.H. 82. An Nawawi.

said, "take these in exchange for what I have eaten belonging to ye two and have received of your food." They then quarreled over it and the owner of the five loaves said, "for me are five dirhams and for thee three," and the owner of the three loaves exclaimed, "I shall not agree unless the dirhams are divided equally between us;" and they took their case before Ali the prince of the Faithful and related to him their adventure, and he said to the owner of the three, "verily thy companion hath offered to thee what he hath offered, and his loaves were more than thine, therefore be content with three." But he replied, "by Allah, I will not be satisfied with him except in my exact due." And Ali said, "in bare right thou shouldst have only one dirham and he seven dirhams." And the man said, "God God! " and Ali answered, "that is so." The other said, "inform me of the grounds of this being my bare right, that I may acqueses in it." Ali answered, "are there not in eight loaves, four and twenty thirds which ye have eaten and ye are three men? and it is not known who is the greatest eater amongst ye and who the least, you will therefore be considered in your eating as equal." He went on, "now thou hast eaten eight-thirds, and verily thou hadst but nine-thirds, and thy companins eat eight-thirds, and he owned fifteen-thirds of which he eat eight-there remain of his, therefore, seven which the owner of the dirhams eat, and he eat of what belonged to thee one out of nine. Therefore for thee is one for thy one, and for him seven." And the man exclaimed "now I am content." A.H.40. A.D.661

Ibn Abi Shaybah records in the Musannaf on the authority of Ata that a man was brought before Ali and two men testified against him that he had committed theft, whereupon Ali took up a certain case in which the people were concerned and threatened false withnesses and said, "a false witness was never brought before me but I did to him such and such a thing." Then he summoned the two witnesses but could not find them, wherefore he let the accused go.

Ibn Asakir records on the authority of an ascription to the father of Jaafar b. Muhammad that the signet ring of Ali was of stamped coin, the impression on it being "excellent is the Omnipotent God."

A.H.40. And from Amr the son of Othman b. Affan that the impression on
A.D.661 the signet ring of Ali was, "the kingdom is the Lord's." And from al Madaini,[1] that when Ali enterend Kufah, one of the wise men o the Arabs went in to him and said, "by Allah, O prince of the Faithful, verily thou hast adorned the Caliphate, but it hath not adorned thee, and thou hast exalted it, but it hath not exalted thee, and it was more in need of thee that thou of it." And from Mujammi', that Ali used to sweep out the public treasure and then pray within it, in the hope that it would be testified in his favour that he did not keep the state property within it withheld from the Muslims.

Abul Kasim al Zajjaji narrates in his Dictation, that he had been told that the father of Abul Aswad said, "I went in unto the prince of the Faithful Ali and found him looking down in deep thought and I said to him "what art thou thinking over O prince of the Faithful ?" He replied, "verily I have heard in this your city a faulty pronunciation of the vowels : I was therefore thinking of composing a work on the principles of the Arabic language." I exclaimed, "I thou doest this thou wilt give us life, and this language will be preserved amongst us." Three days afterwards I went to him, and he threw me a wirtting in which was, "In the name of God, the most Merciful the most Compassionate. Speech consists entirely of nouns, verbs and particles. A noun is that which denotes the thing named, and a verb is that which denotes the action named, and a particle is that which expresses a signification, being neither a noun nor a verb." Then he said, "examine it and add to it what may occur to thee : know, O Abul Aswad, that objects are of three kinds, expressed, understood, and what is neither expressed nor understood, and verily the learned have vied with eath other in the definition of what is neither expressed nor understood." Abul Aswad continues, "then I collected according some parts of speech and showed them to him. Among them were particles governing the

1 Abul Hasan Ali b. Muhammad a native of Madain, a client by enfranchisement (Mawla) to the family of Abd Shams b. Abd Manaf. He was born A.H. 135 (752-3) and died A.H. 225 (839-40). He wrote upwards of twenty works on Muhammad, and a number on the history of the Kuraysh, and the Umayyad and Abbaside Caliphs and other subjects. De Slane, Ibn Khall.

accusative. Oof these I mentioned "verily" and "that,"[1] and "would A.H.40.
that," and "perhaps" and "as if," but I did not include "but." He A.D.661
said to me "why hast thou omitted it ?" I replied, "I did not count it among them." He said, "yes it is among them, therefore add it to them."

Ibn Asakir records on the authority of Rabiih b. Najid that Ali said, "be among men like the bee among birds, for there is none among the birds but thinks them insignificant, but if the birds knew what of good there is in their belliers, they would not think thus of them. Mix with the people with your tongues and persons and separate yourselves from them in deeds and in your hearts, for verily to a man shall be given that which he hath earned, and he shall appear at the day of resurrection with him whom he loveth." And from Ali that he said, "give ye a more urgent heed to the acceptance *before God* of your works rather than to the workds themselves, for verily an action accompanied by the fear of God is not of little account, for how can an action accepted by God, be of light estimation ?"[2]

And from Yahya b. Juadah[3] that Ali said, "O ye bearers of the Qurãn, act ye according to it, for he is a wise man who hath understood and acted according as he hath understood, and whose knowledge hath accorded with his works, and it shall come to pass that there shall be sects carrying a knowledge that goeth not beyond their collar-bones, whose disposition is at variance with their exterior show, and whose workds are opposed to their understanding, sitting in a circle contending for superiority one with another, until a man will be wroth with his neighbour that he should sit by another than himself and leave him-such as these, their works in these their assemblies shall not ascend to God." And from Ali, "the grace of

---

1 The MS. has also لن "certainly not."

2 The text of the printed edition is here incorrect for بقبل read يقل and for متقبل read مُتقبل

3 Of the Kuraysh descended from Makhzum, one of the Tabiis. He was son of Ali's sister. An Nawawi.

A.H.40. A.D.661 God is the best guide, a good disposition the best companion, wisdom the best friends, and good breeding the best inheritance, and there is nothing more hateful than pride." And on the authority of al Harith that a man went to Ali and said, "tell me what is Fate." He replied, "it is a gloomy road-tread it not." He asked again, "tell me what is Fate." He said, "it is a deep sea-enter not upon it." Again he asked, "tell me what is Fate." He replied, "it is a mystery of God's which is hidden from thee, therefore seek not to penetrate it." He asked again, "tell me what is Fate." He exclaimed, "O questioner, hath tha Lord created thee for what he hath willed, or what thou hath willed?" He replied "indeed for what he hath willed." Ali answered, "Then he will use thee as He thinketh fit."

He also records of the sayings of Ali. [1]

"Misfortunes have their terminations. When any one is in misfortune, it must be that it will have an end : therefore it behoveth the wise man when distress cometh upon him, to submit to it until its time is accomplished, for verily in repelling it before the fulfillment of its term, there is an increase to its calamities."

It was said to Ali, "what is generosity ?" He replied, "that from which the iniative proceedeth, for what cometh after a request is liberality and munificence."

A man went to Ali and praised him and spoke extravagantly, and it happened that Ali had heard somewhat of him before that, so he said to him, "verily I am not as thou sayest, yet I am above that which is in thy heart."

"The punishment of sin is lukewarmness in devotion, and straintness of means, and the lessening of enjoyment. A lawful appetite is not *sought to be* gratified, but there cometh that which diminisheth it."

A man said to Ali, and he secretly hated him, "may the Lord

---

1 A collection of one hundred and sixty-nine moral sentences, attributed to Ali is given by Ockley. See. Hist, Sar. P. 339.

make thee firmly established." Ali replied, "upon thy heart," (on the authority of Ibn Rabiih). A.H.40. A.D.661

Abu Bakr, Omar and Othman used to versify,[1] but Ali was the best Poet of the three. (As Shaabi.)

He records likewise on the authority of Nabit al Ashjai that Ali spoke this verse.

"When hearts contain despair,
And the spacious breast is stified by what is within it,
And cares make their abode and repose,
And sorrows anchor in their habitations,
And no way is seen for the dispelling of distress,
And the stratagem of the cunning availeth not,
There shall come to thee in thy despair a helper,
Whom the Answerer of prayer who is nigh, shall bring,
For all sorrows when they have reached their term,
There is linked to them an approaching joy."

And on the authority of as Shaabi, that Ali said to a man to whom the society of another man was displeasing-

"Consort not with a foolish brother, beware of him :
For how many a fool hath corrupted the gentle when he hath fraternized with him !
A man is judged by the man with whom he consorteth ;
For there are comparisons and similitudes for one thing with another.
The measure of a sandal is made when it is matched with it,
And the evidence of *the feeling of* one heart towards another is when they meet."

1 The expression يقول الشعر 'he spoke poetry is used, for poetry was always spoken by the Arabs in classical times, and seldom written if written at all, until after the lifetime of the author. Lane, art شعر

A.H.40. A.D.661 And from al Mubarrad that upon the sword of Ali was inscribed-

"Men lust after the world and plot for it,
Yet its clearness is mingled for thee with impurities.
They do not give thee of it thy portion, according to thy wisdom, when it is distribted :
But men have their allotted shares according to their destinies,
How many there are of the wise and sagacious unprospered :
While a fool hath gained his wealth by his errors,
If it could be acquired by force and rapine,
Falcons would swoop off with the subsistence of sparrows."

And on the authority of Hamzah b. Habib az Zayyat that Ali used to speak this verse :

"Disclose not thy secret but to thyself,
For every confidant, hath a confidant ;
For verily I have seen erring men,
Who do not aspire to a high sense of honour."

He records likewise on the authority of Ukbah b. Abil Sahba, that when Ibn Muljam stabbed Ali, al Hasan who was weeping went in unto him and Ali said, "O my dear son, treasure in thy memory from me four things and yet four." He said, "what are they, father?" He replied, "wisdom is the richest tresure, and folly the greatest poverty, and the most hateful of what is odious is pride, and the noblest excellence a good disposition." Al Hasan said, "and the other four ? He replied, "beware thee of the companionship of a fool, for he will desire to profit thee and will do thee harm, and beware of the friendship of a liar, for he will bring nigh unto thee what is afar off and make distant from thee what is near at hand-and beware thee of the friendship of a miser, for he will withhold from thee what thou art most in need of-and beware thee of the friend-ship of a libertine for he will sell thee for a trifle."

And from Ali that a Jew went to him and said, "when did our

God exist?" and the face of Ali flushed with anger and he said, "creation was not and He was ; He was ; He was while yet there was no being: He existed without a cause-He was, having no beginning and no end-all limits fall short of him, for he is the end of all ends," and the Jew embraced Islam. A.H.40. A.D.661

Ad Darraj, in his well known work, records on an obscure ascription to Shurayh the Kadhi,[1] that when Ali set forth to Siffin, he lost a coat of mail belonging to him, and when the war was over, and Ali returned to Kufah the armour came into the hands of a Jew, and he said to the Jew, "the armour is my armour-I neither sold it nor gave it away." The Jew replied, "it is my armour and in my possession." Ali said, "let us go to the Kadhi," and Ali preceded him and sat by the side of Shurayh and said, "were not my opponent a Jew, I would assuredly sit on a level with him in the court, but I heard the apostle of God say, 'treat them with ignominy, for the Lord hath treated them with ignominy.' Shurayh said, 'proceed, O prince of the Faithful.' And he said, 'yes-this armour which is in the hand of this Jew, is my armour-I neither sold it nor gave it away.' Shurayh cxclaimed, 'what dost thou say, O Jew?' He replied, it is my armour and in my possession.' Then Shurayh said, 'hast thou any proof, O prince of the Faithful?' He said, "yes, Kanbar and al Hasan are witnesses that the armour is my armour." Shurayh replied, 'the evidence of a son is not admissible in favour of a father.' Ali exclaimed, 'what! The evidence of one among the people of Paradise not admissible!' I heard the apostle of God say-'al Hasan and al Husayn are the two chiefs of the youth among the dwellers in Paradise.' The Jew said, 'the prince of the Faithful caused me to appear before the Kadhi and the Kadhi gave judgment against him,-I testify that this is the Truth-I testify that there is no

1 Abu Umayyah Shurayh al Harith b. Kays of the tribe of Kinda. He was an eminent Tabii born before the promulgation of Islam and appointed Kadhi of Kufah by Omar – a post he held with scarcely any interruption for seventy five years. He was one of the four persons called the smooth-faced chiefs (as Sadat at Tuls) the others being Abdullah b-uz Zubayr, Kays b. Saad, and al Ahnaf b. Kays. He died A.H. 87, at the age of one hundred years. Ibn Khall.

A.H.40. A.D.661 God but God, and I testify that Muhammad is the apostle of God and that this armour is thy armour.'"

The discourses of Ali in exposition of the Qurãn are numerous and are fully treated in my commentary supported by their ascriptions. And verily Ibn Saad records on the authority of Ali that he said, "by Allah, a verse of the Qurãn was never revealed, but I knew regarding what it was revealed and where it was revealed and concerning whom it was revealed, for my Lord hath given unto me a wise heart and an eloquent tongue." And he and others on the authority of Abut Tufayl that Ali said, "ask ye me regarding the book of God, for verily there is not a verse but I know whether it was revealed by night or day, in the plains or on the mountains."

Ibn Abi Dauud records from Muhammad b. Sirin that he said, "when the Apostle of God deid, Ali delayed to swear allegiance to Abu Bakr, and Abu Bakr met him and said, 'art thou averse to my holding authority?' He said, 'no, but I have sworn not to put on my mantle except for prayers until I have collected the Qurãn.' And they think that he wrote it according to the order of its revelation." Muhammad b. Sirin adds, "if that book were to be met with, there would be found in it much instruction."

On some of his short sententious maxims worthy of remark.

1. Precaution consists in evil opinion (recorded by Abul Shaykh b. Hiyan).

2. He is near of kin whose kinship is affection though his relation-ship be distant, and he is remote whom enmity hath rendered distant though his kinship be close, for there is nothing nearer to the body than the hand, but when the hand is corrupted it is cut off, and when cut off it is cauterized. (Abu Nuaym).

3. Take ye five *maxims* from me, 1, 'Let none of ye year

anything but his sin. 2. And hope for nothing but his Lord. 3. He who knoweth not, let him not be ashamed to learn. 4. He who knoweth let him to be ashamed when he is asked concerning what he knoweth not, to say "God knows best." 5. Patience is to faith what the head is to be body ; when patience departeth, faith departeth, and when the head goeth the body goeth. (Ibn Mansur in his Sunan.) A.H.40. A.D.661

4. The perfect doctor of the law is he who doth not make men despair of the mercy of God and is not indulgent to them in repect of their sins against God-and doth not proffer them inmmunity from the chastisement of God and doth not willingly forsake the Qurãn for other than it-for there is not profit in devotion in which there is not knowledge, and no knowledge unless accompanied by comprehension, and no proper reading of the Qurãn without meditation upon it. (Dhurays in the Fadhailul Qurãn. (Excelencies of the Qurãn).

5. I make it incumbent upon myself when I am asked what I know not, to say God knoweth best. (Ibn Asakir.)

6. He who seeketh to do justicc unto men, let him desire for them what he desireth for himself. (Ibid.)

7. Seven things are of the devil. 1. Excessive anger. 2. excessive sneezing.[1] 3. Excessive yamning. 4. Vomiting. 5. Bleeding at the nose. 6. Clandestine discourse[2]. 7. Sleeping during devotional exercise.

8. Eat ye the pomegranate for it is a stomachic. (Abullah b. Ahmad in the Zawaidul Musnad.)

---

1 It is also said in a tradition ان يحب العطاس و يكره التثاؤب "He (Muhammad) used to like sneezing and dislike yawning," because the former is accompanied by lightness of body and openness of the pores, whereas in yawning the contrary is the case, but the Arabs used to augur ill from sneezing, so that if a man were journeying and heard a sneeze, it prevented him from going on. With regard to yawning, it is said, اذاتثائب احدكم فليغظ "when any one of you yawns, let him cover his mouth," for it is believed, that the devil leaps into the uncovered yawning mouth. Lane.

2 انما النجوىٰ من الشيطان Qur. LVIII.

A.H.40. A.D.661 9. Thy reading the Qurãn under the tuition of a learned man, and his reading it to thee are equal *in meritoriousness.* (Al Hakim in his History.)

10. A time shall come upon the people when a true believer will be more abject than a female salve. (Said b. Mansur.)

And by Abul Aswad ad Duali is the following, eulogizing Ali.

"And now, O eye, alas for thee! Come to my aid !
Now weep for the prince of the Faithful ;
And let Umm Kulthum[1] weep for him
With her flowing tears, for verily she hath beheld death,
Now say to the schismatics wheresoever they may be :
May the eyes of the envious never be refreshed.
In the month of the Fast have ye made us to grieve
For the best of all men universally.
Ye have slain the best of those that have mounted steeds
And tamed them or put foot upon a vessel,
Of those who wear and adjust sandals :
And of those who read the Qurãn and its perspicuous verses.
And in him were the noblest vitues
And the love of the Apostle of the Lord of created things.
Verily the Kuraysh knew wheresoever they were,
That thou wert the best of them in ancestry and faith.
When I stood[2] before the face of the father of Husayn,
I saw the radiance that shone above his eyes.
And before his death we were happy,
Beholding the son-in-law of the Apostle of God among us,
Establishing the truth in which there was no thought of evil,
And acting equitably between enemies and kinsmen ;

---

1 The daughter of Ali by Fatimah and wife of Omar.

2 I prefer the reading of the first to the second person sing. and in this follow, M. Reynard in the Prairies d 'Or. Tom. IV, p. 436.

Knowledge with him was not hidden, A.H.40. A.D.661

Nor was he created among the proud of heart.

The people became when they lost Ali

Like unto the ostrich bewildered in a country bare of herbage.

Rejoice not, Muawiyah, son of Sakhr :

For verily the continuance of the Caliphs is with us."

Of the distinguished persons who died during the time of Ali whether by natural death or by violence were, Hudayfah b-ul Imam-Az Zubayr b-ul Awam-Talhah-Zayd b. Suhan-Salman al Farisi- Hind b. Abi Halah and Uways al Kurani- Khabbah b-ul Aratt-Ammar b. Yasir- Sahl b. Hanif-Suhayb ar Rumi-Muhammad the son of Abu Bakr as Siddiq-Tamim ad Dari-Khawwat b. Jubayr-shurahbil b. as Samt-Abu Maysarah al Badri-Safwan b. Assal Amr b. Anbasah- Hisham b. Hakim-abu Rafi freedman of the Prophet and others.

AL HASAN-B-ALI-B-ABI TALIB

Al Hasan was the son of Ali, the son of Abu Talib, Abu Muhammad, grandson of the Apostle of God, and his descendant, the last of the Caliphs according to his prediction. [1]

Ibn Saad records on the authority of Imran b. Sulayman that al Hasan and al Husayn were two of the names of the dwellers in Paradise, the Arabs never having been named by those two in the time of Ignorance.

Al Hasan was born in the middle of the month of Ramadhan in the 3rd year of the Flight. It is stated that he heard traditions from

1 Muhammad is reported to have said, "the Caliphate shall continue after me thirty years and then shall be a kingdom." Muhammad died in the 11th year of the Flight and Hasan's abdication was in the year 40 from whence it is plain, says al Bukhari that not only was Muhammad a Prophet but Hasan was his rightful successor, Ock, Hist, Sar, p. 352.

A.H.40. A.D.661

the Prophet: and Ayesha and others of the Tabiis-among them his son al Hasan, and Abu Haura Rabiah b. Shayban, As Shaabi and Abu Wail, have related traditions on his authority. He resembled the Prophet in appearance, and the Prophet named him al Hasan and slaughtered a sheep as a sacrifice for him on the seventh day, and shaved his head and ordered that the weight of his hair in silver should be given in alms, and he was the fifth of the people of the mantle.[1] Al Askari says that this name (*al Hasan*) was not known in the time of Ignorance.

Al Mufadhal[2] says that the Lord concealed the names of al Hasan and al Husayn until the Prophet named his two sons[3] by them, and al Bukhari records on the authority of Anas that no one resembled the Prophet more than al Hasan the son of Ali. The two Shaykhs record on the authority of al Bara that he said, "I saw the Apostle of God, with al Hasan upon his shoulder, and he was saying "O God verily I love him, therefore love Thou him." And al Bukhari from Abu Bakr that he said, "I heard the Prophet, while on the pulpit with al Hasan by his side, looking now upon the people, and now upon him, exclaim, 'verily this son of mine is a prince and perchance the Lord will unite throught his means, the two contending parties of the Muslims.'[4] And from Ibn Omar that the Prophet said, 'they two are my descendants in the world meaning al Hasan and al Husayn.'"

At Tirmidi and al Hakim record on the authority of Abu Sai'd

---

1 When Muhammad went forth to dispute with the ambassadors from the people of Najran on the subject of religion he took with him Ali Fatima, al Hasan and al Husayn, and some say gathered them under his mantle. See Sale, Qur. P. 44.

2 Ibn Khall gives two of the name, both philologers of eminence and authors of numerous works. One, Abu Talib al Mufaddhal b. Salama of the school of Kufah. The other Abul Abbas al Mufaddhal b. Muhammad b. Yala, a native of Kufah author of the Mufaddhal, died A.H. 168.

3 They were always looked upon by him in the light of his children, his own having died at an early age.

4 The Syrians who set up Muawiyah, and the people of Iraq who took the side of al Hasan.

al Khudri that the Apostle of God called al Hasan and al Husayn A.H.40. the two princes of the youth of Paradise. And at Tirmidi from A.D.661 Usamah b. Zayd that he narrates, "I saw the Prophet with al Hasan and al Husayn on either hip, and he exclaimed 'these are my two sons and the sons of my daughter. O God, verily I love them, wherefore love Thou them and love him who loveth them.' And from Anas that the Apostle of God was asked 'which of the people of thy house are dearest to the?' He replied, 'al Hasan and al Husayn.' Al Hakim records on the authority of Ibn Abbas, that the Prophet advanced, carrying upon his neck al Hasan, and a man met him and said, 'an excelleznt steed thou ridest, lad !" the Apostle of God replied, 'and he is an excellent rider.'"

Ibn Saad records on the authority of Abdullah b-uz Zubayr that he said, "the one most resembling the Prophet of his family, and the most endeared to him of them was al Hasan the son of Ali-I saw him come while Muhammad was worshipping and mount upon his neck (or, he says, his back) and Muhammad did not make him get down until he himself got down-and indeed I saw, him in the act of bowing in prayer, separate his legs for al Hasan so that he might pass through from the other side." And from Abu Salimah b. Abdur Rahman[1] that the Apostle of God used to put out his tongue towards al Hasan the son of Ali, and when the boy saw the redness of the tongue, he would be merry with him. Al Hakim records on the authority of Zubayr b-ul Arkam, that al Hasan rose and preached and a man of the tribe of Azd Shanuwwah stood up and said, "I testify verily that I saw the Apostle of God take him in his lap, saying 'he who loveth me, let him surely love him and he that is present, let him inform him who is absent,' and were it not for reverence of the Apostle of God I would have told it to no one."

Al Hasan had many virtues-he was a prince gentle of disposition, grave, reserved and dignified ; generous, greatly extolled, averse from strife and the sword, and given much to marrying-he would bestow upon one man as much as a hundred thousand dirhams.

---

1 A Tabii, son of Abdur Rahman b. Auf, died at Medina A.H. aged 72.

A.H.40. A.D.661 Al Hakim records on the authority of Abdullah b. Ubahyd b. Umayr that al Hasan performed the pilgrimage on foot twenty-five times, his horses being led beside him. And Ibn Saad from Umayr b. Ishaq that he said, "no one ever discoursed before me whom I more wished when he spoke that he should not be silent, than al Hasan the son of Ali, and I never heard from him an improper word except once, when there was verily a dispute between al Hasan and Amr b. Othman regarding some land. Al Hasan proposed a thing which Amr did not approve, and al Hasan said, there is nothing for it then in my opinion but to act in spite of him."[1] He adds, "this was the harshest word of impropriety that I ever heard from him."

He also said, "Marwan was ruler over us and he used to revile Ali every Friday from the pulpit and al al Hasan used to listen without retorting a thing. Then he sent a man to say to him, 'I swear by Ali, and by Ali, and by Ali, and by thee, and by thee, and by thee, and I find not a comparison for thee but that of a mule, which when it is asked, "who is thy father?" replies, "my mother is a mere."' Al Hasan replied to him 'go back to him and say to him *from me*-verily I will not blot out from thee thing that thou hast said by reviling thee *in turn,* but my place of meeting and thine is *before* God, and if thou hast spoken the truth, the Lord will reward thee acoording to thy truth, and if thou hast lied, then the Lord is terrible in vengeance.'"

Ibn Saad records on the authority of Ruzayk b. Sawwar that there passed words between al Hasan and Marwan and al Hasan was silent. Then Marwan blew his nose with his right hand, and al Hasan said to him, "Out upon thee! Dost thou not know that the right hand is for bonour and the left for what is base ? Shame upon thee!" Marwan held his peace. And from Ashath b. Sawwar on the authority of another, that a man sat down by al Hasan, and he said, "Verily thou hast sat down by me as I was about to rise-wilt thou give me permission?" And from Ali-b. Zayd-b. Judaan, that al Hasan gave away his property twice for the sake of God, and

1 Lit, that his nose should cleave to the dust, i.e. render him submissive. 25

three times shared his property with God *by religious donations*, so that he would give a sandal, and keep sandal, and give a boot and keep a boot. And from Ali the son of al Husayn, that al Hasan was given to divorcing his wives, and he never separated himself from a woman but she still continued to love him, and he married ninety women. And from the father of Jaafar b. Muhammad that he said, "al Hasan used to marry and divorce till I feared that he would cause enmity amongst the tribes." Ali one said, "O men of Kufah, give not your daughters in marriage to al Hasan, for he is a man that divorceth frequently:" and a man from Hamadan exclaimed, "by Allah, we will surely give in marriage to him and such as he approves, he may retain, and such as he dislikes, he may divorce." And from Abdullah b. Husayn, that al Hasan was a man much given to taking women in marriage, and they rarely committed a fault towards him, and it was seldom with a woman he married but she loved him and was passionately attached to him.

A.H.40.
A.D.661

Ibn Asakir records on the authority of Juwayyrah b. Asmi that when al Hasan died, Marwan wept over his bier, and al Husayn said to him, "dost thou weep for him and verily thou hast given him to suffer[1] what thou hast given him to suffer." He replied, "verily, I would have done the same to one even more forbearing than he," and he pointed with his hand to the hill.[2] And from al Mubarrad that it was said to al Hasan-"Abu Darr Sayeth-poverty is dearer to me than wealth, and sickness than health." He replied-"may God have mercy upon Abu Darr, but I say, that he who confideth in the good choice of the Lord for him, desireth not to be in any other condition than that which the Lord hath chosen for him, and this is the highest attainment of resignation unto what Fate hath ordained."

Al Hasan assumed the Caliphate after the assassination of his father, according to the allegiance sworn to him by the people of Kufah, and governed it during six months and some days. Then

---

1 Lit. to swallow.

2 As forbearing-or as self-contained–as a hill-is a proverbial comparison Arabic.

A.H.40. A.D.661 Muawiyah marched against him and the affair was left in the hands of God. Then al Hasan sent to him, offering to resign the government to him on the condition that the Caliphate should revert to himself after him,[1] and that he should not call upon any one of the people of Medina, Hijaz and Iraq for anything that had happened during his father's lifetime, and that he should pay his debts. Muawiyah accepted his demands, and they made peace upon this. Thus was made manifest the Prophetical prediction in his words "the Lord will unite through his means, the contending parties of the Muslims." And he abdicated the Caliphate in his favour. Al Balkini[2] indeed has sought to prove from his renunciation of the Caliphate which is the highest of dignities, the lawfulness of the renunciation of offices.

His abdication of the Caliphate took place in the year 41 in the month of Rabiiul Ula, and some say in Rabiiul Akhir (August 661) and Jamadaul Awwal. His Companions used to say to him, "O shame of the Muslims," and he would reply, "shame is better than hell fire." And a man said to him, "peace to thee, O dishonourer of the Muslims." He replied, "I am no dishonourer of the Muslims, but I was loth to have ye slaughtered for sake o a kingdom." Al Hasan then removed from Kufah to Medina and settled there.

Al Hakim records on the authority of Jubayr b. Nufayr[3] that he narrates, "I said to al Hasan, verily the people say that thou desirest the Caliphate." He replied, "the chiefs of the Arabs were under my authority, warring with those with whom I warred, and at peace with those with whom I was at peace-yet I abandoned it, seeking the favour of God, and to spare the blood of the people of Muhammad: shall I then again seize it amid the despondency of the people of Hijaz ?"

Al Hasan died at Medina of poison. His wife Jadah, daughter

---

1 This condition I find in no other author I have consulted.

2 The surname of Jalaluddin, author of a work on the difficulties of science. I best known composition is the Muhimmatul Muhimmat, a commentary on Asnavi great Jurisconsult who died A.H. 882. D'Herb. Art. Balkini.

3 One of the Tabiis.

of al Ashath b. Kays poisoned him. Yazid b Muawiyah suborned her to poison him, *promising* that he would then marry her, and she did so. And when al Hasan was dead, she sent to Yazid claiming the fulfillment of what he had promised, but he replied, "I did not approve thee for al Hasan, shall I then be content with thee for myself?" His death took place in the year 40. Some say, however, *it occurred* on the 5th of Rabiiul Awwal in the year 50, and others in the year 51. His brother endeavoured to make him confess to him who poisoned him, but he would not inform him and said, "the Lord is terrible in His vengeance if it be the one I suppose, and if not, by Allah, let not an innocent man be put to death on my account." A.H.40. A.D.661

Ibn Saad records on the authority of Imran b. Abdillah b. Talhah that al Hasan saw in a dream that there was as if inscribed between his eyes "Say God is One" (Qur CXII) and he announced the good news to the people of his house, and they related it to Sai'd b-ul Musayyab, and he exclaimed "if his dream speak truly, little time remaineth unto his death." And he lived but a few days when he died.

Al Bayhaki and Ibn Asakir record on a line of ascription through the father of Abu Mundir Hisham b. Muhammad, that al Hasan was in straitened circumstances, and they used to give him an allowance of one hundred thousand dirhams a year. One year Muawiyah withheld it from him, and he was in great distress. He himself narrates "I sent for an inkhorn that I might write to Muawiyah to remind him of me, but I refrained, and I saw the Apostle of God in a dream. And he said, 'how art thou, O Hasan ?' I replied, 'well; father,' and I complained to him of my allowance being kept back from me and he said, 'didst thou send for an ink-horn to write to a creature like unto thyself, reminding him of it ?' I answered 'yes, O Apostle of God-what then should I do?" He said 'say-O God, instill into my heart Thy desire, and cut off my hope from all beside Thee, so that I may not hope in any one save Thee, O Lord ! and vouchsafe unto me O Lord of created things that which my strength is too weak to reach, and my striving falleth short of, to which my desire attaineth not nor doth my supplication aspire, and which hath not passed upon my tongue, of what Thou

A.H.40. A.D.661 hast bestowed of certitude upon any one of those that have gone before, and those that have come after.'

He continues, "by Allah, I did not persist with this *prayer* for a week, but Muawiyah sent me 1,500,000, dirhams, and I exclaimed, 'praise be to the Lord who doth not forget him who remembereth Him and disappointeth not him that calleth upon Him.' Then, I saw the Prophet in a dream, and he said, 'O Hasan, how art thou,' and I said, 'well, O Apostle of God,' and I related to him my story and he said, 'thus it is, O my son, with him who hopeth in the Creator and hopeth not in the creature.'"

It is stated in the Tuyyuriyat on the authority of Salim b. Isa, the Qurãn-reader of the people of Kufah, that when al Hasan was nigh unto death, he became affected with violent grief, and al Husayn said to him, "what meaneth, O brother, this lamentation ? Verily thou goest unto the Apostle of God and unto Ali, and they two are thy fathers, and unto Khadijah and Fatimah, and they two are thy mothers, and unto al Kasim and at Tahir, and they two are thy maternal uncles, [1] and unto Hamzah and Jaafar, and they two are thy paternal uncles." Al Hasan said to him, "O brother, verily I am entering upon one of the decrees of the Most High, upon the like of which I have not entered, and I behold a people among the creatures of God, the like of whom I have never seen." Ibn Abdil Barr says, "it has been related to me in different ways, that when al Hasan was near unto death, he said to his brother-"O my brother, verily thy father cast his eyes upon this authority, but the Lord averted it from him, and Abu Bakr held it ; afterwars again he raised his eyes to it, but it was turned from him unto Omar ; then at the time of the Council, he had no doubt that it would not pass from him, but it was turned from him unto Othman, and when Othman was slain Ali was sworn allegiance to : then it was contested until the sword was drawn, and it never rested undisturbed in his possession. And verily, by Allah, I do not think that the Lord will unite in us the Prophetic mission and the Caliphate, and indeed I know not with what indignity the rabble of Kufah have *not* Itreated thee, and cast

1 Sons of Muhammad.

thee forth. And verily I asked of Ayesha that I might be buried with the Apostle of God, and she agreed, therefore when I am dead, ask that of her, and I do not think otherwise of the people but that they will hinder thee, and if they do so, do not dispute with them." And when he was dead, al Husayn went to Ayesha, the mother of the faithful, and she said, "yes ; willingly," but Marwan hindered them, and al Husayn and those that were with him took up their arms until Abu Hurayrah turned him back. Afterwards he was buried in al Bakii by the side of his mother. A.H.40. A.D.661

MU'AWIYAH-B-ABI SUFIYAN

Muawiyah, the son of Abu Sufiyan Sakhr b. Harb b. Umayyah b. Abdis Shams b. Abd. Manaf b. Kusayy al Umawiy-Abu Abdur Rahman, embraced Islam with his brother on the day of the conquest of Mecca. He was present at Hunayn, [1] and was of those hearts were conciliated[2] *by Muhammad*. He became sincerely converted to Islam, and was one of the Secretaries to the Apostle of God. It is said that he had one hundred and sixty traditions from Muhammad. Of the Companions who related traditions on his authority, were Ibn Abbas, Ibn Omar, Ibnuz Zubayr, Abud Darda-Jarir al Bijli, Numan b. Bashir and others. And among the Tabiis, Ibnul Musayyab, Hamid b. Abdir Rahman &c.

He was of those celebrated for acuteness and forbearance, and verily traditions of his merit have been transmitted, which are seldom well established. At Tirmidi records on the authority of the

1 This battle was fought in 8 A.H. in the valley of Hunayn, about 3 miles from Mecca, between Muhammad and the tribes of Hawazen and Thakif. See Sale, Qur. P. 151.

2 These were certain Arabs of name and position whom Muhammad won over to his side by showing them every consideration, in order that their example might be followed by their tribes. The Muntaha'l Arab gives a list of thirty of them.

A.H.41. A.D.661 Prophet, substantiating it from Abdur Rahman b. Abi Amirah the Companion, that he said to Muawiyah, "O God, make him a guide unto others and himself rightly directed." And Ahmad in his Musnad from Irbadh b. Sariyah that he narrates, "I heard the Apostle of God say, 'O God, instruct Muawiyah in writing and accounts, and preserve him from *eternal* punishment.'"

Ibn Abi Shaybah records in the Musannaf, and at Tabarani in the Kabir on the authority of Abdul Malik b. Umayr, that Muawiyah said, "I never ceased to desire the Caliphate since the Aposlte of God said to me, "O Muawiyah, when thou rulest, act with kindness.'"

Muawiyah was a man, tall, fair, handsome and of awe inspiring aspect, and Omar used to look upon him and say, "this is the Caesar of the Arabs." It is recorded of Ali and he said, "be not averse to the rule of Muawiyah, for verily when ye lose him, ye will see heads fall from their shoulders." Al Makburi[1] says, "ye Admire the sagacity of Heraclius and Khusrau, and ye pass over Muawiyah?" He was proverbial for his forbearance. Ibn Abid Dunya and Abu Bakr b. Abi Aasim have severally compsed a work solely on his forbearance. Ibn Aun narrates that a man said to Muawiyah, "by Allah, thou must surely act uprightly with us, O Muawiyah, or wel will assuredly set thee right." He said, "how ;" he replied, "with a stick." Muawiyah answered "Very well-I will act uprightly."

Kabisah b Jabir[2] says. "I was much in company with Muawiyah and I never saw a man of more settled forbearance, and slower to folly and further from indolence than he;-and when Abu Bakr sent me to Syria, Muawiyah set forth with his brother Yazid b. Abi Sufiyan, and Yazid dying, appointed him his successor in Damascus. Omar confirmed him in this, and subsequently Othman, who added to his government the whole of Syria, and he was prefect for twenty years and Caliph twenty years." Kaab al Ahbar said, "no one shall

---

1 Abu Said Kaysan Makburi-a Tabii-he was called Makburi because he lived near a graveyard. Muntaha'l Arab.

2 Abul Ala Kabisah b. Jabir al Asadi a native of Kufah and one of the Tabiis, of respectable authority as a Traditionist. Died a little before 83 A.H. An Nawawi

rule this people as long as Muawiyah." Ad Dahabi says that Kaab died before Muawiyah was made Caliph, and that Kaab was right in what he said, for Muawiyah continued Caliph for twenty years, and none of the princes of the earth contended with him, unlike others who came after him, for they had opponents and portions of their dominions passed out of their sway. Muawiyah went forth against Ali as has preceded, and assumed the title of Caliph. Then he marched against al Hasan, who abdicated in his favour. He therefore became firmly established in the caliphate from Rabiiul Akhir or Jumadal Awwal 41. The year was therefore called the year of Union, on account of the gathering of the people under one Caliph. During this year Muawiyah appointed Marwan b-ul Hakam over Medina. A.H.41. A.D.661

In the year 43 Rukhkhaj[1] and other places in Sijistan were captured and Waddan in Barkah and Kuzaa[2] of the country of the Moors. And in the same Muawiyah appointed as his lieutenant Ziyad "the son of his father," and this is the first instance in Islam in which the command of the Prophet was violated[3]-(at Thaalabi[4] and others).

In the year 45 al Kikan[5] was reduced and in the year 50, Kuhistan conquered. In the same year Muawiyah invited the people of Syria engage for the succession after him of his son Yazid, and

---

1 The printed edition has رجج which is an error. The MS. gives رخج and Ibnul Athir confirms it.

2 The MS. has لورا but I am unable to trace the names in Yakut.

3 Ziyad was the reputed son of Abu Sufiyan by Sumayyah who was married to a Greek slave. According to the Prophetical law the child belonged to his legal father the Greek, but Muawiyah, anxious to secure in his interest so eminent a man, publicly acknowledged him as his brother by the father's side, notwithstanding the remonstrances of his family. The doubtful parentage of Ziyad gained for him the vague distinction of "the son of his father." See Ockley, Abu Fida. D'Herb.

4 Ibn Khall gives two of this surname – both from Naysabur, Abu Ishak, a well known Commentator on the Qurãn-who died A.H. 629 (1035-6), the other Abu Mansur Abdul Malik a voluminous author : died A.H. 350 (961).

5 Yakut places this district between Sind and Khurasan.

A.H.45. A.D.665-6 they made a covenant with him. He was the first who made a compact for the Cliphate to descend to his son, and the first who did so while in sould health.

Afterwards he wrote to Marwan at Median, to take the covenant *from the people*, and Marwan preached and said, "verily the prince of the Faithful hath seen fit to appoint his son Yazid as successor over ye according to the institution of Abu Bakr and Omar," whereupon Abdur Rahman the son of Abu Bakr as Siddik arose and said, "rather according to the institution of Khusran and Caesar, for Abu Bakr and Omar did not do so for their children, nor for any one of the people of their house."

In the year 51, Muawiyah performed the pilgrimage, and took the covenant for his son. Then he sent to the son of Omar and recited the profession of faith and said, "now, O son of Omar, verily thou didst say unto me, that thou in truth wouldst not wish to pass a single dark night without there being over thee during it a ruler-therefore, verily, I warn thee that thou break not the staff of the Muslims nor strive for the disturbance of their harmony." Then the son of Omar praised God and glorified Him and said, "now, verily there were before thee Caliphs who had sons, thy son being no better than their sons, yet they did not regard in their sons what thou regardest in thy son, but they chose for the Muslims the best wheresoever they knew *him to be,* and thou dost caution me lest I break the staff of the Muslims, but I have not been doing so, and indeed I am but a man among the Muslims and when they are agreed upon a thing, then surely I am one of them." And he said, "may the Lord have mercy upon thee," and the son of Omar departed. Then he sent to the son of Abu Bakr and recited the profession of faith, and began his discourse, but the other cut short his speech and said, "verily, thou assuredly hast desired that I should commend thee to God in the affair of thy son, but, by Allah, I shall not do so-by Allah, I will refer this matter to a council of the Muslims, or I will assuredly by circumvention unsettle it upon thee." Then he sprung up and departed. But Muawiyah said, "O God, suffice to me against him in what Thou willest." Then he said, "Softly, O youth-go not within sight of the people of Syria, for verily I fear lest they anticipate me with regard to thee, until I tell them in the evening that thou hast sworn allegiance." Next he sent to the son of az Zubayr and said, 'O son of az Zubayr-verily thou art a crafty fox which whenever it cometh out of one hole goeth into another, and verily thou hast supported these two men and hast blown into their nostrils, and hast carried them against their judgment." The son of az Zubayr replied, "if indeed thou art weary of the government, resign it, and bring us thy son and we will swear allegiance to him. Hast thou considered if we make a covenant for thy son together with thee, which of ye two we must hear and obey ? The covenant can never be made with the ye two conjointly." Then he departed, whereupon Muawiyah ascended the pulpit and praised God and gloried Him and said, "verily, we have heard the sayings of certain misguided men who think that the son of Omar and the son of Abu Bakr and the son of az Zubayr have not sworn allegiance to Yazid, where-as they have heard and obeyed him and made a covenant of allegiance with him." And the people of Syria said, "by Allah, we shall not be content until they swear allegiance to him before witnesses, otherwise we shall smite their necks" but he said, "great God, how prompt are the people to evil against the Kuraysh-let me not hear this speech from any of ye after to-day." Then he descended and the people said, "the son of Omar and the son of Abu Bakr and the son of az Zubayr have sworn allegiance," and the Syrians said, "no ! by Allah," but the people said "yes". And Muawiyah set forth and arrived in Syria. It is stated on the authority of Ibn Munkadir[1] that Ibn Omar said when the covenant was made for Yazid, "if he proveth good we will be content, and if wicked we must be patient."

A.H.51
A.D.671

Al Kharaiti[2] records in the Hawatif ((*Monitors*) on the authority of Hamid b. Wahb that Hind the daughter of Utbah b. Rabiih was the wife of al Fakah b-ul Mughirab, and he was one of the youths of the Kuraysh, and he possessed a banqueting house which the

1 Abu Bakr Muhammad b. Munkadir of the Kuraysh was a traditionist of good authority. He died A.H. 130, (747-8). De Slane, I.K.

2 Abu Bakr Muhammad b. Jaafar, al Kharaiti authority of the Makarimul Akhlak and other works died at Jaffa or Askalon, A.H. 328 9939-40). De Slane, I.K.

A.H.51. A.D.671 people could enter without permission. One day the house was empty, and al Fakah arose, Hind being within, and went forth on some businees of his and a man of those who used to guard the house, came and entered it, bt when he saw the woman he turned fleeing ; but al Fakah observed him, and he went up to her and kicked her with his foot and said, "who was he that was with thee?' She replied, "I did not see any one and I did not wake until thou didst wake me." But he said to her "go to thy family." And the people spoke concerning her, wherefore her father took her apart and said to her, "O daughter-verily people talk much about thee, therefore tell me concerning it, and if the man speak truly, I will suborn one who will slay him and the talk about us will cease, and if he lieth, I will summon him before certain soothsayers of Yaman." The narrator continues, "then she swore to him upon that by which they used to swear in the time of Ignorance that he spoke falsely concerning her, wherefore Utbah said to al Fakah, 'verily thou hast charged my daughter with a grave thing, therefore summon me before certain of the soothsayers of Yaman.' And al Fakah went forth with a party of the Banu Makhzum, and Utbah at the head of a party of the Banu Abd Manaf, and with them Hind and other women along with her in familiar intercourse. But when they drew near the confines, the appearance of Hind was transformed and her countenance changed and her father said to her, 'O daughter, verily I see the change of appearance that hath come over thee, and what is that, but on account of the guilt thou feelest.' She replied, 'no, by Allah, father ! it is not from guilt, but I know that you go unto a mortal who may fail or prove right, therefore I cannot trust him that he brand me not with a stain which will be a reproach to me among the Arabs.' But he said to her, 'verily I will prove him for thee before he look into thy business.' And he whistled to his horse until he staled and he inserted a grain of wheat and bound it with a thong. And they reached the soothsayer in the morning who slew a camel for them, and received them with honour, and when they had finished their morning meal, Uthbah said to him, "verily we have come to thee concerning an affair, and indeed I have concealed from thee a hidden thing that I may prove thee-wherefore see what it is." He replied, "wheat." He said, "I desire what is clearer than this." He answered "a grain of wheat in a clot." And Utbah said, "thou hast spoken truly, see into the business of these women." Then he began to approach each one of them, striking her shoulder and saying "rise," until he came to Hind and he struck her shoulder and said "rise thou undefiled and no adulteress, and verily thou shalt give birth to a king called Muawiyah." Then al Fakah looked upon her and took her by the hand but she withdrew her hand from his hand said,-"go to, for by Allah, I will surely endeavour that it is by another than thee." Abu Abu Sufiyan married her and she brought forth Muawiyah.

Muawiyah died in the month of Rajab of the year 60 (April 680) and was buried between the gate of al jabiyah, and the Little Gate. It is said that he lived seventy-seven years, and he possessed a little of the hair of the Apostle of God and a paring of his nail, and enjoined as his last request that it should be put into his mouth and eyes, and he added, "do this and leave me alone with the Most Merciful of the Merciful."

On some accounts of him.

Ibn Abi Shaybah records in the Musannaf on the authority of A.H.60.
Abu Sai'd b. Jumhan that he narrates, "I said to Safinah, -verily the A.D.680.
Banu Umayyah conceive that the Caliphate is among them." He replied, "verily the fierce-eyed some[1] lie-they are the most rigorous of kings and the first of the kings is Muawiyah." And al Bayhaki and Ibn Asakir from Ibrahim b. Suayd al Armani that he narrates, "I said to Ahmad b. Hanbal,-who are the Caliphs?" He answered, "Abu Bark, Omar, Othman and Ali," I said, "and Muawiyah?" He replied, "no one had more claim to the Caliphate in the time of Ali

---

1 Lit, blue-eyed, which is employed as signifying hostility because the زرقة blueness or lightness of the eye is predominant in the Greeks and the Daylam between whom and the Arabs is a confirmed enmity. Imrul Kays, used this adjective in this sense. Diwan, p. 34, Ar Text. Consult Lane, and Chenery, notes to 10th assembly of al Hariri.

A.H.60. than Ali." And as Silafi in the Tuyyuriyat from Abdullah b. Ahmad
A.D.680. b. Hanbal that he states, :"I asked my father concerning Ali and Muawiyah," and he answered, "know, that Ali had many enemies, and his enemies searched for a fault in him but they found it not, wherefore they went to a man[1] who had fought with him and battled with him, and they praised him extravagantly setting a snare themselves for him." And Ibn Asakir from Abdul Malik b. Umayr,[2] that Jariyah b. Kudamah as Saadi went to Muawiyah who said to him, "who art thou?" He replied, "Jariyah the son of Kudamah." He said, "and what art thou near to being-art thou anything but a bee?" He answered, "dost thou not understand, that verily, thou hast likened me to it, and it protects itself with a sting and is sweet of juice! by Allah, Muawiyah is nothing but a bitch, howling to the dogs, and Umayyah, is but the diminutive of a female slave."[3] And from al Fadhl b. Suayd, that Jariyah b. Kudamah went to Muawiyah who said to him, "thou art the procurator of Ali the son of Abu Talib and the kindler of fire in thy burnings, going round about the villages of the Arabs, shedding their blood."[4] Jariyah replied, "O Muawiyah- put Ali aside from thee, for we have never hated Ali since we loved him, and never acted with dissimulation towards hin since we dealt sincerely with him." He answered, "alas for thee, O Jariyah, how contemptible wert thou to thy family when they named thee Jariyah." He replied, "O Muawiyah, thou wert contemptible to thy

---

1 I.e. Muawiyah.

2 Abu Amr or Abu Omar Abdul Malik b. Umayr was one of the Tabiis and a native of Kufah of which town he was Kadhi. He is considered a good authority by some and doubtful by others, as his memory towards the close of his life failed him. He died about A.H. 136. An Nawawi.

3 Meaning that the names themselves have that signification in Arabic. I know not why he should have likened Jariyah to a bee, the name not bearing that meaning, unless it be for the same reason that a ship is termed Jariyah because it runs or flows on the sea, and thus the bee in the air. Jariyah likewise signifies a female slave.

4 Muawiyah had sent Abdullah b-ul Hedhrami to Basrah to secure that town for him and Ali dispatched Aayan b. Dhabiah for the same purpose. The latter was killed whereupon Jariyah was sent and he besieged Abdullah in his house and set it on fire and burnt him to death. Ibn Hajr.

A.H.60.
A.D.680.

was Muawiyah and that was when his flesh had increased and his stomach had grown large. (Recorded by Ibn Abi Shaybah.) Az Zuhri states that Muawiyah was the first who introduced the discourse before prayers on the Eed. (Abdur Razzak in his Musannaf.) And Sai'd b-ul Musayyab says that he was the first who introduced the call to prayers on the Eed, (Ibn Abi Shaybah) and who diminished the number of the Takbirs. Ali Askari says in his Awail, "Muawiyah was the first to establish post-messengers in Islam, and the first who appointed eunuchs for his personal service, and the first with whom his subjects jested familiarly, and the first to whom it was said *by the Muaddin,* "peace be to thee, O prince of the Faithful and the mercy of God and His blessing-to prayers ! May the Lord have mercy upon thee,"-and the first, who established the office of the Seal, and he appointed to it Abdullah b. Aus al Ghassani, and confided to him the Seal, and upon the stone of it was inscribed, "every work has its reward;" and that continued with the Abbaside Caliphs to the end. The reason of his instituting it was, that he commanded *to be given* to a man one hundred thousand *dirhams*, and he opened the document and made it two hundred thousand, and when the account was taken to Muawiyah, he disavowed it, and established the register of the Seal from that day. "And he was the first who established an enclosure in the great mosque, and the first who permitted the stripping of the Kaabah, for before that its vesture was thrown one over another."

Az Zubayr b. Bakkar records, in the Muwaffikiyat on the authority of the son of az Zuhri's brother, that the narrates, "I said to az Zuhri-who was the first who demanded an oath in the covenant of allegiance ?" He replied, "Muawiyah made them swear by God, but when Abdullah b. Marwan came, he made them swear upon divorce and manumission.[1] Al Askari records in his book of the Awail on the authority of Sulayman b. Abdullah b. Maamar, that Muawiyah went to Mecca or Medina and arriving at the mosque, sat himself down among a circle in which were, Ibn Omar, Ibn

1 That is, that the penalty of the violation of their oath would be divorce of their wives and manumission of their slaves.

Abbas and Abdur Rahman b. Abi Bakr. And they welcomed him, but Ibn Abbas turned from him and Muawiyah said, "I have more claim to his authority than this recusant and the son of his paternal uncle."[1] And Ibn Abbas said, "why ! for priority in Islam, or early *companionship* with the Apostle, or kinship with him?" He answered, "no, but for being the son of the paternal uncle of the murdered *Othman.*"[2] He retorted, "then this one more deserveth it," meaning the son of Abu Bakr. Muawiyah answered, "his father died a natural death." Ibn Abbas replied, "then this one has more claim to it," meaning the son of Omar. He answered, "verily an infidel slew his father." The other rejoined, "then that is the worse for thy argument, for it was the Muslims who were wroth with the son of thy paternal uncle and slew him." A.H.60. A.D.680.

Abdullah b. Muhammad b Ukayl says that Muawiyah arrived at Medina, and there met him Abu Katadah the Auxiliary, and Muawiyah said, "all the people have come unto me except ye, O men of the Auxiliaries." He replied, "we had no riding animals." He said, "where were *your* camels for drawing water?" "We lamed them in the chase after thee and thy father at Badr." After a little Abu Katadah said, "verily the Apostle of God said to us, 'you will see after me a state of calamity,'" Muawiyah asked, "what then did he command you to do ?" He replied, "he commanded us to be resigned." He answered, "then be resigned." This reached Abdur Rahman b. Hasan b. Thabit, and he said-

"Now, give Muawiyah the son of the Harb
The prince of the Faithful, this message from us,

---

2 I, e., Ali-Abbas and Abu Talib being brothers.

1. Umayyah.

Abul Aasi	Harb
Affan	Abu Sufiyan
Othman	Muawiyah

A.H.60.
A.D.680.

'We will then be resigned and will await you
At the day of mutual[1] endamaging and contention.'"

Ibn Abid Dunya and Ibn Asakr record on the testimony of Jabalah b. Suhaym that the narrates, "I went in unto Muawiyah during his Caliphate, and round his neck was a rope and a child was leading him, and I said to him, 'O prince of the Faithful, dost thou do thus?" 'O fool,' he said, 'be silent,' for I heard the Apostle of God say, 'he who hath a child, let him act towards him as a child,'" (recited but by one authority according to Ibn Asakir.) Ibn Abi Shaybah records in the Musannaf on the authority of as Shaabi, that a youth of the Kuraysh went in to Muawiyah and spoke harshly to him, and Muawiyah said to him, "O son of my brother! I warn thee against a king, for a king waxes angry with the *sudden* anger of a child, and seizes with the gripe of a lion." And from as Shaabi that Ziyad said, "I appointed a man as collector and he embezzled *the proceeds* of the taxes and fearing that I would punish him, he fled to Muawiyah, and I wrote to him, *saying,* "verily this is disrespect towards me,"[2] but he wrote to me, *saying,* "verily it is not fitting for me nor for thee to govern men by one kind of polity: if we were to be lenient to them all, we would confound men in iniquity, and we should not be hard with them all for we would drive men to ruin, wherefore, act thou with severity and harshness and I will act with mildness, and clemency." And from the same, I heard Muawiyah say, "a people were never ye divided but the wicked prevailed over the just, save this people." It is recorded in the Tuyyuriyat on the authority of Sulayman al Makhzumi, that Muawiyah gave a general audience to the people, and when the assembly had gathered together, he said, "recite ye to me three

---

1 That is the day of resurrection called يوم التغابن or the day of mutual cheating or overreaching, because the people of Paradise will then overreach the people of hell by their state of enjoyment while the latter will suffer the punishment they deserve or because the former will impute defect to the latter for preferring infidelity to faith. Lane The LXIVth chap. of the Qurãn is no named.

2 The MS. has rightly سوادب which words are improperly inverted in the printed edition.

verses by an Arab, each verse complete in its meaning;" and they A.H.60.
were silent. Then Abdullah b-uz Zubayr rose and said, "This Abu A.D.680.
Khubayb here, is the most eloquent and learned of the Arabs," and Abu Khubayb said, "what is it?" Muawiyah said, "recite to me three verses by an Arab, each verse complete in its meaning;' He replied, "for three hundred thousand *dirhams!*" Muawiyah said, "and will they be worth it?" He answered, "thou hast the choice ; therefore thou art the best judge."[1] Muawiyah said, "out with them:" and he recited to him from Afwah al Azdi[2]

"I have proved men age after age,

And have seen none but dissemblers and praters."

Muawiyah exclaimed "he hath spoken truly, go on."
He continued-

"And I have not seen among evil,s any more calmatious in their fall,

Or more distressing than the enmity of men."

Muawiyah said "he hath spoken truly, go on." He continued-

"And I have tasted the bitterness of all things ;

And there is no favour more bitter than supplicatin."

Muawiyah exclaimed, "he hath said truly," and he ordered him three hundred thousand *dirhams.*

Al Bukhari and an Nasai and Ibn Abi Hatim in his commentary, record with various readings, that Marwan was preaching in Medina, he being then *ruler* over Hijaz on the part of Muawiyah, and he said, "verily God hath shown the prince of the Faithful in regard to his son, an excellent counsel, and if he appointeth him successor,

---

1 Lit. "complete and sufficient."

2 The printed edition has اودى which is incorrect. She the Muntahal Arab art.فره

A.H.60. A.D.680. verily then Abu Bakr and Omar named successors," (and in one reading "according to the institution of Abu Bakr and Omar"). Whereupon Abdur Rahman b. Abu Bakr said, "*rather* according to the institution of Heraclius and Khusrau, for, by Allah, Abu Bakr did not give it to any of his sons nor to any of the people of his house, and Muawiyah hath not done this save from partiality and favour to his son." And Marwan said; "art thou not he who said to his parents 'Fie upon you ?'" (Qur. XVII.) And Abdur Rahman said, "art thou not the son of the accursed, of him thy father whom the Apostle of God curse?" but Ayesha exclaimed, "Marwan hath lied, that[1] was not revealed regarding Abdur Rahman, but it was revealed regarding such a one the son of such one, but the Apostle of God cursed the father of Marwan and Marwan was then in his loins-therefore Marwan is full of the curse of God."

Ibn Abi Shaybah records in the Musannaf on the authority of Urwah, that Muawiyah said, "there is no forbearance without tryings *of temper.*" And Ibn Asakir from as Shaabi that he said, "the most sagacious of the Arabs are four, Muawiyah, Amr b-ul Aas, Mughirah b. Shuubah and Ziyad : but Muawiyah *shows it* in his forbearance and gravity, Amr in difficulties, al Mughirah in swift action, and Ziyad in great and small *things.* The most eminent judges were four, and the most sagacious men four, and the judges were Omar. Ali, Ibn Masaud, and Zayd b. Thabit and the most sagacious, Muawiyah, Amr b-ul Aas, al Mughirah and Ziyad." And from Kabisah b. Jabir that he said, "I have associated with Omar the son of al Khattab and I never saw a man more learned in the book of God, or more profoundly versed in the religion o God than he, and I have associated with Talhah the son of Ubaydullah, and I have never seen a man more munificent in large gifts of wealth unsolicited, than he, and I have associated with Muawiyah and I have never seen a man of greater forbearance or slower to folly or more extreme in gravity than he, and I have associated with Amr the son of al Aas and I have never seen a man purer in ancestry and a gentler companion than he, and I have associated with a

1 I. e. the verse above mentioned. "Fie upon you."

Mughirab the son of Shuubah, and if there were a city with eight gates, out of any gate of which one could not go forth save by cunning, he would assuredly get out by them all." A.H.60. A.D.680.

Ibn Asakir records on the authority of Hamid b. Hilal, that Akil the son of Abu Talib begged of Ali and said, "I am poor and needy, therefore give unto me." He replied, "wait until my stipend cometh with *that of* the other Muslims, and I will give unto thee with them," but he was importunate and Ali said to a man, "take him by the hand and go with him to the shop of the people of the market and say, 'break these locks and take what is in the shops,' Akil said, 'dost thou wish to make me a thief?" Ali retorted, 'and dost thou wish to make me a thief that I should take the property of the Muslims and give it to thee, and not to them?' He answered, 'I shall assuredly go to Muawiyah.' He replied, 'that as thou willest,' and he went to Muawiyah and begged of him, and he gave him a hundred thousand *dirhams* and said, 'get up on the pulpit and mention what Ali hath given thee and what I have given thee.' Then he mounted, and praised God and glorified him, and said, 'O people I tell ye, verily I tempted Ali in regard to his religion and he preferred his religion, and verily I tempted Muawiyah in regard to his religion and he preferred me to his religion.'"

Ibn Asakir records on the authority of the father of Jaafar b. Muhammad, that Akil went in the unto Muawiyah who said, "that is Akil and his paternal uncle was Abu Lahab," and Akil said, "this is Muawiyah and his maternal aunt was the bearer of wood" [1] (Qur. CXI). And from al Auzaai, [2] that Khuraym b. Fatik went unto

---

1 "The hands of Abu Lahab shall perish and he shall perish. His riches shall not profit him nor that which he hath gained. He shall go down to be burned in flaming fire and his wife *also* bearing wood, on her neck a cord of twisted fibres of a palm tree." Qur. CXI. Her name was Umm Jamil, she was the daughter of Harb and sister of Abu Sufiyan. See Sale.

2 Abu Amr Abdur Rahman b. Yuhmid al Auzaai the chief doctor of law among the Syrian Muslims and the most learned in jurisprudence. He dwelt at Bayrut ; Sufiyan at Thauri was his pupil in traditions, with many others. Born al Baalbek A.H. 88 (707) died at Bayrut. His tomb is in a village called Hantus outside the gate of the city. Ibn Khall.

A.H.60. A.D.680. Muawiyah, and his nether garment was tucked up, and he had shapely legs. And Muawiyah said, "if but those legs belonged to a woman;" and Khuraym said "like thy hips, O prince of the Faithful."

There died during the reign of Muawiyah among distinguished persons, Safwan b. Umayyab and Hafsah, Umm Habibah, Safiyyah, Maymunah, Saudah and Juayriyyah mothers of the Faithful,-Labid the poet, Othman b. Talhah al Hajabi, Amr b-ul Aas, Abdullah b. Salam the learned doctor, Muhammad b. Maslamah, abu Musa al Ashari, Zayd b. Thabit, Abu Bakrah, Kaab b. Malik, al Mughirah b. Shuubah, Jarir al Bajli, Abu Ayub al Ansari, Imran b. Hasin, Said b. Zayd, Abu Katadah al Ansari, Fudhalah b. Ubayd, Abdur Rahman b. Abi Bakr, Jubayr b. Mutim, Usamah b. Zayd, Thauban, Amr b. Hassan b. Thabit, Hakim b. Hizam, Saad b. Abi Wakkas, Abul Yusr, Kutham b-ul Abbas, and his brother Ubaydullah, Ukbah b. Aamir, and Abu Hurayrah (in the year 59, for he used to pray "O God, verily I fly to thee for protection against the year 60 and the reign of children," and his prayer was heard)-and others.

YAZID-B-MUAWIYAH

Yazid the son of Muawiyah, Abu Khalid, the Umayyad, was born in the year 25 or 26. He was stout, very corpulent and hairy-His mother Maysun[1] was the daughter of Bahdal al Kalabi. He narrated traditions on the authority of his father, and they are related on his authority by his son Khalid and Abdul Malik b. Marwan. His father made him his heir, and the people were averse to it as hath gone before. Al Hasan of Basrah says, "two men threw into confusion the affairs of the people, Amr the son of al Aas on the day he suggested to Muawiyah the lifting of the Qurãn *on the lances,* and they were upraised (and Ibnul Kara adds, 'and the

1 This Bedouin bride of Muawiyah was a graceful poetess-some of her verses are translated in Carlyle's specimens of Arabian poetry. One song especially is well known and is given in Ockley and in Burton's Pilgrimage. The latter says that the Bedouins never hear it without screams of joy.

schiesmatics asserted that judgment *belongeth to God,* and this judgment will continue *to be maintained* till the day of resurrection,') and al Mughirah b. Shuubah, for verily he was Muawiyah's prefect over Kufah, and Muawiyah wrote to him, *saying,* 'when thou readest this letter, come *to me*-deposed from thy office,' but he delayed about it, and when he arrived, Muawiyah said to him 'what delayed 'thee?' He replied, 'an affair which I was setting and arranging,' and Muawiyah said, 'what was that?' He replied, 'the covenant of allegance for Yazid, after thee." He said, 'and hast thou done it?' He answered 'yes' : Muawiyah replied, 'go back to thy prefecture.' And when he went out his Companions said to him, 'how goes it with thee?' He answered, 'I have placed the food of Muawiyah in the stirrup of error in which it will continue till the day of resurrection.' Al Hasan says, 'for this reason, these have taken covenants of allegiance for their sons, and were it not for that, there would have been a Council *of election* till the day of resurrection.'"

A.H.60.
A.D.680.

Ibn Sirin states that Amr b. Hazm went to Muawiyah and said to him, "I call the Lord to thy remembrance in regard to the people of Muhammad, concerning him whom thou placest as thy successor over them." He replied, "thou hast given me counsel and spoken according to thy judgment, but verily there remain none but my son and their sons, and my son is the most deserving."

Atiah b. Kays says that Muawiyah preached and said, "O Lord, if I have surely made a covenant for Yazid on account of the merit I saw in him, then cause him to arrive at that which I have hoped, and assist him, but if it was indeed the love of the father for his son that hath influenced me, and if he be not deserving of that which I have done for him, then take him away before he arriveth at it." And when Muawiyah died, the people of Syria swore allegiance to Yazid. Then he sent to the people of Medina, one who was to take the covenant of allegiance for him, but al Husayn and Ibn uz Zubayr refused to acknowledge him and they too went forth in the night to Mecca. With regard to Ibn uz Zubayr he neither swore allegiance nor made any pretension on his own account, but as to al Husayn, the people of Kufah had written to him in the time of Muawiyah

A.H.60. A.D.680. soliciting him to come to them and he had refused, but when Yazid was acknowledged he reverted to what had been formerly meditated, at one time to remain and at another purposing to go to them, Ibn uz Zubayr counseled him to set out, but Ibn Abbas used to say "do not do it," and Ibn Omar said to him, "go not forth, for the Lord gave the apostle of God a choice between this world and the next, and he chose the next, and thou art a part of him, and thou shalt not obtain it" meaning the world, and he fell upon his neck and wept and bade him adieu. Ibn Omar used to say, "al Husayn prevailed over us concerning his departure, and by my life, verily he had beheld a warning example in his father and his brother ;" and Jabir b. Abdullah and Abu Sai'd, and Abu Wakid al Laythi used to address him similarly, but he did not yield to any of them and resolved upon the journey to Iraq, whereupon Ibn Abbas said to him, "by Allah, verily, I think thou wilt be slain among thy wives and children as Othman was slain." But he did not acquiesce, and Ibn Abbas wept and said "the eye of the son of az Zubayr hath become refreshed."[1] And when Ibn Abbas saw Abdullah b-uz Zubayr, he said to him, "what thou hast desired hath come to pass-this al Husayn is about to set forth and will quit thee and al Hijaz." Then he quoted appositely-

"O lark ! in this pasture land,
The valley is open to thee, lay thy eggs and sing.
Peck at what thou willest to peck." [2]

---

1 Meaning, that he saw his own way to the Caliphate only through the death of al Husayn whose march to Kufah he had counseled.

2 The verses are Kulayb Wail's of the tribe of Taghlib-the most powerful chief of Najd. The proverbial "guarded domain of Kulayb," was any land he chose to take for pasture, prohibiting others therefrom. It is said, he would put a dog in a field and wherever its bark could be heard, the prohibition of pasturage extended. From this dog, he is supposed to have received the name of Kulayb. Once when he was walking in his domain, a lark flew away from her eggs at his approach, upon which he said, "Fear not, thy eggs are under my protection," and then added the verse quoted which concludes thus : "The fowler is far from thee, so he glad-yet, sure, he will take thee some day, so beware." See Chenery's notes to 19th and 26th Assemblies of al Hariri.

And the people of Iraq, sent messengers and letters to al Husayn, inviting him among them whereupon he set forth from Mecca to Iraq on the 10th of Dul Hijjah, an with him a party of his household, men, women and children. The Yazid wrote to Ubaydullah b. Ziyad, his prefect in Iraq to oppose him and he sent against him an army of four thousand men, commanded by Omar b. Saad b. Abi Wakkas. And the people of Kufah deserted al Husayn, as had been their way with his father before him, and when the troops came up with him he proffered, submission to them and to return and go to Yazid to place his hand in the hand of Yazid, but they refused everything but his death, and he was slain and his head was carried in a platter until it was placed before Ibn Ziyad-may God curse his slayer, and Ibn Ziyad with him and Yazid likewise. A.H.60. A.D.680.

He was slain at Karbala and the narrative of his death is long the mention of which the heart cannot endure, "verily we belong to God, and verily unto Him shall we return." There were slain together with him sixteen men of his family. And when al Husayn was murdered, the world stood still for seven days, and the sun upon the walls appeared as saffron-coloured sheets, and the stars struck one upon the other. His murder took place on the 10th of Muharram, and the sun was eclipsed on that day and the horizon of the sky became red for six months after his death. The rednesd did not ceases to be seen after that, but it had never been beheld before.

It is said that not a stone was turned in Jerusalem on that day but fresh blood was found beneath it, and the saffron that was in their army became ashes, and they slew a camel in their army and they saw in its flesh, as if flames, and they ecoked it and it became like the colocynth, and a man spake some words against al Husayn and the Lord launched at him two stars from heaven and his sight was destroyed.

At Thaalabi says that historians have recounted in several ways on the authority of Abdul Malik b. Umayr al Laythi, that he said, "I saw upon this palace," and he pointed to the royal palace of Kufah, "the head of al Husayn the son of Ali upon a buckler, before

A.H.60. A.D.680. Ubaydullah b. Ziyad ; afterwards I beheld the head of Ubaydullah b. Ziyad before al Mukhtar b. Abi Ubayd; again, - I saw the head of al Mukhtar before Musaab. b-uz Zubayr; next I saw the head of Musaab before Abdul Malik b. Marwan and I related this circumstance to Abdul Malik who was started at it and left the place." [1]

At Tirmidi records on the authority of Salma[2] that she narrates, "I went in unto Umm, Salimah[3] and she weeping and I said, 'what makes thee weep?' She replied, 'I saw the apostle of God in a dream, with dust on his head and beard,' and I said, 'what hath come to thee, O apostle of God?' He replied, 'I withnessed but now the murder of al Husayn.'" And al Bayhaki in the Dalail from Ibn Abbas that he said, "I saw the Apostle of God at midday, with disheveled hair, soiled with dust and in his hand a phial of blood, and I said, 'with my father and my mother, *mayst thou be ransomed,* what is this?' He replied, 'this is the blood of al Husayn and his Companions, I have not ceased to gather it up from to-day;' and they computed the day and found that he was slain on that day."

Abu Nuaym records in the Dalail from Umm Salimah, that she said, "I heard the jinns weeping for al Husayn and lamenting over him." And Thaalab in his Dictations from Abu Janab al Kalabi that he narrates, "I went to Karbala and I said to one of the Arab Chiefs, 'tell me regarding what hath reached me, *viz.,* that ye hear the lamentations of the jinns ;' and he said, 'thou wilt not meet with any one, but he will tell thee that he hath heard it.' I replied, 'then tell me what thou hast heard.' He replied, 'I have heard them saying-

The Apostle stroked his forehead
And he had a radiance in his cheeks ;

---

1 According to Ockely, he commanded the castle to be demolished to avert the ill omen-Masaudi says امربهدم الطاق الذى كان علي المجلس

2 Freedwoman of Muhammad or according to others of Safiyyahd of Abdul Muttalib – she married Abu Rafi,' freedman of Muhammad.

3 See note 1 page 19.

His parents were the noblest of the Kuraysh, A.H.60.

And the grandsire the best of grandsires.'" A.D.680.

And when al Husayn and the children of his father were slain, Ibn Ziyad sent their heads to Yazid who at first rejoiced at their death, but repented afterwards when the Muslims hated him for it, and the people bore him enmity and bore him enmity with justice.

Abu Yala records in his Musnad on a weak ascription to Abu Ubaydah, that the Apostle of God said, "the government of my people shall not cease to be based on justice until the first that shall subvert it shall be a man of the Banu Umayyah called Yazid." Ar Ruyani records in his Musnad on the authority of Abud Darda, that he narrates, "I heard the Apostle of God say, 'the first who will alter my law, will be one of the Banu Umayyah called Yazid.'" Naufal b-ul Furat says, "I was with Omar b. Abdul Aziz, when a mam mentioned Yazid and said, 'the prince of the Faithful Yazid the son of Muawiyah said,' and he exclaimed, 'dost thou call him prince of the Fithful?' and he gave orders regarding him, and he was scouraged twenty lashes."

In the year 63 it reached Yazid, that the people of Medina had rebelled against him and deposed him, wherefore he sent against them a large force and ordered it to attack them and them march to Mecca to engage Ibn uz Zubayr. And they sent out and there took place the batlle of Harrah over against the gate of Taybah, and what shall made thee understand what the battle of Harrah was ! Al Hasan mentions it once and says, "by Allah, scarcely one of them escaped." A large number of the Companions and others were slain in it, and Medina was sacked and a thousand virgins violated. Verily we belong to God and verily unto Him shall we return. The apostle hath said, "he who intimidateth the people of Medina, the Lord shall put him in fear and upon him be the curse of God and his angels and of all mankind" (Muslim relates this). The reason of his deposition by the people of Medina was that Yazid became boundless in iniquities. Al Wakidi records with various lines of ascription, that Abdullah b. Handhalah bil Ghasil said, "by Allah, we did not rebel against Yazid until we feared that we should be stoned from Heaven on account of a man who would marry slave mothers *who had borne* children *to their masters* and daughters and sisters, and drink wine and abandon public prayers." Ad Dahabi says, "when Yazid had done unto the people of Medina what he had done, together with his drinking wine and indulgence in forbidden things, the people became violent against him and more than one rebelled against him, and the Lord did not bless his life and while the army of Harrah marched to Mecca, the commander of the troops[1] died on the way. But he appointed over them a chief to succeed him and they reached Mecca and besieged Ibn uz Zubayr and attacked him and launched engines of war against him, and that in Safar of the year 64. And from the sparks of their fire, the covernings of the Kaabah took fire and its roof and the two horns of the ram, the one by which Ishmael was ransomed[2] and which were in the roof."

A.H.64. A.D.683. The Lord destroyed Yazid in the middle of the month of Rabiiul Awwal of this year (11th November, 683) and the news of his death arrived while the fighting was going on. And Ibnuz Zubayr called out; "O men of Syria, verily your oppressor is dead ;" and they were rounted and broken and the people captured them, and Ibnuz Zubayr invited the covenat of allegiance for himself, and assumed the title of Caliph. But the people of Syria swore allegiance to Muawiyah the son of Yazid, but his reign was not long, as will appear afterwards. Among the verse of Yazid are,

This sorrow hath returned and drawn near,
And embittered sleep and withheld it.
Gazing upon the stars I watched them
And when a planet rose
It circled over until, verily, I saw it
Declining to its fall.

---

1 Muslim b. Ukbah, he died at a place called Harsha having appointed Husayn (حصين) b. Numayr as Sakunit succeed him. Ibn Khall, art. Abu Jaafar.

2 The printed edition should have, with the MS. فُدِىَ for فدّىَ it is well-known that the Muhammadans maintain that Ishmael and not Isaac was taken for Sacrifice by Abraham.

A.H.64.
A.D.683.

And my love in Matirun,[1] what time
The ant eateth[2] of what she hath garnered,
Hath a pleasant abode and when she arriveth,
She alighteth at a temple near Damascus
Under the domes in the midst of cloisters
Round which the olives are ripening.

Ibn Asakir records on the authority of Abdullah b. Omar that he said-"Abu Bakr the witness to the truth, ye have well hit his name-and Omar, the discriminator, a horn of iron, ye have well hit his name, Ibn Affan the possessor of two luminaries, unjustly slain, is given a double portion of divine mercy. Muawiyah and his son are kings of the Holy Land. As Saffah, and Salam,[3] and al Mansur, and Jabir, and al Mahdi, and al Amin and the prince of wrath, are all of them of the Banu Kaab b. Lawayy, all of them virtuous, their like cannot be found." Ad Dahabi says that this is given in various ways, but no one has traced its ascription.

Al Wakidi states on the authority Abu Jaafar al Bakir,[4] that the first who covered the Kaabah with silk brocade was Yazid b. Muawiyah.

There died of distinguished people in the reign of Yazid, beside those who were killed with al Husayn and in the battle of Harrah, Umm Salimah the mother of the Faithful, Khalid b. Urfutah, Jarhad al Aslami, Jabir b. Atik, Burayda b-ul Husayb, Maslamah b. Mukhallad, Alkamah b. Kays an Nakhai the doctor of law, Masruk, Miswar b. Makhramah and others. The number of the slain at Harrah of the Kuraysh and the Auxiliaries, were three hundred and six.

---

1 A village near Damascus.

2 The printed edition has اكمل for اكل The MS. here agrees with Yakut who gives these verses with slight variants under art- الماطرون

3 I am unable to explain the introduction of the names, Salam, Jabir and the prince of wrath. The MS. is in accordance with the text but both are probably in error. Its unintelligibility may account for its lack of ascription.

4 Muhammad b. Ali bal Husayn b. Ali b. Ali Talib called al Bakri, from the profundity of his knowledge. Muntahal Arab.

A.H.64.
A.D.683.

MUAWIYAH-B-YAZID

Muawiyah b. Yazid b. Muawiyah, Abu Abdur Rahman, called also Abu Yazid, and Abu Layla, was acknowledged Caliph according to the covenant of his father in the month of Rabiul Awal 64. He was a virtuous youth, and was suffering in health when appointed Caliph, and continued ill till he died. He never came forth to the people and did not take any part in affairs, nor prayed before the people. The duration of his Caliphate was forty days ; some say two months and others three months. He died being one and twenty years of age. When he was at the point of death, it was said to him, "wilt thou not name a successor ?" He replied, "I have not enjoyed the sweets of it, therefore I shall not take upon myself its bitterness."

ABDULLAH-B-UZ ZUBAYR

Abdullah was the son of az Zubayr bil Awwan b. Khuwaylad, b. Asad b. Abdil Uzza b. Kusayr. His surname was Abu Bakr and he was also called Abu Khubayb, a Companion, son of a Companion. His father was one of the ten unto whom the *attainment of* Paradise was testified, and his mother was Asma, daughter of Abu Bakr as Siddiq, and his father's mother was Safiyyah, paternal aunt of the Apostle of God. He was born at Medina twenty months after the Flight, and it is also said, within the first year, and he was the first child born to the Fugitives after the Flight. The Muslims rejoiced at his birth with an exceeding joy, for the Jews used to say, "we have bewitched them. The Apostle of God rubbed his palate with a date,[1] which he had first chewed and named him Abdullah and gave him the surname of Abu Bakr after the name and surname of his grandfather.

He was a great observer of fasting and devotions and given to

1 A custom with a newly born child to induce it to suck.

long prayer, attached to his kindred and of great intrepidity. He apportioned his time into three *recurring* nights ; on one night he prayed standing till morning, on the next with body inclined, and the next worshipping on his face till the morning. It is said that he had thirty-three traditions from the Prophet, and his brother Urwah, and Ibn Abi Mulaykah, Abbas b. Sahl, Thabit al]ani, Ata, Ubaydah as Salmani and others relate them on his authority. A.H.64. A.D.683.

He was one of these who refused to acknowledge Yazid b. Muawiyah and he fled to Mecca making no pretension *to the Caliphate* for himself but refusing to swear allegiance. And Yazid was wroth against him with exceeding anger, but when Yazid died, he was acknowledge Caliph and the people of Hijaz, Yaman, Iraq and Khurasan obeyed him. He renewed the building of the Kaabah and made for it two gates after the plans of Abraham, and included within it six cubits of the enclosure when Ayesha his aunt related to him *the tradition* from the Prophet.[1] External to his authority were only Syria and Egypt, and Muawiyah b. Yazid was acknowledged in those two places, but his reign was not long, and when he died the people of those two countries obeyed Ibn uz Zubayr and swore him allegiance. The Marwan b-ul Hakam rebelled and took possession of Syria and then of Eypt and remained in possession till he died in the year 65, after having covenanted for his son Abdul Malik.

It is most just what ad Dahabi observes that Marwan is not to be counted amongst the princes of the Faithful,[2] but as a rebel in revolt against az Zubayr, nor was his covenant for his son legal, but

1 This tradition is thus given in al Bukhari, "Muhammad said to Ayesha, 'were it not that thy tribe have been but lately converted from infidelity, I would order the temple to be demolished, and what had been excluded from it I would again adjoin to it, and would make two gates, to the east and west, and thus fashion it after the plan of Abraham.'" The narrator adds, that this tradition induced Ibnuz Zubayr to demolish the temple-see Sahih, p. 206. Delhi editin. 1848.

2 Well omits Ibnuz Zubayr and places the name of Marwan between Muawiyah II and Abdul Malik. Masaudi however, clearly, states that the authority of Ibnuz Zubayr became established even in Syria, (cont..)

A.H.64. A.D.683. the Caliphate of Abdul Malik became rightful from the time that az Zubayr was slain. Ibn uz Zubayr, however, remained at Mecca as Caliph until Abdul Malik obtained the ascendancy who dispatched al Hajjaj to oppose him at the head of forty thousand men, and he besieged him for some months and attacked him with engines of war. The friends of az Zubayr then deserted him and stole secretly to al Hajjaj, who defeated him and slew him and crucified him, and that on Tuesday the 17th[1] of Jumadal Awwal and say Jumadal Akhirah of the year 73 (3rd October 692).

Ibn Asakir records on the authority of Muhammad b. Zayd b. Abdillah b. Omar that he said, "I was *standing* upon the summit of *the hill* of Abu Kubays, at the time the engines were laid against Ibn uz Zubayr when a thunderbolt fell *from heaven,* so that I saw it wheeling round as if it were a red wild ass, and it burnt up of the people at the engine about fifty men. Ibn uz Zubayr was the best horsemen of his time among the Kuraysh-and his exploits are well attested.

Abu Yala records in his Musnad on the authority of Ibn uz Zubayr that the Prophet was bled and when it was over, he said to him, "O Abdullah, go with this blood and pour it out where no one may see thee;" and when he departed he drank it.

On his return the Prophet said to him, "what hast thou done?" He replied, "I designed it for a most secret place and I have put it therein." He said "perhaps thou hast swallowed it." He replied, "Yes." He exclaimed, "woe unto the people from thee, and woe unto thee from the people;" and they used to think that the strength that was in him was from that blood. And from Nauf ul Bikali[2] that

---

(cont.275) and he was publicly proclaimed from all the pulpits of Islam except that of Tiberias, where Hasan b. Malik held for Khalid b. Yazid –see Prairies d'Or. Tom 5, p. 194. Ockely likewise recognizes Ibnuz Zubayr as 9th Caliph, but places Marwan after him as the 10th .

1 Weil, following Masaudi makes it the 14th – as the 14th and not the 17th was a Tuesday.

2 Abu Yazid Nauf b. Fudhalah, a Tabii of the Banu Bikal-Munt. Arab.

he said, "verily I find in the revealed book of God that the best horseman among the Caliphs is Ibnuz Zubayr." A.H.73. A.D.692.

Amr b. Dinar says "I never saw one at prayers more devout than Ibn uz Zubayr, and he was once praying in the enclosure *of the temple* when a *bolt from a* catapult struck the side of his garment, but he did not heed it." Mujahid says, "there was no method of devotion which men *from its hardship* failed to perform, but Ibn uz Zubayr undertook it, and verily a torrent came and flooded the temple, whereupon he went round it swimming." Othman b. Talhah says that Ibn uz Zubayr could not be matched in three things-in bravery, piety or eloquenc, and he had a voice that when he preached resounded in the hills. Ibn Asakir records from Urwah that an Nabighah al Jaadi recited this verse regarding Ibn uz Zubayr.

> Thou didst remind us of Siddik when thou didst rule us ;
> And of Othman and the Discriminator, and the poor rejoiced.
> And thou didst Amininster justice equally amongst the people, and it was undeviating :
> But in the morning returned the dark sable clouds.

And from Hisham b. Urwah and Khubayb, that the first who covered the Kaabah with silk brocade was Abdullah b-uz Zubayr, its covering having been of haircloths and dressed leather. And from Omar b. Kays that he said, "Ibn uz Zubayr had one hundred servants, each servant among them speaking a different tongue, and Ibn uz Zubayr used to speak with each of them in his Own tongue and when I regarded him in his worldly conduct, I used to say, 'this man never turns to God for the twinkling of an eye,' and when I regarded him in his religious conduct, I used to say, 'this man never turns to the world for the twinkling of an eye.'" And from Hisham b. Urwah, "the first word my paternal uncle Ibn uz Zubayr distinctly uttered as a child was 'sword,' and never let it out of his mouth, and his father when he heard that, would say, 'well, by Allah, thou shalt have it for a day and a day and days.'" And from Abu Ubaydah, that Abdullah b-uz Zubayr al Asadi, went

A.H.73. A.D.692. to Abdullah b-uz Zubayr bil Awwam and said, "O prince of the Faithful, between me and thee there is relationship through a certain female." Ibn uz Zubayr replied, "yest, it is a thou sayest, but it thou wilt consider this, thou wilt mark that all men go back to one father and mother." He said, "O prince of the Faithful, my means of subsistence are at end." He replied, "I never was surety to thy family that it would suffice for thee until thous dost return to them!" He answered, "O prince of the Faithful, my camel is footsore." He replied, "help her by cooling her hoof and pasture her on the plant called Subt,[1] and cover her with hair and ride her in the morning and the evening." He exclaimed "O prince of the Faithful, verily I came to thee asking for relief, but I did not come to thee asking for a prescription-the Lord curse the camel that bore me to thee;" and Ibnuz Zubayr replied "and its rider." And al Asadu deoarted, reciting this verse-

"I see that with Abu Khubayb, needs
Are unsupplied, and there is no Umayyad in the land
Among the Banu Aas or the descendants of Harb
Resplendent like the white star of a generous stood.
And I said to my companions, 'draw nigh to my stirrup
For I shall leave the interior of Mecca in the darkness
And when I pass Dat Iraq,[2] there shall be for me
No return to this son of remissness.'"

Abdur Razzak records in the Musnnaf on the authority of az Zuhri, that never was a head brought to the Apostle of God at Medina, not even after the battle of Badr, but a head was once take to Abu Bakr, and he disapproved of it. The first to whom heads were taken was Abdullah b-uz Zubayr.

---

1 Lane makes this to be a plant resembling the *Althea officinalis* or marsh mallow.

2 A place near Mecca where the pilgrims from Irak put on the pilgrims dress before approaching the Kaabah.

During the reign of uz Zuhayr occurred the rebellion of al A.H.73.
Mukhta, the liar, he who pretended to propheey,[1] and Ibn uz Zuhayr A.D.692.
dispatched an army to opposed him until he overpowered him in the year 67 and put him to death-may God curse him.

Of the distinguished men who died during the reign of az Zuhayr, were, Usayd b. Dhuhayr, Abdullah b. Amr bil Aas, an Numan b. Bashir, Sulayman b. Surad, Jabir b. Samurah, Zayd b. Arkam, Abi b. Hatim, Ibn Abbas, Abu Wakid al Laythi, Zayd b. Khalid al Juhni, Abul Aswad ad Dauli and others.

ABDUL MALIK-B-MARWAN

Abdul Malik b.Marwan bil Hakam b. Abil Aas Umayyah b. Abd Shams b. Abd Manaf b. Kusayy b. Kilab,-Abul Walid, was born in the year 26, and was acknowledged Caliph according to the covenant of his father, during the Caliphate of Ibn uz Zubayr, but his Caliphate was not valid, and he continued as a usurper over Egypt and Syria. Subsequently he took possession of Iraq and the adjacent provinces, till Ibn uz Zubayr was slain in the year 73, from which day his Caliphate became valid and his authority established.

During this year, al Hajjaj pulled down the Kaabah and restored

---

1 On what ground this is asserted I cannot find. Neither d'Herbelot, nor Ockley nor Weil, nor Masaudi mention it. The latter says that when his wives were commanded by Musab to curse their dead husband, two of them refused testifying to his piety and his exertions in the cause of God and his Prophet and his avenging the blood of Husayn. One of these two women subsequently relented under threat of death and called al Mukhtar an infidel, adding that she would have abjured Islam likewise under a similar threat. The other died rather than consent to the intimidations of Musab. The aim of al Mukhtar's ambition was to extirpate the murderers of al Husayn, and avenge his death which he amply accomplished by killing, according to Ockely, nearly fifty thousand men. He was slain in the 67th year of his age after having beaten all the generals of Yazid, Marwan and Abdul Malik and made himself master of Baylonian Iraq.

A.H.73. it to the condition in which it now is ; he likewise suborned a man to
A.D.692. strike Ibn Omar with a poisoned javelin, of which he sickened and died.

In the year 74 al Hajjaj went to Medina and began to oppress its people and humilties the remnant of the Companions of the Apostle of God therein, and sealed them in their necks and hands, thereby bringing them into contempt, such as Anas, Jabir b. Abdillah, and Sahl b. Saad as Saadi-verily we belong to God and unto God do we return.

In the year 75 the Caliph Abdul Malik made the pilgrimage with the people, and he sent al Hajjaj as governor to Irak.

In the year 77 Heraclea was taken, and Abdul Aziz b. Marwan demolished the principal mosque at Cairo and enlarged it on all four sides.

In the year 82 the fortress of Sinan in the district o Masisah,[2] was captured, and the expedition to Armenia and Sinhajah in northern Africa took place.

In the year 83 the city of Wasit was founded by al Hajjaj.

In the year 84 Masisah was occupied and the valleys of Mauritania.

In the year 85 the city of Ardabil was founded and the city of Bardaah,[3] both by Abdul Aziz Abi Hatim bin Numan al Bahili.

In the year 86 the forts of Taulak and Akram were taken. During the same occurred the Pestilence of the Girls, so called

---

1 Lane says that the "sealing of the neck" (ختم الاعناق) is mentioned in the Risaluh Yusufiyah thus-Omar sent Ibn Hunayf to seal the علوج or unbelievers of the Sawad, and he sealed 5,00,000 of them in classes ; that is, he marked them twelve dirhams and twenty-four and forty-eight, tying a thong upon the neck of each and putting upon the knot a seal of lead.

2 On the north frontier of Syria.

3 In Adarbijan.

because it began with the women : in the same died the Caliph Abdul Malik in the month of Shawwal leaving seventeen sons. A.H.86. A.D.705. Ahmad b. Abdillah al Ijli says that Abdul Malik was foul of breath, and that he was a six months child. Ibn Saad says that he was pious and virtuous when at Medina before the Caliphate, and Yahya al Ghassani mentions that Abdul Malik was often in the company of Ummud Darda,[1] and she said to him on one occasion, "it was reached me, O prince of the faithful, that thou drinkest wine after all thy piety and devotion." He replied "yes, by Allah, and it is the pleasantest liquor I have tasted." Nafi says, "verily I have been Medina and there is not in it a youth more zealous nor more learned in the law, nor more virtuous nor more versed in the book of God than Abdul Malik the son of Marwan," and Abuz Zanad observes that the jurists of Medina are four, Sai'd b-ul Musayyab Abdul Malik b. Marwan, Urwah b-uz Zubayr and Kabisah b. Duayb. Ibn Omar remarks that men beget a son, but Marwan begot a father,[2] and Abbadah b. Lubni, that it was said to Ibn Omar, "verily ye are a body of elders, and it will soon be that ye will pass away, whom then shall we consult after ye?" He replied, "verily Marwan hath a son learned in the law, consult him." Suhaym the freedman of Abu Hurayrah narrates that Abdul Malik, when he was a lad went in to Abu Hurayrah who said, "this man shall govern Arabia." And Ubaydah b. Riyah al Ghassani, that Ummud Darda said to Abdul Malik, "I never ceased thinking that this authority would come to thee since I saw thee." He replied, "how so?" She answered, "I never saw any one better than thou art as a narrator of traditions nor one more intelligent as a listener to them." And as Shaabi, "I never associated with any one, but I found in myself a superiority over him, save Abdul Malik b. Marwan, and verily I never related

---

1 Abud Darda the Companion had two wives of this name-the first Khayrah died during his lifetime, the second Hujaymah is here alluded to. On her husband's death she vowed to remain a widow, and refused Muawiyah's offer of marriage, saying that she hoped to marry her husband again in Paradise. She ended her days in great piety between Jerusalem and Damascus. An Nawawi.

2 Meaning one more illustrious than himself.

A.H.86. A.D.705. a tradition to him but he added to it, and never a verse o poetry but he capped me in it."

Ad Dahabi says that Abdul Malik heard traditions from Othman and Abu Hurayrah and Abu Sai'd and Umm Salimah, Barirah,[1] Ibn Omar and Muawiyah; and Urwah, Khalid and others have related them on his authority.

Bakr b. Abdullah al Muzani narrates "a Jew whose name was Yusuf embraced Islam, and he had read the scriptures, and he passed by the house of Marwan and said, 'woe to the people of Muhammad from the people of this house,' and I said to him for how long?' He replied, 'until the black standards come from Khorsan.' Abdul Malik had a friend who slapped him on the shoulder and said 'fear God in *thy charge of* the people of Muhammad when thou relest them.' He replied, 'leave me ! fie on thee, what hath such as I am to do with that dignity!' The other answered 'fear God in what concerneth them.'" The narrator continues, "Yazid dispatched an army against the people of Mecca and Abdul Malik said, 'God preserve me, is it sent against the sanctuary of God?' and Yusuf slapped his shoulder and said, 'thy army against them shall be greater.'"

Yahya al Ghassani relates, "when Muslim b. Ukbah[2] arrived at Medina, I entered the mosque of the Apostle of God and sat down by the side of Abdul Malik, and he said to me, 'art thou of this army?" I said 'yes.' He replied 'may thy mother be childless of thee! dost thou not know against whom thou goest?-against the first-born in Islam and against the son of the disciple of the Apostle of God and against a son of the Possessor of the Girdles,[3] against him whose palate the Apostle of God rubbed with a date! By Allah, if thou goest to him in the daytime, thou wilt find him fasting, and if

---

1 Barirah was the daughter of Safwan and the freedwoman of Ayesha. An Nawawi.

2 He commanded the army dispatched by Yazid against Medina, and after wards to engage Ibnuz Zubayr at Mecca. (See p. 271)

3 See Note 1, Page 107.

thou goest to him at night, thou wilt find him praying-and if the A.H.86. A.D.705.
people of the earth combine to slay him, the Lord will assuredly fling them headlong into hell-fire.' And when the Caliphate fell to Abdul Malik, he sent us with al Hajjaj until we slew him."

Ibn Abi Ayesha says that *the announcement* of the government having devolved upon him reached Abdul Malik when the Qurãn was in his lap, and he closed it and said, "this is *my* last time with thee;" and Malik narrates, "I heard Yahya b. Said say 'those who prayed in the mosque between midday and the afternoon were Abdul Malik and certain youths with him-when the Imam had read the midday prayers they used to stand praying till the afternoon; and it was said to Sai'd b-ul Musayyab, if we could but stand and pray as those pray !' He replied, 'devotion lieth not in much prayer and fasting, but verily devotion consisteth in meditation on the commands of God and abstaining from the things that God hath prohibited.'" Musab b. Abdullah says, that the first who was named Abdul Malik in Islam, was Abdul Malik b. Marwan. And Yahya b. Bukayr narrates, "I heard Malik say that the first who coined dinars was Abdul Malik and he inscribed on them *a verse* of the Qurãn." Musab states that Abdul Malik inscribed on the dinar, "Say God is One" (Qur. CXII) and on the reverse, "there is no God but God;" and its circumference was a rain of silver, and he inscribed outside the rim, "Muhammad is the Apostle of God, whom He hath sent as a guide unto salvation and the true faith."

It is stated in the Awail of al Askari with its ascription, that Abdul Malik was the first who wrote at the headings of letters "Say there is one God, "together with the mention of the Prophet and the date, and the Grecian emperor wrote, saying, "verily you have introduced in your epistles some what of the mention of your Prophet, therefore abandon it, otherwise there will reach you on our dinars the mention of what you will not like." And this pressed sorely upon Abdul Malik and he sent to Khalid b. Yazid b. Muawiyah and consulted him, who said 'forbid their money and strike for the people coins upon which shall be the praise of God and His Prophet and do not forego for them that which they dislike in your epistles." He therefore coined dinars for the people in the year 75, And the

A.H.86. first Caliph who was parsimonious was Abdul Malik, and he was
A.D.705. named "Sweat of a stone," and obtained the surname of the "Father of flies" from his foul breath. He was the first in Islam who acted treacherously and the first who forbade speaking in presence of the Caliphs, and the first who prohibited exhortation to uprightness of conduct. [1]

He than records with its ascription on the authority o Ibnul Kalabi, that Marwan b-ul Hakam had named Amr b. Sai'd bil Aas to the succession after his own son, but Abdul Malik slew with, and his assasinaiton was the first act of treachery in Islam. One has said-

> O people ! be not prevailed over in your judgments, for verily
> Ye have experienced perfidy from the sons of Marwan.
> And verily they slew Amr and did not act uprightly,
> Asserting treachery and fraud to be the command of God;
> And they slay men ripe of judgment, in sound mind
> That they may give children to rule over the affairs of men.
> They jest with the Book of God and take
> Their desires in iniquities against the Lord, to be a means of approaching him.

He has also recorded with an ascription, (in which comes al Karimi who is suspected of falsehood) on the authority of the father of Jurayi, that he said, "Abdul Malik preached to us in Median after the death of Ibn uz Zubayr, in the year of his pilgrimage, the year 75, and after praising and glorifying God, he said "now, I am not a weak Caliph, to wit Othman, nor a Caliph a hypocrite, to with Muawiyah, nor a Caliph weak in understanding, to wit Yazid-now,

---

1 I.e. venturing to suggest to the Caliph a particular course of conduct or condemning any that he might have adopted, a not unfrequent practice with holy fanatics in early times-compare يامرهم بالمعروف (Qur. VII.)

verily the Caliphs before me used to consume and enjoy this property *of the State*-now forsooth, I will not heal the diseases of this people save with the world until your spears rise erect for me. Ye thrust upon me the needs of the Fugitives, but ye do not yourselves according to their works-therefore you will add only to your punishment until the sword shall decide between me and between ye. This Amr, his kinship was such as it was and his position such as it was-he said with his head-thus, and I said with my sword-thus. Now, I will endure anything from you but attacking a governor or raising a standard-verily the collar which I put upon the neck of Amr b. Yazid is with me-by Allah, no one shall do his deed, but I will put it upon his neck-by Allah, no one shall enjoin upon me the fear of God after this my rising *to-day* but I will smite his neck"-then he descended. A.H.86. A.D.705.

Al Askari then continues that Abdul Malik was the first that altered the public registers from Persian to Arabic and the first that raised up his hands on the pulpit. I remark that ten innovations are thus summed up in him of which five are reprehensible.

Ibn Abi Shaybah records with its ascription in the Musannaf on the authority of Muhammad b. Sirin, that the first who introduced the call to prayers on the festivals of Fitr and Adhha were the children of Marwan, either Abdul Malik or one of his sons. Abdur Razzak records from Ibn Juryj that he said, "more than one person has told me that the first who covered the Kaabah with silk brocade was Abdul Malik, but verily those among the jurists who have been best acquainted with that subject, say, 'there hath reached us what we know regarding the covering of the Kaabah more exact, than that.' Yusuf b-ul Majishun[1] says that when Abdul Malik sat down

---

1 Abu Yusuf Yakub, the father of Yusuf, was the son of Abu Salama Dinar, a client of the Banu Taym. He was a Mawla of the Munkadirs, a family of Medina. He pretended to have been ravished to heaven in spirit, and to have seen Muhammad with Abu Bakr and Omar at his right and left hand and Omar b. Adil Aziz at his feet. He died at Baghdad under the Caliphate of al Mahdi, A.H. 164 (780-1). Ibn Khall says that Majishun signifies rose colour or tinged with red and white, and the name was given him by Sukaynahd of Husayn b. Abi Talib. Another explanation is (cont...)

A.H.86. A.D.705. to administer justice, men stood at his head with swords. And al Asmai, that it was said to Abdul Malik, greyness is hastening upon thee,' he replied, 'and how could it be otherwise when I give forth my *whole* intellect to the people every Friday.'" Muhammad b. Harb az Ziyadi narrates that it was said to Abdul Malik "who is the best of men?" he replied, "he who is humble in a lofty station, devout though in authority and just though in power." And Ibn Ayesha, that Abdul Malik when a man from any of the remote countries came in to him, used to say, "spare me four things-and say after that what thou pleasest-do not lie to me for liars have no judgment, and do not answer me regarding what I do not ask thee for it is a distraction from what I do ask thee, and do not be extravagant in my praise for I know myself better than thou, and do not incite me against my subjects for verily clemency unto them is more needful for me."

Al Madaini says that when Abdul Malik was made aware of his *approaching* death, he said, "by Allah, I would that from the time I was born until to-day, I had been a porter;" then he commended unto his sons, the fear of God, and warned them against dissension and discord, and said, "be ye as sons of a virtuous mother, and be brave in war, and as a beacon in doing good for verily war doth not bring death before its time, and as to goodness, its reward and its fame endure, and be ye sweet in bitterness and lenient in severity, and be ye as Ibn Abd al Aala as Shaybani says-

'Verily arrows when they are gathered together, and hath sought
To break them, a stong man full of rage and might.
They resist and cannot be broken, but it they be separated
Then rupture and weakness belong to what is dispersed.'

O Walid, fear God in that in which I leave thee to succeed me; and he went on to say-:look to al Hajjaj, and honour him, for verily,

(Cont.285) that as they were originally from Ispahan, they saluted each other when they met with "Shuni-Shuni" and were therefore called Majishun. The etymology is not satisfactory.

he it is who hath coerced for you the pulpits, and he is thy sword, O Walid, and thy *right* hand against those who oppose thee,- therefore hear not the word of any one against him, for thou art more in need of him than he of thee-end summon the people when I die to the covenant of allegiance, and he who said with his head-thus-say with thy sword-thus." A.H.86. A.D.705.

Another relates that when Abdul Malik was on the point of death, his son al Walid went in unto him, and Abdul Malik recited appositely-

How many a visitor hath a *sick* man, who doth not visit him
But to learn whether he shall see him die.

Al Walid wept ; and Abdul Malik said, "what is this ? dost thou whine with the whining of a slave girl? When I am dead gird up thy loins and go forth and put on the skin of a leopard and lay thy sword upon thy shoulder, and whosoever showeth himself against thee smite him on the neck, and he who submits shall die a natural death." I remark that if the crimes of Abdul Malik had been only the appointing of al Hajjaj over the Muslims and the Companions, bringing them into contempt and degrading them by death, stries, reproach and imprisonment-and verily he slew of the Companions and the greatest of the Tabiis what is beyond count, to say nothing of others besides them, and sealed the neck of Anas and others of the Companions with a seal, intending thereby their humiliation,- then, *for these alone,* may God not have mercy upon him nor pardon him.

The following are lines of Abdul Malik's-

By my life, verily, I have lived a long space in the world.
And the world hath come night to me with the striking of sharp swords.
That which delighted me hath gone
Like a flash that hath passed among enduring remains.
And O would that I had never busied myself with the kingdom for a moment.
Nor diverted myself amidst the joyous pleasures of life.

A.H.86. A.D.705.

And that I had been as one clad in rags, living on a little
For a time until he visited the narrowness of the tombs.

In the history of Ibn Asakir it is stated on the authority of Ibrahim b. Adi that he said, "I saw Abdul Malik at a time when four events were announced to him during the night and he was not moved nor did his face alter-to wit the death of Ubaydullah b. Ziyad, the death of Hubaysh b. Daljah[1] in Hijaz, the rupture between himself and the Greek Emperor, and the rebellious march of Amr b. Said to Damascus." And in the same it is stated on the authority of Asmai that four men never spoke incorrectly either in earnest or jest-as Shaabi, Abdul Malik, al Hajjaj b. Yusuf and Ibnul Kirriyyah.[2]

As Silafi mentions in the Tuyyuriyat with its ascription, that Abdul Malik went forth one day and a woman me him an exclaimed, "O prince of the Faithful !" He said, "what is thy business ?" She replied, "my brother died and left six hundred dinars, and there was given to me of his inheritance but one dinar, and it was said to me, 'this is thy due;' and the thing was incomprehensible to Abdul Malik and he sent to as Shaabi and asked to him, who said, 'yes, this *man* died and left two daughters and they had two-thirds, four hundred, and a mother who had a sixth, one hundred, and a wife who had an eighth, seventy-five, and twelve brothers, who had twenty-four, and for this woman remineth one dinar.'"

Ibn Abi Shaybah relates in the Musannaf from Khalid b. Muhammad of the Kuraysh, that Abdul Malik said, "he who desireth to take a female slave four his amusement, let him take a native of

---

1 The only mention I can find of this name is in the Muntaha'l Arab where he is mentioned as a traditionist.

2 Abu Sulayman Aiyub al Hilali. Al Kirriyyah which signifies-the crop of a bird, was given to Jamaa, mother of Jusham, one of his ancestors. He was an untutored Arab of the desert, but the elegance and precision of his language gave him the reputation of one of the best orators of that people. He was summoned by al Hajjaj to his court and honored so far as to be entrusted by him with a mission to Abdul Malik. He was put to death afterwards in A.H. 84 by that tyrant for having allowed himself to be compelled to join in the rebellion of Ibnul Ashath. Ibn Khall.

Barbary, and who needs one for the sake of children, let him have a Persian, and who desireth to have one for service, let him take a Greek." A.H.86. A.D.705.

Abu Ubaydah narrates that when al Akhtal recited to Abdul Malik his verse in which he *says of the Umayyads-*

The Most inveterate enemy ends by submitting[1] to them
And they are greatest of men in meekness when they are in power.

He said, "O slave, take him by the hand, and lead him forth and put upon him robes of honour as many as will cover him up-then he said, "verily every tribe hath a poet, and the poet of the Banu Umayyah is al Akhtal."[2] Al Asmai says that al Akhtal went Abdul Malik who said, "come now, describe intoxication to me." He replied, "its beginning is pleasure and its end a headache, and between that there is a moment, the crisis of which I will not describe to thee." He said "and what is its crisis?" He replied, "verily thy kingdom, O prince of the Faithful, *then* is of less account to me than the latchet of my shoe," and he versified, saying,

When my boon Companion giveth me to drink and giveth yet again
Three globets of bubbling *wins*
I go forth trailing my garment behind me as if
I were lord over thee, O prince of the Faithful.

At Thaalabi narrates that Abdul Malik used to say, "I was born in the month of Ramadhan, and weaned in Ramadhan, and

---

1 For يستفاد read يستقاد the verse will be found in the Kitabul Aghani, Vol. 7.

2 The life of al Akhtal is given by M. Caussin de Perceval in the Journal Asiatique for April 34. His real name was Ghyath b. Ghauth and belonged to the Banu Malik, a branch of the Taghlabites. He was a Christian like the greater number of the tribes of Bihra, Taghlib, and Tanukh and remained attached to his faith, notwith-standing the many seductive offers made to him to abandon it for Islam. He died at an advanced age recommending Farazdak with his last breath, to cover his rival Jarir with ridicule.

A.H.86. completed learning the Qurãn by heart in Ramadhan, and I reached
A.D.705. the age of puberty in Ramadhan, and the Caliphate fell to me in Ramadhan, and I fear lest I die in Ramadhan," and when he entered upon the month of Shawwal and felt safe, he died. (8th October 705).

Of those of note who died in the reign of Abdul Malik were Ibn Omar, Asma, daughter of as Siddik , Abu Sai'd b-ul Mualla, Abu Sai'd al Khudri, Rafi b. Khadij, Salimah b-ul Akwa, Irbadh b. Sariyah, Jabir b. Abdillah, Abdullah b. Jaafar b. Abi Talib, as Saib b. Yazid, Aslam the freedman of Omar, Abu Idris al Khaulani, the Khadhi Shurayh, Aban b. Othman b. Affan, al Aasha the poet, Ayub b-ul Kirriyah, proverbial for eloquence, Khalid b. Yazid b. Muawiyah, Zirr b. Hubayah, Sinan b. Salimah bil Muhabbik, Suwayd b. Ghaflah, Abu Wail Tarik b. Shihab, Muhammad b-ul Hanafiyah, Abdullah, b. Shaddad bil Had, Abu Ubaydah b. Abdillah b. Masaud, Amr b. Harith, Amr b. Salimah al Jirmi and others.

AL WALID-B-ABDIL MALIK

Al Walid b. Abdil Malik, Abul Abbas, was brought up effeminately, says as Shaabi, by his parents and he grew up without culture. Ruh b. Zinbaa narrates, "I went in one day to Abul Malik, and he was meditating, and he said, 'I was thinking to whom I should commit the government of Arabia, and I cannot find any one.' I said, 'what dost thou think of al Walid ?" He replied, "verily he is not well versed in grammar." Walid heard this and he rose at once and assembled the grammarians, and sat with them in his house for six month and then came forth more ignorant than before, and Abdul Malik said, "verily he is excusable." Abuz Zinad[1] states

1 A native of Medina, a doctor of law and one of the Tabiis. His varied information and his erudition gained him preeminence among the learned of his day. He died A.H. 130. (A.D. 748). Aged 66. De Slane, I.K. At age 220 the name is misspelt Zanad.

that al Walid mispronounced to a great degree ; he exclaimed from the pulpit of the Prophet's mosque, "O people of al Medina."[1] A.H.86. A.D.705.

Abu Akrinah ad Dhabi says that al Walid read from the pulpit, "O that death had made an end of me."[2] (Qur. LXIX), and below the pulpit stood Omar b. Abdil Aziz and Sulayman b. Abdil Malik, and Sulayman exclaimed, "by Allah, I would it had." Walid was despotic and tyrannous.

Abu Nuaym records in the Huliyah from Ibn Shaudab that Omar b. Abdil Aziz said, "al Walid in Syria, al Hajjaj in Iraq, Othman b. Habbarah[3] in Hijaz and Kuraah b. Sharik in Egypt, have filled the earth, by Allah, with tyranny." And Ibn Abi Hatim in his Commentary, from Ibrahim b. Abi Zuraah, that al Walid said to him, "will the Caliph be judged *at the resurrection?*" He replied, "O prince of the Faithful, art thou more honoured of the Lord, or David ? Verily the Lord united in him the Prophetic mission and the vicegerency, yet hath he threatened him in His Book and said, "O Daiv," &c. (Qur. XXXVIII.)[4]

Al Walid, however, stirred up religious wars in his time and great conquests were made under his Caliphat-and withal he used to circumcise orphans and appointed teachers for them and assigned for those crippled by disease, persons to attend them and for the blind those who should lead them, and he embellished the mosque of the Prophet and enlarged it and settled a daily allowance on the doctors of law and the infirm and the poor and forbade their begging of the people, and assigned for them what would suffice *for their maintenance* and regulated affairs by a thorough administration ;

---

1 It is impossible to reader the error in a translation as it consists in a misplacement of the diacritical points. He said "Ya ahlul Medinah" instead of "Ya ahla'l Medinah," the vocative requiring the objective case when the noun is in construction.

2 Misplacing the vowel-points again. "Yalaytu ha for Ya layta ha.

3 The MS. has Janadah.

4 "O David ! verily we have appointed thee a sovereign prince in the earth-judge therefore between men with truth and follow not thy own lust, lest it cause thee to err from the way of God." Qur. XXXVIII.

A.H.86. A.D.705. and Ibn Abi Aylah says, "the Lord have mercy on al Walid, and where is the like of Walid who conquered India and Spain and built the mosque of Damascus, and who used to give platters of silver which I divided among the readers[1] of the Qurãn of the mosque at Jerusalem?"

Al Walid assumed the Caliphat according to the covenant of his father in the month of Shawwal in the year 86, and in the year 87, he set about the building of the mosque at Damascus and ordered the enlargement of the mosque of the Prophet and its *thorough* construction. During the same Bikand[2] was taken by force of arms and Bukhars, and Sardinia and Matmurah,[3] Kumaykim and the Persian Gulf. And Omar b. Abdil Aziz, governor of Medina made the pilgrimage with the people, and performed by mistake the ceremony of standing[4] on Mount Arafah on the Day of Victims and was sore grieved thereat.

In the year 88 Jurthumah[5] and Tuanah[6] were taken-and in the year 89, the islands of Majorea and Minorca. In the year 91 were Capturel Nasaf[7] and Kash, Shuman, and other towns and forts by the Caspian Sea. In the year 92 the whole of Spain was subdued and the cities of Armail[8] and Katarbun-and in 93 Daybal and other places were conquered, and Kirakh, Barham, Bajah, al Baidha,

---

1 Both the MS. and the printed edition have [illegible] (readers of the Qurãn.) but it is possible that ! فقرا (the poor) might have been the original word and the elision of the ف taken place through the error of a copyist.

2 A town between Bukhara and the Oxus.

3 On the frontiers near Tarsus. Kumaykim, according to the Muntahal Arab is the name of a stream, but it does not say where.

4 The Wakf or standing on Mount Arafah should take place on the second day of the pilgrimage, 9th of Dul Hijjah, and the ceremony of the Day of Victims on the third day, 10th of Dul Hijjah.

5 In Najd.

6 On the Frontiers of Masisah, north of Syria.

7 Nasaf is a large town between Samarkand and the Oxus, and Kash is three Parasangs from Jurjan.

8 Both these places are in Sind : Ibnul Athir writes the second name Kannazbur and in some readings Firbur, Kirnur and Fabryur. Daybal (cont..)

Khuwarazm, Samarkand, and Sughd. In 94 Kabul, Farghanah, Shash and Sandarah were taken and in 95, Mukan[1] and Darband. In 96, Tus and other places. A.H.86. A.D.705.

In this year died the Caliph al Walid in the middle of Jumadal Akkirah at the age of fifty-one. (23rd February 715). Ad Dahabi says that religious wars were continuous throughtout his reign, and great conquests were made as in the time of Omar b-ul Khattab. Omar b. Abdil Aziz says, "when I put al Walid in his grave, behold he kicked in his shroud,-that is, he struck the earth with his foot." Among the sayings of al Walid is *the following,* "if God had not mentioned the family of Lot in the Qurãn, (VII, XV, XXVIL, LXVI) I would have thought that any one would act thus."

Of persons of note who died in the reign of al Walid, were Utbah b. Abdur Sulma, al Mikdam b. Madi Karb, Abdullah b. Bashr als Mazini, Abdullah b. Abi Aufa, Abul Aaliyah, Jabir b. Zayd, Anas b. Malik Sahl b. Saad, as Saib b. Yazid, as Saib b. Khallad, Khubayb b. Abdillah biz Zubayr, Bilal b. Abid Darda, Sai'd b-ul Musayyab, Abu Salimah b. Abdir Rahman, Abu Bakr b. Abdir Rahman, Said b. Jubayr martyred, slain by al Hajjaj may the Lord curse him, Ibrahim an Nakhai, Mutarrif, Ibrahim b. Abdir Rahman b. Auf, al Ajjaj the poet and others.

(cont.292) is in Sind. Of Barham I can find no mention, but Ibn Athir speaks of a place, Brahmanabad in Sind, taken and destroyed at this time. Bajah, Yakut places in Africa, and al Baidha so called from its white citadel, in the district of Persepolis. Kirakh is written Kiraj by Ibn Athir and he states that Muhammad b-ul Kasim who commanded the army in Sind, hearing at Multan of the death of his uncle al Hajjaj, returned at once to Rori Bakkar and thence proceeded to Kiraj. I am inclined to think that this must be Karachi, as Daybal or Dewal is stated by Elphinstone to have been probably close to that scapart. See Elph. India, p. 263, where will be found a sketch of Kasim's conquests.

1 Mukan is in Adarbijan. Tus had already been conquered in the time of Othman. Another reading is Tuways which I cannot find, but Yakut mentions a district Tawawis, near Bukhara. The MS. is here wanting.

A.H.96.
A.D.715.

SULAYMAN-B-ABDIL MALIK

Sulayman b. Abdil Malik, Abu Ayub, was among the best of the kings of the Banu Umayyah, and he assumed the Caliphate according to the covenant of his father in succession to his brother, in Jumadal Akhirah of the year 96. He was related a few traditions on the authority of his father and Abdur Rahman b. Hubayrah, and his son Abdul Wahid and uz Zuhri have transmitted them from him.

He was eloquent fluent of speech, preferring justice, a lover of war. He was born in the year 60. It is to be accounted among his merits that Omar b. Abdil Aziz was as his prime minister, and he used to follow his beneficial counsels ; and he deposed the revenue collectors of al Hajjaj and released those who were in the prisons of Iraq, and restored public prayers to their original appointed times, the Banu Umayyah having suffered them to lapse into dilatoriness. Ibn Sirin says, "the Lord have mercy on Sulayman who inauguared his Caliphate by the restoration of prayers to their, stated times, and closed it by appointing as his successor Omar b. Abdul Aziz." Sulayman forbade singing, and he was among those famed as large eaters, for he eat at a sitting seventy pomegranates, a lamb, six fowls, and a Makkuk[1] of Taif currants. Yayha al Ghassani says that Sulayman looked into a mirror and his youthfulness and beauty surprised him, and he said, "Muhammad was the Prophet, and Abu Bakr Witness to the Truth, and Omar the Discriminator, and Othman the Bashful, and Muawiyah the Forbearing, and Yazid the Patient, and Abdul Malik the Administrator, and Walid the Tyrant, and I am the Young King ;" but the month *in which he thus spoke* did not pass over him but he died, and the day of his death was Friday the 10th of Safar in the year 99 (22nd Sept. 717). During his regin were conquered Jurjan, and the Iron Fortress,[2] and Sarda, and Shakka,

---

1 About 11 pounds and a quarter. It is not astonishing that after this feat, he had an attack of indigestion which proved fatal.

2 I do not find any such name in Yakut, it is probably some local name given to a strong fort, unless Darband is meant, which was defended by Anushirwan by an iron gate. Neither Sarda or Shakka are given, nor a they noticed by Ibnul Athir.

and Tabristan and the city of as Sakalibah.[1] A.H.99. A.D.717.

Of persons of note that died during his time were, Kays b. Abi Hazim, Mahmud b. Labid. Al Hasan bil Husayn b. Ali, Kurayb freedom of Ibn Abbas, Abdur Rahman bil Aswad an Nakhai and others.

Abdur Rahman b. Hassan al Kanani, says, that Sulayman died at Dabik,[2] engaged in leading an expedition. When he sickened, he said to Raja b. Hayat, "who is to succeed me in this authority ? shall I appoint my son ?" He replied, "he is absent." He said, "then my other son?" He answered, "he is a child." He said, "then whom dost thou advise?" He replied, "I think that thou shouldst appoint Omar b. Abdil Aziz." He said, "I fear that my brothers will not consent." He rejoined, "appoint Omar, and after him Yazid b. Abdil Malik and write a document and seal it and summon them to take a covenant regarding it sealed." He replied, "verily thou hast conceived *wisely.*" Thereupon he called for paper and wrote the covenant therein and gave it Raja, and said, "go forth unto the people and let them make a covenant regarding that which is within it, sealed as it is." And he went forth and said, "verily the prince of the Faithful hath cammanded ye to make a covenant of allegiance for him *whose name is* in this document." They said, "who is in it?" He answered, "It is sealed-ye cannot be infored concerning the one who is in it until the Caliph dieth." They said, "we will not swear allegiance." And he returned to Sulayman and informed him of it, and he said, "go to the commander of the gurards and the

1 So likewise Ibnul Athir, Tabari calls it Sakalie. Weil says that it should be Sakalibah which he considers a district to the N. and N.W. of Constantinople. He can find no town of that name. Yakut makes as Sakalibah a (slav) district "between Bulgaria, and Constantinople." The word city I imagine, must be an error, or must refer to the then capital city of the Thracian towns of the Propontis, round which Maslamah wheeled his army after the passage of Abydus, to invest Constantinople defended by Leo the Isaurian. An Army of Bulgaraians from the Danube at the call of Leo fell upon the Saracen army and slaughtered twenty-two thousand. See Gibbon, Ch. LII.

2 Near Chalcis. He was preparing, according to Gibbon, to lead against Constantinople the remaining forces of the East.

A.H.99. A.D.717. watch, and assemble the people and order them to take the oath, and he who refuses smite his neck." And they swore allegiance. Raja relates, "while I was returning, behold *I met* Hisham and he said to me, O Raja, verily thou knowest thy credit with me, and verily the prince of the Faithful hath done a thing and I know not what it is, and verily I fear that it may be that he hath put the Caliphate from me, and if it be indeed that he hath put it side from me, tell me while there is yet time in the affair, that I may see *what to do*;" and I said, "good God ! the prince of the Faithful hath asked me to conceal a thing; and shall I tell it to thee? that can never be." Then I met Omar b. Abdil Aziz and he said to me, "O Raja, a grave thought has occurred to my mind concerning this man, I fear lest it be that he hath put the Caliphate upon me and I am not equal to this position, therefore tell me while there is yet time in the affair, perchance I may escape from it as long as I live." I said, "good God ! the prince of the Faithful asked me to conceal a thing and shall I tell it to thee?" Shortly after Sulayman died and the document was opened, when lo ! within was the covenant for Omar b. Abdil Aziz, and the faces of the sons of Abdul Malik changed, but when they heard that after him was to be Yazid the son of Abdul Malik, they returned and came to Omar and did homage to him as Caliph ; but he was stupefied at it, and was not able to rise until they took him by the arms and brought him to the pulpit and helped him to mount it. He sat a long time without speaking, at last Raja said to them, "do ye not stand up to the prince of the Faithful to swear allegiance to him?" Then they made the covenant with him, and he stretched out his hand to them. Then he arose and praised God and glorified Him and said, "O people, I am not one who decideth but one who executeth, nor one who beginneth but one who followeth-and verily the countries and cities round about ye, if they submit as ye have sumitted then I am your ruler, but I they refuse then I am not a ruler for ye." Then he descended, and there came to him the master of the horse, and he said, "what is this?" The man replied, "the Caliph's charger." He said, "I have no need of it-bring me my mule," and they brought him his mule and he proceeded to his house. Then he called for an ink horn and wrote with his own hand to the prefects of the provinces. Raja says, "I thought that he would soon lack strength, but when I saw his actions in his correspondence, I knew that he would become powerful." It is related that there fell some words between Marwan b. Abdul Malik[1] and Sulayman during the Caliphate of Sulayman, who said to him "O so, of an uncircumcised woman!" and Marwan opened his mouth to answer him, when Omar b. Abdil Aziz stopped his mouth and said, "I conjure thee for God's sake-he is thy Imam and thy brother and he is thy elder in years." And Marwan held his peace, and said, "thou hast slain me, by Allah, verily thou hast put within me that which is hotter than fire," and he died before the evening.

A.H.99.
A.D.717.

Ibn Abid Dunya records on the authority of Ziyad b. Othman that he went in unto Sulayman b. Abdul Malik when his son Ayub died, and said, "O prince of the Faithful, verily Abdur Rahman b. Abi Bakrah used to say 'he who desireth the things that are eternal, let him habituate himself to misfortunes."

OMAR-B-ABDIL AZIZ

Omar b. Abdul Aziz b. Marwan-the good Caliph-Abu Hafs, was the fifth of the orthodox Caliphs. Sufiyan at Thauri says that the five Caliphs are Abu Bakr, Omar, Othman, Ali, and Omar b. Abdil Aziz (Abu Dauud). Omar was born at Hulwan, a village in Egypt, of which his father was governor in the year of the Flight 61, or as some say 63. His mother was Umm Aasim, daughter of Aasim b. Omar bil Khattab. On Omar's face was a scar, a horse having kicked him in the forehead when he was a boy. His father wiping the blood off him said, "if thou art he of the Scar of the Banu Umayyah, verily thou art fortunate." (Ibn Asakir.) Omar b-ul Khattab used to say, "of my posterity there shall be a man with a scar in his face who shall fill the earth with justice" (at Tirmidi). The opinion

---

1 It must be remembered that Abdul Malik had seventeen sons.

A.H.99. A.D.717. of his father regarding him proved true. Ibn Saad records that Omar b-ul Khattab said, "would that I knew which of my posterity shall be the possessor of the letter, Shin[1] in *in his name*-he who is to fill *the earth* with justice as it hath been filled with tyranny." And from Ibn Omar that he said, "we used to say that the world would not pass away until a man of the posterity of Omar should rule, doing according to the works of Omar, and Bilal b. Abdillah b. Omar had a mole upon his face, and they used to think that it was he until the Lord sent Omar b. Abdil Aziz."

Omar b. Abdil Aziz related traditions on the authority of his father and Anas and others; and az Zuhri, Muhammad b-ul Munkadir, Yahya b. Said the Auxiliary, Maslamah b. Abdil Malik, Raja b. Hayat and many more related them on his.

He learnt the Qurãn when he was yet a child, and his father sent him to Medina to be instructed there, and he used to attend Ubaydullah b. Abdillah,[2] studying science under his tuition. When his father died, Abdul Malik sent for him to Damascus and married him to his daughter, Fatimah. Even before his Caliphate he walked in virtue save that he was over given to luxury, and the envious that found fault with him did not reproach him same for excess in luxury and haughtiness in his gait. When al Walid assumed the Caliphate, he made Omar governor of Medina and he ruled it from the year 86 to the year 93 when he was removed, and he went to Syria. After this, verily, al Walid determined to set aside his brother Sulayman from the succession, and to appoint his own son ; and many of the principal men, willingly or unwillingly obeyed him, but Omar b. Abdil Aziz objected, and said, "the covenant unto Sulayman is upon our necks," and he was firm, and al Walid immured him, but he was interceded for after three days and they found him with

1 The word 'scar' or fracture begins with that letter.

2 Abu Abdullah Ubaydullah b. Abdillah b. Utbab, was one of the seven great jurisconsults of Medina. Az Zuhri called him an ocean of knowledge, and Omar b. Abdil Aziz used to say that an evening with Ubaydullah was worth a thousand pieces of gold out of the public treasury. He died at Medina A.H. 102 (720-1) One of his poems is given in the Hamasah. Ibn Khall.

his neck drooping *from exhaustion.* Sulayman learnt this regarding him and nominated him to the succession in the Caliphate. A.H.99. A.D.717.

Zayd b. Aslam narrates that Anas said, "I never prayed behind an Imam after the Apostle of God, resembling the Apostle of God more in the manner of his praying, than this youth *i.e.,* Omar b. Abdil Aziz-while he was governor of Medina." Zayd b. Aslam adds, "he used to dwell long in his bending and prostrations, and shortened the time of standing and sitting," (this tradition has several lines of ascription to Anas-recorded by al Bayhaki and others).

Muhammad b. Ali bil Husayn was asked regarding Omar b. Abdil Aziz, and he said, "he is the noblest of the Banu Umayyah and verily he will be raised up at the day of resurrection, unequalled and alone."

Maymun b. Mihran said that the learned in comparision with Omar Abdil Aziz were mere students. Abu Nuaym records on the authority of Riyah b. Ubaydah by a sound ascription, that he said, "Omar b. Abdil Aziz went forth to prayers, and an old man was leaning on his arm, and I said to myself, 'verily this old man is rude;' and when he had prayed and entered *his house,* I joined him and said, 'may God prosper the Amir, who was the old man that was leaning on thy arm?' He replied, O Riyah didst thou see him?' I said 'yes.' He answered, 'I do not hold thee to be other than a virtuous man-that was my brother al Khidhr[1] who came to me and told me that I shall rule this people, and shall act with justice unto them.'" And from Abu Hashim that a man went to Omar b. Abdil Aziz and said, "I saw the Prophet in a dream, with Abu Bakr on his right hand and Omar on his left, and lo ! two men were disputing and thou wert seated before him, and he said to thee. 'O Omar when thou rulest, do according to the works of these two, of Abu Bakr and Omar.' And Omar b. Abdil Aziz made

---

1 This person as is well known, is regarded as a Prophet, and was supposed to have been the minister of an ancient king of Persia. By some he is said to be Elias, and by others St. George of England. His aid is frequently invoked by Muhammadan story-tellers whether the knot be worthy of his untying or otherwise.

A.H.99. A.D.717. him swear before God, *saying* 'didst thou see this ?' And he swore, and Omar wept."

He was acknowledge Caliph according to the covenant of Sulayman in the month of Safar 99 as hath gone before, and he continued in the Calipate for two years and five months about *the duration of* that of Abu Bakr, filling the earth with justice, removing grievances and establishing good laws. When the writing of the covenant was read contaning his name, he was stupified and said, "by Allah, verily I never asked for this authority of God." The master of the horse brought him the Caliph's charger, but he refused it, and said, 'bring me my mule." Hakam b. Omar relates, "I was present with Omar b. Abdil Aziz when the equerries came demanding of him provender *for the horses* and the atipends of their attendants. He exclaimed, 'send them to the Syrian towns, and let any one buy them who listeth, and put the prices of them with the property of the Lord-this grey she mule sufficeth for me.'" Omar B. Darr says, that when Omar returned from the funeral of Sulayman, his freedman said to him, "why do I see thee sad ?" he replied, "one should grieve to be in the station that I am in,-there is not on of this people, but I wish to give him his due without his writing to me about it or demanding it from me." And from Amr b. Muhajir and others, that when Omar was appointed Caliph, he stood up before the people and praised God and glorifed him and said, "O people ! there will be no *revealed* Book after the Qurãn and no Prophet after Muhammad,-now verily I am not one who decideth but one who executeth, nor one who beginneth but one who followeth, and I am not better than any one of ye but I am more forbearing in meekness, and verily a man that fleeth from a tyrannous Imam, doeth not wrongfully-surely there is no obedience due from the creature to what is sinful before the Creator." And from az Zuhri, that Omar b. Abidl Aziz wrote to Salim b. Abdillah[1] to describe to him the practice of Omar b-ul Khattab concerning the poor-rate, and he wrote to him regarding what he asked telling him, "verily if thou doest unto thy age and thy people according to

1 Grandson of Omar b-ul Khattab.

the works of Omar unto his age and people, thou will be greater A.H.99.
before the Lord than Omar." And from Hammad[1] that when Omar A.D.717.
was appointed Caliph he wept and said *to a certain person.* "O ! such a one, dost thou fear on my account?" He replied, "how is thy desire with regard to money ?" He said, "I have no love for it." He answered, "then fear not for the Lord will assist thee." And from Mughirah, that at the time Omar succeeded to the Caliphate, he assembled the sons of Marwan and said, "verily the Apostle of God possessed *the estate of* Fadak, from which he derived funds and supported by it the children of the Banu Hashim and gave in marriage their orphans by its means, and verily Fatimah asked him to bestow it upon her and he refused, and it continued thus during the lifetime of Abu Bakr and Omar. Afterwards Marwan assigned it away, and it hath come into the hands of Omar B. Abdil Aziz. Now I think that a thing forbidden to Fatimah by the Apostle of God is no right of mine, and verily I call ye to witness that I have restored it to what it was in the time of the Apostle of God." And from al Layth, that when Omar became Caliph, he began with his kindred and the people of his, house, and confiscated what was in their hand, and called their substance, exactions.

Asma b. Ubayd narrates that Anbasah b. Said bil Aas went in to Omar b. Abdil Aziz and said, "O price of the Faithful ! the Caliphs before thee used to bestow gifts but thou hast forbidden them to us, and I have a family and an estate-wilt thou permit me to go to my estate to improve *the circumstances* of my family?" He replied, "the most beloved of ye *to me* is he who spares me his keep." Then he added, "be frequent in the remembrance o death, for if thou be in straitened circumstances it will enlarge them for thee, and if in affluence it will straiten it upon thee."

1 Abul Kasim Hammad b. Abi Layla Sapur (nor Maysara) a Daylamite born at Kufah called ar Rawiyah (the narrator) because he was able, according to his own account to the Caliph al Walid b. Abdil Malik, to recite the poems of more poets than the Caliph had never read or heard of. In one sitting he recited two thousand poems by poets who flourished before Muhammad, and it was he who united in one collection the seven "Muallakat." He was treated by the Umayyads with preference and honour. He was born A.H. 95 (713-4) and died in 155 (A.D. 772). Ibn Khall.

A.H.99. A.D.717. Furat b-ul Saib narrates that Omar b. Abdil Aziz said to his wife Fatimah, daughter of Abdul Malik who possessed a jewel which her father had given her, the like of which had never been seen, "choose whether thou wilt give up thy jewel to the public treasury, or suffer me to separate from thee, for verily I am loth that I and thou and it should be in one house." She replied, "I prefer thee to it, and to double *its value.*" He therefore gave orders and it was taken away and placed in the public treasury of the Muslims ; and when Omar died, and Yazid succeeded to the Caliphate, he said to Fatimah, "dost thou wish that I should return it to thee ?" she answered, "no, by Allah, I did not care for it during his life and shall I take it again after his death?" Abdul Aziz says that one of the prefects of Omar b. Abdil Aziz wrote to him *saying*- "verily our city is in ill condition-if the prince of the Faithful thinketh fit to assign us money that we may repair it, let him do so:" and Omar wrote to him, *saying,* "when thou readest this letter, fortify it with justice and *purify* its streets from oppression-for verily that is its restoration, and peace *be to thee.*" Ibrahim as Sakuni states that Omar b. Abdil Aziz said, "I never lied from the time that I knew that a lie was a disgrace to its utterer." And kays b. Jubayr says that Omar among the Banu Umayyah is like the true believer of the family of Pharaoh.[1] And Maymun b. Mihran, that the Lord used to be regardful of His people by means of a succession of Prophets, but that verily the Lord now watcheth over His people through Omar b. Abdil Aziz. And Wahb b. Munabbah, "if there be a guide among this people it is Omar b. Abdil Aziz."

Muhammad b. Fadhalah narrates that Abdullah b. Omar b. Abdil Aziz passed by *the dwelling of* a monk in Mesopotamia, and the monk went down to him, and he had never visited any one before, and said, "knowest thou why I have come down to thee?" He replied, "no." He answered, "on account of the merits of thy father, I find him among the just Imams in the position of the month of Rajab among the sacred months;" Ayub b. Suwayd has interpreted this to mean that the three consectuve months Dul

---

1 See page 45, Note 1.

Kaadah, Dul Hijjah, and al Muharram, are Abu Bakr, Omar and Othman, and Rajab, separate from them is Omar b. Abdil Aziz. Hasan al Kassab says, "I saw wolves grazing with sheep is the desert during the Caliphate of Omar b. Abdil Aziz and I said, 'good God ! a wolf among sheep and not injuring them!' the shepherd answered, "when the head is sound, there is no harm to the body.'" Malik b. Dinar narrates that when Omar b. Abdil Aziz ruled, the shepherds said, "on account of this good man who rules the people as a just Caliph, the wolves restrain themselves from our flocks." And Musa b. Aayan, "we were tending sheep in Kirman during the Caliphate of Omar b. Abdil Aziz, and the sheep and the wolf used to pasture in one place, but meanwhile one night, behold, a wolf attacked a sheep, and I said, 'I cannot but think that the just man is dead,' and they enquired and found that he had died that night." Walid b. Muslim states that he had heard that a man in Khurasan related, *saying,* "a stranger came to me in my sleep and said, 'when he of the Scar among the sons of Marwan rules, go and swear allegiance to him for he is a just Imam,' and I began whenever a Caliph arose, to ask regarding him until Omar Abdil Aziz succeded, and the stranger came to me three times in my sleep, so I set out and swore allegiance to him." He also states on the authority of Habib b. Hind al Aslami that he said, " Sai'd b-ul Musayyab said to me, 'verily the Caliphs are three, Abu Bakr, Omar, and Omar b. Abdil Aziz,' I replied, Abu Bakr and Omar, verily we know them, but who is Omar? He answered, 'if thou livest thou wilt attain to *his time,* and if thou diest *before that* he will come after thee.' I remark that Ibnul Musayyab died before the Caliphate of Omar."

A.H.99.
A.D.717.

Ibn Aun says that when Ibn Sirin was asked regarding wine, he said, "the Imam of salvation that is, Omar b. Abdil Aziz has forbidden its use." And al Hasan declared, that if there is a Mahdi,[1]

1 "The directed" the surname of the twelfth and last Imam of the race of Ali. His name was Abul Kasim Muhammad son of Hasan al Askari the eleventh Imam. He was born at Sarramanra 255. A.H. and he descended into a cistern in presence of his mother at 9 years of age, whence he is expected to return towards the end of the world to join the Messiah in combating Antichrist and establishing one faith. See D. Herb. And Ibn Khall.

A.H.99. A.D.717. it is Omar b. Abdil Aziz and if not he, then there is no other than Jesus to son of Mary." Malik b. Dinar said-"people assert that Malik is an ascetic, whereas the ascetic is Omar b. Abdul Aziz, for the world came to him and he abandoned it." And Yunas b. Abi, Shabih, "I saw Omar b. Abdil Aziz and verily the waist-band of his drawers was hidden in the folds of fat of his stomach : I saw him again after he had become Caliph, and if I had wished to count his ribs without touching them I could have done so."

His son Abdul Aziz said, "Abu Jaafar al Mansur enquired of me, *saying*, "what was the income of thy father when he succeeded to the Caliphate?" I replied "forty thousand dinars ?" He asked, "and how much when he died?" I replied, "Four hundred dinars, and if he had lived longer it would have been less." Maslamah b. Abdil Malik narrates, "I went in to Omar b. Abdil Aziz to visit him in his illness, and lo, he was wearing a dirty shirt and I said to Fatimah the daughter of Abdul Malik, "dost thou not wash his shirt?" she replied, "by Allah, he has no other."

Abu Umayyah, the eunuch, the slave of Omar said, "I went in one day to my mistress, and she gave me a meal of lentils, and I said, "every day lentils!" she replied, "O my son, such is the meal of thy master the prince of the Faithful." When death was approaching, he sent me with a dinar, to the people of the monastery *of Simaan*[1] to say-"if ye sell me a place for my grave, *it is well* otherwise I will turn from ye *elscwhere :* and I went to them and they answered "were it not that we are averse to his leaving us we would not conset." Al Aun b-ul Muammar narrates that Omar went to his wife and said, "O Fatimah, hast thou a dirham that I may buy some grapes with it?" She said, "no" and added, "and thou, the prince of the Faithful, dost thou not possess a dirham where-with to buy grapes ?" He replied, "this is easier for me than to labour under manachles in hell."

---

1 In the District about Damascus-a pleasant spot says Yakut surrounded by gardens and buildings-Omar b. Abdil Aziz was buried here but the site of his grave is unknown.

Sahl b. Sadakah says that when Omar was appointed Caliph, lamentation was heard in his house and they enquired about it and people said, that Omar had given his female slaves a choice, saying, "verily business hath come upon me that will keep me engged from ye; therefore she that wishes that I should free her, I hereby free her, and she that desires that I should retain her, I will retain her though I have no need of her"-and they wept in despair at it. According to his wife Fatimah, when he entered the house, he used to throw himself down at his place of prayer and would not cease to weep and pray until *the drowsiness of* his eyes overpowered him and when he awoke, he would do the same thing throughout the night. A.H.99. A.D.717.

Al Walid b. Abil Musayyab said, "I never knew any one more in fear *of the Lord* than Omar." And Said b. Suayd, that Omar prayed before the people on a Friday, wearing a shirt patched at the collar in front and behind, and a man said to him, "O prince of the Faithful, verily God hath given unto thee, and wert thou but to clothe thyself properly!" Omar looked down awhile, then raised his head and said, "modcration is most meritorious in affluence, and pardon most praiseworthy in power."

Maymun b. Mihran narrates, "I heard Omar say, 'if I remained among you fifty years, I should not perfect justice amogst you- verily I desire a thing, but fear lest your hearts endure it not, I therefore leave the world with that in my desire *unfulfilled* wherefore if your hearts are averse to this thing, they must rest content with the other.'"

And Ibrahim b. Maysarah, "I said to Taus[1] is Omar Abdul Aziz the Mahdi ?' He replied, 'he is a Mahdi but not *the* Mahdi, for he hath not entirely perfected justice.'" Omar b. Usayd says, "it was

---

1 Abu Abdur Rahman Taus b. Kaysan al Khaulani one of the most eminent of the Tabiis, was of Persian extraction. He died at Mecca A.H. 106 (725) and the crowd at his funeral was so great that the governor had to send a guard to clear the way. Abul Faraj al Jouzi says that he was called Taus because he was the peacock of the Qurãn readers, but it is the general opinion that it was his real name. Ibn Khall.

A.H.99. before Omar's death that a man used to come to us with a
A.D.717. considerable sum of money and say, 'use this as ye think fit.' And he continued until he had brought all his property : *thus* Omar verily provided for the wants of the people." And Juwayriyah,[1] "we went in to Fatimah, the daughter of Ali b. Abi Talib, and she praised Omar b. Abdil Aziz and said, 'if he had remained with us, we should have needed none after him.'"

Ata-b-Abi Rabah[2] narrates, narrates, "Fatimah the wife of Omar, told me that she went in to him, and he was at his place of prayer, his tears streaming over his beard, and she said, 'O prince of the Faithful, has anything happened ?' he replied, 'O Fatimah, verily I am invested with authority over the people of Muhammad, the Arabs among them and the foreigners, and I was meditating upon the poor that are starving and the sick that are destitute, and the naked that are in distress, and the oppressed that are stricken, and the stranger that is in prison and the venerable elder, and him that hath a large family and small means, and the like of them in the countries, of the earth and the distant provinces, and I felt that my Lord would ask an account of them at my hands on the day of resurrection, and I feared that no defence would avail me, and I wept.'" Al Auzaai says that Omar b. Abdil Aziz was seated in his house and with him were the chiefs of the Banu Umayyah, and he said, "do ye wish that I should give each one of you to rule over a province ?" and one of them said, "why dost thou propose to us what thou wilt not perform?" he replied, "do ye see this carpet of mine, verily I know that it will fall to ruin an decay, yet verily I am loth that ye should soil it with your feet-therefore how can I place ye in authority over my administration-in authority over the property of the Muslims and their persons ? this cannot be for you-it cannot be!" And they said to him, "why, have we not kinship-have we not

1 The traditionist, a member of the Dubaiah tribe-died A.H. 173, (A.D. 789-99) De Slane, I.K.

2 He was a Mulatto born at a Janad and Mawla to the Fikr Family at Mecca. He held a high rank as a Tabii, a jurisconsult and ascetic and he and al Mujahid were the muftis of Mecca. He died A.H. 115 (73304) at the age of 88. Ibn Khall.

a claim?" he replied,-"ye and the most remote of the Muslims are A.H.99. but equal in my sight in this matter, save that a long journey's distance A.D.717. keeps *that* man of the Muslims from me."

Hamid narrates, "al Hasan dictated to me a letter *addressed* to Omar b. Abdil Aziz, in which he employed all his powers of persuasion and lamented his needs and his *large* family, and Omar ordered him a present." And al Auzaai, that when Omar desired to punish a man, he kept him in confinement for three days and then punished him, not wishing to be hasty in the first impulse of anger. And al Juayriyah b. Asma, that Omar b. Abdil Aziz said, "my heart is most covetous-nothing of worldly goods is given to it but it desires something still better, and when I was given that than which nothing in the world is greater, my heart longed for that which is better than it-namely, heaven." According to Amr b. Muhajir the expenditure of Omar every day was two dirhams. Yusuf b. Yakub al Kahili says that Omar used to wear at night a cloak of camels hair and the lamp in his house was placed on the top of three reeds upon which was some clay. Omar ordered his servant to heat some water for him and he went and heated a vessel in the public kitchen, whereupon Omar ordered him to take a dirhams worth of wood and place it in the kitchen. (Ata al Khurasani.) He used to light a was-candle for himself when engaged in the needs of the Muslim, and when he had finished their business, he would extinguish it and light his own lamp. (Amr b. Muhajir.) The Caliph was always attended by three hundred guards and three hundred armed attendants, but Omar said to the guards, "verily I have among ye Fate as a defender and Death as a guard-he among ye who remains, shall have ten dinars, and whoso wishes may go to his family." (Al Hakam b. Omar.) Amr b. Muhajir relates, "Omar once longed for an apple, and one of the people of his house made him a present of one, and he said, 'how sweet is its odour, and how beautiful it is ! take it O slave ! to him who sent it, and give him greeating and say to him "verily thy present hath pleased us very much." I said to him, 'O prince of the Faithful, he is the son of thy uncle, and one of thy own house, and verily I have heard that the Prophet used to eat such presents ;' he replied, 'fie on thee-verily a present to the Prophet was a present,

A.H.99. A.D.717. but to us in these days it is a bribe.'" "I never knew Omar during his Caliphate," says Ibrahim b. Maysarah, "strike any one but one man who had received presents from Muawiyah, and he struck him three stripes." When Omar discontinued to the people of his house, the special allowance which used to be issued to them, they murmured against it, but he said, "my property will not be enough for ye all, yet as for this money, your claim to it is as the claim of a man *dwelling afar at Birkul Ghimad.*"[1] (Al Auzzi.) He also wrote to cancel such orders of al Hajjaj as were opposed to public opinion. Yahya al Ghassani says, "when Omar made me prefect of Mosul, I found theft and house-breaking more common there than in the majority of cities, wherefore I wrote to inform him of the state of the city and asked him whether I should take men up on suspicion and chastise them on mere accusation, or arrest them on clear proof and according as the law directed ; he wrote to me i*nreply* that I should arrest them only on clear proof and as the law directed, for if justice would not make them honest, then may God not reform them. I therefore acted accordinly and I did not leave Mosul until it had become one of the most orderly of cities and least frequent in theft and house-breaking." And Raja b. Hayat narrates, "I was conversing one night with Omar when the lamp grew dim and near it was an attendant *asleep.* I exclaimed, "shall I rouse him?" He said, "no," I said, "shall not I get up them ?" He replied, "It is not polite for a man to exact service from his guest;" and he went to the oil flask and trimmed the lamp and returned and said, "I arose as Omar b. Abdul Aziz and have returned as Omar B. Abdil Aziz." According to Nuaym, Omar's secretary, Omar said, "fear of vainglory verily prevents me from speaking much." Makhal observes, "if I were to swear *to it* I would but speak the truth, that I never saw any one more pious and good-fearing than Omar b. Adil Aziz."

When the mention of death was made, Omar, says Said b. Urubah, would tremble in all his joints. He used to assemble every night the doctors of law and coverse with them on death and the

1 Or Birkul Ghamad a town at the extreme corner of Yaman. Yakut M.B.

resurrection, and they would weep as if a bier were before them. A.H.99.
(Ata.) Ubaydullah b. Ayzar narrates, "Omar preached to us in Syria A.D.717.
from a pulpit of clay and said, 'O people purify your inner thoughts and your exterior conduct will be amended-direct your actions with regard to the world to come, and your wordly concerns will not be amiss-and know that a man between whom and Adam there is no living ancestor, has assuredly a hereditary portion in death,[1] peace be to ye.'"

The Banu Marwan assembled at Omar's gate and said to his son Abdul Malik-"say to thy father that the Caliphs before him used to make grants to us and recognized our station, but verily thy father hath prohibited to us that which is in his hands;" and his son went in to him and informed him, and he replied, "tell them forsooth my father says to ye-'verily I fear, if I should rebel against my Lord, the punishment of the Great Day.'" (Qur. VI,) (Wuhayb b-ul Ward.)

Omar said, "take ye for counsel that which those before ye approved to be good and take not that which is opposed to them, for they were better than ye and wiser."[2] Jarir once came and took his post for a long time at the gate of Omar who would not notice him, whereupon he wrote to Aun b. Abdillah who was a confident of Omar's-

O reader with the flowing turban,
This is thy day, verily my day hath passed.
Tell our Caliph if thou meetest him
I am at the gate like one chained to a pillar.

(Al Auza'ai).

When Omar succeeded to the Caliphate, Bilal b. Abi Bardah went and congratulated him and said, there have been those whom

---

1 Lane mentions this (art عريق)as a tradition.

2 Abu Hazrah Jarir b. Atiyah-the poet-the great rival of Farazdak and al Akhtal-for his history consult Ibn Khall. Kitabul Aghani-and the Journal. Asiatique for April 34.

A.H.99. the Caliphate ennobled, but thou hast ennobled it, and there have
A.D.717. been those whom it has graced it, but thou hast lent a grace to it and thou art as Malik b. Asma says :

"Thou addest a sweet odour to the most delicious fragrance
If thou but touch it-where is thy like? Where?
For lo! The pearl gives luster to the beauty of the face
But the beauty of thy face gives luster to the pearl."

(Juayriyah.)

When Abdul Malik b. Omar b. Abdil Aziz died, Omar began to praise him whereupon Maslamah[1] said, "O prince of the Faithful, if he had lived thou wouldst have made him heir." He said, "no." He answered, and why not, for thou wert but now praising him." Omar said, "I fear that there might have been a consideration in my regard towards him, such a consideration as a son holds in the eye of his father," (Juunah). A man said to Omar-"leave me a charge." He said, "I commend to thee the fear of God and the preferring of His *above all things,* and afflicting will be withheld from thee and help will be vouchsafed to thee from God" (Ghassan). The daughter[2] of Usamah b. Zayd went in to Omar and he arose before her and advanced towards her, and made her sit down in his seat, and he sat down before her and left her no wish ungratified. (Abu amr.) The sons of Marwan assembled together and they said, "if we went in to the prince of the Faithful, we might make him favourably disposed towards us by pleasantly ;" anα they entered and one among them spake and jested, and Omar regarde him then another added his jest to the other's, and Omar said, "is it for this ye have assembled-for the lowest kind of discourse and that which breeds enmities? When ye assemble, betake yourselves to the Book of God, and if ye go beyond that, then to the laws of the Apostle of God, and if ye go again beyond that, then employ

1 Son of Abul Malik b. Marwan.

2 Her name was Fatimah : she resided at the village of Mizzah near Damascus after the death of her father, the well known Mawla of the Prophet who was dispatched at the head of an army to Syria at the time the Prophet was dying. (See page 74) Usamah died at Medina, and some say at Wadil Kura about A.H. 54.

yourselves in *the interpretation of the* meanings of the traditions." (Al Hajjaj b. Anbasah.) A.H.99. A.D.717.

Iyas b. Muawiyah b. Kurrah says, "I liken Omar to none but an excellent workman who has no tools with which to work-that is, he has none to help him." And Omar b. Hafa narrates, "Omar said to me, 'when thou hearest a word from a Muslim, do not impute to it aught of evil as long as thou canst find for it a good motive.'"

Omar used to dissuade Sulayman b. Abdil Malik from putting the Haruriyah sectarians[1] to death and he would say to him, "imprison them until they show repentance." And a Haruri was brought before Sulayman who said to him, "well now!" The Haruri replied, "what shall I say, O villain, son of a villain?" Sulayman exclaimed-"send for Omar Abdil Aziz ;" and when he came, he said, "listen to the speech of this man," and he Haruri repeated it, and Sulayman said, "what dost thou think *should be done to* him?" but he was silent. He said again "I command thee to tell me what thou thinkest regarding him." He answered, "I think with regard to him that thou shouldst revile him as he hath reviled thee." He replied, "the matter *ends* not thus," and he commanded regarding him, and his head was struck off, and Omar departed. But Khalid the captain of the guard, overtook him, and said, "Omar, how couldst thou say to the prince of the Faithful-'I do not see anything for him but that thou shouldst revile him as he hath reviled thee? verily I was expecting that he would command me to strike off thy head." He replied, "and if he had commanded thee, wouldst thou have done it?" He answered, "Yea, by Allah." Now when the Caliphate fell to Omar, Khalid came and stood up in the place of the captain of the guard and Omar said, "O Khalid put this sword from thee" and he added, "O God, verily I have humbled Khalid for thy sake, therefore raise

---

1 A sect of schismatics called after Harura, a town two miles distant from Kufah because they first assembled there and taught that government belongs only to God. They consisted of Najdeh and his Companions holding their tenets. They were also called Mubayyadhah because their ensigns in war were white. They dived so deeply, says Lane, into matters of religion that they became heretics-and hence the appellation is applied also to any who do thus. Lane, art. حر

A.H.99. A.D.717. him up never again." Then he looked upon the faces of the guard, and summoned Amr b. Muhajir the Auxiliary and said, "O Amir, verily thou knowest that there is no kinship between me and thee save the kinship of Islam, but I have heard thee diligently reading the Qurãn, and I have seen thee praying in a place when thou didst think that none observed thee, and I saw thee pray with devotion and thou art one of the Auxiliaries-take this sword therefore, for verily I give thee the command of my guard." (Yahya al Ghassani). Shuayb says, "I have been told that Abdul Malik b. Omar b. Abdil Aziz went in to his father and said, "O prince of the Faithful what wilt thou say unto thy Lord hereafter when he questioneth thee?" and added, "thou hast witnessed heresies and hast not erushed them, and laws *fallen into disuse* and thou hast not revived them." And his father answered, "may the Lord have mercy upon thee and reward thee for a good son-may child, verily thy tribe have bound this authority knot by knot and loop by loop, and were I to seek to oppose them by taking away what they possessed, I would not be safe from their making a rupture with me in which much blood would be shed-by Allah, the loss of worldly goods would be easier unto me than that a cupping-glass of blood should be spilt on my account, yet art thou not content that a single day in the world should come to thy father, except he crush a heresy therein and revive a law."

Omar said, "he is happy who is preserved from disputation, anger and convetousness." (Ma'mar.) It was said to Omar, "if thou wert to appoint a bodyguard and to be careful in thy food and drink."[1] He replied, "O God if thou knowest that I fear aught except the day of resurrection believe not in my fear." (Artah b. Mundir.) Adi b-ul Fadhl narrates, "I heard Omar preaching to the people, and he said, 'fear ye God, O people! And proceed with moderation in your quest *of worldly goods,* for if he destined portion of any one be upon the summit of a mountain or in the depths of the earth, it will reach him.'" And Azhar says, "I saw Omar preaching to the

1 Such sentences where the apodosis is wanting to complete the period are common enough in the Semitic languages and may be found frequently in the Bible, e.g. Gen. iii. 22.

people wearing a patched garment." And Abdullah b-ul Ala. I heard A.H.99.
Omar preaching on a Friday a single discourse which he kept A.D.717.
repeating and beginning it with these seven sentences-'Praise be to God, we glorify Him and implore His help and His pardon, and we fly toGod for protection against the wickedness of our passions and the evil of our deeds ; whom God directeth, none can misguide, and there is no guide for him whom God alloweth to go astray-and I testify that there is no god but one God who hath no copartner-and I testify that Muhammad is His servant and His apostle ; -he who obeyeth God and His apostle, verily he followeth the right path-and whose rebelleth against God and His apostle, verily goeth astray." Then he commended *unto them* the fear of God and continued to preach, and he concluded his final discourse with these verses "O my servants who have transgressed" (Qur. XXXIX) to the conclusion of the section. Hajib b. Khalifah al Burjumi says, "I was present when Omar being then Caliph, was preaching, and he said in his discourse, 'verily that which the apostle of God and his two companions have ;instituted, is the faith which we conform to and follow out and that which others besides those two have established we may put aside.'" (Abu Nuaym gives with their ascriptions in his Huliyah all that I have advanced.)

Ibn Asakir records on the authority Ibrahim b. Abi Aylah that he said, "we went in to Omar on the day of the festival,[1] and the people were greeting him, and saying, "the Lord be propitious unto us and unto thee O prince of the Faithful." And he returned it to them and did not disapprove their conduct. I remark that this is an excellent precedent for a congratulatory salutation for *the day of* the festival, and for the year and for the month. He records also from Juunah, that Omar gave Amr b. Kays as Sakuni the command of an expedition *against the Greeks* and said, "receive graciously those among them that do good and forgive those of them that do evil-and be not the foremost among them, lest thou be slain, nor yet

---

1 By the term Eed is meant one of the two principal religious festivals of the Muslims. Eedul Adha (festivals of the victims) held on the 10th of Dul Hijjah or the Eed ul Fitr the festival of the breaking of the fast after the Ramadhan.

A.H.99. the hindermost lest thou appear cowardly, but be in the middle so
A.D.717. that thy place may be seen and thy voice heard." And from Saib b. Muhammad, that Abdul Jarrah b. Abdillah wrote to Omar, *saying,* "verily the people of Khurasan are a race whose community is unruly and verily nothing will mend them but the sword and the scourge, therefore if the prince of the Faithful see fit to permit their use to me?" And Omar wrote, "now, verily thy letter hath reached me, saying, that the people of Khurasan are a community that are unruly, and that nothing will mend them but the sword and the scourge, but in truth thou hast spoken falsely for justice will mend them ant truth-therefore spread these amongst them and peace *be to thee."* And from Umayyah b. Zayd, of the Kuraysh that he said, "when Omar dictated his correspondence to me, he would say, 'O God I fly to thee for protection from the eveil of my tongue.'" And from Salih b. Jubayr that he said, "I have often times discoursed with Omar on a subject and he would get wroth and I would say-'it is written in a book,-fear the wrath of a youthful king and be gentle with him until his anger departeth ;'and he would say to me afterwards, 'let not what thou seest in me, O Salih, hinder thee from recurring to the subject with me when thou seest it *fit.'"* And from Abdul Hakim b. Muhammad al Makhzumi that Jarir b-Ful Khatafi went before Omar and was about to recite *poetry* when Omar checked him, but he said, "indeed I am about to make mention of the Apostle of God." Omar replied-"well if it be the Apostle of God, then mention him"- and Jarir went on.

Verily He who sent the Prophet Muhammad
Hath conferred the Caliphate on a just prince,
Who hath restored extortions with exactness to their just owners
From their urrighteouness, and made straight the erring of the deviator.
Verily I seek of thee a present bounty
For the heart clings to the love of the present.

Omar said to him "I find nothing due to you in the book of God," He replied, "yes, O prince of the Faithful-verily I am a wayfarer." He therefore ordered him fifty dinars from his privy purse. A.H.99. A.D.717.

It is recorded in the Tuyyuriyat that Hariz b. Othman ar Rahbi went in with his father to Omar who asked the latter regarding his son, and then said, "teach him the great science." He answered, "and what is the great science?" Omar replied, "contentment, and abstaining from molesting *others.*" Ibn Abi Hatim records from Muhammad b. Kaab al Kardhi that he narrates, "Omar, summoned me and said, 'define justice to me.' I said, 'well, thou askest regarding a momentous thing-be to the little ones among men as their father-to the great as their son-to your equals among them as a brother and the same towards women, and punish men according to the degree of their faults and the measure of their bodily *endurance,* and strike not, be sure, a single blow of a scourge in anger lest thou exceed *justice* and be of those who oppress.'"

Abdur Razzak records in his Musannaf from az Zuhri that Omar used to make his ablutions after *eating* anything that had touched the fire, so that he would make his ablutions after *eating* sugar. And from Wuhayb that Omar said, "he who considers his words as a part of his actions will be sparing of his conversation."

Ad Dahabi says that Ghaylan[1] professed a denial of predestination during the Caliphate of Omar, who sought to make him abjure, wherefore he said, "verily I was in error but thou hast directed me aright." Omar exclaimed, "O God-if he be sincere, forgive him otherwise crucify him and cut off his hands and feet." And his prayer concerning him took effect, for he was seized in the Caliphate of Hisham b. Abdil Malik and his limbs were cut off and he was crucified at Damascus for the denial of predestination. Some other author says that the Banu Umayyah used to vilify Ali b. Abi Talib in the Khutbah, and when Omar ruled, he abolished

---

1 Ghaylan of Damascus according to Sale, (p. 112) together with Mabad al Juhni and Jonas al Aswari, broached heterodox opinions concerning predestination shortly after the rise of the first heresy in Islam, that of the Kharijites under the Caliphate of Ali. Their opinions were followed by Wasil b. Ata the founder of the Muatazalites.

A.H.99. A.D.717. this and wrote to his prefects to discontinue it, and he read in its palce "verily God commandeth justice and the doing of good." (Qur. XVI) and the rest of the verse, and the reading of this was continued to this day.

Al Kali says in his Dictations on the authority of Ahmad b. Ubayd that Omar before his Caliphate versified.

"Restrain thy heart from love
And from subservience to passion,
For by the life of thy Lord, verily in
The greyness of thy head and its baldness
Is an admonisher if thou canst
Take warning as he is admonished who is wise.
Till how long wilt thou not forbear ?
Till how long and how long !
After thou hast been called of mature age
Dost thou still snatch at the name of youth!
Youth is worn out and thou
If thou live, will be a hostage to calamity.
That sufficeth as an admonisher
To a man from wandering astray."

At Thaalabi says in the Lataiful Maarif (Curiosities of Knowledge) that Omar b-ul Khattab, Othman, Ali, Marwan b-ul Hakam and Omar b. Abdil Aziz were bald, and after that, baldness ceased *to be seen* among the Caliphs. Az Zubayr b. Bakkar says that a poet said of Fatimah, daughter of Abdul Malik b. Marwan and wife of Omar b. Abdil Aziz.

Daughter of a Caliph-a Caliph her grandsire,
Sister of Caliphs and her husband a Caliph."

He continues "no other woman but herself can claim in her behalf this verse up to my time," and I add up to mine.

His sickness and death.

A.H.99.
A.D.717.

Ayub states that it was said to Omar Abdul Aziz, "if thou wert to go to Medina and wert to die there, thou wouldst be buried in the place of the fourth grave with the Apostle of God." He replied, "by Allah, that the Lord should chastice me with every torture save hell-fire, would be preferable to me than that the Lord should conceive that I deemed myself worthy of that place." Walid b. Hisham says that it was said to Omar in his sickness, "wilt thou not get thyself a remedy?" he answered- "verily I knew the moment in which I was given to drink *poison,* and if my cure were but to touch the lobe of my ear or were I brought a perfume which I had only to raise to my nose, I would not do it." Ubayd b. Hasan narrates that when Omar was on the point of death, he said, *to those present-* "depart from me," and Masalamah and Fatimah sat down by the door and they heard him saying, "welcome these faces that are not the faces of men or genii." Then he said, "as to this future mansion *of paradise,"* (Qur, XXVIII) and the rest of the verse : then the sound grew faint, and they went in and found him dead. Hisham says that when the news of Omars death went abroad, Hasan al Basri said, "the best of men is dead :" and Khalid ar Rabii, "I find in the Pentateuch that the heavens and the earth shall weep over Omar b. Abdil Aziz for forty mornings." Yusuf b. Mahak says, "while we were leveling the earth over the grave of Omar, lo! there fell upon us a scroll of parchment from the sky in which was *written,* 'In the name of God the most Merciful, the Compassionate, Immunity from God for Omar b. Abdil Aziz from hellfire.'"

Katadah narrates that Omar wrote to the heir who was to succeed him, "In the name of God the most Merciful the Compassionate."

From Omar b. Abdil Aziz, to Yazid b. Abdil Malik.

"Peace be to thee! Verily I glorify God unto thee, besides whom there is no other God. And now, verily, I write *to thee,* being nigh unto death through my sickness, and insooth I know that I shall be questioned regarding the things that I have governed, the King of

A.H.99. this world and the next taking account of me concerning it, and I
A.D.717. am unable to hide from him a tittle of my deeds. If therefore He be content with me verily I shall be happy and shall excape from enduring contempt, but if he be displeased with me, then woe unto me for that which I shall become. I ask of God, of Him besides whom there is no other God, to save me through His mercy from hell-fire and to vouchsafe unto me His approbation and Paradise. Let the fear of God be upon thee-and the people-the people-*be thy care,* for verily thou will remain after me but a little while." (Abu Nuaym has given all this with their ascriptions in the Huliyah).

Omar died at Dayr-Simaan, in the district about Emessa[1] on the 20th or as some say the 25th of Rajab of the year 101 (5th or 10th February 720), he being at that time thirty-nine years and six months old. His death was caused by poison. The Banu Ummayyah hated him on account of his severity to them and his confiscating from them much that they had plundered. He neglected to take precautions and they gave him poison to drink. Mujahid narrates, "Omar said to me, 'what do people say about me?' I replied 'they say thou art disordered in mind' He replied, 'I am not disordered in mind: verily, I knew the moment in which they gave me *poison* to drink.' Then be summoned one of his slaves and said –'alas ! for thee-what brought thee to give me poison to drink ?' He replied, 'one thousand dinars that I was given and *the promise* that I should be liberated.' Omar said, 'bring them here.' Mujahid adds that he brought them and Omar put them into the public treasury and said to him, 'go that no one may see thee,'"

Among people of note who died in Omar's reign were, Abu Imamah b. Sahl b. Hunayf, Kharijah b. Zayd b. Thabit, Salim b. Abil Jaad, Busr b. Said, [2] Abu Othman and Nahdi, and Abu's Saha.

---

1 Yakut says Damascus : it is probably somewhere between those two towns. Another of the same name was in Mount Lebanon and a third near Antioch. Simaan is Simon, and Yakut says that the convent was named, it is supposed, after Simon Peter, "one of the great doctors of the Christians !"

2 Ibnul Athir, says Busr b. Saad. The name Abu's Saha is probably wrong-I have never met a name of the kind and, it is not mentioned in the Kamil. Abu Salih Zakwan died in the time of the Omar and also Abu Salih Saman.

YAZID-B-ABDIL MALIK

A.H.99.
A.D.717.

Yazid b. Abdil Malik bil Hakam, Abu Khalid, of the house of Umayyah, a native of Damascus, was born in the year 71 and ruled the Caliphate in succession to Omar b. Abdil Aziz, according to the covenant of his brother Sulayman, as hath gone before. Abdur Rahman b. Zayd b. Aslam says that when Yazid ruled he said *to the people* "take as your rule of life, the conduct of Omar b. Abdil Aziz ;" and there were brought to him forty Shaykhs and they testified to him *saying*-"for the Caliphs there is neither *a day of* reckoning nor punishment."

When Omar died, Yazid exclaimed, "by Allah, Omar was not more in need of the Lord than I,"-and for forty days be continued to follow the example of Omar, and then abandoned it. (Ibn ul Majishun). When Omar was on the point of death, he wrote to Yazid b. Abdil Malik *saying,* "peace be to thee ! now, verily I do not see myself other than what I am-I commend to thee in God's name the people of Muhammad-for verily thou wilt leave the world to one who will not praise thee, and wilt go unto one who will not hold thee excused-and peace *be to thee !"* (Sulaym b. Bashir).

In the year 102 Yazid b-ul Muhallab rebelled against the Caliphate, and Muslamah b. Abdil Malik b. Marwan was dispatched against him, and Yazid was defeated and slain, and that at Akr[1] a place near Karbala. Al Kalbi says, "I was a youth when people used to say that the Banu Umayyah slaughtered religion on the day of Karbala and clemency[2] on the day of Akr. Yazid died towards the end[3] of Shaaban in the year 105 (28th January 724).

---

1 The printed edition has Akir which is incorrect.

2 By the Caliph's orders 300 Irakian prisoners were put to death at Kufah. This inhumanity was not however confined to one side, for Muawiyah, Yazid's son, according to Weil, on leaving Wasit slaughtered 32 of the prisoners he had taken. Among them Adi b. Artah and his son. See Weil, Gesch, Caliph, and Ibn Khall, who has a long article on Yazid b. Muhallab. The family of Muhallab were as celebrated under the Umayyads for generosity as the Barmekides under the house of Abbas.

3 On the 25th according to Ibnul Athir.

A.H.101. Of people of note who died during his geign were, ad Dhahhak
A.D.720. b. Muzahim, Abi B. Artah, Abul Mutawakkil an Naji, Ata b. Yasar, Mujahid, Yahya b. Wathab the Qurãn reader of Kufah, Khalid b. Maadan as Shaabi the scholar of Iraq, Abdur Rahman b. Hassan b. Thabit, Abu Kilabah al Jarmi, Abu Burdah b. Abi Musa al Ashari, and othes.

HISHAM-B-ABDIL MALIK

Hisham b. Abdil Malik, Abul Walid was born after the year 70[1] and succeeded to the Caliphate according to the covenant of his brother Yazid. Musaab az Zubayri says that Abdul Malik had a dream regarding which he questioned Sai'd b-ul Musayyab, who interpreted it *to mean* that four of the issue of his lions would bear sway. Hisham was the last of these. He was discret and wise. He would never allow any money to enter his treasury until forty people had testified upon oath that it had been rightfully exacted, and that to every just claimant had been given his due.

A man once addressed Hisham abusively, and he said to him, "O such a one, it doth not befit thee to revile the Caliph." And once he was wroth with a man and said-"By Allah, verily I intended to scourge thee !" (Al Asmai.) Sahbal b. Muhammad says, "I never saw one of the Caliphs to whom *the shedding* of blood was more hateful and upon whom it was more grievous, than Hisham." It is recorded on Hisham's authority that he said, "there is not one remaining of the pleasures of the world, but I have enjoyed it, save one-a friend regarding whom I can dispense with the trouble of being vigilant concerning what is between me and him."

When Hisham built ar Rusafah[2] near Kinnisrin, he desired to retire there for one day during which no care should approach him,

1 In the year 72 according to Ibnul Athir.

2 About four parasangs west of Rakkah towards the desert. He built it when the plague desolated Syria and used to reside in it during the (cont...)

but the day was not half spent when there floated towards him a feather covered with blood from some part of the frontier and was borne to him, and he exclaimed, "not a single day !" A.H.. A.D.724.

It is said that the following line is his and no other of his is recorded.

"If thou dost not rebel against concupiscence, it will lead thee

To what will occasion evil speaking against thee.

He died in Rabbiul[1] Akhir of the year 125. (6th February 743).

In the year 107 of his reign Kaysariyah in Asia Minor[2] was taken by the sword.

In the year 108 Khanjarah[3] was taken by al Battal the famous hero.

In the year 112 Kharshanab[4] near Malatiyah was captured.

Of persons of note who died in the reign of Hisham, were, Salim b. Abdillah b. Omar, Taus, Salayman b. Yasar, Ikramah Mawla of Ibn Abbas, al Kasim b. Muhammad b. Abi Bakr is Siddik , Kuthay

---

(Cont.320) summer. One of Yakut's authorities (Ibn Butlan) asserts it to have been originally a for built of stone in which was a large Christian Church built by Constantine the son of Helena. Beneath the Church was a cistern on marble pillars paved with marble and full of rain water. The people living in its neighbourhood were mostly Bedouin Christians. The word Rasafah رصفة signifies a dam constructed for the purpose of obstructing or retaining water-hence the place was so called after the cistern in the fort, no other water nearer than the river Euphrates being procurable.

1 On the 6th according to Weil.

2 Yakut spells this word قيساريه and not قيصريه as in the text.

3 The printed edition and MS. both have Hanjarah. Yakut does not give it, but names Khanjarah as a portion of the Grecian territory. Abdullah al Battal was one of the Generals of Muawiyah b. Hisham who commanded the troops in Asia Minor. In 739-al Battal was defeated in one of his expeditions and slain. See Weil, p. 638, Vol. I, and Ibnul Athir for the year A.H. 122.

4 Harsanah in the printed edition and MS. but Ibnul Athir and Yakut make it Kharshanah.

A.H.125. A.D.743. the poet *lover of* Azza, Muhammad b. Kasl al Karadhi,[1] al Hasan al Basri, Muhammad b. Sirin, Abut Tufayl Aamir b. Wathilah the last of the Companions, Jarir, Farazdak, Atiyah al Aufi, Muawiyah b. Kurrah, Makhul, Ata b. Abi Rabah, Abu Jaafar al Bakir, Wahab b. Munabbih, Sukaynah daughter of al Husayn, al Aaraj, Katadah, Nafi Mawla b. Omar, Ibn Aamir the Qurãn reader of Syria, Ibn Kathir Qurãn reader of Mecca, Thabit al Bunani, Malik b. Dinar, Ibn Muhayyasah[2] the Qurãn reader, Ibn Shihab az Zuhri, and others.

Among the narratives concerning Hisham, Ibn Asakir records on the authority of Ibrahim b. Abi that he said, "Hisham desired to place me over the finanaces of Egypt, but I declined and he grew wroth so that his countenance was agitated and there was a fierceness in his eye, and he cast upon me a forbidding look and said, 'thou shalt assuredly take charge willingly or against thy will;' but I restrained myself from speaking till his anger had calmed down, and I said, 'prince of the Faithful, may I speak?' He replied, 'yes'. I said, 'verily God hath spoken in His glorious Book, "we proposed the faith unto the heavens and the earth and the mountains and they refused to undertake the same &c." (Qur. XXXIII) now, by Allah, O prince of the Faithful, He was not wroth with them when they were loth, and I do not deserve that thou shouldst be angered against me because I refused, or that thou shouldst force me when I am unwilling'-and he laughed and forgave me." And from Khalid b. Safwa[3] that he said, "I visited Hisham and he said, 'say, what is it? O son of Safwan,'-I began-one of the Kings set forth on a pleasure excursion to al Khaurnak[4] and he was a man

---

1 Ibnul Athir writes this name Kurti قرطي but Ibn Khall confirms the reading of the text ; al Karadhi signifies a dealer in Karadh. قرظ The leaf of the salam tree used in tanning. See Ibn Khall, De, S. Vol. 3, p. 373.

2 Net Myhayyasan as in the text. See Ibnul Athir for the spelling of this name, under the year 113 A.H.

3 His father was the chief of the Banu Tamim and a great orator. Khalid was equally distinguished in his oratory and his avarice and his frequent divorces. No night, he used to say, was so pleasant as the one wherein he had dismissed his wives. Ibn Kutaybah K.M.

4 This was an Nuaman b. Imr ul Kays b. Abi descended (cont.)

of wisdom as well as of wealth and power, and he looked round and said to his, courtiers-'unto, whom doth this belong? And they said-'unto the king.' He exclaimed, 'have ye seen any who hath been favoured as I have been favoured ?'" Now there was with one of the most excellent of those versed in lore and he said, "verily thou hast enquired regarding a certain matter-dost thou give me leave to reply?" The king answered, "Yes." He said,-"hast thou regarded the condition in which thou art? Is it a thing in which thou wilt continue or rather a thing which hath come to thee by inheriatance, and which shall pass from thee to another as is hath come to thee?" He answered-" such is the case." He continued, "dost thou then pride thyself on a trifling thing which thou dost possess but for a short time and from which thou must sever for a time that will endure, and *of which* account will be demanded of thee?" The king exclaimed, "alas! Then-where is there a refuge and where a haven of retreat?" and a cold shodder seized him. The other said, "either thou must continue in thy sovereignty and act in obedience to God in regard to what displeaseth or gratifieth thee, or thou must relinquish thy kingdom and lay down thy crown and cast from thee thy worn garments and worship thy Lord." He answered, "I will reflect to-night and will go to thee in the morning." And when it was morning, he knocked at his door and said, "I have chosen tis mountain and these solitudes and have put on my garments of sackeloth, and if thou wilt be my companion-do not deny me." And they dwelt upon the mountain until they died- A.H.125. A.D.743.

Adi b. Zayd b. Hammad[1] says on this subject :
"O thou who rejoicest at other's affliction and scoffest
At fortune ! art thou exempt and perfect ?

(Cont. 322) from Kahtan-the palace of Khaurnak built by him was near Kufah. It was designed by a Greek called Sinimmar and finished in sixty years. The architect was thrown from its summit by order of Nuaman for boasting that by the removal of a secret part of the masonry the building would fall. The story in the text is given much the same in Yakut.

1 Not a Himar as in the text. He was a poet of the time of Ignorance. He and his family professed the Christian religion. For his life consult Kitab ul Aghani. Tom, II. P. 18, and the Journal Asiatique for November '38.

A.H.125.
A.D.743.

Or hast thou a firm covenant with time?
Nay ! thou art an arrogant fool !
Whom hast thou seen whom Death hath suffered to endure ?
Or who hath over him a defender to save him from being wronged ?
Where is Khusrau-king of kings-father of
Sasan, and where Sabur before him ?
And the fair1[1] illustrious race, monarchs
Of Rum ? no mention of them remains.
And the Lord of Hadhr[2] when he founded it and when
The Tigris and the Khabur, went back towards it-
He built it strongly of marble and covered it with cement,
And now birds have their nests in its pinnacles.
Death hath not respected him and perished
Hath his kingdom, and his gate is deserted.
And remember the Lord of Khaurnah the day
That he gazed from an eminence and be the memory a guide to thee !
His wealth gladdened him and the plenty
That he possessed-and the river lay before him and Sadir.[3]
And his hear repented and he said,
What is the happiness of a creature that is about to die?

---

1 Called also Banul Asfar from Asfar, son of Rum, son of Esan, son of Isaac, son of Abraham. See Lane, for other derivations of this word.

2 Between Mosul and Takrit. The name of a certain king Satirun is connected with this city's early history-it was built of cut stone and was of great magnificence which is still attested, according to Yakut, by the remnants of its ruined walls. It afterwards fell into the possession of a chief called Dhayzan and being built under talismanic influence, it could not be taken save by the breaking of the spell. For the story consult Yakut. The heronic was the daughter of Dhazan, who had been so delicately nurtured that a crumpled myrtle leaf disturbed her sleep. Ibn Khall says that Satirun and Dhazan were the same person. See under "art" Muhammad b. Jabir.

3 A river near Hirah-also a palace built near Khaurnak by Nuaman the Great for a Persian king-consult Yakut.

And after prosperity and empire and dominion A.H.125.
The graves have concealed them there, A.D.743.
And they become like unto a withered leaf
That the east and west winds whirl away."

The narrator continues, "and Hisham wept until his beard was wet, and he commanded his two daughters to take up his couch and he secluded himself[1] in his palace. And his servants and his retinue went to Khalid b. Safwan and said, 'what hast thou desired with the prince of the Faithful? Thou hast ruined his happiness.' He replied, 'begone from me-I have verily made a covenant with God, that I would never be alone with a king, but I would remind hira of the Most High.'"

AL WALID-B-YAZID-B-ABDIL MALIK

Al Walid b. Yazid b. Abdil Malik b. Marwan bil Hakam,-the profligate Caliph, Abul Abbas was born in the year 90. When his father was on the point of death, he was unable to appoint him successor as he was but a chold ; he therefore covenanted for his brother Hisham, and named him heir after Hisham. He assumed the government on the death of Hisham in Rabiiul Akhir in the year 125. He was a libertine and a wine-drinker and a breaker of the divine commands. He wished to make the pilgrimage in order that he might drink upon the summit of the Kaabah. The people abhorred him for his profligacy, and rose up against him and he was slain on (27th) Jamadal Akhirah of the year 126. (16th April 744).

It is recorded on his authority that when he was besieged he said to the people. "have not I increased your largesses ? Have not I removed your grievances ? Have not I given unto the poor among

---

2 For لَزَمَ read لَزَم I believe the text here to be corrupt. The MS. has امر بابفقيه وضم فرشه ولذم قصره

A.H.126. ye ?" they replied, "we do not reproach thee for ourselves, but we
A.D.744. find fault with thee for thy transgressions against the prohibitions of God, and the drinking of wine and marriage with the concubines of thy father who have borne children to him, and thy comtempt for the commands of the Lord." And when he was slain and his head was cut off and taken to Yazid an Nakis, he placed it on a spear, and his brother Sulayman b. Yazid looking upon it said-"away with it-I testify that he was a wine drinker, licentious and profligate and he sought to seduce me into immorality."

Al Muafa al Jariri[1] says, "I have collected some particulars regarding the life of al Walid and his verses which contain the wickedness he committed through his folly and weakness of mind and the heresies he openly expressed regarding the Qurãn, and impiety towards God." Ad Dahabi observes that the impiety and atheism of al Walid are not clearly established, but he was notorious for drinking and profligacy, and for that reason they rebelled against him.

Mention of al Walid was once made in the *presence* of al Mahdi and a man said that he was an atheist, and al Mahdi replied, "go to, the Vicegerency of God in his charge is too sublime *an office* that he should have given it to an atheist." Al Walid was one of the most comely of men as well as one of the most violent and he was among the most polished of poets. Marwan b. Abi Hafsah az Zuhri was always reviling al Walid and finding fault with him to Hisham, and saying, "it is not lawful for thee *to do other* than put him aside," but Hisham was not able to do so, and if az Zuhri had fived until al Walid reigned, the latter would have put him to death. (Abu'z Zinad.)

Hisham desired to put aside al Walid and bestow the succession upon his son, but al Walid said,

---

1 Probably Abu Masud al Muafa b. Imran, a native of Mosul of the tribe of Azd, who studied jurisprudence under Sufiyan at Thauri. He was remarkable for his learning and piety, died A.H. 184. I.K. De Slane.

Thou hast been ungrateful for the favours of *thy* benefactor-wert thou but thankful A.H.126. A.D.744.

The most Merciful would requite thee with favour and bounty.

I have seen that thou that planned industriously to set me aside,

If thou wert wise, thou wouldst annul what thou has designed.

I behold thee working enmity upon those that remain,

Happy for them wert thou to die from the evil thou workest !

I am as one among them to-day, while their frequent exclaimation is

O would that we had been in happier circumstances[1] or that thou hadst never lived.

ad Dhakhak b. Othman).

Hammad ar Rawiyah narrates, "I was one day with al Walid and two astrologers came in to him and said, 'we have looked into what thou hast commanded us, and we have found that thou wilt reign for seven years. I was desirous,' continues Hammad, 'to deceive him so I said falsely-"I too am learned in signs and the systems of knowledge, and verily I have looked into this and have found that thou wilt reign forty year." And he looked down in thought and then said, 'what they have declared will not afflict nor what thou hast said make me over-confident. By Allah, I will assuredly gather in the revenue lawful like unto the gathering of him who was to live forever, and I will surely disburse it according to its just claims, as he would disburse it who was to die tomorrow.'"

In the Musnad of Ahmad verily there hath come down a tradition-"there shall be over this people, a man called al Walid ; he will assuredly be more hard upon this people than Pharaoh upon his subjects."

---

1 I read with the MS. خير of the word حين in the printed edition. I can make no sense.

A.H.126. A.D.744. Ibn Fadhlillah says in the Masalik (Ways).[1] "Al Walid was an inexorable tyrant, a tittle that does not wrong him- a path which he trod, but which did not guide him aright-the Pharaoh of this transitory age-of this world filled with calamities. He will come at the day of resurrection at the head of his tribe, bringing them into hell-fire and delievering them over to shame. Miserable the station where they alight-and hateful their place of return on that plain of assemblage. He hath shot arrows at the holy Book, and hath been licentious and hath not feared[2] sins."

As Suli records on the authority of Said b. Salim that Ibn Miyadah repeated to al Walid the verse of his in which he says :

"You have surpassed the Kuraysh, save the family of Muhammad

Save the Banu Marwan, the eminent.

Al Walid said to him, "I see that thou hast put before us the family of Muhammad." He replied, "I do not think it is lawful to do otherwise." And this Ibn Miyadah is he who says of al Walid also in his long poem.-

"I purposed to say a true speech,
And verily I shall say it in spite of enemises.
I have seen al Walid the son Yazid blessed,
His shoulders strong under the burdens of the Caliphate."

---

1 مسالك الابصارفي اخبار ملوك الامصار Vice oculorum de historia principum magnarum urbium-in twenty folies by Shihabuddin Ahmad b. Yahya b. Muhammad, al Kirmani, ad Dimishki, as Shafii known as Ibn Fadhlillah died 749 (1348). A supplement to this work was written by the author's son. Haj, Khal.

2 It may be also translated-" hath not concealed his sins"-according as the verb may be taken from the root خرف or خفى

YAZID-AN-NAKIS-B-UL WALID

A.H.126.
A.D.744.

Yazid the Retrencher, Abu Khalid b-ul Walid b. Abdil Malik was surnamed the Retrencher because he cut down the allowances to the troops. He usurped the Caliphate and slew his nephew al Walid and took possession of the government. His mother was Shahfarand daughter of Firuz son of Yazdajird, and the mother of Firuz was daughter of Shiruyah son of Khusrau, and the mother of Shiruyah was daughter of Khakan the Turkish chief and the grandmother of Firuz was the daughter of the Roman Emperor-for this reason Yazid says boastingly :

"I am the son of Khusrau, my ancestor was Marwan
Caesar was my grandsire and my grandsire was Khakan."

At Thaalabi says that he was the most noble in descent on both sides as well in regard to the monarchy as the Caliphate, and when he had put al Walid to death he stood up to preach and said, "now verily, by Allah, I have not rebelled out of insolence or ingratitude, nor seeking after worldly advantage, nor aiming at sovereignty and verily I have been but an oppressor unto my own soul if the Lord have not mercy upon me-but I came forward out of zeal for God and His religion as a summoner to His Book and the laws of his Prophet, at a time when the banners of right guidance wee defaced, the light of peity extinguished and a tyrant appeared making lawful, things that are forbidden and indulging in heretical innovations.[1]And when I beheld that, I feared that a darkness had come over ye which would not be removed for the multitude of your transgressions and the hardness of your hearts,-and I feared lest he should seduce many of the people to follow his course, and that they would consent, wherefore I asked of the Lord a blessing upon my purpose, and I summoned those of my family and under my authority who obeyed my call, and the Lord freed the people and the cities from him by the jurisdiction that is from God and there is no power or strength but from God. O ye people ! verily I promise ye, if I rule your affairs, that I shal not lay a brick upon a

1 He himself was a Muatazalite. See Masaudi.

A.H.126. A.D.744. brick, nor a stone upon a stone, nor carry away revenue from any city until I have fortified its frontier and expended for its welfare what will suffice to make ye secure, and if any balance should remain, I will transfer it to the city that is next to it, in order that the means of subsistence may be duly provided for, and that you may all be on an equality therein. If therefore ye desire to swear allegiance to me on the conditions I have proposed, I am yours, and if I deviate *from my word,* allegiance to me will not be binding upon ye. And if ye see any one more capable than I am for this authority, and ye desire to make a covenant with him then I will be the first to swear him allegiance and ask pardon of God for myself and for ye."[1]

Othman b. Abil Aatikah says that the first Caliph who came forth armed on the two festivals was Yazid b-ul Walid : he came forth then between two ranks of armed horsemen from the gate of the fort to the place of prayer.

And on the authority of Abu Othman al Laythi, that Yazid said, "O children of Umayyah, beware of singing, for it lessens shame, increases concupiscence and destroys manliness and indeed it takes the place of wine and doth that which intoxicating liquor effects, but if needs be that ye do it, then restrain your women therefrom, for song is an incentive to incontinence."

Ibn Abdil Hakam narrates, "I have heard as Shafii say that when Yazid assumed the government, he summoned the people to deny predestination and seduced them to it and honoured the followers fo Ghaylan. Yazid did not long enjoy the Caliphate but died in the same year on the 7th of Dul Hijjah:[2] thus his Caliphate lasted not quite six months, he being thirty-five years old, some say forty-six. It is said he died of the plague."

---

1 This discourse is translated by Weil from Tabari and it is given by Ibnul Athir. They differ slightly, but much less so from each other than either of them from the text of as Suyuti.

2 According to Weil the end of that month.

IBRAHIM-B-UL WALID-B-ABDIL MALIK

A.H.126.
A.D.744.

Ibrahim b-ul Walid b. Abdil Malik was acknowledged Caliph after the death of his brother Yazid an Nakis who as some say made a testament inhis favor, while others assert that he did not. Burd b. Sinan narrates, "I was with Yazid b-ul Walid when he was on the point of death, and Katan[1] came to him and said, 'I am a messenger from those who are behind thy gate asking of thee in the name of God's justice why thou hast appointed over their affairs thy brother Ibrahim.' But he grew wroth and said 'I appoint Ibrahim?'-then he said *to me* 'O father of the learned, whom dost thou think that I should appoint?' I replied, 'I shall not counsel thee regarding the conclusion of what I warned thee against entering upon.' Then a faintness came over him so that I thought that he was dead. Then Katan sat down and forged a testamentary document *as if* them the dictation of Yazid and summoned some people and asked them to bear witness to it-but no, by Allah, Yazid made no testament at all."

Ibrahim continued in the Caliphate seventy days[2] and was then deposed, for Marwan b. Muhammad set forth against him *and* received the covenant of allegiance and Ibrahim fled. Afterwards he came and abdicated the government and resigned it to Marwan and Voluntarily swore him allegiance and Ibrahim lived after that till the year 132 and he was killed among those of the Banu Ummayyah who were slain in the massacre perpetrated by a Saffah.

It is related in the history of Ibn Asakir that Ibrahim heard traditions from az Zuhri and narrated them on the authority of his paternal uncle Hisham, and his son Yakuq recited them from him. His mother was a slave concubine,[3] and he was the brother of Marwanul Himar by his mother. His deposal took place on Monday

---

1 Perhaps Katan b. Mudrik al Kilabi governor of Basrah.

2 Lit. nights, but the world ليل is often used to signify a period of twenty four hours counted from the sunset of one day to the sunset of the next.

3 Umm-Walad, signifies a slave who has borne a child to her master. After she has become a mother, she can no longer be sold, and is considered as married to her master though no marriage ceremony may have been performed.

A.H.127. A.D.744. the 14th of Safar in the year 127 (23rd November 744). Al Madaini says that his authority was never completely established, one party acknowledging him as Caliph and another acknowledge his temporal government, and another refusing altogether to swear him allegiance, and one of the poets of that time has said-

> We swear Ibrahim[1] allegiance every Friday-
> Verily a government must perish that hath thee for its ruler.

It has been said by some one that the impression on his signet ring was, "Ibrahim relies upon God !"

MARWAN AL HIMAR

Marwan the Ass, Abu Abdul Malik b. Muhammad b. Marwan bil Hakam was the last of the Caliphs of the Banu Umayyah. He was surnamed al Jaadi after his preceptor al Jaad b. Dirham,[2] and the Ass, because he was never weary of fighting those who rose up against him, and he would make march after march and was patient under the hardships of war. It is a proverbial expression- "such a one is more patient than an ass in war," and for that reason he was so named.' Another reason given is, that the Arabs name every hundred years an ass, and when the rule of the Banu Umayyah was nigh upon a hundred yars, they called Marwan the Ass, on the account.

Marwan was born in Mesopotamia of which his father was administrator in the year 72 and his mother was a slave concubine. Before his Caliphate he had the government of several important prefectures and took Iconium in the year 105. He was famed for his horsemanship, intrepidity, manliness, sagacity and recklessness. When al Walid was slain and the news reached him, he being in

---

1 For تبايع ابراهيم of the text, I read with Masaudi. نبايع ابراهيم

2 Ibnul Athir says that Jaad had the reputation of being an atheist, and he indoctrinated Marwan with his own heresies, teaching the creation of the Qurān and the denial of predestination.

Armenia, he summoned such of the Muslims as approved him, to do him allegiance, and the swore fealty to him. As soon as he heard of the death of Yazid, he disbursed sums of money and set out and fought Ibrahim and put him to flight. Marwan was then acknowledged Caliph and that occurred in the middle of Safar in the year 127 and his authority was firmly established.

A.H.132.
A.D.750.

The first thing he did was to command the exhuming of Yazid an Nakis, and he took him out of his grave and crucified him for his murder of al Walid. However he found little repose in the Caliphate on account of the number of those that rose against him on every side up to the year 132. Then the banu Abbas rebelled against him, and at their head Abdullah b. Ali, the paternal uncle of as Saffah. He set out to engage them, and the two armies me near Mosul. Marwan was routed and he returned to Syria, but Abdullah followed him and Marwan fled to Egypt. Salih, the brother of Abdullah pursued him and they met at the village of Busir[1] and Marwan was slain in Dul Hijjah of the same year. (5th August 750).

Of people of note who died during his reign were, as Suddi, the elder, Malik b. Dinar, the ascetic, Aasim b. Abin Najud, the Qurãn reader, Yazid b. Abi Habib, Shaybah b,Nisah the Qurãn reader, Muhammad b-ul Munkadir, Abu Jaafar Yazid bil Kakaa the Qurãn reader of Medina, Abu Ayub as Sikhtiyani, Abuz Zinad, Hamman b. Munabbih, and Wasil b. Ata the Muatazalite.

As Suli records on the authority of Muhammad b. Salib, that when Marwan was slain, his head was cut off and sent to Abdullah b. Ali, who gazed upon it, and it was removed, when a cat came and tore out the tongue and began to gnaw it ; whereupon Abdullah b. Ali said, "if the world had shown us none other of its wonders but the tongue of Marwan in the mouth of a cat, it would have been sufficient for us."

---

1 Four several places all in Egypt—says Gibbon bore the name of Busir or Busiris, so famous in Greek fable. The first where Marwan was slain to the west of the Nile in the province of Fium or Arsince, the second in the Delta, the third near the Pyramids, the fourth, which was destroyed by Diocletian, in the Thebais. Chap. XII, Decline and Fall.

A.H.132.
A.D.750.

AS SAFFAH

First Caliph of the House of Abbas.

As Saffah, the first Caliph of the House of Abbas, Abul Abbas, Abdullah b. Muhammad b. Ali b. Abdillah b. Abbas b. Abdil Muttalib b. Hashim, was born in the year 108 (some say 104) at Humaymah in the district of Balka,and there grew to manhood. He was acknowledged Caliph at Kufah. His mother was Raitah of the tribe of Harith. He related traditions on the authority of Ibrahim b. Muhammad the Imam, and his paternal uncle. Isa b. Ali related them on his. He was younger than his brother al Mansur.

Ahmad records in his Musnad on the authority of Abu Sai'd al Khudri that the Apostle of God said, "there shall come forth from the people of my house, after the lapse of time and the appearance of seditions, a man called as Saffah, and it shall come to pass that his largesses of money shall be by handfuls."

Ubaydullah al Ayshi narrates-"my father relates 'I heard the Shaykhs saying-by Allah, verily the Caliphate hath come to the children of Abbas, and there is not upon the earth any more learned in the Qurãn, nor more distinguished for piety nor more devout that they.'" The origin of the authority of the Banu Abbas was that the Apostle of God told his uncle Abbas that the Caliphate would descend to his posterity, and his descendants continued in expectation of it (Ibn Jarir at Tabari). *The latter relates* from Rishdin b. Kurayb, that Abu Hashim Abdullah b. Muhammad bil Hanafiyah went to Syria, and met Muhammad b. Ali b. Abdillah b. Abbas and said, "O cousin, verily I have information which I wish to lay before thee, but be sure tell no one of it-verily this authority which people hope for, shall be with you." The other replied, "verily I was aware of it, but let no one hear of it from thee."

Al Madaini[1] narrates on the authority of a number of people, that the Imam Muhammad b. Ali b. Abdillah b. Abbas said, "we have three opportunities-the death of Yazid b. Muawiyah, the beginning of the century, and the rupture in Africa. At that time the summoners shall summon *the people* in our behalf, and our allies from the east shall come until their horsemen shall reach the west." A.H.132. A.D.750.

And when Yazid b. Abi Muslim was slain in Africa and the Berbers were reduced, Muhammad the Imam sent a man to Khurasan and commanded him to invite *the people* to approve one of the posterity of Muhammad and not to name any one. Then he dispatched Abu Muslim al Khurasani and others, and wrote to the principal men who received his letters favourably, but it came to pass that Muhammad died, leaving the succession to his son Ibrahim. On the news of this reaching Marwan, he imprison Ibrahim and put him to death. Ibrahim had bequeathed the succession to his brother Abdullah as Saffah and his followers gathered about him and he was acknowledged as Caliph at Kufah on the 3rd Rabiiul Awwal in the year 132. He read prayers to the people on the Friday and said in his discourse, "praise be to God who hath chosen Islam for Himself and hath honored it and exalted it and magnified it and hath chosen it for us and strengthened it by us, and made us its people, its asylum and its defence to maintain and protect it." Then he went on to mention the kinship *of the Banu Abbas alluted* to in the Qurãn until he said, "and when the Lord took to Himself His Prophet, his companions stood up in authority until the Banu Harb and Marwan usurped it, and they were tyrannous and appropriated every thing to themselves. And God bare with them for a time until they angered Him, wherefore He took vengeance upon them by our hands, and restored unto us our right, that He might be bountiful

1 Abul Hasan Ali b. Muhammad al Madaini was a Mawla of the family of Abd Shams b. Abd Manaf. He was born A.H. 135 (752-3) and died A.H. 225 (839-40). He was a disciple of the Muatazalite doctor Mamar b-ul Ashath. He wrote upwards of twenty works on Muhammad and many others biographical and historical treatises. De Slane I.K.

A.H.132. A.D.750 through us upon those who are outcast[1] throughout the earth, and he hath ended with us as He began with us and we of the *Prophetical* house have no grace but through God. O ye people of Kufah ye are the seat of our regard and the abiding place of our affection-ye have not been remiss in this, nor hath the rigour of the tyrannous turned ye from it-for ye are the most favored people unto us and of those who most honour us ; wherefore verily I have increased your largesses by a hundred *dirhams* eash. Therefore be prepared, for I am the justifying shedder of blood and the destroying avenger."[2]

Isa b. Ali[3] when he mentioned their setting out from Humaymah[4] for Kufah, used to say, "fourteen men departed from their homes, seeking what we sought throught the greatness of their resolution, the steadfastness of their hearts."

When news of the allegiance sworn to as Saffah reached Marwan, he set forth to encounter him, but was defeated as hath gone before, and afterwards slain. At the ceremony of allegiance sworn to as Saffah, a countless number[5] of the Banu Ummayyah and their followers were put to death and his dominions were firmly settled under his authority to the furthest confines of the West.

Ad Dahabi says that in his reign the unity of the State was dissolved and all between Tahart and Tubnah as far as the Soudan

---

1 For أستَضعفوا read أُستضعفوا

2 This discourse which is here considerably shortened, is given in full by Ibnul Athir. During its delivery as Saffah was seized with an attack of fever and sat down. His uncle Dauud b. Ali rose and continued the oration which will be found in the Kamil.

3 The uncle of the Caliph al Mansur and of as Saffah.

4 The Kamil has erroneously جهيمة

5 Sulayman b. Ali put to death a number of them at Basrah, and had their bodies flung to the dogs. Abdullah b. Ali, in Palestine massacred about ninety of them. "The laws of hospitality were violated by a promiscuous massacre, the board was spread over their fallen bodies and the festivity of the guests was enlivened by the music of their dying groans." The surprising accuracy of Gibbon can only be known to those who consult his authorities. Though the Kamil is not one of them, the above passage is almost a literal translation from it.

fell from his obedience, as well as the entire kingdom of Spain, and A.H.136.
there come forth in these provinces, those[1] who took possession of A.D.754.
them, and that so continued.

As Saffah died of small-pox in Dul Hijjah in the year 136 (9th June 754) bequeathing the succession to his brother Abu Jaafar. In the year 136 he removed to Anbar and made it the seat of government.

Redarding accounts of as Saffah, Suli relates among his sayings, "As power becomes great, concupiscence grows less. It is rare that bounty is given unasked but a just claim is destroyed thereby. Verily they are the basest and meanest of men who account avarice prudence, and clemency ignoble. When forbearance is mischievous, to pardon is weakness. Patience is praiseworthy save in what prejudices the faith or renders sovereignty contemptible, and moderation is commendable except at the season of opportunity. As suli adds that as Saffah was the most generous of men-he never made a promise and delayed its fulfillment at its appointed timc, nay hc ncvcr rosc from his scat without pcrforming it.

Abdullah b. Hasan once said to him, "I have heard of a million dirhams but have never seen them," whereupon he ordered concerning them and they were brought, and he commanded him to take them with him to his house.

As Suli says that the impression on his signet-ring was, "God is the reliance of Abdullah and on Him he confideth." Scarcely and poetry of his has been handed down.

Said b. Muslim al Bahili narrates that Abdullah b. Hasan went in unto as Saffah and the assembly was full of the Banu Hashim and their followers and the chiefs of the people and with him he carried the Qurãn and he said, "O prince of the Faithful, give us our right which God hath vouchsafed unto us in this book." He replied, "verily thy great-grandfather Ali, who was better than I am and more just, held this authority, and he gave unto thy progenitors

---

1 The Edrisites of Mauritania and the Futimites of Africa and Egypt.

A.H.136. al Hasan and al Husayn somewhat, and it would be but right did I
A.D.754. give thee the same, and if I have done that, verily I have given thee thy due, and if I have done more, then this should not be my reward from thee." And Abdullah departed and returned no answer, and the people were astonished, at the reply of as Saffah. Historians say that under the House of Abbas the unity of Islam was dissolved, and the Arab name lapsed from the registers, and the Turks were installed in public offices and the Daylamites came into power, and afterwards the Turks, and a mighty empire belonged to them, and the dominions of the earth were parceled out and on every side was a usurper, doing violence to the people and ruling them with tyranny. They say that as Saffah was quick to shed blood and his prefects in the east and west followed his example in that, but withal he was liberal with his wealth.

Of people of note who died in his reign were Zayd b. Aslam, Abdullah b. Aslam, Abdullah b. Abi Bakr b. Hazm, Rabii ar Rai,[1] jurisconsult of Medina; Abdul Malik b. Umayr, Yahya b Abi Ishak al Hadrami, Abdul Hamid the welknown scribe slain with Marwan at Busir, Mansur b-ul Muatamir, and Hammam b. Munabbih.'

AL MANSUR

Al Mansur Abu Jaafar, Abdullah b. Muhammad b. Ali b. Abdillah b. Abbas (whose mother was Salamah a Berber slave concubine) was born in the year 95 and had known his grandfather but had no traditions from him. He narrated them on the authority of his father and Ata b. Yasar ; and his son, al Mahdi, from him.

He was acknowledged Caliph according to the bequest of his

1 Or the Rationalist, so called, because he drew many of his legal decisions from the fourth source of Muhammadan law, which is entitled Rai (private judgment) or Kiyas (analogy). This system was followed by the Hanafites who were called Ashabur Rai, or Rationalists. See De Slane, I.K. notes to Rabii ur Rai.

brother and was the foremost among the Banu Abbas in Majesty of demeanour, bravery, prudence, judgment and haughtiness-a hoarder of wealth, averse to pastime and frivolity, of cultivated mind, of excellent converse in science and literature and with a natural taste for jurisprudence. A.H.136. A.D.754.

He put a multitude of people to death until his power was established, and it was he who scourged Abu Hanifah on account of *his refusal to accept* the office of Kadhi, and then put him in prison where he died after some days. It is also said that he despatched him by poison because he had passed a judicial sentence authorizing rebellion against him. He was polished in language, eloquent and fluent, well fitted, for governing but excessively avaricious. He was surnamed Abud Dawanik[1] on account of his scrutiny of the accounts of intendants and artificers even to fractions of dirhams and grains.

Al Khatib records on the authority of the Prophet that he said, "from us shall arise as Saffah and from us al Mansur, and from us al Mahdi," (ad Dahabi states this to be unacknowledged and its ascription interrupted). He and Ibn Asakir and others states on the ascription of Said b. Jubayr that Ibn Abbas said, "from us *shall come* as Saffah, from us al Mansur and from us al Mahdi." The ascription of this is pronounced by ad Dahabi to be sound. Ibn Asakir records from Abu Sai'd al Khudri that he narrates, "I heard the apostle of God say, 'from us *shall arise* al Kaim, from us al Mansur, from us as Saffah and from us al Mahdi. As to al kaim, the Caliphate shall come to him, and during his reign not a cupping-glass of blood shall be spilt, as to al Mansur, his standard shall not be turned back : as to as Saffah, he will lavish treasure and blood and with regard to al Mahdi, he shall fill the Caliphate with justice as it hath been filled with tyranny.'"

And from al Mansur, that he said, "I beheld myself as it were in the precincts of the temple and the Apostle of God was in the Kaabah the door of which was open and a crier cried out, 'where

---

1 A Danik is the sixth part of a dirham.

A.H.136. A.D.754. is Abdullah ?' and my brother Abul Abbas arose and stood upon the step and was taken within, and it was not long before he became forth with a spear upon which was a black pennon measuring four cubits. Then there was cried out, 'where is Abdullah ?' And I stood upon the step and was made to ascend and lo ! there was the Apostle of God and Abu Bakr, Omar and Bilal, and he invested me with authority and commended to me his people, and put on my head a turban, the windings of which were twenty and three and he said, 'take this unto thyself, O father of the Caliphs, until the day of resurrecton.'"

Al Mansur assumed the Caliphate in the beginning of the year 137. The first thing he did was to put to death Abu Muslim al Khurasani, the author of their call and the founder of their dynasty. In the year 138 Abdur Rahman b. Muawiyah b. Hisham b. Abdil Malik b. Marwan the Umayyad entered Spain and conquered it. His reign was long and Spain continued in the hands of his descendants until after the fourth century. This Abdir Rahman was a man of learning and justice. His mother was a native of Barbary.

Abu Mudhaffar al Abiwardi says that people used to say that the two sons of two Berber women ruled the world-al Mansur and Abdur Rahman b. Muawiyah.

In the year 140 he laid the foundation of the city of Baghdad. In the year 141 appeared the Rawadiyah[1] sectaries the asserters of metempsychosis and al Mansur put them to death. During the same, Tabaristan was conquered.

Ad Dahabi says that in the year 143 the doctors of Islam began at this period to compose works on traditions, jurisprudence and the interpretation of the Qurãn. Thus Ibn Juraij[2] wrote at Mecca,

---

1 Weil is in accordance with Ibnul Athir who calls them "Rawandiyah, a people of Khurasan, followers of Abu Muslim and believing in metempsychosis." Masaudi calls the sect Khurramiyah-in one MS. (خرميه) and in two others جربية and جرميه Yakut places Rawan between Kashan and Ispahan. The text ريونديه is incorrect.

2 Abu Khalid Abdul Malik of Mecca, by adoption a member of the Kuraysh. It is said he was the first in Islam to compose books, died A.H. 149. (766). Ibn Khall. For جريح read جريج

Malik compose the Muwatta at Medina, al Auzaai wrote in Syria, A.H.143.
Ibn Abi Arubah, [1] Hammad b. Salamah[2] and others in Basrah, A.D.760.
Mamar, in Yaman,[3] Sufiyan at Thauri in Kufah, Ibn Ishak drew up his Maghazi (wars of Islam). Abu Hanifah wrote treatises on law and the theory of private judgment. Very soon after Hushaym,[4] al Layth, and Ibn Lahiah composed their works. Then followed Ibnul Mubarak and Abu Yusuf and Ibn Wahab, at which period the collection of works of science and their classification increased greatly and treatises on the Arabic language and idiom were drawn up and also on history and the encounters of the desert Arabs. Before this period, the learned used to discourse from memory or lectured on science from manuscripts, accurate, but unsystematically arranged."

In the year 145 occurred the rebellion of the brothers Muhammad and Ibrahim, the two sons of Abdullah b. Hasan bil Hasan b. Ali b. Abi Talib, but al Mansur defeated and slew them and a large number of the descendants of the *Prophetical* House. Verily we belong to God and verily unto Him shall we return. Al

---

1 A tranidionist of Basrah, died A.H. 156, (772-3) De Slane I.K.

2 Abu Sulamah hammad b. Salamah, a traditionist of the highest order, descended from an enfranchised slave of this Banu Tamim, died A.H. 167. Ibid.

3 Mamar b. Abi Urwah Rashid a Mawla to the tribe of Azd, learned traditions from az Zuhri a native of Basrah and settled in Yaman, died A.H. 153. De Slane I.K.

4 Abu Muawiyah, Hushaym the Traditionist was a native of Basrah died A.H. 183, De Slane in translating this passage of ad Dahabi (Introduction to Vol. I,) gives "Ibn Hisham," for "Hushaym." Ibn Hisham's family was also of Basrah though he was born at old Cairo. He is the author of the history of the Prophet drawn from Ibn Ishak's work and called Sirat Ibn Hisham. He died A.H. 218 I have not the work of ad Dahabi to consult : the Nujum, of Abul Mahasin from which De Slane cites, has "Hisham" without any prefix. De Slane is incorrect in his translation of the word الراى in his Introduction, (p. xxiv) as will be seen on a reference to the original in Abul Mahasin where the name Rabii does not occur. Moreover after the words الراى in the Nujum follows بالكوفه Now Rabii was jurisconsult of Medina and Ibn Khall mentions nothing of his ever having been at Kufah whereas it was Abu Hanifah's native town. For the biographies of those authors not mentioned in the notes, consult Ibn Khall.

A.H.145. Mansur was the first who occasioned dissensions between the
A.D.762. Abbassides and the Aliites for before that they were united. He persecuted many of the learned who had risen with them or counseled rebellion, by putting them to death and scourging them and in other ways-among them Abu Hanifah and Abdul Hamid b. Jaafar, and Ibn Ajlan. Among those who pronounced on the legality of rebelling with Muhammad against al Mansur, was Malik b. Anas. It was said to him-"upon our necks is the oath of allegiance to al Mansur !" He replied-"ye swore allegiance under compulsion and an oath is not binding upon one who is forced.

In the year 146 occurred the expedition against Cyprus. In the year 147 al Mansu removed his paternal uncle Isa b. Musa from the succession to which as Saffah had appointed him after al Mansur. Isa was he who fought for him against the two brothers and defeated them and he rewarded him by setting him aside against his will and nominating his own son al Madhi.

In the year 148 the whole empire was firmly established under the authority of al Mansur, and awe of him waxed great in the minds of men. The provinces submitted to him and Spain alone was excluded from his sway, for Abdur Rahan b. Muawiyah, the Umayyad, of the house of Marwan, had taken possession of it, but he was not called prince of the Faithful but "the price" only and in the same way, his posterity.

In the year 140 al Mansur completed the building of Baghdad. In the year 150, the Khurasan troops under their leader Ustad Sia[1] revolted from his authority and seized the greater part of Khurasan, and calamities increased and evils waxed great and affairs grew serious with al Mansur, for the strength of the army of Khurasan amounted to 3,00,000 warriors horse and foot. Ajtham[2] al Marwazi engaged them in battle but he was slain and his army destroyed. Then al Mansur despatched Khazim[3] b. Khuzaymah to attack them

---

1 So Ibnul Athir and Weil. The text gives اسفاد سيس which is incorrect.

2 Ibnul Athir has "Ajsham" اجشم

3 For حازم read خازم

at the head of a prodigious force that obstructed the plains, and the two armies met and fought obstinately. It was a famous battle. It is said that seventy thousand men were slain in it and Ustad Sis was routed and he fled to the mountains. The general, Khazim, gave orders in the following year regarding the prisoners, and their heads were struck off and they were in number 14000. Then they besieged Ustad Sis for some time, until he surrendered. They kept him in confinement and dismissed his troops who numbered.30,000. A.H.158. A.D.775.

In the year 151 al Mansur built ar Rusafah (*of Kufah*) and made it a strong and lofty construction.

In the year 153, al *Mansur* complelled his subjects to wear tall caps-they used to make them of need and paper, and cover them with black.

Abu Dulamah,[1] says-

> We desired an increase from the Imam.
> And the chosen Imam gave us an increase to our caps.
> Thou mayest behold them on the heads of men as if
> They were wine jars of the Jews covered with the burnus.

In the year 158 al Mansu commanded the governor of Medina to imprison Sufiyan at Thauri and Abbad b. Kathir and they were put into confinement, and the people feared that al Mansur would put them to death when he came from the pilgrimage, but the Lord did not suffer him to reach Mecca in health, for he arrived ill and died, and the Lord was sufficient for them against his wicked purpose. His death occurred at Batn[2] in Dul Hajjah (6th) (7th October

1 Abu Dulamah was an Abyssinian slave celebrated for his wit, his amusing adventures and his talent for poetry. He died A.H. 161 (778-9). His real name was Zand. Some amusing stories regarding him, may be found in Ibn Khallikan.

2 Batn Murr or Marr, five miles from Mecca. This name is not mentioned by Weil or Ibn Athir : Masaudi says that death overtook him at the Bustan of the Band Aamir on the Iraq road. Al Hajun is a hill overlooking Mecca.

A.H.158. A.D.775. 776) and he was buried between al Hajun and Bir Maymun. Salm[1] al Khasir says,

> The pilgrims returned and left the son of Muhammad
> As a pledge at Mecca in the niched tomb.
> They witnessed the entire ceremonies while their Imam
> Beneath the broad stone, purposing to perform the pilgrimage, witnessed them not.

Regarding accounts of al Mansur, Ibn Asakir records with its ascriptions, that Abu Jaafar al Mansur used to travel for the purpose of acquiring knowledge, before his Caliphate. Once when he was about to enter a place of resort, the guardian seized him and said, "pay down two dirhams before thou enterest." He replied, "loose me for I am one of the Banu Hashim." Then man said, "pay down two dirhams." He replied "loose me, for I am one of the descendants of the uncle of the Prophet." The man went on, "pay down two dirhams." He replied, "loose me for I am a man versed in the book of God.: The man repeated "pay down two dirhams." He exclaimed "loose me for I am a man skilled in Jurisprudence and the law of inheritance." He replied "pay down two dirhams." When at length the man's insistence wearied him, he paid the two dirhams and returned and set himself to amassing money and to scrupulous niggardliness therein, until he received the nickname of Abud Dawanik. And on the authority of Rabibi b. Yunus the chamberlain, who narrates, "I heard al Mansur say, 'the Caliphs are four, Abu Bakr, Omar, Othman and Ali, and the kings are four, Muawiyah, Abdul Malik, Hisham and I." And from Malik b. Anas, "I went in unto al Mansur and he said, 'who are the most excellent of men after the apostle of God!' I replied, 'Abu Bakr and Omar.' He said, 'thou hast hit it-and such is the opinion of the prince of the Faithful.'" And from Ismail al Fihri, "I heard al Mansur on the day of Arafah,

---

1 A native of Basrah, a poet notorious for his profligate life. He lived at Baghdad and received his epithet (the loser) because he sold a copy of the Qurãn to bujy a book of poetry or else because he squandered his patrimony. He died about 186 A.H. De Slane I.K.

saying ir. his discourse from the pulpit at Arafah, 'O ye people ! verily I am the Lord's ruler upon His earth and I govern ye through His grace and guidance and I am His treasurer over His tribute which I divide according to his pleasure and bestow with His permission. And verily the Lord hath made me as a lock upon it : When He willeth to open me, He openeth me that I may give unto ye, and when it pleaseth Him to fasten me, he fasteneth me. Wherefore turn ye to the Lord, O ye people ! and ask of Him on this glorious day in which he hath given unto ye of His grace, as he hath made known to ye in His Book when he saith, "this day I have perfected your religion for ye and have completed my mercy upon ye, and I have chosen for ye Islam to be your religion" (Qur. V),[1] that He may vouchsafe unto me justness of conduct, and guide me to rectitude and inspire me with clemency unto and kindness towards ye, and open me to be bountiful unto ye, and the distribution of your allowances in equity, for he hearkeneth and granteth.'" As Suli records this and mentions further at the beginning of it, that the reason of this discourse was that the people esteemed him niggardly, and he adds at the end, "and people said 'the prince of the Faithful transfers to his God the responsibility of withholding *his bounty.*'" And he records on the authority of al Asmai and others that al Mansur ascended the pulpit and said, "praise be unto God : I glorify Him and implore His aid, and I believe in Him and put my trust in Him and I testify that there is no god but one God who hath no equal." Then there arose before him a man who said, "O prince of the Faithful, be thou mindful of Him whom thou art praising." He answered, "welcome, welcome, verily thou hast admonished me by One that is great and put me in fear of One that is mighty-God forbid, that I should be as one who when it is said to him, 'fear God,' his pride takes it as an offence, but the exhortation began with me and proceeded from me ; and thou ! thou speaker, I swear by Allah. it was not God thou thoughtest of, but thou soughtest that

A.H.158.
A.D.775.

---

1 This passage it is said was revealed on Friday evening, being the day of the pilgrimas visiting aount Arafat the last time Muhammad repaired to the temple of Mecca, therefore called the pilgrimage of Valediction. Sale, p. 81.

A.H.158. A.D.775 it should be said-he arose and spake and was punished but bore it patiently. But the thing is not worthy of notice from such a speaker, and take this as a favourable opportunity from God.[1] Have a care. Verily I have pardoned it. Beware, ye men, of the like of it ; - and I testify that Muhammad is His servant and His apostle." He then returned to his discourse *as fluently* as though he were reading it from paper.

He also records with various ascriptions that al Mansur said to his son al Mahdi-"O Abu Abdullah, nothing maketh a Caliph virtuous but piety, nor well disposeth a monarch but obedience, nor reformeth a people but justice ; and the best of men to pardon is he who is the most powerful of them to chastise, and the feeblest of men in intellect is he who oppresseth him that is beneath him. Do not proceed with an affair until thou hast reflected upon it, for the meditation of a wise man is a mirror which showeth him his faults and his merits. O son, seek the continuance of bounty by gratitude, and of power by pardon, and of obedience by conciliating affection, and of victory by humility and forgiveness of men." And from Mubarak b. Fudhalah that he said, "we were with al Mansur when he summoned a man and sent for a sword, and Mubarak said, 'O prince of the Faithful, I heard al Hasan declare that the Apostle of God said, "when the day of resurrection cometh, a crier of the Lord's shall rise and shall cry out-arise those whose reward is with God, and none shall stand up but he who hath pardoned." And al Mansur said-let him go his way.'"

And from al Asami, that a man was taken to al Mansur whom he was about to punish, but the man said, "O prince of the Faithful, vengeance is but justice, but forgiveness would be super-eminent virtue and may God preserve the prince of the Faithful from choosing for himself the less noble of two courses without being able to attain to the higher degree;" and he pardoned him. And from the same, that al Mansur met a desert Arab in Syria and said to him, "praise God, O Arab, who hath taken from ye the plague under the

1 The Kamil has اغتنمها اذعفوت

government of us of the prophetical house;" He replied, "verily God hath not overwhelmed us with both bad dates and bad measure, your government and the plague." A.H.158. A.D.775.

And from Muhammad b. Mansur al Baghdadi, that a certain devotee[1] stood up before al Mansur and said, "verily the Lord hath given unto thee the whole earth, redeem then thy soul, with a portion of it. Remember the night which thou shalt pass in the grave,-a night thou hast never before so passed, and remember the night which shall bring forth the day that hath no night after it." And al Mansur was silenced and commanded money to be given to him, but he said, "If I needed thy money, I should not have admonished thee." And from Abdus Salam b. Harb, that al Mansur sent for Amr b. Ubayd who came to him, and *he* commanded money to be given to him but he refused to accept it, and al Mansur said, "by Allah, thou shalt accept it." He replied, "by Allah, I will not accept it." Al Mahdi *who was present* said to him, "verily the pricne of the Faithful hath taken his oath." He replied, "the prince of the Faithful is more able to pay the expiation of broken oaths than is thy uncle."[2] Al Mansur said to him, "ask for what thou needest." He replied, "I ask thee not to send for me until I go to thee, and not to give unto me until I ask of thee." He said, "dost thou know I have made this *al Mahdi* my heir?" He replied, "the supreme power will come to him the day it comes to him, and thou wiit be

1 This was Amr b. Ubayd whose mention follows in the next anecdote. Both of them are related in his life in Ibn Khallikan. He was a celebrated ascetic and scholastic theologian; his devotion was proverbial though his orthodoxy is disputed by nearly all but his own sect of the Muatazalites of which he was the chief. He was born A.H. 80 (699) and died A.H. 144 (761-2). Al Mansur composed an elegy on his death and praised him as an orthodox believer and saint.

2 In Ibn Khallikan, he addresses al Mahdi, as "son of my brother" and therefore calls himself his uncle, not of course meaning that there existed the remoted relationship, for Amr's father acted as lieutenant to the successive chiefs of police at Basrah and had been one of the prisoners taken at Kabul. The expiation for breaking an path consists in granting freedom to a slave or in once feeding and clothing ten paupers-if this cannot be done, a fast for three days is obligatory. De slane, I.K. Vol, I, p. 53.

A.H.158. otherwise employed *than in providing for it.*" And from Abdullah
A.D.775. b. Salih that al Mansur wrote to Sawwar Kadhi of Basrah, *saying*, "look to the piece of land regarding which a certain officer and a certain merchant have disputed and give it to the officer ;" and Sawwar wrote, "verily it was proved to me that it belonged to the merchant, and I cannot withdraw it from his possession except on clear evidence." Then al Mansur wrote, "by Allah, save whom there is not God, thou shalt give it to the officer;" Sawwar replied to him, "by Allah, save whom there is no God, I shall not withdraw it from the possession of the merchant except lawfully." When this letter reahed al Mansur, he exclaimed, "thou hast filled *thy office* with justice and my judges are now turning me to justice." And from anther source that Sawwar was denounced to al Mansur who summoned him, and al Mansur happened to sneeze and Sawwar did not bless him, and al Mansur said, "what prevented thee from saying a blessing?" he replied, "because thou didst not praise God."[1] Al Mansur said, "indeed I praised God to myself," and he answered "I prayed for a blessing on thee to myself." The Caliph exclaimed, "go back to my office, for verily if thou payest no regard to me, thou wilt pay none to any other."

And from Numyr al Madani who narrates, "al Mansur arrived at Medina, and Muhammad b. Imran at Talhai was holding judgment as Kadhi and I was his scribe. And certain camel-owners sought justice against al Mansur in some affair, and Muhammad ordered me to write to him to appear, and to do them justice ; but I asked to be excused, but he would not excuse me, wherefore I wrote the summons and sealed it." He said-"by Allah, no one shall go with it but thyself." Wherefore I carried it to ar Rabii who went in unto al Mansur. Shortly after he came forth and said to the people, "verily the prince of the Faithful saith to ye-"I have been summoned to the judgment-seat, but let no one go up with me." Then he and ar Rabii went, but the Kadhi did not rise before him, nay he lossed his mantle and wrapped it round his legs and back, and then summoned the

1 The prayer for the sneezer (which is, may God avert from thee what may make the enemy rejoice at thy affliction) is uttered, when he has in obedience to an injunction of the Prophet said الحمد لله praise be to God, Lane, art. شمت

plaintiffs. They made their plaint and he decided in their favour against the Caliph ; and when he had finished, al Mansur said to him, "may God reward thee for thy judgment, with the best of rewards-verily I have commanded to be given to thee, ten thousand dinars." A.H.158. A.D.775.

And from Muhammad b. Hafa al Ijli, that a son was born to Abu Dulamah, who went early in the morning to al Mansur and informed him and recited-

"If there sat above the sun, on account of their liberality
A people, it would be said-sit ye O children of Abbas.
And ascend upon the rays of the sun, all of ye
Unto heaven, for ye are the most bountiful of men.

Then Abu Dulamah drew out a purse and al Mansur said, "what is that ?" He replied, "I mean to put into it what thou orderest for me." He said, "fill it for him with dirhams," and it held a thousand dirhams. And from Muhammad b. Sallam al Jimhi, that it was said to al Mansur, "is there any yet left of the pleasures of the world that thou hast not enjoyed ?" He replied, "one thing is still wanting-that I should sit upon a bench, and round me the traditionists, the disciple writing from dictation, saying, 'whom didst thou mention[1] may the Lord have mercy on thee ?'" The next morning the courtiers and the sons of the ministers came with their ink-horns and tablets, but al Mansur said, "ye are not they-for they are of soiled garments, weary of foot, long of hair, the couriers, of the earth, the transmitters of tradition." And from Abdu's Samad b. Ali, that he said to al Mansur, "verily thou hast applied punishment as if thou hadst never heard of pardon." He answered, "because the Banu Marwan, their bones have not yet decayed and the swords of the descendants of Abu Talib have not been sheathed, and we are among a people who sawus subjects yesterday and Caliphs to-day, and the fear of us will not take possession of their hearts save by ignoring pardon and the adoption of chastisement." And from

1 That is, of course, asking for the names of the authorities whom the traditionist mentions in the ascriptions of any tradition.

A.H.158. A.D.775 Yunas b. Habib that Ziyad b. Abdillah al Harithi wrote to al mansur, petitioning for an increase to his allowances and stipends, and employed all his eloquence in *the composition of* hid letter but al Mansur noted on the case *saying*, "verily wealth and eloquence when combined in one individual, make him vain-glorious, and the prince of the Faithful hath compassion on thee one that account ; therefore be content with eloquence." And from Muhammad b. Sallam, that a slave girl saw a Mansur with a patched tunic, and she exclaimed-"the Caliph with a patched tunic!" He replied, "fie on thee, hast thou not heard the words of Ibn Harmah : [1]

> Verily a youth may attain honour though his mantle
> Be thread-bare, and the collar of his tunic, patched."

Al Askari says in the Awail that al Mansur among the sons of Abbas, was like Abdul Malik among the Banu Umayyah, in niggardliness. One of the people saw upon him a patched tunic, and said, "great is He who hath tried Abu Jaafar with povety in his own kingdom."

Salm the camel-driver once drove al Mansur's camel, singing to it, and al Mansur was so excited with delight, that he nearly fell from the animal, and he rewarded him with half a dirham. The man said, "I drove Hisham and he rewarded me with ten thousand." The Caliph replied, "He had no right to give thee that from the public treasury. O Rabii,[2] appoint some once to take it from him;" and they did not finish with him until al Mansur made him drive the camel, going and coming for nothing.

---

1 Abu Ishak Ibrahim b. Ali B. Maslamah b. Aamir b. Harmah died A.H. 176. Al Asmai says of him that he was the last of the poets, and his life has been written by as Suli (probably not now extant). This is the only information regarding him furnished by De Slane in his life of as Suli. I.K.

2 Abul Fadhl Rabii b. Yunas was chamberlain to al Mansur, and later, on the deposition of Abu Ayub, al Muriani, became his vizier, and continued in the service of al Mahdi in the same capacity. The Caliph treated him with signal favor. He died in A.H. 170 (786) in the reign al Hadi, poisoned according to some, by that Caliph, Ibn Khall.

In the Awail of al Askari it is stated that Ibn Harmah was A.H.158.
much addicted to wine, and he went into al Mansur, and versified, A.D.775.
saying,

"His glances from both sides of his throne
When he launches them contain punishment or favour.

On the one hand he to whom thou grantest *protection*, thou protectest, from destruction,[1]

On the other, he whom thou wishest to be bereft of a child, he is bereft.

And al Mansur was pleased with him and said, "What is they need?" He replied, "write to thy prefect at Medina not to punish me, if he finds me drunk." Al Mansur answered, "I will not abate a single restrictive ordinance of the ordianaces of God." He said "contrive some expedient for me." And al Mansur wrote to his prefect, *saying*, "whoever bringeth before thee Ibn Harmah drunk, scourge him with a hundred stripes and scourge Ibn Harmah with eighty." Wherefore when the watch used to pass by Ibn Hrmah when he was drunk, he would exclaim, "who will buy a hundred for eighty," and then leave him and pass on. Al Mansur gave him on this occasion ten thousand dirhams and said to him, "take care of them, O Ibrahim, for there is nothing for thee like it again, with me." He replied, "verily I will meet thee on the bridge of as Sirat with it, with the seal of the court treasurer."[2]

Among the lines of al Mansur, and they are few, is the following–

When thou hast formed an opinon be steadfast in it,
For verily it is an ill-judgment that is vacillating.
Nor grant thy enemies respite in power for a single day

---

1 This line is faulty ; in the text the word امنة as it stands has no meaning and will not scan-I suggest and adopt the following emendation فام الذي آمنتَ امنتهُ الردي

2 The word جهبذ is used by Masaudi in this same, in his life of al Mahdi. Speaking of Sharik, he says, كتب له بارزاقه الي الجهبذ transltated by M.De Meynard, "le Khalife lui ayant donne un bon sur le payeur de la cour."

A.H.158. A.D.775. But be beforehand with them, lest they obtain the same tomorrow.

Abdur Rahman b. Ziyad b. Anum al Ifriki narrates, "I was pursuing my studies with Abu Jaafar al Mansur before his Caliphate, when he took me into his house and placed some food before me, wherewith there was no flesh-meat. The he called out, 'girl! Hast thou any sweetmeats?' She said, 'no'. 'Nor any dates?' 'No.' Then he laid himself down and read 'peradventure your Lord will destroy your enemy,' &c. (Qur. VII.) And when he succeeded to the Caliphate, I visited him, and he said, 'how is my government compared with that of the Banu Umayyah?' I replied, 'I see no oppression under their rule, but I find it also under thine.' He exclaimed, 'we have no helpers.' I answered, 'Omar b. Abdil Aziz said that a monarch is like a market that attracts to itself what will sell freely in it: if he be virtuous, they bring him the virtuous among them; if he be wicked, they bring him the wicked among them,' whereupon al Mansur lowered his eyes."

Among the sayings of al Mansur are, [1] "kings can tolerate every thing but three practices-revealing a secret, an outrage on his harem, or a blow aimed at his power. When thy enemy stretches out his hand to thee, cut it off if thou art able, otherwise kiss it." The ascriptions of these are given by as Suli who also records on the authority of Yakuq b. Jaafar as one of the instances related of the quick apprehension of al Mansur, [2] that he entered Medina and said to ar Rabii, "find me a man who will point out to me the *chief* mansions of the people." And a man came to him and began to inform him about the houses, save that he never began to speak until al Mansur questioned him. And when he left him he ordered him a thousand dirhams. The man asked ar Rabii for it, but he replied, "he said nothing to me about it, but he will soon ride round again when you can remind him." Al Mansur continued his ride a second time, and the man began to give him information *regarding*

1 This is told by Masaudi of al Mamun.

2 This story will be found in Ibn Khallikan's life of ar Rabii b. Yunas.

the houses, but found no opportunity of speaking *on the subject of his reward*. At length when the Caliph desired to leave him, the man said, beginning of his own accord, "and this, O prince of the Faithful, is the house of Aatikah of whom al Ahwas[1] says A.H.158. A.D.775.

"O dwelling of Aatikah which I avoid

Through dread of foes, upon thee may heart is fixed.'

Al Mansur was displeased at his beginning to speak unasked, but he went over the poem in his mind, and behold there was in it,

"I see that thou performest what thou dost promise

But there are some insincere of speech who promise what they never perform."

Al Mansur laughed and said-"confound thee ! Rabii give him a thousand dirhams."

As Suli records on an ascription from Ishak of Mosul that al Mansur never joined his courtiers in convivial drinking bouts or musical entertainments, but when he sat, a curtain was between him and them, a distance of twenty cubits being between it and then and he the same distance from it. Then first of the Banu Abbas who mixed with his courtiers, was al Mahdi. And from Yakut b. Jaafar, that al Mansur said to Kutham b-ul Abbas b. Abdillah bil Abbas, who was his prefect over Yamamah and Buhrayn, "what is *the meaning of* Kutham and whence is it derived ?" He replied, "I do not know." Al Mansur exclaimed, "thy name a Hashimite name, and thou not understand it ! by Allah, thou art ignorant." He replied, "will the prince of the Faithful deign to enlighten me regarding it ?" Al Mansur said, "the Kathim is he who broacheth *a cask of wine* after eating and "yekthimu al ashiya" means, he takes the things and breaks them."

---

1 Abdullah b. Muhammad al Ansari, surnamed al Ahwas (and not al Akhwas us the text and all the MSS, of Ibn Khall except the autography have it) was a descendant of one of the Ansars. He cultivated poetry and such was the virulence of his satires that Omar B. Abdil Aziz banished him to the island of Dahlak in the Red Sea. Omar's successor recalled him, and he died A.H. 179 (795-6). De Slane, I.K. Vol. I, p. 526.

A.H.158. A.D.775 It is related that a fly was worrying al Mansur, whereupon he sent for Mukatil b. Sulayman[1] and asked him why God had created flies ? He replied, "to humble the mightly by their means." Muhammad b. Ali al Khurasani says that a Mansur was the first Caliph who admitted astrologers into his society, and acted according to the dictates of the stars, and the first Caliph for whom Syrian and Persian books were translated into Arabic, such as the apologue of Kalilah and Damnah,[2] and Euclid. He was the first who appointed his freedom to offices and preferred them before Arabs, and this custom became frequent after his time, until the Arab sway and preeminence declined. He was also the first who sowed disccensions between the Banu Abbas and the descendants of Ali for before that they were united in interest.

Traditions from the narration of al Mansur.

As Suli says that al Mansur was the most learned of men in tranditions and genealogy, famous for his research. Ibn Asakir in his history of Damascus gives the ascription of a tradition told by al Mansur from Ibn Abbas, that the Prophet were his signet ring on his right hand. And as Suli mentions as ascription through al Mansur from Ibn Abbas that the Apostle of God said, "the people of my house are like unto the ark of Noah ; who saileth in it is saved, who remaineth behind perisheth." And through al Mansur from the father of Ibn Abbas that the apostle of God said, "when I appoint a

1 Abul Hasan Mukatil b. Sulayman b. Bashir; he was distinguished as an eminent commentator on the Qurãn. As a traditionist his authority is disputed, and the general opinion is unfavorable to his veracity. He died at Basrah, A.H. 150 (767-8, Ibn Khall.

2 Translated by Abdullah Ibnul Mukaffa the Kitab renowned for the elegance of his style. He was a Persian by birth, and a Magian but made the profession of Islam ; his orthodox however was always suspected. He was put to death under al Mansur's orders.

governor and fix for him his stipend, whatever else he may acquire A.H.158.
over and above, is unlawful plunder." And from the father of A.D.775.
Yahya b. Hamzah al Hadhrami that he narrates, "al Mahdi appointed me to the office of Kadhi and said, "be fearless in thy judgments for my father told me on the authority of al Abbas that the Apostle of God said, "the Lord saith-by my majesty and glory, I will take revenge upon the oppressor in his present life and in his lfe to come, and I will take vengeance upon him who seeth one oppressed, being able to succour him and yet doth it not.'" And through al Mansur from Ibn Abbas that the Prophet said, "every connection and every affinity shall be sundered at the day of resurrection, save connection with me and affinity to me. And from the same that he said, "I heard Ali b. Abi Talib say, 'journey not in the last three nights of the lunar month nor when the sun is in Scorpio.'"

Of people of note who died in the reign of al Mansur were Ibnul Mukaffa', Suhayl b. Abi Salih, al Ala b. Abdir Rahman, Khalid b. Yazid al Misri the Jourisconsult, Dauud b. Abi Hind, Abu Hazim Salimah b. Dinar al Aaraj (the lame), Ata b. Abi Muslim al Khurasani, Yunus b. Ubayd, Sulayman al Ahwal (the one-eyed), Musa b. Ukbah, author of the Maghazi, Amr b. Ubayd al Muatazali, Yahya b. Said al Ansari, al Kalbi, Ibn Ishak Jaafar b. Muhammad as Sadik , al Aamash, Shibl b. Abbad the Qurãn reader[1] of Mecca, Muhammad b. Ajlan, al Madani the jurisconsult, Muhammad b. Abdir Rahman b. Abi Layla, Ibn Juraij, abu Hanifah, Hajjaj b. Artat, Hammad ar Rawiyah, Rubah the poet, al Jariri, Sulayman at Tamimi, Aasim al Ahwal, Ibn Shirmah ad Dhabbi, Mukatil b. Hayyan, Mukatil b. Sulayman, Hisham b. Urwah, Abu Amr bil Ala, Ashab at Tammaa,' the avaricious, Hamzah b. Habih az Zayyat, al Auzaai and others.

---

1 The difference between a "Kari" and a "Mukri," is that the first reads the Qurãn to his pupils, the second makes them read and corrects them where they err De Slane, I.K. P. 675, Vol. 1.

A.H.158.
A.D.775.

AL MAHDI

Al Mahdi Abu Abdullah Muhammad bil Mansur was born at Aidaj[1] in the year 127 or as some say 126. His mother was Umm Musa, daughter of al Mansur a descendant of the Himyarite[2] princes. He was munificent, much extolled, of handsome countenance, beloved by his subjects and of orthodox belief. He persecuted the Zindiks[3] and destroyed a considerable number of them. He was the first who commanded the writing of polemical works in refutation of the Zindiks and the heretics. He related traditions on the authority of his father and Mubarak b. Fudhalah; and Yahya b Hamzah, and Jaafar b. Sulayman al Dhabai, and Muhammad b. Abdillah ar Rakashi, and Abu Sufiyan Said b. Yahya the Himayarite, have narrated them from him. "I have never known it said," Observed ad Dahabi, "that there was any invalidation or correction of his testimony." Ibn Adi records from a trandition of Othman ascribed to the Prophet, "al Mahdi shall be of the descendants of my uncle Abbas." Muhammad b-ul Walid the Mawla of the Banu Hashim is the single authority for this, and he was one who fabricated traditions. Ad Dahabi in this place adduces a tradition of Ibn Masaud ascribed to the Prophet, "the name of al Mahdi shall correspond with mine and the name of his father with that of my father."

When al Mahdi grew up, his father appointed him governor of Tabaristan and its dependencies, and he was taught polite literature and associated with the learned and distinguished himself. Subseqently his father named him to the succession and when his

---

1 Between Khuzistan and Ispahan.

2 His genealogy according to Masaudi, al Mansur b. Abdillah b. Di Sahm b. Abi Sarb, descended from Du Ruayn a Himyrite prince.

3 The precise religious or irreligious code of this free-thinking commune of sectarians, is nowhere satisfactorily given, but the broad principles of their school seems to have been a denial of the existence of a Supreme Being, the rejection of all religious systems, but a strict observance of the laws of nature as imprinted in the heart of man and the profession of the love of humanity in its widest sense. A practical application of this last, permitted incestuous marriages. Consult Weil, p. 105, under al Mahdi.

father died, he was acknowledge Caliph. The new reached him at A.H.158.
Baghdad and he preached before the people and said, "verily the A.D.775.
prince of the Faithful is a servant-he hath been summoned and hath answered to the summons, and he hath been commanded and hath obeyed." Then his eyes filled with tears and he said, "verily the apostle of God wept at separating from his friends, and indeed, I have suffered a great separation and have been invested with a weighty charge, but the prince of the Faithful reckons upon a reward from God and I implore His assistance upon the Caliphate of the Muslims. O ye people ! be inwardly, as ye appear outwardly, obedient to us, and we will grant ye security and ye will be made worthy of commendation in the end. Lower ye the wings of submission unto him who hath diffused justice amongst ye, and hath put away coercion from ye and hath shed peace over ye since the Lord hath approved him as a promoter of these things. By Allah, I will consume my life between chastising and favouring ye." Niftawayh says that when the public treasure came into the hands of al Mahdi, he set about the removal of grievances and took a considerable part of the public stores and distributed them and treated generously his kindred and his clients. Another author observes that the first who congratulated al Mahdi on his accession to the Caliphate and condoled with him on his father's death was Abu Dulamah who said

"Of my eyes one of them is seen joyful
Glad for its lord, while the other sheds tears.
Weeping and smiling by turns, for saddens it
That which it takes ill, and that which it experiences, makes it glad.
Now the death of the Caliph in the inviolable state of pilgrimage, grieves it,
And that this most clement one has arisen, gladdens it.
I have never before beheld what I have now seen nor do I experience
My combing one hair while plucking out another.
The Caliph is dead, alas for the religion of Muhammad !

A.H.160. A.D.776-7

But there comes to ye after, one that succeeds him.

God hath granted to this, the honor of the Caliphate

And to the other the beauteous gardens of delight."

In the year 159 al Mahdi made a covenant for the succession in favour of his son Musa al Hadi and Harun ar Rashid after him. In the year 160, Barabd[1] in India was taken by force. During the same al Mahdi made the pilgrimage and the guardians of the Kaabah informed him that they feared its breaking in from the number of coverings over it, and he gave orders regarding it, and it was stripped and restricted to the covering of al Mahdi. Snow[2] was carried to al Mahdi at Mecca. Ad Dahabi observes that this was never arranged for any sovereign before.

In the year 161, al Mahdi commanded the construction of the Mecca road, and built houses along it and made reservoirs, and he ordered the abandonment of the reserved places for Imams in the mosques of Islam and lessened the size of the pulpite and restricted them to the measure of the pulpit of the Apostle of God.

In the year 163 and the following years, conquests in the Grecian provinces were numerous. In the year 166 al Mahdi removed to Kasrus Salam[3] and he ordered to be established for him a postal service of mules and camels from the prophetical city (Medina)

---

1 So the word is given both by Ibnul Athir and Weil. The latter cannot determine the position of the town, but supposes it to have been on the sea coast or on one of the arms of the Indus. The expeditionary fleet was commanded by Abdul Malik b. Shihab al Masmai. The troops before setting sail on their return were attacked by a disease in the mouth of which about a thousand died. Shipwreek added to their discomfiture and a similar attempt was not repeated.

2 "A pious and charitable motive may sanctify the foundation of cisterns and caravanseras which he distributed along a measured road of 700 miles, but his train of camels laden with snow could serve only to astonish the natives of Arabia and to refresh the fruits and liquors of the royal banquet." Decline and Fall. Chapter LII.

3 "The palace of peace" –Yakub states this to have been erected at Rakkah, by ar Rashid the son of al Mahdi-Rakkah is the ancient Nicephorium.

and from Yaman and Mecca to the royal residence. Ad Dahabi A.H.169.
says that he was the first who established a post from al Hijaz to al A.D.785.
Iraq. During this and the following years al Mahdi was energetic in the persecution of the Zindiks and in exterminating them and hunting then down throughout the provinces and putting *people* to death on mere suspicion. In the year 167 he ordered a great enlargement of the sacred mosque (of Mecca)[1] and brought a number of buildings within its enclosure. In the year 169 al Mahdi died : he had given chase to an animal, and the quarry rushed into a ruined building ; the horse following, al Mahdi struck his back against the doorway and died on the spot. This took place on the 22nd Muharram. (4th August 785). It is also said that he died of poison. Salm al Khasir laments him as follows :

"There weeps over al Mahdi one that weeps
As if frenzy were on her, yet she is not insane.
Yea- she tears her countenance and discovers
Her locks and reveals her tresses.
Verily, if the Caliph has passed away after his exaltation,
Surely he has left deeds which have not passed away.
The peace of God throughout each day
Be upon al Mahdi from the time when he remained a pledge *of the grave.*
We have left religious peace and worldly happiness all
Where the prince of the Faithful lies buried."

Among accounts of al Mahdi, as Suli says that when he covenanted for the succession of his son Musa, Marwan b. Abi Hafsah said,

"Allegiance hath been covenanted for Musa at Rusafah
By which God hath made fast the loops of Islam.
Musa, he whose merit the Kuraysh know

---

1 Burton is an error in giving the year 163, as the date of this enlargement. See Mecca, p. 151.

A.H.169. And unto them is preeminence among the tribes.
A.D.785. Through Muhammad (*Musa*) after the Prophet Muhammad
All lawful things have sprung to life, and all that is forbidden hath perished.
The guide of his people-who are through him
Protected from ignominy and deprivation.
Musa sways the rod of the Caliphate after him (*al Mahdi*)
And with that are dried up the records of pens !" [1]
Another says-
"O son of the Caliph, verily the people of Ahmad (*Muhammad*)
Their desires incline to the in obedience.
Thou shalt fill the earth with justice, like unto that
Which the learned of the people used to related to them,
Until their dead shall desire to witness
Of the justice of thy rule what the living behold.
Then upon thy father now be the gladness of their empire
And hereafter upon thee its garment and its mantle."

As Suli records with its ascription that a woman advanced before al Mahdi, and said, "O sinew[2] of the Apostle of God! see to my need." He exclaimed, "I have never heard that *epithet* from any one-(turning to his attendants), do what she wants and give her ten thousand dirhams." Kuraysh als Khuttali says that Salih b. Abdil Kuddus al Basri was brought before al Mahdi on the charge of being a Zindik, and Salih exclaimed, "I repent before God," and he recited to him regarding himself.

---

1 جفت القلم is an expression that signifies an unalterable fact, the ink of the pen that decreed it having dried up-so the tradition جف القلم بما انت لاق that is, all that a man meets with in the world has already been destined and cannot be avoided or altered. See the Sahih of Bukhari, Chapter on Fate, p. 976, Folio and Kirmani's notes on this expression.

2 It may also mean-"heir." The word signifies also the heirs of a person who has left neither parent nor offspring, and can be applied to a single person as well as to a pl. number.

"Enenies suffer not at the hands of a fool A.H.169.
What a fool suffers at his own. A.D.785.
And an old man will not abandon his habits
Until he is hidden in the dust of his grave."

In Madhi therefore let him go, but when he was about to depart, he called him back and said, "didst thou not say that an old man will not abandon his habits ?" He replied, "yes," "In the same way then," said he, "thou wilt not abandon thy ways until thou diest," whereupon he ordered him to be put to death. Zahir states that ten traditionists were brought before al Mahdi, among them Faraj b. Fudhalah and Ghyath b. Ibrahim. Now al Mahdi took pleasure in piegeons and when Ghiyath was introduced, it was said to him, "recite a tradition unto the prince of the Faithful." Whereupon he related from so and so on the authority of Abu Hurayrah from the Prophet, "there shall be no wager except on a hoof[1] or an arrow or lance head" and he added to it, "or a wing." Al Mahdi then ordered for him ten thousand dirhams," but as he arose, al Mahdi said, "I declare that the nape of thy neck is as the nape of the neck of a liar. Surely thou hast interpolated that." Then he gave orders regarding the pigeons and their throats were wut. It is related that Sharik went in unto al Mahdi who said to him, "one o three things thou must do-either thou must take the office of Kadhi, or thou must instruct my sons and relate traditions to them or eat a meal with me." He considered a moment and said, "to eat with thee will be least inconvenient to me." Whereupon al Mahdi ordered dishes of marrow mixed with sugar and other things, of which he eat ; but the cook said, "he will not prospher after it." The narrator adds that after this Sharik taught traditions to them and accepted the office of Kadhi.[2]

1 The tradition is not here given entire, it should be في خف او حافر او نصل "except in the hoof of *a camel,* or that of a horse, mule or ass, or in the case of an arrow or lance head"- (shooting or throwing the lance), because all these are used in fight with the enemy. Lane. Art. سبق

2 Masaudi adds to this story that the Caliph having given Sharik an order on the paymaster, Sharik made some difficulty on the subject of payment, upon which the paymaster said-"you have not been selling cloth?" "No," said Sharik, "but something more precious, my religion." Murujud Dahab, Vol. VI.

A.H.169.
A.D.785

Al Baghawi records in the Jadiyat on the authority of Hamdan al Isbahani that he narrates, "I was with Sharik when there came to him the son of al Mahdi, who learning *against the wall* asked him concerning a tradition, but Sharik did not take any notice of him, so he repeated *his question* and Sharik repeated *his conduct,* when the former said to him, "it seems as though thou thinkest lightly of the sons of the Caliph!" He replied, "no so, but knowledge is too precious in the estimation of its possessors, for them to throw it away." The other them sank down upon his knees and then put his question, whereupon Sharik said, "thus should knowledge be sought."

Among the verses of al Mahdi recited by a Suli *are the following-*

"The people will not restrain themselves from us,
The people do not weary of us,
Verily their endeavour is
To dig up what we have buried.
If we dwell in the bowels of the earth
They would come where we were."[1]

As Suli records with its ascription to Muhammad b. Umarah, that al Mahdi had a slave girl of whom he was passionately fond, and she likewise of him, save that she avoided him not a little, whereupon he sent one clandestinely to her who knew what was in her mind, and she said *to him,* "I fear lest he should weary of me and leave me and I should die."

Al Mahdi then said concerning this,

"A girl fresh as a new moon
Hath conquered my heart.
Whenever my love is assured to her

1 The next line I have omitted to translate as I can make no sense of it and believe it to be corrupt. I give it for the benefit of those who may succeed better. وهم ان كاشفونا ـ في الهوىٰ يوما محتنا The first two lines only of the verse are given by Masudi but differently to those in the text. They are placed in the mouth of Abu Zakkar a singer performing before the Caliph Harun ar Rashid.

A.H.169.
A.D.785.

She bringeth but excuses ;
Separation is not pleasing to me
Nor our refraining from meeting.
Nay, I will continue in my affection
For her, keeping in fear, satiety."

The following is by him on his boon-Companion, Omar b. Bazli'.

"O God ! prefect unto me my joy
Through Abu Hafs my Comrade :
For the pleasure of my life
Is in song and wine,
And perfumed slave girls
And music and enjoyment.

I observe that the poetry of al Mahdi is much smoother and more graceful than that of his father or of his sons.

As Suli also states with ascription to Ishak of Mosul, that al Mahdi at the beginning of his reign, like al Mansur, kept himself secluded from his courtiers for about a year, after which he mixed with them. It was suggested to him that he should withdraw himself more, but he said, "verily the enjoyment consists in their being present." And on the authority of Mahdi b. Sabik, that a man called out to al Mahdi while he was among his cortage.

Say to the Caliph, Hatim is a traitor to thee,
Then fear God and save us from Hatim.
For when a virtuous man asks the assistance of a traitor
He becomes a partner in his guilt.

Whereupon al Mahdi said, "let every one of my prefects who is named Hatim, be deprived of office." And from Abu Ubaydah that he said, "al Mahdi used to read to us the five appointed services of prayer in the mosque of Basrah when he came there. One day prayers were being begun when a desert Arab exclaimed, 'I am not in a state of legal purification, and verily I desire to join the

A.H.169. A.D.785. prayers behind thee.' Whereon he ordered them to wait for him, and they waited for him and al Mahdi entered the arched niche of the mosque and stayed until it was said that the man had come, upon which he recited the takbir, and the people wondered at the considerate courtesy of the Caliph." And from Ibrahim b. Nafi that some of the people of Basrah carried a dispute concerning one of the streams about Basrah before al Mahdi, and he said, "verily the earth belongeth to God being in our hands for *the benefit of* the Muslims, therefore that regarding which there hath been no purchase, its value, reverts to all of them and for their advantage. Therefore no one individual hath any claim upon it." Then the deputation said, "this stream is ours by the direction of the apostle of God, for he said, 'he who cultivatecth waste land it belongeth to him,' and this land is waste." Al Mahdi threw himself forward at the mention of the Prophet, until his cheek touched the ground, and he exclaimed, "I hearken unto what he hath said and obey." Then he continued, "I remains now to be shown that this is waste land, so that I may make no objection, and yet how cant it be waste when the water surrounds it on all sides-now if they can establish the proof of this, I will assent."

And on the authority of al Asma'I, I heard al Mahdi from the pulpit at Basrah say, "verily the Lord hath laid upon ye a command, in *the performance* of which He Himself set the example and made His angels follow His for He hath said, 'verily God and his angels bless the Prophet &c.' (Qur. XXXIII.) He hath distinguished him by means of it among the apostles inasmuch as He hath distinguished ye by it among nations."

I have to observe that he was the first to speak thus in a discourse, and preachers unto this day have been guided by it as an example.

When al Mahdi died, and sackcloths were, hanging from the

cupolas of the Caliph's harem, Abul Atahiyah[1] said- A.H.169. A.D.785.

"At eve, they went in dyed garments,
And in the morning they were clad in sackcloth.
Unto every butting ram in the world
Shall come a day when there shall be one butting against him.
Thou art not immortal
Didst thou live to the age of Noah :
Weep for thyself, hapless one
If thou art to weep."

Traditions from the narration of al Mahdi.

As Suli give a tradition through al Mahdi from Abu Sai'd al Khudri who said, "the apostle of god preached a discourse to us from the afternoon until sunset which some remember and some have forgotten, and he said *in it,* 'now verily the goods of this world are sweet and refreshing'and the rest of the tradition in full."

And through al Mahdi from Abbas, that a deputation of Persians visited the apostle of God, and they had shaved their beard and allowed their moustaches to grow long, and the Prophet said-"do the contrary of what they do-let your beards grow long and shave your moustaches," and the shaving of the moustache means the

---

1 Abu Ishak Ismail b-ul Kasim was born at Ainut Tamr in A.H. 130, brought up at Kufah and settled at Baghdad. He was surnamed Abul Atahiyah, and also al Jarrar, because he sold Jars. He was among the principal of the poets who flourished in the early times of Islam and ranked in the same class with Bashshar and Abu Nawas. His passion for Utba, a female slave of al Mahdi and his numerous odes to her, added to his nortoriety, but did not advance his suit, for though the Caliph was willing to bestow her upon him, she disbelieved in his affection and abhorred his face. He died at Baghdad in 211 (A.D. 826). Ibn Khall.

A.H.169. A.D.785 removal of as much of it as falls upon the lip," and al Mahdi placed his hand upon his upper lip.

Mansur b. Muzahim and Muhammad b. Yahya b. Hamzah, narrate of Hamzah b. Yahya that he said, "al Mahdi read to us the evening prayer and called out in a high voice, 'In the name of God, the most Merciful, the most Compassionate.' I exclaimed, 'O prince of the Faithful what means this!' He replied, 'my father related to me, on the authority of Ibn Abbas, that the Prophet called aloud-In the name of God, the most Merciful, the most Compassionate'-I said to al Madhi, 'may I transmit this on thy authority?' He replied, 'yes'."

Ad Dahabi says, "this ascription is unbroken in continuity but I never knew any one adduce al Mahdi, or his father as authority for religious ordinances." Muhammad b-ul Walid, client of the Banu Hashim is the only authority for this, and Ibn Ali states that he fabricated traditions. I remark that he is not alone in this, for I have noticed another that follows him.

Of people of note who died in the reign of al Mahdi were Shulah b-ul Hajjaj. Abu Bistam, Ibn Abi Dib, Sufiyan at Thauri, Ibrahim b. Adham the ascetic, Dauud at Tai the ascetic, Bashshar b. Burd the most eminent of the post-classical poets, Hammad b. Salamah, Ibrahim b. Tahman and Khalil b. Ahmad, author of the treatice on prosody.

AL HADI.

Al Hadi Abu Muhammad, Musa b-ul Mahdi il Mansur, whose mother was a Berber slave concubine called al Khayzuran, was born at Rai in the year 147 and was acknowledged Caliph after his father, in accordance with the latter's deed of succession. Al Khatib says that no one ruled the Caliphate before him at his age. He continued in it for a year and some months. His father charged him as his last bequest to exterminate the Zindiks and he pursued them actively and put to death a large number of them. He used to be called Musa Atbik, because his upper lip was contracted, and his father placed a servant in charge over him when he was a child, who whenever he saw his mouth open would say, "Musa, draw *your lips* together !" (Atbik), whereon he would recover himself and compress his lips. He was therefore thus distinguished. A.H.170. A.D.786.

Ad Dahabi says that he was addicted to drinking and frivolous amusement, and used to ride a brisk-going donkey, and did not uphold the dignity of the Caliphate ; yet withal he was eloquent, with a great command of language, well enducated, an aspect of awe encompassed him and he possessed intrepidity and hardiness. Another author describes him as a despot, and as being the first before whom men marched with sharp scimitars and staves and strung bows. His prefects imitated him in this and the *wearing of* arms prevailed much in his time.

He died in Rabiiul Awwal[1] in the year 170, (15th Sept. 786). Accounts are conflicting regarding the manner of his death. Some say that he pushed one of his courtiers over a precipitous bank upon the stumps of a reed bed that had been cut, but the courtier clung to him and he fell and a reed entered his nostril and they were both killed. It is said too that he had an ulcer in his stomach. Anthor account is, that his mother al Khayzuran poisoned him, when he sought to murder ar Rashid in order to confer the succession on his own son.

It is said that his mother was an imperious woman, assuming absolute direction of affairs of state. A line of persons attended at her gate every morning, but he forbade them doing so, and addressed her in rough Ianguage, and said,[2] "verily, if there attendeth a noble

1 The text has "Akhir." This is an error probably of the copyist as in the life of ar Rashid, as Suyuti places al Hadi's death in Rabii I. All other authorities concur in the mouth being Rabii' I, except Tabari, who says Jumada I, and a Makin Rabii' II, but this latter is a mere slip of the pen, as he himself states the duration of al Hadi's reign to be one year and 52 days, which fits in with 14th Rabii' I. Weil fixes the date at the 16th Rabii I. See Gesh, der. Cal.

2 This speech is not accurately given by as Suyuti and is marred in the telling. Ibnul Athir and Masaudi concur in their narratives of it.

A.H.170. A.D.786. at thy gate, I will assuredly strike off his head-but as for thee, hast thou not a spindle to employ thee, or a Qurān, or beads to engage thee in devotion?" And she arose beside herself with anger, and it is reported that he sent her poisoned food, but she caused some of it to be given to a dog which was *immediately* affected[1] by it. She therefore conspired to put him to death when he was prostrate with fever and they smothered him with the bed coverning and sat upon its sides. He left seven sons.

Of the verses of al Hadi, are the following on his brother Harun when he refused to renounce the succession.

I couselled Harun, but he rejected my counsel,
And every man that taketh not advice, repenteth ;
I invite him to a deed that will restore harmony between us,
But he turneth from it, and in that he doth wrong.
And were it not for my expectation of his *consent* from day to day
He should do what I say under compulsion.

Among the events of al Hadi's reign, it is recorded by Al Khatib on the authority of al Fadhl that al Hadi was wroth with a man, and they interceded for him with the Caliph, upon which he was pacified towards him, and the man went to make his excuses, and al Hadi said to him, "my approval exempts thee from the pain of apology." And on the authority of Musaab, that Marwan b. Abi Hafsah went in unto al Hadi and recited to him a panegyrie on him, until he came to the following verse,

His bounty and intrepidity are to-day so evenly balanced
That no one knows with which the superiority lies.

Al Hadi said to him, "which dost thou prefer, thirty thousand dirhams down, or one hundred thousand paid through the accountant's office?" He replied "give the thirty thousand dirhams

---

1 The verb انتثار has not this meaning in the Lexicons, but it is plain that this is the sense intended which would be usually expressed by تأثر

down and let the hundred thousand come round to me *through the office.*" Al Hadi said "nay, both shall be paid down together," and the sun was taken to him. A.H.170. A.D.786

As Suli observes that no woman is known to have given birth to two Caliphs, except al Khuzayran, the mother of al hadi and ar Rashid, and Walidah, daughter of al Abbas, of the tribe of Abs,[1] wife of Abdul Malik b. Marwan, who bore al Walid and Sulyaman; and Shahim[2] daughter of Firuz son of Yazdajird, son of Khusrau, who bore to al Walid b. Abdil Malik, Yazid and Nakis and Ibrahim, both of whom succeeded to the Caliphate. I remark that there may be added to these, Bai Khatun, the concubine of the last al Mutawakkil who gave birth to al Abbas and Hamzah, who both ruled the Caliphate ; and Kazl a concubine of the same who bore Dauud and Sulayman who governed it likewise.

As Suli also says that no Caliph was ever known to ride post, except al Hadi *who rode* from Jurjan to Baghdad,[3] He adds that the impression on his signet ring was, "the Lord is the reliance of Musa and in him he confides."

The following, according to as Suli is by Salm al Khasir eulogizing al Hadi.

Musa is a rain-a cloud that riseth early,-and is then discharged-he appropriates power to himself-how hath he foreibly seized- and waxed strong!--and then pardoned!-just in disposition-of enduring renown-*for* good and evil-weal and woe-the best of moratle-of the race of Mudhar-a moon that is at full-unto him who beholdeth-He is the refuge-of them that are nigh-and they glory-of those that remain.

As Suli says, "this detached verse-is of the measure Mustafilun-

---

1 There are two of this name ; one a branch of the Kays Aylan, the eponymous head of which was Abs b. Baghidh b. Rayth, and the other of the Banu Kudhaah sprung from Abs b. Baghidh b. Rayth, and the other of the Banu Kudhaah sprung from Abs b Khaulan. Muntaha'l Arab.

2 See page 329. The name there given is "Shahfarand."

3 This took place when the death of his father was announced to him and he accomplished the distance according to Ibnul Athir, in twenty days.

A.H.169. A.D.785 Mustafilum;[1] he was the first to employ it and I have never heard poetry of this detached character by any one else."

He traces an ascription to Said b. Salm who is reported to have said, "verily I trust that the Lord will be merciful unto al Hadi on account of an act of his which I witnessed. I was present with him one day when Abul Khitab, as Saadi was reciting a poem to him in his praise *continuing* till he came to,

"O best of those whose hands tie the waist band,
O best of those whom *the race of* Mudhar hath invested with their authority.'"

Al Hadi said to him, "have a care! Whom *dost thou mean?* Shame on thee!" For he excepted no one in his verse ; whereupon I exclaimed, "O prince of the Faithful, surely, he means of the people of this age.'" The poet then reflected and said,

"Save the Prophet, the Apostle of God[2] to whom
Belongeth preeminence and thou, in that preeminence, doth glory."

Al Hadi said, "now thou hast hit it and hast done well," and he ordered fifty thousand dirhams to e given to him.

Al Madaini, says, that al Hadi condoled with a man on account *of the loss* of his son, and said, "he made thee glad when he was *to thee* a temptation[3] and an evil, and now grieveth thee when he

---

4 A variety of the Rajaz, dimeter acatalectic, the third epitrite

--- --- --- Varied by the diiam --- --- ---

O carminum | dulces notae,
Quas ore fun | dis melleo.

1 Who was eighteenth in direct descent from Mudhar b. Nizar b. Maad b. Adnan ; the generation between Adnan and Ishmael are uncertain, some enumerating eight, others (and among these, Muhammad himself) counting no more than three. See Sale's Genealogical Tables.

2 This is said with reference to Qur. VIII, "Know that your wealth and your children are a temptation to you" وَاعلَمُوا اَنَّمَا اَموَالُكُمْ وَاَولَادُكُمْ فِتنَةٌ and it is mentioned in a tradition that the death of a child is the occasion of a storing of reward unto the father.

hath become unto thee a reward and a mercy!" A.H.170. A.D.786.

As Suli narrates that Salm al Khasir recited on al Hadi the following verse coupling condolence and congratulation.

"Verily Musa hath assumed the Caliphate and guidance unto salvation,

And Muhammad (*al Mahdi*) prince of the Faithful, is dead.

He is dead whose loss the people suffer in common

And he hath arisen who will suffice thee for him who is gone."

And Marwan b. Abi Hafash says similarly-

"Verily there pride themselves in every city

On account of the grave of the prince of the Faithful, the cemeteries.

And had they not been consoled in his son after his death,

Never would the pulpits have ceased to weep over him.

And if Musa had not arisen upon them, they would have wailed.

With a yearning cry, as the tribes yearn for the best portions of plunder."

Traditons from the narration of al Hadi.

As Suli narrates from al Mutalib b. Ukkashah al Marri that he said, "we went to al Hadi as evidence against a man who had reviled one of the Kuraysh and passed on even to the disparagement of the Prophet-whereupon he covened an assembly for us, to which he summoned the chief jurisconsults of his time, and had the man brought into his presence; and we gave evidence against him. The countenance of al Hadi changed, and he hung down his head, and then raised it, and said, 'I heard my father al Madhi relate on the authority of Ibn Abbas, that he said-he who desireth to put scorn upon the Kuaysh, may the Lord put scorn upon him, and thou, O enemy of God, wert thou not satisfied in desiring that for the Kuraysh

A.H.170. A.D.786. but thou must pass on to disparage the Prophet ? Strike off his head :" (recorded by al Khatib from the ascription of as Suli) : and the tradition in this narration stops thus *withIbn Abbas,* but one with another ascription traced to the Prophet, hath also come down.

Of people of note who died in the reign of al hadi were, Nafi, Qurãn reader of the people of Median and others.

HARUN UR RASHID

Ar Rashid Harun, Abu Jaafar b-ul Mahdi Muhammad bil Mansur Abdillah b. Muhammad b. Ali b. Abdillah bil Abbas succeeded as Caliph by the covenant of his father on the death of his brother al Hadi on Friday night the 16the Rabii I, in the year 170. As Suli mentions that on this night al Mamun was born to him, and in the whole course of time there has never been a night but this, in which a Caliph died, a Caliph succeeded, and a Caliph was born. He used to be called Abu Musa but took benceforth the surname of Abu Jaafar. He related traditions on the authority of his father and grandfather and Mubarak b. Fudhalah, and his son al Mamun and others have related them on his. He was one of the most distinguished of Caliphs and most illustrious of the princes of the earth. He undertook many military expedtitions as well as pilgrimages, as Abul Ala al Kilabi has said concerning him-

"He who seeketh or desireth ot meet thee
Will find the either in the two sacred cities or on the most distant frontier.
If in the country of the enemy, it will be on a high-mettled charger,
If in the land of the desert, on a camel's saddle."

His birth took place at Rai when his father was Prefect over it

and over Khurasan in the year 148. His mother was a slave concubine called Khuzayran who was also the mother of al Hadi, and Marwan b. Abi Hafsah[1] has said regarding her : A.H.170. A.D.786

"O Khuzayran, rejoice thee and again rejoice !
For thy two sons have come to rule the universe."

Ar Rashid was very fair, tallm handsome, of captivating appearance, and eloquent. He was verse in science and literature. During his Caliphate, he used to pray every day a hundred "rakaats," until he died, never neglecting them save for some special cause, and he used to give in charity from his private purse every day a hundred dirhams.

He loved science and its professors, and held in reverence the sacred shrines of Islam and abhorred disputation in religion an controversy on established points of doctrine. The opinion of Bishr al Marrisi[2] on the creation of the Qurãn was reported to him, and he exclaimed-"if I cated him, I will strike off his head."

He used to weep over his own extravagance and his sins, especially when an exhortation was addressed to him. He loved panegyrie and would bestow large sums in raward for it. There are likewise verses attributed to him.

---

1 He was descended from Abu Hafsah Yazid, according to some a Jewish convert, according to others one of the captives taken at Istakhar. He was purchased by Othman, given to Marwan bal Hakam who married him to one of his own concubines by whom he had a daughter called Hafsah. This girl was brought up by Yazid as his own and he received the surname of "father of Hafsah" Marwan, the subject of this notice, was extremely avaricious and asked 1000 dirhams for every verse he wrote in praise of the Abbaside Caliphs. De Sacy Chrest, Arab. Tom. III. P. 518.

2 Abu Abdur Rahman Bishr b. Ghiath al Marrisi a theologian and jurisconsult of the school of Hanifah. He taught openly the creation of the Qurãn and he belonged to the sect of the Murgains which is called after him the Marrisian, and he held that it was not an *act* of infidelity to bow down to the sun and moon but only a token of it. He died at Baghdad A.H. 218. (833-4). Ibn Khall. De Slane writes incorrectly "Marisi" for Marrisi."

A.H.169. A.D.785 On one occasion Ibnus Sammak[1] the preacher went in unto him and he exerted himself to the utmost to do him honor, and Ibnus Sammak said to him-"thy humility in thy greatness is nobler than thy greatness :" then he addressed him an exhortation and made him weep. He was also in the habit of going in person to the house of al Fudhay b Iyadh.[2]

Abdur Razzak says, "I was with al Fudhyal at Mecca when Harun passed by and al Fudhayl said, "the people dislike this man, but there is not on earth any more esteemed by me than he-were he to die, thou wouldst surely behold most serious events occur."

Abu Muawiyah ad Dharir[3] says, "I never mentioned the Prophet before ar Rashid, but he said, 'may God bless my lord;' and I related to him his tradition of his, 'I would that I might do battle for the sake of God and be slain, and be brought to life and slain again,' and Harun wept until he sobbed aloud ; and I once related to him the tradition, 'Adam and Moses entered into a disputation,' and there was by him one of the chiefs of the Kuraysh, and the Kurayshi said,-but where did he meet him?- At this ar Rashid grew wroth and exclaimed-the leather mat and the sword!-shall a Zindik impugn a tradition of the Prophet!'- But I continued to pacify him and to

---

1 Abul Abbas Muhammad b. Sabih surnamed al Madkur (or as Ibnul Athir says al Mudakkar) and known as Ibnus Sammak, (son of the seller or catcher of fish). He was a native of Kufah and a professional narrator of anecdotes. His devotion, his pious exhortations and the elegance of his language acquired him great celebrity. He died at Kufah, A.H. 183 (799-80) Ibn Khall.

2 Abu Ali al Fudhayl b. Iyadh a celebrated ascetic. Drew his origin from a family of the tribe of Tamim which had settled at Talakan in Khurasan. He was born at Abiward or Samarkand, passed his youth at Abiward and then went to learn traditions at Kufah, from thence he removed to Mecca where he dwelt tell his death in 187 A.H. (803). It is said that his commenced life as a highway robber and was converted by hearing a sentence of the Qurãn pronounced, when he was about to climb a wall to see a girl whom he loved. Ibn Khall.

3 Abu Muawiyah Muhammad b. Khazim, ad Dharir (the blind) adopted member of the tribe of Minkar, born at Kufah A.H. 113. He was a traditionist of eminence, died A.H. 185 (811) De Slane, I.K.

say, 'O prince of the Faithful, it came from him unpremeditatedly,' A.H.170.
until he was appeased. I was *once* taking a meal with ar Rashid, A.D.786.
when a man whom I did not perceive poured water upon my hand, and ar Rashid said, 'dost thou know who is pouring water upon thee?' I said, 'no.' He replied, 'it is I, out of reverence for *thy* knowledge.'" Mansur b. Ammar[1] says "I never say any more copious it tears when engaged in devotional exercises than three men, al Fudhayl b. Iyadh, ar Rashid, and another."

Ubaydullah al Kawariri narrates that when ar Rashid me al Fudhayl, the latter said to him, "O thou with the handsome face! art thou he who is answerable *before God* for this people ? Layth related to me on the authority o al Mujahid, *that the verse,* 'and the cords *of relation* between them shall be cut asunder,' (Qur. II) signifieth the connection that was between them in the world, and Harun began to weep and sob."[2] As an instane of his good qualities, *it is said* that when the news of the death of Ibnul Mubarak[3] reached him, he gave an audience of condolence and commanded his nobles to condole with him on the loss of Ibnul Mubarak.

Niftawayh says that ar Rashid followed in the footsteps of his grandfather Abu Jaafr save in covetousness, for no Caliph before him, had been as munificent as he. He bestowed on one occasion on Sufiyan b. Uyaynah[4] one hundred thousand dirhams, and on

---

1 A native of Khurasan (or of Basrah as some say) celebrated for his wisdom piety and eloquence as a preacher. He also delivered traditions. He resided at Cairo and died A.H. 225 (839040) De Slane, I.K.

2 This story is related differently and probably more correctly in Ibn Khall.

3 Abu Abdur Rahman Abdullah al Marwazi, a Mawla to the tribe of Handhalah, a man of profound learning and of mortified life. He loved retirement and was extremely assiduous in the practice of ascetic devotion. He died at Hit on the Euphrates on his return from a military expedition in A.H. 181 (797). The nausous details of his funeral are given by Masaudi. Ibn Khall.

4 He was an Imam of learning and piety and distinguished for the exactitude of his traditions. His parents lived at Kufah where he was born A.H. 107. He made the pilgrimage seventy times. He died at Mecca, A.H. 198 (814). Ibn Khall. In the text for عينيه read. عيينه

A.H.170. A.D.786. another, two hndred thousand on Ishaq[1] of Mosul, and he gave Marwan b. Abi Hafsah for a poem, five thousand dinars, a robe of honour, a horse from his own stud and ten Greek slaves.

Al Asama'i narrates, "ar Rashid said to me, 'O Asma'i, what hath made thee neglect me and keep aloof from me?' I replied, 'by Allah, O prince of the Faithful, the provinces, after thee could not attach me *to them,* until I came to thee.' And he was silent but, when the people dispersed he said 'what means could not attach me,' (alakatni).[2] I said,

'Of thy two hands, one keepeth not within it a dirham
Through munificence, while the other sheddeth blood with a sword.'

He replied, 'thou hast said well and continue to be thus ; honor us in public and instruct us in private,' and he ordered for me five thousand dinars."

In the Murujud Dahab (*Meadows of gold*) of Masaudi, the author says that ar Rashid desired to unite the Mediterranean and the Red Sea at a point adjacent to Farama,[3] but Yahya b. Rashid

---

1 Abu Muhammad Ishak known by the name of Ibnun Nadim al Mausli (son of the boon companion from Mosul a member by adoption of the tribe of Tamim and born al Arrajan. He was a constant companion of the Caliphs in their parties of Pleasure: he was well versed in pure Arabic and the history of the poets, in jurisprudence and tradition, and as a singer was without a rival. Born A.H 150, died 235 (A.D. 850). Ibn Khall.

2 The verb ilakat means to bind to one's self or to put raw silk into an inkstand as is the oriental custom, to prevent the reed-pen being overcharged with ink. Al Asmai who had a marvelous command of the Arabic language and knowledge of the poets and their works, purposely used an uncommon word to attract the attention of Harun, and then illustrated it by a verse which instructed the Caliph in its meaning as well as in the needs of the speaker. The Arabic verse in the printed edition is incorrect. The word كَفاك should be pointed كَفّاكَ and the second hemistich should begin with the word جودا which has been omitted, but which is in the MS. The metre is Rajaz.

3 Near what is now el Arish on the Mediterranean : the town of Farama has diappeared and not trace of it remains. See Yakut for its history.

the Barmecide said to him that the Greeks would carry off the people from the sacred mosque (*at Mecca*) and that their ships would come up to al Hijaz ; he therefore abandoned it. A.H.170. A.D.786

Al Jahidh[1] observes that there were assembled round ar Rashid *such a company as* were never united under any other *Caliph, to wit,* his ministers the Barmecides, his Kadhi Abu Yusu, his poet Marwan b. Abi Hafsah, his boon companion al Abbas b. Muhammad the paternal uncle of his father, his chamberlain al Fadhl bur Rabii one of the most celebrated and remarkable of men, his musician Ibrahim of Mosul, and his wife Zubaydah. Another author says that all the days of ar Rashid were as happy in their joyousness as if they had been marriage-feasts, and ad Dahabi states that a narrative of the adventures of ar Rashid would extend to great length and his good actions are numerous. There are accounts of him also in his diversions, forbidden pleasures and musical entertainments,-may god exalted him.

Of people of note who died in his reign were Malik b. Anas, al Layth b. Saad, Abu Yusuf the disciple of Abu Hanifah, al Kasim b. Maan Muslim, b. Khalid al Zanji, Nuh al Jami', the Hafidh Abu Uwanah al Yeshkuri, Ibrahim b. Saad az Zuhri, Abu Ishak al Fazari, Ibrahim b. Abi Yahya the master of as Shafii, Asad al Kufi one of the most eminent of the disciples of Abu Hanifah, Ismail b. Ayyash, Bashir b-ul Mufadhdhal, Jarir b. Abdil Hamid, Ziyad al Bakkai, Sulaym the Qurãn reader, the disciple of Hamzah,[2] Sibawayh the great master of Arabic, Dhaygham the ascetic, Abdullah al Umari, the ascetic, Abdullah al Umari the ascetic, Abdullah b-ul Mubarak Abdullah b. Idris ad Kufi, Abdul Aziz b. Abi Hazi, ad Darawardi, al Kisai master of the Qurãn readers and grammarians and

---

1 Abu Othman Amr b. Bakr known as al Jahidh (the Starer) and al Hadaki (The goggle-eyed) on account of the prominence of his eyes. He was a native of Basrah, celebrated for his learning and author of numerous works on every branch of science. One of his best works is the Book on Animals. Numerous anecdotes are told of his by Ibn Khall whom the reader may consult. He died at Basrah A.H 255 at the age of ninety.

2 Probably Hamzah b. Habib az Zayyat one of the seven readers of the Qurãn and master of al Kisai, died at Hulwan A.H. 156 (772-3). Ibn Khall.

A.H.170. A.D.786. Muhammad b-ul Hasan the disciple of Abu Hanifah both on the same day ; Ali b. Mushir, Ghunjar, Isa b. Yunas as Sabii'I, al Fudhayl b. Iyadh, Ibnus Sammak the preacher, Marwan b. Abi Hafsah the poet, al Muafa b. Imran al Mawsili, Muatamir[1] b. Sulayman, al Mufadhdhal b. Fudhalalh Kadhi of old Cairo, Musa al Kadhim (the forbearing), Musa b. Rabbih Abul Hakam al Misri one of the saints, an Nuaman b. Abdi's Salam al Isbahai, Hushaym, Yahya[2]b. Abi Zaidah, Yazid b. Zuray', Yunus b. Habib the grammarian, Yakub b. Abdir Rahman, the Qurãn reader of Medina, Sasaah bus Sallam, the learned doctor of Spain, one of te disciples of Malik, Abdur Rahman b-ul Kasim the most eminent of the disciples of Malik al Abbas b-ul Ahnaf, the famous poet, Abu Bakr b. Ayyash, the Qurãn reader, Yusuf b-ul Majishun and others.

The following are among the events of his reign. In the year 175 Abdullah b. Mussab az Zubayri falsely accused Yahya b. Abdillah b. Hasan, the descendant of Ali of having invited him to rebel with him against ar Rashid, whereupon Yahya imprecated with him the curse of God upon which ever of them spoke falsely, in the presence of ar Rashid and locked his hand in the hand of the other, and exclaimed, "say-O God, if thou knowest that Yahya did not invite me to oppose and rebel against the prince of the Faithful here, then commit me to my own power and strougth, and utterly destroy me by a chastisement from thee. Amen Lord of created things." Az Zubayri stammered hesitatingly but repeated it, and Yahya did the like, and they arose *and departed* and az Zubayri died the same day.

In the year 176 the city of Dubsah[3] was captured by the Amir Abdur Rahman b. Abdil Malik b. Salih al Abbasi. In the year 179 ar Rashid performed the lesser pilgrimage in the month of Ramadhan and remained in the state of Ihram[4] until he made the greater pilgrimage and went on good to Arafah from Mecca.

---

1 "Mua'mmar" according to Ibnul Athir.معمربن سليمان بن طرخان التيمي

2 "Zakariya." Ibnul Athir.

3 Ibnul Athir has Dalsah or Dulsa, for the word is not pointed, but Dulsah is stated in a note to be a variant. I cannot find the name of the map. He places this event in the year 190.

4 I.e. abstaining from all acts which are unlawful at that season.

In the year 180 occurred the great earthquake in which the top of the minaret at Alexamdira fell. In the year 181, the fort of Safsaf[1] was captured by force of arms, the captor being ar Rashid. In the year 183 the Khazars[2] burst upon Armenia and fell upon the true believers and made great slaughter and carried away captive more than a hundred thousand souls. Thus a grievous calamity fell upon Islam, the like of which had not been heard of before. A.H.180. A.D.796.

In the year 187, there came a letter to ar Rashid from Nicephorus[3] the Roman Roman Emperor breaking the truce which had been established between the Muslims and Irene Empress of Rome. The letter ran as follows: "from Nicephorus, the Roman Emperor, to harun, sovereign of the Arabs : After preliminaries- verily the Empress who preceded me gave thee the rank of a rook and put herself in that of a pawn, and coveyed to thee many loads of her wealth, and this through the weakness of women and their folly. Now when thou hast read this letter of mine, return what thou hast received of her substance, otherwise the sword shall decide between me and thee." When ar Rashid read the letter, he was so inflamed with rage, that no one durst look upon his face, much less speak to him, and his courtiers dispersed from fear, and his ministers speechless forbore from counsel. Then ar Rashid sent for an inkhorn and wrote upon the back of the letter. "In the name of God, the most Compassionate the most Merciful, from Harun the prince of the faithful to Nicephorus the Roman dog. Verily I have read thy letter, son of an unbelieving mother, and the answer thou shalt behold and not hear." Thereupon he set out the same day and did not stay until he reached Heracles, and there took

---

1 On the frontier of Syria between Antioch and the Grocian territory.

2 A Turkish tribe north of Derbend, their eponymous ancestor being Khazar the son of Japhet, the son of Noah-for a particular account of them, consult Yakut. The cause of there irruption was the death of the Khakans daughter whom the Barmecide Fadhl b. Yahya had wooed. The Khakan had been informed that the Muslims had put her to death. According to another account the murder of the Khakan himself by an Arab provoked the calamity. See Weil, Vol. V. p. 158.

3 The printed edition has يقفور for نقفور

A.H.180. A.D.796. place a famours battle and a manifest victory, and Nicephorus implored peace and engaged to pay a tribute which he would transmit to him every year and it was accepted. But when ar Rashid returned to ar Rakkah, the dog violated the engagement, deeming impossible the return of ar Rashid in the winter, and no one durst tell ar Rashid of the violation, but Abdur Rahman b. Yusuf at Tamimi versified, saying,

"Nicephorus hath violated what thou didst concede to him,
Therefore around him the circle of destructon shall revolve
Give the good news to the prince of the Faithful,
Verily he is a spoil that the great God hath vouchsafed thee."

And Abul Atahiyah made some verses which were shown to ar Rashid, and he said-"indeed hath he done do?" He therefore set out on his return march in the face of the greatest hardships until he caused his camel to kneel in the Emperor's courtyard, and continued until he attained his purpose and accomplished *the object* of his holy war : and coucerning this, Abul Atahiyah says,

Now hath Heraclea perished in war
At the hand of the king who is guided to success.
Harun hastened thundering with death,
And lightening with bright cutting swords ;
And his standards upon which victory alrights
Speed by as though they were broken masses of cloud.

In the year 189 he ransomed his people in captivity with the Romans, so that there did not remain a single Muslim captive in their territories. In the year 190 he took Heraclea and spread his troops over the Roman terriotories. Shurabil b. Maan b. Zaidah captured the fortress as Sakaliyah, and Yazid, b. Makhlad,[1] Malakuniyah.[2] Humayd b. Mayuf set out against Cyprus, and

---

1 Read مُخْلَد for مُخَلَّد

2 The printed edition has erroneously at Kuniyah. Malakuniyah (cont...)

devastated and wasted it by fire and carried away into captivity sixteen thousand of its people. A.H.192. A.D.807

In the year 192 ar Rashid marched towards Khurasan, and Muhammad bus Sabah at Tabari mentions that his father accompanied ar Rashid to an Nahrawan, and he used to enter into conversation with him on the road, until he said *one day,* "O Sabah I do not think that thou wilt see me again after this,"[1] I replied, "nay-may the Lord bring the back in safety." He continued, "I do not think thou knowest what I have." I answered, "no-by Allah." Ar Rashid said "come till I show thee." and he left the road and signed to his attendants who retired. Then he said "the faithfulness of God, O Sabah, *be thy oacth*, that thou keep it secret concerning me," and he uncovered his stomach, when lo! there was silken bandage round about his stomach, and he said, "I have concealed this disease from all men, fro each one of my sons hath a spy upon me; Masrur is the spy of al Mamun, and Gabriel the son of Bakhtishuu'[2] is the spy of al Amin, and I have forgotten the third. There is not one of them but counts my breathings, and reckons my days and finds my life too long, and if thou wishest to know this, I will at once send for a horse and they will bring me one every lean in order to increase my malady *by its roughness."* And he sent for a horse and they brought one such as he described, and he glanced at me ans then mounted and did me farewell, and set out for Jurjan. Shortly after he left in the month of Safar of the year 193, while still suffering, for Tus, and continued there till he died.

Ar Rashid had covenanted for the succession of his son Muhammad in the year 175 on account of his mother Zubaydah's great eagerness for it and surnamed him al Amin, he being at the time five years of age. Ad Dahabi says that this was the first

---

(Cont.380) is stated by Yakut to be near Iconium. According to Theophanes, the Arabs took Thebasa (Dubsah or Dalsah ?) Malacopaea, Sideropolis, and Andrasus. Neither Yakut nor Weil fix the position of as Sakaliyah. See Weil's notice of these names, Tom, II, p. 160.

1 The narrative here passes from the third to the first person with the usual قال

2 His physician.

A.H.192. A.D.807 unsettlement that came upon the Muslim state as regards the Imamate. He afterwards covenanted for his son bestowed on him the government of all the provinces of Khurasan. Next he covenanted for the succession of his son al Kasim after his two brothers, in the year 186 and surnamed him al Mutamin, and made him governor of Mesopotamia and the frontiers while he was yet a child. When he had thus partitioned the world among these three, it was observed by one of the learned, that he had thrown among them what would be their injury, and that the evil of it would work mischief to his people. The poets recited congratulatory poems on the covenantof allegiance, and he after wards suspended copies of the covenant in the temple of Mecca, and regarding this Ibrahim of Mosul and said-

"The best of affairs in their issue,
The most just of ordinances in their completion,
Is a dead, the decrees of which hath promulgated
The most Merciful in the Sacred Temple."

And Abdul Malik b. Salih says :[1]

"The love of the Caliph is a love to which submit themselves not
The sinner against God, and the schismatic who promoteth discord.
God invested Harun with this Jurisdiction
When He chose him, He verified or faith and our laws.
And Harun through this benignity unto us, hath given jurisdiction over the earth
Unto al Amin, al Mamun, and al Mutamin."

It has been stated by some authorities that ar Rashid withheld the Caliphate from his son al Mautasim on account of his being illiterate, but the Lord caused it to come to him and made all the

1 Abu Abdur Rahman Abdul Malik b. Salih b. Ali b. Abdillah bil Abbas b. Abdil Muttablib. He was the most elegant speaker of the surviving descendants of al Abbas. The town of Manbij which he held as appanage, was his place of residence. He died at Rakkah A.H. 193. Ibn Khall.

Caliphs succeeding him, to be of his descendants, and did not establish a Caliph from among sons of ar Rashid, save of his stock. A.H.193. A.D.808-9.

Salm al Khasir says regarding the covenant in favour of al Amin-

"Say to the dwellings on the white sand-hills
Watered by the morning rain-clouds,
Verily men and spirits have sworn allegiance to the guide unto salvation
Unto Muhammad, the son of Zubaydah, daughter of Jaafar.[1]
Verily God prospered the Caliphate, when he built
The House of Vicegerency, for the nobly born, the illustrious,
For he is the Caliph through his sire and grandsire

Who bear testimony unto him *by evidence of* sight and report."

Upon this Zubaydah stuffed his mouth with jewels which he sold for twenty thousand dinars. (£10,000)

Some particulars of the life of ar Rashid.

As Salifi records in the Tuyyuriyat with ascription to Ibnul Mubarak, that when ar Rashid succeded to the Caliphate, one of the slave girls of al Mahdi made an impression on his and he sought her hand, but she said, "I am not lawful unto thee, since thy father used to visit me." But he grew violently enamoured of her and sent to Abu Yusuf, [2] and asked of him, *saying,* "hast thou any remedy

1 Son of the Caliph al Mansur.

2 The Kadhi Abu Yusuf Yakub al Ansari. He was a native of Kufah and one of Abu Hanifah disciples, a legist, a learned scholar and a Hafidh. While at Baghdad, he acted as Kadhi to al Mahdi, al Hadi and Harun by the latter of whom he was treated with great honor and respect. He was the first who bore the title of Kadhiul Kudhat (or Chief Justice) and it is said that he was the first who changed the dress of the ulema (learned) and (cont.)

A.H.193. A.D.808-9. for this case ?" He replied, "O prince of the Faithful-what ! is a slave girl to be believed whenever she makes an assertion ? do not credit her-for verily she is not to be trusted."Ibnul Mubarak observes *on this* "I know not at whom I should most wonder in this affair-whether at this man who steeped his hands in the blood of the Muslims and *seized* their goods, or at this slave girl who of her own accord shrunk from the prince of the Faithful, or at this jurisconsult and judge of the eath who said, 'violate the honour of thy father and gratify thy lust and put it upon my shoulders ?" As Silafi records also on the authority of Abdullah, b. Yusuf that ar Rashid said to Abu Yusuf, "I have bought a slave and wish to take her at once before the legal period of abstention be passed-hast thou a device to offer?" He replied, "Yes-give her to one of thy sons and then marry her."[1] And from Ishak b. Rahwayh that ar Rashid sent for Abu Yusuf one night, who gave him his judgment *on the case required.* Ar Rashid then ordered one hundred thousand dirhams (£2,500) to be given to him. "Abu Yusuf exclaimed if the prince of Faithful sees good, he will order it to be given at once before morning." Ar Rashid said *to his attendants,* "bring it immediately:" but one of his suite exclaimed "the Treasurer is at his house and the doors *of the Treasury* are locked." Abu Yusuf retorted "verily the doors were locked when he sent for me." They were therefore opened *and the money given.*

As suli records with ascription to Yakub b. Jaafar, that ar Rashid set out in the year in which he aussumed the Caliphate, in order to ravage the outlying Roman provinces and returned in Shaaban and performed the pilgrimage with the people at the close of the year, and distributed great sums among the Sacred Cities. He had previously seen he Prophet in a dream who had said to him, "this authority will come to thee during this month ; make war therefore and perform the pilgrimage and give largely to the people of the Sacred Cities:" all of which he carried out. And from Muawiyah

---

(Cont. 383) gave it the form which it retains to this day. The anecdotes told of him by Ibn Khall are numerous. He was born 113 A.H. and died at Baghdad A.H. 182 (789) holding the Kadhiship till his death.

1 This legal period of abstention not being required in cases of marriage.

b. Salih on the authority of his father, that the first verse composed by Ar Rashid was when he made the pilgrimage in the year of his accession to the Caliphate ; he entered a house and lo! at the head of a chamber in it was a line of a verse written upon the wall. A.H.193. A.D.808-9.

"Now, O prince of the Faithful, dost thou not see
(I ranson thee) that separation from a friend is a momentous thing?"

Whereupon he sent for an inkhorn and wrote beneath it with his own hand-

"Yes ; and the camels marked for sacrifice, and what moves
In Mecca wearied, at a hurried pace."

And from Said b. Muslim that the understanding of ar Rashid was as the understanding of the learned. An Numani versified to him in describing a horse,

"As if his two ears when he raises his head
Were the first feather of a wing or an obliquely-nibbed pen."

Ar Rashid said "omit كان (As if) and say "thou wouldest think his two ears." So that the verse may run smoothly.[1]

And from Abdullah b-ul Abbas bil Fadhl bir Rabii that ar Rashid swore that he would not approach a female slave of his for a certain number of days, and he was much attached to her. And when the period had clasped, she did not seek to make him reconciled to her, whereupon he said,

"He[2] shunned me when he saw me infatuated

---

1 The Caliph's emendation does not touch the scansion which is the same with either word. The metre is Rajaz.

2 This mode of appealing to a mistress under the mark of an address to one of the other sex is common in oriental poetry. It is from a Jealousy of making public the circumstances of life, or the attractions of those whom Eastern custom rigidly excludes from the gaze of men. According to De Slane this is still carried so far in Cairo that public singers dare not amuse their auditors with a song in which the beloved indicated is a female.

A.H.193. A.D.808-9.

And prolonged his patience, when he discovered it.
He was my slave and hath not become my master
Verily this is among the wonders of the age."
Then he sent for Abul Atahiyah and said "Cap these lines" who said,
"The potency of love hath disclosed to him my humiliation
In my love for him, and he hath a comely face :
And through the one I have become his slave
And through the other hath appeared and become manifest what I feel."

Ibn Asakir records on the authority of Ibn Ulayyah that ar Rashid seized a Zindik, and gave orders that this head should be struck off, and the Zindik said, "why dost thou strike off my head?" He replied "I shall free the people from thee." He replied "and where art thou against the thousand traditions which I have falsely ascribed to the Apostle of God, not one word of which he spoke ?" Ar Rashid answered, "and where art thou, O enemy of God, before Abu Ishak al Fazari, and Abdullah b-ul Mubarak who can sift and eject them letter by letter ?"

As Suli records on the authority of Ishaq al Hashimi that he said, "we were with Ar Rashid when he exclaimed, 'I hear that the people suspect me of hatred towards Ali b. Abi Talib, whereas, by Allah I love no one with the love I bear to him, but these people are the most violent in hating and reviling us, and in attempting to excite discord in our kingdom, notwithstanding that we hage their blood-revenge, and shared withthem what we possess, so that they are more favourably inclined to the children of Umayyah than towards us. But as to the descendants of his loins, they are indeed the chiefs of the people and the first in merit, and verily my father al Mahdi related to me on the authority of Ibn Abbas that he heard the Prophet say regarding al Hasan and al Husayn-whoso loveth those two, verily loveth me, and whoso hateth those two, verily he hateth me ; - and he likewise heard him say-Fatimah is the chief of the women of the universe, save Miriam the daughter of Imran[1] and Asyah daughter of Muzahim.'" A.H.193. A.D.808-9.

It is related that Ibnus Sammak went in unto ar Rashid who called for *water to* drink, and a goglet was brought to him, and when he took hold of it, Ibnus Sammak said "gently ! O prince of the Faithful ! if thou wert forbidden this draught, at how much wouldst thou purchase it?" He answered "with the half of my kingdom." The other said-"drink, may the Lord make it wholesome to thee." And when he had drunk, Ibnus Sammak said, "I ask of thee, if its emission from thy body wee forbidden thee, at how much wouldst thou purchase its emission?" He replied "with the whole of my kingdom." He continued "verily a kingdom whose price is a draught of water and its emission, is not worth contending for." And Harun wept bitterly.

Ibnul Jauzi relates that ar Rashid said to Shayban, "give me an admonition." He replied, "that thou shouldst consort with one who will terrify thee until security cometh upon thee, is better than that thou shouldst consort with one who will inspire thee with a feeling of security until fear cometh upon thee." Ar Rashid said, "explain this to me." He replied, "he who said to thee, 'thou art ansereable for thy people,' is a better counselor unto thee than one who saith-ye people of the Prophetical house-your sins are forgiven ye-for ye are the kinsfolk of your Prophet." And ar Rashid wept until those who were around him had compassion on him.

In as Suli's work of the Aurak *it is stated* with its authorities, that when ar Rashid assumed the Caliphate, and installed Yahya b. Khalid as first minister, Ibrahim of Mosul said,

"Didst thou not see that the sun was wan,
But when Harun came its rays shone forth.
The world has become clothed with beauty through his sovereignty,

1 This is the name give in the Qurãn to the father of the Blessed Virgin. (Qur. III, See Sale's notes, p. 39). Asyah was the wife of Pharaoh who saved the life of Moses from the anger of her husband. (Qur. XX, Sale, p. 257).

A.H.193.
A.D.808-9.

For Harun in its monarch and Yahya its minister."

Whereupon ar Rashid made him a present of one hundred thousand dirhams and Yahya gave him fifty thousand.

The following is by Dauud b. Razin of Wasit on Harun.

"Through Harun the light hath shone over every city,

And in the justice of his disposition the ways of rectitude are through him established.

The Imam whose works are directed to the service of God,

And what most frequently occupy him to that end, are war and pilgrimage.

The eyes of the people are blinded by the light of his face

When his shining countenance appeareth before me.

Hopes grow ample through the munificence of his hand.

For he giveth unto him who hopeth from him beyond what he hopeth."

The Kadhi al Fadhil[1]observes in one of his Epistles. "I know of no journey ever undertaken by a monarch in search of knowledge, save that by ar Rashid, who journeyed with his two sons al Amin and al Mamun to study the Muwatta[2] under Malik : the original of the Muwatta heard by ar Rashid was in the library of the Egyptians. Afterwards the Sultan Salahuddin b. Ayub traveled to Alexandria

---

1 Abu Ali Abdur Rahim al Lakhmi, al Askalani, known as the Kadhi al Fadhil (the excellent Kadhi) was the son of the Kadhi al Ashraf (the most noble) and grandson of the Kadhias Said (fortunate). He was born at Ascalon in A.H. 529 and was Vizir to al Malik an Nasir Salahuddin by whom he was treated with great favour. He was pre-eminent as a writer of epistles and surpassed every predecessor. Such is the Judgment of Ibn Khall confirmed by the opinion of his contemporaries but to a European taste, his style is turgid, and the specimens of his correspondence given by Ibn Khall, show the conventional mannerism and the hackneyed tropes of all Oriental letter writers. He died at Cairo A.H. 596, (1200).

2 The famous work on tradition by Malik b. Anas, which is part of the basis on which the Malikite system of Jurisprudence is founded.

and studied the Muwatta under Ibn Tahir[1] b Auf-I do not know of A.H.193.
a third *that can be added* to these two." A.D.808-9.

The following is by Mansur an Namari[2] on ar Rashid-

"He made the Qurãn his Imam and his guide
When the Qurãn chose him as a defence."

And from a poem of his is this verse-

"Noble qualities and beneficence are valleys,
God hath caused thee to dwell in them where they meet."

It is said that ar Rashid reward him for this with a hundred thousand dirhams.

Al Husayn b. Fahm narrates that ar Rashid used to say-" among the most pleasing to me of what has been said in my praise, is-

The father of al Amin, al Mamun and al Mutamin
"How generous is he as an affectionate father! and how *generous* those whom he hath begotten."

Ishak of Mosul says, "I went in unto ar Rashid and recited to him,

'A woman enjoined thrift, I said to her, Stay thee

---

1 The printed edition has incorrectly the name Ali for the Preposition ala (علي) and Ibn (بن) for Abi (ابي) The MS. has not these faults. Abu Tahir Ismail b. Makki b. Ismail b. Isa b. Auf Az Zuhri was a doctor of the school of Malik and a Mufti of the highest consideration. The Hafidh as Silafi attended his lectures and as the text rightly says, the Sultan Salahuddin studied the Muwatta under him. He died A.H. 581 (1185).

2 Mansur b-ul Zibrikan b. Salmah called in Namari because descended from Namar b. Kasit. He was a native of Mesopotamia and brought by al Fadhl b. Yahya to the notice of ar Rashid. This poet adroitly copied Marwan b Abi Hafsah in joining to his eulogies of the Caliph the disparagement of the family of Ali, by which he intended to show that he did not recognize their claim to the Imamate. A practice pleasing to the Caliph, notwithstanding his professions of love towards Ali and his affected kindness to his descendants. Mansur died at Rasul Ayn in the reign of Harun ; consult Kitabul Aghani, Tom. 12.

A.H.193.
A.D.808-9.

For that is a thing to which there is no way.

I see that men are friends of the munificent and I see not

A miser in the universe that hath a friend.

And verily I have seen that avarice bringeth contempt on those that practice it.

And my spirit is too generous that it should be called avaricious.

And the best of circumatances for a youth-if thou knowest it,

Is when he hath acquired a thing, that he be in the habit of giving to others.

My gift is as the gift of the abundant in generosity.

And I have not, as thou verily knowest little.

And how should I fear poverty and be deprived of wealth

While the judgment of the prince of the Faithful is so excellent.'"

Ar Rashid exclaimed-"No indeed-how ? if it please God. O Fadhl, give him one hundred thousand dirhams. To God be attributed the flow of the verses he hath brought us ! How admirable is their point and how beautiful their arrangement !" I said, "O prince of the Faithful, thy words are better than my verse." He replied, "O Fadhl, give him another hundred thousand."

In the Tuyyuriyat with its ascription to Ishak of Mosul, *it is stated* that Abul Atihiyah said to Abu Nawas[1] I would that I had been before hand with thee in the verse in which thou didst praise ar Rashid.

"Verily I used to fear thee, but what freed me

From fearing thee was thy fear of God."

Muhammad b. Ali al Khurasani says that ar Rashid was the first Caliph who played with hockey stick and hall and shot arrows at a

---

1 The ready wit and brilliant powers of extempore versification of ar Rashid' famours poet may be sought for in D'Herbelot's meager sketch of his life, by the reader who may be unacquainted with Arabic. The Arabic scholar needs no reference to the life of one of the best known figures of his time.

target, and the first Caliph of the sons of al Abbas that played at chess, and as Suli states that he was the first who appointed degrees and classes for singers. Of the verses of ar Rashid in lament over his female slave Haylanah, (Helen) as Suli quotes the following " A.H.193. A.D.808-9.

"I endured afflictions and sorrow
When death took Haylanah to itself.
I parted from my happiness when I lost her
And care not now what it may be.
She was my world : and when she sank
Into her grave, I parted from my world.
Verily people have multiplied, but I
Behold no creature after her.
By Allah, I shall not forget thee
As long as the wind shaketh the boughs on the uplands."
And quoted by as Suli is this verse by him-
"O, mistress of the mansion in Firk,
And mistress of the Sultan and his kindom
For God's sake, spare to slay me
For I am neither Daylam nor Turk."

Ar Rashid died at Tus in Khurasan while leading a military expedition, and was buried there on the 3rd Jumada II, 193[1] (23rd March 809) at the age of forty-five, and his son Salih read prayers over him.

As Suli says that ar Rashid left one hundred million dinars, and furniture and jewels and bullion and beasts of kinds, to the value of one hundred and twenty-five thousand dinars.

---

1 It is as Weil remarks, a strange fact that notwithstanding the full and splendid court kept by ar Rashid and the learned doctors, authors, traditionists and poets that attended it, the date of his death, as that o his birth, is uncertain. According to Wakidi, he died on Friday night, 3rd Jumada II, according to Hisham, Sunday night in the beginning of Jumada II, According to others Jumada I. The duration of his Caliphate is also a matter of dispute-Weil follows Wakidi whose narrative accords with that of as Suyuti.

A.H.193. A.D.809. Another author states that Gabriel the son of Bakhtishuu erred[1] in his medical treatment of ar Rashid which was the cause of his death, and ar Rashid purposed to have him quartered, but he said, "give me time till to-morrow and thou wilt enter upon the morning in health." But he died the same day.

It is said that ar Rashid dreamed that he was leading the prayers as Imam at Tus, and he wept, and said "dig me a grave;" and one was dug for him, and he was born in a covered litter upon a camel, and it was driven along until he beheld the grave, and he said, "O son of man, thou art about to come to this." And he gave orders to a party who set him down, and they read over him the entire Qurãn while he was in the little on the edge of the grave. When he died allegiance was sworn in the army to al Amin, he being at that time in Baghdad. When the new reached him, he prayed before the people on the Friday and preached a discourse and announced the death of ar Rashid unto the people, and they swore allegiance to him. Raja the eunuch took the mantle, scepter and signet ring and rode post from Marw will he reached Baghdad in twelve days in the middle of the month of Jumada II, and deposited them with al Amin.

The following is by Abush Shis[2] lamenting ar Rashi-

"A sun hath set in the East
And for it my eye weepeth;
We have never before seen a sun
That set where it riseth."

Abu Nuwas has the following partly in condolence and partly in congratulation.

---

1 The MS. has غلظ (was rough or harsh) instead of غلط (erred) of the printed text.

2 Muhammad b. Abdullah b. Razin al Khuzaai surnamed Abush Shis. He composed poems in honour of as Rashid, al Amin and that Caliph's son and successor, and wrote elegies on the death of ar Rashid. He died A.H. 196. Ibn Khall.

“The stars revolve in fortunate and sinister aspects. A.H.193. A.D.809.
And we too are in grief and joy.
The heart weeps while the eye smiles
For we are in gloom and in glandness.
The rising al Amin makes us smile
And the death yesterday of the Imam makes us weep.
They are two moons. One hath appeared at Baghdad
In al Khuld,[1] and a moon at Tus *hath sunk* in the grave.”

Of the traditions recited by ar Rashid, as Suli mentions one related by him on the autority of Anas that the Apostle of God said, “fear hellfire, though it be but *for the value of* a split date.” And from Ali b. Abi Talib that the Prophet said, “purify your mouths, for they are the pathways of the Qurãn.”

AL AMIN

Al Amin Muhammad, Abu Abdullah, son of ar Rashid was the heir of his father and assumed the Caliphate after him. He was one of the finest of youths in appearance-fair, tall, handsome, possessed of great strength and vigour and of renowned bravery. It is said that he once killed a lion[2] with own hands. He was eloquent, polished in speek well-educated and accomplished, but defective in judgment, of great prodigality, weak in mind, apathetic and unfit for government.

As soon as he was acknowledged Caliph, on the following day, he ordered the construction of a level piece of ground near the palace of al Mansur for playing at ball. In the year 194 he removed[3]

1 “Paradise” the name of the palace at Baghdad, built by al Mansur. Yakut.

2 The narrative of the feat is given by Masaudi.

3 That is Mesopotamia, but allowed him to retain the governorship of Kinnarsin and command of the fortresses of the marches. Weil.

A.H.193. A.D.809 his brother al Kasim from *the government* to which ar Rashid had appointed him, and there occurred an estrangement, between him and his brother al Mamun.

It is said that Fadl b. Rabii, being aware that when the Caliphate came to al Mamun, he would have no mercy on him,[1] instigated al Amin and urged him to set him aside and give the succession to his son Musa. When the disgrace of his brother al Kasim reached al Mamun, he cut off all communication will al Amin and omitted his name from the uniforms[2] and the coinage. Shortly after al Amin sent to him desiring him to yield Musa precedence *in the succession to the Caliphate* before himself and stated that he had named him Natik bil Hakk. (proclaimer of the truth). But al Mamun rejected it and refused him. The messenger[3] (of *al Amin)* joined the party of al Mamun, and did homage to him as Caliph in secret. Afterwards he used to keep him informed of news and sent him advices from Iraq.

And when he returned and informed al Amin of the refusal of al Mamun, he struck out his name from the succession and sent for the deed which ar Rashid had written and deposited in the Kaabah. They therefore brought it to him and he tore it in pieces and the estrangement *between the brothers* was thus increased. His counselors urged their advice on him and Khuzaymah b. Khazim[4] said, "O prince of the Faithful, he who lieth to thee, giveth thee no good counsel, and he who speaketh the truth to thee, doth not betray

---

1 He was the prime minister of al Amin and altogether wedded to his interest. He had also suffered the maltreatment of one of al Mamun's messengers in his presence by one of his suite, and allowed him to speak harshly of that prince of which al Mamun was informed by the messenger himself on his return. Ibnul Athir.

2 So Weil translates this word طرز The MS. has "khutbah" (خطبه) Ibnul Athir has طرز with the printed text.

3 His name was Abbas b. Musa, one of four delegates dispatched by the Caliph to al Mamun.

4 The printed text and MS. have –Hazim b. Khuzaymah, but this is an error- Masaudi Ibnul Athir Ibn Khaldun and Weil who follows them, write the name as I have given it.

thee. Do not encourage[1] the officers to call for deposal, for they will *some day* depose thee, and do not incite them to violate a compact, for they will violate their covenant of Allegiance to thee, for verily he who deceive shall be deceived, and he who perjures himself shall be betrayed." But he would not listen to advice, and set about conciliating to officers with presents, and had the covenant of sucession taken for his son Musa who was at that time a child in arms, and surnamed him Natik bil Hakk. One of the poets has said regarding this.[2] A.H.194. A.D.810

"The Caliphate is ruined by the treachery of the vizier,
The profligacy of the prince and the folly of his counselor;
For Fadhl is the vizier and Bakr the councilor,
Seeking that in which lieth the perdition of the prince.
And stranger thatn either one or the other
Is that we should swear allegiance to a little child,
One[3] that is unable to blow its nose
And is never out of the lap of its nurse
And[4] what is this, but that Fadhl and Bakr
Seek to deface the Illustrious Book.
And were it not for the vicissitudes o Fortune, these two
Would never be among princes and leaders."

When al Mamun was assured of his having been set aside, he

---

1 For تُجرِ of the printed text, read, as in Masaudi and Ibnul Athir. تجرّي The MS. has also تجري but without the Tashdid.

2 This, according to Masaudi was a blind poet of Baghdad called Ali b. Abi Talib. Some of the lines I have omitted for reasons obvious to those who can read the original.

3 So this line runs in Masaudi من ليس يحسن مسح انفه ـ ولم يخل متنه من حجر ظفر The one in the text is probably the correct one, but it is untranslatable.

4 Masaudi has و ماذاك إلايا غ و غلو He also gives a closing line which is not in the text, ولكنها قنن كالجبال ترفّع فيها بضيع الحقير But it hath summits like hills upon which worthless things are flung up.

A.H.195. A.D.811. assumed the tittle of the prince of the Faithful and was thus addressed. Al Amin appointed Ali b. Isa Mahan to the mountainous districts of Hamadan, Nahawand, Kumm and Ispahan in the year 195. Ali b. Isa then set forth from Baghdad in the middle of Jumada II, at the head of an army forty thousand strong, the like of which had not been seen to engage al Mamun, and he took with him a silver chain,[1] in order as he thought to bind him with it. Al Mamun dispatched against him Tahir b-ul Husayn at the head of less than four thousand men. He was victorious and Ali was slain and his army routed. His head was taken to al Mamun and sent through Kurasan and al Mamun was saluted as Caliph. The news reached al Amin while he was engaged in fishing, and he said to him who brought the report, "Confound thee ! Leave me, for Kauthar (*his counch*) hath taken two fish, and I have not taken anything as yet."

Abdullah b. Salih al Jarmi[2] says, that when Ali was slain, the people in Baghdad raised a great tumult and al Amin repented of having set aside his brother. The nobles too, sought to obtain what they could of him, and dispatched their troops to demand pay of al Amin, and the contest continued between him and his brother. The affairs of al Amin daily grew worse through his abandonment to frivolity and follies, while those of al Mamun improved till the inhabitants of the Sacred Cities and the greater part of Iraq swore allegiance to him. The circumstances of al Amin at length became desperate, the discipline of the army was destroyed, and his treasures dissipated, by reason of which the condition of the people fell into a grievous state. Meanwhile violence, devastation and ruin waxed great and increased through the continuance of hostilitiesand the play of the engines of war and the liquid naphatha, till the

1 This, according to Tabari, was given to Ali by al Amin, according to Ibn Khaldun by Zubaydah. Weil.

2 In the text this name is marked Jurmi, but I think this is an error. Ibn Khal in his life of Abu Omar al Jarmi (so De Slane writes the name) says that there are several tribes so called. The Muntahal Arab gives the name Jarm, but not Jurm, nor is there such a town in Yakut who, however, mentions Jirm as a place near Badakhshan.

splendours of Baghdad were obliterated and dirges were sung over it. And among the pieces recited regarding it, is the following- A.H.198. A.D.813-14.

"I[1] wept tears of blood over Baghdad when
I lost the delights of a happy life ;
The eye of the envious fell upon it
And destroyed its people by the engines of war."

The siege of Baghdad continued for fifteen months, and the greater number of the Abbasides and ministers of State joined the forces of al Mamun and none remained with al Amin to defend him, but the rabble and the vagabonds[2] of Baghdad, and this lasted till the beginning of the year 198. Then Tahir b-ul Hasuyn entered Baghdad at the point of the sword, and al Amin fled with his mother and family from the palace to the city of al Mansur,[3] and all his troops and servants dispersed, and food and water became scarce among them.

Muhammad b. Rashid narrates, "Ibrahim b-ul Madhi[4] told me that he was with al Amin in the city of al Mansur, and added, "he sent for me one night, and I went to him and he said, 'dost thou not observe the beauty of the night, the splendour of the moon and its radiance on the water ? What sayest thou to a bout of wine ?' I replied 'do as thou wilt.' Then we drank together and he sent for a slave girl whose name was Dhaaf (*weakness*) and I was struck

---

1 Ten more lines of this poem may be found in Masaudi.

2 Kazimirski gives two plurals to this word *viz.*, حرافيش and حرفشه The text and Ms. have حرافشه Lane does not give it.

3 The old city called also the city of Abu Jaafar. Masaudi. See M. De Meynard's translation, Tom VI., p. 471.

4 Brother to Harun ar Rashid. He had great talent as a singer and was an agreeable companion at parties of Pleasure. He was surnamed at Tinnin or the dragon, from his large frame. He was proclaimed Caliph at Baghdad during the absence of al Mamun in Khurasan, and so continued for nearly two years. His flight and adventures have been given by Tabari and others and are well known. He died at Sarr-man-raa. A.H. 224 (839). Ibn Khall.

A.H.198. with the ill-omen of her name. He commanded her to sing and she
A.D.813-14. sang a verse of an Nabighah al Jaadis.[1]

'By my life, Kulayb had more allies,
Had more numerous followers[2] than thou, and yet was stained with blood.'

The Caliph felt this as in ill augury and said 'sing something else.' So she sang-

'Their departure hath made mine eye to weep and hath rendere it sleepless,
For separation is a cause of weeping unto friends.
The adversity of fortune continued to attack them
Until they destroyed one another, for the adversity of fortune is imimical.
And to-day I weep for them greatly and lament them
Until I return so incessantly that no tears are left in my eyes.

He exclaimed-'may Allah curse thee ! knowest thou nothing but that ?

She replied, 'I thought that thou didst like this.' Then she sand again-

'But, by the Lord of repose and movement,
Verily death hath many snares.
Days and nights do not recur nor
Do the stars revolve in the sky and the firmament,

---

1 Hassan b. Kays a member of the tribe of Jaad b. Kaab known as an Nabighah al Jaadi was one of the most celebrated of the poets contemporary with Muhammad. He was born before the promulgation of Islamism and fought on Ali's side at Siffin. He died during the reign of Abdullah b-uz Zubayr. He was surnamed an Nabighah because he did not given any proofs of poetical talent till after his 30th year. De Slane. Ibn Khall.

2 So I venture to translate ايسرزنيا The phrase عقيل طويلة الذنب means Okayl has numerous horsemen, مذندب a man having many dependents. Masaudi has ايسر حزما and Ibnul Athir the same.

Save to take a king from his kingdom. A.H.198.
Verily his authority passeth to another monarch, A.D.813-14.
But the kingdom of the Lord is everlasting,
It decayeth not neither is it shared.'

He exclaimed-'Begone-Allah curse thee !' and she arose and stumbled over a crystal goblet of price and broke it. He said, 'alas, Ibrahim ! – dost thou not see ? by Allah. I cannot but think that my time is drawing near !' I replied 'nay-may Allah prolong thy life and render glorious thy kingdom.' Then I heard a voice from the Tigris, saying-'the case is judged regarding which ye two called for a judicial decision'-at which Muhammad al Amin sprung up in great trouble. A night or two after this, he was slain. He was taken and imprisoned in a house and a party of Persians were let in upon him, and they struck him with their swords, and cut him throught the nape of his neck and went with his head to Tahir, who placed it upon a wall of a gardon, and it was proclaimed by the crier, 'This is the head of the deposed Muhammad,' and his body was dgragged by a rope."

Tabir then sent the head, the mantle, the scepter and the praying carpet which was of palm branches lined, to al Mamun. The assassination of his brother weighted sorely on al Mamun for he would have preferred that he should have been sent to him alive in order that he might consider his intention regarding him. He therefore hated Tahir and neglected him with total oblivion till he died in distant exile.[1] Thus were verified the words of al Amin, for he had written a letter with his own hand to Tahir b-ul Husayn when he was summoned to war aginst him in which *he said* 'O Tahir, no assertor of our rights hath ever arisen in our behalf, since we come to power, but his reward from us was the sword-therefore

1 His splendid banishment to the almost independent government of Khurasan may well have consoled his for the loss of the society of a capricious master from whose tardy remorse he did not feel himself safe. D'Herbelot says that al Mamun could not look upon Tahir without weeping. He became the founder of the dynasty that bears his name.

A.H.198. A.D.813-14. look to thyself or meddle not-consider Abu Muslim and such as he, who spent themselves in serving *the Abbasides,* and their end was death at their hands." Regarding the murder of al Amin, is the following by Ibrahim al Mahdi.

"Turn to the mansion on the hills, effaced by the blowing winde
At Khuld, formed of stone and tile,
And the polished marble with which it was faced
And its gate, a gate of resplendent gold.
And convey for me a message to
The prince, concerning[1] the ruled and him who rules.
Say to 'O son of the prinee of right guidance,
Cleanse the cities of God from *the presence* of Tabir ;
It was not enough for him that he sould cut[2] the jugular vein of al Amin
Like the slaughter of sacrificial offerings, with cutting blades,
But he must[3] drag his limbs
With a rope, meaning thereby to act as a merciless avenger[4];
Verily death hath settled on his eyelids
And his eye hath a troubled glance.'"

And among the verses that were composed is also-

"Why should I lament thee ? why ? for thy mirth,
O Abu Musa and thy continual frivolity ?
And for thy neglect of the five devotions at their appointed times
Through, thy passion for wine ?

---

1 Ibnul Athir has علي for عن of the text.

2 The text makes this and another verb in the next line passive without any occasion. The sense is made clearer by allowing them to stand simply as transitive verbs which from Ibnul Athir, it is evident they are.

3 حتي اتي يسحب Ibnul Athir.

4 هذا مدي السائر Ibid/

For Shanif[1] I shall not mourn A.H.198. A.D.813-14.

Nor care I for the retribution that hath befallen Kauthar.

Thou wert incapable of rule nor

Was obedience rendered unto thee in the Arabian kingdom.

Why should we mourn for thee ? for what thou hast exposed us to

At one time to the engines of war, and at another to pillage ?"

There is a poem by Khuzayumah b-ul Hasan supposed to be recited by Zubaydah, in which he says:[2]

"Tahir came, may the Lord not purify Tahir from sin,

For Tahir was impure in the purpose for which he came.

He turned me forth with uncovered head and unveiled,

And plundered my goods and destroyed my dwellings.

What I have suffered will afflict Harun,

And what hath befallen me from the basest and most corrupt of mankind.

Remember, O prince of the faithful my kinship :

I ranson thee with my life, thou who are revered and remembered,

Ibn Jarir says that when al Amin assumed the government, he purchased eunuchs and gave excessive prices for them, and admitted them to his intimacy and abandoned the society of his wives and slave girls. Another author observes that on is accession he sent into the districts in quest of buffoons, and allowed them stipends and procured a number of wild beasts, and animals of prey and birds, and kept apart from his family and his nobles, and treated them with contempt. He wasted what was in the public

---

1 These were two of his minions.

2 This poem is omitted in the MS, but it will be found in Masaudi where it is stated to be written by Zubaydah herself to al Mamun. There are several additional lines in Masaudi and some variants from those in the text, the last line especially being altogether different.

A.H.198. A.D.813-14. treasuries and squandered jewels and objects of price in profusion and built numerous palaces in *various* places for purpose of amusement, and on one occasion he gave a boat full of gold as a present to one who sang to him the following verse-

"I kept retired from thee till thou sadist, 'he knoweth not *the distress* of aversion.'"

And I visited thee so often that thou sadist, 'he hath no self restraint.'"

He also built five barques in the shape of a lion, an elephant, an eagle, a serpent and a horse, and spent great sums on their construction, regarding which Abu Nuwas said,

"The Lord hath subjected unto al Amin
Animals for his riding which have never been subjected to Solomon.
For whenever his riding camels go by land,
He goeth upon the water mounted on a lion[1] of the forest.
A lion with outstretched limbs ready to spring
With wise jaws and terrible teeth."

As Suli relates on the authority of Muhammad b. Amr ar Rumim that Kauthar the eunuch of al Amin went forth to watch the fighting and a missile struck him in the face. Al Amin set about wiping the blood from his face and said-

"They have struck the apple of my eye,
And on account of me, have they struck him.
May Allah punish for my heart's sake
Those who have set it on fire."

But he was unable to add to these *lines,* so be summoned Abdullah but Taymi the poet and said to him "Cap these two." Upon which he exclaimed-

---

1 For لَيثُ read لَيثَ

A.H.198.
A.D.813-14.

"There is no equal to him whom I love,
The whole world is dazed in him.
Union with him is sweet, but
Parting is bitter and hateful.
Those who see in him his
Speriority over them, are envious of him.
In the same manner as the monarch that reign is envied by the brother."

Upon which al Amin gave him three mule-loads of dirhams. But when al Amin was slain, at Taymi went to al Mamun and vaunted his praises, but he would not allow him *an audience,* whereupon he betook himself to al Fadhl b. Sahl who introduced him into al Mamun's presence, and when he had made his salutation, the Caliph said, "Come, O Taymi, some more of-"

In the same manner as the monarch tha reigns
Is envied by his brother.
At Taymi said,[1]
"Abdullah al Mamun was succored
When they oppressed him.
The covenant was violated
Which they had formerly made with him.
His brother did not deal with him
As his father had directed."

Upon this he pardoned him and ordered ten thousand dirhams to be given to him.

It is said that Sulayman b. Mansur complained to al Amin that Abu Nuwas had satirized him and he replied, "O uncle, can I put him to death after his saying-

---

1 To the reader who is not acquainted with the Arabic it may be as well to mention that this is continued in the same metre and rhymes with the preceding lines to al Amin.

A.H.198.
A.D.813-14.

I offer praise unto Muhammad al Amin,
And beside it there is no commodity so desired.
Praise speaketh truly of Muhammad al Amin,
Though of praise there is much that is false and lieth.
Verily the bright moon waneth after it hath reached its fullness,
But he splendour of the light of Muhammad waneth not :
And if the pebbles of the sone of al Mansur be counted
The Muhammad among them is like a picked sapphire"

Ahmad b. Hanbal observes "verily I truth that the Lord will be merciful unto al Amin for his repudiation of Ismail b. Ulayyah, who was brought unto him, and the Caliph said-son of an adulteress-it is thou that sayest that the Qurãn is created !"

Al Masaudi says, "no one up to my time hath ruled the Caliphate being a Hashimite and the son of al Hashimite woman, save Ali b. Abi Talib, his son al Hasan, and al Amin whose mother was Zubaydah daughter of Jaafar b. Abi Jaafar al Mansur : her name was Amatul Aziz (handmaind of the Almighty) and Zubaydah[1] was a surname given to her."

Ishaq of Mosul states that there were qualities in al Amin to be found *united* in no other-he was one of the handsomest of men in face and one of the most generous; the noblest of the Caliphs by his father's and mother's side, skilled in letters, verse in the art of poetry, but enslaved by sensuality and frivolity, and notwithstanding his extravagance in money, a nigged in his table.

Abu Hasan al Ahmar says, "I used often to forget a verse by which a point of grammar might be illustrated, and al Amin would adduce it for me, and I have never met among the sons of a monarch any quicker of apprehension than he and al Mamun. His assassination occurred on (*the 24th or 25th*) Muharram of the year 198, (24th or 25th *September,* 813) he being twenty-seven years of age,"

---

1 Zubaydah is diminutive of "Zubdah" cream or fresh butter. See her life in Ibn Khall. And De Slan's note.

Of people of note who died during his reign were : Ismail b. Ulayyah, Ghundur, Shakik al Balkhi the ascetic, Abu Muawiyah ad Dharir (the blind) Muwarrij[1] as Sadusi, Abdullah b. Kathir the Qurãn reader, Abu Nuwas the poet, Abdullah b. Wahb, disciple of Malik, Warsh the Qurãn reader, Wakii and others. A.H.198. A.D.813-14.

Ali b. Muhammad an Naufali and others say that neither as Saffah nor al Mansur nor al Mahdi nor al Hadi nor ar Rashid were prayed for in the pulpits by their surnames, nor so addressed in epistolary correspondence until al Amin reigned, and he was prayed for as al Amin in the pulpits, and correspondence was conducted in his name *thus,* "From the servant of God Muhammad al Amin prince of the Faithful," and to the same effect al Askari observes in his Awail, *viz.,* that the first who was prayed for by his surname in the pulpits was al Amin.

Among the verses of al Amin addressed to his brother al Mamun, reviling him on account of *the base descent of* his mother, on hearing that al Mamun was in the habit of recounting his vices and asserting his own superiority over him, are the following quoted by as Suli-

"Be not vain-glorious for thyself in the absence of the choicest *of thy race.*

For vaunting is justified alone in a perfect man.

And if thou exaltest thyself over men through their merit,

Then pause, for thou art not pre-eminent.

Thy grandsire hath bestowed upon thee what thou didst desire, yet forsooth

Thou wilt find the reverse of thy wishes with Marajil,[2]

Thou ascendest the pulpit each day, hoping

For that which thou shalt not obtain after me.

---

1 The text has erroneously "Muwarrakh" but the MS. is correct. Muwarrij was a grammarian of Basrah. See his life in Ibn Khall.

2 The name of his mother who was a slave concubine.

A.H.198.
A.D.813-14.

And thou reproachest one who is above thee in merit
And repeatest vain words regarding me."

I remark that this verse is of approved merit, and if it is really his, it is better than the poetry of his brother and his father. And Suli says, that the following lines on his eunuch Kauthar who was serving wine to him while he was reclining on a couch of narcissus flowers, and the moon had just risen are ascribed to him, but others, ascribe them to al Husayn bud Dhahhak[1] al Khalii, a boon companion of his who was never separate from him.

"The full moon hath so portrayed thy beauty of thy face that
I deemed I saw thee and yet saw thee not.
Whenever the tender narcissus breathes,
I think it the sweet breath of thy brightness.
An illusion of my desires hath occupied me with thee
In the splendour of the one and the fragrance of the other.
I will abide while I live, in thankfulness
Unto the one and the other while they resemble thee."

By him also are these lines on his eunuch Kauthar-

"What seek the people of a lover
Afflicted for one he loves ?
Kauther is my faith and my worldly fortune,
Both my sickness and my physician ;
The most despicable of men is he who reproveth
A lover on account of his beloved."

---

1 Generally known by the appellation of al Khalii (the libertine). He was born at Basrah in 162. A.H., descended from a native of Khurasan. He was a writer and a poet, and was admitted to the society of the Caliphs and enjoyed their favour to an extent almost unequalled by any other save Ibrahim of Mosul. He had some amusing adventure with Abu Nuwas. He died A.H. 250 (864) having nearly attained his hundredth year. Ibn Khall. An account of him will be found in the Kitabul Aghani. Fol. 6, p. 170-but the verses in the text are not cited therein.

The following was composed by him when he despired of his kingdom, and Tahir obtained the mastery over him. A.H.198. A.D.813-14.

"O soul ! now must thou beware
For where is there a refuge from Fate ?
Every man, of what he feareth
And hopeth, is in peril.
He who sippeth the sweets of life
Shall one day be choked by affliction."

As Suli records with its ascription that al Amin said to his scribe, "Write *as follows* : From the servant of God, Muhammad, prince of the Faithful, to Tahir b-ul Husayn-Greeting to thee! And now, verily, things have proceeded between me and between my brother even to the rending of veils, and the disclosure of what is inviolable, and I am not sure but that he may covet this authority which is distant and remote *from him,* through the differences in our friendship and the opposition of our interests. Yet, verily, I am content that thou shouldst write me a safe conduct to my brother, and if he be generous towards me, such conduct is worthy of him, but if he put me to death, then hath manliness destroyed manliness, and the sword cloven the sword, for, verily, I would rather that a lion should rend me than that a dong should bark at me," but Tahir refused his request. And on the authority of Ismail b. Abi Muhammad al Yazidi, that he said, "my father used to discourse with al Amin and al Mamun on subjects in which they displayed their eloquenc, and he used to say, "the children of the Caliphs of the House of Umayyah used to be sent out to the desert, that they might gain purity of speech, but ye are even more chaste in language than they." As Suli says, "I know not of any relation of a tradition by al Amin save this one. Al Mughirah b. Muhammad al Muhalabi said to me, 'I saw a compay of the Banu Hashim, among whom was one of the sons of al Mutawakkil, with al Husayn bud Dhahhak, and they asked him regarding al Amin and his acquirements. Al Husayn described his accomplishments as considerable. 'And in theological law?' asked they. He replied 'that al Mumun was more profoundly versed in it than he.' 'And in tradition ?' they said. He answered 'I

A.H.198.
A.D.813-14.

never heard a tradition from him but once, when it was announced to him that a slave of his had died in Mecca, when he exclaimed-my father related to me a tradition, heard from Abbas, who said-I heard the Prophet say-he who dies engaged in the functions of the pilgrimage, shall be raised giving the salutation Labayk.'"[1]

At Thaalabi in the Lataiful Maarif observes that Abdul Ayna[2] used to say, "were Zubaydah to let loose her braided locks, they would fasten upon nothing but Caliphs or heirs to the Caliphate, for al Mansur was her grandsire and as Saffah the brother of her grandsier, and al Mahdi her paternal uncle, and ar Rashid her husband, and al Amin her son, and al Mamun and al Muatasim the sons of her husband, and al Wathik and al Mutawakkil her husband's grandsons, and as for the heirs-apparent, they are numerous. Like her, *in this respect*, of the House of Umayyah was Aatikah, daughter of Yazid b. Muawiyah. Yazid was her father, Muawiyah her grandfather, Muawiyah b. Yazid her brother, Marwan b-ul Hakam her father in law, Abdul Malik her husband, Yazid her son, al Walid her sons son, al Walid, Hisham and Sulayman the sons of her husband, and Yazid and Ibrahim the two sons of al Walid, grandsons of her husband.

---

1 This Talbiyat or cry of supplication (which signifies, "here I am at thy service") is incumbent upon the pilgrim. To use it frequently is meritorious and is a sunnat or practice, a single Talbiyat is a "shart" or positive condition. The refrain is لبيك الهُمَّ لبيك لاشريك لك لبيك

ان الحمد و النعمة لك و الملك لاشريك لك لبيك

See Burton's Mecca, p. 232.

2 Abu Abdullah Muhammad b. al Kasim, Maula to the Calipha al Mansur was a blind man remarkable for his repartees, verses and literary knowledge. He was born at al Ahwaz A.H. 131 and bred at Basrah. He received the surname of Abul Ayna from his having asked Abu Zayd al Ansari, the diminutive of Ayna (a large-eyed female) to which he received the answer 'Uyayna O Abul Ayna, which nickname clung to him ever after. He died, according to some in 283, according to others 282 A.H. Some of his witty replies are given by Ibn Khall from whom the above extract is taken.

AL MAMUN

A.H.198.
A.D.813-14.

Al Mamun Abdullah Abdul Abbas the son of ar Rashid was born in the year 170 on Thursday night[1] in the middle of Rabii I, the same night on which al Hadi died, and on which his father ar Rashid, succeeded him. His mother was a slave concubine named Marajil who died in giving birth to him. In his childhood he applied himself to learning. He heard traditions from his father and Hushaym and Abbad b-ul Awam, Yusuf b. Atiyah, Abu Muawiyah ad Dharir, Ishmail b. Ulayyah, Hajjaj al Aawar (the one-eyed) and men of their class.[2]

Al Yazidi instructed him in polite accomplishments and he assembled the jurisconsults from all quarters, and became a proficient in jurisprudence and the Arabic language, and *the history of* the encounters of the desert Arabs. When he grew up he applied himself to philosophy and the sciences of the ancients and became profoundly versed in them, and it was that which seduced him into asserting the creation of the Qurãn.[3] Jaafar b.Abi Othman at Tayalisi and others have related traditions on his authority. He was the most distinguished of the House of Abbas for his prudence, his determination, his clemency and judgment, his sagacity and aweinspiring aspect, his intrepidity, majesty and liberality. He had many emiment qualities, and a long series of memorable actions

---

1 In the life of ar Rashid, this event is given as having occurred on Friday night. See page. 290.

2 For طبقيم read as in the MS. طبقتهم

3 The orthodox Muslims maintain, if I may venture upon a definition of their belief, that the Qurãn, the uncreated Logos, was from the beginning,-co-eternal with the Deity, not of His essence in hypostatic union, but an inseparable inherent quality of it, like His Unity. Al Mamun adopted the opinions of the Muatazalites (whom Weil terms the Protestants and Rationalists of Islam) who asserted the necessity of its creation by the Deity. They believed the word of God to have been created *in subjects,* and to consist of letters and sound, copies thereof being written in books to express the original. They also went further and affirmed, that whatever was created *in subject* was an accident and liable to perish. See their doctrines in Sale. The arguments of al Mamun in defence of his opinions will afterwards appear in a latter to his Prefect at Baghdad.

A.H.198. A.D.813-14. *are rescorded of him* were it not *that he mared them by* what he did in foreing men to an interrogation regarding the creation of the Qurãn. Of the House of Abbas none wiser than he ever ruled the Caliphate. He was eloquent and fluent of speech, and he used to say, "Muawiyah ruled through his Amar, and Abdul Malik through his Hajjaj, but I by myself." It used to be said that the Banu Abbas were distinguished by a beginning, a middle and an end, for the beginning was as Saffah, the middle al Mamun, and the end al Muatahid.

It is related that in one of the faste of the Ramadhan, he read the Qurãn through thirty-three times. He was notorious for his attachment to the Shiite doctrines which indeed led him to exclude his brother al Mutamin and confer the succession upon Ali ar Ridha[1] as we shall shortly mention. Abu Maashar,[2] the astrologer, says that al Mamun was wont to govern with justice, possessed a natural turn for jurisprudence, and deserved to be accounted among the greatest doctors. Of ar Rashid, it is reported that he said, "verily I recognize in Abdullah (*al Mamun*) the prudence of al Mansur, the piety of al Mahdi, and the majesty of al Hadi, and if I chose to mention him in connection with a fourth (meaning himself), I might do so, and yet I gave precedence to Muhammad (*al Amin*) before him, although I knew him to be a slave to his passions, lavishly profuse of what he possessed, and calling into counsel with him his concubines and wives, and had it not been for Umm Jaafar (*Zubaydah*) and the affection of the Banu Hashim for him, I would have palced Abdullah before him.'

Al Mamun assumed the supreme power after the assassination of his brother in the year 198, while he was in Khurasan and he took the surname of Abu Jaafar. As Suli says that the Abbassides preferred this surname, because it was the surname of al Mansur,

---

1 The son of Musa, the sixth in descent from Ali b. Abi Talib.

2 Abu Maashar Jaafar b. Muhammad, al Balkhi the celebrated astrologer was the great master of his age in that art. He composed a number of words on the science of the stars, such as the Mudkhil (*Introduction*) the Zij (*astronomical* tables). He was very successful in his divinations. He died A.H. 272 (885-6). Ibn Khall.

and it possessed in their minds a majesty and an suspiciousness on account of the longevity of those who were so named, such as a Mansur and ar Rashid. A.H.198. A.D.813-14.

In the 201 he excluded hia brother al Mutamin from the succession and appointed as heir after him Ali ar Ridha the son of Musa al Kadhim (*the meek*) the son of Jaafar as Sadik (*the upright*). His extravagant attachement to th Shiite deoctrines induced him to this, so that it was even said, that he himself purposed abdicating and resigning the government to him. It was he who named him ar Ridha (the accepted *of God and men*), and he coined money in his name, gave him his daughter in marriage and promulgated this in the various quarters of his empire. He likewise commanded the abandonment of black garments[1] and the adoption of green. This was highly displeasing to the Banul Abbas, and they rose up against him and swore allegiance to Ibrahim the son of al Mahdi who surnamed al Mubarak (*blessed*). Al Mamun prepared to oppose him and various affrays and engagements took place and al Mamun set out for Iraq. Now it came to pass that Ali ar Ridha died[2] in the year 203, whereupon al Mamun wrote to the people of Baghdad telling them as they were angered against him on account of his having taken the covenant of allegiance for Ali, that he was now dead, but they returned him a rough answer, so al Mamun began his advance. Now Ibrahim the son of al Mahdi heard that the people had withdrawn from their engagement to him, wherefore he did himself in the month of Dul Hijjah. Thus his reign

---

1 According to Ibn Khaldun, the Abbasides adopted black as mourning for the slaughter of so many of the Hashimites under the Umayyad dynasty. The followers of Ali who rose against the Abbasides took the opposite colour, white. The adoption of green by al Mamun, Weil supposes to have been suggested by an ides of a mixture of the two colours, as significant of an alliance between the two-the word خضر meaning grey as well as green. The rebel Aliites in the reign of al Mansur wore yellow according to Tabari. Al Mamun, however, soon recalled the order, and the cherished black was again resumed. See Weil. Tom II, P. 216.

2 It was strongly suspected that he died of poison administered at the instigation of al Mamun : Masaudi attributes his death to indigestion from eating grapes, but alludes to the remour that he was poisoned.

A.H.204. lasted two years all but a few days, and he remained in concealment
A.D.819. for the space of eight years. Al Mamun arrived at Baghdad in Safar 204, and the Abbasides and others entreated him to return to the wearing of black and the abandonment of green ; he at first hesitated but afterwards consented.

As Suli records with its ascription that one of the women of his family said to al Mamun. "verily thou art generous to the descendants of Ali b. Abi Talib, but the government in thy hands is more powerfully employed against thy interests for their benefit than it would be in their hand *for thine,*" but he replied, "verily I have done what I have done because Abu Bakr when he ruled, did not appoint any of the Banu Hashim to office, and so with Omar and Othman ; than Ali succeeded to the government and he appointed Abdullah b. Abbas to Basrah, Ubaydullah to Yaman, Maabad to Mecca and Kutham to Bahrayn, and he left none of them without naming them to some post. This therefore was upon our shoulders, until I recompensed him in his posterity by what I have done."

In the year 210, al Mamun married Buran daughter of al Hasan b. Sahl[1] and her outfit amounted to many thousand *dinars.* Her father presented the chief officers of State with robes of honour and entertained them for the space of nineteen[2] days, and wrote on slips of paper the names of estates belonging to him, and scattered them among the generals and the Abbassides, and into the hand of whomsoever a slip fell with the name of an estate in it, he received it, and he showered before al Mamun a tray full of pearls when the bride was conducted to him.

In the year 211 al Mamun commanded it to be proclaimed that whosoever should speak well of Muawiyah should be outlawed

---

1 His prime minister. The cost of the nuptials is stated by Ibn Khall to have been 50 million dirhams (about £1,200,000). Buran's grandmother presented the Caliph with 1000 pearls-and on the marriage night a candle of ambergris weighting 80th was placed in a candlestick of gold. The Caliph himself protected against this wild extravagance. In compensation for his expenses he gave al Hasan one years revenue of Fars and al Ahwaz. Ibn Khall.

2 For سبعة in the text which is a misprint, read تسعة.

and that Ali b. Abi Talib was *to be considered* the best of men A.H.204. after the Apostle of God. In the year 212 al Mamun made public A.D.819. his doctrine on the creation of the Qurãn conjoined with *the declaration of* the superiority of Ali over Abu Bakr and Omar, but the people shrunk from it with aversion and the country was near being involved in rebellion, but he did not obtain by this what he desired, wherefore he desisted from it until the year 218. In the year 215 al Mamun undertook an expedition against the Byzantines and captured by force of arms the fortress of Kurrah, and the fortress of Majidah,[1] and then returned to Damascus. In the year 216 he again adanced into the Roman territory and took a number of fortresses and agains retired to Damascus. Afterwards the proceeded to Egypt and entered it, and was the first who entered it of the Abbaside Caliphs. In the year 217 he returned to Damascus and *repeated his incasion of* the Roman territory.[2]

In the year 218 he submitted the people to an inquisition regarding the doctrine of the creation of the Qurãn, and he wrote to his prefect in Baghdad, Ishak b. Ibrahim al Khuzaai cousin of Tahir b-ul Husayn regading the interrogation of the learned, a letter in which he says *as follows* :

"Verily the prince of the Faithful is aware that the public at large, and the general herd of the rabble and vulgar mob who have no insight nor knowledge, nor seek illumination from the light of wisdom and its demonstration, are a people ignorant of God and blind in regard to Him, and in error as to the truth of his doctrine, and fail to estimate Him according to the reality of HIS

1 So Ibn al Athir and Weil : the text has Majid. Both these places are in the neighbourhood of Tarsus.

2 As Suyuti omits to mention the conquest of Crete and Sicily. "Under the reign of al Mamun, at Baghdad, of Michael the Stammerer at Constantinople, the islands of Crete and Sicily were subdued by the Arabs. The former of these conquests is disdained by their own writers who were ignorant of the fame of Jupiter and Minos, but it has not been overlooked by the Byzantine historians." Decline and Fall, (C. Iii). The history of Sicily under the Muslims may be read with interest in the pages of Amari-Storia dei Musulmani di Sicilia.

A.H.218. A.D.833. transcendence, and to arrive at a true knowledge of Him and to distinguish between Him and His creature, and that inasmuch as they have formed as ill opinion of the difference between Him and His creation and what He hath revealed in the Qurãn, for they are agreed upon its being from the beginning, not created by God nor produced by Him ; yet, verily, the Most High hath said, 'verily we have made the same an Arabic Qurãn (Qur. XLIII). Now, indeed whatever He hath made, He hath created, as the Most High hath said, 'and hath created the darkness and the light,' (Qur. VI) and, 'do we relate unto thee of the histories *of the Apostle,'* (Qur. XI), *viz.,* of what had previously occurred-wherefore He announceth that He relateth events subsequent to which He produced the Qurãn. Again He says, '*this book,* the verses of which are guarded against corruption, and are also distinctly explained,'[1] (Qur. XI). Therefore is God the guardian of His book and its expounder, He is therefore its maker and its originator. Further, they pretend to adhere to the Prophetical traditions and that they are the people of orthodoxy and of the church, and all besides them are in error and infidelity, and they pride themselves on this and seduce the ignorant by it, so that a number of persons following a false course and yielding submission to other than God, have inclined to agreement with them. Thus they wrest the truth to the side of their win words and make of other than God a channel to their own error." He goes on to say, "the prince of the Faithful therefore considereth these to be mischievous people who would hinder a portion of the divine unity, and vessels of ignorance and beacons of falsehood and the tongue of Satan speaking amon his accomplices and terrifying his enemies-the people of God's word. It is right, therefore, that the sincerity of such a one should be suspected and his testimony rejected, for he is not to be trusted who is ignorant as to his true course and his portion in the divine unity, and hath been moreover in exceeding error and hath wandered astray from the right path. And by the life

1 So distinctly explained that this single passage alone has received many different interpretations on account of the ambiguity of the words أحكمت and فصلت The difficulties of private judgment are not confined to the churches of the West.

of the prince of the Faithful, the greatest liar among men is he who speaketh falsely of God and of His revelations, and who inventeth untruths and doth not comprehend God with a real comprehension of Him. Assemble. Therefore, the Kadhis that are with thee and read to them my latter and question them as to what they maintain, and discover from them what they believe in regard to the creation of the Qurãn and its being called into existence,and inform them that I seek no assistance in my service, nor do I put my confidence[1] in one who is untrustworthy in his faith. And if they allow it and are of accord, then command them to interrogate those witnesses that come before them and to question them as to their belief[2] in the matter of the Qurãn, and to reject the testimony of those who do not allow it to be created, and write to me regarding what cometh to thee concerning the Kadhis of the people under thy jurisdiction in their interrogation, and orders about them will be issued accordingly." Al Mamun likewise wrote to him to send seven individuals to him, and they were, Muhammad b. Saad Katibul Wakidi, Yahya b. Main, Abu Khaythamah, Abu Muslim disciple[3] of Yazid b. Harun, Ismail b. Dauud, Ismail b. Abi Masaud, and Ahmad b. Ibrahim ad Dauraki. They were accordingly sent to him and he questioned them on the creation of the Qurãn and they admitted it, wherefore he sent them back from Rakkah to Baghdad. The reason of their having been summoned was that they at first hesitated, but afterwards admitted it through fear. He wrote again to Ishak b. Ibrahim to summon the jurisconsults, the Skykhs and the tradidionists and to inform them of what the seven had admitted.

A.H.218.
A.D.833.

---

1 The MS. has لاواثق in place of the لاأُوثّق of the text.

2 The MS. has عن the text. من

3 Lit, one who writes at the dictation of another. It was the custom for the disciples of a master of any science to sit round him and write down the information he gave them : these manuscript records were termed Amali or dictations. Yazid b. Harun was a famous traditionist of Baghdad. It was through dread of his opposition that al Mamun hesitated for some time to assert publicly his doctrine on the creation of the Qurãn, a doctrine which Yazid strenuously opposed. He was born A.H. 118. died 206. See De Slane I.K. regarding further particular of his life. The lives of the others mentioned (except the last) will be found in Ibn Khall.

A.H.218. A.D.833. He did so, and some joined in agreement, while others were recusant and Yahya b. Main said, "we consented through fear of the sword." Afterwards he wrote another letter to Ishak, after the manner of the first, and commanded him to summon those who were recusant. He therefore summoned a number among whom were Ahmad b. Hanbal, Bishar b-ul Walid al Kindi, Abu Hassan az Ziyadi, Ali b. Abi Mukatil, al Fadhl b. Ghanim, Ubaydullah b. Omar al Kawariri (the flask-seller), Ali b-ul Jaad, Sajjadah, ad Dayyal b-ul Haytham, Kutaybah b. Said, Saadawayh al Wasiti Ishaq b. Abi Israil, Ibnul Haras,[1] Ibn Ulayyah the elder, Muhammad b. Nuh al Ijli, Yahya b. Abdur Rahman al Omari, Abu Nasr at Tammar (the date-seller) Abu Mamar al Katiai, Muhammad b. Hatim b. Maymun and others, and he showed them the letter of al Mamun, but they hung back and dissembled, neither admitting nor denying. Then he said to Bihar b-ul Walid "what dost thou say?" he answered "verily I have informed the prince of the Faithful more than once." The other continued, "and *what is thy opinin* now ? for verily a letter has newly arrived from the prince of the Faithful." He answered, "I say, it is the word of God." He rejoined, "I do not ask thee that-is it created ? Bishar replied, "there is nothing better to say than what I have told thee, besides I have a stipulation with the prince of the Faithful that I need not discuss it." Then Ishak addressed Ali b. Mukatil, "what dost thou say ?" He replied, "the Qurãn is the word of God, but if the prince of the Faithful lay on us a command, we hear and obey." Abu Hassan az Ziyadi replied to the same effect. Next he questioned Ahmad b. Hanbal "what dost thou say ?" He answered "it is the word of God." He asked, "is it created ?" He replied, "it is the word of God, I shall not say more than this." Then he interrogated the rest and recorded their answers. Ibnul Baka said, "I declare that the Qurãn was made and brought into exitense on the authority of the revealed text to that effect." Ishak said to him "and what is made is created." He replied "yes." "Therefore," said Ishak, "the Qurãn is created." He answered, "I do not say it is created." Then Ishak sent their answers to al

---

1 MS. and Ibnul Athir. Harash هرش

Mamun, and a letter from al Mamun reached him, *saying,* "what the pretenders to orthodoxy and the seekers after an authority for which they are unfitted have replied, hath reached me. Now whoso doth not admit that the Qurãn is created, suspend his exercise of judicial powers and authority to relate tradition." He goes on in his letter. "As to what Bishar sayeth, verily he lieth, for there passed no stipulation between the prince of the Faithful and him,[1] more than he accounts which the prince of the Faithful has of his belief and sincere profession and assertion that the Qurãn is created. Summon him before thee therefore, and if he recanteth, publish his case abroad, but if he persisteth in his infidelity and denieth, in his impiety and heresy, that the Qurãn is created, smite him on the neck and send his head to me. The same with Ibrahim b-ul Mahdi: question him, and if he assents, *it is well,* if not cut off his head. As for Ali Abi Mukatil, say to him, 'art thou not be who said to the prince of the Faithful that thou verily canst absolve and blind?' As to ad Dayyal, inform him that the grain which he stole from the granaries is what distracts him *from other affairs.* With regard to Ahmad b. Yazid bil Awam and his saying that he cannot give a better answer concerning the Qurãn, tell him that he is a child in mind thoug not in years-he is ignorant-he will find an answer to his liking when he is better taught ; if he doth not do so, the sword is behind it. As to Ahmad b Hanbal, inform him that the prince of the Faithful is aware of the matter of his argument and draws an inference from it, of his ignorance and falsehood. As to Fadhl b. Ghanim, tell him that it is not unknown to the prince of the Faithful what he was about in Egypt and what wealth he acquired to less than a year-to wit in his office of Kadhi. As for az Ziyadi tell him that he used falsely to claim clientship with a spurious son."[2] (But Abu Hassan az Ziyadi denied that he was client *by descent* of

A.H.218.
A.D.833 .

1 MS. في ذلك "in this matter."

2 See note 4, page 198. It will be remembered that Muawiyah attempted to procure the recognition of Ziyad as the son of Abu Sufiyan by Summayya the wife of a Greek slave whom he met in a tavern and in a fit of drunkenness seduced. The truth of the affiliation, however, was doubtful and Ziyad was known or unknown as the "son of his father."

A.H.218. A.D.833. Ziyad "the son of his father," but that he was called az Ziyadi for other reasons.) As to Abu Nasr the date-seller, verily the prince of the Faithful likeneth the meanness of his intellect to the baseness of his trade. With regard to Ibn Nuh and Ibn Hatim inform them that they employ themselves in taking usury, to the hindrance of their knowledge of the divine unity, and if nothing justified the prince of the Faithful in hostility to them in the cause of God, but their usury and what hath been revealed regarding such as they, that alone would justify it, but how much the more when they have added infidelity to usury and have become like the Nazarenes. As to Ibn Shujaa inform him that the prince of the Faithful was with him but a short time since, and took from him what he took of the property which he authorized unto Ibn Hisham from the substance of the prince *of the Faithful.* As for Saadawayh of Wasit, say to him-"may the Lord bring to shame that man whose pretentiousness in tradition and the craving for uthority therein have led him to lie at the time of interrogation. With regard to him known as Sajjadah and his denial that he had heard from those who had conversed wih the learned, of the doctrine that the Qurãn is created, tell him that his occupation, and the counting of beads (*date stones*) and his directions for the adjustment of his prayer-carpet and the deposite made with him by Ali b. Yahya and others, are what cause him to forget the divine unity. As to the flask-seller, what is manifest of his circumstances and taking of bribes and presents, sufficiently reveals his religious profession, his evil course of life and the weakness of his understanding and of his faith. As to Yahya al Omar, if he be a descendant of Omar b-ul Khattab, the answer to him is apparent. With regard to Muhammad b-ul Hasan b. Ali Aasim, if he followeth his ancestors who have passed away, he cannot have professed adherence to the doctrinal school which is mentioned in connection with him, besides, he is but a lad in need of being instructed. And verily the prince of the Faithful sent to you one known as Abu Mushir, after the prince of the Faithful sent to you one known as Abu Mushir, after the prince of the Faithful had subjected him to inquisiting on the subject of the Qurãn –he faltered and hesitated about it, until the prince of the Faithful called for the sword for him when he abjectly yielded. Now interrogate him in

the matter of his assent, and if he standeth by it, publish it abroad A.H.218.
and proclaim it, and such as do not draw back from their heresy of A.D.833.
those thou hast named after Bishar and Ibnul Mahdi, send them bound to the camp of the prince of the Faithful, that he may question them, and if they recant not, he will put them to the sword." The narrator says-"but all of them yielded upon this, save Ahmad b. Hanbal, Sajjadah, Muhammad, b. Nuh and the flask-seller, whereupon Ishak gave orders regarding them and they were put in fetters. Then he questioned them the following day, they being in fetters, and Sajjadah yielded. Again he interrogated them a third time, and the flask-seller submitted, and he sent Ahmad b. Hanbal and Muhammad b. Nuh to the Roman territories.[1] Afterwards it came to al Mamun's ear that these had really yielded under compulsion, wherefore he was enraged and summoned them to him, and they were being taken to him when the news of the death of al Mamun reached them before their arrival in his presence. Thus the Lord was merciful to them and banished their fear."

Now al Mamun fell sick in the Roman territories and when his illness became serious, he sent for his son Abbas to be brought to him, and he feared that he would not reach him *in time,* but he arrived when al Mamun was in the last distress. And verily, letters had been already despatched to the provinces containing *the following,* "From Abdullah al Mamun, and his brother Ishak the Caliph after him, under authority of these pesents." Some say that this occurred by order of al Mamun, while others assert that they wrote this at a time when a swooning fit was on him.

Al Mamun died on Thursday the 18th Rajab, 218 (9th August 883) at Badandun in the Roman teeritories and was carried to Tarsus and there buried.[2] Al Masaudi relates that he encamped on the stream of Badandun and its coldness and limpidity, the beauty

---

1 Where the Caliph with his army was at the time.

2 Known to the Byzantines under the name of ñoóavóov or ñoóavîos. Yakut places it at a day's march from Tarsus. Within the fortification of which is the tom of al Mamun. According to him one of the gates of the town is called the gate of Badandun.

A.H.218. A.D.833. of the place and its abundant verdure pleased him. He saw in the stream a fish *glittering* like silver which struck him with admiration, but no one could swim in the stream on account of the intensity of its coldness. He therefore offered a sword[1] to any one who would bring it out. An attendant went in and caught it and came out, but it struggled and got away into the water, and the chest and throat of al Mamun were splashed and his garments drenched. The attendant went in a second time and caught it. And Al Mamun said "let it be fried at once." Shortly after an ague seized him and he was covered up with blankets while he was shivering and crying out.[2] Then they lighted a fire round him and the fish was brough, but he could not touch it in his distraction regarding his own condition. After a little he rallied from his suffering and asked the interpretation *of the name* of the place in Arabic. They said, "stretch out thy feet,"[3] and he regarding it as an evil omen. Then he asked the name of the country and they said "Rakkah." Now according to the horoscope drawn at his birth, it was foretold that he would die at Rakkah, wherefore he always avoided making a stay at Rakkah, but when he heard this *reply* from the Romans he knew *his fate* and despaired and said "O Thou whose kingdom never endeth, have mercy on one whose kingdom hath passed away." When the news of his death reached Baghdad, Abu Sai'd al Makhzumi said-

"Hast thou seen the stars protect
Mamun and his kingdom firmly established ?
They have abandoned him between the two valleys of Tarsus
As they abandoned his father at Tus."

At Thaalabi observes, "there are not known of any father and son among the Caliphs any more distant graves than those of ar Rashid and al Mamun." He adds, "similarly the sepulchers of five of the sons of al Abbas are separated by a wide interval of space, the like of which men have not seen for the tomb of Abdullah is in Taif, that of Ubaydullah at Medina, that of al Fadhl in Syria, of Kutham in Samarkand, and of Maabad in Africa."

---

1 Masaudi, ha سبقا "a prize."

2 "The cold! the cold!البرد البرد Masaudi.

3 Podendon-from wooa and reivw.

On some accounts of al Mamun

A.H.218.
A.D.833 .

Niftawayh[1] says that Hamid b-ul Abbas bil Wazir related to me *as follows :* "We were in the presence of al Mamun when he sneezed, but we did not pray for a blessing upon him, whereupon he said, 'why do ye not pray for a blessing upon me ?' We replied, 'we held thee too exalted, O prince of the Faithful.' He answered, 'I am not one of those monarchs who thinketh himself above prayer.'" Ibn Asakir records on the authority of Muhammad al Yazidi that he said, "I used to instruct al Mamun, and one day I went to him but he was in privacy, wherefore I sent to him one of the attendants to inform him of my arrival, but he delayed, and I sent again to him and still he tarried, so I said 'this youth often diverts himself with idle trifling.' They repliec, 'yes, and withal when he leaves thee, he is ill-tempered with his attendants and they meet with great annoyance from him, therefore set him right with correction.' And when he came out, I ordered him to be brought up and I struck him seven blows with a scourge, and he was rubbing his eyes which were in tears when they called out, 'Jaafar b. Yahya[2] is coming.' So he took a kerchief and wiped the tears from his eyes and gathered up his garments and went to his carpet, sat down cross-legged and after a little, said, 'let him come in.' He then entered and I withdrew from the assembly, fearing that he would complain to him of me. Jaafar then advanced in front of him and coversed with him and made him laugh and went out again. Then I came up and said, 'verily I feared that thou wouldst complain of me to Jaafar.' He replied, 'O Abu Muhammad, I would not have told ar Rashid of this, how then Jaafar ! indeed I am much in need of correction.'"

And from Abdullah b. Muhammad at Taymi that he relates- "Ar Rashid designed to make a journey, wherefore he commanded the people to prepare for it and informed them that he would set

---

1 This famous grammarian was a native of Wasit where he was born in A.H. 244, he resided at Baghdad and died there A.H. 323. Ibn Khall.

2 For the life and unhappy end of this famous minister of ar Rashid consult Ibn Khall, and D'Herbelot.

A.H.218. out at the end of the week, but the week passed and he did not go
A.D.833. so they gathered round al Mamun and asked him to obtain information concerning it, wherefore al Mamun wrote to ar Rashid, who did not know that he could versify, the following lines :-

"O best of those whom a beast of burden coveyeth,
And of those whom a saddled charger followeth,
Is there an appointed time for the march that we may knew it,
Or is our order for the march to remain obscure ?
There is no knowledge of this save with the king,
From his luster we borrow light in the darkness.
If thou go forth, good guidance will set out following thee
And if thou remain, good guidance will be detained *with thee.*"

Ar Rashid read them and was pleased with them, and wrote upon them, "O my little son! What hast thou to do with verse-making,[1] which is the highest qualification of the base, but the last of the accomplishments of the noble." He also records on the authority of al Asami that the impression on the signet ring of Mamun was, "the servant of God son of the servant of God." And on that of Muhammad b. Abbad, that none of the Caliphs knew the Qurãn by heart except Othman b. Affan and al Mamun. I observe, that I have already refuted this limitation in the remarks that have preceded. He records likewise on the authority of Ibn Uaynah,[2] that al Mamun assembled the learned and held a public andience, when there came forward a woman and said, "O prince of the Faithful, my brother died and left six hundred dinars-they have given me but one dinar, saying, "this is thy share." Al Mamun computed and made the fractional division of the inheritance and said to her, "this is thy portion." The learned said to him, "how dost thou know, O prince of the Faithful?" He said to her, "this man left two daughters." She answered, "Yes." He proceeded, "then they have two-thirds, *viz.,* four hundred, and he left a mother, and she

1 الشعرا MS.

2 In the printed text for. عيينه Read عيينه The MS. is here correct.

has one-sixth, *viz.*, one hundred, and he left a wife and her share is an eighth, *viz.*, seventy-five-and, by Allah, hast thou twelve brothers?" She said, "Yes." He went on-" they get two dinars a piece and one dinar comes to thee." And from Muhammad b. Hafs al Anmati (*the carpet merchant*), that he narrates, "we were breakfasting with al Mamun on a festival day and there were piaced upon the table more than three hundred dishes, and every time a dish was served, al Mamun looked upon it and observed. "this is good for such a thing and hurtful for such another. Now if thee be among you one who is phlegmatic, let him another. Now if there be among you one who is phlegmatic, let him avoid this, and he among you, who has the yellow bile[1] let him eat of this, and he who is subject to atrabiliousness, let him not partake of this, and he who desires to eat but little, let him restrict himself to this." Upon this Yahya b. Aktham[2] said to him, "O prince of the Faithful, if we were to enter upon *the discussion of* medicine thou wouldst be a Galen in the knowledge of it, or of the stars, a Hermes in their computation, or of jurisprudence an Ali b. Abi Talib in its comprehension, or should liberality be spoken of, thou wouldst be a Hatim Tai in its description, or the truth of tradition, an Abu Darr in its proof, or generosity a Kaab Mamah[3] in his deeds, or good faith, a Samuel b. Aadiya in Fidelity."[4] Al Mamun was pleased at this speech and said, "verily, man is distinguished by his intellect, and

A.H.2
A.D.8

1 According to early notions on this subject the four constituent homours of the body were: بلغم phlegm, الصفرا yellow, bile, السوداء black bile, and الدم the blood. See Lane, Art. سود

2 Yahya b. Aktham was appointed Kadhi of Basrah by al Mamun in A.H. 202. See I.K. Life of Ibn Abi Duwad.

3 One of the principal chiefs of the tribe of Iyadh, noted for his liberality. De Slane, I. K. under Yakut al Hamawi.

4 Samuel the son of Aadiya, proverbial among the Arabs for his good faith. His name is introduced in the 23rd Assembly of al Hariri. The story of his fidelity is briefly as follows : Imrul Kays having fled from the pursuit of the king of Hira took refuge with Samuel in his castle of al Ablak in Tayma. Thence he proceeded to the court of the emperor Justinian to implore aid against his enemies, leaving with Samuel his daughter and several suits of mail. After various adventurers at the Greek court, he died at (Cont..)

A.H.218. A.D.833. were it not for that, no flesh would be better than other flesh, nor blood than other blood."

And from Yahya b-ul Aktham-"I never saw a more perfect man than al Mamun-I once passed a night with him and he awoke and said, 'O Yahya, see what there is near my foot.' I looked but saw nothing. He then called for a candle and the attendants hastened up, and he said, 'search' and they search and lo ! beneath his quilt was a snake as long as his body, and they killed it, and I said 'verily the knowledge of the unseen is a further addition to the accomplishments of the prince of the Faithful !" He replied-'God preserve me! No-but a secret monitor called to me but now when I was sleeping and said-

"O, thou who sleepest at night-awake!
For calamities travel by night.
The reliance of a youth on his fortune
Is Like trusting to loosened fastenings."

And I awoke and knew that something had happened either near or at a distance, and I reflected on what might be near and it was what thou hast seen.'" And from Umarah b. Ukayl, "Ibn abi Hafsah[1] the poet said to me, "dost thou know that al Mamun doth not understand poetry ?" replied "who is there that hath a quicker perception of it than he ? by Allah, verily did we recite the first line

---

(Cont. 423) Aneyra. On his death the prince of Ghassan determined to seize the armour of the warrior poet and besieged Samuel in his castle. Samuel's infant son was by some accident, captured outside the gate and Samuel was offered the choice of surrendering the armour or seeing his child slain. On his refusal to betray his trust the alternative was carried out before his father's eyes. The siege was raised and Samuel had the satisfaction of delivering the armour to the heirs of Imrul Kays at the fair of Ukadh. See Chenery's Hariri. Abul Feda. Anteislam Hist. p. 133.

1 Marwan b. Abi Hafsah a native of al Yamama and grandson of Abu Hafsah the Mawla of Marwan b-ul Hakam, born, A.H. 105, died at Baghdad A.H. 182. He ranked as a poet with the first of his age and his best piece is considered his Kasida rhyming in –I-(al Larmiyh) composed in honor of Maan b. Zaida as Shaybani. Ibn Khall.

of a verse he would anticipate the end of it without ever having A.H.218.
heard it." Ibn Abi Hafash replied, "verily I recited to him a line A.D.833 .
which I had well expressed, but I did not see his moved by it-and it was this-

The Imam of right guidance, al Mamun, is employed
In the concerns of religion, while men are busy about the world."

I said to him, "thou hast done no more than make of him an old woman in her closet with beads in her hand, for who can rise to the transaction of worldly affairs, when he is diverted from them by other things and trammeled by them ? Thou hast not spoken as thy uncle spoke of al Walid-

He doth not loss his portion in the world
Nor do the things of the world distract him from religion."

Ibn Asakir states that he had heard that an Nadhr b. Shumayl[1] related *as follows :* I went to al Mamun when he was at Marv, wearing worn out garments and he said to me, "O Nadhr, dost thou come into the presence of the prince of the Faithful in such garment?" I replied, "O prince of the Faithful verily the heat of Marv cannot be kept out except by wearing old garments like these." He said, "nay, but thou livest in a miserable way." We then spoke on tradition. At length al Mamun said, " I heard a tradition from Hushaym b. Bushayr[2] on the authority of Ibn Abbas who related that the apostle of God said, 'when a man marries a woman for her piety and beauty, it is a prevetive (sadad) against want.'" I replied

---

1 Abul Hasan, at Nadhr b. Shumayl b. Kharashah b. Yazid, at Tamimi was a native of Basrah and celebrated as a grammarian. He was skilled as a jurisconsult and traditionist and well acquainted with poetry and the battles of the desert Arabs. He left Basrah, where he found not means of support and settled al Marv and acquired great wealth. The story in the text is given in Ibn Khall, with some variation. An Nadhr died A.H. 204 (A.D. 820).

2 Hushaym b. Bushayr a native of Wasit acquired a high reputation as a traditionist at Baghdad. He knew by heart twenty thousand of them. Died. A.H. 183 (799) at the age of 79. De Slane : Ibn Khall.

H.218. D.833. "the words[1] of the prince of the Faithful have reported truly *the tradition* from Hushaym. It was related to me by Auf al Aarabi[2] on the authority of al Hasan that the Prophet said, 'when a man marries a woman for her piety and beauty, it is a preventive (sided) against want.' Al Mamun was at the time lecturing, but sat up then and exclaimed, 'is sadad a mispronunciation, O Nadhr ?' I said, 'yes here, but undoubtedly a mispronunciation of Hushaym's, for he was an incorrect speaker.' He asked, 'what is the difference between the two ?' I answered, 'Sadad means, following a right course of action, and sided, what is necessary to support life and whatever thou mayest stop up a thing with.' He said, 'do the Arabs (*of the desert*) know this *distinction ?'* I replied 'yes, al Arji,[3] a descendant of Othman b. Affan, says as follows-

They have left me to perish and what a youth have they left to perish

One who could have helped them in an evil day or in the defence (sided) of a breach.'"

Al Mamun looked down for a little and then said, "the Lord confound those who have no education." After a little he said, "recite to me, O Nadhr the most captivating verse composed by the Arabs." I replied the lines of Ibn Baidh[4] one al Hakam b. Marwan.

---

1 Ibn Khall's version has here صدق يا امير المؤمنين هشيم and the Kitabul Aghani, (in the life of Hamzah b. Baidh) صدقوك يا امير المؤمنين without the mention of Hushyam.

2 Auf b. Abi Jamila sirnamed al Aarabi (the desert Arab) bore a fair reputation as a traditionist.

3 Abdullah b. Amr al Arji, a grandson of the Caliph Othman : his life extracted from as Suyuti's Sharb Shawahidul Mughni, is given by De Sacy in his Anthologic Grammaticale, p. 453. De Slane : Ibn Khall. A notice of him will also be found in the Kitabul Aghani.

4 Hamzah b. Baidh al Hanafi was one of the best poets of the Umayyad dynasty as well as one of the most licentious. He was a native of Kufah and eulogized al Muhallab and his son, also Aban b-ul Walid and the Kadhi Bilal b. Abi Burdah. He received large rewards from them. A long notice of him will be found in the Kitabul Aghani, where the verses in the text are also given. He did not live till the accession to power of the Abbaside dynasty.

A.H.218.
A.D.833.

"She says to me with sleepy eyes
Stay with us ; but I did not stay,
'Which of the chiefs hast thou visited ?' I said to her
'What chief but al Hakam !'
Whenever the two chamberlains[1] of his sent, say
'This is Ibn Baidh at the door,' he smiles :
Verily I paid in advance in regard to thee, as a pledge-
Come,[2] let him enter and give me my earnest money."

He continued-"recite to me the verse expressive of the greatest justice of conduct, which the Arabs have spoken." I repeated the lines of Ibn Arubah[3] of Medina-

"Verily, though the son of my uncle were to chide,
I would thrust away such as came behind and after him.
And my wealth[4] should aid him, even were he a man
Far remote in his land and sky.
And I should be the lord of his secret and preserve it
Until there seized me a yearning[5] for the time of its fulfillment.
And if misfortunes injured his camels at pasture
My healthy camels should join his afflicted with mange.
And were he to call me by name to ride a steed
That was refractory, I would sit on his back for him.
And were he to come on his way and on his own affairs
I would not look into what was behind his tent.
And were he to wear a handsome garment, I should not say

---

1 For حاجنا read حاجنا

2 The text and MS. are here in error. It should be as in the Kitabul Aghani
هات ادخلن ذاواعطني سلمي

3 For المديني read المدني as in the K.A. De Slane states that he was a traditionist of Basrah. Died A.H. 156.

4 For بصري read (as in the MS. and Kitabul Aghani) نضري

5 حتى يحيي علي Kitabul Aghani.

A.H.218. A.D.833. Would that upon me were the beauty of his mantle."

He said, "now recite to me a verse of the Arabs, most expressive of content." Upon which I quoted the lines of Ibn Abdal *Al Asadi*-

"Verily I am a man who continues (and that
By the favour of God) being well instructed, to teach polite learning.
I remain at home while home is free from disquiet to me,
And if I am far away, I am cheerful.
I grasp not at the friendship of a friend nor
Make my mind desire a thing after it hath passed away.
I seek myself what a generous man seeketh
Of the means of subsistence and am moderate in my desire *thereof.*
Verily I behold a generous man when
I seek a benefit of him, eager to grant it.
But the slave pursueth not what it lofty nor
Giveth ought to thee save in fear.
Like an ass, galled in the back[1] and vicious,
Which is good for nothing until it is beaten.
And I have found no firm stay[2] save
Religion, from what I have experienced, and nobility of race.
Verily he who stays tranquilty at home is nourished, who never
Hath bound pack or saddle on his camel.
While support of existence is withheld from the owner of the camel and pack.
And one who never ceases to travel."

---

1 The MS. and Kitabul Aghani have in the first hemistich مثل الحمار الموقّع السؤلا. The text is here is here in error. In the second hemistich the K.A. has يحمل for يحسن

2 عروة is the loop-shaped handle of the water skin and علاقة its suspensory thong.

Al Mamun exclaimed, "thou hast said well, O Nadhr !" He then took a piece of paper and wrote something I know not what : then he observed, "How do you form the imperative from *turab*?" (earth or dust). I said *"atrib,"*[1] *(cover him with earth or dust).* "And of *tin ?" (clay).* I said, *"tin" (plaster or seal up).* He went on, "what then would a writing be ?" I said *"mutrab*, (sprinkled with dust) or *matin,"* (plastered or sealed with clay). He exclaimed, "better and better," and he wrote for me an order for fifty thousand dirhams. Then he commanded an attendant to take me to al Fadhl b. Sahl, and I went with him and when al Fadhl read the writing, he exclaimed, "O Nadhr, didst thou charge the prince o the Faithful with a mispronunciation ?" I said, "by no means, but Hushaym spoke very incorrectly and the prince of the Faithful did but follow his words." Then he ordered me on his own account thirty thousand dirhams, thus I set forth for my house with eighty thousand." A.H.218. A.D.833 .

Al Khatib records on the authority of Muhammad b. Ziyad the desert Arab, that he relates as follows : "Al Mamun sent for me and I went to him, and he was in the garden walking with Yahya b. Aktham, and I saw the two moving with their faces turned from me, so I set down, and when they came forward, I arose and saluted him as Caliph and I heard him say to Yahya, 'O Abu Muhammad how good are his manners ! He saw us turned from him and sat down, and then seeing us advance, he arose and returned me my salutation." Then he aid, 'tell me regarding the verse of Hind the daughter of Utbah[2]

---

1 The text points the word "itrab," but the simple trilateral form ترب is intransitive and the transitive derived conjugation (IV.) is here meant (افعال) as is clear from Ibn Khallikan's narrative where after the words 'better and better,' al Mamun says boy, earth, him, and plaster him ياغلام اتربه و طنه The text has likewise erroneously "mutayyan for matin.

2 Wife of Abu Sufiyan and mother of Muạwiyah. The words were used by her on the day of Ohud, quoting proverbially the saying of az Zarka al Iyadhiyah when Kisrah warred with Iyadh. Lane gives the following version; نحن بنات طارق لانثني لوامق نمشي علي المارق We are the daughters of the morning star, we bend not to a love &c. Two other lines with variations of the others will be found in Ibn Hisham used by Hind as an encouragement to the youths going to battle at Ohud. إن تقبلوانعانق ان تدبرو انقارق If ye advance we shall embrace ye. If ye fly, we shall abandon ye.

A.H.218. A.D.833.

We are the daughters of Tarik
Moving upon cushion with the walk of the desert grouse.'

'Who is this' Tarik ? for I have looked in her pedigree and found him not.' I replied, 'O prince of the Faithful I do not know of him in her pedigree.' He answered 'assuredly she meant by it the star, claiming, descent from it on account of her beauty-according to the words of the Most High. "By the heavens and the nocturnal star.'" (Qu. LXXXVI.) I said, 'corroborate that *by proof,* O prince of the Faithful.' He rejoined, 'I know it perfectly well.' Then he threw to me a piece of amber which he was turning about in his hands and I sold it for five thousand dirhams."

And from Abu Ubadah[1] who says, that al Mamun, was one of the *greatest* sovereigns of the earth and that this title was justly due to him.

And from Ibn Abi Dauud that one of the schismatics came before al Mamun, and he said to him, "what induced thee to oppose us ?" He answered, "a verse of the Book of God." Al-Mamun said "and which is that ?" He replied, "the words of the Most High, 'and who so judgeth not according to what God hath revealed, they are infidels' (Qur. V)." The Caliph asked "hast thou any certain knowledge that this was revealed ?" He replied "Yes." "And what is thy proof?" "The consensus of the people." Al Mamun replied "then as thou art content with their agreement concerning the revelation, be content witht their unanimity in the interpretation thereof." The other said, "thou has spoken truly, peace be to thee. O prince of the Faithful."

Ibn Asakir records on the authority of Muhammad b. Mansur that al Mamun said, "one of the signs of a man of distinction is that he will ill-treat one who is above him, and will suffer one who is beneath him to ill-treat him." And from Said b. Muslim that al Mamun said, "I would that those who commit crimes were aware

1 Probably Abu Ubadah al Buhturi the poet, the friend and contemporary of Abu Tammam the author of the Hamasah : his life will be found in Ibn Khall.

of my conception of pardon, that fear might leave them and joy be unmixed in their hearts." And from Ibrahim b. Said al Jauhari, that a man stood before al Mamun who had committed a crime, and he said to him, "by Allah, I will slay thee !" He replied, "O prince of the Faithful at gently in regard to me for compassion is the half of mercy." He replied, "how can I ? now that I have sworn to slay thee." He answered, "it is better to meet God as a perjurer than to meet Him as a slayer,"-upon which al Mamun let him go his way. A.H.218. A.D.833.

Al-Khatib records from Abus Salt Abdus Salam bis Salih that he narrates as follows, "I passed the night with al Mamun and the attendant who used to trim the lamp went to sleep, and al Mamun arose and trimmed it and I heard him say, 'I am sometimes in the bath-room when the servants are reviling and traducing me, not knowing that I hear them but I forgive them.'" As Suli records on the authority of Abdullah b-ul Bawwab that he said, "al Mamun was so forbearing that he used to enrage us. On one occasion he sat cleaning his teeth behind a curtain on the banks of the Tigris and we were standing before him, when a boatman passed and said- 'do ye imagine that this al Mamun hath any worth in my eyes, when verily he hath put to death his own brother?'-and, by Allah, he did nothing more than smile and say to us, 'what contrivance have ye that I may have merit in the eyes of this excellent man?'"

Al Khatib merit on the authority of Yahya b. Akhtham that he narrates as follows, "I never knew a man more noble than al Mamun. I passed a night with him and he was seized with coughing and I saw him close him mouth with his sleeve, so that I might not awake, and he used to say that the beginning of equitable dealing is that a man should be just to his intimate friends, then to those who are nearest to them in succession, until he reaches the lowest grade."

Ibn Asakir records from Yahya b. Khalid al Barmaki that he relates, "Al Mamun said to me, O Yahya take every opportunity of satisfying the needs of men, for the heavens are too inconstant and fortune too unjust, to leave a man in one condition and continue unto him his enjoyments."

And from Abdullah b. Muhammad az Zuhri,-"al Mamun said,

A.H.218. A.D.833. 'superiority in argument is more pleasing to me than superiority of force, for superiority of force vanishes by its decay, while superiority in argument nothing can destroy.'" And from Utbi, "I heard al Mamun say, 'he who praiseth thee not for goodness of intention will not thank thee for excellence of deed.'" And from Abul Aaliyah, "I heard al Mamun say, 'how odious is contentiousness in monarchs, and more odious than that is vexation in judge, before comprehension *of what is before them,* and more odious than it, is the shallowness of jurisconsults in religion, and more odious still is avarice in the rich, jesting in old man, idleness in youths and cowardice in soldiers.'"

And from Ali b. Abdir Rahim al Marwazi, that al Mamun said, "he, of all men is most unjust to himself, who draweth near to one who keeps him at a distance, and abaseth himself before one who honoureth him not and receiveth the praise of one whom he doth not know." And from al Mukharik,[1] "I recited to al Mamun the words of Abul Atahiyah."

> "I am in need of the protection of a master.
> Who is compassionate and who is unruffled though I trouble him."

He said to me, "repeat it," and I repeated it seven time, whereupon he exclaimed, "O Mukharik, take the Caliphate from me and give me such a master."

And from Hudbah b. Khalid, "I was at breakfast with al Mamun, and when the table was taken away, I began to gather up what was on the ground, and al Mamun looked at me and said, 'hast thou not hat engouh ?' I replied, 'yes, but Hammad b. Salamah told me on the authority of Anas that he had heard the apostle of God say,-whose eateth what is under the table is secure from poverty :

---

1 He was one of the first singers of his time. He once sung in the presence of the Caliph ar Rashid who was so delighted, that he caused the curtains usually placed between himself and the musicians to be removed, and ordered him to draw near and sit on the throne by his side. He was afterwards attached to the service of al Mamun and accompanied him to Damascus. He died A.H. 230 (844-5) He was surnamed Abul Hina. De Slane, I.K.

whereupon he ordered me a thousand dinars.'" And from al Hasan b. Abdus as Saffar (*the brazier*), that when al Mamun married Buran, the daughter of al Hasan b. Sahl, the people sent presents to al Hasan, and a poor man sent him two wallets in one of which was salt and in the other glasswort and wrote to him at the same time, *saying,* "May I be sacrificed for thee-these goods of little worth fall short of the extent of my desire, but I was unwilling that the scroll of the beneficent should be folded up and no mention of my name within it, therefore have I sent unto thee what is commenced with,[1] on account of the auspiciousness and blessing of it, and what is concluded with, by reason of its goodness and cleansing properties." Al Hasan took the two wallets and went with them to al Mamun, who was pleased thereat and ordered them to be emptied and filled with dinars. As Suli records on the authority of Muhammad b-ul Kasim that he had heard al Mamun say, "by Allah, I delight in pardon to such an extent, that I fear I may not be rewarded on account of it, and if men knew the extent of my love of pardoning, they would come to me guilty of crimes." A.H.218. A.D.833 .

Al Khatib records on the authority of al Mansur al Barmaki, that ar Rashid possessed a slave girl whom al Mamun loved, and once while she was pouring out water for ar Rashid from a vessel she held, al Mamun who was behind him, made a sign of a kiss to her, and she reproved him with her eyebrows and delayed in pouring out the water. Harun looked at her and said, "what is this?" and she faltered in her answer to ar Rashid. Whereupon he said-"if thou dost not tell me, I will certainly put thee to death." She replied, "Abdullah made a sign to me of a kiss." Harun looked towards him, and lo! shame and fear so fell upon him that it made Harun take pity on him, and he embraced him and said, "dost thou love her?" He said, "Yes." He answered, "rise and take her into that room."

And, he arose and as he went, ar Rashid said to him, 'say a verse on this' and he recited-

1 The Arabs beginning their meals by tasting salt and using glasswort to was their hands with.

A.H.218.
A.D.833.

"A gazelle, I hinted with my glance
As to my feelings to her.[1]
I kissed her from afar,
But she made excuses with her lips,
And returned the best of answers
By the contraction of her eye-brows.
But I did not quit my place
Before I obtained possession of her."

Ibn Asakir records on the authority of Abu Kahlifah al Fadhl b. Habab, that he narrates, "I heard a slave dealer say as follows 'I showed a slave girl to al Mamun, skilled in versifying, eloquent, well-bred and a good chess-player, and I asked of him a thousand dinars as her price, and he said, "if she can cap a verse I will recite to her by a verse of her own, I will purchase her for what thou askest, and will give thee over and above the bargain," and al Mamun recited-

'What wilt thou say regarding one whom sleeplessness hath emaciated

Through the strength of his love for thee, so that he became distracted.'

And she capped it thus-

'When I find a lover whom hath smitten
The sickness of love, I will show him kindness.'"

As Suli from al Husayn al Khalii that he narrates as follows, "when al Mamun was angered with me and stopped my stipend, I composed a poem wherein I praised him and gave it to one who coveyed it to him."

The beginning of it is-

"Reward me, for I thirst for the promise :
When wilt thou fulfil the promise confirmed by vow ?

---

1 The pronoun is here in the masculine, the reason of which has been before explained.

I fly to thee for protection from the breach of faith of princes, and verily thou seest. A.H.218. A.D.833.

That I die for love of thee.

Will he who is incomparable in goodness, grudge me

A slender gift ? and verily I alone have give him an incomparable love." &c., until he says-

"The Lord found Abdullah the best of His servants,

And he gave him sovereignty and God knoweth His servants best.

Now surely al Mamun is a defence unto his people

Distinguishing between error and right guidance."

"Al Mamun observed 'verily he hath done well, save that he is the author of the following :

'O mine eyes ! rain abundantly and weep over Muhammad *(al-Amin)*

And spare not thy tears over him and give your aid.

May public affairs fail of success after Muhammad

And the unity of the kingdom not cease to be divided.

May al Mamun not enjoy the kingdom after him.

And not cease to be an exile in the world and a fugitive.'

This then is against the other and I have nothing for him." The chamberlain said, "where, then, is the prince of the Faithful's practice of pardon ?" He replied, "well as to that, why yes," and he ordered him a present and retored to him his stipend.

And from 'Ulayyah Hammad b. Ishak, that when al Mamun went to Baghdad, he held inquiry into wrongful exactions every day until noon. And from Muhammad b-ul Abbas, that al Mamun was very fond of chess and used to say, "this sharpens the intellect," and he originated some moves in it. He used to say, "I will never hear any one say, 'come let us play,'-but, 'let us fall on, let us press one another.'" However he did not excel in it, and he would exclaim,

A.H.218. "I have the administration of the world and am equal to it, whereas
A.D.833. I am straitened in the ordering of a space two spans by two spans."

And from Ibn Abi Sai'd, that Dibil[1] satirized al Mamun saying :

"I belong to the same tribe as those whose swords

Slew thy brother and raised thee to the throne.

They exalted thy fame after its long abasement

And drew thee forth from the depth of thy degradation."

When al Mamun heard it, he did no more than say "what little shame hath Dibil ! when was I obscure who indeed have been reared in the lap of Caliphs ?" and he did not punish him. As Suli states also from various source that al Mamun used to drink date-wine. And on the authority of Jahidh, that the associates of al Mamun used to assert that the colour of his face and of his body was the same except his legs which were yellow as if anointed with saffron.

And from Ishak of Mosul, that al Mamun said, "the sweetest of songs is that which, the hearer, whether it be well or ill sung, rejoiceth over. And from 'Ali bil Husayn that Muhammad b. Hamid[2] was standing over al Mamun while he was drinking, when Gharib broke forth and sang a verse of an Nabighah al Jaadis.-

---

1 Abu Ali Dibil b. Ali Khuzaai, was a good poet, but addicted to satire and scurrility, always ready to slander men of merit, not sparing even the Caliphs. Ibrahim b-ul Mahdi was so irritated at one of his cutting verses, that he complained to al Mamun who counselled him to put up with it in silence as he himself had done in regard to the lines quoted in the text which are given by Ibn Khall. Dibil was born A.H. 148, and died at Tib near Wasit A.H. 246. Ibn Khall. His life will also be found in the Kitabul Aghani.

2 De Slane in a note to the life of Abu Tammam mentions a Muhammad b. Hamid at Tusi, a son of one of al Mamun's principal generals who fell in battle against Babak al Khurrami in Adarbijan A.H. 214. He is mentioned as renowned for his liberality and that his death gave great pain to al Mamun. It is probably the same person, the accent on the name being misplaced in one or other version.

"Like the hem of the striped garment of Yaman." Whereupon al Mamun suspected that she did not begin without a reason and the company were silent. He therefore said, "may I be repudiated by ar Rashid ! but if I am not told truly regarding this, I will cause *the culprit* to confess with grievous blows and will punish him heavily, but if I am told the truth, I will forward the true speaker's desire." Whereupon Muhammad b. Hamid replied, "my lord, I made signs of a kiss to her." He rejoined, "now comes the truth, thou hast spoken truly, dost thou wish that I should marry thee to her?" He answered, "yes," Then al Mamun said, "praise be to God the Lord of all creatures, and may God bless our chief Muhammad and his offspring-verily I give in marriage unto Muhammad the son of Hamid, my freedwoman Gharib and I assign her as a dowry from him four hundred dirhams with the blessing of God and by the ordiance of the Prophet. Take her hand," and she arose with him. Then al Muatasim went to the threshold and said to Ibn Hamid, "the brokerage !" He replied, "it is thine"-The other said-"my brokerage is that she mout sing to me during the night." And she continued to sing to him till the morning and Ibn Hamid at the door. Then she arose, took his hand and departed with him. And from Ibn Abi Dauud, that the Roman Emperor sent a present to al Mamun of two hundred pounds of musk and two hundred skins of sable, and al Mamun said, "double the gift, for him that he may know the splendour of Islam." And from Ibrahim b. ul Hasan that al Madaini told al Mamun that Muawiyah said, "the Banu Hashim are lions and swift to wrath, but we are more numerous in chiefs." Al Mamun replied, "verily he hath made an admission and adduced a claim ; he is therefore, in his claim, a plaintiff, and in his admission a defendant." A.H.218. A.D.833 .

As Suli likewise records on the authority of Abu[1] Usamah that he narrates as follows,-"one of my companions told me that Ahmad

1 The MS. has Ibn Abi Usamah, of which name there are two, at Tamimi, a traditionist and al Halabi, a disciple, of the poet an Nami. Abu Usamah Junadah was a philologer of distinction who died A.H. 399.

A.H.218. b. Abi Khalid[1] was once reading stories to al Mamun and said, "a
A.D.833. certain at Tharidi"[2] (it being al Yazidi) and al Mamun laughed and called out Ho! Page, bring some food to Abu al Abbas for verily he is hundrey'-and he was ashamed and said, 'I am not hungry but the author of the story is a dunce, for he has pointed the *ya (ي)* with the points of the *th (ث)*.' Al Mamun exclaimed, 'never mind.' And they brought food and he eat until he had done. Then he went on and came to the story of a certain al Hamsi, instead of which he said, al Khabisi[3] whereupon al Mamun laughed and called out, 'ho! boy, a dish of Khabis,' Ahmad said, 'verily the author of the story was a fool, for he hath made an open mim (م), and it is as, if there were two dots.' Al Mamun laughed and said, 'were it not for the incorrectness of those two words, thou wouldst have remained hungry.'"

And from Abu Abbad that he said, "I do not think that God ever created a disposition more excellent than that of al Mamun nor one more generous, and it truth he was aware of the gluttony of Ahmad b. Abi Khalid, so that whenever he sent him on any business, he gave him his breakfast before he sent him. It was represented to him in a case that if he, the prince of the Faithful, saw fit to settle some provision upon Ibn Abu Khalid, *it would be well,* as he was in the habit of favouring the more powerful party for the sake of his entertainment, wherefore al Mamun settled upon him a thousand dirhams a day for his table, yet notwithstanding, he would desire greedily to eat at the expense of thers. 'Dibil the poet has said regarding this-

"We thank the Caliph for the settlement
Of a maintenance upon the son of Abu Khalid.

---

1 Ahmad b. Abi Khalid al Ahwal was vizier to al Mamun and al Muatasim, succeeding al Fadhl b. Suhl in that post. He was a man of great intelligence and foresight and expressed himself elegantly in speech. He died A.H. 240. See De Slane's correction of D'Herbelot's error regarding this Wazir. Vol. I, p. 20.

2 Tharid signifies sliced bread in milk or broth with meat.

3 Khabis is a kind of sweetmest.

Thus he hath restrained his tyranny over the Muslims A.H.218.
And given him his occupation at home." A.D.833.

And from Ibn Abi Dauud,[1] "I heard al Mamun say to a man whether thy conduct be marked with perfidy or with token of good, I will not hold thee responsible for either ; thou wilt not cease to do evil, and I to do good, and thou to be in fault and I to forgive until it shall be pardon itself that shall amend thee.'" And from al Jahidh that Thumamah b-ul Ashras[2] said, "I have never seen any one more eloquent than Jaafar b. Yahya al Barmaki and al Mamun."

As Silafi records in the Tuyyuriyat on the authority of Hafs al Madiani, that a negro who pretended to the gift of prophecy was brought before al Mamun and said, "I am Moses the son of Imran," and al Mamun said to him, "verily Moses the son of Imran drew forth his hand from his bosom white, therefore draw forth thy hand white, that I may believe in thee." The negro replied, "surely that was done by Moses when Pharaoh said to him, 'I am thy most High God.' Therefore say as Paraoh said, that I may draw out my hand white, otherwise it will not become white." Also that al Mamun said, "a revolt has never broken out against me, but I found the cause of it in the tyranny of the prefects." Ibn Asakir records on the authority of Yahya b Aktham, that al mamun used to preside at a disputation on questions of Jursiprudence every Tuesday, and there came a man wearning a garment which he had tucked up, and holding his shoes in his hand and he stopped on the border of the carpet and said "peace be to you." Al Mamun returned his salutation and the other said, 'tell me regarding this seat which

---

1 I am of opinion that this name should be Ibn Abi Dauud, the Kadhi who died in 240 A.H. Ibn Abi Dauud the Hafidh died in 316. It is scarcely probable that he could have heard and remembered speeches of al Mamun's in 218.

2 Abu Maan Thumamah b-ul Ashras surnamed al Majin or the licentions for his disorderly life. Al Mamun met him once in the street in a state of intoxication and said to him, "is it you Thumamah ?" "Yes!" "Are you drunk ?" No. "Do you know me?" "Yes." "Who am I ?" "I don't know." This threw the Caliph into such a fit of laughter that he nearly fell off his horse. He died A. H. 213. De Slane, I.K.

A.H.218. thou occupiest-dost thou sit there[1] with the unanimous consent of
A.D.833. the people or by violence and force ?" He replied, "neither the one nor the other, but one who governed the affairs of the Muslims bequeathed it to me and to my brother, and when the authority devolved upon me, I felt that I needed the unanimous consent of the Muslims in the east and the west in accepting me, but I saw that if I abandoned the government, the security of Islam would be disturbed, and their affairs fall into confusion, and that they would contend in strife one with another, so that holy wars and pilgrimages would be neglected, and the hightways infested with robbers, wherefore I arose in defence of the Muslims, until they should be of accord upon one man whom they should approve, and I would then resign the government to him : now when they agree upon a man, I will abdicate in his favour." The man replied, "peace be to you and the mercy of God and his blessing," and he departed. And from Muhammad b.ul Mundir al Kindi, that ar Rashid, being upon the pilgrimage entered Kufah and summoned the Traditionists, and none stayed away but Abdullah b. Idris, and Isa b. Yunas. He sent al Amin and al Mamun to them, and Idn Idris related to them one hundred traditions, and al Mamun said, "O uncle ! Suffer me to repeat them by heart." He answered, "do so," and he repeated them and Ibn Idris marveled at his memory. Some author states that al Mamun took away books of philosophy and works of Greeian writers from the island of Cyprus. This much ad Dahabi briefly narrates. Al Fakahi says that the first who covered the Kaabah with white brocade was al Mamun, and this continued to be the custom after him till the time of the Caliph an Nasir, save when Mahmud the son of Sabaktagin durng the interval, covered it with yellow brocade.

The following are among the sayings of al Mamun. "There is no pleasure greater than that of observing the intellects of men. Stratagem is of no avail to turn back an affair when it advances, or to advance it where it is retrogressing. The best of conference is where one gets an insight into men. Men are of three classes.

---

1 I prefer to read, جلسته as in the MS. for جلسة

Those who are as nourishment, necessary under all circumstances; those who are like medicine, necessary on occasion of sickness, and those who are like disease, hateful under every condition. The answer of none has ever embarrassed me, as he answer of a man of the people of Kufah embarrassed me, whom its inhabitants sent to me and he complained against their governor. I replied, "hou liest, for he is a just man." He said, "the prince of the Faithful hath spoken truly and I have exclusion of other cities, now appoint him to another city that he may encompass them with his equity and justice as he hath encompassed us." I said, "rise, and be off, verily I shall remove him from over you." A.H.218. A.D.833 .

The following are among the lines of al Mamun "

"My tongue concealeth your secrets
And my tell-tale tear is an informer of my secret.
Were it not for my tears, I should conceal my love,
Yet were it not for love, I should have no tears."

And on chess-

"A square field of red-dressed leather
Between too friends known for generosity ;
They call war to mind and invent stratagems therein,
Without being guilty of shedding blood there.
This one attacks that, and that
Falls upon this, and they eye of caution sleepeth not.
See then the ingenious *foes* moving with skill
Among two armies without drum or banner."

As Suli records on the authority of Muhammad b. Amr, that Asram b. Humayd[1] presented himself before al Mamun with whom was al Muatasim, and the Caliph said "describe me and my brother and give no preference to either over his fellow ;" whereupon he versified after a little :

1 This individual is mentioned in Ibn Khall's life of Abdullah b. Tahir, as the author of some verses quoted, but no other information is given of him.

A.H.218. A.D.833.

"I saw a ship sailing upon a sea,
Towards two seas, beyond which are other seas,
Towards two prince whose splendours both,
Are equal, at whom the beholder is confounded.
They are two Princes ; this resembles that,
And that this, and that and this are chiefs ;
If this were that and that this
In this and that together would be my delight.
A canopy of glory is extended over the one
And the face of the other is a shining moon."

Traditions related on the authority of al Mamun.

Al Bayhaki mentions on the authority of Jaafar b. Abi Othman at Tayalisi that he relates as follows, "I was praying the afternoon prayer at ar Rusafah behind al Mamun in the enclosed space of the mosque on the day of Arafah, and when he pronounced the salutation the people responded with the Takbir, and I saw al Mamun behind the railing exclaiming, "no, O people ! no O people ! tomorrow is the day prescribed by Abul Kasim (*Muhammad*)." And when the day of Adha (10th *dul Hijjah*) arrived, I went forth to prayers and he ascended the tribune and praised God and glorified Him and said, "God is exceeding great, and frequent be the praise of God, and I extol the perfections of God morning and evening !" Hushaym b. Bushayr related to me on the authority of Abu Burdah b. Dinar that the apostle of God said, "he who performeth sacrifice before he prayeth, assuredly it is a flesh offering which he hath anticipated before its time, but who so performeth sacrifice after he hath prayed, verily he fulfilleth the ordianace. God is exceeding great, and frequent be the praise of God and I extol the perfections of God morning and evening. O Lord, amend me and seek to render me virtuous, and amend others through me." Al Hakim says, "I have copied this tradition only from Abu Ahmad who is in my opinion

a trustworthy authority, and it continued to occupy my thoughts A.H.218.
until I mentioned it to Abul Hasan ad Darakutni who observed, A.D.833.
'this relation is, in my opinion, soudly transmitted from Jaafar'. I said, 'does any corroborative authority follow our Shaykh Abu Ahmad in this?' He said, 'yes' and recited a tradition from the Wazir Abul Fadhl Jaafar b-ul Furat through Jaafar at Tayalisi to Yahya b. Main[1] who said that he had heard al Mamun and mentioned the discourse and the tradition."

As Suli states the Yahya b. Main says as follows : "Al Mamun preached to us at Baghdad on a Friday which happened to coincide with the day of Arafah, and when he came to the salutation, the people shouted the Takbir, but he disapproved of the Takbir and he leaped up and seized the wooden rail of the enclosure and said, 'O people, this Takbir should not be said out of its place. I have heard from Hushaym on the authority of Ibn 'Abbas that the apostle of God used to continue the Talbiyat until he had thrown stones at the Jamrat[2] ul Akabah, and the Takbir was pronounced on the morrow at midday at the close of the Talibiyat, if God so willeth."

And that Ibrahim al Mosuli says, "we were with al Mamun when a man stood before him and said, 'O prince of the Faithful,

---

1 Abu Zakariya Yahya b. Main was a native of Baghdad, a celebrated Hafidh and noted for the exactitude of his traditional information. On his death, he left one hundred and thirty cases and four water-jar stands filled with looks. Ahmad b. Hanbal used to declare that any tradition unknown to Ibn Main was not a true tradition, and that he was created for the express purpose of exposing false ones. He said of himself that he had written quantities of traditions under the dictation of liars and made use of the paper for heating his oven. I thus obtained, he added, one advantage that of having bread well-baked. He died A.D. 233.

2 Vulgarly called the Shaytanul Kabir or Great Devil. Another pillar is the Wusta or central place of stoning built in the middle of Muna and there is a third at the eastern and called al Ula. These mark the successive spots where the devil in the shape of an old Shaykh appeared to Adam, Abraham and Ishmael and was driven back by the throwing of stones, of size of a bean, as enjoined by Gabriel. This Jamratul Akabah is a dwarf buttress of masonry about 8 feet high by 2½ placed, against a rough wall of stones at the Meccan entrance to Muna. Burton's Mecca, p. 282.

A.H.218. A.D.833. the apostle of God said-creatures are the household of God, and the most pleasing of the servants of God unto God (may He be honored and glorified) is he who most profiteth His household.' Al Mamun cried out and said, 'be silent, I am more learned in tradition than thou art : Yusuf b. Atiah, the brazier told me on the authority of Thabit b. Anas that the Prophet said- creatures are the household of God, and the most pleasing of the servants of God unto God, is he who most profiteth His household.'"[1] Ibn 'Asakir records this by the same ascription.

As Suli also mentions that he had heard a tradition on the authority of Abdul Jabbar b. Abdullah who relates-" I heard al Mamun preaching and he spoke in his discourse of modesty and he described and praised it and said, 'Hushaym told me on the authority of Abu Bakrah[2] and Imran b. Husayn that the apostle of God said- modesty is a part of faith and fiath hath its portion in Paradise, while obscenity is brutishness, and brutishness hath its portion in hell fire.'" Al Hakim mentions on the authority of Yahya b. Aktham the Kadhi, that he says as follows- "Al Mamun said to me one day, 'O Yahya, I wish to relate traditions." I replied, 'and who is fitter for this than the prince of the Faithful ?" He said, 'let them place a tribune for me,' and he ascended it and the first tradition he gave us was through Hushaym from Abu Hurayrah that the Prophet said-'Imrul Kays is the leader of the poets in hell :' then he related about thirty traditions and afterwards descended and said, 'O Yahya what dost thou think of our lecture ?' I replied, 'a most excellent lecture, O prince of the Faithful thou hast instructed high and low.' He answered, 'no ! thy life ! I observed no pleasure that you took in it : a lecture is for men with thread-bare garments and ink-horns."

Al Khatib says that he was told on the authority of Ibrahim b.

---

1 The parenthetical sentence of the first speaker was apparently an incorrect transmission.

2 Abu Bakrah Nufai b-ul Harith was a companion of Muhammad's, who named him Abu Bakrah or the father of the pulley, because he let himself down by a pulley from the castle of Taif when it was attached by the Muslims in A.H. S. Imran b. Husayn al Khuzaai was also a Companion, became Kadhi of Basrah and died there A.H. 53. De Slane : I.K.

Sai'd al Jauhari that when al Mamun conquered Egypt, a person said to him, "praise be to God, O prince of the Faithful who hath sufficed thee against thy enemies, and subjugated to thee the two Iraks and the Syrian provinces and Egypt and withal thou art the descendant of the uncle of the apostle of God." Al Mamun replied,[1] "well said, now there is one condition still wanting to me, and that is, that I should sit in an assembly and below me a disciple who should say 'whom didst thou mention, may the Lord be well pleased with thee ?' and I should reply-the two Hammads, Hammad b. Salamah and Hammad b. Zayd[2] narrated to me on the authority of Anas b. Malik that the Prophet said, 'he who supporteth two daughters or three or two sisters, until they die, or he is taken from them by death, shall be with me in Paradise like these two', and he pointed to his fore and middle fingers. Al Khatib remarks that there is a glaring error in this story and he suppose it probable that al Mamun related his on the authority of some person who had it from the two Hammads, and that, because the birth of al Mamun occurred in the year 170, and Hammad the son of Salamah died in the year 167, three years before al Mamun was born, and Hammad b. Zayd died in the year 179."

A.H.218.
A.D.833 .

Al Hakim mentions that he was told on the authority of Muhammad b. Sahl b. Askar that he narrates as follows : "Al Mamun one day stood waiting for the call to prayers and we were standing before him, when there came up to him a stranger with an ink-horn in his hand, who said, 'O prince of the Faithful, I am a master of tradition, devoted to it." Al Mamun said, 'what dost thou remember on such and such an article?' and he could not mention a word about it, while a Mamun continued, 'Hushaym told me who had it from Hajjaj, who had it from such and such a one &c., until he mentioned the article, then he questioned him on a second article,

---

1 For فقالت read فقال

2 Abu Ismail Hammad b. Zayd surnamed al Azrak (blue-eyed) a native of Basrah who receive his knowledge from the first doctors of his age under some of whom his namesake b. Salamah studied. He held a high repute as a jurist, traditionsit and Hafidh died A.H. 179. D. Slane I.K.

A.H.218. A.D.833. and he could not say a word about it, and al Mamun gave it and then turning to his companions said, 'one of these searches for traditions for three days and then says-I am a traditionist. Give him three dirhams."

Ibn Asakir quotes from Yahya b. Aktham as follows : "I passed a night with a Mamun and I awoke in the middle of the night, being thirsty and I tossed about and al Mamun said, 'Yahya, what is the matter with thee?' I replied, 'I am thirsty.' He leaped up from his couch and brought me a goglet of water. I said, 'O prince of the Faithful, with thou not call a servant ? wilt thou not summon a page? He replied, 'no my father told me on the authority of Ukbah b. Aamir that the apostle of God said, 'the chief of the people is their servant.'[1] Al Khatib mentions a similar tradition from Yahya b. Akhtham save that he traces it up to Jarir b. Abdullah who heard the apostle of God say, "the chief of the people is their servant." Ibn Asakir gives the ascription of a tradition through Abu Hudayfah of Bukhara and al Mamun to Ibn Abbas that the Prophet said, "the prince of a people is of them."

Muhammad b. Kudamah states that it reached al Mamun that Abu Hudayah related this tradition on his authority, whereupon he ordered ten thousand dirhams to be given to him. During the reign of al Mamun the descendants of al Abbas were numbered and they were thirty-three thousand males and females and that in the year 200 A.H.

Of people of note who died in his time were, Sufiyan b. Uaynah, the Imam as Shafii, Abdur Rahman b. Mahdi, Yahya b. Said al Kattan (*the cotton-spinner*), Yunas b. Bukayr the historian of the wars, Abu Matii al Balkhi the disciple of Abu Hanifah, Maruf al Karkhi the devotee, Ishak b. Bashr, author of the Kitabul Mubtada, Ishak b-ul Furat Kadhi of old Cairo one of the most eminent of the disciples of Malik, Abu Amr as Shaybani, the philologer, Ashhab the disciple of Malik, al Hasan b. Ziyad al Lului disciple of Abu Hanifah, Hammad b. Usamah the Hafidh, Ruh b. Ubadah, az Zayd

---

1 Compare Matt. xx. 27. Luke xxii. 26.

b-ul Habab, Abu Dauud at Tayalisi, al Ghazi b. Kays one of Malik's disciples, Abu Sulayman ad Darani, the famous devotee, Ali ar Ridha b. Musa al Kadhim, al Fara the great master of the Arabic language, Kutaybah b. Mihran author of the Imalah, Kutrub the grammarian, al Wakidi, Abu Ubaydah, Maamar b-ul Muthanna, an Nadhr b. Shumayl, as Sayyidat Nafisah, Hisham, one of the grammarians of Kufah, al Yazidi, Yazid b. Harun, Yakub b. Ishak al Hadhrami the Qurãn reader of Basrah, Abdur Razzak, Abul Atahiyah the poet, Asadus Sunnat, Abu Aasim an Nabil, al Faryabi[1] Abdul Malik b-ul Majishun, Abdullah b-ul Hakam, Abu Zayd al Ansari the professor of Arabic philology, Al Asmai and others. A.H.218. A.D.833.

AL MUATASIM BILLAH

Al Muatasim Billah, Abu Ishak Muhammad the son of ar Rashid was born in the year 180, so says ad Dahabi, but according to as Suli, in the year. 178. His mother was a slave concubine of Kufah of foreign extraction : her name was Maridah,[2] and she held in the highest favour by ar Rashid. He related traditions on the authority of his father and his brother al Mamunm and Ishak of Mosul and Hamdun b. Ismail and others related them on his. He was a brave man, of great personal strength and of high spirit, but destitute of education. As Suli relates on the authority of Ibrahim b. Muhammad al Hashimi that there was a page studying at the *same* school with al Muatasim. The page died, and al Muatasim's father, ar Rashid, said to him, "Muhammad thy page is dead." He replied, "yes, my lord, and is at rest from school." Ar Rashid exclaimed, "is this what school gets from thee ? (*turning to his attendants)* let him alone,

1 The text has incorrectly Faryani. His name was Muhammad b. Yusuf b. Wakid b. Abdillah ad Dhabbi, and he was one of the Traditionists of Bukhars. "Ibnul Athir."

2 According to Masaudi, she was the daughter of Shabib ; no other particular is given.

A.H.218. A.D.833. do not teach him." "Ibrahim," he adds "therefore, used to write and to read but indifferently."

Ad Dahabi says that al Muatasim would have been one of the greatest and most awe-inspiring of the Caliphs were it not for the inquisition of the learned regarding the creation of the Qurãn which has left a stain upon his glory. Niftawayh and as Suli say that al Muatasim had many good qualities, and he was called the Octonary because he was the eighth Caliph of the house of Abbas, and the eighth in descent from 'Abbas, the eighth of the children of ar Rashid, succeeded to the government in the year 218, reigned eight years and eight months and eight days, his birth occurred in 178, he lived forty-eight years. His horoscope was the Scorpion which is the eighth sign of the Zodiac, he was victorious in eight expeditions, slew eight of his enemies, left eight male and the same number of female children, and he died in the month of Rajab I, eight nights thereof still remaining unelapsed.[1] Many laudable actions are ascribed to him, and some eloquent saying and tolerate verses, but when he was enraged, he was reckless in the destruction of life.

Ibn Abi Duad[2] says, "al Muatasim would put out his arm to me and say, 'Abdullah ! bite my arm with all your force;' I would decline and he would say, 'it will not hurt me,' and I would try it, but, lo the points of spears would make no impression upon it much less teeth." Niftawayh observes that he was one of the most powerful of men in bodily strength and would take a man's elbow between his fingers and break it. Others remark that he was the first of the Caliphs to introduce Turks into offices of state. He affected to imitate the Persian monarchs and to adopt their manners; his Turkish slaves amounted to over ten thousand.

Ibn Yunas says that Dibil satirized al Muatasim ; subsequently fearing its consequences he became terrified and fled until he reached Egypt. Afterwards he proceeded to Mauritania. The verses in which he satirized him were these :

---

1 In another account he had also 8,000 slaves and 8 millions of gold.

2 Not Dauud as in the text.

"The kings of the sons of 'Abbas in history are seven, A.H.218. A.D.833 .
And history doth not show us an eighth among them.
So the people of the cave[1] in the cave were seven.
On the morn they took up their abode therein and the eighth was a dog.
And verily I hold their dog in greater esteem than thee,
For thou art a man of sin, and it was sinless.[2]
And verily the affairs of the people have been ruined since there ruled over them
Wasif and Ashnas, and afflictions have increased.
And verily I hope that there will be seen after their setting
The risings of a sun through which thou mayst be straitened.
And thy heart's desire is a despicable[3] Turk
To whom thou art a father and a mother.

He was acknowledged as Caliph in sucession to al Mamun in the month of Rajab in the year 218. He followed the course adopted by al Mamun in regard to questioning the people on the creation of the Qurãn and continued in it to the end of his life. He wrote to the provinces on the subject, and commanded the teachers to instruct the children accordingly, and the people suffered much tribulation on the account, and he put to death many of the learned therefore, and he scourged the Imam Ahmad b. Hanbal whose scourging took place in the year 220.

During the same al Muatasim removed from Baghdad and founded Surra man raa, and this because he was solicitous to enlist Turks *in his service.* Wherefore he sent into Samakand, Farghanah and the adjacent countries to purchase them and lavished wealth upon them and clothed them in various kinds of brocade and belts

---

1 The seven sleepers.

2 Or tailless, a pun intended. In the first half of this line the Kitabul Aghani (ar, Dibil, fol. 18), has واني لاعلي كلبهم عنك رفعة The last tow lines are not in the K.A.

3 For مهابة read مهانة as in the MS.

A.H.218. of gold. And they used to gallop their horses through Baghdad and
A.D.833. harass the people, and the city was reduced to extremities through them. Then the people of Baghdad assembled round al Muatasim and said, "if thou goest not forth from among us with thy troops, we will attack thee," and he said "how will ye attak me?" They replied "with the arrow of enchantments." He replied, "I have no power against that." And this was the cause of his founding Surra man raa and his removal to it.

In the year 223 al Muatasim led an expedition against the Byzantines and slaughtered[1] them with a great slaughter, the like of which hath not been heard of under any other Caliph. He dispersed their collected troops and ravaged their country and carried Amorium[2] by the sword, massacreing therein thirty thousand and taking a like number captive. When he was engaged in the preparation for its attack, the astrologers pronounced that the aspect of the stars was sinister, and that he would be defeated, but it proved amongst his most conspicuous victories and successes. It was upon this subject that Abu Tammam[3] wrote his well known poem which runs thus :

"The sword is more truthful in prophecy than documents,
In its edge, a sharpness between earnest and jest.
And divination lies in the flaming fires of glittering lances
Between the set battalions, not in the seven planets.
Where now is their fabling-and where *the predictions* of the stars and all
The fictions and falsehood they fabricated !
Delusion and lying asseverations

---

1 The MS. has فانكافيهم the text فانكاهم but this verb does not possess the 4th conjugation. I would therefore emend as follow فنكاهم.

2 For the name and site of Amorium. See Gibbon, Cap. LII.

3 Abu Tammam Habib the celebrated poet and author of the Hamasah. His life will be found in Ibn Khall. He died at Mosal about A.H. 231. (845-6) Consult also Kitab al Aghani, Fol. 15, p. 99.

That come not to fulfillment[1] when computed, nor is it strange." A.H.227. A.D.842.

Al Muatasim died on Thursady the 19th of Rabii I , 227, (5th *January 842)*. He had in truth humbled his enemies round about, and it is said that he exclaimed in his last sickness-"Until while they were rejoicing for that which had been given to them, we suddenly laid hold on them." (Qur. VI.) And when death was night at hand he began to say, "artifice is exhausted and there is no evading (*death*)." It is related also that he began to say, "I have been taken from among this people" and it is also said that he exclaimed, "O God, verily thou knowest that I fear Thee on my own account and I do not fear Thee in respect of Thyself, and I hope in Thee in respect of Thee, and I do not hope in Thee from my deserts."

Among his verses are the following –

"Bring my steed and be quick, page,
And place the saddle and bridle upon him.
Tel! the Turks that I am about to plunge into
The sea of death, then let who will, arise."

He had purposed marching to the uttermost parts of the west to conquer the proviness which had not come under the authority of the House of 'Abbas on account of the occupation of them by the Umayyads, for as Suli narrates that al Muatasim said, "the sons of Umayyah ruled and none of us had any territory, and now we have authority and yet this Umayyad holds Andalusia, for them." He therefore appointed what was necessary for the expedition, and made due arrangements, but his sickness increased and he died. As Suli states that he had heard al Mughirah b. Muhammad observe that it was stated that kings were never gathered together at the court of any one in such numbers as in the court of al Muatasim, and that no monarch had ever made conquests like his, for he took prisoner the king of Adarbijan, the king of Tabaristan,

1 The MS. has نبغ for ينبغ

A.H.227. A.D.842. the kind of Astisan, the king o Ashyasih,[1] the king of Farghanah, the king of Astisan, the king of Takharistan, the king of Suffah and the king of Kabul." As Suli also states that the impression on his signet ring was-"Praise be to God who hath no like."

Regarding personal accounts of al Muatasim, as Suli records on the authority of Ahmad al Yazidi that when al Muatasim had finished the building of his palace in the plain and held audience within it, the people came to him and Ishak of Mosul wrote a poem on it, the like of which in beauty no one had heard, save that he began it with these words-

"O mansion ! misfortune hath altered and defaced thee :
Would that I knew what[2] hath afflicted thee !"

And al Muatism and the people took an ill omen at this and they looked at each other and wondered, *saying,* "how hath this happened with Ishak with his penetration and intelligence and long attendance upon kings." After this al Muatasim destroyed the palace. He also records on the authority of Ibrahim b-ul Abbas that when al Muatasim discoursed, he attained whatever he desired to effect and even went beyond it. He was the first who was bountiful in his table and increased *its expenses* till they reached the sum of one thousand dinars a day. And from Abu Uaynab, "I heard al Muatasim say 'when passion is in the ascendant, reason is dulled.' And from Ishak, that al Muatasim used to say, 'he who seeketh the truth with all its duties and responsibilities, is sure to attain to it.' And from Muhammad b. Omar ar Rumi, "al Muatasim had a page called Ajib, the like of whom men had never seen, and to whom he was attached, and he composed some verses on him and then summoned me, and said, 'thou knowest that I am inferior to my brothers in polite learning on account of the affection of the prince

---

1 The MS. has "Ashyah," which is mentioned by Yakut as the name of a lofty and impregnable fort in the mountains of Yaman. Astisan and Suffah are unnoticed by him, and I have not found them in Ibnul Athir. The text has Tukharistan but Yakut's authority points the word Takharistan or Takhiristan.

2 The MS. has مالذى for بالذي

of the Faithful (*my father*) for me, and my inclination to amusements, A.H.227.
and I am but a youth and cannot reach to what they have attained, A.D.842.
yet verily I have composed some verses on Ajib and if they are good, *its well,* otherwise tell me truly that I may suppress them,' then he recited-

'Verily I behold Ajib
Resembling a reared gazelle :
His face is like a moon,
And his stature like a wand,
And when he snatches a sword,
I behold a lion robbed *of his prey.*
And when he shoots arrows,
He does it excellently and hits the mark.
He is a physician for all that I suffer in love.
May I never be without such a physician,
Verily I love Ajib
With a love which I find wonderful.

Thereupon I swore to him by the oath of allegiance that *it might be accounted* a graceful composition among the verses of such of the Caliphs who were not poets, at which he was pleased and ordered me 5,000 dirhams."

As suli records on the authority of Abdul Wahid b-ul Abbas ar Raiyashi, that the Roman Emperor wrote to al Muatasim a letter threatening him, and when it was read to him, he said to the secretary, "write-In the name of God, the most Merciful, the most Compassionate. Now, I have read thy letter, and heard thy address, and the answer is what thou shalt see; not hear, 'and the infidels shall surely know whose will be the rewards of paradise.'" (Qur. XIII.) And from Fadhl al Yazidi, that al Muatasim sent to the poets in attendance, *saying,* 'who among you is capable of versifying on me as well as did Mansur an Namari on ar Rashid as follows :

"Noble qualities and munificence are valleys,

A.H.227. A.D.842.

God hath caused thee to dwell in them where they meet.
He who relieth not upon the trusted of God,
Obtaineth no profit from his five daily prayers.
If rain withholds itself. His bounties are not corrupted,
And if an affair is straitened to us, if we remember Him, it is unloosed."

Upon which Abu Wuhayb said, "there is one among us who can do better than that, "and he continued."

"Three things there are by the beauty of which the world is resplendent.
The noonday sun, Abu Ishak and the moon.
In every calamity, his actions resemble
A lion, rain, and a sharp sword."

When he died, his Wazir Muhammad b. Abdil Malik mourned him in verse partly elegiac, partly congratulatory, and said,

"I exclaimed when they buried thee, and there were tossing
Above thee hands full of earth and clay.
Go, for thou wert an excellent protector in things temporal,
And an excellent defender of the faith.
May the Lord make not amenda to the people who have lost
The like of thee, save by the like of such as Harun (*al Wathik*)."

Traditions related by al Muatasim.

As Suli narrates a tradition through al Muatasim from Ibn 'Abbas that the Prophet observed a body of men of a certain tribe moving proudly in their galt, and a flush of anger rose to his face, and he recited, "and the tree cursed in the Qurãn" (Qur. XVII). It was said to him, "what tree is that, O apostle of God, that we may avoid it?" He said, "it is not a tree of vegetable growth, but the children of Umayyah, who when they rule, will be tyrannous, and when trusted in, will betray;" and he slapped his hand upon the shoulder of his uncle al 'Abbas and said, "the Lord will bring forth from thy loins, O uncle, one whose hand shall accomplish their destruction." I am of opinion that this tradition is not genuine but fabricated by al 'Alai. Ibn 'Asakir records a tradition from Ishak b. Yahya b. Maad that he said, "I was once visiting al Muatasim when he was sick and I said to him 'art thou better ?' he replied, 'how can that be, when verily I have heard ar Rashid relate a tradition from the Prophet-whoso is cupped on a Thursday and sickens on that day, dies in it." Ibn Asakir observes that the names of two authorities between and Dhabii'I and Ishak have been omitted from this ascription. A.H.227. A.D.842.

Of people of note who died during the reign of al Muatasim were al Humaydi, Shaykh al Bukhari, Abu Nuaym al Fadhl b. Dukayn, Abu Ghassan an Nahdi, Kalun and Khallad the Qurãn readers. Adam b. Abi Ayas, Affan, al Kanabi, Abdan al Marwazi, Abdullah b. Salih, the secretary of al Layth, Ibrahim b-ul Mahdi, Sulayman b. Harb. Ali b. Muhammad al Madaini, Abu Ubayd al Kasim b. Sallam, Kurrah b. Habib, Aarim, Muhammad b. Isa, the sword culter and Hafidh, Asbagh b-l Faraj, the Jurisconsult, Saadawayh of Wasit, Abu Omar al Jirmi, the grammarian, Muhammad b. Sallam of Baykand, Sunayd, Said b. Kathir, Ufayr, Yahya b. Yahya at Tamimi and others."

AL WATHIK BILLAH

Al Wathik billah, Abu Jaafar (and it is also said, Abul Kasim) the son of al Muatasim, the son of ar Rashid whose mother was a Greek slave concubine name Karatis, was born on the 20th Shaaban in the year 196 and assumed the Caliphate according to the testament of his father.

Allegiance was sworn to him on the 19th of Rabii I in the year

A.H.231 A.D.845. 227. In the year 228 he appointed Ashnas the Turk, regent (Sultan) of the kingdom and decorated him with a jeweled double girdle, and a jeweled crown, and I believe him to have been the first Caliph who appointed a Sulatan[1] for verily the Turks became numerous only in the time of his father.

In the year 231 his instructions reached the governor of Basrah commanding him to question the Imams and callers to prayer regarding the creation of the Qurãn, and he followed his father in this, but retracted towards the close of his reign. In this year he put to death Ahmad b. Nasr[2] al Khuzaai. He was one of the traditionists and assumed authority[3] to enjoin to good and to prohibit from evil. He sent for him from Baghdad to Samarra in fetters and questioned him regarding the Qurãn, but he said "it is not created," and in regard to the vision of God at the Day of Judgment, he said, "thus goes the narration and he related the tradition."[4] Al Wathik said to him "thou liest," but he replied to al Wathik, "nay, it is thou that dost

---

1 Se Freitag in the notes to Halebi, p. 84.

Anno 223 Watsikus Aschnasum tuream in imperio vicarium sibi creavit quem primum chalifarum vicarium sibi constitueit fuisse puto." Weil, Note 2, p. 344. Al Wathik billah.

2 D'Herbelot. Ibnul Athir, Weil, and the Muruj and Dahab all have Nasr and not Nadhr as in the text.

3 That this is the meaning here, appears to be evident from Weil's statement that Ahmad b. Nasr in his conspiracy to dethrone the Caliph meant either to usurp the government himself or place therein a Caliph of his own choice. This is confirmed by the words of the kamil &c. فبايعوه علي امربالمعروف used by D'Herbelof.

4 ترون ربكم يوم القيامه كماترون القمره "Ye shall see your Lord at the Day of Judgment as ye see the moon." The Muatazalites hold this to attribute a corporeal from to the Godhead, but they assert that men after death will see God with their spiritual eyes that is with their reason. Another tradition runs قلب ابن آدم المؤمن بين اصبعين من اصابع الرحما يقليه "God will turn about between two of his fingers the heart of a son of Adam a true believer." The orthodox believe that the Essence of God's corporeal form is different from that of man's; but the Muatazlites, of whom the Caliph was one, allowed not the existence of matter, and gave this an allegorical interpretation. See the Kamil and Weil' note. If the latter copies the Kamil, I think he is in error in putting the last tradition and speech into the mouth of Ahmad.

lie." The Caliph said, "what! will He be seen, as is seen a circumscribed and corporeal form which space can contain and the eye graps ! verily I deny a God with such attributes-what say ye ?" And some of the Muatazalite doctors who were about him, said, "it is lawful to put him to death." Wherefore he ordered the sword to be brought and said, "when I rise against him, let no one rise with me, for verily I throw the burden of my sins[1] upon this infidel who worshippeth a God I do not worship, and whom I do not recognize with those attributers with which he investeth Him." He then commanded the executioner's carpet to be brought, and *the prisoner* was placed upon it while still fettered, and he walked towards him and smote off his head, and ordered the head to be taken to Baghdad where it was impaled, and his body was impaled at Surra man raa. It remained in that state for six years until the reign of al Mutawakkil, who caused it to be taken down and buried. When he was impaled, and inscription was written and attached to his ear, which ran thus : "This is the head of Ahmad the son of Nasr, the son of Malik. The servant of God, the Imam Harun invited him to affirm the creation of the Qurãn and to deny the similitude of God to human form, but he refused except to continue in his obstinacy, therefore may God hasten his descent into hell fire." A man was placed on guard over the head, to turn it *from looking* towards the kiblah, with a spear, but the guard who was over it narrated that he saw it one night, turn its face towards the Kiblah and recite the Surah Y.S. (XXXVI) with a fluent tongue. This narration is given in other ways.

A.H.231.
A.D.845 .

During this year al Wathik engaged for the ranson of sixteen hundred[2] Muslim prisoners from the Romans, but Ibn Abi Duadi[3]

---

1 Meaning that he hoped for the forgiveness of God for his offences through the merit of slaying such an infidel.

2 According to Ibn Ath. 4,400 men, 800 women and children, and 100 of the non-Muslims (Ahlud Dimmah) living under a Muslim government.

3 Not Dauud as in the text. Ibn Abi Dauud was the well known Hafidh of Baghdad who died in A.H. 316. "Ibn Abi Duad was made chief Kadhi by al Muatasim and continued in high favor with that Caliph and his successor. In the reign of al Mutawakkil he was struck with paralysis (cont...)

A.H.231. (may the Lord reprobate him) said, "such of the prisoners as
A.D.845. acknowledge the creation of the Qurãn, let us release and bestow upon them two dinars, but whoso refuseth let us leave him in captivity." Al Khatib says that Ahmad b. Abi Duad influenced al Wathik and urged him to severity in the inquisition, and summoned the people to confess that the Qurãn is created. It is said that al Wathik retraced his steps before his death. One author relates that one of those who were brought in fetters from the provinces, was taken before the Caliph, and when he entered,. Ibn Abi Duad being present, the prisoner said : "Inform me regarding this belief which you summon the people to accept-did the apostle of God hold it and yet not call the people to believe in it, or was it a thing which he held not ?" Ibn Abi Duad replied "yest he did hold it." The other said 'then he was at liberty not to call the people to believe in it, and you are not so!" The narrator says, That *those* present were confounded and al Wathik laughed, and arose holding his mouth and entered a chamber and threw himself down at length, exclaining, "the Prophet was at liberty to be silent about it and we are not !" He then ordered that the man should be given three hundred dinars, and should be sent back to his city, and he did not question any one after this, but held Ibn Abi Duad in aversion from that day. Then man alluded to was Abu Abdur Rahmad Abdullah b. Muhammad al Azadi, the Shaykh of Abu Dauud and an Nasai.

Ibn Abid Dunya says that al Wathik was of fair complexion in which sallowness prevailed, with a handsome beard, and a spot in his eyes.[1] Yahya b. Aktham states that no one was as generous to the posterity of Abu Talib as was al Wathik. There was not one among them in distress, when he died, Another author observes that al Wathik was well versed in polite literature and was a graceful poet. He was much attached to a slave who had been sent to him as a present from Egypt, and one day al Wathik annoyed him, and

---

(Cont. 457) and his office conferred on his son and he died in A.H. 240 (854). See his life in Ibn Khall. The mistake in the name is made in the Kamil, doubtless by a copyist and passed unnoticed by Weil who has followed it."

1 The terrible eyes of al Wathik are noticed by D'Herbelot and figure in Beckford's famous romance.

afterwards, he heard him say to another slave, "by Allah, al Wathik has been wishing since yesterday that I would speak him but I will not,"-and al Wathik said- A.H.231. A.D.845.

"O thou who dost glory in punishing me
Thou art but a tyrant, tyrannous when in power.
Were it not for my infatuation, we would meet according to our respective positions.
And if I recover from this some day, thou shalt see !"

Among the verses of al Wathik are the following: -

"A heart that ruleth hearts[1]
With the repose of a languishing dark eye,
Beautiful of form, ravishing,
Full of conquttishness, and arch glances :
It is not possible for an eye when
She glanceth, to turn away from her."

As Suli says that al Wathik was called al Mamun the Younger on account of his polite learning and accomplishments, and al Mamun used to honour him and give him precedence before his son. Al Wathik was one of the most proficient of men in every thing; for he was a poet and the most versed in music among the Caliphs, there being about a hundred melodies and airs composed by him. He was also skilled in the lyre and in reciting poetry and narratives.

Al Fadhl al Yazidi observes that there was none of the Caliphs of the House of Abbas that could recite more poetry than al Wathik and having been asked whether al Wathik could recite more than al Mamun, he replied, "yes, for al Mamun mixed up with Arabian learning, the learning of the ancients in astrology, medicine and logic, and al Wathik adulterated Arabian science with nothing." Yazid al Muhallabi says that al Wathik was a very grater eater, and

---

1 Read مُهجَ for مُهجَ

A.H.231. A.D.845. Ibn Fahm,[1] that al Wathik had a table of gold made up of four-pieces, each piece requiring twenty men to carry it, and everything y upon the table, dishes, plates and saucers were of gold. Ibn Abi Duad begged of him not to eat from it on account of the Prophetical prohibition against it, whereupon he ordered it to be broken up, coined and taken to the treasury.

Al Husayn b. Yahya narrates that al Wathik dreamed that he asked for paradise of God, and a speaker said, "no one shall perish before God, save he whose heart is 'mart (مرت) In the morning he asked his companions regarding that, and they knew not the meaning of it. Then he sent for Abu Muhallim[2] and caused him to be brought into his presence and enquired of him regarding the dream and *the word* "mart". Abu Muhallim replied, 'mart' is a desert which produces no herbage, and the meaning of it is, that no one will perish before God except he whose heart is barren of faith, like the barrenness of a desert of herbage." Then al Wathik said to him, "I should like a proof from poetry of this 'mart';" whereupon one who was present hastily interposed and recited a line from the Banu Asad.

"She passed deserts which the sand-grouse avoids
Did a wise man enter into day break in them, he would lose his senses."

Abu Muhallim laughed and said "I shall not depart until I have recited to thee;" and he recited from the desert Arabs a hundred well, known verses from a hundred distinguished poets in every verse of these being the mention of the word 'mar', and al Wathik ordered him one hundred thousand dinars. Hamdun b. Ismail says that there was none among the Caliphs more fobearing than al Wathik nor more patient under annoyance and opposition than he. And Ahmad b Hamdun narrates that his tutor, Harun b. Ziyad went to him and he received him with the greatest deference, and it was

1 Abu Ali al Husayn b. Muhammad b. Fahm, a learned traditionist and a native of Baghdad, died A.H. 289 (902), aged 78. De Slane ; I.K.

2 The MS, has Abu Mujlim, but I can find no celebrity bearing either of these names.

said to him, "who is this, O prince of the Faithful to whom thou dost this thing?" He replied, "he is the first who unloosed my tongue to recite the praise of God and brought me within the Compass of His mercy." A.H.232. A.D.847 .

The following eulogy on him is by Ali b. Jahm :-

"The minds of men confide
In the monarch Wathik billah.
A monarch through whom wealth suffers,
But his companions suffer not.
A lion at whose fierceness smiles
Stern war.
The sword is friendly with him
But he dainty gazelle is in fear.
O sons of Abbas, the lord hath forbidden
But that ye only should rule."

Al Wathik died at Surra man raa on Wednesday the 24th of Dul Hijjah in the year 232, (11th *August* 847). When he was on the point of death, he began repeating these two lines "

"Death is common to all mankind
Neither prince nor subject is spared.
Their poverty[1] hurteth not the poor
And princes are not[2] profited against God by what they possess."

It is related that after he was dead, he was left abandoned and the people set about swearing allegiance to al Mutawakhil and a lizard came and pulled out his eyes and eat them.

Among distinguished persons who died during his reign were

---

1 For تفارهقم read as in Ibnul Athir تفاقرهم,

2 Compare Qur. III, 8, and LVIII 18 لن تعني عنهم اموالهم. "Their possession will not suffice them in lieu of (or defend them) against God."

A.H.232. Musaddad, Khalaf b. Hisham, the cloth merchant and Qurãn reader,
A.D.847. Ismail b. Said as Shalakhi the Shaykh of the people of Tabaristan, Muhammad b. Saad Katibul Wakidi, Abu Tammam at Tai the poet, Muhammad b. Ziyad bil Aarabi the grammarian, al Buwayti the disciple of as Shafii in prison and in manacles on account of the inquisition on the Qurãn, Ali b-ul Mughirah al Athram (*broken tooth*) the grammarian and others.

Regarding personal accounts of al Wathik, as Suli records that Jaafar b. Ali bir Rashid narrates as follows :

"We were in presence of al Wathik who had just taken his morning draught, when his eunuch Mahaj brought him a rose and a narcissus. The next day he recited the following regarding this :

"God preserve thee with thy narcissus and rose,
Thou shapely of figure and form.
His eyes have inflamed love
And increased desire and passion.
I sought by my sovereignty proximity to him,
But my sovereignty is the cause of my remoteness.
The intoxication of love hath dazed him,
And in union he turneth to repulsion.
If a favour is asked of him he turneth aside
And the tears pour down his cheeks.
He glories over the injuries his glances have done,
And he knoweth not the fulfilling of promises.
The master complains of the tyranny of the slave
Wherefore do justice to the master against his slave."

He adds "and they were agreed that by no other Caliph were there verses equal to these." As Suli also records that Abdullah b-ul Muatazz said, "one of my companions recited to me the following verse by al Wathik who was attached to two slaves, one of whom served him one day and the other the next."

A.H.232
A.D.847.

"My heart is divided between two persons :
Who has ever before seen one soul in two bodies ?
This one is angry if the other is kind
Thus my heart is occupied by a double grief."

And from Khirbil, that a verse of al Akhtal was sung in presence of al Wathik as follows :-

"A jovial singer joined me in my cups
Neither abstemious nor ye quarrelsome (sawwar) over his wine."

Some said it was 'sawwar" and others "saar," Whereupon he sent to Ibnul Aarabi questioning him on the point. He replied, "Sawwar means assaulting": one says, "he does not assault his boon companions" and saar is one who leaves a residue (suran) in the cup, and verily both readings are given." Upon this al Wathik ordered Ibnul Aarabi twenty thousand dirhams. He records likewise from Ahmad b.ul Husayn b. Hisham that he says, "al Husayn bud Dahhak and Mukharik were disputing one day at an assembly in presence o al Wathik regarding Abu Nuwas and Abul Atahiyah as to which was the better poet, and al Wathik said, 'lay a wager between ye,' and they staked between them two hundred dinars and al Wathik said, 'who among the learned is here?' They replied, 'Abu Muhallim;' whereupon he summoned him and he was questioned on the subject. He said, 'Abu Nuwas is the better poet and the most profoundly versed in Arabian science and the most copious of us in his variety of the kinds of verse.' Upon this al Wathik commanded that the stakes by paid to al Husayn.'"

A.H.234.
A.D.848-9.

AL MUTAWAKKIL ALAL LAH

Al Mutawakkil Alal lah Jaafar Abul Fadhl the son o al Muatasim then son of ar Rashid, whose mother was a slave concubine name Shujaa', was born in the year 205 and according to some. 207. He was acknowledged Caliph, in succession to al Wathik in Dul Hijjah 232. He evinced his partiality for the Sunnite doctrines and favoured' its professors and abolished the inquisition and wrote to the provinces to that effect, and that, in the year 234.

He summoned the Traditionist to Samarra and loaded them with presents and honoured them and commanded them to bring forward tradtitions on the attributes[1] of God and His personal vision at the day of Judgment. Abu Bakr b. Abi Shaybah taught in the mosque of Rusafah, there gathering round him about thirty thousand people, and his brother Othman lectured in the mosque of al Mansur, about thirty thousand also being collected under him. The prayers of the people for a Mutawakkil were frequent and they were vehement in his praise and honor to such an extent that one of them said, "The Caliphs are but three-Abu Bakr for his waging war on the apostates, Omar b. Abdil Aziz for his removal of abuses, and al Mutawakkil for his revival of traditional doctrine and abolition of servere measure. Regarding this, Abu Bakr b-ul Khabbazah says-

"And now to-day orthodoxy has become
Honoured, as if it never had been in reproach.
It overpowers and subdues since its pinnacle has been set up,
While the pinnacle of falsehood and lying is overthrown from its height.
And the innoators in religion have fled
Into hell fire disgraced and unaccepted of God.
The Lord hath made amenda for them by his Caliph Jaafar
His Vicegerent, the holder of orthodoxy and trusting in Him.

---

1 Which were rejected by the Muatazalites, the true doctrine of Wasil b. Ata their founder being that whoever asserted an eternal attribute, asserted that there were two gods. See Sale, p. 113, on their tenets.

The Vicegerent of my Lord and the descendants of His Prophet's uncle. A.H.234. A.D.848-9 .

The best of those of the sons of Abbas who have borne rule.

The gatherer of the scattered portions of the faith after their dispersion,

And the cleaver of the heads of apostates with the sword.

May the Lord of mankind preserve him long

Safe from dangers and unreplaced.

And grant him, for his protection to religion, an abode in paradise

In the familiar society, among its gardens, of the best of the Apostles."

In this year Ibn Abi Duad was seized with paralysis which made him like a fallen stone; may God not reward him! Among the wondrous events of this year, was a wind that blew in Iraq, an intensely hot wind, the like of which had not been known. It burnt up the sown fields of Kufah, Basrah and Baghdad, and destroyed travellers, continuing for fifty days. It reached Hamadan and burnt up the fields and cattle and came upon Sinjar and Mosal, preventing the people from frequenting the market places and walking in the streets, and killed a large number. In the previous year a tremendous earthquake occurred in Damascus, the houses of which fell and killed the people within them, and it extended to Antioch and destroyed it, and to Mesopotamia and laid it waste and even to Mosal, and it is said that fifty thousand persons were killed.

In the year 235 al Mutawakkil ordered the Christians[1] to wear collars round their necks.

In the year 236 he ordered the tomb of al Husayn to be

1 Ibnul Athir makes no mention of this word "ghul" which means a collar of iron, wood or leather worn round the neck, but he says that the non-Muslim population were compelled to wear yellow head coverings and girdles, to use stirrups of wood, and among other things to have the figures of devils put in front of their dwelling houses; the women and slaves had also distinct dresses assigned to them. See also Weil, p. 351, Vol. II.

A.H.245. destroyed, and the destruction likewise of the houses round about
A.D.859. it, and that it should be turned into cultivation, and he forbade the people to make pilgrimages to it; it was therefore destroyed and it remained a waste.

Al Mutawakkil was notorious for his Nasabi[1] tenets, and the Muslims were grieved on this account, and the people of Baghdad wrote upo the walls and mosques reviling him and the poets satirized him. Among what has been said on the subject is the following –

> "By Allah, if the Umayyads
> Went to slay the son of the Prophet's daughter unjustly put to death,
> Verily the sons of his ancestor have come against him likewise.
> See, by my life, his tomb destroyed !
> The grieve that they did not share
> In his assassination wherefore they pursue his mouldered bones."

In the year 237 he sent to the prefect of Egypt to shave the beard of Abu Bakr Muhammad b. Abil Layth, the chief judge of Egypt and to scourge him and to have him carried round the city on an ass. This was done, and indeed done well for Abi. Bakr was an oppressor, and one of the leaders of the Jahmite[2] following. He appointed to the judical office in his stead al Harith b. Miskin one of the disciples of Malik notwithstanding his declining it, and he disgraced the deposed Kadhi by scourging him with twenty stripes every day in order to return their oppression upon the doers thereof. In this year a conflagration broke out in Ascalon and burnt down houses and granaries, and it continued burning for a third of the night, when it ceased. During the same he invited Ahmad b. Hanbal

---

1 اهل المنصب was the name given to the adversaries of the Caliph Ali.

2 Ibnul Athir mentions four persons who encouraged al Mutawakkil in his persecution of the followers of Ali, viz., Ali b-ul Jahm the poet, of the Banu Shamah, Omar b. Farakh, Abus Samt and Abdullah b. Muhammad b. Dauud al Hashimi.

to come to see him, and he went, but he had no interview with him, A.H.245.
obtaining audience only of his son al Muatazz. A.D.859.

In the year 238 the Romans attacked Damietta and plundered and burnt it, and took thence six hundred women prisoners, and made good a hasty retreat by sea. In the year 240, the people of Khilat[1] heard a loud shriek from the vault of Heaven, and a large number of people died therefrom, and hail fell in Iraq, like hen's eggs, and thirteen village were swallowed up in the earth in Mauritania.

In the year 241, there was a commotion of the stars in the heavens, and the heavely bodies were falling the greater part of the night like locusts ; a disturbing occurrence such a had not been known.

In the year 242 there was a great earthquake at Tunis and its dependencies, and at Rai, Khurasan, Naysabur, Tabaristan and Ispahan, the hills were rent asunder, and the earth opened to an extent that would have admitted a man into the cleft. The village of Suwayda on the confines of Egypt was stoned from heaven, and one of the stones was weighed and it came to ten ratls (*pounds*). A mountain too in Yaman on which were the tilled fields of its owners, moved until it came to the tilled lands of others, and in Aleppo there came down a white bird somewhat smaller than the white vulture, in the month of Ramadhan, and it screamed out, "O ye people, fear the Lord, the Lord, the Lord," and it called out thus forty times, and then flew away but returned on the morrow and did the same again: the post brought word to this effect and five hundred men who had heard it, testified to it.

During the same year Ibrahim b. Mutahhar the secretary made the pilgrimage from Basrah in a carriage drawn by camels at which the people wondered. In the year 243 al Mutawakkil went to Damascus which greatly pleased him and he built himself a palace at Darayya and resolved to dwell there, upon which Yazid b. Muhammad al Muhallabi said-

---

1 In Central Armenia.

A.H.245.
A.D.859.

"I think that Syria will rejoice over the sorrow of Iraq
Since the Imam hath resolved to quit it.
For it thou quittest (O prince) Iraq and its inhabitants
Verily thou wilt afflict the fail one with divorce."

Upon which he changed his mind and returned after two or three months. In the year 244 al Mutawakkil put to death Yakub bus Sikkit[1] the great master of the Arabic language whom he had invited to teach his sons, and one day looking upon his two sons al Muatazz and al Muayyad, he said to Ibnus Sikkit, "which are the more endeared to you, these two or al Hasan and al Husayn?" He answered "Kanbar," (meaning the freedman of Ali) is better than these two." Upon this he gave orders to the Turks who trampled upon his belly till he died. It is also said that he commanded his tongue to be torn out, after which he expired, and he sent his blood-money to his son. Al Mutawakkil was a Nasabi.

In the year 245 erthquakes occurred over the world universally and cities and forts and bridges were destroyed, and a mountain at Antioch fell into the sea. In the heavens there were heard dreadful sounds : Egypt was convulsed by an earthquake and the inhabitants of Bilbis[2] heard a terrible shriek from the direction of Cairo[3] from which many of them died. The springs at Mecca dried up and al Mutawakkil sent one hundred thousand dinars to have water conveyed to it from Arafah. Al Mutawakkil was very liberal and much enlogised. It is said that no Caliph gave in bounty to a poet as much as was given by al Mutawakkil and regarding this Marwan b. Abi Janub said-[4]

"Stay the munificence of thy hands from me and add not more

---

1 He was the author of the work Islabul Mantik. Muntahal Arab.

2 Not Bulbays as in the text, though Yakut says it is vulgarly called Bilbays.

3 The phrase من ناحيه مصر may be also taken to mean that Bilbis was in the district of old Cairo, but I do not think that is here intended.

4 The text has يقول which must here be taken to imply a past sense. Ibn Khall has no notice of this poet beyond mentioning one of his verses in praise of Ibn Abi Duad.

For verily I fear lest I become haughty and insolent." A.H.245. A.D.859.

He replied, "no, I shall not refrain till my bounty overwhelmeth thee." He bestowed on him for one poem, a hundred and twenty thousand dirhams and fifty robes. One day Ali b-ul Jahm visited al Mutawakkil who held in his hand two pearls which he was turning about, and Ali recited to him a poem, upon which he threw him a pearl. Ali turned it about and al Mutawakkil said, "dost thou think little of it, while, by Allah, it is worth more than a hundred thousand dirhams?" He answered, "no, but I was thinking over some verses that I am composing in order that I may have the other too." The Caliph exclaimed, "say them." He recited-

"At Surra man raa is the Imam of justice,
From whose ocean the seas lap their waters.
May the kingdom be with him and with his children,
As long as night succeedeth day.
In every continguency he is hoped in and feared
As if he were heaven and hell.
His two hands in bounty are as rival wives,
For both of them are jealous of him.
His right hand giveth nought
But the left giveth the like to it."
Upon this, he threw him the other pearl.

One author observe that eight persons the father of each of whom was a Caliph acknowledged al Mutawakkil as Caliph, namely, Mansur, the son of al Mahdi, Abbas the son of al Hadi, Abu Ahmad the son of ar Rashid, Abdullah the son of al Amin, Musa the son of al Mamun, Ahmad the son of al Muatasim, Muhammad the son of al Wathik, and his son al Muntasir, Al Masaudi remarks that no one was known to be distinguished for any accomplishment, whether grave or gay, but had a share in al Mutawakkil's favour, and received considereable sums of money, and further that he was addicted to sensual pleasures and wine and had four thousand concubines.

Ali b-ul Jahm relates that al Mutawakkil was much attached

A.H.245. to Kabihah[1] the mother of his son al Muatazz, and was constantly
A.D.859. in her society. She stood before him one day having written upon her cheek in musk and ambergris the word "Jaafar," whereupon he looked at her meditatingly and versified as follows :-

> "She hath written Jaafar upon her cheek with musk,
> I would give my life for the spot where it has left a trace.
> If she hath engraved lines of musk upon her cheek
> Verily she hath inscribed lines of love upon my heart."

In the work on Inquisitions by as Salami, it is stated that Dun Nun[2] was the first who discoursed in old Cairo on the methods of ecstatic communion with the Deity and the degrees of the contemplative life among the mystics. Abdullah b-ul Hakam, who was one of the principal men of old Cairo and among the most eminent of the disciples of Malik, opposed him on the ground of his introducing a doctrine which none before him had advanced, and accused him of impiety. The governor of Egypt then sent for him and questioned him as to his belief which he explained. The governor approved his conduct and wrote regarding him to al Mutawakkil who commanded him to be summoned. He was accordingly sent, travelling post, and when the Caliph heard his discourse, he was enraptured with him and held him in high favour and honoured him, so that he used to say, "talking of pious men, give me Dun Nun !"

Al Mutawakkil covenanted for the succession, first for his son al Muntasir, then for al Muatazz, and next for al Muayyad. He subsequently sought to give al Muatazz, and precedence out of his love for his mother, and he asked al Muntasir to renounce the

---

1 The text "Fatihah" is wrong, all authorities together with the MS. have قبيحه Masaudi has قينه (a slave) in one copy and قبيخه in another, and the story is told differently, the verses being ascribed to Mahbubah another slave girl of the Caliph's and two other lines are added.

2 Abul Faydh Thauban b. Ibrahim surnamed Dun Nun (or he of the Fish, an epithet of the prophet Jonas) the well-known Muslim saint and ascetic ; his life will be found in I.K. He died A.H. 245 or 246 in Old Cairo, buried in the lesser Karafa one of its cemeteries.

succession, who refused. Al Mutawakkil thereupon summoned him A.H.245.
to a public audience, degreaded him from his position, and A.D.859.
threatened, reviled and menaced him. It happened that the Turks had withdrawn their countenance from al Mutawakkil on account of certain affairs, wherefore they conspired with al Muntasir to slay his father, and five men went in to him at dead of night when he was at a festive meeting and they slew him and his minister Fath b. Khakan on the 5th of Shawwal in the year 247 (10th *Dec.* 861.)

Some one saw him in a dream and said to him, "what hath God doe to thee?" He replied, "He hath pardoned me for the sake of the few orthodox traditionary doctrines that I have revived." When he was slain the poets mourned him, and among these are the following verses of Yazid al Muhallabi.

"His death came while his eye was sleeping,
Why came not death to him where lances are in splinters?"[1]
A Caliph who obtained what none hath received :
Never were there created a body and a soul like his."

Among his concubines was a girl called Mahbubah, a poetess, and possessing many accomplishments, and very skilful with the lute. When he was slain, she came into the possession of Bugha the elder, and he summoned her one day to a carousal. She sat down sorrowfully and he asked her to sing. She excused herself, but he adjured her and sent for the Jute and she placed it on her lap and sang extempore.

"How can life delight me
When I see Jaafar no more ?
This monarch whom I have seen
Covered with blood and dust.
All who are sick with love[2]

---

1 This word should be printed قِصَدٌ plur of قِصْدَةٌ a fragment.

2 Masaudi has خيال for هيام

A.H.247.
A.D.861.

Or disease may be indeed cured,
Save Mahbubah who
If she knew that Death were to be purchased,
Would purchase it with all
That her hands possessed, that she might be borne to the grave.
For a melancholy death
Is preferable to life prolonged."

Bugha was angry with her at this and ordered that she should be imprisoned, and this is the last that was heard of her.

Among curious coincidences it is stated that al Mutawakkil said to al Buhturi,[1] "speak a verse regarding me and Fath b. Khakan for I desire that he should continue in life with me, and that I should not lose him for my joy would then depart, nor he lose me. Say therefore something to this effect,"-and al Bukturi said,

"O my prince, how hast thou broken thy promise to me
And abstained from the fulfillment of thy engagements with me.
May the days not show me thy loss O Fath,
Nor announce my loss unto thee while thou livest :
The greatest of calamities would be that thou should'st precede me,
And yet a calamity, shouldst thou remain after I am gone.
Beware of taking another friend than myself
Since I have made thee alone the object of my love."

They were both slain together as hath gone before.

Regarding personal accounts of al Mutawakkil, Ibn Asakir

---

1 Abu Ubadah al Walid b. Ubayd of the tribe of Tai, al Buhturi was born at Manbij about A. H. 206 (812-2). He was accounted a poet of the first rank and was considered by some superior to Abu Tammam and al Mutanabbi. He returned to Manbij after the death of al Mutawakkil and died there in A.H. 284 (897-8). Consult Ibn Khall.

reecords that al Mutawakkil saw in a dream a piece of sugar of the kind called Sulaymani falling upon him from heaven upon which was written ; Jaafar al Mutawakkil alallilah (*who confideth in God*). When he was saluted Caliph, the people deliberated about giving him a name, and some said "let us call him Muntasir." Then al Mutawakkil related to Ahmad b. Abi Duad what he had seen in his dream, who found it a suitable name. He therefore adopted it and wrote to that effect to the provinces. A.H.247. A.D.861.

He records also from Hisham b. Ammar that he narrates, "I heard al Mutawakkil exclaim, 'alas ! for Muhammad b. Idris as Shafii ! how glad should I have been had I lived in his days ; I would then have beheld him, and witnessed his life and received instruction from him, for I saw the apostle of God in a dream, and he was saying-O people ! Muhammad the son of Idris, the descendant of al Muttalib hath departed to the mercy of God and hath left behind with ye an excellent doctrine, wherefore follow it and ye shall be rightly guided.' Then al Mutawakkil continued, 'O God ! vouchsafe unto Muhammad, the son of Idris a large share of Thy mercy and render easy unto me the remembrance of his doctrines, and profit me thereby.' I remark that from this we may infer that al Mutawakkil was attached to the Shafii school. He was the first of the Caliphs who followed its teaching."

He also records on the testimony of Ahmad b. Ali al Basri that al Mutawakkil sent to Ahmad b-ul Madil and others of the learned and assembled them in his palace ; he then went out to them and all the company arose before him except Ahmad b-ul Madil, and al Mutawakkil said to Ubaydullah,[1] "does not this man consent of allegiance ?" He said, "yes, O prince of the Faithful, but there is a defect in his eyesight." But Ahmad exclaimed, "prince of the Faithful, there is no defect in my eyesight, but I have preserved thee from the wrath of God, for the Prophet hath said, 'whose desireth that men should stand up before him, let him take up his abode in hell-fire;'" thereupon al Mutawakkil went and sat down by his side.

---

1 Ubaydullah b. Yahya b. Khakan who succeeded Muhammad b. Fadhl as Wazir in that post till the Caliph's death. Mur. Dahab, Vol. VII, p. 197.

A.H.247. A.D.861. And from Yazid al Muhallabi, "al Mutawakkil said to me, 'O Muhallabi, the Caliphs oppressed their subjects to compel their obedience, but I have been gentle with them that they might submit to and obey me.'" And from Abdullah b. Hammad at Tarmusi that he relates as follows: "I went to al Mutawakkil and he said-' O Abu Yahya, what hath kept thee from me, I have not seen thee for three days ! I purposed to give thee something but have transferred it to some one else.' I replied, 'O prince of the Faithful ! may the Lord requite thee with good for this intention. Shall I give thee a couple of verses on this subject ?' He replied 'yes,' so I versified-

'I thank thee indeed for the favour tha thou didst intend.
For thy solicitude in granting favours is well known.
And I shall not reprove thee since destiny hath not brought it about.
For one's lot is apportioned according to fixed decree.'
Upon this he ordered me one thousand dinars."

He records also from Jaafar b. Abdul Wahid the Hashimite as follows : "I visited al Mutawakkil when his mother died, and he said, 'O Jaafar, I often repeat this single verse, and when I wish to go on to the next, I get confused-and this is what I say.'

'When the world part us, I call to mind
And console myself with the *memory of the* Prophet Muhammad.'

One of the company present capped it with-

'And I say to it-verily death is our road
And he who dieth not to-day, dieth to-morrow.'"

And from Fath b. Khakan that he says, "I went in one day to al Mutawakkil and I saw him looking down and abstracted in thought and I said,-'Prince of the Faithful! Why this thoughtfulness ! for by Allah, there is not upon the face of the earth any one possessing greater happiness nor one more fortunate than thou art.' He answered, 'O Fath,-he enjoyeth greater happiness who hath a spacious house, a virtuous wife, and a present sufficiency, one who knoweth us not lest we injure him and hath no need of us, lest we disdain him.'" And from Abul Uayna that a slave girl who was a poetess and named Fadhl was given as a present to al Mutawakkil who said to her, "art thou a poetess ?" she replied, "so think they who sold and bought me?" He contimued-"recite me some of thy verses," she versified- A.H.247. A.D.861.

"The Imam of right guidance assumed the sovereignty
In the year thirty and three.
The Caliphate passed to Jaafar
When he was seven and twenty.
I hope, indeed, O Imam of right guidance
That thou mayest rule the kingdom for eighty years.
May God not bless the man who sayeth not
At the time of my prayer fot thee-Amen."

Ibn Asakir further records that Ali b-ul Jahm narrates as follows: "There was given to al Mutawakkil a slave girl called Muhbubah. She had been brought up in Taif, instructed in polite learning and could compose verses. Al Mutawakkil was much enamoured of her, but she fell subsequently under his displeasure, and he forbade the salve girls of the palace to speak to her. I visited him one day and he said to me, 'verily I had a dream of Muhbubah that I had become reconciled with her and she with me.' I answered, 'a happy omen, O prince of the Faithful.' He rejoined, 'come with us and let us see what she is about.' We proceeded until we reached her chamber, when lo! she was touching her lute and saying,

'I wander round the palace and behold none
To whom I can complain or who will respond to me.
So that I am as if I had committed a sin
For which there is no repentance which will release me,
Then[1] wo will be my intercessor with a monarch

---

1 The Murujud Dahab has من for هل

A.H.247. A.D.861.

Who visited me in his slumber and made peace with me.
But when the morning dawned upon us
He reverted to his disdain an forsook me.'"

Then al Mutawakkil called and she came forth, and she fell at his feet, an I kissed them, and murmured, "O my Lord, I dreamt of thee this night that thou wert reconciled with me." He replied, "and I too, by Allah, dreamt of thee." He then restored her to her former place in his favour. When al Mutawakkil was assassinated, she fell to the lot of Bugha, and the preceding[1] verses have already been recorded in their place.

Ibn Asakir mentions on the authority of Ali b-ul Jahm that al Buhturi praises al Mutawakkil for having abolished the Inquisition and satirizes Ibn Abi Duad in the following lines :

"Prince of the Faithful verily me thank
Thy ancestors the illustrious and noble.
Thou hast restored to the faith its unity, after
I had seen it in two hostile factions.
Thou hast overthrown oppressors over the whole earth
And the place of tyranny is known no more.
And in the space of a year which hath smitten their proud ones
According to their deserts by a sudden descending calamity.
And it hath left nothing of Ibn Abi Duad
Save a punishment which speaks with signification.
Sabur b. Sahl[2] was confounded at it
And granted him respite and afford him protection.
When his companions carouse at night
They prolong vain discourse on the creation of the Qurãn."

And from Ahmad b. Hanbal, that he says, "I was wakeful one

---

1 Page 471.

2 I can find no mention of this name in any work I have consulted and cannot explain the allusion.

night but afterwards fell into a slumber and in my dream I saw, as it were, a man ascending to heaven, and a speaker, saying, A.H.247. A.D.861.

'A king who is led to a just king
Eminent it mercy and not an oppressor.'

Afterwards when I awoke at dawn, there arrived at Baghdad from Surra man raa a messenger announcing the death of al Mutawakkil."

And from Amr[1] b. Shayban al Jubni "I saw in the night in which al Mutawakkil was slain, in my dream a speaker, saying,

'O thou whose eye sleepeth in regard to the things of the body,
Shed[2] thy tears, O Amr, son of Shayban.
Seests thou not the youths guilty of shameful deeds, what they have done
Unto the Hashimite and Fath b. Khakan.
He hath departed to God unjustly dealth with, and there call out to him
The dwellers in the heavens by twos and ones.
And there shall come unto ye others distinguished[3]
Whom ye may expect possessing dignity upon dignity.
Then weep for Jaafar and mourn for your Caliph
For verily men and jinns weep for him.'

Again I dreamt of al Mutawakkil after some months, and I said, 'what hath the Lord done unto thee ?' He answered, 'He hath pardoned me for the sake of the few traditionary doctrines I have revived,' I continud, 'what then dost thou do here?' He replied, 'I wait for Muhammad, my son, that I may plead for him to God.'"

---

1 Probably the son of the grammarian and philologer Abu Amr Ishak, Sukul Jubn is the name of a street in Damascus, which has given its name to several individuals.

2 These verses are different in Ibnul Athir and only two couplets are given.

3 Compare الخيل المسومة Qur. III, 9. And read ياتيكم for تاتيكم The line is obscure.

A.H.247.
A.D.861.

Traditions related through al Mutawakkil.

Al Khatib, narrates a tradition through al Mutawakkil from the Prophet that he said, "whoso refuse to be compassionate, declines a good action." Ibn Asakir records in a tradition from Ali b-ul Jahm that he relates as follows : 'I was with al Mutawakkil when they were discoursing with him on the subject of beauty, and he said, 'fine hair is undoubtedly a beauty :" then he recited a tradition from Ibn Abbas, who said,-'the apostle of God had tresses of hair that fell to the lobes of his ears like strings of pearls. He was one of the most comely of men, and was of a delicate tawny colour, erring neither on the side of excess nor of deficiency. Abdul Muttalib also had locks falling to the lobes of his ears and Hashim likewise.' Ali goes on to say that al Mutawakkil had the same and adds, 'al Matawakkil told me that al Muatasim likewise wore long locks, and so too al Mamun, ar Rashid, al Mahdi and al Mansur and his father Muhammad, his grandfather Ali and his great-grandfather Abdullah b. Abbas.'"

I remark that this tradition is continuous in three ways-by the mention of the hair, by the mention of the genealogical tree of descent, and the enumeration of the Caliphs-and in the ascription six Caliphs occur.

Of distinguished persons who died during the reign of al Mutawakkil were : Abu Thaur, Ahmad b. Hanbal, Ibrahim b-ul Mundir, al Hizami, Ishak b. Rahwayh, Ishak the Caliphs boon Companion, Ruh the Qurãn reader, Zuhayr b. Harb, Sahnun, Sulayman as Shadkuni, Abu Masaud al Askari, Abu Jaafar an Nufayhi, Abu Bakr b. Abi Shaybah and his brother, Dikul Jinn the poet, Abdul Malik b. Habib the Imam of the Maliki school, Abdul Aziz b. Yayha al Ghul, one of the disciples of as Shafii, Ubaydullah b. Omar al Kawariri, Ali b-ul Madini, Muhammad b. Abdullah b. Numayr, Yahya b. Main, Yahya b. Bukayr, Yahya b. Yahya, Yusuf al Azrak the Qurãn reader, Bishr b.ul Walid al Kindi al Maliki, Ibn Abi Duad that dog, may God not have mercy on him, Abu Bakr al Hadalli al Allaf Shaykh of the Muatazalite school and head of those who err from the true faith, Jaafar b. Harb one of the head of the

Muatazalites, Ibn Kilab the orator, the Kadhi Yahya b. Aktham, al Harith al Muhasibi,[1] Harmalah a disciple of as Shafii, Ibnus Sikkit, Ahmad b. Manii, Dun nun al Misri the ascetic, Abu Turab an Nakhshabi, Abu Omar ad Duri the Qurãn reader, the poet Dibil, Abu Othman al Mazini the grammarian and others. A.H.247. A.D.861.

AL MUNTASIR BILLAH

Al Muntasir Billah Muhammad Abu Jaafar, called also Abu Abdullah was the son of al Mutawakkil the son of al Muatasim, the son of ar Rashid. His mother was a Greek slave named Habshiyah. He was of comely countenance, of a tawny colour, large-eyed, with an anquiline nose, of middling stature, robust of body, corpulent, and of engaging and yet aweinspiring exterior. He was a man of great capacity, well-inclined, with little of the tyrant in him, a benefactor to the followers of Ali, and generous to them. He removed from the posterity of Abu Talib the threats and persections which they suffered by being forbidden to visit the shrine of al Husayn, and restored to the posterity of al Hasayn, the domain of Fadak.[2] Yazid al Muhallabi says, regarding this,

> "Thou has been generous to the descendants of Abu Talib after they
> Had suffered reproach age after age.
> And thou hast restored concerd in the house of Hashim
> I behold them as brothers after hostility had divided them."[3]

He was acknowledged Caliph after the assassination of his brother in Shawwal 247. He set aside his brothers al Muatazz and al Muayyad from the succession after him covenanted for them by al Mutawakkil. He display justice and equity towards his subjects,

1 See his life in Ibn Khall. He was an ascetic and called al Muhasibi, because he frequently called himself to account (yuhasib) for his actions.

2 See life of Omar b. Abdil Aziz, p. 300.

3 Two mor couplets are given by Masaudi.

A.H.247. A.D.861. wherefore all hearts were inclined towards him notwithstanding the great awe in which they held him, and he was moreover munificent and forbearing. Among his sayings are the following : "The pleasure of pardoning is sweeter than the delight of gratifying anger, and the worst of deeds in the powerful is revenge." When he assumed the government, he began to reproach the Turks, saying, "these are the assassins of the Caliphs." Therefore they conspired against him and sought to do away with him, but they failed in their purpose, because he was formidable, brave, sagacious and circumspect. Then they went cunningly to work until they sent secretly thirty thousand dinars to his physician Ibn Tayfur[1] to cause a malady. He therefore proposed to bleed him and he hled him with a poisoned lancet of which he died. It is also said that Ibn Tayfur forgetting this and falling ill himself, ordered his slave *to bleed him,* who bled him with the same lancet and he died also. It is likewise stated that he was poisoned by a pear, and according to another account, that he died of the quinsy. When he was on the point of death, *he exclaimed,* "O mother, this world and the next have gone from me: I shortened the days of my father, and my own end is now hastened."

Al Muntasir died on the 5th of Rabii, II, 248, *(7th June 862)* at the age of 26 or less, having enjoyed the Caliphate for a term computed at somewhat under six months. It is said that one day he sat down to a convivial meeting, and some capets having been brought out from his father's treasuries, he ordered them to be spread at the banquet and he beheld on one of the carpets a circle in which was *figured* a Persian, and on his head a crown, and round it a Persian inscription. He sent for some one who could read it, and a man was brought, who looked at it and frowned, and the Caliph said, "what is this?" He replied, "it has no meaning," but the Caliph insisted, whereupon the man read. "I am Shiruyah the son of Khusrau the son of Hurmuz, I slew my father, but I did not enjoy the sovereignty for more than six months." The face of al Muntasir changed colour and he ordered the carpet which was woven with gold, to be burnt.

1 Masaudi and the Kamil have at Tayfurii.

In the Lataiful Maarif (*Curiosities of Knowledge*) of at Thaalabi, it is stated that the most nobly born of the Caliphs who governed the Caliphate was al Muntasir, for he and his five immediate ancestors were Caliphs, as well as his brothers Muatazz and al Muatamid. I remark that even more nobly born than he was al Muatasim, whom the Tartars slew, eight of whose immediate ancestors were Caliphs. At Thaalabi further observes that the noblest by birth of the Persian monarchs that reigned was Shiruyah who slew his father and survived him only six months and the noblest of the Vicegerents that ruled the Caliphate was al Muntasir who likewise slew his father and enjoyed the succession but six months.

A.H.248.
A.D.862.

AL MUSTAIN BILLAH

Al Mustain Billah Abul Abbas Ahmad the son of al Muatasim, the son of ar Rashid and the brother of al Mutawakkil was born in the year 221. His mother was a slave concubine named Mukharik. He was comely, fair, pock-marked in the face, and had a defective pronunciation. When al Muntasir died, the generals assembled and took counsel together and said, "if you should appoint to the government any of the sons of al Mutawakkil, there will remain none of us alive." Wherefore they said, "there is nothing for it but Ahmad the son of our master al Muatasim." They therefore swore him allegiance, and he continued in power till the beginning of the yer 251. The Turks became alienated from his cause when Wasif and Bugha put to death[1] Baghir the Turk, he who murdered al Mutawakkil.

Al Mustain in the hands of Wasif and Bugha lost all authority, so that it was said on this subject –

---

1 The text is here incorrect, the words و نفي (not in the MS.) should be omitted : the words of Masaudi are identical with the MS. لماقتل و صيف و بغاباغر التركي the name Wasif and Bugha should therefore stand in the nominative case.

A.H.248.
A.D.862.

"A Caliph in a cage
Between Wasif and Bugha
Says that they tell him
As speaks a parrot."

And when the Turks became estranged from him, he feared and fled from Samarra to Baghdad, and they sent to him pleading excuses and tendering submission, begging of him to return, but he refused, whereupon they went to the prison and released al Muatazz billah and swore him allegiance and deposed al Mustain. Al Muatazz then fitted out a large force to attack al Mustain, but the people of Baghdad espoused the cause of al Mustain and many engagemens took place between the two factions. The war lasted for some months and the slaughter was great. Prices also rose and disorders increased, and the cause of al Mustain began to decline. They endeavoured to bring about a peace founded on the deposal of al Mustain, and Ismail the Kadhi and others proposed with this object definite conditions. Al Mustain therefore abdicated in the beginning[1] of the year 252 and the Kadhi and others testified to it. He was removed to Wasit and remained there nine months imprisoned under the charge of a nobleman,[2] but was subsequently brought back to Samarra. Al Muatazz then seat to Ahmad b. Tulun to overtake al Mustain and slay him, but the said, "by Allah, I will not slay the sons of the Caliphs." He next incited to it Said (*b. Salih*) his chamberlain who slew him on the 3rd of Shawwal of the same year, he being 31[3] years of age.

He was virtuous, of distinguished merit, accomplished and eloquent, and he was the first who set the fashion of wearing loose sleeves, for he made their breath about three spans, and he diminished the height of the caps which were excessively tall before his time.

Among persons of note who died during his reign were: Abd b.

1 11th Dul Hijjah, 4th Janurary 866.

2 Ahmad b. Tulun Afterwards governor of Egypt. Masaudi.

3 Masadi says 35.

Hamid, Abut Tahir b. Sarh, al Harith b. Miskin, al Bazzi the Qurãn reader, Abu Hatim al Sijistani, al Jahidh and others. A.H.252. A.D.866.

AL MUATAZZ BILLAH

Al Muatazz billah Muhammad called also az Zubayr, Abu Abdullah the son of al Mutawkkil, the son of al Muatasim the son of ar Rashid, was born in the year 232. His mother was a Greek alsve called Kabihah.[1] He was acknowledged Caliph on the abdication of al Mustain in the year 252, at the age of nineteen, none ever having ruled the Caliphate before him at an earlier age than his. He was exceedingly beautiful. Ali b. Harb .one of he teachers of tradition to the son of al Muataaz says, "I never saw a Caliph more comely than he." He was the first Caliph who set the fashion of appearing on horseback with ornaments of gold, for the Caliphs before him used to ride with but trifling ornamnents of silver. In the fist year of his reign died Ashnas he whom al Wathik had appointed Regent of the kingdom, leaving 500,000 dinars. Al Muatazz took possession of them, and he invested with the robes of office Muhammad b. Abdillah b. Tahir and girded him with two swords. Subsequently he deposed him and bestowed the viceregal robes upon his brother, that is the brother of al Muatazz, Abu Ahmad, and crowned him with a diadem of gold and a jeweled cap and *gave him* two jeweled girdles and belted him with two swords. He deposed him, however, the same year and banished him to Wasit and invested Bugha[2] the cup-bearer and placed upon him the viceregal crown; but he rebelled aginst al Muatazz the following year and was slain and his head brought to the Caliph.

In th month of Rajab of this year, al Muatazz set aside his brother al Muayyad from the succession, and scourged him and put him in prison where he died after a few days. Al Muatazz

---

1 See page 470.

2 This was Bugha the younger.

A.H.252. fearing, however, lest it should be said of him that he had put him to
A.D.866. death or had artfully contrived it, summoned the Kadhis in order that they might behold him, and there was no mark of violence[1] found on him.

Al Muatazz was impotent in the hands of the Turks. It happened that a number of the chiefs went to him and said, "O prince of the Faithful give us our pay and we will slay Salih the son of Wasif."[2] Now al Muatazz feared him wherefore he sent to his mother for money to distribute among them, but she being extremely covetous, refused him and there was nothing left in the public treasuries. Then the Turks straightway agreed to depose him, and Salih b. Wasif and Muhammad b. Bugha joined with them, and they armed themselves and went to the palace and sent to al Muatazz, *saying,* "come out to us." He returned as answer, saying, "verily I have taken medicine and am weak." Then a number of them set upon him ad dragged him by the foot, and beat him with clubes and made him stand in the sun in the fierce heat of the day and smote him on the face, saying, "abdicat". Then they summoned the Kadhi Ibn Abi Shawarib and witnesses and deposed him. Next they sent for Muhammad the son of al Wathik (*al Muhtadi*) from Baghdad to the capital which was then at Samarra, for al Muatazz had removed him to Baghdad, and al Muatazz resigned the Caliphate to him and swore him allegiance. Then the mob seized al Muatazz five nights after his abdication and put him into a hamman and when he had bathed he became thirsty, but they forbad him water. Then he was taken out[3] and they gave him snow water which he

---

1 Masaudi says he had been enveloped in a fur robe, the sides of which were fastened, so that he was smothered within it.

2 This promise was only a blind to induce the Caliph to give them money, for Salih, was one of the three principal promoters of this insurrectionary demand. Together with the other two, *viz,* Babkial and Muhammad the son of Bugha, he subsequently took the Caliph prisoner and forced him to abdicate.

3 The MS. has not the word اول which here has no meaning and should be omitted from the text. Ibnul Athir relates the manner of his death altogether differently.

drank and dropped dead. This occurred in the month of Shaaban the honoured, in the year 255 (*July* 869). His mother Kabihah concealed herself, but subsequently appeared in public in Ramadan and gave up immese treasures to Salih the son of Wasif. Among these were 1,300,000 dinars,[1] and a casket in which was eleven and a quarter pounds weight of emeralds, and a casket in which was a similar measure of pearls of large size, and a measure of three pounds and three quarters of rubies, besides other things. The caskets were valued at two thousand dinars. When Salih b. Wasif beheld all this, he exclaimed, "may God bring evil upon her. She exposed her son to be murdered for the want of 50,000 dinars, while she had this in her possession." He appropriated the whole and banished her to Mecca where she remained until the reign of al Muatamid who brought her back to Samarra where she died in the year 264. A.H.255. A.D.869.

Of persons of note who died in the reign of al Muatazz were, Sarri as Sakti, Harun b. Said al Ayli, ad Darimi author of the Musand, al Utbi author of the Masailul Utbiyah on the doctrine of Malik, and othcrs.

AL MUHTADI BILLAH

Al Muhtadi billah, the good Caliph, Muhammad Abu Ishak, called also Abu Abdullah, the son of al Wathik, the son of al Muatasim, the son of ar Rashid whose mother was a slave concubine named Wardah[2] was born during the Caliphate of his grandfather about the year 210 and odd,[3] and was acknowledged Caliph on the 29th Rajah 255 (13th *July* 869).

1 The dinar of that period, according, to De Slane, had an intrinsic value of about ten shillings British.

2 According to Ibnul Athir, her name was Karab or Kurb.

3 "Or it may be translated, between the years 213 and 219." See the discussion on this point in Lane, art. بضع

A.H.255. A.D.869. He would not accept the oath of allegiance[1] from any one until they had brought al Muatazz, whereupon al Muhtadi rose and saluted him as testified against al Muatazz that he was unequal to the Caliphate, and he himself acknowledged it and stretched out his hand and tendered allegiance to al Muhtadi. From that day al Muhtadi was raised to the throne.

Al Muhtadi was of a light tawny complexion, comely of countenance, chaste, pions, just, firm in carrying out the commands of God, intrepid, and brave, but he found none as an ally or a helper. Al Khatib says that he did not cease to fast from the time he began his reign till he was assassinated.

Hashim b-ul Kasim relates as follows : I was once in presence of al Muhtadi one evening in the Ramadhan, when I started up to depart,but he said "sit down," and I sat down, and he advanced and prayed before us. Then he called for food, and an earthen[2] vessel was brought in which were round flat cakes of white bread, and on it were vessels in which were salt, vinegar and olive-oil, and he invited me to eat. I began to eat, thinking that they would presently bring the viands, but he looked at me and said, "dost thou not fast?" I replied, "Yes." He continued, "hast thou not the intention[3] of fasting?" I answered, "how not ! since it is Ramadhan !" He said, "eat and satisfy thyself, for there is no other food than what thou seest here." I was astonished, and after a little I exclaimed, "and why, O prince of the Faithful ? for the Lord hath given thee amply of his benefits!" He replied, "verily the thing is as thou sayest, but I considered that there was indeed among the Banu Umayya, Omar b. Abdil Aziz, and he lived on scanty food and poorly as thou hast heard, therefore I was jealous for the Banu Hashim, and I adopted the life thou dost witness."

Jaafar b. Abdil Wahid[4] says, "I was conferring with al Muhtadi

---

1 For بيعته read بعية as in the MS. it would read therefore. بعية احمد

2 For حلاف read جلاف the Kamil has خلاف (a kind of willow the *Saliz Egyptia*) and حلاب in another reading.

3 See note page 68.

4 A member of the Abbaside family whom al Mutawakkil appointel to succeed Yahya b. Aktham, as Kadhi. He died in 258 (871-2) some say 268. Ibn Khall, life of Yahya b. Aktham.

regarding a certain point, and I said to him, 'Ahmad b. Hanbal used to maintain, it,' but he was averse to my alluding to any of his departed ancestors, and he said, 'may God, have mercy upon the son of, Hanbal, if it were permitted to me to hold myself clear of my father, I would have no part with him.'[1] Then he said, 'assert the truth and maintain it, for the man who asserts the truth is noble in my eyes.'" A.H.255. A.D.869.

Niftawayh relates as follows : "One of the Hashimites told me that he found in al Muhtadi's possession a coffer containing a woollen tunic and a coarse garment which he used to wear at night and pray in. He put down all wanton pastimes and forbade singing, and checked the oppression of the Regent's myrmidons. He was particularly zealous in the administration of the public registers, himself sitting down and making the secretaries sit down in front of him, and they would work at the accounts. He also never failed to hold audience on Mondays and Thursdays. He to Baghdad abhorring his presence, because he considered him attached to Rafidhite tenets."

In his time Musa the son of Bugha set out with his followers from Rai for Samarra to put to death Salih b. Wasif in revenge for the murder of al Muatazz and the spoliation of his mother's treasures, and the populace called out against Ibn Wasif, *saying,* "O tyrant, verily Musa hath come against thee." Then Musa b. Bugha sought admission to the presence of al Muhtadi but he would not grant it, upon which he forced an entrance with his followers while the Caliph was seated in the Hall of Justice and took him away upon a sorry mare and they sacked the palace and lodged al Muhtadi in the palace of Najud[2] who kept saying, "O Musa, fear God. Alas for thee! what dost thou want ?" He replied, "by Allah, we seek nothing but what is *for thy* good,-now swear to us that thou wilt not follow the guidance of Salih b. Wasif." He took this oath to

1 On account of his persecution of Ahmad b. Hanbal and others on the question of the creation of the Qurãn.

2 Ibnul Athir has ياجور Yajur. Najur and Bajur are also variants. Ibn Khaldun, likewise according to Weil gives the name of this Turk as Yajur.

A.H.255. them and they renewed the oath of allegiance to him at the same
A.D.869. time. They next sought Salih to bring him to account for his deeds, but he hid himself and al Muhtadi invited them to a mutual reconciliation. They then suspected that he knew his place of concealment and a discussion arose about this. Subsequently they talked of deposing al Muhtadi, but the next day al Muhtadi came out to them girt with his sword, and said, "verily, your intentions have come to my knowledge, but I am not like those who have preceded me, such as al Mustain and al Muatazz. By Allah, I have not come forth to you save well considering what I do.[1] I have made my last testament and this in my sword. By Allah, I will wield it as long as I can grasp its hilt in my hand. Have ye no religion, no shame, no gentleness left? How long[2] will there continue this opposition to the vicegerents and this audacity against God?" Then he continued, "I have no knowledge of Salih." On this they were appeased and dispersed and Musa b. Bugha issued a proclamation that whoever should bring Salih, should receive ten thousand dinars, but no one was able to lay hold of him. I happened, however, that a certain boy entered a lane at noontide and he saw a door ajar. He entered and crossed the vestibule which was dark and beheld Salih asleep. He recognized him and there being no one with him he went to Musa and informed him, and he sent a party who seized him and cut off his head which was carried round the city and al Muhtadi was inwardly grieved at this.

Subseqently Musa accompanied by Bakyal[3] set out for Sinn against Musawir.[4] Al Muhtadi hereupon wrote to Bakyal to put to

---

1 In Ibnul Athir, the word is متحنط "prepared for death."

2 The MS. has كم and so Ibnul Athir-it is a better reading than the لم of the text : the accidental oversight of the oblique stroke of the ك has no doubt caused the error.

3 One of the Turkish leaders.

4 Musawir b. Abdul Hamid b. Musawir in revenge for the maltreatment of his son by the prefect of Mosul, attacked Mosul at the head of a band of Bedouins and Kurds, released his son from prison, defeated the Turkish generals and for a time occupied the greater part of the province. See Ibnul Athir and Weil, p. 406. Vol. II.

death Musa as well as Muflih one of the Turkish chiefs or to arrest them, and himself assume the leadership of all the Turks. Bakyal acquainted Musa with the purport of his letter and said, "I am not pleased with thism for indeed it toucheth us all." They then agreed to put al Muhtadi to death, and set out against him. On the side of al Muhtadi fought the men of the west and of Farghanah and of Ushrusanah,[1] and there were slain of the Turks in one day, four thousand, and the fighting continued until the troops of the Caliph were put to flight. He was taken prisoner, put to the torture and died. This occurred in Rajab (18th) in the year 256, (21st *June* 870). Thus his Caliphate lasted one year all but fifteen days.[2] A.H.256. A.D.870.

When the Turks rose against him, the people rose in tumult and wrote on slips of paper and threw them in the mosques, "O ye Muslims ! pray for your Caliph, the just, the approved, who resembleth Omar the son of Abdul Aziz,[3] may the Lord defend him against his enemies."

AL MUATAMID ALAL LAH

Al Muatamid alal lah Abul Abbas, called also Abu Jaafar, Ahmad, the son of al Mutawakkil, the son of al Mutasim, the son of ar Rashid, was born in the year 227. His mother was a Greek named Fityan.

When al Muhtadi was slain, al Muatamid was lying in prison at al Jausak,[4] and they brought him out and swore allegiance to him. He then appointed his brother *Abu Ahmad* Talhah *surnamed* al

---

1 Not Usrus, as in the text. The MS. is here correct. It is the name of a district beyond the Oxus, lying between Samarkand and the Jaxartes. Yakut.

2 The date of his abdication was the 15th of Rajab. Ibnul Athir.

3 The Kamil has,—but I think incorrectly –Omar b-ul Khattab.

4 There are various places of this name, some in the vicinity of Baghdad. Consult Yakut.

A.H.256. Muwaffak *billah, (the directed of God)* ruler over the East and
A.D.870. nominatied his son Jaafar to the succession and gave him the government of Egypt and the West and surnamed him al Mufawwadh ilallah *(recommended to God).* Al Muatamid now gave himself up to pastime and sensual pleasures, and neglected the care of his subjects, the people therefore regarded him with dislike, and became attached to his brother Talhah.

During his reign the Zanj[1] entered Basrah and its dependencies and laid waste and slaughtered and burnt and ravaged and made prisoners. Many engagements took place between them and the Caliph's troops, which during most of them, were commanded by his brother al Muwaffak.

This event was followed by the plague which never fails to follow blood. shed in Iraq, and countless people died therein. This was succeeded by convulsions and earthquakes, and thousands of people perished in falling ruins, and hostilities with the Zanj continued from the accession of al Muatamid in 256 till the year 270. In that year the chief of the Zanj-may God curse him-whose name was Bihbud,[2] was slain. He pretended that he had been sent from God to the people but had rejected the mission, and that he was congnizant of hidden things.

As Suli says that he slew 1,500,000 Muslims, three hundred thousand having been slain in a single day at Basrah. He had a

---

1 The leader of the Zanj was, according to Ibnul Athir, Ali, b. Muhammad b. Ahmad who was 5th in descent from Ali b. Abi Talib : according to another account his grandfather was Abdur Rahim (not Abdur Rahman as Weil has it) of the tribe of Kays. He rallied round his standard the African salves (known by the generic name of Zanj) and kept his ground against the Caliph's troops till the year 270. The Arabic historians name him "al Khabith," "the impure," "or the reprobate." Consult Weil, pp. 452-4, Vol. II, and Ibn Athir p. 139, and D'Herbelot.

2 This is certainly incorrect, the chief of the Zanj was Ali al Khabith as above stated. Bihbud was one of his generals, and took a considerable part in the defence of the Zanj stronghold of Mukhtarah. Ibnul Athir does not give the date of his death and rarely mentions him, and Well not at all. All Khabith was slain on 3rd Safar 270, after he had been for more than 14 years the terror of Islam.

pulpit in his city which he used to ascend and revite Othman Ali, Muawiyah, Talhah, Zubayr and Ayesha, and he used to sell by the public crier an Aliide woman at two or three dirhams, and one of the Zanj had ten Allide women whom he employed in his service. A.H.256. A.D.870.

When this reprobate was slain, his head and brought into Baghdad on a spear, and pavilions of triumph were erected and the people called down blessings on al Muwaffak, and the poets praised him and it was "a day upon which men are assembled" (Qur XI). The people *thenceforth* reposed in security and returned to the cities which the Zanj had taken and there was many such, as Wasit and Ramahurmuz.

In the year 260 of this reign a great scarcity prevailed in Hijaz and Iraq, and a *Kurr*[1] of wheat in Baghdad rose to one hundred and fifty dinars. During the same year the Byzantines captured the town of Luluah.[2]

In the year 266 al Muatamid covenanted for the succession after him of his son Jaafar al Mufawwadh ilallah and next, for his brother Talhah al Muwaffak. He appointed his son over Mauritania and Syria, Mesopotamia and Armenia, and placed his brother over the East and Iraq, Baghdad, Yaman, Parthia, Ispahan, Rai, Khurasan, Tabaristan, Sijistan and Sind. He appointed also for each of them two banners, black and white, and stipulated that if anything should happen to him, the government should go to his brother, should his son not be of age, and he set the agreement in writing and sent it in charge of the chief Kadhi Ibn Abi Shawarib to hang it in the Kaabah.

In the year 266 the Byzantine troops entered Diyarbakr and ravaged it, and the inhabitants of Mesopotamia and of Mosul fled. During the same year the Bedouine plundered the covering of the Kaabah and carried it away.

In the year 267 Ahmad b. Abdillah al Hijabi made himself master of Khurasan, Kirman and Sijistan and even purposed subjugating Iraq. He struck the coinage in his own name, and one the reverse

---

1 About 7100 Ibs. Ibn Athir gives the price as 120 dinars.

2 According to Yakut a fortress near Tarsus.

A.H.269. A.D.882-3. side the name of al Muatamid, a strange circumstance. His own slaves put him to death at the close of the year, thus God sufficed for his evil deeds.

In the year 269 al Muatamid conceived strong suspicions against his brothr al Muwaffak who had risen against him in the year 264, but they had subsequently become reconciled. When in this year these suspicious again strongly possessed him, he wrote to Ibn Tulun his prefect in Egypt and they agreed upon a certain course. Ibn Tulin set out until he reached Damascus and al Muatamid left Samarra on the pretext of a change of air, his intended destination beig Damascus. When this reached al Muwaffak, he wrote to Ishak b. Kundaj[1] to turn him back, and Ibn Kundaj rode from Nasibin to al Muatamid and met him between Mosul and al Hadithah and said, "O prince of the Faithful, thy brother is opposing the enemy and thou hast come forth from thy residence and the capital of thy empire, and when this becomes authentically known to him, he will return from engaing the rebels, and they enemies will take possession of the dominion of thy ancestors," and other words to the like effect. Then he placed a party in charge of al Muatamid, and gave orders respecting his suite of attendants.[2] Then he sent to al Muatamid, saying, "this is no place for thee, therefore return." Al Muatamid said "swear to me that thou wilt go down to Samarra. There Said b. Mukhallad the Secretary of al Muwaffak met him and Ishak delivered the Caliph up to him who took him to the house of Ahmad b. Khasib and would not suffer him to enter the palace and placed over him five hundred men who forbade all access to him.

When this reached al Muwaffak, he sent Ishak a robe of honour and presents, and bestowed upon him the estates of the chiefs who were with al Muatamid and gave him the title of Du's Sanadayn (*Lord of the two Sanads*) and surnamed Said, Dul Wizaratayn (*Possessor of the dignity of the two ministries of state*). Said continued to serve under al Muatamind, but al Muatamid had no

1 In the Kamil followed by Weil, this name is written Kundajik. He was governor of Mosul. Ibn Khall, accords with the text.

2 Placed them in chains according to Ibn Athir.

real authority in the administration and he himself says regarding this: A.H.269. A.D.882.3.

"It it not strange that one like myself
Should see that there is not a little that is denied him.
The whole world is under the authority of his name
And yet of all this he hath nothing in his possession.
The entire wealth of the state is carried to him
Yet he is denied much of what is exclusively his own."

He was the first Caliph who had force put upon him was restrained and kept under ward.

Al Muatamid was then brought to Wasit, and when this reached Ibn Tulun, he assembled the Kadhis and the nobles, and said, "verily al Muwaffak hath rebelled against the prince of the Faithful, therefore set him aside from the succession." They thereupon removed him from the succession, all save the Kadhi Bakkar b. Kutaybah who exclaimed, "thou didst bring me from al Muatamid a deed appointing him to the succession, bring me therefore, another deed excluding him." He replied, "but al Muatamid is under restraint and compulsion." He answered, "I do not know it." Then Ibn Tulun said, "the people have beguiled thee with their saying that there is no one in the world like Bakkar! Thou art old and dotest." He then imprisoned him and put him in chains and confiscated from him all the gifts he had received for years past which amounted to ten thousand dinars, and they say that this sum was found in the house of Bakkar with the seals *unbroken.*[1] Al Muwaffak hearing of this caused Ibn Tulun to be cursed from the pulpits.

Subsequently in the month of Shaaban 270, al Muatamid, was brought back to Samarra and entered Baghdad, Muhammad b.

---

1 Ibn Khall in his life of Bakkar states that Ibn Tulun used to give Bakkar every year 1000 dinars in addition to his salary. The Kadhi made no use of this, neither did he break the seal placed on the purse which contained it. Eighteen such purses were delivered up to Ibn Tulun, to his great confusion with the seals unbroken.

A.H.269. A.D.882-3. Tahir accounted, preceding him and the troops in attendance on him as if he were not under constraint.

Ibn Tulun[1] died in this year, and al Muwaffak appointed his son Abul Abbas to his government and sent him with the army of Iraq to Egypt, but Khumaruwayh the son of Ahmad b. Tulun had succeeded to his fathers possessions, wherefore there took place between him and Abul Abbas the son of a Muwaffak a great battle, so that the earth ran with blood. The victory remained with the Egyptians.

In this years a breach took place in the Isa canal and the water reached Karkh and destroyed seven thousand houses.

During the same, the Byzatines came down upon Tarsus with one hundred thousand men, but the victory remained with the Muslims who took in plunder what could not be computed, and it was a great and unparalleled victory.[2]

In the same year was made public the mission of al Mahdi Ubaydullah b. Ubayd the ancestor of the Banu Ubayd the heretic Caliphs of Egypt, in Yaman;[3] and he continued in the prosecution of this design until the year 278, in which year he made the pilgrimage to Mecca and joined with a tribe of the Banu Kutamah.[4]

---

1 The good effects of Ibn Tulun's administration of Egypt, his reforms and endowments, the splendour of his court, and the vast wealth he bequeathed, may be read with interest in Weil, who draws a parallel between him and Muhammad Ali the destroyer of the Mamelukes in our own times.

2 This expedition, according to Weil, was led by Stypiotis : Ibn Athir mentions it and states that, according to report, 70,000 Byzantines fell including the commander of the forces, seven crosses of gold were taken, and one large one of the same metal studded with jewels, 15,000 beasts and mules, besides considerable plunder in silver articles and brocade and 10,000 standards !

3 The establisher of this mission or "call was abu Abdullah al Husayn the Shiite a native of Sanaa in Yaman. Consult his life in Ibn Khall, and Weil, p. 511.

4 Not "Kananah" as in the text. The MS. is in accordance with all the other authorities and has Kutamah. According to Weil, it was the missionary Abu Abdullah, not Ubaydullah that made the pilgrimage and secured the Banu Kutamah.

His pretension satisfied them, and he went with them to Egypt and saw that there was in them devotion and vigour. He accompanied them to Mauritania and this was the beginning of al Mahdi's rise. A.H.270. A.D.884.

In the year 271, says as Suli, Harun the son of Ibrahim al Hashimi, took the office of Muhtasib, and issued orders that the people of Baghdad should transact business with the copper coins called "fulus," but they employed them reluctantly and afterwards abandoned them.

In the year 278 the Nile in Egypt fell so low that nothing remained of it and prices rose. During the same year, died al Muwaffak, and al Muatamid was thus freed from him. In the same year, the Carmathians appeared in Kufah. They are a sect of heretics who assert that no ablution is necessary after being in a state of ceremonial uncleanness, and that the use of wine is lawful, and they add *words* to the call to prayers and maintain Muhammad b-ul Hanifa to be the apostle of God, and that fasting is obligatory in the year on two days only, on the festival of the Nauroz (*New Year's Day*) and that of Mihrjan,[1] that the place of pilgrimage and that towards which the face should be directed in prayer shold be Jerusalem, and the like, and their opinions spread among the foolish and the dwellers in the deserts and the people were troubled by them.

In the year 279, the power of al Muatamid declined through the usurpation by Abul Abbas the son of al Muwaffak of the administration of affairs, and the devotion of the troops to him. Al Muatamid held a public audience and before it took himself to witness that he set aside his son al Mufawwadh from the succession and he took the covenant for Abul Abbas and surnamed him al Muatadhid. During this year al Muatadhid ordered that no astrologer and no story-teller should sit by the roadside, and he took an oath

1 These were two Persian festivals held in honor of the sun. The first took place on the 1st of Farwardin (March) when the sun entered Aries, and the second on the 16th of Mihr (September) the time of the autumnal equinox.- For an account of the Carmathians, consult Ibn Athir, Weil, D'Herbelet, Ibn Khall &c.

A.H.279. A.D.891 from booksellers that they would not sell works on philosophy and polemies.

Al Muatamid died suddenly after a few months of this year had clasped. Some say he was poisoned, other that he was smothered in his bedding when he was asleep ; and this on Monday the 19th of Rajab 279 (14th *October* 892). His Caliphate lasted twenty-three years, but he was under subjection to his brother al Muwaffak through the latter's usurpation of the government, and when al Muawaffak died, he was for several reasons kept under ward by al Muatadhid in like manner.

Among persons of note who died in the reign of al Muatamid were al Bukhari, Muslim, Abu Dauud as *sijistani,* at Tirmidhi, Ibn Majah, ar Rabii al Jizi, ar Rabii al Muradi, al Muzani, Yunas b. Abdul Aala, az Zubayr b. Bakkar, Abul Fadhl ar Riashi, Muhammad b. Yahya ad Duhli, Hajjaj bus Shair, the Hafidh al Ijli, the chief Kadhi Ibn Abi's Shawarib, as Susi the Qurãn reader, Omar b. Shaybah, Abu Zarah ar Razi, Muhammad b. Abdillah b. Abdil Hakam, the Kadhi Bakkar, Dauud at Tahiri, Ibn Darah Bakii b. Mukhallad, Ibn Kutaybah, Abu Hatim ar Razi, and others.

The following are among the verses of Abdullah the son of al Muatazz on al Muatamind :

"O best of those with whom riding camels travel swiftly,
Of those the rope of whose covenant is bound firm,
The reins of sovereigny were unwillingly forced
Into thy hands, which thou didst grasp and abandon.
Subject then to thyself the world and its inhabitants
As long as the arrow is turned aside of which thou art the target." [1]

Of the verses of al Muatamid when he was under ward, are these:

"I am so placed that I am unable to ward off
What I suffer of indignity and contempt.

1 For موفقه read as in the MS موقفه.

The affairs of men proceed without me A.H.279. A.D.891.
And little mention of them is made to me.
When I desire a thing, they take it from me
And say, herein is harm *to thee*.'"

As Suli says that he had a scribe who used towrite his verses in water of gold, and Abu Sai'd al Hasan b. Sai'd an Nisaburi mourned him as follows :

"Verily the eye of avaricious fortune hath brightened
After the had been blurred, him sighted and blear.
Misfortunes have attained their desires
By the death of the Imam of right guidance, al Muatamid.
And since he has gone, no vigilant guardian is left me
And we strive our best against misfortunes."

AL MUATADHID BILLAH

Al Muatadhid billah Ahmad, Abul Abbas son of the heir apparent al Muwaffak Talhah b-ul Mutawakkil b-ul Muatasim bir Rashid was born in Dul Kaadah in the year 242, but according to as Suli in Rabii, I 243. His mother was a slave concubine called Sawab, but some say, Hirz, and others Dharar, and he was acknowledged Caliph in succession to his paternal uncle al Muatamid in the month of Rajab 279.

He was comely, intrepid, of a grave exterior, majestic in presence, of considerable intellectual power, and the fiercest of the Caliphs of the house of Abbas. He once had the courage to engage a lion single-handed. He was little prone to mercy ; when enraged with one of his generals, he ordered him to be thrown into a pit, and to be covered over with earth. He possessed great talents for administration.

Abdullah b. Hamdun relates as follows : "Al Muatadhid set out

A.H.279. for the chase and dismounted by the side of a cucumber bed, I
A.D.891 being with him. The keeper called out loudly, and al Muatadhid said, 'bring him to me.' He was brought and the Caliph questioned him *as to the reason of his shout,* and he answered, 'there youths came upon the cucumber bed and plundered it.' They were brought before him and he decapitated them in the cucumber bed on the following day. Some time subsequently discoursing with me, he said, 'tell me truly why the people dislike me!' I replied, 'for shedding blood.' He said, 'by Allah, I have never shed blood unlawfully since I assumed the government.' I rejoined, 'why then didst thou put to death Ahmad b-ul Tayyib.' He replied, 'he sought to lead me into heresy.' I said, 'well then, the three who came down upon the cucumber bed.' He replied, 'by Allah, I did not lawlessly shed their blood, but I executed robbers who had been guilty of murder, and I had been made to believe that these were they.'"

The Kadhi Ismail b. Ishak[1] says : "I visited al Muatamid upon one occasion and he pushed a book towards me. I glanced into it and lo ! there was collected for him in it the ordinanaces of indulgence from legal observances, granted by the erroneous opinions of the learned. I exclaimed, 'the author of this is a Zindik.' He said, 'is he a fabricator ?' I replied, 'no, but[2] he who permits the use of intoxicating liquor will not hold temporary marriage lawful, and he who holds temporary marriage lawful, will not permit singing, and there is no learned man but has some error, and he who holds all the errors of the learned, his religion is gone,' where-upon he gave orders concerning the book and it was burnt."

Al Muatadhid was bold, active, and distinguished for manliness, indeed he had been present in military expeditions, and his capacity was acknowledged. He administered the government admirably and the people stood in awe of him and feared him with a great fear. Dissensions were lulled during his days through the excessive dread he inspired, and his reign was happy and full of peace and prosperity. He diminished the taxes and diffused justice and freed

---

1 He was appointed Kadhi of Baghdad A.H. 262 (875-6). De Slane, I.K.

2 The words ولكن are not in the MS.

his subjects from oppression. He used to be called as Saffah the A.H.279.
second, because he restored the power of the House of Abbas A.D.891.
which had become effects and weak and was approaching its decay, for it had been rudely shaken from the time of the assassination of al Mutawakkil. On this subject Ibn ar Rumi[1] says eulogizing him-

"Hail sons of Abbas, for your Imam
Is the Imam of right guidance, power and liberality, most worthy of praise.[2]
As with Abul Abbas (*as Saffah*) rose your power,
So with Abul Abbas likewise is it restored.
The Imam *towards* whom yesterday turns
Lamenting with grief and for whom tomorrow yearns."

To the same effect, says likewise Ibn al Muatazz-

"Dost thou not see the dominion of the House of Abbas
Hath returned triumphant after its decline.
O thou that seekest power, do like him
Be worthy of sovereignty or otherwise, *seek it* not."

In the first year during which he became Caliph he forbade booksellers from selling works on philosophy and the like of them, and prohibited story-tellers and astrologers from sitting by the wayside. He also read the prayers of the festival of Adha and pronounced the takbir in the first *Rakaat* six times, and in the second once, but the Khutbah was never heard to be delivered by him.

---

1 Abdul Hasan Ali was the son of al Abbas the son of Juraij or Jurgis (Georgius). He was considered an admirable poet, and his poems were transmitted down early by al Mutannabi who learned them from himself. He was born at Baghdad A.H. 221 (836) and died there, A.H. 283 (896). The cause of his death was poison administered by al Muatadhid's minister who feared his satirical tongue. A poisned biscuit was given to him while he was in the minister's company. The poet ate it and perceiving that he was poisoned rose to withdraw, on which the minister asked him whither he was going. "To the place you are sending me." "Present my respects to my father." "I am not taking the road to hell," retorted the poet who retired to his house and died a few days after. Ibn Khall.

2 His name, Ahmad, has this interpretation.

A.H.280. A.D.893 In the year 280, the missionary of al Mahdi entered Cyrene. His designs became spread abroad and a battle took place between him and the ruler of Africa and his authority grew apace.

In the same year came advices from Daybul that the moon had been eclipsed in the month of Shawwal, and that darkness had spread over the country till the afternoon when a black storm began to blow which continued for a third of the night, followed by a mighty earthquake which destroyed the whole city, and the number of those taken out from the ruins was one hundred and fifty thousand.

In the year 281, Makuriyah[1] in the Byzantine territory was taken. During the same the waters of Rai and Tabaristan subsided into the earth, so that water sold at three pints for the dirham, and the people were famished and fed on corpses. In the same al Muatadhid demolished the Hall of Assembly[2] at Mecca and coverted it into a place of prayer adjoining the Sacred Mosque.

In the year 282 he cancelled what had been instituted regarding the burning of fires and the pouring of water upon the people on the day of the new year and abolished the Magian year. During the same Katrun Nada (*the dew-drop*) daughter of Khumaruwayh b. Ahmad b. Tulun was led in bridal procession to his house and he consummated his marriage with her in Rabii' I. Her portion consisted of four thousand jeweled waistbands[3] and ten coffers of jewels.

In the year 283 he prescribed throughout his dominious that

---

1 I do not trace this name in Ibn Athir, and Yakut does not give it.

2 The Bab al Nadwah still exists at Mecca under its later name of Babul Atik, the Old Gate. The Hall of Assembly was built by Kusayy and contained the great tribal standard. : see page 30, and Burton's Mecca, p. 180. The new year's day was altered from the Persian date to the 11th of Huzayran the Syrian month of June, called thenceforth. النيروز المتعضدي Ibn Ath.

3 Ibn Khall says that she received one thousand mortars of gold. De Slane notes that mortars were used or pounding perfumes and were an important article of the female toilette. Ibn Khall relates on hearsay that the Caliph by marrying her purposed reducing the Tulun family to poverty.

relation[1] called Duul Arham should be capable of inheritance, and he abolished the Court of Inheritances *lapsed to the Crown* and the benedictions of the people on al Muatahid rose louder. A.H.284. A.D.897.

In the year 284 a great redness showed itself in Egypt, so that when a man looked upon the face of another, he beheld him quite red, and in the same way appeared the walls. The people supplicated the Most High in prayer, and this redness continued from the afternoon till night.

Ibn Jarir[2] relates that in this year al Muatadhid resolved upon having Muawiyah cursed from the pulpits. His minister Ubaydullah endeavoured to dissuade him by the fear of a public disturbance, but he gave no heed to him, and drew up a latter on the subject in which he mentioned many of the virtues of Ali and impugned the character of Muawiyah. The Kadhi Yusuf said to him, "Prince of the Faithful, fear a disturbance at the hearing of this." He replied, "If the populace move, I will put them to the sword." He continued, "what will thou do then, with the followers of Ali, who in every province have rebelled against thee? for when the people hear all this of the merits of the Prophetical House, they will be more inclined to them." Upon this al Mutadhid withdrew from it.

In the year 285, a yellow looking storm blew in Basrah ; it next turned green and then grew black and extended to the provinces. It was followed by hail, the weight of a hailstone being one hundred and fifty dirhams and the wind uprooted about five hundred palm trees and it rained in one village black and white stones.

In the year 286, Abu Sai'd[3] al Karmati appeared in Bahyran

---

1 ذووالارحام means in law any relations that have no portions of the inheritances termed فرائض and are not such heirs as are indicated by the term عصبة see Lane arts. ذو And رحم

2 Not Jurayr as pointed in the text. Ibn Jarir at Tabri is the author of the great commentary on the Qurãn and the celebrated history. He was born A.H. 224 (838-9) at Amul in Tabaristan and died at Baghdad 310 (923). Ibn Khall.

3 For a sketch of the Carmathians under Abu Said and his son Abu Tahir, see Ibn Khall under art. Al Jannabi, and for the history of the (cont...)

A.H.284. and his power increased. He was the father of Abu Tahir Sulayman
A.D.897. he who, as will follow, carried off the Black Stone. Engagements took place between him and the Caliph's troops. He descended upon Basrah and its environs and defeated the army of the Caliph on several occasions.

Of personal accounts of al Muatadhid recorded by al Khatib and Ibn Asakir, is the following on the authority of Abul Husayn al Khasibi who relates that al Muatadhid sent to the Kadhi Abu Hazim, saying, "verily I have a claim upon the goods of a certain person, and I have heard that his creditors have appeared before thee, and that thou hast divided his property amongst them; therefore put us down as being one of them." Abul Hazim replied, "tell him that the prince of the Faithful-may the Lord lengthen his days- when he conferred with me at the time of investing me with office, said that he put off its responsibility from his own shoulders and placed it upon my shoulders, and it is not permitted to me to pass judgment on the property of an individual in favour of a claimant without evident demonstration." *The messenger* returned and informed the Caliph who said, "tell him such a one and such a one are withnesses, alluding to two repectable persons." The Kadhi replied; "let them give testimony before me and I will examine them, and if they are just I will accept their testimony otherwise I will execute what is in my judgment established." Those persons, however, refrained from giving testimony fearing *the result* and nothing was given to al Muatadhid.

Ibn Hamdun the boon companion[1] says that al Muatadhid spent sixty thousand dinars on the construction of al Buhayrab whither he sued to retire with his slave girls, among them his favourite Durayrah.

Durayrah died during the reign of al Muatadhid, and he grieved

---

(Cont.501) Carmathians, Abul Fida, Ibn Ath, Weil, M. de Sacy's Expose de l'histoire des Druzes, and Gibbon's short but picturesque narrative.

1 Hamdun b. Ismail b. Dauud the Katib was the first of his family who followed the profession of a Nadim or boon companion. His son Ahmad was an oral transmitter of poetry and historical narrations. De Slane ; I.K.

over her with exceeding grief, and said, mourning her loss- A.H.286. A.D.899.

"O beloved ! none can equal her
As a loved one to me.
Thou art far from my sight,
But near to my heart.
Since thou art gone I have
No share in pleasures.
Thou hast in my heart, over my
Heart, though thou be away, a watcher.
And my thoughts have been of thee since
Thou hast departed, thoughts that are never absent.
Would that thou couldst see how since
Thou hast left, I lament and mourn.
An my heart ! a flame hath filled
It with burning grief.
Thou mayst truly know that I
Am disconsolate and afflicted for thee.
I do not find my soul, though I console it
For thy loss, become cheerful.
I have tears that do not resist me
And resignation that will not obey."

One author praises al Muatadhid thus, in detached sentences-

A vision approached-in the land of the Mimosa-amongst the tents-wandering about the hills : an auspicious neighbour-healing the sickness-of whomsoever it kisseth-or clingeth to. It hath a slender waist-when clasped-wearing long tresses. Then it departed, I did not sleep-for love and anxiety. Reproach censureth-how long and yet how long-a day of calamity. I labour to collect-all learning[1]-it hath therefore not perished. He is a beacon-and a place of protection-the best of mortals-by female or male descent-who

---

1 The MS. لثم has for علم

A.H.286. containeth all high resolves-and how full of manly vigour. Firm and
A.D.899. dignified-liberal of nature-who illumineth darkness-like the full moon-whose rights are protected-and what should be inviolate, guarded – wherefore he hath not sought *what is forbidden.* He distinguisheth specially and generally-in what he lavisheth. With him are favours –and punishments. Good things abound-when he smiteth-and water becometh blood-when he taketh revenge.

In Rabii, II of the year 289, al Muatadhid fell it of a grievons sickness, for his constitution was injured by the excess of his sensuality, but after a little he recovered, and Ibn al Muatazz said-

"My heart fluttered with trembling wings
Bemoaning the mishaps of calamities,
And in fear lest they should wish thee evil
Who art the lion of the kingdom and the Sword of War."

He, however, again relapsed and died on Monday the 22nd of the same month (*5th April* 902). Al Masaudi relates that they doubted whether al Muatadhid was dead and the physician drew near and felt his pulse,whereupon be opened his eyes and kicked the physician with his foot, flinging him away several yards so that the physician died and al Muatadhid died immediately after. During his last moments he thus versified :

"Enjoy the world ; for, verily, thou shalt not-live,
And snatch its brightness while it is brights, and lay aside retirement,
And be not confident of fortune, for verily I trusted to it
And it hath not left me any place nor regarded my due.
I have slain heroes among men and have not left
An enemy and given none a respite, in his own conceit. [1]
I have cleared the habitations of the kingdom of every rival.
Scattered them in the west and dispersed them in the east.
And when I reached unto the stars in glory and power,

---

1 Ibn Ath, has طغية a better reading. See his variants on this poem.

And the necks of all the people were abased before me in submission, A.H.286. A.D.899.

Death smote me with an arrow and extinguished the spark of my life.

And now am I fallen, hastening to the grave.

I have lost this world and the next through my folly.

Who is there more miserable than I am in his abasement ?

Would that I knew whether after death I shall behold

The mercies of God or be cast into hell fire."

Among the verse of al Muatadhid are the following :

"O thou who regardest me with a languishing dark eye

And slayest me with coyness and glances of love,

I complain to thee of what I have suffered

Through love : have I no relief to expect from thee ?

By thy glance and thy beauty thou hast taken

Among men the place of their eyes and thcir souls."

As Suli relates the following by him :

"None hath ever suffered from the burning of separation

What I have undergone from it.

O thou who askest me regarding its taste !

I have found it bitter of flavour.

My body is dissolved and my eye

Weeps and my heart it aflame.

Since thou art gone I have no companion

But sadness and longing.

May God watch over you both

When I am with you and without you."

Ibn al Muatazz mourns him in these lines "

"O world-shame on thee-thou hast left me no one,

And thou art a parent of evil that devourest thy children.

I ask pardon of God-this all is destiny.

I resign myself to God, this all is destiny.

A.H.289. A.D.902

I resign myself to God, the Lord, One, Eternal.

O thou dweller in the tomb in the dark earth
Of Tahiriyah, alone, in a distant abode !

Where are the armies thou wert wont to lead ?

Where the treasures whose number thou wet wont to count over ?

Where is the throne thou wert wont to fill

With awe so that the eye of him who beheld it trembled?

Where are the enemies of old whose stubbornness thou didst abse ?

Where the champions thou didst catter abroad?

Where the swift steeds whose fetlocks thou didst die with blood,

And which bore in thee a raging lion ?

Where the lances which thou didst feed on hearts ?

Since thou hast died, they have reached neither heart nor liver !

Where are the gardens whose rivulets flow[1] murmuring

And answer to them the warbling birds ?

Where are the handmaids wandering at pleasure like gazelles

Trailing coloured robes fresh from the loom ?

Where the wanton pastimes and where the red wine thou didst deem

A ruby clothed in silver mail ?

Where the assaults on thy enemies, seeking

The welfare of the kingdom of the sons of Abbas, when it had fallen into disorder ?

Thou didst not fail to subdue every mighty one among them

And to overthrow the lofty and the powerful who were

---

1 تجرَي read تجرُي

trusted in, A.H.289. A.D.902.

And now thou hast passed away, and neither trace nor vestige remains

So that thou art as if thou hadst never been."

Among the persons of note who died during the reign of al Muatadhid were Ibnul Mawwaz al Maliki, Ibn Abid Dunya, the Kadhi Ismail, al Harith b. Abi Usamah, Abul Uayna, al Mubarrad, Abu Sai'd the Cobbler the Sufi Shaykh, al Buhturi the poet and others.

Al Muatadhid left four male and eleven female children.

AL MUKTAFI BILLAH

Al Muktafi billah Abu Muhammad Ali the son of al Muatadhid was born in the beginning of the month of Rabia II, in the year 264. His mother was a Turkish woman named Jijak. His comeliness was proverbial so that one author has said :-

"I compared her beauty and her deeds

But he beauty equals not her deceit,

By Allah, I never addressed her, though verily she

Is like the sun, the full moon or Muktafi."

His father made him his heir and he was acknowledged as Caliph during his father's sickness on Friday afternoon the 19th of Rabia II 289. As Suli observes that none of the Caliphs had his name of Ali, save he and Ali b. Abi Talib, and none the surname of Abu Muhammad save al Hasan the son of Ali, al Hadi, and al Muktafi.

When he was acknowledged Caliph on the death of his father,

A.H.289. A.D.902 he was absent at Rakkah, and he Wazir Abul Hasan al Kasim b. Ubaydullah undertook the duties of receiving the oath of allegiance and wrote to him and he arrived in Baghdad on the 7th of Jumada I, and passed down the Tigris in a ship and it was a great day. The Kadhi Abu Omar fell through the bridge by reason of the crowd but was taken out unhurt. Al Muktafi alighted at the palace and the poets spoke their poems, and he bestowed seven robes of honour upon the Wazir al Kasim, and destroyed the underground prisons which his father had established, turning them into mosques. He ordered the gardens the shops which his father had taken from the people whereon to build his palace, to be restored to their owners, and he showed an excellent disposition, and the people loved him and invoked blessings upon him. During this year Baghdad was convulsed by a great earthquake which lasted for days, and also in the same, a furious wind blew at Basrah uprooting all its palm trees, the like of which had been never heard of.

In the same year rose Yahya b. Zakaruyah the Carmathian, and engagements took place between him and the troops of the Caliph until he was killed in the year 290. His brother al Husayn succeeded him and shewed the mole upon his face[1] and pretended that it was his token. He was joined by his cousin Isa b. Mahruyah[2] who asserted that al Husayn was entiled "al Mudaththir," and that he it was who was intended in the Sura (LXXIV) and he surnamed a page of his "al Mutawwak bin Nur (*Colared with Light*). He overran Syria and destroyed and ravaged and assumed the titles of al Mahdi prince of the Faithful, and prayers were made for him in the pulpits. All the three were, however, killed in the year 291.

---

1 A mark of the Imamate ; for an account of this sect of the Ismailites, their belief and mode of initiation, see Weil, Vol. II. P. 493. They are discussed at sufficient length in D'Herbelot, art. Carmath, and by Gibbon, cap LII.

2 Ibnul Mahdi, according to Ibn Ath. Who gave himself out as great-grandson of the Imam Ismail. Al Mudaththir signifies "the Covered" and the 74th Sura of the Qurãn is so entitled. Ibn al Mahdi himself gave al Husayn the title of al Mudaththir and named him his heir. Ibn Ath.

In this year Antaliyah[1] (with anl) was taken by storm, and the booty captured therefrom was beyond computation. A.H.292. A.D.904.

In the year 292 the Tigus, rose so high that the like of it had never before been seen, for it did much injury in Baghdad, the rise reaching twenty-one cubits.

The following is by as Suli eulogizing al Muktafi and mentioning the Carmathians-

"Al Muktafi the Caliph was made sufficient
For the emergency he was provident against.'"

And he goes on until he comes to

"Sons of Abbas-ye
Are the chiefs and the first of men.
Allah ordained that ye
Should be rulers over the people.
And those among ye who hold rule
Are the brightest and best of Gods creatures.
He who obeyeth you is a true believer,
And whoso rebelleth hath turned infidel.
Allah hath revealed that regarding ye
Before in the perspicuous chapters of the Qurãn."

As Suli says, "I heard al Muktafi saying during his illness, 'I grieve not but for seven hundred thousand dinars which I expended

---

1 Ibn Ath. Has I in one copy, k in another. In Yakut Antaliyah is called one of the great Byzantine cities, and its position is marked by the words of al Balkhi who says that when you pass Kalamiyah (near Tarsus) and Lamas you get to Antaliyah. Ibn Batutah fixes its position with precision. He traveled from Latakia to Alaia, thence to Antaliyah (Adalia, in the gulf of that name) proceeding onwards inland to Buldur and Isbarta. The Greek writers mention the sack of Thessalonica at this time and the coincidence of their accounts with that of the Arabs in the number of prisoners and body leads Weil to the conclusion that this place must be meant, but I believe it to be a coincidence and nothing more, as the difference of sites and names will not easily support the notion of mistaken identity.

A.H.292. from the funds of the Muslims on buildings of which I had no need
A.D.904. and which I might have done without, and verily I ask pardon of this from God.'" Al Muktafi died in the prime of life on Sunday night the 12th of Dul Kaadah in the year 295 (13th *August* 907) leaving eight male and eight female children.

Among persons of note who died during his reign were : Abdullah b. Ahmad b. Hanbal, Thaalab the great master of the Arabic language, Kunbal the Qurãn reader, Abu Abdullah al Busanji the jurisconsult, al Bazzar the author of the Musnad, Abu Muslim al Kajji, the Kadhi Abu Hazim, Salih Jazarah,[1] Muhammad b. Nasr al Marwazi, the Imam Abul Husayn an Nuri the Sufi Shaykh, Abu Jaafar at Tirmidi, the Shafii Shaykh in Irak.

I read in the History of Nyasabur by Abdul Ghafir regarding Ibn Abid Dunya that he says as follows-"when the Caliphate fell to al Muktafi I wrote to him these two couplets."

"The right of correction is a right of paternal authority
According to men of intelligence and honour.
And the most deserving of men to maintain this
And to regard it are those of the prophetical House."

The narrator adds "upon this he brought me ten thousand dirhams." This is a proof that Ibn Abid Dunya lived till the reign of al Muktafi.

AL MUKTADIR BILLAH

Al Muktadir billah, Abul Fadhl Jaafar the son of al Muatadhid was born in Ramadhan of the year 282. His mother was a Greek but some say a Turkish woman, her name Shaab, and according to another account, Gharib. When the illness of al Muktafi became

1 The MS. has icorrectly, "the son of Jazarah" whereas Jazarah was his surname. The Muntahal Arab calls him-Salih Hafidh b. Muhammad.

serious, he enquired about him, and on being assured that he had A.H.295.
reached the age of puberty, he made him his heir. None ever A.D.907.
governed the Caliphate at an earlier age than he for he was thirteen years old when he assumed power. The Wazir al Abbas b-ul Hasan regarding him as a child, sought to depose him and a party conspired with him to place Abdullah the son of al Muatazz upon the throne. The son of al Muatazz agreed to it on the condition that no blood should be spilt, but al Muktadir on hearing of this bettered the condition of al Abbas and lavished wealth upon him that contented him, upon which he reverted from his design. The rest of the conspirators, however came upon al Muktadir on the 20th of Rabii I, 296 when he was playing at ball.[1] He fled and the doors were locked, and the Wazir with a number of others were slain. The son of al Muatazz was sent for, and he came, and the generals assembled together with the Kadhis and principal men, and they swore homage to him as Caliph, and gave him the title of Ghalib billah.[2] He appointed Muhammad b. Dauud bil Jarrah his Wazir and Abul Muthanna Ahmad b. Yakub to the office of Kadhi, and letters were dispatched as issued under the Caliphate of the son of al Muatazz.

Al Muafa b. Zakariya al Jariri[3] relates as follows : "When al Muktadir was deposed and allegiance was sworn to the son of al Muatazz, people went to visit my Shaykh Muhammad b. Jarir at Tabari. He asked what the news was. He was told that the son of al Muatazz had been acknowledged Caliph. He asked who was appointed to the office of Wazir. They told him Muhammad b.

---

1 For الاكرة read بالكرة as in Ibn Ath.

2 According to Ibn Ath. "al Murtadha billah" and Weil gives also, "al Munsif billah."

3 The Kadhi Abul Faraj Muafa surnamed b. Tarara al Jariiri was a jurisonsult, a philologer, a poet, and a scholar versed in every branch of science. He held the post of Kadhi in that quarter of Baghdad called Babut Tak. He was considered also a faithful transmitter of tradition. He was born in A.H. 303 (916) and died at Nahrawan in 390 (A.D. 1,000). He was called al Jariri because he adopted the religious opinions of Ibn Jarir at Tabari, consult both names in Ibn Khall.

A.H.295. Dauud. He then enquired who was named to that of Kadhi ; he
A.D.907. was told, Abul Muthanna. Thereupon he looked down in thought, and then said, 'this affair will not succeed.' He was asked why it should not. He replied, 'every one name that you have mentioned is eminent, in its meaning high in dignity, but fortune shifts and prosperity turns its back, and I behold in this but its decline, and I cannot think that its season will endure.'"

Ibn al Muatazz now sent to al Muktadir commanding him to depart to the house of Muhammad b. Tahir in order that he himself might remove to the palace. He submitted, for there were with him only a few retainers but they said one to another, "shall we, O brethren, yield the government, and shall we not exert ourselves to avert what hath befallen us ?" And they girded on their arms and made for the quarter of al Mukharrim in which resided Ibnul Muatazz. When he beheld them surrounding him, the Lord put fear into the hearts of those with him, and they retired in disorder without fighting. Ibn al Muatazz together with his Wazir, and his Kadhi fled, and there was rapine and slaughter in Baghdad. Al Muktadir made prisoners of the jurisconsults and nobles that had deposed him, and made them over to Munis[1] the treasurer who put them to death save from death. Ibn al Muatazz was placed in confinement from which he was shortly after taken out dead. The authority now reverted to al Muktadir who appointed Abul Hasan Ali b. Muhammad al Furat his Wazir. He pursued a most praiseworthy course, brought abuses to light, and invited al Muktadir to justice. The Caliph, on account of his won inexperience, committed the administration to his care and devoted himself to amusement and frivolity and dissipated the public treasure. During this year al Muktadir ordered that Jews and Christians should be employed in menial service, and that they should ride only one packsaddles. During the same, the affairs of al Mahdi throve in Africa : he was saluted as Imam and the Caliphate was claimed as his right. He extended justice and beneficence to the people and they inclined to

1 For يونس read مونس as in Ibn Ath.

him. Africa fell under his power and his dominion increased, and the city of al Mahdiyah was founded. A.H.296. A.D.908.

Ziyadatullah b. Aghlab, the ruler of Africa, fled to Egypt,[1] but afterwards repaired to Irak. From this date Africa passed from the sway of the children of Abbas, the term of their rule over the whole of the dominions of Islam having been one hundred and sixty and odd years, and from this period dates their decline. Ad Dahabi says that the administration became disorganized under al Muktadir by reason of his youth.

In the year 300[2] a mountain near Dinawar subsided into the earth and a large quanity of water issued from beneath it and overwhelmed willages. During the same year a mule gave birth to a colt-and God is powerful to do what He willeth.

In the year 301 Ali b. ISa became Wazir. He followed a course of virtue, justice and piety. He abolished the use of wine and diminished the taxation by the amount it had been increased in the year, *viz.*, five hundred thousand dinars. During the same thc Kadhi Abu Omar was restored to the judicial office and al Muktadir rode from his palace to al Shamsiyah,[3] and this was the first ride he had made and in which he showed himself to the people. During the same al Husayn the weaver was brought into Baghdad exposed to the public gaze, on a camel. He was crucified alive,[4] and it was

1 After his decisive defeat at Arbes in Jumada II, 296 (Feb, 909) by Ubadullah's missionary and general Abu Abdullah. This last prince of the Aghlabite dynasty died according to Ibn Asakir in A.H. 304 at Ramla. The duration of the power of his House was 212 years, 5 months and 14 days. Ibn Khall, see also Weil, p. 584.

2 It was in this year also as well as in 290 that disturbances of the stars and the failure of the Nile were remarked in Egypt, as related by Abdul Latif, and troubles arose which in the latter year occasioned the fall of the House of Tulun. See his Hist. Egypt, Cap. I. Lib. II.

3 A part of Baghdad.

4 From early morning till midday for three days. According to Ibn Ath this Husayn b. Mansur denied that he pretended to the powers the vulgar accused him of claiming and he held himself to be a devout worshipper of God. Some believed in his sanctity and miraculous powers and asserted that he even raised the dead ; others condemned him as an (Cont...)

A.H.301. A.D.913. proclaimed over him-"This is one of the missionaries of the Carmathians, therefore recognize him." He was then kept in prison till he was put to death in the year 309. It was given out that he claimed divine power, and that he asserted the descent of the divinity upon eminent persons and that he wrote to his associates with long rays of light. He was questioned but found not to possess any knowledge of the Qurãn, nor of the Traditions, nor of Jurisprudence.

During the same year al Mahdi the Fatimite set out at the head of 40,000 Berbers to attack Cairo, but the Nile interposing as a barrier between him ad the city, he turned towards Alexandria and ravaged and slaughtered and then returned. The troops of al Muktadir marched against him to Barkah and several engagements took place, the Fatimite afterwards made himself master of Alexandria and Fayyum in this year.[1]

In 302 al Muktadir caused five of his children to be circumcised, and expended on the festival of their circumcision six hundred thousand dinars, and he circumcised at the same time a number of orphans and treated them with great kindness. During the same al Muktadir read the prayers for the Eed in the principal mosque of Cairo, and before this time the prayers for the Eed had never been made in it. Ali b. Abi Shaykhah read his discourse to the people from a book, and it happened that by an inaccuracy, he said, "Fear God with His true fear and die not unless ye be also infidels."[2] (Qur. III).

(Cont.513) imposter. On examination he was found to maintain nothing opposed to the law of Islam, but the Wazir Hamid was determined on his death, and catching at a hasty expression of Abu Omar's the Kadhi, that the shedding of his blood was lawful, he was barbarously scourged with a thousand stripes, his hands and feet cut off and his body burnt and the ashes thrown into the Tigris. Ibn Ath.

1 This account is confused and incorrect in order of time. Mahdi with his son, Abul Kasim first marched and took Barkah, next occupied Alexandria and Fayyum and some other towns, and was then attached by the Caliph's troops under Munis al Khadim and driven back to Africa. Ibn Ath.

2 Instead of infidels he should have said "true believers."

During this year also the Daylamites were coverted to Islam by al Hasan b. Ali[1] al Alawi al Utrush (the deaf) and before this they wee Magians. A.H.304. A.D.916.

In the year 304 Baghdad was in consternation regarding an animal called Zazbad. People said that they saw it at night upon the flat roos of the houses, and that it eat children and tore off the breasts of women. They used to watch and beat upon their drinking vessels that it might be scared and they set up covered pens for their children, and this continued for many nights.

In the year 305 the ambassadors arrived from the Roman Emperor with presents seeking to conclude a peace. Al Muktadir prepared a grangd display, and assembled the army and set them in ranks under arms, 160,000 strong, extending from the Shamasiyah gate to the palace. Behind them came the royal retinue 7,000 in number, and after them the chamberlains who were 700. The coverings that were placed upon the walls of the palace were 38,000 and were of brocade, and there were 22,000 carpets, and in the courtyard were one hundred wild beasts in chains besides other things.

In this year there arrived presents from the prince of Oman, and among them a bird, black in colour, which spoke in the languages of Persia and of India more fluently than a parrot.

In the year 306, the mother of al Muktadir opened a hospital, and the sum expended on it yearly was seven thousand dinars.[2] During the same the supreme authority fell into the hands of the Caliph's harem and his women through his imbecility, and things

---

1 He was another partisan of the Aliide cause and received the surname of an Nasir al Utrush (the deaf conqueror). He won the Daylamites to his side, converted many of them to Islam and took possession of Tabaristan from the Samanides, and his descendants ruled in parts of Daylam, Tabaristan and Ghilan to the middle of the 4th century.

2 So the text and MS. The words of Ibn Athir are : In this year al Muktadir ordered the building of a hospital ....and it was named the Muktadiri Hospital.

A.H.304. A.D.916. came to such a pass that the mother of al Muktadir governed like a queen-regent, holding audience to redress wrongs and looking into the petitions of the people every Friday. She held public audiences and used to summon the Kadhis and nobles and issue state edicte signed under her hand.

In the same year al Kaim Muhammad bal Mahdi the Fatimite returned again towards Egypt, and made himself master of a great portion of Upper Egypt. In the year 308 prices rose exceedingly high in Baghdad, and the people were starving, through the Wazir Hamid b-ul Abbas having undertaken the administration of the royal domains in the Sawad[1] and renewed wrongful exactions. The people fell to plundering and the troops rode among the populace, but they dispered them and the fighting continued some days. The mob set fire to the prison and opened the cells and plundered the citizens and stoned the Wazir and the affairs of the House of Abbas fell into great disorder. During the same year the troops of al Kaim took possession of the Delta from Fustat and the distress of the people of Cairo became grievous and they prepared for war and hostilities took place.

In the year 309 al Husayn the weaver was put to death by the sentence of the Kadhi Abu Omar and the jurisconsults and the doctors, who declared that it was lawful to shed his blood, and there are accounts of the extraordinary circumstances regarding him which authors have separately compiled.

In the year 311 al Muktadir ordered the restoration of the inheritances inherited by those who are Duul Arham,[2] to the condition from which they had been altered by al Muatadhid.

---

1 The Sawad extends in length from Hadithat ul Mausil to Abbadan and in breadth from al Udhayb to Hulwan. Hamid took their administration from Ali b. Isa whom he wished to ruin with the Caliph and who had been endeavouring to subvert Hamid's power, and in order to fill the Caliph's purse without ruining himself, he was obliged to purchase corn &c. at a high cost and instead of sending it to Baghdad, sold it in other places where he obtained a better price. This reacted on the Baghdad market and caused the popular tumult. See Weil, p. 552.

2 See Note 1, p. 501.

In the year 312, Farghanah was conquered by the ruler of Khurasan. In the year 314 the Byzantines captured Malatiyah by the sword. During the same, the Tigris was frozed over at Mosal and cattle crossed over and such a thing was never before heard of. In the year 315, the Byzantines entered Damietta and took the inhabitants prisoners with all the property therein, and sounded their bells for worship in the mosques of that town. During the same the Daylamites made their appearance in Rai and the mountainous districts, and people were slain and children slaughtered. A.H.308. A.D.920.

In the year 316, the Carmathian established a residence which he called the House of Pilgrimage.[1] It was during these years that his evil doings increased, and his conquest of towns and attacks on the Muslims, and through him calamities multiplied, and fear of him fell upon all hearts. His followers became more numerous and he sent his bands in every direction, and the Caliphate was convulsed by him, and the troops of al Muktadir were routed on several occasions. During these years the pilgrimage to Mecca was interruptec through fear of the Carmathians and the people of Mecca quitted the town. The Byzantines marched against Khalat,[2] tore down the pulpit from the principal mosque and set up the cross in the place. In the year 317 Munis al Khadim surnamed al Mudhaffar rebelled against al Muktadir because he heard that he purposed conferring on Harun b. Gharib the office of Amir ul Umara, (*chief of the Amirs*) in place of Munis himself. The whole of the military force and the nobles and the confederates advanced with him against the palace. The attendants of al Muktadir fled and al Muktadir was brought out from his palace after his evening repast on the night of the 14th of Muharram together with his mother, his

1 It was in the Katamah country near the mountaineers district of Ankijan in Barbary the head quarters of Abu Abdullah the missionary of al Madi. The account is here incorrect. The House of Pilgrimage in the Valley of the Good ذ الاخيار was established in 280 or 88 (for Ibn Ath, has a variant in the date) by Abu Abdullah who was put to death by al Mahdi in 298. The "Carmathian" in the year 316, refers to Abu Tahir. See Ibn Ath under these years.

2 In Armenia.

A.H.317. A.D.929. maternal aunt and his women and 600,000 dinars were taken from his mother. His abdication was testified to[1] and they sent of Muhammad the son of al Muatadhid, and Munis, and the nobles swore allegiance to him and surnamed him al Kahir billah (*conquering through God*). The office of Wazir was entrusted to Abu Ali b. Muklah on the Saturday and al Kahir took his seat on Sunday and the Wazir wrote informing the provinces of this. On Monday the royal procession was to be held and the troops came demanding their largesse for their covenant of allegiance and their pay for the year, Muni not being present. Voices were then loudly raised and they slew the chamberlain and made for the house of Munis demanding al Muktadir to restore him to the Caliphate. They bore him on their shoulders from the house of Munis to the palace and al Kahir was seized and he was brought out weeping and crying "Allah ! Allah ! protect me !" Al Muktadir desired him to approach and embraced him, and said, "O brother, by Allah thou art not in fault-by Allalh, no harm shall ever befall thee from me-therefore be of good cheer." The people were silent and the Wazir returned and wrote to the provinces announcing the restorating of the Caliph to the Caliphate and al Muktadir lavished sums of Money on the troops.

In this year al Muktadir sent the Mecca caravan in charge of Mansur ad Daylami. They arrived safely at Mecca. But on the day of Tarwiyah,[2] Abu Tabir the Carmathian, the enemy of God, fell upon them and slew the pilgrims in the holy temple with a swift slaughter and threw the slain into the well of Zem Zem and smote the Black Stone with an iron mace and broke it and then they dug it up. They remained at Mecca eleven days when they departed, and the Black Stone remained in their possession for more than twenty years, (50,000 dinars being offered to them for it which they refused) until it was restored in the Caliphate of al Mutii. It is said that when they carried it away, forty strong[3] camels sunk under

1 By Abu Omar the Kadhi احضروالقاضي اباعمريشهد عليه بالخلع Ibn Ath.

2 The first of the three days of pilgrimage, i.e., the 8th of Dul Hujjah.

3 Ibn Khall says three. Life of al Jannabi.

its weight from Mecca to Hajar and when it was brought back, it was borne by a lean young camel which grew fat on the road. Muhammad bur Rabii b. Sulayman relates as follows : "I was at Mecca in the year of the Carmathians when a man *of them* ascended *the temple* to tear down the water-spout,[1] I was observing him and losing patience, I cried, 'O God! what hath induced thee !" and the man fell upon his head and died on the spot" The Carmathian *(Abu Tuhir)* ascended to the door[2] of the Kaabah calling out. A.H.317. A.D.929.

"We, by Allah, and by Allah, we
Create creatures and destroy them, we.

Abu Tahir did not prosper after this, and his body was eaten up with small – pox.

During this year a great tumult arose in Baghdad regarding the saying of the Most High, "Peradventure the Lord will raise thee to an honorable station." (Qur. XVII). The Hanbalites asserted the meaning of it to be that God would place Muhammad upon His throne *beside Him,* while others maintained that this meant only the power of intercession. The Controversy continued, and they fell to blows until a great number were slain.

In the year 319 the Carmathians fell upon Kufah and the people of Baghdad feared their entry into Baghdad itself. They implored aid and lifted up their Qurãns and reviled al Muktadir.

During the same, the Daylamites entered Dinawar and took prisoners and made great slaughter.

In the year 320 Munis marched against al Muktadir, the greater part of the troops of Munis, being composed of Berbers. When the contending armies met, a Berber struck al Muktadir with a javelin by which he fell to the ground. He then slew him with a sword and

1 This was of gold, a span in width and stands out about the distance of two cubits. Ibn Batoutah. Defremery, Vol. I, 312.

2 There is only one door according to Burton, that affords entrance to the Kaabah,. It is opened only two or three times a year and is seven feet from the ground.

A.H.320. A.D.932. placed his head upon a spear. The body was stripped and remained naked until it was covered over with dry grass. A grave was dug for him on the spot and he was there buried, and this on Wednesday the 27th of Shawwal (31st October 932).

It is said that his Wazir took his horoscope on that day and al Muktadir said to him, "at what time was that ?" He replied, "at the hour of sunset." The Caliph took it as a bad omen and purposed turning back, but the horsemen of Munis approached and the battle began. As to the Berber who slew him, the people called out against him, and he rode on towards the palace to bring out al Kahir when he encountered a stack of brambles which threw him violently over his bridle, a prog caught him and the horse passed from under him in his gallop and he was killed. The people pulled him down and burnt him with the bramble stack.

Al Muktadair had good sense and sound judgment, but was addicted to sensuality and drinking and profuse in his expenditure. His women had entire influence over him, and he lavished upon them the whole of the crown jewels and precious objects and bestowed upon one of his concubines a matchless pearl, the weight of which was three mithkals,[1] and he gave Zaydan the Comptroller of the Haren a string of jewels, the like of which were never seen, and he wasted immense wealth. He had in his palace eleven thousand eunuch boys, besides slaves and Greeks and negroos. He left twelve male children, three of whom ruled the Caliphate, *viz.*, ar Radhi, al Mutakki and al Mutii. The same occurred with al Mutawakkul and ar Rashid, but it the instance of Abdul Malik four of his children held sway-and there is no parallel to this except among temporal sovereigns. Thus observes ad Dahabi. I note, however, that in my time, five of the sons of al Mutawakkil held the Caliphate, al Mustain al Abbas, al Mautadhid Dauud, al Mustakfi Sulayman, al Kaim Hamzah, and al Mustanjid Yusuf, which is unparalleled.

---

1 A mithkai is one dinar's weight or 1 3/7 of a dirham equal to about four and a half drams.

In the Latiful Maarif of at Thaalabi is the strange fact that none of the name of Jaafir governed the Caliphate, save al Mutawakkil and al Muktadir, and they were both put to death-the former on the night[1] preceding the fourth day of the week, the latter on the fourth day itself. A.H.320. A.D.932.

Among praiseworthy actions of al Muktadir is the following related by Ibn Shahin, namely, that his Wazir Ali b. Isa desired to effect a reconciliation between Ibn Said[2] and Abu Bakr b. Abi Dauud as Sijistani and the Wazir said, "O Abu Bakr, Abu Muhammad (*b. Sai'd*) is older than thou, wert thou then to make the advance to him, *it would be fitting.*" He replied, "I will not." The Wazir said, "thou art a vain old man." He replied, "nay, the vain old man is he-the liar against the apostle of God." Saying this Ibn Abi Dauud rose, and exclaimed, "thou thinkest that I am inferior to thee because my stipend cometh to me from thy hand-by Allah, I will never take anything at thy hands." Al Muktadir hearing of this weighed out his daily allowance with his own hand and sent it one a platter by his servant.

Of distinguished persons who died during the reign of al Muktadir were, Muhammad b. Abi Dauud ad Dhahiri, Yusuf, b. Yakub the Kadhi, Ibn Sarih the Shafii Shaykh, al Junayd the Sufi Shaykh, Abu Othman al Hiri the devotee, Abu Bakr al Birdiji, Jaafar al Kariyani,[3] Ibn Bassam the poet, an Nasai the author of the Sunan, al Hasan b. Sufiyan author of the Sunan, al Jubbai the Muatazalite Shaykh. Yamut b. Muzarra'[4] the grammarian : Ibnul Jala the Sufi Shaykh, Abu Yala al Mausili author of the Musnad, al Ashnani the Qurãn reader, Ibn Sayf one of the great Qurãn readers of Cairo, Abu Bakr ar Ruyani author of the Musnad, Ibnul Mundir the Imam, Ibn Jarir at Tabari, az Zajjaj the grammarian, Ibn Khuzaymah, Ibn

---

1 It must be remembered that the Muhammadan day begins at sunset.

2 Yahya b. Muhammad b. Said al Baghdadi an eminent traditionist died in A.H. 318, at the age of 90. Ibn Ath.

3 Ibnul Ath. has two variants, al Faryabi and al Gharyani.

4 The next is here incorrect, the life of this grammarian will be found in Ibn Khall.

A.H.320. A.D.932. Zakariya the physician, al Akhfash the Less, Bannan al Jammal, Abu Bakr b. Abi Dauud as Sijistani, Ibnus Sarraj the grammarian, Abu Auanah the author of the Sahih,[1] Abul Kasim al Baghawi al Musnid,[2] Abu Ubayd b. Harbubah, al Kaabi the Muatazelite Shaykh, Abu Omar the Kadhi, Kudamah the Secretary and others.

AL KAHIR BILLAH

Al Kahir billah Abu Mansur Muhammad was the son of al Muatadhid b. Talbah b. Mutawakkil. His mother was a slave concubine called Fitnab. When al Muktadir was slain, he was summoned together with Muhammad the son of al Muktafi, and they asked the son of al Muktafi whether he would accept the government. He replied, "I have no need of it, and my uncle here has a better right to it." Al Kahir was then addressed and he accepted, and the oath of allegiance was sworn to him and he was surnamed al Kahir billah, as he had been thus surnamed in 317.

His first act was to despoil the family of al Muktadir and to maltreat them, and he scourged the mother of al Muktadir till she died under the punishment.

In the year 321 the army was unfavorable to him, and Munis and Ibn Muklah,[3] and others conspired to dethrone him in favour of

---

1 More properly speaking author of a Musnad extracted from the Sahih of Muslim. See Ibn Ath, anno, 312.

2 I do not find this personage mentioned by Ibn Ath., but De Slane mentions a traditionist named, as in the text, who died in 317, the author of a Mujam or catalogue of the Companions of Muhammad. Musnid signifies a reader of isnads or ascriptions. De Slane elsewhere makes it synonymous with Hafidh.

3 The life of this celebrated scribe and minister may be read in Ibn Khall whose narrative throws light on the events of this and the succeeding reign. He was the inventor (or his brother, for the question is in dispute) of the style of writing termed Sharki or Oriental, derived from the characters used by the people of Kufah.

the son of al Muktafi, but al Kahir intrigued with them till he seized their persons and put them to death and immured the son of al Muktafi between two walls. As for Ibn Muklah, he concealed himself, but his house and the houses of the conspirators were burnt down. Al Kahir now discharged the pay of the troops who were the quieted, and his authority became firmly established, and awe of him filled the minds of men. To his titles was added that of "Chastiser of the enemies of God," which was engraved upon the coinage. A.H.321. A.D.933.

In this year he issued a prohibition against female musicians,[1] and the use of wine, and arrested all singers and forbade the employment of infamous persons, and he broke all instruments of idle diversion, but permitted the sale of female singers on the condition of their being of rustic and simple manners, yet withal he did not relinquish intemperance himself nor desist from listening to music.

In the year 322 Daylamites grew in power and this because the followers of Mardawij[2] entered Ispahan, and among their leaders was Ali b. Buwayh who gaining considerable resources, detached himself from his chief Mardawij. Subsequently he engaged Muhammad b. Yakut the Caliph's governor *of Ispahan ;* Muhammad was defeated and Ibn Buwayh occupied Fars. Buwayh himself had been in very poor circumstances and employed himself in catching fish. He saw himself in a dream, as it were a whale, and there came forth from his person a column of fire, and the column dispered until it filled the earth. This was interpreted to mean that his posterity would rule the world, and that their dominion would reach to the limits embraced by the fire. Years passed by and events resulted in his becoming a general under Mardawij Ziyad

1 The MS. has قيان Ibn Ath. states that the Caliph's object in all this was not to reform morals, but to purchase at a cheap rate for his own amusement, the singing girls whom he forbade his subjects to entertain. "Heaven preserve us," he pathetically adds, "from such morals as these."

2 Of Ghilan, one of the soliders of fortune who figured in the wars between the Aliides and the Samanides in Tabaristan. See Weil, pp. 651-2-3, and 657.

A.H.322. ad Daylami who despatched him to obtain resources from Karaj.[1]
A.D.934. He wrung out of it five hundred thousand dirhams and marched to occupy Hamadan. The inhabitants closed the gates against him, but he attacked them and took it by storm, though some say, by treaty, and then set out for Shiraz. Subsequently his resources ran short, and one day when he was lying asleep on his back, a serpent crept out of the roof of the hall *where he was.* He ordered it to be pulled down and there were taken from it chests of gold which he distributed amongst his troops. *At another time* he sent for a tailor to sew something for him : the man was deaf and imagined that information had been laid against him, whereupon he exclaimed, "by, Allah, I have nothing but twelve chests and I know not what is in them." They were sent for and there were found in them vast sums of money. On another occasion as he was riding, the legs of his horse sunk into the earth, which on digging up they found to contain treasure. He made himself master of the provinces, and Khurasan and Fars passed away from the rule of the Caliph.

During this year al Kahir put to death Ishak b. Ismail an Naubakhi, he who had counseled the elevation of al Kahir to the Caliphate. He, cast him down head foremost into a well and filled it up. His crime was, that before the Caliphate of al Kahir, he had outbid him for a female slave and bought her, for which reason he bore him a grudge. During the same the army was incited against him because Ibn Muklah during his concealment put them in dread of him, saying, "he has built dungeons for you to imprison you" and the like, and they assembled to assault him and forced an entrance upon him, sword in hand, but he fled. They, however, overtook him and seized him on the 6th of Jumada I[2] (25th *April* 934) and swore allegiance to Abul Abbas Muhammad the son of al Muktadir and surnamed him ar Radhi billah. Then they dispatched to al Kahir his

---

1 Not Karkh as in the text. The MS. is here correct. Karaj is between Ispahan and Hamadan

2 The text and MS. have Jumada II, but this is wrong. All the other authorities give Jumada I, and the duration of al Kahir's reign which was I year 6 months and 8 days, proves it.

Wazir and the Kadhis Abul Husayn the son of the Kadhi Abu Omar, A.H.322.
and al Hasan b. Abdillah b. Abis Shawarib, and Abu Talib b-ul A.D.934.
Buhlul. They accordingly went and al Kahir was asked what he had to say. He replied, "I am Abu Mansur Muhammad the son of al Muatadhid and the covenant of allegiance to me is upon your necks and upon the necks of the people, and I will not release nor absolve ye from it-therefore depart." They retired and the Wazir said, "he must be deposed and there is not need of reflection[1] on his deeds which are notorious." The Kadhi Abul Husayn thus continues the narration. "I then went to ar Radhi and recounted to him what had passé and informed him that I considered his assumption of the Caliphate as a bounden duty." He replied, "depart and leave me and him." He then directed Sima the commander of the guards to blind him, who therefore seared his eyes with a red hot needle. Mahmudal Ispahani says : "The cause of al Kahir's deposition was the depravity of his nature and his shedding of blood. He refused to abdicate, they therefore branded his eyes till they came out upon his cheeks." As Suli observes that he was violent and blood-thirsty, of a depraved disposition, volatile and inconstant, and addicted to intemperance, and that had it not been for the munificence of his chamberlain Salamah, the whole country[2] would have been ruined. He had also made for him a javelin which he carried about, and he never cast it aside until he had slain a man with it. Ali b. Muhammad al Khurasani, narrates as follows. "Al Kabir sent for me one day, and the Javelin was before him, and he said, "I wish to ask you regarding the Caliphs of the House of Abbas-as to their qualities and dispositions." I replied, "with regard to as Saffah-he was quick to shed blood and his prefects imitated him in that respect, but he was withal munificent and liberal with money." He said, "and al Mansur ?" I continued, "he was the first who threw dissension between the descendants of al Abbas and the descendants of Abu Talib who before that were united, and he

1 I prefer the reading of the MS. here which is يخلع ولاتفكرفيه افعاله مشهورة and which would run. "He should be deposed and do not reflect about it-his deeds are notorious."

2 Literally, the soil and its products.-See Qur. II.

A.H.322. A.D.934. was the first Caliph who gave access to astrologers, and the first who had translated for him Syrian and Persian works like the book of Kalilah and Damnah and the book of Euclid and *other* Greek works, and the people read them and took to them. And when Muhammad b. Ishaq observed this, he compiled his work on battles and military expeditions. Al Mansur likewise was the first who employed his slaves in service and preferred them over the Arabs." He asked, "and al Mahdi?" I replied, "he was generous, just and equitable. He restored what his father had taken by violence from the people, and was zealous in rooting out the Zindiks. He also re-fashioned the sacred temple of Mecca and the mosques of Median and Jerusalem." He exclaimed "and what of al Hadi?" I answered, "he was a proud tyrant, and his prefects walked in his way during his short reign." He went on, "and ar Rashid?" I said , "He was devoted to war and pilgrimage, and he established house and reservoirs of water on the road to Mecca and fortified the frontier positions of Kadanah, Tarsus, Masisah and Marash. His bounty embranced the people at large, and during his days flourished the Barmecides with their renowned munificence. He was the first Caliph who played at polo and who shot arrows at a target and who played at chess." "And al Amin ?" I said, "he was bountiful but absorbed on sensuality, and affairs fell into disorder."

"And al Mamun ?"

I said, "astrology and philosophy had too much influence over him, but he was forbearing and munificent."

"And al Muatasim ?"

I replied, "he followed in his footsteps, but the love of horsemanship and the imitation of foreign potentates unduly swayed him, and he occupied himself in war and conquest."

"And al Wathik ?"

I replied, He walked in the ways of his father."

"And what of al Mutawakkil ?"

I said, "he was opposed to the course of conduct of all Mamun and al Muatasim and al Wathik in the matter of religious belief, and prohibited contention and controversies and disputes and punished them, and he commanded the reading and hearing of traditions, and forbade the doctrine of the creation of the Qurãn, wherefore the people loved him." Then he asked concerning the rest of the Caliphs, and I answered him in what regarded them, and he said to me, "I have heard thy discourse, and it is as if I saw the actors themselves." Then he arose and departed. A.H.322. A.D.934.

Al Masaudi says that al Kahir confiscated an immense amount of property from Munis and his followers, and when he was deposed and blinded, he was asked for it, but he refused compliance, and he was tortured in various ways, but would not confess anything. Then al Radhi billah took him and caused him to approach and broght him close and said to him, "verily thou seest the demands of the army for money, and I possess nothing and what thou hast, doth not profit thee, therefore confess where it is." He replied-"well, if thou doest this,[1] why then the money is buried in the garden." For he had formerly laid out a garden in which were trees of various kinds brought to him from the provinces and he had embellished it and built therein a pavilion and ar Radhi was much attached to the garden and the pavilion, and he said, "in what part of it is the treasure?" He replied, "I am blind and cannot be a guide to the place but dig up the garden and you will find it." Ar Rashid dug up the garden, and the foundations of the pavilion, and rooted up to trees but found nothing, and he said to al Kahir "where is the treasure?" Al Kahir replied, "have I any treasure ? my only regret was thy sitting in the garden and thy enjoyment of it, and I therefore wished to grieve thee through its loss."

Ar Radhi repented *of what he had done* and put him in prison where he remained till the year 333 when they released him and left him at liberty. He was standing one day in the mosque of al Mansur among the ranks *of the worshippers* wearing a lined garment of white, when he exclaimed-"Give me alms for I am one whom ye know :" and this was in the reign of al Mustafi and *done*

---

1 I read with the MS. اذا for اذ.

A.H.322. in order to dishonour him. For this he was forbidden to appear in
A.D.934. public till he died in the year 339 on the 3rd Jumada I, (18th *October* 950) at the age of three and fifty. The sons he had were Abdus Samad, Abul Kasim, Abul Fadhl and Abdul Aziz.

Of persons of note who died in his reign were at Tahawi the Hanafite Shaykh, Ibn Durayd, Abu Hashim al Jubbai and others.

AR RADHI BILLAH

Ar Radhi Billah, Abul Abbas Muhammad the son of al Muktadir was born in the year 297. His mother was a Greek slave concubine called Dhalum. He received the oath of allegiance on the day of the deposition of al Kahir and he commanded Ibn Muklah to draw up a document containing the misdemeanour of al Kahir and to read it to the people.

During the year of the Caliphate, that is 322-died Mardawij[1] the Daylamite chief in Ispahan. His power had grown great, and they say that he even purposed marching against Baghda, and that he cultivated the friendship of the chief of the Magians-and he used to declare that he would restore the Persian monarchy and annihilate the Arab power.

In the same year Ali b. Buwayh sent to ar Radhi proposing the retention of the provinces he had conqurred as a fief of the Caliphate

---

1 According to Ibn Ath. he was murdered by the Turks in his service in 323. He used to assert that the spirit of Solomon, dwelt in him, and that the Turks were devils who could be made submissive only by violent measures-which he consistently resorted to. A little before his assassination, which was instigated by Tuzun who became afterwards the commander in chief at Baghdad-he had made for himself a golden throne on which he sat surrounded by his nobles on silver seats, and he wore a crown of gold after the manner of the Khusroes. He purposed, to rebuild Madain and the palace of the Persian kings, and to have himself saluted as king of kings. Ibn Athir's narrative will repay perusal.

on the yearly paymen of 800,000[1] dirhams. The Caliph therefore sent him a standard and a robe of honour. Ibn Buwayh subsequently put off indefinitely the payment of the money. A.H.322. A.D.934.

During the same year died al Mahdi the ruler of Africa. His reign was twenty-five years in duration. He was the ancestor of the Egyptian Caliphs whom the vulgar call the Fatimites, because this al Mahdi claimed to be a descendent of Ali, while in truth his ancestor was a Magian.

The Kadhi Abu Bakr al Bakilani says-"the grandfather of Ubaydullah surnamed al Mahdi was a Magian. Ubaydullah entered Egypt and gave out that he was a descendant of Ali, but none of the genealogists would acknowledge him as such. He was a Batini-a reprobate, thirsting to extirpate the religion of Islam. He got rid of the learned and the jurisconsults that he might be able to seduce the people and his posterity followed his example. They made wine-bibbing and fornication lawful and disseminated heresy. After his death his son al Kaim Biamrillah Abul Kasim Muhammad Succeeded him. In this year appeared Muhammad b. Ali al Shalmaghani known as Ibn Abi Azakir.[2] It was reported that he claimed divine power and raised the dead to life. He was put to death and crucified, and a number of his companions were put to death with him. In the same Jied Abu Jaafar as Sajzi one of the Chamberlains. It is said that he reached the age of 140 and that all his senses were in sound condition. From this year the pilgrimage to Mecca from Baghdad was interrupted[3] until the year 327.

In the year 323 ar Radhi billah ruled in paramount authority

---

1 The MS and text here have 800,000,000 - but this sum would be equivalent to about £20,000,000 sterling which is of course absurd, Ibn Ath. mentions that he offered the Caliph a lump sum of a million dirhams (about £25,000) but says nothing of an annual tribute. One (الف) (thousand-therefore omitted in the text would bring the amount approximately to that mentioned by Ibn Ath.

2 Ibn Khall. Notices this individual in his life of Ibn al Mukaffa, and says that he was burnt by fire and his disciple Ibn Abi Aun crucified after being beheaded.

3 By the Carmathians.

A.H.322. A.D.934. and conferred the east and west on his two sons Abul Fadhl and Abu Jaafar.

During the same occurred the well known affair of Ibn Shanabud[1] and the recantation he was called upon to make regarding his unorthodox reading of the Qurãn, and his declaration that was taken down and that in the presence of the Wazir Abu Ali B. Muklah.

In the same year in Jumada I, a violent storm blew in Baghdad- the earth was darkened and the darkness contined from the afternoon till sunset.

During the month of Dul Kaadah of the same, the stars kept falling all night with extraordinary frequency, the like of which has been never recorded.

In the year 324 Muhammad b. Raik, governor of Wasit and its dependencies obtained supreme predominance in the state. He issued orders to the provinces, and the offices of the minister of state and of the controllership of the public registers were abolished, and he and his scribes took charge of the whole, and all monies were taken to him and the state treasuries were abolished and ar Radhi remained with him as a mere plantom, having nothing of the Caliphate but the name. In the year 325 affairs fell into great confusion. The provinces became a prey either to a rebel that seized them or to a prefect who would not pay the state revenues, and they became separate independent princes and nothing remained in the possession of ar Rashi but Baghdad and the Sawad on account of the hand of Ibn Raik being upon him.[2]

---

1 Abul Hasan Muhammad a famous reader of the Qurãn, but whose readings deviated from the received orthodox text. Ibn Khall gives various instances of his misreadings, and adds that he was reported to be a man of little knowledge. When he was being scourged by order of Ibn Muklah, he cursed him and prayed that God would cause his hand to be cut off which actually took place. He died at Baghdad in 328 (939).

2 Basrah appertained to Ibn Raik, Khuzistan was held by al Baridi, Fars by Imadud Dawlah Ibn Buwayh. Kirman by Abu Ali Muhammad (Con..)

When the power of the Caliphate in these times waxed feeble, and the pillars of the Abbaside dominion tottered to their fall, and the Carmathians and other heretics became supreme in the provinces, the spirit of the Amir Abdur Rahman, the descendant of Umayyah and Marwan, ruler of Spain, became emboldened, and he said, "I am the most worthy of men for the Caliphate." He called himself prince of the Faithful, the Defender of the religion of God. He held ruler over the greater part of Spain. He inspired great awe and carried on religious wars, and commanded military expeditions, and possessed many eminent qualities, and he overthrew all rivals, and captured seventy fortresses. There were thus three personages calling themselves princes of the Faithful, the Abbaside at Baghdad, this one in Spain, and al Mahdi at Cyrene. A.H.324. A.D.936.

In the year 326 Bahkam[1] rose against Ibn Raik and prevailed over him and Ibn Raik concealed himself. Bahkam entered Baghdad and ar Radhi received him with honour, raised him in dignity and gave him the title of Amirul Umara and invested him with the government of Baghdad and Khurasan.

In the year 327, Abu Ali Omar b. Yahya, the descendant of Ali, wrote to the Carmathian leader with whom he was on friendly terms, soliciting him to open the road free to pilgrims, and that he would give him five dinars for every camel. Permission was accorded and the people performed the pilgrimage, and this was the first year that mail was levied from pilgrims.

(Cont. 530) b-ul Yas Rai, Ispahan and the mountainous districts were fought for by Ruknud. Daulah another son of Buway's and Washmagir brother of Mardawij ; the Hamdanites ruled in Mesopotamia, the Ikshides in Syria and Egypt, the Fatimites in Africa, the Umayyads in Spain, the Samanides in Khurasan and the trans Oxus country, the Daylamites in Tabaristan and Jurjan and the Carmathians in Yemamah and Bahrayn. Such is the picture drawn by Ibn Ath of the now distracted Caliphate.

1 Or Bajkam. He was a Turk and originally a slave of the Daylamite Wazirs and afterwards of the Daylamite prince Makan under whom he commanded a troop of horse. He afterwards served under Mardawij, and eventually offered his services to the Caliph, and Ibn Raik called him with his Turkish and Daylamite following to Baghdad. See Weil, p. 664.

A.H.329. In the year 328, Baghdad was swamped by a terrible
A.D.940. inundation,so that the rise of the water reached nineteen cubits and men and animals were drowned and houses destroyed.

In the year 329, ar Radhi fell ill and died in the month of Rabii I,[1] at the age at of thirty-one and a half. He was beneficent, liberal and accounplished, skilful in versifying, eloquent and a patron of men of learning, and a collection has been made of his poetry. He heard tradtions from al Baghawi and others. Al Khatib observes that some notable particularities distinguished him ; among these-that he was the last of the Caliphs whose verses were collected together, and the last of the Caliphs who undertook the sole direction of the army and the finances, the last who preached on Fridays, and the last who sat with boon companions. His largesses and his state surroundings were after the manner of the former Caliphs, and he was the last of the Caliphs who journeyed in the fashion of his predecessors.

Among his verses are the following-
"All that is pure tends to defilement[2]
And all things to decay.
And the march of youth towards
Death-is in death or affliction.
May hoariness be abundant
As a monitor to warn mortals.
O thou who entertainest hope and
Art confounded in an occan of deception,
Where are they that were before us ?
Their forms and traces have disappeared.
O God, pardon my sin,
Thou who art the best of those who pardon."

---

1 Abul Fida and Ibn Ath have Rabii I. Weil gives one authority that writes Rabii II, but as the justly observes, this date does not coincide with the duration of ar Radhi's reign which was 6 years 10 months, and (according to Ibn Ath.) ten days. Abul Fida makes him 32 year old. Ibn Ath. 33 and some months. They both say that he died in the middle of the month which would be about (18th Dec. 940).

2 Ibn Ath, and Abul Fida give these verse with variants.

Abul Hasan b. Zarkuyah relates on the autority of Ismail al A.H.329.
Khatabi,[1] that he said : "Ar Radhi sent for me on the eve of the A.D.940.
close of the Ramadhan fast. I went to him and he said, 'O Ismail, I purpose tomorrow to pray before the people-what shall I say when I come to the supplication for myself ?' I looked down in though for a little while, and I exclaimed, 'say, O prince of the Faithful ! "O Lord excite me, that I may be thankful for thy favour wherewith thou hast favoured me and my parent,'" &c., (Qur. XXVII). He replied, 'that will suffice.' Afterwards a servant followed me and gave me four hundred dinars."

Of people of note who died in his reign were : Niftawayh, Ibn Mujahid the Qurãn reader, Ibn Kas the Hanafite, Ibn Abi Hatim, Mabraman, Ibn Abd Rabbih author of the Ikd[2] (*necklace*) al Istakhari, the Shafiite Shaykh, Ibn Shanabud, Abu Bakr al Anbari and others.

AL MUTTAKI LIL LAH

Al Muttaki lil lah Abu Ishak Ibrahim was the son of al Muktadir. He was acknowledged Caliph on the death of his brother ar Radhi, being thirty-four years old. His mother was a slave girl called Khalub or as some say, Zuhrah. He never made any changes *in his establishment* nor secretly visited a female slave that he had. He used to fast and pray much, and he never drank wine, and he used to say, "I need no boon companion but the Qurãn." He had nothing of authority but the name, and the administration was in the hands

---

1 I cannot find this name in Ibn Khall : both the MS. and text have خطبي a form I have not before met-it should be, perhaps خطيبي or خطابي

2 See his life in Ibn Khall. The Ikd contains much important information on the manners of ancient Arabs of which some-extracts have been given by M. Fresnel in his letters.

A.H.330. A.D.941. of Ibn[1] Abdullah Ahmad b. Ali al Kufi the secretary of Bahkam. In this year the green dome of the city of Mansur[2] which was the crown of Baghdad and a memorial of the house of Abbas, fell in. It was one of the edifices crected by Mansur. Its height was eighty cubits, and below it was a hall, its length twenty cubits by twenty cubits, and over it was the statue of a horsemen with a spear in his hand, and when he turned facing towards any direction, it was known that a rebel had risen up in that quarter. The summit of this dome fell in during a night of rain and thunder.

In this year Bahkam[3] the Turk was slain and Kurtakin the Daylamite succeeded him in the office of Amirul Umara. Al Muttaki took possession of the treasures of Bahkam that were in Baghdad and they were more than a million dinars. Subsequently in this year Ibn Raik,obtained predominance and fought Kurtakin al Baghdad.[4] Kurtakin was routed and he concealed himself while Ibn Raik became Chief Amir in his place.

In 330 there occurred a scarcity in Baghdad so that a "kur" of wheat fetched 316 dinars. Distress was in consequence very severe and people fed on corpses, and it was a famine the like of which had never been seen in Baghdad.

During the same year Abul Husayn Ali Ibn Muhammad al Baridi[5] raised the standard of revolt and the Caliph and Ibn Raik

---

1 Abu Abdullah. Ibn Ath.

2 Baghdad, because built by him. Yakut, on the authority of al Khatib, mentions the horsemen that stood on it, and which pointed in the direction of any rebellion as it occurred,-but adds that he considers it a most preposterous falsehood. Neither the dome nor the horsemen existed when Ibn Batutah visited it about 1330 A.D. Let the horsemen with his spear be considered- what it may have been – a simple weather-cock, and the wonder vanishes, for from "a" the airts the wind can blaw" came daily tidings of disaster and rebellion.

3 During a hunting excursion he came upon a troop of Kurds who had amassed considerable plunder. He followed them up, and in the melee he was fallen upon from behind and transfixed with a spear. Ibn Ath.

4 This engagement took place according to Ibn Ath. at Ukbarah, a town on the Tigris ten parasangs from Baghdad.

5 Not Yazidi as in the text. The family of Baridi were masters of Khuzistan during ar Radhi's reign.

set out to engage him, but they were defeated and fled to Mosal, and Baghdad and the royal palace were sacked. A.H.331. A.D.942-3

When the Caliph arrived at Takrit he found there Sayfud Daulah Abul Hasan Ali b, Abdillah b. Hamdan and his brother al Hasan. Ibn Raik was treacherously assassinated, and the Caliph appointed al Hasan b. Hamdan to his office and gave him the title of Nasirud Daulah (*Defender of the State*) and to his brother a robe of honour and surnamed him Sayfud Daulah, (*The Sword of the State*). He then returned to Baghdad accompanied by these two, upon which al Baridi fled to Wasit. Subsequently advices arrived in the month of Dul Kaadan that al Baridi was marching on Baghdad, whereupon the people were alarmed and the principal men of Baghdad fled. The Caliph set forth in order to be with Nasirud Daulah, while Sayfud Daulah marched to meet al Baridi.[1] A desperate engagement took place between the two near Madain. Al Baridi was defeated and returned in disheartened mood to Wasit. Sayfud Daulah pushed on to Wasit and al Baridi retreated to Basrah.

In the year 331 the Byzantines made a raid as far as Arzan, Mayyafarikin and Nisibin and slaughtered and took prisoners. Then they demanded the handkerchief preserved in the church of Edessa with which they believe the Messiah to have wiped his face by which its image was impressed upon it, engaging in turn to release all those they had taken captive. It was sent to them and the prisoners were set free.

During the same the nobles of Wasit rose against Sayfud Daulah who fled on relays of post horses making for Baghdad. His brother Nasirud Daulah then set out for Mosal in fear on account of the the flight of his brother. Tuzun[2] left Wasit and marched on Baghdad from which Sayfud Daulah had fled to Mosal. Tuzun entered Baghdad in Ramadhan and al Muttaki presented him with a robe of honour and appointed him chief of the Amirs. Soon afterwards

1 Several consecutive engagements took place continuing for some days in one of which Sayfud Daulah was worsted. He was reinforced by his brother and succeeded in routing al Baridi.

2 See Not 2. p. 511.

A.H.331. A.D.942-3. there fell a mutual distrust between al Muttaki and Tuzun. Tuzun sent Abu Jaafar b. Shirzad from Wasit to Baghdad which he governed (*in Tuzun's absence*) issuing his commands and prohibitions. Al Muttaki then wrote to Ibn Hamdan to come to him, who advanced at the head of a considerable force. Ibn Shirzad concealed himself and al Muttaki and his family set out for Takrit and Nasirud Daulah moved forward with a large army consisting of Arabs and Kurds to engage Tuzun. The two armies met at Ukbara[1] and Ibn Hamdan and the Caliph retreated in disorder to Mosal. A second engagement afterwards took place and Ibn Hamdan and the Caliph fled to Nisibin, upon which the Caliph wrote to al Ikhshid[2] the ruler of Egypt to come to him.

Subsequently he received at the hands of the House of Hamdan much annoyance and vexation upon which he proposed a reconciliation with Tuzun who consented and confirmed his words by oath. Later al Ikhshid repaired to al Muttaki who was at Rakkah and the news of the reconciliation with Tuzun having already reached him, he said, "Prince of the Faithful, I am thy slave, and verily I know the Turks and their evil deeds and their treacher-then ten Lord protect thee-come with me to Egypt for it is thine and be in safety for thy person." He would not however consent, and al Ikshid returned to his dominions, and al Muttaki set out from Rakkah

---

1 Us Suyuti seems in error here and is confusing this engagement with that between Ibn Raik and Kurtakin (p. 413). Ibn Ath. says that a series of actions between Nasirud Daulah and Ibn Hamdan took place during three days at 2 parasangs below. Takrit and Takrit is 30 parasangs from Baghdad and therefore 20 from Ukbara.

2 This family was descended from the princes of Farghanah. The Caliph al Muatasim billah drew into his service a number of soldiers from Farghanah among whom was Juff, grandfather of Abu Bakr Muhammad al Ikhshid father of Tughj. See Ibn Khall, and Abul Mahasin Nujum, Part I, page 251. Or Tulun and Ikhshid, Gibbon says, "The founders of these two potent dynasties confessed either in words or actions the vanity of ambition. The first on his death-bed implored the mercy of God to a sinner ignorant of the limits of his own power : the second in the midst of 400,000 soldiers and 8,000 slaves concealed from every human eye the chamber where he attempted to sleep." Chap. LII. Ikhshid signifies according to Abul Mahasin, king of kings in the Farghanian tongue.

to Baghdad on the 4th of Muharram, 433. Tuzun went forth to meet A.H.331.
him and they met between Anbar and Hit. Tuzun dismounted and A.D.942-3.
kissed the ground, and al Muttaki commanded him to remount, but he would not do so and walked on foot before him to the camp he had pitched for him. When the Caliph alighted, Tuzun seized him together with Ibn Muklah and those that were with him. Shortly after the blinded the Caliph with a hot iron, and he was taken into Baghdad with his eyes seared, his ring mantle and scepter having been taken from him. Tuzun then sent for Abdullah the son of al Muktafi and swore allegiance to him as Caliph and he was surnamed al Mustakfi billah (*contening himself with God*). Then the blinded Muttaki swore him allegiance and thus testified to his own abdication on the 20th of Muharram, or as it is said of Safar, [1] (12th *October,* 944)

When he was blinded, al Kahir (*the deposed Caliph*) said-

"I and Ibrahim (*al Muttaki*) are two blind old men,

There must be to the two old men but one common end.

As long as Tuzun holds sway

Which is implicity obeyed, the blinding iron will be the chafing dish."[2]

But a year did not elapse before Tuzun died. As for al Muttaki, he was conveyed to an island opposite Sindiyyah[3] where he was imprisoned. He remained in prison twenty-five years till his death in Shaaban 357. In the reign of al Muttaki lived Hamdi the robber to whom Ibn Shirzad when he governed Baghdad accorded the license of robbing therein on the payment to him of 25,000 dinars a

1 All the other authorities give the latter date.

2 The MS. has جمر for مجمر which is perhaps a better reading.

3 Sindiyyah was a village situated on the Isa Canal between Anbar and Baghdad. Yakut.

A.H.333. A.D.944. month.[1] He used to fall unawares upon the houses of the people with torches and lights and carry off their property. Ishuraj the Daylamite who held the post of chief of police in Baghdad, caught him and sawad him in half, and this in the year 332.

Of distinguished persons who died during the reign of al Muttaki[2] were Abu Yakub an Nahrjuri one of the disciples of Junayd, the Kadhi Abu Abdillah al Mahamali, Abu Bakr al Farghani the Sufi, the Hafidh Abul Abbas b. Akadah, Ibn Wallad the grammarian and others.

When al Kabir heard that al Muttaki was blinded, he said,"We are now two, needing a third," – and so it turned out, for al Mustakfi was also blinded.

AL MUSTAKFI BILLAH

Al Mustakfi billah Abu Kasim Abdullah was the son of al Muktafi b-ul Muatadhid. His mother was a slave concubine called Amlah un Nas (*the most beautiful of mankind*). He was acknowledged Caliph on the deposal of al Muttaki in the month of Safar 333 at the age of forty-one. During his reign Tuzun died. His secretary Abu Jaafar b. Shirzad was with him at the time and he thereupon sought the viceroyalty for himself and obtained the concurrence of the army, and the Caliph invested him with a robe

---

1 Ibn Hamdi, according to Ibn Ath. who places the hush-money at 15,000 dinars. The name of the prefect of police he gives as Abul Abbas. The terrible scarcity then prevailing at Baghdad, and the heavy and incessant rains had half depopulated the city. Private houses and public edifices, mosques, baths and palaces had fallen into ruin, and were abandoned by the famishing people.

2 During this reign the Russians made their first appearance in Arab history. They sailed down the Qur and attacked and took the town of Bardaah on the confines of Azarbijan in 332. They put to death a great number of the inhabitants, but were afterwards expelled by the Daylamite general.

of honour. Subsequently Ahmad b. Buwayh entered Baghdad and Ib Shirzad concealed himself, and Ibn Buwayh entered the palace. The Caliph stood before him and gave him a robe of honour and the title of Muizzud Daulah and his brother Ali that of Imadud Daulah, and their brother al Hasan that of Ruknud Daulah and engraved their titles on the coinage. Al Mustakfi took for himself the title of the Imam of the Truth, and caused this to be struck on the coinage. Muizzud Daulah now waxed in power. He placed the Caliph under ward and appointed for him every day by way of maintenance five thousand dirhams and no more. He was the first of the Daylamites who was supreme in Iraq. He was the first who exhibited *trials of speed between* runners in Baghdad and unduly encouraged wrestlers and swimmers, wherefore the youth of Baghdad gave themselves up to learning to wrestle and to swim, so that a swimmer would swim holding in his hand a chating dish upon which was a vessel, and he would swim until the meat in it was cooked. After a time Muizzud Daulah began to suspect al Mustakfi, and he visited him in Jumada II of the year 334. He stood in waiting and the people were likewise standing according to their degrees when two of the Daylamites stepped forward towards the Caliph, who stretched forth his hand thinking that they wished to kiss it, but they pulled him from his throne and threw him on the ground and dragged him by his turban, and the Daylamites thronged through the palace into the Haren and plundered it until nothing was left therein. Muizzud Daulah repaired to his own residence and they drove al Mustakfi on foot to him and he was deposed and his eyes seared on the same day (*22nd Jumada,* II 334 = 29th *January* , 946). His Caliphate lasted year and four months, and they summoned al Fadhl the son of al Muktadir and swore allegiance to him. Then they brought forward his cousin al Mustakfi who acknowledged him as Caliph and testified to his own abdication. He was then imprisoned till he died in the year 338 at the age of forty-six. He professed the Shiite doctrines.

A.H.333.
A.D.944.

A.H.333.
A.D.944.

AL MUTII' BILLAH

Al Mutii'billah Abul Kasim al Fadhl was the son of al Muktadir. His mother was a slave concubine called Mashghalah. He was born in the year 301 and was acknowledged Caliph on the abdication of al Mustakfi in Jumada II, 334, and Muizzud Daulah appointed him a stipend of but one hundred dinars a day. In this year of his Caliphate the scarcity in Baghdad became excessive, so that men ate corpses and ordure and died by the roadside and the dogs devoured their flesh. An estate was given in exchange for loaves of bread, and among the very destitute, children were found roasted *for food.* A "kur" of flour was purchased for Muizzud Daulah at 20,000 dirhams[1] and a –"kur" is equivalent to seventeen kintars of Damascus.

During this year a dissension arose between Muizzud Daulah and Nasirud Daulah b. Hamdan and Muizzud Daulah marched to engage Nasir taking al Mutii with him.. He afterwards returned accompanied by al Mutii almost as a prisoner.

During the same, died al Ikshid, ruler of Egypt, Muhammad b. Tughj[2] al Farghani, and the meaning of al Ikshid is king of kings, and this was the title of each prince of Farghanah, as al Isbahbad[3] is the title of every prince of Tabaristan, and Sul of the prince of Jurjan, and Khakan of the chief of the Turks, and Ifhshin[4] that of the prince of Ushrusanah, and Saman of the prince of Samarkand. Al Ikshid was brave and awe-inspiring. He governed Egypt on the

---

1 This would be about £42 a bushel.

2 Next Tufj as in the text. His life will be found in Ibn Khall.

3 The text has Isbahand ; Abul Mahasin from whom this information is probably taken, writes the word Isbahand, and this is confirmed by the words of Yakut و كانت ملوك الفرس يولونطا ـ رجلا و يسمونه الا صبهبذ

4 So Abul Mahasin : though the word in the Leyden edition is printed Afshin, the Muntahal Arab points it as I have done. The Ikshin of the text must be incorrect.

part of Kahir (*A.H.* 321). He had eight thousand slaves and was the master of Kafur.[1] A.H.334. A.D.946.

During the same, died al Kaim al Ubaydi, ruler of the West, and he was succeeded by his son and heir Ismail al Mansur billah. Al Kaim was more wicked than his father, an accursed Zindik who openly reviled the Prophets. His criers used to call out-"Curse the Cave[2] and what it contained" and he put to death many of the learned.

In the year 335 Muizzud Daulah renewed protestations of mutual confidence with al Mutti, freed him from close ward and lodged him in the palace once more.

In the year 338, Muizzud Daulah solicited permission to associated with him in his government his brother Ali Buwayh Imadud Daulah in order that he might enentually succeed him, to which al Mutii consented, but it so happened that Imadud Daulah died the same year, upon which al Mutii appointed Ruknud Daulah the father of Adhudud Daulah.

In the year 339 the Black Stone was restored to its place and a silve band was fixd to it to secure it,[3] its weight being 3777 dirhams and a half.

Muhammad b. Nafi al Khuzzai says, "I looked carefully at the Black Stone when it was dug up, the blackness was only on the surface, the whole of it being white *beneath*,[4] and its length was about the measure of a cubit."

---

1 Abul Misk (*father of Musk*) Kafur (*Camphor*) was a negro slave sold to Muhammad al Ikshid, by whom he was appointed guardian of his two sons, upon whose death he virtually succeeded to supreme power. Ibn Khall.

2 Meaning Muhammad and Abu Bakr-who took refuge in a cave on their flight to Medina.

3 Ibn Batutah says that the Stone is in four pieces, having been broken by the Carmathians. According to Burton, it appears to be composed oi a dozen small stones of different sizes joined together as if the whole had been broken to pieces by a violent blow and then reunited. The silver band was afterwards changed into a massive arch of gold or silver gilt. Consult Burton's Mecca.

4 See Burton p. 159, note.

A.H.339. A.D.950. In the year 341 a sect of metempsychosists appeared, and among them a youth who asserted that the soul of Ali had passed into him, and his wife who pretended that the sould of Fatima had entered her, and another who gave out that he was Gabriel. They were scourged but they gloried in their kinship with the Prophetical House, wherefore Muizzud Daulah ordered them to be released through his partiality to the people of the House, and this was one of his accursed deeds.

In the same year died al Mansur al Ubaydi the ruler of the West at Mansunyah which he had founded. He was succeeded by his son and heir Saad in the government and surnamed Muizz li dinillah (*the glorifier of the religion of God*). He it was who founded Cairo. Al Mansur succeeding his father, displayed benevolence of disposition, for he but down oppressions and the people loved him. His son too was of an amiable character and the West acknowledged his undisputed sway.

In the year 343 the prince of Khurasan named al Mutii in the Khubah, before which time the khutbah had not been read in his name. Upon this al Mutii sent him a standard and a robe of honour.

In the year 344, old Cairo was convulsed by a dreadful earthquake which overthrew houses, lasting for three hours and the people called out to the Lord in supplication. In the year 349 the sea sunk eighty cubits, and there appeared within it hills and islands and things such a hand never been beheld.

About Rai and its dependencies occurred a dreadful earthquake. The town of a Talikan sunk into the earth, and there escaped of its inhabitants only about thirty persons, and one hundred and fifty of the villages of Rai were swallowed up. The calamity extended as far as Hulwan, the greater part of which was engulfed and the earth vomited up the bones of the dead, and waters burst forth from it. A mountain in Rai was cleft asunder, and a village with its inhabitants was suspended between heaven and earth during the half of a day, then it was swallowed up. The earth was rent in a mighty chasm and fetid waters came forth from it and volumes of smoke. This is the narration of Ibnul Jauzi.

In the year 347, the earthquakers recurred at Kumm and Hulwan and in the mountainous districts, and great umbers of people perished, and locusts came and overspread the earth and settled upon all the crops and the trees. AH350. AD961.

In the year 350 Muizzud Daulah built in Baghdad a vast stupendous palace, its foundations being thirty-sx cubits deep in the earth.[1] During the same, he invested with the office of Kadhi, Abul Abbas Abdullah b. Hasan b. Abis Shawarib, who rode wearing the robe of honour from the palace of Muizzud Daulah preceded by drums and trumpets and accompanied by the troops, and he undertook to convey every year to the treasury of Muizzud Daulah two hundred thousand dirhams writing a judicial record to that effect, but al Mutii refused to invest him and to allow him audience, and[2] he commanded that he should not be authorized on any occasion to have access to him.

During the same, Muizzud Daulah farmed the, offices of market inspector and chief of police in Baghdad, and all this was after an indisposition from which he suffered and was restored to health-but may God not preserve him from punishment for his sins. During the same, the Byzatines took the island of Crete from the Muslims which had been conquered by the latter about the year 230.[3]

In the same year died the ruler of Spain an Nasir li dinillah (*Defender of the religion of God*) and was succeeded by his son al Hakim.

---

1 The cost of this was 13,000,000 dirhams, about £3,25,000 a great part of which he extorted from his followers. He was at this time suffering from gravel and he supposed that a lofty house and purer air would benefit him. Ibn Ath.

2 This word 'and' (و) should be inserted in the text, as it stands in the MS.

3 This would make it in the reign of al Wathik, whereas it was taken by the Arabs under Abu Hafs Omar b. Isa al Andalusi surnamed the Cretan, in the Caliphate of al Mamun A.H. 210, and in the reign of Michael the Stammerer (A.D. 823). It was retaken by Nicephorus Phocas, according to Yakut in the 13th of Muharram 350 (7th *March* 961). Ibn Ath. is incorrect in giving the year as 351.

A.H.352. A.D.963. In the year 351, the Shiites wrote upon the doors of the mosques "Curse upon Muawiyah and cursed be he who took from Fatima her right of Fadak[1] and upon those who forbade al Hasan to be buried with his grandfather, and a curse upon him who banished Abu Darr."[2] This was however rubbed out in the night. Muizzud Daulah wished to re-inscribes it, but his minister al Muhallabi suggested that he should write in place of what had beed effaced. "May God curse the oppressors of the family of the apostle of God," and they particularized Muawiyah alone in the curse.

In the year 352 on the 10th day of the Muharram, Muizzud Daulah forced the people to close the market-places and forbade the cooks from cooking. They set up cupolas in the public squares and hund sackeloths over them, and they made the women come forth with disheveled hair, beating their breasts and mourning for al Husayn. This was the first day in which lamentation had been made over him in Baghdad, and this innovation continued for some years. On the 12th of Dul Hijjah of the same was held the festival of Ghadir Khumm[3] and drums were beaten.

During this year one of the Arman Chiefs sent to Nasirud Daulah b. Hamdan, twins coupled together, their ago being twenty-five. The junction was at the side and they had two bellies and two nevels and two stomachs. Their times of hunger and thirst &c.

---

1 She gave out that it had been granted to her as a marriage portion by Muhammad but the shrewd Abu Bakr needed some further testimony than her own word.

2 Othman. Muawiyah induced that Caliph to recall Abu Darr from Syria to Medina for inciting the people to give alms in larger proportion than was legally incumbent upon them. Othman reproved him for this and Kaab al Ahbar interfering in the discussion, the hasty Abu Darr smote him for a meddling Jew, and requested the Caliph's leave to retire from men: he was permitted to select Rabadah three miles from Medina on the Hijaz road. See Tabari, Zotenberg, Tom III, p. 567.

3 Ghadir is a valley between Mecca and Medina wherein is a pool (Ghadir) where Muhammad once preached. See the various derivations of this name in Yakut. The discourse of this occasion was in favour of Ali. According to Weil this festival was on the 18th and according to Abul Fida on the 8th of Dul Hijjah.

were different. Each had two palms, two arms two hands, two thinghs, and two shanks. One of them died and so remained for days, while his brother was yet living and he began to putrefy. Nasirud Daulah assembled the physicians to decide if they were able to sever the dead from the liviag, which they could not do. Soon after he who was alive, sickened from the smell of the dead and died. A.H.357. A.D.968.

In yhr year 353 a vast tent was made for Sayfud Daulah, the height of its poles being fifty cubits. In the year 351 died the sister of Muizzud Daulah, and al Mutii went down to his residence in a fast sailing boat, to condole with him. Muizzud Daulah went forth to meet him but would not put him to the inconvenience of leaving the boat, but kissed the earth several times before him and the Caliph returned to his palace.

During the same, Nincephorus[1] (*Phocus*) Emperor of Rome fortified[2] Cesarea near the frontier towns of the Muslims, and took up his abode in it that he might pursue his depredation at all seasons.

In the year 356, Muizzud Daulah died and his son Bakhtyar succeeded him in the government and al Mutii surnamed him Izzud Daulah.

In the year 357, the Carmathians seized Damascus,[3] and during it no one made the pilgrimage either from Syria or from Egypt. They then determined to march to old Cairo and take possession of it; but the Ubaydites came and mastered it, and the heretic rule was supreme in the countries of the West, and in Egypt and Syria.

---

1 The text has 'Jacob'. Ibn Ath. Nakfur, which is Nicephorus Arabecized. Reiske (Abul Fed.) gives the name in full.

2 The word is بنا which cannot mean "founded" as Cesarea was one of the conquests of Omar, 19 A.H. The words of Ibn Ath. are بنا بقيشاريه مدينة "He built near or at Cesarea, a town," &c.

3 From the Fatimite General Jaafar b. Falah who was acting under the orders of Jauhar the Commander-in-Chief of the African Muizz. The Carmathians pressed on against Cairo, but reinforcements sent to Jauhar enabled him to hold it and the alliance of the Carmathian was bought by the prudent policy of Muizz.

A.H.357. A.D.968. And this because when Kafur al Ikshidi died, affairs fell into disorder and the largesses to the troops diminished, whereupon a faction wrote to al Muizz (*the Fatimite Caliph*) solicting from his a force in order that they might surrender old Cairo to him. He sent his freedman Jauhar,[1] al Kaid a (*the generallissimo*) at the head of one hundred thousand horsemen, who took possession of it. He encamped at the spot which is now Cairo and traced out its position and built a palace for al Muizz now known as al Kasarayn. He abolished the khutbah for the House of Abbas, and the wearing of black, and caused the preachers to wear white, and he commanded that in the Khutbah should be said, "O God, bless Muhammad the chosen, and Ali the Accepted, and Fatima the virgin, and al Hasan and al Husayn the grandsons of the Apostle, and bless the Imams the predecessors of the prince of the Faithful al Muizz billah." All this took place in the month of Shaaban 358.

Afterwards in Rabii II of the year 359 they introduced into the call to prayers, at old Cairo-"Hasten to an excellent work,"[2] and they began the construction of the principl mosque of al Azhar (*the splendid*) and completed it in Ramadhan 361. and in the year 359 a huge meteor fell in Iraq by which the whole country was illumined as though it were with the rays of the sun, and after its fall was heard a sound like a peal of thunder.

In the year 360 the callers to prayer in Damascus introduced into the call to prayers. "Hasten to an excellent work" by command of Jaafar b. Falah the prefect of al Muizz billah at Damasucs and no one dared to oppose it.

In the year 362 Bakhytary exacted money from al Mutii, who said, "I have nothing *of sovereignty* left now but the khutbah *in my name* and if ye desire it, I will abdicate," but he pressed him so

---

1 Ibn Khall may be consulted for the life of this General.

2 The words of the Adan after the invocation of the Deity Muhammad are حی علی الصلوة حی علی الفلاح "hasten to prayers-hasten to the attainment of ever, lasting life," to which were added the words in the context, used by the Shiiahs to this day.

that he sold his own furniture and gave him 400,000 dirhams, and it was bruited about on men's tongues that the Caliph had been mulcted. A.H.362. A.D.978.

During the same, one of the attendants of the Police Magistrate[1] at Baghdad was killed, whereupon the Wazir Abul Fadhl as Shirazi sent people to throw inflammable materials from the quarter of the copper smiths to that of the fish-mongers, and a huge conflagration occurred, the like of which had not been seen, and considerable property was burnt and many people *perished* in their houses and in the baths. The Wazir died in the same year-may God not have mercy upon him. In Ramadhan of this year al Muizz entered old Cairo with the coffins of his ancestors.

In the year 263 al Mutii invested with the office of Kadhi, Abul Hasan Muhammad b. Umm Shayban al Hashimi after his having declined the office, and he stipulated for himself certain conditions. Among them, that he should not receive any stipend for the judicial office, nor be invested with a robc of honour, nor be petitioned regarding things which were contrary to law. And he appointed for his secretary three hundred dirhams, monthly, and for his chamberlain one hundred and fifty, and to the official at his gate, skilled in the division of inheritances, one hundred-and to the treasurers of the judicial court and the assistants six hundred, and he wrote him a charge which ran as follows : "This is what the servant of God al Fadhl al Mutii lillah prince of the Faithful, hath commissioned unto Muhammad b. Salib the Hashimite what time he called him to those things appertaining to the judicial office over which he hath appointed him, among the dwellers in the city of peace, the city of al Mansur and the castern city from the east side and the west side-and Kufah-and the districts watered by the Euphrates-and Wasit-and Karkhi-and the course of the Euphrates

---

1 The text should have Wali (والي) as in the MS. which term is equivalent to the Sahih ul Maunat which Ibn Ath. employs. This conflagration according to the latter took place at Karkh and 30 mosques were burnt down.

A.H.362. and the Tigris-and the road to Khurasan-and Hulwan,-and
A.D.973. Karmisin,[1] and Diyar Mudara[2]-and Diyar Rabiah- and Diyar Bakr-and Mosal-and the two sacred citites-and Yaman-and Damascus-and Emessa-and the district opf Kinassrin-and al Awasim-and Cairo-and Alexandria-and the province of Palestine-and the Jordan and all their dependencies-and the supervision consequent therefro over such as he may prefer of the Abbasides in Kufah and the districts watered by the Euphrates and their dependencies-and the duties of the chief judicial office with which he hath invested him-and inquiry into the condition of the judges-and the consideration of all that the course of judicial decisions involves-in all the provinces and countries which the empire comprehends and within which the Abbaside prerogative determines-and the maintaining of such whose method and conduct he approves, and the removal of those whose character and disposition he reprehends-watchful over private and public interests, embracing those of the faith and those tolerated under its protection, from the Caliph's knowledge that he is the chief of his house, of eminent continuence of life, pure in his faith and his trust-renowned for his virtue and stainless conduct-a cynosure for his erudition and sagacity-acknowledged for his forbearances, and intelligence-for removed from *association with* the base-clothed in the most beauteous-garment of virtue-the pure-the beloved-rejoicing in supernatural serenity-learned in worldly affairs-congnizant of the things which imperil the salvation to come. The Caliph hath enjoined him the fear of God, for verily it is a covering shield-and that he should make the Book of God his study in all that he does-and order his decisions and decrees in accordance with it-his guide to which he should tunr for aid his prop upon which he must rely-and that he should take the law of the apostle of God as the beacon to which he must advance-the exemplar which he must follow-and that he should observe the consensus of teaching and follow the orthodox Imams-and use his own discretionary faculties in cases which are not found in the Book, the Low and the general concurrence of the faithful-and that he should sommon

---

1 Not Farmisin-as in the text. The MS. is correct.

2 This is the plain country to the cast of the Euphrates towards Harran. The text and MS. have مصر without the discritical points. For the limits of these three Diyars, consult Yakut.

to this Council those on whose wisdom and judgment he can rely, and be the same in look and word to two litigants whehn they come before him-and accord to both of them of his justice and his equity, so that the weak shall be secure from his tyranny and the powerful despair of his partiality. He hath further enjoined him to regard with solicitous affection his assistants and coadjutors, and those of his supervisors and instruments upon whom he relies, withdrawing them from the evil adoption of reprehensible condust and checking any tendencies to unlawful gain," –and he continued a long discourse to the same effect. I here remark that the Caliphs used to nominate the Kadhi resident within their metropolis, over the judicial service throughout the whole of the territories and provices under their sovereignty, and the Kadhi would appoint as deputy under his authority whomsoever he pleased in every district and in every town, and for this reason he was entitled the Kadhi of the Kadhis, and no one was so named save such as were thus distinguished, and others besides him were Kadhi simply or Kadhi of such a town. But now a days in a simple town there are four conjointly, and each of them called Kadhi of the Kadhirs-and perhaps a single one of the subordinates of the former ones had a jurisdiction twice as large as any of the chief Kadhis now possesses, and indeed the chief Kadhis then held a more extensive authority than is enjoyed by sovereigns of this our time.

A.H.363.
A.D.974.

In this year, namely 363, al Mutii was struck with paralysis and he lost the power of speech. Sabuktagin ; chamberlain of Izzud Daulah smmoned him to abdicate and to resign the government to his son at Taiilillah (*obedient to God).* And this he did and made over the government to him on Thursday the 13th[1] of Dul Kaadah (*5th August,* 974). The duration of the reign of al Mutii was twenty-nine years and some months, and his abdication was attested by the Kadhi, Ibn Umm Shayban. After his abdication he went by the name of the virtuous Shaykh.

Ad Dahabi says that al Mutii and his son were powerless in the hands of the House of Buwayh, and the authority of the Caliphate

1 The text has 23rd. but this is an error. The MS. is in accordance with ibn Ath who makes it the 13th.

A.H.363. A.D.974. continued to decline until the accession of al Muktafi when it recovered a little, but the sway of the heretical House of Ubayd in Egypt was pre-eminent and their commands universally obeyed and their power contested the Abbaside sovereignty in their time.

Al Mutii went to Wasit with his son ad *there* died in the month of Muharram 364. Ibn Shahin remarks. "He voluntarily abdicated as far as I can ascertain." Al Khatib relates a tradition on the authority of Muhammad b. Yusuf al Kattan through al Mutii lillah, that Ahmad b. Hanbal said, "when the friends of a man die,he becomes humbled."

Of distinguished persons who died in the reign of Mutii were al Khirki the Hanbalite Shaykh, Abu Bakr as Shibli the Sufi, Ibnul Kadhi the Shafiite Imam, Abur Raja al Uswani, Abu Bakr as Suli, al Haytham b. Kulayb as Shashi, Abut Tayyib as Saluki, Abu Jaafar the coppersmith and grammarian, Abu Nasr al Farabi, Abu Ishak al Marwani the Shafiite Imam, Abul Kasim az Zajjaji the grammarian, al Karkii the Hanafite Shaykh, ad Dinawari author of th Majalisat (*Conference)*, Abu Bakr al Dhabai, the Kadhi Abul Kasim at Tanukhi, Ibnul Haddad author of the Faruu' (*development of Law*). Abu Ali b. Abi Hurayrah one of the most eminent of the Shafiite doctors, Abu Omar the devotee, al Masaudi author of the Meadows of gold, Ibn Darastwayh, Abu Ali at Tabari the first who wrote on controversy in the abstract, al Fakihi author of the history of Mecca, al Mutanabbi the poet, Ibn Habban author of the Sahih, Ibn Shaaban one of the Malikite elders, Abu Ali al Kali, and Abul Faraj author of the Aghani.

AT TAII LILLAH

At Taii lillah Abu Bakr Abdul Karim was the son of al Mutii. His mother was a slave concubine called Hazar. His father abdicated in his favour, he being forty-three years of age. He rode in procession wearing the royal mantle accompanied by the troops and preceded by Subuktagin. On the following day he invested Subuktagin with the office of Sultan, fastened for him a banner *to a spear* and gave him the title of Nasirud Daulah (*Defender of the State*). Shortly after a misunderstanding occurred between Izzud Daulah and subuktagin. The latter invited the Turks to his aid who answered to his call, and hostilities took place between him and Izzud Daulah. In Dul Hijjah of this year *i.e.,* 363, the khutbah and the prayer for al Muizz the Ubaydite were read in the sacred cities. A.H.363. A.D.974.

In the year 364 Abhudud Daulah marched on Baghdad to aid Izzud Daulah against Subuktagin. Baghdad and its possession excited his cupidity and he set about acquiring it. He won the favour of the troops and thy turned against Izzud Daulah, who now retired from public life.[1] Adhudud Daulah wrote to the provinces under the authority of at Taii announcing the nomination to supreme authority of Adhudud Daulah. Upon this a quarrel arose between at Taii and Adhudud Daulah on which account the khutbah in the name of at Taii was discontinued in Baghdad and other places from the 10th Jumada I, until it was restored on the 10th of Rajab.

In this year and subsequently, heresy became rampant and spread in Egypt and Syria and in the East and the West, and the cessation of the prayers called at Tarawih was proclaimed on the part of the Ubaydite. In the year 365 Ruknud Daulah b. Buwayh renounced in favour of his son the dominions he held in his possession, conferring on Adhudud Daulah, Fars and Kirman, and Kirman, on Muayyidud Daulah, Rai and Ispahan, and on Fakhrud Daulah, Hamadan and Dinawar. In the month of Rajab a judicial session was held in the palace of Sultan Izzud Daulah and the chief Kadhi b. Maruf took his seat and adjudicated cases, because Izzud Daulah had requested it, that the might witness how the procedure of his court was conducted. During the same a breach occurred between Izzud Daulah and Adhudud Daulah during which a Turkish page belonging to Izzud Daulah was imprisoned. He longed to recover him and his sorrow overpowered him, and he refused to eat and took to weeping, shunning society and ceasing to hold audience in his court. He wrote to Adhudud Daulah entreating him to restore the boy to him, and he demeaned himself till he became

---

1 اغلق باب داره و صرف كتابه و حجابه Ibn Ath.

A.H.365. the ridicule of the people. He was reproved for his conduct, but
A.D.975. would not forbear from it, and he proffered in ranson for the boy two slave girls skilled in the lute for one of whom,[1] a hundred thousand dinars had been paid on his account, and he said to the messenger- "if he is reluctant to restore him, add what thou thinkest fit and do not hesitate, for verily I would be content to have him even if I had to go to the ends of the earth,"-and Adhudud Daulah restored the youth to him.

During the same, the Khutbah in the name of Izzud Daulah was discontinued in Kufah and was read for Adhudud Daulah. In the same, died al Muizzli din illah the Ubaydi ruler of Egypt and the first of the Ubaydites that conquered it. His son Nizar succeeded him in the government and was surnamed al Aziz.

In the year 366 died al Mustansir billah al Hakam b. Nasir li din illah, the Umayyad ruler of Spain. His son al Muayyid billah Hisham succeded him. In the year 367 an engagement took place between Izzud Daulah and Adhudud Daulah. The latte was victorious, and he took Izzud Daulah prisoner and afterwards put him to death. At Taii then invested Adhudud Daulah with the royal robe and crowned him with a jeweled crown and decked him with a collar and bracelet and girt a sword about him, and fastened for him two banners with his own hand, one ornamented with silver after the fashion of nobles, and the other with gold after the manner of regents designate, and the second banner had never been bound for any one before him. He also wrote him a diploma of investiture which was read in his presence, and there was none but was astonished, for this had never been the custom, the diploma being given only to the successors to the Sultanate in the presence of the prince of the Faithful, and when he received it the prince of the Faithful would say"this is my diplima, act therefore according to it."

In the year 368 at Taii commanded that the drums should be sounded at the gate of Adhudud Daulah, in the morning, at sunset and at night fall and that the Khutbah should be read in his name in

---

1 After الواحده read منهما as in the MS.

the pulpits of the metropolis. Ibn al Jauzi observes that these two orders were never issued before his time nor sanctioned for regents designate, for Muizzud Daulah desired that the drums should be sounded for him in Baghdad, and he solicited it of al Mutii who would not permit it, and Adhudud Daulah would not have enjoyed this privilege except for the impotence of the Caliphate. A.H.369. A.D.979.

In the year 369 the ambassador of al Aziz ruler of Egypt arrived in Baghdad, and Adhudud Daulah solicited at Taii to add to his titles that of Tajul Millat (*Crown of the Faith*) and to present him anew with a robe of honour and to crown him. At Taii consented and took his seat upon the throne, and around him stood a hundred men with swords and bravely appareled, and before him was placed the Qurãn of the Caliph Othman, and upon his shoulders the Apostolic Mantle and in his hand the scepter, and he was girt with the sword of the Apostle of God. A curtain, sent by Adhudud Daulah had been set up, and he had requested that it might be placed as a veil before at Taii, in order that the eyes of none of the troops should behold himself. The Turks and Daylamites then entered, but none of them in mail, and the nobles and officers of State stood ranged on either side. Then permission was given to Adhudud Daulah to enter, and he entered, and the veil was raised and Adhudud Daulah kissed the earth. The general Ziyad was struck with awe and he said to Adhudud Daulah, "What is this ? O king,[1] is he the Almighty?" He looked towards him, and replied, "This is the Vicegerent of the Almighty upon earth,"-and he continued moving onwards kissing the ground seven times. Then at Taii looked towards Khalis the eunuch and said, "let him approach." And Adhudud Daulah ascended and kissed the ground twice, and the Caliph said to him-"come near to me," and he approached and kissed his foot and at Taii stretched out his right hand to him and commanded him *to sit down,* and he sat down upon a seat after the Caliph had repeatedly requested him to be seated, and he excusing himself, till the Caliph said, "I adjure thee to be seated"

1 Adhud ud Daulah was the first prince according to Ibn Khall who since the promulgation of Islamiam, had received the title of Malik.

A.H.369. A.D.979. whereupon he kissed the throne and sat down. Then at Taii said to him, "verily I think it meet to entrust to thy care what God hath committed to me of the affairs of my subjects in the east of the earth and the west thereof, together with their direction in all their aspects, with the exception of what appertains to my special and personal effects-wherefore assume charge of them." He replied, "may God aid me in obedience to the prince of the Faithful and in his service." Then the Caliph bestowed upon him a robe of honour and took his departure.

I remark that I took upon this fact *as a proof* that he was a Caliph so impotent that the Caliphate was never so feeble in the time of any other as it was in his, nor was the authority of any Sultan so powerful as that of Adhudud Daulah, and things have come to such a pass in our time that the Caliph visits the Sultan to congratulate him, at the beginning of each month, and the utmost that the Sultan condescends in his favour, is to come down from his dais and the two sit down together beyond the dais ; then the Caliph arises and departs like an ordinary person, and the Sultan seats himself in the Hall of State. Indeed, I have been told that Sultan al Ashraf Barsabai[1] when he marched to Amida to engage the enemy, the Caliph accompanied him riding before him and acting as his chamberlain while all dignity and honour were reserved for the Sultan, the Caliph appearing as one of the nobles in the suite of the Sultan.

In the year 370, Adhudud Daulah left Hamadan and marched to Baghdad, and at Taii went out to meet him, though it had never been the custom for the Caliphs to go forth to meet any one, for when the daughter[2] of Muizzud Daulah died, al Mutii went to visit

---

1 Abur Nasr Sayfud din surnamed Malik al Ashraf, eighth Sultan of Egypt of the second dynasty of the Mamelukes called Burjites-who began his reign in 825 A.H. (1421 A.D.,) and died 841 after a reign of 7 years. D'Herbelot says that he was so modest that he would not force his subjects to kiss the earth or prostrate themselves before him. His life will be found in Weil's Hist. of the Abbaside Caliphs in Egypt, Vol. II.

2 He had before said "sister." See page 545.

and condole with him, and Muizzud Daulah kissed the ground On this occasion the messenger of Adhudud Daulah went to request at Taii to meet him who was unable to decline. A.H.370. A.D.980.

In the year 372, Adhudud Daulah died and at Taii appointed to the Sultanate in his place, his son Samsamud Daulah, and he gave him the little of Shamsul Millat (*Sun of the Faith*). He bestowed upon him seven robes of honour and crowned him and fastened for him two banners.

Subsequently in the year 373 died Muayyidud Daulah brother of Adhudud Daulah. In the year 375 Samsamud Daulah proposed to put a tax upon stuffs of silk and cotton woven in Baghdad and its envirous, the farming of which brought him a million dirhams a year, but the people assembled in the mosque of al Mansur and determined to stop the Friday prayers and the city was almost in an uproar whereupon he remitted this monopoly.

In the year 376, Sharafud Daulah marched against his brother Samsamud Daulah. He was victorious over him and blinded him. The army now favoured Sharafud Daualh who marched to Baghdad. At Taii rode out to meet him and to congratulate him on *his conquest of* the provinces and gave him a diploma of investiture in the dignity of the Sultanate, and crowned him. The diploma was read out while at Taii listened. In the year 378, Sharafud Daulah ordered an observation of the seven heavenly bodist[1] and their orbits as a Mamun had done. During the same a great scarcity prevailed in Baghdad and deaths occurred therein, and the people of Basrah sufferen from a violent heat and from a burning wind under which men dropped down. A strong wind blew at Famus Silh[2] which dried up the Tigris so that it was said that the bottom appeared, and many ship were overwhelmed, and it carried down a boat full of cattle which it cast in the land of Jukha[3] where it was seen after some time.

1 The sun, moon, Venus, Mercury, Mars, Jupiter and Saturn.

2 A large canal above Wasit.

3 The name of a stream in the Sawad of Baghdad upon which a large town was situated rich enough to yield a revenue of eight million dirhams. It was destroyed, says Yakut, by the Tigris altering its course and a plague completed its ruin. Yakut.

A.H.379. A.D.989. In the year 379 died Sharafud Daulah who bequeathed the succession to his brothe Abu Nasar, and at Taii went to the palace to condole with him, and the latter kissed the earth several times. Afterwards Abu Nasr rode to visit at Taii. The nobles were present and at Taii bestowed seven robes of honour upon Abu Nasr, the upper one being of black, and a black turban and placed a collar round his neck and two bracelets upon his arm and the chamberlains preceded him with *drawn* swords. Then he kissed the ground before at Taii and sat upon a chair of state. His diploma of investiture was read out, and at Taii surnamed him Bahaud Daulah wa Dhiyaul Millat. (*The Glory of the State and the luster of Faith*).

In the year 381 at Taii was arrested. The cause of this was that he had imprisoned one of the suite of Bahaud Daulah. Upon this, Bahaud Daulah went to at Taii who was seated in the pavilion girt with a sword, and as he approached he kissed the ground and seated himself one a chair. His myrmidons advanced and dragged at Taii from his throne, and the Daylamites pressed upon him and enveloped him in a mantle and he was taken up to the Sultan's palace. The city was in commotion and Bahaud Daulah returned and dictated an oath to at Taii that he would abdicate and resign the government to al Kadir billah, and the nobles and principal men testified to this. This took, place on the 19th of Shaaban (1st *November* 991) and a dispatch was sent to al Kadir billah who was at al Batihah[1] to summon him. At Taii dwelt in the palace of Kadir billah, respected and honoured in most confortable circumstances-(as an instance of which-a candle was one night taken to him the half of which had been burnt, and he refused it and they brought him another)[2]-until he died on the night of the Eedul Fitr 393, (2nd

---

1 Between Wasit and Basrah.

2 On another occasion al Kadir sent him a dish of lentils. He asked the messenger if that was the kind of food the Caliph ate. On being answered in the affirmative, he desired the man to tell his master that if such fare contented him, he need not have aspired to the dignity of the Caliphate. From that time al Kadir appointed a girl from his own kitchen to cook whatever he asked for. Ibn Ath.

August, 1002). Al Kadir, prayed over him and the noblest and attendants followed him and the Sharif ar Ridha[1] moured in a poem. He was particulary hostitle to the descedants of Abu Talib. Reverence for his authority had so declined in his reign, that the poets satirized him. A.H.381. A.D.991.

Of persons of note who died in the days of at Taii were Ibn Sunni the Hafidh, Ibn Adi, al Kaffal the elder, as Sirafi the grammarian, Abu Sahl as Saluki, Abu Bakr as Razi al Hanafi, Ibn Khalawayh, al Azhari the great philologist, Abu Ibrahim al Farabi author of th Diwanul Adad, ar Raffa the poet, Abu Zayd al Marwazi as Shaffi, ad Dariki, Abu Bakr al Abhari the Malikite Shaykh, and Abul Layth as Samarkandi, the Hanafite Imam, Abu Ali al Farisi the grammarian, and Ibnul Hallab al Maliki.

AL KADIR BILLAH

Al Kadir billah Abul Abbas Ahmad b. Ishak bil Muktadir was born in the year 336. His mother was a slave girl called Tamanni and some say Damnah. He was acknowledged Caliph on the abdication of his brother, being then absent, but he arrived on the 10th of Ramadhan and gave public audience the next day and received congratulations and the poets recited their poems before him. Among these was the following by as Shari far Ridha-

"Sons of Abbas, the honour of the Caliphate,
This day Abul Abbas hath renewed.
May fortune log preserve as a store for time of need, this rock

---

1 Abul Hasan Muhammad the son of at Tahir Dul Manakib directly descended from Ali b. Abi Talib. His poetical works fill a large diwan of four volumes and at Thaalabi considers him the ablest poet of all the descendants of Ali b Abi Talib. His life in Ibn Khall. Will repay perusal. He was born at Baghdad 359 A.H., (969-70) and died there 406 A.H. (1015).

A.H.381. A.D.991 Of that mighty immoveable mountain, (*the Abbaside dynasty*)."

Al Khatib says that al Kadir was distinguished for his rectitude and nobility of character, for long watching and much alms-giving, and an admirable course of conduct in accordance with the accounts reported of him. He studied the science of the law under the learned Abu Bishar al Harawi the Shafiite, and he composed a treatise on the fundamental principles of faith I which he introduced the merits of the Companions and accused of impiety the Muatazalites and those who maintained the creation of the Qurãn, and this work used to be read every Friday, in an assembly of Traditionists in the mosque of al Mahdi, and in presence of the people. (Ibnus Salah[1] records this in his Classes of the Shafiites).

Ad Dahabi states that in the month of Shawwal of the year of his accession, a public audience was held at which at Kadir and Bahaud Daulah pledged their faith to each other and al Kadir invested him with authority wheresoever the Abbaside dominion was acknowledged outside his own gate. During the same Abul Futuh[2] al Hasan b. Jaafar the Aliide, the governor of Mecca claimed sovereignty for himself, and assumed the surname of ar Rashid billah and he was saluted Caliph. The sovereign of Egypt was uder much apprehension thereat, but after a little the authority of Abul Futuh declined, and he returned to his allegiance to al Aziz the Ubaydite.

In the year 382 the Wazir Abu Nasr Sabur Ardashir purchase

---

1 Abu Omar Othman as Shahrozuri was a jurisconsult of the Shafii school. He was one of the most eminent of his time in Qurãnic interpretation, traditions, Jurisprudence, biographies of traditionists and other branches of knowledge. He was professor of the school for teaching traditions founded at Damascus by al Malik al Ashraf. He died in 643. A. H. (1245).

2 An account of the pretension of this person will be found in Ibn Khallakan's Life of the Wazir al Maghribi-but Ibn Khaldun places this rebellion in the time of al Hakim instead of al Aziz who died in 386-and this is confirmed by Ibn Khallakan.

a house at karkh and fitted it up and named it the House of Learning devoting it to the use of the learned and he bequeathed it many volumes. A.H.381. A.D.991

In the 384 the pilgrims from Iraq returned, for the Bedouin (*Chief*) Usayfar[1] forbade their advance save under his pass, wherefore they returned and did not perform the pilgrimage, neither did the people of Syria or Yaman make it, but those of Egypt did so. In the year 387 Sultan Fakhrud Daulah died. He was succeeded by his son Rustam in the government of Rai and its dependencies at the age of forty, and al Kadir gave him the little of Majdud Daulah (*Glory of the State*).

Ad Dahabi remarks among strange occurrences,the death of nine sovereigns in a series during the years 387 and 388-*among them,* Mansur b. Nuh lord of Trans-Oxiana, Fakhrud Daulah prince of Rai and the mountainous tracts and al Aziz the Ubaydite ruler of Egypt.

And regading them Abu Mansur Abdul Malik at Thaalabi says-
"Hast thou not seen the kings of our time in the past two years,
That a caller summoneth them to death and slaughter.
The hand of death hath grasped Nub the son of Mansur[2]
With the regrets that his heart contained.
Alas ! for the calamity of Mansur (*b. Nuh*) on the day of Sarkhas.
His kingdom was torn from him and he about to perish.
His repose was disturbed by this being blinded and he became
A sightless prince whom calamites had attacked.

---

1 The reason given by Ibn Ath is that Usayfar complained of the debasement of the coin in which the mail he levied had been previously paid by the Sultan. During the correspondence that ensued on this, the time for the pilgrimage passed by.

2 Nuh b. Mansur of the Samani dynasty died in 387, and was succeeded by his son Abul Harith Mansur b. Nuh in the government of Bukhars. He was seized at Sarkhans in Khurasan by two of his rebellious nobles, Bukhuzun and Faik and blinded, Consult Ibn Ath. anno 389.

A.H.387. A.D.997

And the lord of Egypt hath gone his way,

And the prince of the mountains whom the sepulchres have concealed.

And the ruler of Jurjan in his vain regret,

Whom the regardant eye of death was watching.

And the king of Khwarazam[1] the face of whose felicity hath become darkened,

And to whom the day of his evil destiny hath appeared.

And Abu Ali[2] was exalted upon earth seeking to gain it

Until misfortunes destroyed him.

And the lord of Bust[3], that lion whose

Claws were the keys of the East and West.

A quick messenger from adversity alighted near him,

And when fate presents itself it cannot be averted

By armies thoug they exceed in number the pebbles

And though the plains and level grounds are thronged with them.

Upon Samsamud Daulah the Buwide came

Destroying calamities whose spoils are afflictions,

And verily the prince of Juzjan[4] hath crossed

The bridge of life, and the fates that had long regarded him, approached."

Ad Dahabi saya that al Aziz the sovereign of Egypt died in 386 and the conquests made by him beyond those of his predecessors, were Emessa, Hamat and Aleppo. The Khutabah was said for him in Mosal and Yaman. His name was impressed upon the coinage and the stardards, and he was succeeded in the government by his

---

1 Put to death by the ruler of Jurjan Mamun b. Muhammad.

2 Rule of Khurasan succeeding his father Simjur. He was imprisoned by Subuktagin and died in prison.

3 Between the ancient Drangians. (Sijistan) Ghazni and Heart. Subuktagin is probably meant here as he died in 387 A.H.

4 A city in Khurasan.

son al Mansur who was surnamed al Hakim bi amrillah. A.H.394. A.D.1003-4

In the year 390 a gold mine was discovered in Sijistan and they extracted red gold from the soil.

In te year 393 the governor of Damascus al Aswad the Hakimite[1] gave an order regarding a certain Mauritanian, and he was paraded upon an ass, and it was cried out, "This is the retribution for him who loveth Abu Bakr and Omar." Then they struck off his head-may God have mercy upon him, but not upon his slayer or his master al Hakim.

In the year 394 Bahaud Daulah invested the Sharif Abu Ahmad al Husayn b. Musa al Musawi with the office of chief Kadhi and the superintendency of the pilgrimage and of the court for the redressal of abuses, and the chief jurisdiction over the descendants of Abu Talib,[2] and wrote him from Shiraz a commission to that effect, but he did not assume the office of Kadhi through the refusal of al Kadir to sanction it.

In the year 395, al Hakim put to death a number of the principal men of old Cairo by confining them till they died, and commanded that writings reviling the Companions should be palced on the doors of mosques and in the public roads, and he gave orders to his prfects to revile them. In the same he ordered that all dogs should be killed, and forbade the use of beer, of *malukhya,*[3] and Prohibited *the sale of* fish without scales, and he put to death a number of people who sold them after their prohibition.

In the year 396 he ordered the people in old Cairo and the Sacred Cities to rise and bow down in the streets and places of public assembly when the name of al Hakim was mentioned.

---

1 Because appointed by al Hakim biamrillah who gave him in addition the command of his troops in Syria.

2 Ibnul Athir has علويين for طالبيين -but the latter expression is used by Ibn Khall. See his life of the Shari far Ridha son of Abu Ahmad al Husayn.

3 A species of mallows. De Slane gives the botanical name as *Corchorous oliterius.* Al Hakim also forbade lupin pellets to be eaten with the *malukhya.*

A.H.399. A.D.1008. In the year 398, an open rupture occurred between the Shiias and Sunnis at Baghdad in which the Shaykh Abu Ahmad al Asfaraini was nearly killed, and the heretics (*Shiias*) in Baghdad called out, "O for Hakim, O for Mansur." Al Kadir was enraged at this and sent mounted the hose-guards in attendance at his gate to the assistance of the Sunnis, and the heretics were dispersed. During the same, al Hakim demolished the church of the Resurrection[1] at Jerusalem and ordered the destruction of all the churches in Egypt. He also commanded that the Chirstians should place crosses upon their necks, the length of the cross to be a cubit and its weight five Egyptian ratls,[2] and that the Jews should carry on their necks logs of wood equal in weight to the crosses and wear black turbans, whereupon a number of them embraced Islam. Shortly afterwards he permitted the restoration of the churches and temples and suffered those who had embraced Islam, since it had been forced upon the, to return to their faith.

In the year 399 Abu Amar the Kadhi of Basrah was removed from office and Abul Hasan b. Abis Shawarib assumed the post of Kadhi. The poet al Usfari wrote as follows regarding this—

"I have a pleasant story
Such as those which are sung,
Of two Kadhis one of whom is condoled with
And the other congratulated.
This one says, 'I was forced' *to accept it*
The other says, 'I was well rid of it.'

1 Ibn Khall. Places this even in 408. The word Kumamah (*sweepings*, says De Slane, is used by the Muslims contemptuously for Kiyamah (*Resurrection*). Yakut however, does not bear out this statement of its contemptuous application by the Muslims. He allows that it is called Kiyamah, but says that the proper word is Kumamah as the place used to be the refuse repository outside the city, where in the earliest times malefactors were executed. *After* the death of the Messiah, he continues, it became the place of reverence it now is.

2 De Slane makes this equal to ten pounds. Lane gives the Baghdad ratl of one pound.

And both of them lie.
Which of us will believe them ?"

A.H.399.
A.D.1008.

In the same year the supremacy of the House of Umayyah in Spain sunk into feebleness and their authority declined.[1]

In the year 400 the Tigris fell to an extent never before witnessed and agricultural leases were granted on account of the island that appeared in it, and this had never before happened.

In the year 402 al Hakim forbade the sale of dates,[2] and caused them to be burnt, and also the sale of grapes and destroyed many vineyards.

In the year 404 he prohibited the women from going out on the roads night or day, and this continued till his death.

In the year 411 (27th Shawwal, 13th February) al Hakim (may God curse him) was slain at Hulwan a village in Egypt and his son Ali succeeded him and was surnamed ad Dhahir liizazi din illah, (*the aider in exalting the religion of God*), but their supremacy declined in his reign, Aleppo and a great part of Syria being lost to them.

In the year 422 died al Kadir billah on Sunday night, the 11th of Dul Hijjah (29th November 1031) at the age of eighty-seven, and the duration of his Caliphate was forty-one years and three months.

Of persons of note who died during his reign were : - Abu Ahmad al Askari the professor of general literature, ar Rummani the grammarian, Abul Hasan al Masarjisi the Shafiite Shaykh, Abu Ubaydillah al Marzabani, the Sahib Ibn Abbad the minister of Muayyidud Daulah, the fist of the minsters who was called the Sahib, ad Darakutni, the well known Hafidh, Ibn Shahin, Abu Bakr al Audani the Shafiite Imam, Yusuf bus Sirafi, Ibn Zulak[3] al Misri,

1 An account of the deposition of Mahdi and the restoration of Hisham II, and the history of these troublous times will be found treated at length by Dozy (Hist. des. Musalm. D'Esp. Vol. III, p. 299) and more briefly by Ibn Ath, anno 400.

2 Ibn Khall says "Raisins" (زبيب)

3 The text should have be corrected.

A.H.422. A.D.1031. Ibn Abi Zayd al Maliki, the Malikite Shaykh, Abu Talib al Makki author of the Food for the Heart,[1] Ibn Battah al Hanbali, Ibn Samaun[2] the preacher, preacher, al Khattabi, al Hatimi the philologist, al Udfui Abu Bakr, Zahir al Sarkhasi the Shafiite Shaykh, Ibn Ghalbun the Qurãn reader, al Kushmayhani the reciter of the Sahih, al Muafa b. Zakariya and Nahrawani, Ibn Khuayz Mandad, Ibn Jinni, al Jauhari author of *the Arabic lexicon called* as Sahah, Ibn Faris author of the Mujmil *fil Loghat (Collection of Philological observations),* Ibn Mandah the Hafidh, al Ismaili the Shafiite Shaykh, Asbagh b-ul Faraj the Malikite Shaykh, Badiiuz Zaman the first who composed Makamas (*Discourses*) Ibn Lal, Ibn Abi Zumnayn,[3] Abu Hayyan at Tauhidi, al Wawa, [4] the poet, al Harawi author of the *Kitabul* Gharibayn, Abul Fath al Busti the poet, al Halimi the Shafiite Shaykh, Ibnul Faridh, Abul Hasan al Kabisi, the Kadhi Abu Bakr al Bakilani, Abut Tayyib as Saluki, Ibnul Akfani, Ibn Nubatah author of the Khutbahs (*sermons*), as Saymari the Shafiite Shaykh, al Hakim author of the Mustadrak *alas Sahihayn (strictures on the two Sahihs),* Ibn Kajj, the Shaykh Abu Hamid al Asfaraini, Ibn Furak, as Sharifar Ridha Abu Bakr ar Razi author of the Alkab (*Titles*),[5] the Hafidh Abul Ghani b. Said, Ibn Mardawayh, Hibbatullah b. Salamah, the blind Commentator, Abu Abdur Rahman as Salami the Sufi Shaykh, Ibnul Bawwab the Caligraphist, Abdul Jabbar al Muatazali, al Mahamili the Shafiite Imam, Abu Bakr al Kaffal the Shafiite Shaykh, the master Abu Ishak al Asfaraini,[6] al Lalakai, Ibnul Fakhkhar the scholar of Spain,

---

1 Intended as a guide to novices entering the Sufi or contemplative life. De Slane, I.K.

2 The text has incorrectly Shamaun. See Ibn Ath. and Ibn Khall.

3 I cannot find this name in any author I have consulted and am ignorant of its true pronunciation.

4 The text should have a second aliph.

5 This is an error. He died in 311. In Ibn Khall the word is Aktab (اقطاب) of which De Slane remarks that the knows neither the true pronunciation nor the meaning. Haji Khalifa does not mention it neither does Abul Mahasin though he notes the death of this eminent physician.

6 The text wrongly points this name.

Ali b. Isa ar Rabai the grammarian and others. Ad Dahabi says that in this age lived the principal doctor of the Asharites[1] Abu Ishak al Asfaraini, the head of the Muatazalites the Kadhi Abdul Jabbar, the head of the Radifhites (*schismatics*) the Shaykh al Mufid, the head of the Kiramites Muhammad b-ul Haysam, the head of the Qurãn readers Abul Hasan al Hammami, the head of the Traditionists the Hafidh Abdul Ghani b. Said, the head of the Sufis Abu Abdur Rahman as Salami, the Chief of the poets Abu Omar b. Darraj, the the first of Calipgraphists Ibnul Bawwab, and the first among sovereigns Mahmud b. Subuktagin. I observe that there may be added to these al Hakim biamrillah the chief among the impious, al Jauhari' the first of philologists, Ibn Jani the first of grammarians, al Badii the first of eloquent speakers, the first of Khatibs Ibn Nubatah, the first of commentators Abul Kasim b. Habib an Naysaburi, and the first of Caliphs al Kadir billah for he was one of the most learned of them, having studied law and composed treatises therein and let it suffice thee that the Shaykh Takkiud din bis Salah counts him among the Shafiite doctors and has introduced him in the classes of them-further his reign was one of the longest in duration. A.H.422. A.D.1031.

AL KAIM-BI-AMRILLAH

Al Kaim bi amril lah, (*who stands by the order of God*) Abu Jaafar Abdullah the son of al Kadir was born about the middle of Dul Kaadah in the year 391. His mother was an Armenian slave concubine named Badrud Duja (*the full moon of darkness*) and some say Katrud Nada (*dewdrop*). He assumed the Caliphate on the death of his father in 422 having been his heir presumptive during his lifetime and it was his father who surnamed him al Kaim bi amrillah.

1 For the opinions of these various sects, consult Sale's preface to his translation of the Qurãn.

A.H.422. A.D.1031. Ibnul Athir states that he was comely, of an attrctive countenance, austere in life, pious, devout, learned, full of confidence in God, charitable, patient. He was assiduous in the cultivation of litereature and skilled in writing, prompt to justice and benevolence, attending to all claims and undesirous to refuse anything that might be asked of him. Al Khatib observes that his authority continued firm until he was arrested in the year 450. The cause of this was that the Turk Arslan al Basarisi[1] came into power and in the absence of any rivals, his authority increased and the Emirs of the Arabs and other tribes stood in awe of him and prayers were offered for him upon the pulpits. He levied money and desolated whole villages, al Kaim being unable to determine anything without him. At length he discovered his evil designs , for he heard that it was his intention to plunder the palace and to arrest the Caliph himself. Upon this the Caliph communicated with Abu Talib Muhammad Mikayil[2] the chief of the Ghuzz, know as Toghrul Bek who was at Rai, requesting him to march to his relief. Subsequently the palace of al Basasiri was .burnt down and in the year 447 Toghrul Bek arrived and al Basasiri retired to Rahbah where he was joined by a number of Turks and he wrote to the sovereign of Egypt (*al Mustansir billah*) who assisted him with money. He also corresponded with Inal[3] the brother of Toghrul Bek inciting him by the offer of his brother's dignisties Inal accordingly revolted and engaged the attention of Toghrul Bed. Afterwards al Basasiri marched to Baghdad in the year 450 accompanied by the Egyptian standards and engagements took place between him and the Caliph. Public prayers were offered up for the Egyptain monarch al Mustansir in the great mosque of al Mansur and to the call to prayers was added "Haste to an excellent work."[4] Subsequently he was prayed for in all the mosque except

---

1 Abul Harith Arslan the general of the Turkish troops at Baghdad. He had been a Mamluk to Bahaud Daulah b. Buwayh. His life may be found in I.K.

2 Not Mikyal as in the text. Toghrul Bek was the first monarch of the Seljuk Dynasty. See I.K.

3 The text has incorrectly تبال

4 See note 1, p. 545.

that of the Caliph, and hostilities continued for some months. At length al Basasiri seized the Caliph in the month of Dul Hijjah and removed him to Aanah[1] and confined him there. Toghrul Bed in the meantime defeated his brother and put him to death. Then he wrote to the prefect of Aanah to send back the Caliph with honour to his palace, and the Caliph arrived at the royal palace on the 25th of Dul Kaadah in the year 451 entering with great pomp, the nobles and chamberlains preceding him. Toghrul Bed next dispatched an army which encountered al Basasiri and defeated him and he was slain and his head carried to Baghdad. After the Caliph returned to his palace, he never slept save upon his prayers-carpet and gave himself up to fasting and prayer. He forgave all who had injured him and he accepted the restoration of what had been plundered from him only on payment for the same, saying, "I count upon obtaining for these things, a reward from God," and after this he never laid his head upon a pillow. When his palace was plundered there were not found in it any instruments of music. It is related that when al Basasiri placed him in confinement, he wrote his own story and sent it to Mecca where it was hung up in the kaabah. It contained the following-"To the most High God from his lowly servant. O Lord, thou knowest all secrets and readest all hearts ! O Lord, verily thou art self-sufficing in Thine own knowledge and understanding of Thy creatures, needing not my telling. This slave hath been ungrateful for Thy benefits and hath not given thanks for them and hath put aside the consequences thereof and hath not remembered them. Thy forbearance hath led him astray, so that he hath rebelled against us and hath done evil to us in insolence and malice. O Lord, the Defender hath been humbled and the Tyrant exalted, but thou art the All-knowing, the Wise, the Just, the Supreme Ruler. Through thee shall we overcome him and to Thee we fly from his hands. Verily he hath been exalted over us by means of creatures, but we shall overcome by Thy aid and verily we summon him, in judgment before Thee, and we trust to Thee for justice

A.H.422.
A.D.1031.

1 Above Hit, on the Euphrates and near Hadithah. The text incorrectly points the word.

A.H.451. against him and we carry this oppression of us to Thy sanctuary
A.D.1059. and trust to Thy mercy to remove it-therefore judge between us for Thou art the best of judges."

In the year 428, al Dhahir the Ubaydite Sovereign of Egypt died and was succeeded by his son al Mustansir who was of the age of seven, and he reigned as Caliph sixty years and four months. Ad Dahabi says, "I know of no one in Islam, whether Caliph or Sultan, the reigned for this period. During his days there was a famine in Egypt, the like of which had not been known since the time of Joseph. It continued seven years so that people devoured each other, and it is said even that a small load was old for fifty dinars.

In the year 443 al Muizz b. Badis[1] suppressed the Khutbah for the Ubaydite in Mauritania and established in the name of the House of Abbas.

In the year 451, a peace was concluded between Sultan Ibrahim b. Masaud b. Mahmud b. Subuktagin prince of Ghazni and Sultan Jughri Bed b. Saljuk[2] the brother of Toghrul Bek ruler of Khurasan after long hostilities. Jughri Bed died the same year and was succeeded by his son Alp Arslan.

In the year 454 the Caliph betrothed his daughter to Toghrul Bek after doing his utmost to avoid it. He was much perturbed and wished that it should be withdrawn but at last he yielded against his will. This was a concession never obtained by any of the Buwide princes with all their subjection of the Caliphs and their power over them. I observe that now the Caliph of our time hath married his daughter to one of the slaves of the Sultan-to say nothing of the

---

1 Nadis in the text and MS. is incorrect. He was of the Sanhaj, one of the oldest and purest Berber tribes claiming descent from Himyarite Arabs. He ruled Africa for the House of Abbas, and the Khutbah was never again read in that country for any Egyptain sovereign. Ibn Khall.

2 Not حفرى as in the text. He was the son of Mikaylil and brother of Toghrul Bek. The word Toghrul signifies a kind of falcon and Bek a commander Ibn Khall.

Sultan-"Verily we belong to God and verily unto Him shall we return." Subsequently in the year 455 Toghrul Bek arrived and visited the daughter of the Caliph[1] and he restored the inheritances[2] and the taxes and farmed the revenues of Baghdad for one hundred and fifty thousand dinars. He then returned to Rai and died in the month of Ramadhan-may the Lord not forgive him. He was succeeded by his nephew Adhudud Daulah Alp Arslan prince of Khurasan to whom al Kaim sent a robe of honour and the investiture. Ad Dahabi says that he was the first called the Sultan on the pulpits of Baghdad. He reached an eminence which none other of the sovereigns attained and he conquered many of the cities of the Christians and appointed Nidhamul Mulk his Wazir who abolished what his predecessor Amidul Mulk had done regarding the reviling of the Asharis,[3] and he gave his countenance to Shafiites, and honoured the Imamul Haramayn[4] and Abul Kasim al Kushayri[5] and founded the Nizamiyah College. It is said that this was the earliest College[6] founded for jurisconsults. A.H.455. A.D.1059.

---

1 This was a mere visit of ceremony and frequently repeated, she receiving him seated on a throne of gold and never lifting her veil or rising. Weil says that the marriage contract alone was celebrated and that Toghrul Bek died on the 8th Ramadhan (18th according to I.K.) 455, (4th *September*, 1063) before the nuptials were completed, Ibn Ath. seems to bear out this view. The Caliph demanded as the price of his hand from 100 to 300,000 dinars and the revenues of Wasit.

2 The words of Ibn Ath. and Ibn Khaldun are here identical فاعاد ماكان اطلقه رئيس الاراقيهين من المواريس و المكوس

3 Many Shafiite doctors were attached to the teaching of al Ashari (See Sale's preface to the Qurãn for their doctrines) which led them into controversy with the Hanbalites on points of faith. See I.K.'s life.

4 Abul Maali Abdul Malik surnamed Dhiyauddin (*Splendour of Religion*), called the Imamul Haramayn from his long residence in the two Sacred Cities. He was considered the most learned doctor of the Shafiites in later times. The list of many of his works will be found in his biography by Ibn Khall. He died in A.H. 478.

5 Likewise a Shafiite doctor of eminence and one of the most learned in Jurisprudence, Qurãnic Exegesis and Traditions &c., he held the first rank as a preacher. Born A.H. 376 (986) and died 465 (1072). Ibn Khall.

6 The Nizamiyah College was founded for the express purpose of establishing him in it as a professor. This is controverted by ad Dahabi. See de Slane's preface to Vol. I of his translation of Ibn Khall.

A.H.459. A.D.1066. In the year 458 a little girl was born at Babul Azaj[1] with two heads and two faces and two necks upon one body, and during the same, a heavenly body of great brilliancy appeared like a halo round the moon on a night when it was at its full, and it terrified the people, continuing during ten nights when its light waned and it disappeared.

In the year 459, the Nizamiyah College at Baghdad was completed and the Shaykh Ibn Ishak as Shirazi[2] was appointed professor. The people assembled *to hear him,* but he did not appear and concealed himself and Ibnus Sabbagh[3] the author of the Shamil lectured. Subsequently they pressed Abu Ishak with friendly solicitations until he consented and opened a course of teaching.

In the year 460 a tremendous earthquake occurred at Ramlah[4] which destroyed it, and even the water rose over the mouths of the wells and twenty-five thousand of its inhabitants perished. The sea retreated from the shore the space of one day's journey, and the people went down to its bed gathering the fish and the waters returned upon them and destroyed them.

In the year 461 the great mosque of Damascus caught fire and its beauties were effaced and its appearance rendered unsightly and its golden roofs destroyed. In the year 462 an envoy from the Emir of Mecca came to Alp Arslan informing him that he had established the Khutbah for the Abbasides and discontinued it for the Egyptian al Mustansir and had omitted from the Adan "Hasten to an excellent work," whereupon the Sultan bestowed upon him

1 A quarter in Baghdad.

2 Another eminent Shafiite doctor whose life will be found in Ibn Khall. He was born at Firuzubad. A.H. 393 (1003) and died at Baghdad 476 (1083) and the Nizamiyah College was closed for a year as a token of mourning for his death.

3 Abu Nasr Abdus Sayyid, - (*the son of the dyer*) was chief Shafii jurisconsult, of Persian and Arabian Irak. His work the Shamil (*Comprehensive*) is one of the best Shafiite treatises on their system of Jurisprudence. He was reinstated as professor of the Nizamiyah College on the death of Abu Ishak as Shirazi. Born at Baghdad 400 A.H., (1009-10) and died there 477 (1084). Ibn Khall.

4 In Palestine, Ibn Ath. says that the Shock was felt throughout Palestine and Egypt.

thirty thousand dinars and a robe of honour. This was caused by the fallen state of the Egyptians through severe famines in successive years so that people fed upon each other and an irdabb[1] of *wheat* fetched one hundred dinars and a dog was sold for fifty dinars and a cat for thirty. A.H.466. A.D.1073.

The author of the Mirat[2] relates that a woman went out of Cairo with a *mudd (about two pounds)* of jewels, crying out, "Who will take this for a mudd of wheat ?"

One of the poets congratulating al Kaim says-

"Verily the Egyptian knew that within his armies
Were the famine years of Joseph and the plague of Emmaus.
They remained there till he was anxious for his safety

1 An Egyptian measure equal, according to Kazimirski, to about five bushels. Lano fixes it at 24 Saa صاع this latter being about four times the quantity of corn that fills the two hands. Al Akhtal describing miserly people, says,

الخبز كا لعنبر الهندى عندهم
و القهع سبعون اردبابدينار

"Bread is like Indian amber to them
While wheat is seventy irdabbs for a dinar."

"Since writing the above I have met with an account of the famine that desolated Darfur, Kordofan and other provinces of Central Africa, in 1877; by Dr. Daniel Comboni, Vicar Apostolic of that region. The Austrian Consul, he writes, paid £10-3 for an ardeb (so the word is commonly pronounced) of flour, the ordinary price being 15 shilliings. Later on, at Khartoum, flour could not be obtained at any price and in the kingdom of Kordofan £20 could not purchase a single ardeb." This measure he gives as equivalent to a sack containing about '2' cwt. 100 dinars would be equal to about £45, double the price of the ardeb in the famine of 1877, which was terrible enough.

2 Probably the Mirat uz Zaman, the Mirror of the Age by the learned Professor Imam and historian Shamsuddin Abul Muzaffar Yusuf b. Kizaghli grandson of Abul Faraj b-ul Jauzi. He was born at Baghdad 597. A.H. (12001-1), died 654 A.H. (1257). His great historical work the Mirat extends to forty volumes and Abul Mahasin acknowledges his indebtedness to it when composing his annals. De Slane, I.K.

A.H.466. A.D.1073. And he feared them with an exceeding fear."

In the year 463 the khutbah was read for al Kaim and the Sultan Alp Arslan in Aleppo when the people there beheld the supremacy of their authority and the decline of the sway of al Mustansir.

During the same a great battle[1] was fought between the Muslims and the Byzantines, and the Muslims were victorious, praise be to God. They were led by Alp Arslan who took the Emperor prisoner but afterwards released him for a large sum and concluded a peace for fifty years. When he was released he said to Alp Arslan-"In what direction is the Caliph ?" He pointed to it and the Emperor uncovered his head and bent in submission in that direction.

In the year 464, a great murrain, in sheep broke out.

In 465, Alp Arslan was slain and was succeeded in the government by his son Malik Shah who was surnamed Jalalud Daulah. He restored the administration of the Empire to Nidhamul Mulk and gave him the title of Atabek. He was the first so called and it means "the Father[2] Emir."

During the same the famine was so severe in Egypt that a woman ate a small loaf *purchased* for a thousand dinars and the plague reached its height.

In the year 466 there was a great inundation in Baghdad. The Tigris rose thirty cubits, the like of which had never occurred and property and lives and cattle were destroyed. The people went about it boats and the Friday prayers were twice held on sailing vessels on the face of the waters, and the Caliph arose supplicating

---

1 This was fought on 26th August, 1071 near Metazkerd, midway between Van and Erzeroum. Romanus Diogenes was taken prisoner and released on a ranson of 1,500,000 dinars. The intrepidity of the captive and the courtesy of the conqueror may be read with pleasure and instruction in the picturesque and accurate narrative of Gibbon. Cap. LVII.

2 In Ibn Khall's life of Jakar Nasiruddin, the meaning of Atabek is given as الزي يربى اولاد الملوك the educator of princes-from the Turkish Ata father and Bek Emir.

the Lord. Baghdad was leveled at a stroke, one hundred thousand houses or more being destroyed. A.H.466. A.D.1073.

In the year 467, on Wednesday night the 13th of Shaaban (2nd *April,* 1075) the Caliph al Kaim bi amrillah died. This happened in consequence of his having been bled. He went to sleep and the place where he was bled became unbound. A great loss of blood ensued and he awoke, his strength being much diminished. He sent therefore for his grandson and heir Abdullah the son of Muhammad and bequeathed the succession to him and then died. The duration of his Caliphate was five and forty years.

Of persons of note who died during his reign were Abu Bakr al Birkani, Abul Fadhl al Falaki, at Thaalabi the commentator, al Kuduri the Hanafite Shaykh, Ibn Sina (*Avicena*) the philosopher, Mahyar the poet, Abu Nuaym author of the Hulyah, Abu Zayd ad Dabusi, al Bardai the Malikite, author of the Tahdib, Abul Husayn al Basri the Muatazalite, Makki author of the Irab[1] (*grammatical inflexions*), the Shaykh Abu Muhammad al Juayni, al Mahdawi author of the commentary, al Ifllili, at Thamanini, Abu Amr ad Duwani, al Khalil author of the Irshad *fi maarifat Ulamail Balad (Directory of information respecting the learned of all countries)*, Salim ar Razi, Abul Ala the Qurãn reader, Abu Othman as Sabuni Ibn Battah the Expounder of al Bukhari, the Kadhi Abu Tayyib at Tabari, Ibn Shita the Qurãn reader, al Mawardi the Shafiite, Ibn Babshad, al Kudhaai author of the Shihab (*Flambeau on the merits of as Shafii),* Ibn Burhan the grammarian, Ibn Hazm ad Dhahiri, al Bayhaki, Ibn Sidah author of the Mukham (*fixed*) Abu Yala b-ul Farra the Hanbalite Shaykh, al Hadhrami one of the Shafiite school, al Hazli author of the Kamil (*Perfect*) on the reading of the Qurãn, al Furani, al Khatib al Baghdadi Ibn Rashik author of the Umdah (*Column as the art of poetry and poetical criticism*) and Ibn Abdil Barr.

---

1 This is probably the work entitled, "Kitab uz Zahiful Lumaad dallat ala Mustamalat il Iirab," "The blooming, a treatise on the lights which indicate the grammatical inflexions in general use." This Qurãn reader was the author of many voluminous works, the list of which is given by Ibn Khall.

A.H.467.
A.D.1075.

AL MUKTADI BI-AMRILLAH

Al Muktadi bi amril lah (*Directing himself by the command of God)* Abul Kasim, Abdullah was the son of Muhammad the son of al Kaim. His father died during the lifetime of al Kaim while his mother was pregnant with him, and he was born six months after his father's death. His mother was a slave concubine called Arjawan. He was acknowledged Caliph on his grandfather's death, he being nineteen years and three months old. The oath of allegiance was taken in the presence of the Shaykh Abu Ishak as Shirazi, Ibnus Sabbagh and ad Damaghani.[1] During his reign many good works and excellent deeds were done in the provinces, and the ordinances of the Caliphate during his days were noble and honorable in contradistinction to those of his predecessors. Among his good deeds, he proscribed female singers and evil doers in Baghdad, and ordered that no one should enter the baths without drawers, and he destroyed the towers of the baths with a view to securing public decorum. He was pious, virtuous, firm of purpose, magnanimous and one of the noblest of the House of Abbas. In this year of the Caliphate the Khutbah was restored in Mecca in the name of the House of Ubayd. During the same, Nidhamul Mulk assembled the astronomers and they made the New Year's day the first point of the suns entry into Aries, and before this it was held at the meridian of his passage through Pisces, and this act of al Nidham was the origin of *the reformation* of the Calendar.[2]

---

1 Abu Jaafar Muhammad a Hanafite jurisconsult Kadhi of Karkh (a suburb of Baghdad). He resigned that office and entered the Caliph's service as chamberlain and proved an able statesman. De Slane, I.K., died 518 A.H.

2 "In Persia" says Gibbon "since the age of Zoroaster the revolution of the sun has been known and celebrated as an annual festival, but after the fall of the Magian empire, the intercalation had been neglected : the fractions of minutes and hours were multiplied into days; and the date of the spring was removed from the sign of Aries to that of Pisces. The reign of Malak was illustrated by the Jelalean era (from Malak Shah's surname Jalalud Daulah) and all errors either past or future were corrected by a computation of time which surpasses the Julian and approaches the accuracy of the Gregorian Style." *Decline and Fall*, Cap. LVII.

In the year 468 the khutbah was read for al Muktadi at Damascus, and the words "Haste to an excellent work," in the call to prayers were discontinued at which the people rejoiced. In 469, Abu Nasr son of the Master Abul Kasim al Kushayri al Ashari arrived at Baghdad and preached at the Nizamiyah college. A great dissension arose with the Hanbalites because he discoursed in favour of the Ashari doctrine and disparaged *them*. His followers and partisans increased in number and a tumult ensuing, a number were killed. Fakhrud Daulah b. Jahir was removed from the office of Wazir of al Muktadi because he separated himself from the Hanbalities. A.H.474. A.D.1083.

In the year 475 the Caliph sent Shaykh Abu Ishak as Shirazi as an envoy to the Sultan with a complaint against Amid Abul Fath.[1]

In the year 476, prices fell in all the provinces and the scarcity ceased. During the same, the Caliph nominated Abu Shujaa Muhammad b-ul Hasan to the office of Wazir and gave him the title of Dhahirud din (*Defender of the Faith*). I believe that this was the first introduction of surnames coupled with the word "din."

In the year 477, Sulayman the son of Kultumish the Saljuk prince of Konich and Akserai[2], set out with his troops for Syria and took Antioch which had fallen into the possession of the Byzantines

---

1 The words of Abul Fida are : The Caliph sent Abu Ishak to the Sultan Malak Shah and to Nidham ul Mulk. He left Baghdad for Khurasan with a complaint against Amid of Irak Abul Fath b. Abil Layth. He returned with the acceptance by the Sultan of the Caliph's request and Amid was forbidden to exert any authority over the Sultan's private establishment. Reiske, takes Amid (*Columen*) to signify here not a proper name but metaphorically- procuratorem commissarium. An account of Abu Ishak's mission is given by him in a note taken form the classes of the Shafiites (Tabakat us Shafiiah) "auctors Sebekaco,"- and the Caliph's charge to his envoy is to complain that the people of the city (Baghdad) suffer much annoyance at the hands of Abul Fath. See Abul Fida, anno 475. From Ibn Athir it appears that the mission was for the purpose of reinstating Abu Shujaa' as minister who had succeeded Fakhrud Daulah and had been displaced by the Sultan.

2 I have spelt the names as they are marked in Keith Johnston's Atlas.

A.H.479. A.D.1086. in the year 353,[1] and he sent to Sultan Malak Shah to communicate the good tidings.

Ad Dahabi says that the posterity of Saljuk were sovereigns of a portion of Byzantine territory. Their ascendancy continued for a considerable time and a remnant of them existed up to the reign of al Malik ad Dhahir Baybars.[2]

In the year 478 a dark storm swept over Baghdad-the thunder pealed and the lightning flashing luridly and sand and dust fell like rain and many thunderbolts fell, and the people thought that it was the day of resurrection, and it continued for three hours past the afternoon. This occurrence was witnessed by the Imam Abu Bakr at Turtushi[3] who has related it in his Amali (*Dictations*).

In the year 479 Yusuf b. Tashifin[4] prince of Ceuta and Morocco sent to al Muktadi requesting that he would confirm his authority and invest him with the sovereignty of the provinces he possessed. The Caliph accordingly sent him a robe of honour and standards and gave him the title of prince of the Muslims at which he was much pleased, and the jurisconsults of Mauritania rejoiced. It was he who founded the city of Morocco.

During the same, Sultan Malak Shah entered Baghdad for the first time and took up his residence at the palace and played at ball.

---

1 The text has by some mistake 358. In the MS. the unit is omitted. A masterly sketch of these events will be found at the close of Gibbon's 57th chapter.

2 This dynasty of the Saljuks of Rum dates from the year 480 and closes in 700 A. II., continuing 220 years under fifteen sovereigns whose names are recorded by the diligence of D'Herbelot. The Iranian and Kermanian branches will be found noticed by the some author.

3 He was a native of Tortosa in Spain and a Malikite doctor noted for his ascetic life. He studied at Seville, at Baghdad and at Basrah. He died in 520 A.H. (1126). Ibn Khall.

4 The text makes an N of the initial instead of T. The MS. is correct-the particulars of this event will be found in Ibn Khall, under Muatamid b. Abbad.

He met the Caliph *with reciprocal*[1] civility and shortly after he returned to Ispahan. During the same, the Khutbah for the Ubaydite sovereign (*al Mustansir billah*) was discontinued in the Sacred Cities and was read for al Muktadi. A.H.479. A.D.1086.

In the year 481 the sovereign of Ghaznah al Muayyid Ibrahim b. Masaud b. Mahmud b. Subuktagin died and his son Jalaud din Masaud succeeded him.

In the year 488 a College was built at Baghdad by Tajul Mulk Mustawfiud[2] Daulah at the gate of Abraz and Abu Bakr as Shashi[3] lectured there.

In the year 484 the Franks conquered the whole of the island of Sicily which had been first conquered by the Muslims after the year 200[4] A.H. The Aghlabites retained possession of it uninterruptedly till al Mahdi the Ubaydite conquered Africa. During the same, Sultan Malak Shah arrived in Baghdad and ordered a large mosque to be built. The nobles also erected mansions round about it, to dwell in *when they visited Baghdad.* He then returned to Ispahan but again repaired to Baghdad in 485 A.H. with evil intent. He sent to the Caliph informing him that he must quit Baghdad and that he might go to any other city he pleased. The Caliph was much perturbed and replied, "Give me a respite though it be for a month." He answered, "Not a single hour." The Caliph then sent to

1 Or it may mean "He played against the Caliph." The Sultan and the Caliph were on the most friendly terms and interchanged visits and presents. The MS. has تقادم for تقاوم of the text.

2 Tajul Mulk Abul Ghanaim was the favourite of Turkan Khatun wife of Malak Shah. At her instigation Nidhamul Mulk was deposed. Tajul Mulk succeeded him and put him to death. See Weil, Ibn Ath. De Slane, I.K.

3 The College was called the Tajiyah after its founder. Abu Bakr was surnamed the glory of Islam, and was considered the first Jurisconsult of the age of the Shafiite school. He died 429 A.H., (1037). His life will be found in Ibn Khall.

4 212 A.H., 827-8 A.D See Gibbon's 52nd chapter. The descent of the Saracens of Africa was invited by the revengeful Euphemius who had been sentenced by the Emperor to the loss of his tongue for the abduction of a nun. The Arabic name of the island in the text should be spelt with a ص for a س.

A.H.485. A.D.1092. the Wazir of the Sultan begging for a delay of ten days. At this juncture occurred the illness and death of the Sultan which was ascribed to the miraculours powers of the Caliph. It is said that the Caliph fasted and when he had broken his fast, he sat upon ashes and called down a curse upon Malak Shaa. The Lord heard his prayer and Malak Shah departed to hell-fire.[1]

When he died, his wife, Turkan concealed his death and sent to the nobles secretly, requesting their allegiance to his son Mahmud who was then five years old. They swore fealty to him whereupon she sent to al Muktadi to invest him with the dignity of the Sultanate. He assented and gave him the tittle of Nasirud dunya wad din (*Defender of Spirituals and Temporals*). His brother Barkyaruk, son of Malak Shah, however, opposed him and the Caliph invested him with authority and surnamed him Ruknuddin and that in Muharram of the year 487. The Caliph signed the diploma of investiture and died suddenly the next day (15th *Muharram, 4th February* 1094). It was said that his female slave Shamsun Nahar (*the sun of day*) poisoned him. His son al Mustadhir billah was acknowledged as his successor in the Caliphate. Of persons of note who died during his reign were Abdul Kahir al Jurjani, Abul Walid al Baji, the Shaykh Abu Ishak as Shirazi, al Aalam (*the hare-lipped*) the grammarian, Ibnus Sabbagh author of the Shamil, al Mutawalli, Imamul Haramayn, ad Damaghani the Hanafite, Ibn Fadhdhal al Mujashii, and al Bazdawi the Hanafite Shaykh.

---

1 الي حيث القت رحلها أم قشعم is an Arabic proverb, said to be a saying of Zuhayr expressive of the meaning I have given. It is said that Umm Kasham (*Death*) was the name of a camel that had fled from its owner and passing by a large fire, it shied and flung its saddle into the middle of it. The expression is now used as an imprecation. The text would therefore be literally rendered-"and Malak Shah want to where her saddle was thrown *by Umm Kasham.*" She the Durrat al Yatimah bil Amthal il Kadimah (*the matchless pearl on ancient proverbs*) by Ibrahim Sarkis of Lebanon.

AL MUSTADHIR BI'LLAH

A.H.487.
A.D.1091.

Al Mustadhir billah (*Imploring help of God*) Abul Abbas Ahmad son of al Muktadi was born in Shawwal of the year 470. He was acknowledged Caliph on the death of his father, being sixteen years of age. Ibnul Athir says that he was of gentle manners, of generous disposition, zealous in good works, a fine penman, shilful in he dispatch of the royal rescripts in which no one could approach[1] him, indicating considerable[2] merit and extensive knowledge. He was humane and liberal and a patron of the learned and the virtuous. His tenure of the Caliphate was not free from trouble for the times *he liked in* were turbulent and occupied with frequent wars.

During this year of his reign died al Mustansir the Ubaydite sovereign of Egypt and was succeeded by his son al Mustaali Ahmad. During the same, the Byzantines took Valencia.

In the year 488, Ahmad[3] Khan prince of Samarkand was slain, as it seemed that he held impious tenets. The nobles seized him and the jurisconsults were summoned and pronounced sentence of death against him and he was put to death-may God not have mercy upon him-and they gave the government to his cousin *Masaud.*

In the year 489 the seven planets with the exception of Saturn met in the sign of Pisces and the astronomers predicted a deluge similar to the deluge of Noah and it came to pass that the pilgrims encamped at Darul Manakib[4] when a flood overtook and drowned the greater number of them.

In the year 490, the Sultan Arslan Arghun son of Alp Arslan the Saljuk, ruler of Khurasan was assassinated. The country was seized by Sultan Barkyaruk and its cities and people yielded obedience to him. During the same the khutbah was read for the

---

1 Ibnul Athir has يقاريه not يقارنه

2 For عريز read غريز as in Ibn Ath.

3 Not احد as in the text.

4 Ibnul Athir has مياقت and a variant مفاقت -but none of these places are to be found in Yakut. See the M.B. under مناقت

A.H.492 Ubaydite (*Mustaali*) in Aleppo, Antioch and Maarrah and Shayzar
A.D.1099. for the space of one month and afterwards restored for the Abbassides. During the same the Franks advanced and captured Nice which was the first city they took and they reached Kafartab[1] and devastated and adjacent country. This was the first appearance of the Franks in Syria. They passed the Bosporus in vast numbers, and princes and their subjects were in consternation and terrible were their depredations. It is said that when the ruler of Egypt behold the supremacy of the Saljuke and their predominanace in Syria, he wrote to the Franks inviting them to enter and conquer Syria, and from every quarter there was a general summons of the Frankish people.

In the year 492, the mission summons of the Batini[2] sectaries spread into Ispahan, During the same the Franks took Jerusalem after a siege of a month and a half, and slaughtered more than seventy thousand, among them, many learned, devout, and pious men. They destroyed the places of religious visitation and collected the Jews together in a church and burnt it over their heads. The refugees arrived at Baghdad and recounted tales that brought tears to the eyes. But the rival Sultans were at variance with each other, wherefore the Franks subdued all Syria.

Abul Mudhaffar al Abiwardi[3] says regarding this-

"I have mixed blood with flowing tears.
For none is left among us to be a mark for the catapults.
A poor weapon for a man is the tear that he sheds
When war kindles its flame with keen-edged swords.
O sons of Islam ! behind ye

---

1 Between Maarrah and Aleppo.

2 See note 1, p. 5.

3 He was a direct descendant from Muawiyah the less, and a poet of great celebrity and an eminent genealogist and was a native of Abiward. His collected works are classed under various heads, such as Irakiyah, (pieces relative to Iraq) Najdiyah (relative to Najd) and Wajdiyah (amatory pieces). He died at Ispahan 507 A.H. Ibn Khall.

Are battles which will bring death upon your paths. A.H.492 A.D.1099.

O thou fair sleeper in the shade of security and ease
And pleasure like the delicate flower of the grove !
How can the eye slumber whose lids are filled
With dust that awaketh every sleeper ?
Your brethren in Syria take their midday rest
On the backs of well grown steeds or in the maws of vultures.
Rome beateth them with contumely, and ye
Trail the skirts of submission like those who seek peace.
How much blood has been shed with impunity,
And how many fair women veil with shame their beauty with their hands !
So that the glittering swords have their curved blades red with blood for their sakes,
And the tall lances bear their points[1] blood dyed.
It may soon be that he who lies buried in Medina
Will call out with a loud voice, "O sons of Hashim !
Do I see my people not speeding towards the foe
Their spears, while the pillars of the faith are tottering !
And choosing hell-fire for fear of death
And counting not the inevitable shame ?
Are the chief of the Arabs content with ignominy
And submit they to the scorn of barbarian lords ?
Would that it they fight not in defence
Of their faith, they would be jealous for the honour of their homes."

During the same, Muhammad the son of Malak Shah rose against his brother Barkyaruk and vanquished him, wherefore the

---

1 Ibn Ath. has this word with a ز instead of ر -thus making it an adjective, sharp, penetrating. See his variants of this poem.

A.H.492 Caliph invested him with the supreme authority and gave him the
A.D.1099. title of Ghiyathuddunya wad din (*Redresser of wrongs in spirituals and temporals*) and his name was read in the khutbah at Baghdad. Many engagements subsequently took place between them. The Qurãn of Othman was brought this year from Tiberius to Damascus for fear *of an accident* to it, and the people went out to meet it and they placed it in the treasury in the reserved space of the principal mosque.

In 494 the power of the Batinis in Irak increased and their assassination of the people, and the terrors they occasioned were such that the nobles wore armour under their garments and they slew many people, among them ar Ruyani[1] author of the Bahrul Madhab (*occan of doctrine*). In this year the Franks took the town of Saruj[2] and Hayfa, Ursuf and Cesarea.

In the 495 died al Mustaali ruler of Egypt and was succeeded by his son a child of five years, Mansur al Amir biahkam allah (*Ruling according to the commands of God*).

In the year 496 seditions occurred against the authority of the Sultan, and the preachers omitted the prayer for him, and restricted themselves to the prayer for the Caliph and no other.

In 497 a pace was concluded between the two Sultans Muhammad and Barkyaruk. The occasion of it was, that after hostilities had been protracted between them and discussions had become universal, and property plundered and blood spilt and the provinces ravaged during which the Sultanate was the coveted prize, and princes after being victorious were in their turn subdued, men of understanding interfered in the interests of peace, and

---

1 Abul Mahasin Abdul Wahid a Shafiite jurisconsult of eminence in great favour with Nidham ul Mulk. His work, the Badr, was a voluminous treatise on the Jurisprudence of his school. He was killed at Amul and owed his death to sectarian intolerance. Ibn Khall. He was born 415. A.H., (1025) and slain 502 (1108).

2 Sharuj is near Harran N.E. of Aleppo. Hayfa is in the bay of Acre and Ursuf on the coast between Cesarea and Juffa.

treaties and oaths and compacts were drawn up and the Caliph bestowed the viceregal robe of honour upon Barkyaruk and the Khutbah was read for him in Baghdad. A.H.498 A.D.1104-5.

In the year 498 Sultan Barkyaruk died and the nobles set up his son Jalalud Daulah Malka Shah in succession to him. The Caliph invested him and his name was read in the khutbah in Baghdad. He was under five years of age. His uncle Muhammad, however, opposed him and as the general voice was in the favour, the Caliph placed him in the dignity of the Sultanate and he returned to Ispahan, a powerful Sultan much feared and at the head of a numerous army.

During the same year the small-pox broke out with great virulence Baghdad, and a countless number of children died and it was followed by a great plague.

In the year 499, a man arose in the neighbourhood of Nahawand claiming the gift of prophecy. The people followed him but he was taken and put to death. In the year 500, the fort *of Shahdiz*[1] in Ispahan of which the Ismailites had taken possession, was recaptured and destroyed and the defenders slain. Their leader (*Ahmad b. Abdil Malik b. Attash*) was flayed alive and his skin stuffed with straw. This was done by Sultan Muhammad after a close siege. Praise be to God.

In the year 501 the Sultan removed the imposts and taxes in Baghdad and many blessings were invoked on him and he increased in justice and beneficence.

In 502 the Ismailites returned and occupied Shayzar when its inhabitants were off their guard and took possession of it and captured the citadel and shut the gates. Its governor was at the time abset on a tour of pleasure, but he returned and quickly exterminated them.

During this year the Shafiite Shaykh ar Ruyani author of the Bahr was slain by the Ismailites as hath already gone before.

---

1 Ibn Ath. Weil writes the name incorrectly Shahdurr. See Yakut.

A.H.498 A.D.1104-5. In the year 503, the Franks took Tripoli after a siege of some years.

In 504 the troubles of the Muslims increased by reason of the Franks, and being convinced of their ultimate conquest of the whole of Syria, the Muslims sought to conclude a peace which the Franks rejected, but proposed a truce on the condition of the payment of many thousand dinars. A truce was therefore concluded which they afterwards broke-may the Lord confound them.[1]

During the same a dark storm swept over old Cairo which prevented people breathing and a man could not even see his hand, and sand fell upon the people and they believed their destruction was upon them. After a short time it cleared a little and them turned yellow and this went on from the afternoon till past sunset. A bloody battle also took place this year between the Franks[2] and Ibn Tashifin ruler of Spain in which the Muslims were victorious, and they slew and made captive and plundered to an extent which cannot be described and the bravest of the Franks fell.

In the year 507, Maudud governor of Mosal advanced with an army against the Frankish king of Jerusalem[3] (*Baldwin*) and a terrible engagement took place between them. Shortly after Maudud returned to Damascus, and one day while he was reading the Friday prayers, lo! a Batini sprung upon him and stabbed him and he died on the spot. The Frankish king upon this wrote to the governor of

---

1 This pious wish is not echoed by Ibn Athir who does not state in terms that the truce was broken. Its duration was limited to the harvest time. The Crusaders after this, plundered a fleet of merchant ships conveying a rich cargo from Egypt but it is not stated whether this was done during the truce. The silence of the Arab Historian speaks in acquittal of the Frank. Aleppo purchased this truce at 32,000 dinars besides horses and garments, Tyre contributed 7,000, Shayzar 4,000, and Hamat 2,000.

2 Under Alfonso of Toledo according to the Kamil.

3 Godfrey of Bonillon was succeeded in the government of Jerusalem by the two Baldwins, his brother and cousin. Baldwin was defeated in this battle (30th June 1113) which took place near Tiberias, with great loss.

Damascus,[1] a letter which runs as follows ; "Verily a people that slays its chief, on a festival day in the temple of Him whom they worship, the Lord must necessarily destroy." A.H.512 A.D.1118.

In the year 511 a great flood swept over Sinjar[2] and its fortifications and a great number of people were destroyed. The flood carried away the gate of the city several parasangs, and it lay hidden under the soil which the stream took with it, and it was discovered two years after. A little child escaped safely in its cot which the flood carried away. The cot lodged in an olive tree. The child afterwards lived and grew to manhood.

In the same year died the Sultan Muhammad who was succeeded by his son Mahmud at the age of fourteen.

In the year 512 died the Caliph al Mustadhir billah on the 16th Rabii II.[3] He reigned 25 years. Ibn Ukayl the Hanbalite Shaykh washed his body and his son al Mustarshid read the prayers over him. Shortly after his death died his grandmother Arjawan thc mother of al Muktadi. Ad Dahabi says that no other Caliph is known whose grandmother outlived him but this one. She saw her son a Caliph, her grandson and her great-grandson.

The following verses are by al Mustadhir-

"The warmth of love dissolved in my heart what was frozen
On the day thou didst stretch out thy hand in farewell.
How can I tread the path of patience while verily
I behold the way through the defiles of love are various ?

---

1 The Atabak Tughtakin, who it is conjecture instigated the deed, the fruits of which he enjoyed.

2 Near Mosal.

3 The text has 23 Rabii I, and so also the MS., but this must be an error as Suyuti himself admits that the Caliph's son al Mustarshid succeeded *on the death* of his father in *Rabii* II. Both Ibnul Athir and Ibn Khaldun give the date to be the middle of Rabii II. The former specifies it with exactitude, namely, the 16th of that month (8th *August* 1118) and gives the duration of his reign at 24 years 3 months and 11 days, with which Abul Fida exactly accords.

A.H.512 A.D.1118.

If I break my plighted troth, O my delight !
In time to come, may I never behold thee again."
The following is by Sarim al Bataihi-
"I dwelt with Mustadhir the son of Muktadi
Billah, the son al Kaim, the son of al Kadir,
Under his protection. I hope of the bounty of his hands
That he will be a guardian to my family.
May my abode be with him in my advancing years
And may he obtain from my praise, verses of world-wide fame."

Al Mustadhir wrote an order thereupon giving him the choice of receiving a present and departing, or remaining with him with a yearly stipend. As Silafi narrates that Abul Khattab bil Jarrah said to him. "I was praying with al Mustadhir in the Ramadhan, and I read as follows : 'Verily thy son hath been called a thief.' (Qur. XII), a reading which I had from al Kasai, and when I came to the concluding benediction, he said, 'This reading is a good one because it clears the children of the Prophets from having spoken falsely.'"[1]

AL MUSTARSHID BI'LLAH

Al Mustarshid billah (*Taking God for a Guide*) Abu Mansur al Fadhl b-ul Mustadhir was born in Rabii I, in the year 485 and was acknowledged Caliph on the death of his father in Rabii II, 512. He was a man of high resolves and great courage, spirit, intelligence and of awe-inspiring presence. He assumed the affairs of the Caliphate and administered them in an admirable manner. He revived its ancient customs, and put life into its bones,

1 The ordinary reading is-'thy son hath committed thefty' by a charge of the diacritical points. The passage refers to the finding of the cup in Benjamin's sack and Reuben addressing his brethren, refuses to return to Egypt without Benjamin and tells the rest to say the above words to Jacob.

strengthening the pillars of the law and ornamenting its sleeves. A.H.512
He personally undertook the direction of hostilities and marched on A.D.1118.
several occasions to Hillah and Mosal and the road to Khurasan, until the last march he undertook when his army was defeated near Hamadan and he was taken prisoner to Adarbijan. He heard traditions from Abul Kasim b. Bayyan, and Abdul Wahab b. Hibbat illah as Sabti. Muhammad b. Omar b. Makki al Ahwazi, and his Wazir Ali b. Tirad *az Zaynabi* and Ismail b. Tahir al Mausili, related them on his authority. This is mentioned by Ibnus Samaani.[1]

Ibnus Salah notices him in the classes of the Shafiites and let that be sufficient for thee *as a testimony of his merit* and he says that he it was for whom Abu Bakr as Shashi composed his work the Umdah *fi Farunus Shafiyah (the Pillar on the derivative institutes of the Shafii doctrine*) on jurisprudence. The book being known by his surname, for al Mustarshid[2] had at that time the title of Umdatuddunya waddin (*Pillar in spiritual and temporals*). As Subki[3] also speaks of him in his classification of the Shafiite doctors and says that in the beginning of his reign, he was devout and wore hair-cloth and used to retire alone into a room to pray : that he was born on Wednesday the 18th of Shaaban in the year 486 and that his father included him in the khutbah as his heir and engraved his name on the coinage in Rabii I, 488.

He wrote a beautiful hand which none of the Caliphs before him equaled. He used to correct his secretaries and rectify the errors in their documents. As for his nobility of mind, awe-inspiring presence, his courage and intrepidity, they were as clear as the sun. His reign continued to be troubled by many dissessions and

---

1 The Hafidh Abu Saad surnamed Tajul Islam a Shafiite doctor born 466, (1074) died 510 (1116). A list of his works is given by Ibn Khall.

2 See Haji Khalifah under عمده

3 Abu Nasr Abdul Wahab surnamed the crown of religion, chief Kadhi of Damascus. His work on the Shafiite doctors was in three parts called at Tabakat al Kubra (*the greater*) al Wusta (*the medium*) and al Sughra (*the less*). He was born at Cairo, A.H. 728 (1327-8), and died of the plague at Damascus, A.H. 771 (1369-70) De Slane, I.K.

A.H.525 A.D.1131. enemies. He used to march in person to put them down until his final expedition to Iraq when he was defeated, taken prisoner and suffered martyrdom.

Ad Dahabi says that Sultan Mahmud son of Muhammad Malak Shah died in 525 and was succeeded by his son Dauud. His uncle Masaud son of Muhammad opposed him and an engagement took place, but after a short time they made peace on the condition of an equal partition, each of them retaining sovereign authority. Masaud was named Sultan in the Khutbah at Baghdad and Dauud as his successor, and they both received robes of honour. Afterwards an estrangement occurred between the Caliph and Masaud and the Caliph marched against him. The two armies met, but the greater part of the Caliph's troops played false and Masaud was victorious and took him and his suite prisoners and confined them in a fort near Hamadan. When the people of Baghdad heard this, they filled the streets in a state of commotion, having dust upon their heads, and wept and lamented and the women came forth with uncovered faces mourning the Caliph, and they abstained from public prayers and the reading of the khutbah.

Ibnul Jauzi says that Baghdad was convulsed by frequent earthquakes, continuing five or six times each day, and the people fell to supplicating the Lord. Sultan Sinjar[1] thereupon wrote to his nephew Masaud saying, "As soon as my son, the Redresser of Spirituals and Temporals, is informed of this latter, let him present himself before the Caliph, and kiss the ground before him and ask his paradon and forgiveness and make the humblest supplications for his indulgence, for verily signs from the heavens and the earth have appeared to us, the like of which we are unable to listen to

---

1 Sixth Sultan of the elder branch of the Saljuks. He was son of Malak Shah. He governed Khurasan for 20 years under his brothers. Barkyaruk and Muhammad, to whose possessions he succeeded, after foreing Sultan Masaud to acknowledge his paramount authority. He conquered Transoxiana and compelled tribute from the Ghaznevide kings. He was taken prisoner by the Ghuz a Turkish tribe and remained with them for five years. He effected his escape, but died in 552 when on the point of recovering his kingdom. See D. Herbelot art, Sangiar. Gibbon, Cap. LIX and Ibn Khall.

much less witness, such as hurricanes, lightnings and earthquakes, A.H.525
and their continuance for twenty days, together with dissensions in A.D.1131.
the army and confusion in the provinces, for verily I fear for myself before the Lord. And the appearance of his signs and the abstention of the people from praying in the mosques and the discontinuance of the Khutbah *are things* I am not able to bear, therefore I conjure thee by Allah to mend thy affairs and restore the Caliph to his residence of honour and carry before him the housings of State as hath been our custom and the custom of our ancestors." And Masaud did all that was commanded him and kissed the ground before the Caliph and stood before him asking pardon. Sinjar subsequently sent another messenger accompanined by an armed force, urging Masaud to restore the Caliph to his capital. With this force were seventeen Ismailites and it is said that Masaud was ignorant of their presence, but others affirm that it was he who secretly introduced them. They attacked the Caliph in his tent and treacherously slew him and murdered with him a number of his attendants. The troops were not aware of their presence until they had effected their purpose, when they captured them and put them to death under the curse of God. The Sultan Masaud publicly mourned him and affected grief for this, and there was lamentation and weeping, and when the news reached Baghdad the people felt it sorely and they went forth bare foot rending their garments, the women with disheveled hair, beating their breasts and lamenting over him, for al Mustarshid was much beloved among them for his bravery and justice and for his goodness towards them. The assassination of al Mustarshid took place at Maraghah[1] on Thursday the 16th of Dul Kaadah 529, (27th *August* 1134).

The following is by him-

"I am he, ruddy of visage, sought for in battle,
Who can conquer the world without opposition.
My horsemen shall sweep over the Roman empire
And my glittering sword shall be wielded in the furthest ends of China."

---

1 In Adarbijan, Accounts vary as to the exact date of the Caliph's death.

A.H.529 A.D.1134.

The following also are among his lines written during imprisonment-

"It is not strange the lions should be wounded
By dogs of enemies, human beings and brutes.
For the javelin of Wahshi made Hamzah drink of death
And Ali was slain by the sword of Ibn Muljam."

By him also are these verses when he was defeated and counselled to fly, but refused and held his ground till he was captured:

"They said, 'dost thou stand while
The enemy surround thee, and fly not ?'
I answered them, 'the man who will not be counseled
By admonition, deceiveth himself ;
May I never acquire good while I live
And may Fortune never avert evil from me,
If I have ever thought that other
Than God can profit or injure me.'"

Ad Dahabi says that he preached to the people on the festival of Adhha and said, "God is great while the stars move in their orbits and the light breaks in the East, and the sun rises and the heavens cover the earth. God is great, while the clouds shed rain, and the mirage gleams, and what is sought is successfully accomplished, and the returning wanderer is glad as he returns-" and he spoke a long discourse and then sat down. Again he rose and preached and said-O God, be beneficent to me in my posterity and aid me in what Thou hast given me to rule and inspire me with thanks for Thy benefits and give me Thy grace and help me." When he had pronounced this and was about to descend, Abul Mudhaffar the Hashimite advanced to him and recited as follows :

"The peace of God be upon thee thou best of those who have ascended

The pulpit and whose standards victory attends !

And most excellent of those who, bearing rule, A.H.529 A.D.1134.

Art an Imam to thy people and benefitest them universally by thy virtuous conduct !

Best of men in the world in the east and west.

And he whose ancestor was he for whom the rain came upon earth ![1]

Verily, thy discourse and true eloquence which would soften a stone

Hath bedecked our ears with ear-rings.

Thou hast filled all heart with dread,

And verily the whole city with trembled with the fear of its threatening

Thou hast added by it to the glory and nobility of the descendants of Adnan,[2]

And by it amongst men is renown for the won.

Thou art the chief of the Abbas

In whom the lowly and the wise glory.

Unto God we owe the age in which thou art our Imam,

And unto Him the faith of which thou art to us the chief.

Mayst thou continue reigning through time

While age succeeds to age possessing thee !

Mayest thou be present at this happy festival with our good wishes

And thy prayers and sacrifies exalt us in honor."

His Wazir Jalaluddin al Hasan b. Ali b. Sadakah thus praises him-

"I have found men as water in sweetness and delicacy,

But the prince of the Faithful is its perfect purity.

I figured to myself the personification of Wisdom,

---

1 The Muhammadans ascribe the creation of the earth and all its blessings, to their Prophet's advent and that they were for his sake alone, brought into existence.

2 The Kuraysh.

A.H.529 A.D.1134.

And verily the prince of the Faithful is its likeness.
And were it not for religion and the divine law and a sense of piety
I would say in reference to him, may his glory be exalted."[1]

In the twenty-fourth year of his reign, a cloud ascended and rained down fire upon the city of Mosal, through which many houses and places in the city were burnt. In the same year the sovereign of Egypt al Amir bi Ahkamillah Mansur was slain and left no issue. His nephew al Hafidh, Abdul Majid b. Muhammad bil Muntasir succeeded him. During the same also, flying scorpions with two stings made their appearance in Baghdad, and men were in fear of them for verily they killed a number of children.

Of persons of distinction who died during his reign were Shamsul Aimmat Abul Fadhl the Hanafite Imam, Abur Raffa b. Ukayl al Hanbali, the chief Kadhi Abul Hasan al Damaghani, Ibn Bulaymah[2] the Qurãn reader, at Tughrai author of the Lamyatul Ajam,[3] Abu Ali as Sadafi the Hafidh, Abu Nasr al Kushayri, Ibnul Kattaa the philologer, Muhius Sunnat al Baghawi (*al Farra*). Ibnul Fiham the Qurãn reader, al Hariri author of the Makamat, al Maidani author of the Amthal (*Proverbs*),[4] Abul Walid b. Rushd al Maliki, the Imam Abu Bakr of Tortosa, Abul Hajjaj of Saragossa. Ibnus Sayyid of Badajos *the grammarian and philologist,* Abu Ali al Fariki of the Shafiites, Ibnul Tarawah the grammarian, Ibnul Badish *the grammarian,* Dhafir al Haddad the poet, Abdul Ghafir al Farisi and others.

---

1 An expression applied to God alone.

2 I can find no trace of such a name in any work I has have consulted and do not know its true pronunciation.

3 This has been repeatedly published in Europe and been edited by Pocock. This poet was Wazir to the Sultan Masaud and was put to death by Mahmud's Wazir (after the former Sultan had been defeated near Hamadan by his brother Mahmud) on the suspicion or accusation of being an atheist (*A.H.* 513, or 14). Tughrai signifies a tughra writer, the tughra being a flourish at the beginning of official papers over the word Bismillah and containing the titles of the prince. See Ibn Khall.

4 A Latin translation of which has been published by Professor Freytag of Bonn.

AR RASHID BI'LLAH

A.H.529
A.D.1134.

Ar Rashid Billah (*Directed aright by God*) Abu Jaafar Mansur son of al Mustarshid was born in the year 502. His mother was a slave concubine. It was said that there was an obstruction at his birth. The physicians were consulted and they recommended the enlargement of the passage with a golden instrument which was done and proved beneficial. His father introduced his name in the Khutbah as his heir in the year 513, and he was acknowledged Caliph on the assassination of his father in Dul Kaadah 529. He was eloquent, verse in literature and a poet ; brave, beneficent, generous, of a virtuous disposition, choosing justice and hating iniquity. When Sultan Masaud returned to Baghdad the Caliph departed for Mosal. The Kadhis, the principal men and the learned were then summoned *by Masaud* and they drew up an indictment containing the evidence of certain people one the tryranny of ar Rashid, his confiscating of property, shedding of blood and wine drinking and the jurists were asked whether the doer of these things was deserving of the supreme administration and whether, should his guilt be established, it were lawful for the Sultan for the time being, to depose him and substitute for him one more worthy. They gave sentence on the lawfulness of his deposition, and the Kadhi of the city, Ibnul Karkhi pronounced his deposal. And they swore allegiance to his uncle Muhammad the son of al Mustadhir who was surnamed al Muktafi liamrillah (*Following the commands of God). This occurred on the 16th*[1] Dul Kaadh 530 (16th *August* 1135). When the news of his deposition reched ar Rashid, he set out from Mosal for the provinces of Adarbijan with his adherents, and they levied a sum of money from Maraghah and acted there with great injustice and passed to Hamadan where they committed violence and slew a number of people and crucified others and shaved off the beards of some of the learned.

Subsequently they advanced on Ispahan and laid siege to it and

1 18th Ibn Ath.

A.H.530 A.D.1135. ravaged the villages. Ar Rashid fell ill of a grievous sickness[1] outside Ispahan and some Persians who were in his service as chamber attendants, went in to him and slew him with knives, but were afterwards themselves all put to death. This took place on the 16th[2] of Ramadhan 532. Al Imad[3] Katib says that ar Rashid possessed the beauty of Joseph and the Liberality of Hatim.

Ibnul Jauzi observes-"according to as Suli the general opinion is that every sixth Caliph was deposed. I have looked into this statement and observed it with wonder." I remark that I have continued the rest of his observations in the introduction. (page 18.)

The mantle and sceptre were not taken from ar Rashid till be was assassinated when they were brought after his death to al Muktafi.

AL MUKTAFI LI AMRILLAH

Al Muktafi li amrillah Abu Abdullah, Muhammad the son of al Mustadhir billah was born on the 22nd Rabii 489. His mother was a

1 Neither Ibn Khaldun nor Abul Fida mention his illness. This vague account of ar Rashid's movements after leaving Mosal may be supplemented by Weil's (pp. 238 and 9, Vol. III), narrative taken from Ibn Ath. and Ibn Khaldun, and Reiske's Latin version of Abul Fida, Vol. III, p. 477.

2 Ibn Ath, and Abul Fida, have 25th Ibn Khaldun, 15th.

3 Abu Abdullah Muhammad Imamuddin (*Pillar of religion*) Katib al Ispahani (*the scribe of Ispahan*) was a Shafiite doctor and author of many poems and epistles. He was honoured with the friendship of Saladin and served him as Secretary of State till the monarch's death, (A.H. 589-1193) which reduced him to ruin and deprived him of all influence. He was born 519 (1125) and died at Damascus 597 (1201). A list of his works will be found in Ibn Khall- the principal being the Kharidat ul Kasr wa Jaridatul Asr (*virgin of the palace and volume of palm branch of the age*) containing an account of the poets between the years 500 and 572, in 10 vols. Of which De Slane speaks slightingly and apparently with much reason. He has also written a history of the Saljuk dynasty, the conquest of Jerusalem and a historical and authobiographical work entitled the "Syrian Lightning."

Nubian. He was acknowledged Caliph on the deposal of his nephew, at the age of forty. The reason of his being surnamed al Muktafi was that, six days before his elevation to the Caliphate, he dreamt that he saw the Apostle of God saying to him, "This authority shall come to thee, therefore follow the commandments of God."He therefore received the title of "the follower of the commandments of God." Sultan Masaud after he had dealt even-handed justice and set Baghdad in order, next took the whole of the cattle and furniture and gold, and curtain and pavilions that were in the palace of the Caliph and left in the stables of the Caliph but four horses and eight mules[1] for the conveyance of water *from the Tigris.* It was therefore said that al Muktafi was acknowledged Caliph on the condition of his possessing neither a horse nor traveling furniture. A.H.530 A.D.1135.

In the year 531 Sultan Masaud seized al the possession of the Caliph and left him nothing but his personal estate and he sent his Wazir to demand of the Caliph one hundred thousand dinars. Al Muktafi replied, "I have never know anything stranger than thy conduct. Thou knowest that al Mustarshid went to thee with all his wealth and what followed, followed, next ar Rashid ruled and acted as he acted and departed and took what remained,[2] and nothing was left but the furniture, the whole of which thou hast seized, and turned to thy use in the mint and thou hast possessed thyself of inheritances and the proceeds of the poll tax. For what reason then should I give thee this money ? Nothing remains but that I should quit the palace and deliver it up, for I have vowed to God that I would not take a grains's worth from the Muslims unjustly." The Sultan then abandoned his demands on the Caliph and turned to taxing the property of the people and he imposed fines on the merchants, and the people suffered severely through this.

---

1 The version of Ibn Ath. is very different. The Sultan sent to the Caliph informing him of the settlement of certain personal estates for his maintenance. He replied that he had eighty mules in his palace for the conveyance of water from the Tigris and that the Sultan should see to the necessities of the person who drank this water. It was therefore agreed that he should receive the same allowance as al Mustadhir.

2 Read. تَبَقَّي

A.H.532 A.D.1138. Subsequently in Jumada I the estates of the Caliph and his domains and inheritance were restored to his control. During this year the new moon was looked for on the night of the 30th Ramadhan, but it was not seen, and the people of Baghdad entered upon morning, fasting in completion of the term. On the following day they looked again for the new moon but did not see it though the sky was bright and clear, the like of which has not been heard of in history.

In the year 533 there was a great earthquake at Khubzah,[1] felt for a distance of ten parasangs and multitudes perished, after which Khubzah was swallowed up, and black water rose in the place where the town had stood. During the same the nobles took possession of the revenues of the provinces and Sultan Masaud was helpless, nothing being left him but the name power. The supremacy of Sultan Sinjar also declined for the Lord is the humbler of tyrants, but the Caliph al Muktafi became powerful : his influence increased and his authority grew great, and this was the beginning of the restoration of the Abbaside power, for which, praise be to God.

In the year 541 Sultan Masaud arrived at Baghdad and set up a mint, but the Caliph imprisoned the coiner who occasioned the establishment of the mint, whereupon Masaud arrested the chamberlain of the Caliph, who was greatly incensed and closed the principal mosque and the other mosques for three days. Upon this the chamberlain was released whereon the coiner was set free and the affair ended peaceably.

During the same Ibn ul Abbadi[2] held his discourses. On one occasion Masaud was present and the preacher addressed himself to the mention of the tax on sales, and what the people had undergone and he said, "O Lord of the world ! thou givest in one

---

1 This is a fort near Mecca according to Yakut, but Ibn Ath. and Abul Fida speak only of the effects of this earthquake in Syria and especially at Aleppo.

2 Ibn Ath. states that he was a preacher who came as an envoy from Sultan sinjar. So great was the influence of his discourses that not only the court, but the common people left their occupations and went eagerly to hear him.

night to a musician as much as this that thou takest from the Muslims, wherefore bestow on me that musician and give him to me and make of him a thank-offering to God for what He hath bestowed upon thee." And he consented and proclamation was made in the city of its remission, and placards were sent round, preceded by drums and trumpets, on which the remission of the tax was inscribed, and they were nailed up *on the doors of the mosques*[1] and there remained until an Nasirli dinillah commanded the placards to be pulled down, saying, "we have no need of Persian memorials."

A.H.533
A.D.1138-9.

In the year 543 the Franks[2] besieged Damascus, but Nuruddin Mahmud b. Zinki governor of Aleppo and his brother *Sayfuddin* Ghazi lord of Mosal advanced to its relief. The Muslims were victorious, praise be to God, and the Franks were routed. Nuruddin continued the war with the Franks and recovered what they had taken of the cities of the Muslims.

In the year 544 died the sovereign of Egypt al Hafidh li dinillah (*Protector of the religion of God*) and his son al Dhafir Ismail succeeded him. During the same a great earthquake occurred and Baghdad was convulsed about ten times, and a mountain in Hulwan was shattered by it. In the year 545 it rained blood in Yaman and the earth was sprinkled with blood and its traces were left upon the garments of the people.

In the year 547 Sultan Masaud died. Ibn Hubayrah who was the Wazir of al Muktafi relates that when the followers of Masaud behaved arrogantly towards al Muktafi and treated him with disrespect, and he was not powerful enough to proceed from undisguised enmity into open war, it was decided to pray for the

---

1 So Ibn Ath. who places this in the year 533, and does not state that it was in consequence of al Abbadi's intervention.

2 "Under the king of Germany"-writes Abul Fida. This was Conrad III. See Reiske's note to this passage. Conrad marched with St. Louis of France and Baldwin "sed re infecta domun redierunt, seditione inter obsidentes exorta." "The fruitless siege of Damascus," says Gibbon, "was the final effort of the second crusade." See his LIX Chapter.

A.H.547 A.D.1152. curse of God upon Masaud for a whole month as the Prophet called down curses during a month upon Ril and Dakwan.[1] Whereupon he and the Caliph secretly, each one in his place, began to pray at daybreak from the night of the 29th Jumada I and this continued every night. And whon the month was completed Masaud died upon his throne,[2] not a day beyond the month and not a day under it. The army agreed upon the elevation to the Sultanate of Malak Shah,[3] and Khasbek[4] undertook the administration in his name, but he afterwards arrested Malak Shah and sent for his brother Muhammad from Khuzistan who arrived and the Sultanate was resigned to him. At this juncture the Caliph assumed the supreme administration and his commands were universally obeyed, and he removed the professors whom the Sultan had appointed to the Nidhamiyah College. It was reported to him, also that the district of Wasit was in a state of anarchy whereupon he marched at the head of his army and set the provinces in order and entered Hillah and Kufah and returned to Baghdad confirmed in power and victorious and the city was decorated *for his entry.* In the year 548 the Ghuzz[5] rose up against Sultan Sinjar and took him prisoner

---

1 Ril and Dakwan were two tribes descended from Sulaym, who put to death seventy of the Auxiliaries whom Muhammad had sent at their request to aid them against one of the hostile tribes. These 70 were termed Kurra and were apparently in the service of Muhammad as catechists and expounders of the Qurãn : when they reached Bir Maunah, they were met by the Banu Ril and Dakwan and treacherously slain. Two other tribes, that of Usayyah and Lahyan were associated in this murderous deed and in the curse of Muhammad. The Story and ascriptions will be found in the Sahih of Bukhari, pp. 585-6.

2 The more prosaic narrative of Ibn Ath. makes him die of a fever which carried him off in a week. Ibn Khall, states the cause of his death to have been an attack of vomiting and a flow of liquied from the mouth, apparently caused by the intemperate, life he led. In I.K.'s life of Ibn Hubayrah there is no mention of this circumstance.

3 Nephew of Masaud.

4 Of Turkoman origin who as a boy entered the service of Masaud and rose to pre-eminence over the Emirs. He was afterwards put to death by Muhammad for conspiring to obtain the Sultanate for himself. Abul Fida. Ibn Ath.

5 A Turkoman horde consisting of about 40,000 families, on the banks of the Oxus between Balkh and Bukhara. Weil ; see also Abul Fida.

and treated him with – contumely and overran his dominions, but left the khutbah in his name. He remained in their power a shadow without reality and he wept for himself over his nominal authority and his stipend was as much as that of one of his own grooms. A.H.547 A.D.1152.

In the year 549 the sovereign of Egypt ad Dhafir billah al Ubaydi was slain at Cairo and was succeeded by his son al Faiz Isa a little child, and the affairs of the Egyptians fell into a ruinous state. Upon this al Muktafi wrote a diploma of investiture for Nuruddin b. Zinki[1] and entrusted to him the government of Egypt, and ordered him to march thither. He was at the time engaged in hostilities with the Franks, pushing on vigorously the holy war, for he had captured Damascus in the month of Safar of this year, and had taken possession of a number of forts and strongholds of the Byzantines by the sword and by treaty. His dominions increased and his fame spread, and al Muktafi sent him the investiture of authority and commanded him to proceed to Egypt and gave him the title of al Malik al Aadil (*the Just King*). The power of al Muktafi now reached its zenith : his authority was established, he was victorious over his foes and he determined to march for the provinces in rebellion against his government, and his affairs continued in prosperity and success till he died on Saturday night, the 2nd Rabii, I 555 (12th *March* 1160).

Ad Dahabi days that al Muktafi was one of the most eminent of the Caliphs, learned, well-read, brave, forbearing, of easy disposition, supreme in the qualities of a prince, worthy of the Imamate, matchless among Imams, no order however insignificant, being issued in his administration except under his transcript. He wrote out during his Caliphate three-fourths of the Qurãn. He heard tranditions from his master Abul Barakah b. Abil Faraj bus Sunni.[2]

---

1 His character and conquests are sketched by Gibbon in his 59th chapter.

2 This is apparently the same person as Abul Barakah b-ul Anbari whose life is given by Ibn Khall. The dates and circumstances of both, accord, the surname is somewhat different, Ibn Khall writing Abul Wafa for Abul Faraj. He was a philologist and grammarian of repute and studied at the Nidhamiyah the Shafiite jurisprudence. He was born in 513 (119) and died at Baghdad in 577 (1181).

A.H.549 A.D.1154. Ibnus Samaani states that, with his brother al Mustarshid, he heard traditions from Jaz b. Arafah on the authority of Kasim b. Bayyan. Traditions are related on his authority by Abu Mansur al Jawaliki[1] the philologer his Imam, Ibn Hubayrah his Wazir and others.

Al Muktafi gave a new gate to the Kaabah and made a coffin of cornelian for his own burial.

He had a praiseworthy disposition, his reign was deserving of commendation, *as he* occupied himself with religion, learning, virtue, good counsel, and administration of the State. He restored the *defaced* memorials of the Imamate and re-established the *ancient* customs of the Caliphate and applied himself personally to public affairs and more than once headed military expeditions, and his reign was long protracted.

Abu Talib Abdur Rahman b. Muhammad b. Abdi's Samii al Hashimi in his work on the excellencies of the Abbasides, says that the reign of al Muktafi was distinguished for justice and notable for good works. Before his accession to the Caliphate, he was of pious conduct. In the beginning of his reign he applied himself to religious exercises and the transcription of scientific works, and reading the Qurãn. And there was never seen since al Muatasim, a Caliph who combined such beneficence, gentleness of manner and kindness of heart as his, with his intrepidity, firmness and bravery, together with the sobriety, piety and devotion that particularly characterized him. His armies were likewise victorious wherever they advanced. Ibnul Jauzi observes that from the days of al Muktafi, Baghdad and Iraq returned under the power of the Caliphs and no contending rival was left to dispute them, while before that period from the reign of al Muktadir to his time the supreme authority was in the hands of royal tyrants under whom nothing but the nominal direction of the Caliphate remained to the Caliphs.

---

1 Born 466 (1073) died 525 (1134). Jawaliki signifies a maker and seller of mats. Relative adjectives of this form are rare being derived from the plural of the noun and not from the singular. The life of this great scholar may be consulted in Ibn Khall.

Among the Sultans of his time were Sultan Sinjar lord of Khurasan, and Sultan Nuruddin Mahmud sovereign of Syria. A.H.555 A.D.1160.

He was liberal, munificent, a lover of tranditions and of the hearing of them, diligent *in the acquisition of* knowledge and revering its professors.

Ibnus Samaani relates a tradition through al Muktafi with ascription to the Apostle of God that he said, -"the nobles will increased but in violence and the people in covetousness, and the day of resurrection will come *finding* only the wicked among mankind, *left.*"

When al Muktafi sent for the Imam Abu Mansur al Jawalil, the grammarian, in order to make him his chaplain to read the prayers before him, *the latter* said nothing more to him on entering than-" To the prince of the Faithful greeting and the mercy of God." Ibnut Talmid[1] a Christain physician was standing by, and said, "This is not the way of saluting the prince of the Faithful, Shaykh !" Ibnul Jawaliki paid no attention to him, but said, "Prince of the Faithful, my salutation is, that enjoined by prophetical tradition," and he repeated the tradition and added, "Prince of the Faithful ! if any one were to swear that no kind of knowledge can enter into the heart of a Christain or a Jew in a proper manner, he would not be obliged to make expiation for perjury, for God hath put a seal upon

---

1 His name was Hibat ullah b. Abi Ghanaim, and he was reputed the first physician of the age. The Katib Imaduddin calls him the Galen and Hippocrates of his day, which in Oriental imagery may not mean much, but what is more to the purpose, the sweetness of his disposition, his judgment, his elevated sentiment, his powerful intellect, his modesty of deportment and his charity are praised by his enemies who wonder that with his extraordinary intelligence, he should allow himself to be deprived of the blessings of Islamism. This is disinterested and sincere eulogy. He died at Baghdad in 560, (1164-5) at the age of nearly 100 and Ibn Khall relates that all the inhatbitants of Baghdad, whether dwelling on one side of the river or the other attended his funeral to *the church* which sufficiently disposes of Abdul Latif's statement (*autobiography, see De Slan's extract*) that he died a Muslim.

A.H.555 A.D.1160. their hearts[1] and the seal of God is not broken but by faith." Al Muktafi answered, "thou hast spoken truly and done well." Ibnul Talmid with all his extensive erudition *remained silent* as if bridled with a stone.

Of distinguished persons who died during the reign of al Muktafi were Ibnul Islam Abrash the grammarian, Yunus b. Mughith, Jamal ul Islam b-ul Muslim as Shafii, Abul Kasim al Ispahani, author of the Targhib (*Instigation*). Ibn Barrajanm al Mazari al Maliki author of the Mulim *bi fawaid kitab Muslim (indicator of the instructive passges in the book of Muslim*), as Zamakshari, ar Rushati author of the Ansab (*Genealogies*), al Jawaliki the Caliph's Imam, Ibn Atiyah author of the Commentary, Abus Saadat bus Shajari, the Imam Abu Bakr b-ul Arabi, Nasihuddin al Arrajani the poet, the Kadhi, Iyadh, the Hafidh Abul Walid b-ul Dabbagh, Abul Asaad Hibbat ur Rahman al Kushayri, Ibn Alam al Furs the Qurãn reader, ar Raffa the poet, as Shahrastani author of the Milal wan Nihal (*Sects and Rligions*), al Kaysarani the poet Muhammad b. Yahya the disciple of la Ghazzali, Abul Fadhl b. Nasir the Hafidh, Abul Karam as Shahrozuri the Qurãn reader, al Wawa the poet,[2] Ibnul Khall the Shafiite Imam and others.

AL MUSTANJID BI'LLAH

Al Mustanjid billah (*Seeking assistance in God*) Abul Mudhaffar the son of al Muktafi was born in 518. His mother was a Georgian slave concubine called Taus (*Peacock*). His father caused his name to be read in the khutbah as his heir in the year 547 and he was acknowledged Caliph on the day of his fathers death. He was distinguished for justice ad clememy. He remitted the taxes to a large extent, so that he left Iraq without any taxation.

---

1 ختم الله على قلوبهم (Qur. II).

2 Of Aleppo-another of the name, called ad Dimishki (*of Damascus*) died in the reign of Kadir billah.

He was severe upon all promoters of disorder. He imprisoned for a A.H.555 A.D.1160.
long time a man who used to bring calumines against people *before the Magistrate.* A person presented himself before the Caliph and offered him ten thousand dinars for his release : he replied, "I will give thee ten thousand dinars wouldst thou but show me another like him that I may imprision him and avert his mischief from the people."

Ibnul Jauzi says that al Mustanjid was distinguished for his penetrating intellect, sound judgment, powerful understanding and eminent merit. He wrote excellent verse and eloquent prose, and was skilful in the use of astronomical instruments such as the astrolabe and the like. Of his verses are the following :

"She reproached me for my greyness which is venerable,
Would she had reproached me with what is dishonour.
If my forelocks are becoming white *what then ?*
For the moons are the glory of the night."

And on a miser-

"A miser lit in his house
A candle as a respect towards us on his part.
Not a tear fell from its eyes
But a tear fell also from his."

And on Ibn Hubayrah his Wazir, whose administration of the affairs of the Muslims he had witnessed with admiration.

"Two merits are transparently clear that characterize and abound in thee,
By mention of which thou shalt be remembered to the day of resurrection,
Thy presence while the world is needing thy help,
And thy bounty, while beneficence is repudiated by men.

A.H.562 A.D.1166-7. Abu Yahya,[1] if Jaafar sought thy place

And Yahya, both Jaafar and Yahya would refrain from taking it.

Nor have I seen any one purposing to do thee harm, O Abu Mudhaffar

But thou dost overcome him."

He died on the 8th[2] of Rabii II 566 (22nd *December* 1170) and it was during the first year of his Caliphate that al Faiz sovereign of Egypt died and was succeeded by al Aadhiduddinillah (*Aider of the religion of God*) the last of the Ubaydite Caliphs.

In the year 562 Nuruddin dispatched the Emir Asaduddin Shirkuh at the head of two thousand horse to Egypt. He encamped at al Jazirah[3] and besieged Cairo for about two months. Its governor (*Shawar*) applied to the Franks for assistance who marched from Damietta to his aid whereon Asaduddin retired to Upper Egypt. Afterwards a battle took place (*at Babayn*) between him and the Egyptians (*and Franks*) where he gained the victory despite the fewness[4] of his troops and the numerical superiority of the enemy and thousands of the Fransk were slain. Asaduddin then collected the tribute of Upper Egypt while the Franks marched against Alexandria which had been taken by Salahuddin (*Saladin*) Yusuf b. Ayub nephew of Asaduddin, and besieged it for four months.

---

1 Abu Yahya and Abu Mudhaffar are both surnames of Ibn Hubayrah. Yayha and Jaafar are the two Barmecides, father and son, famed for their generosity and misfortunes in the time of Harun ar Rashid.

2 All the other authorities agree in the date being the 9th.

3 A quarter of Fustat, so called because when the Nile is full, it is surrounded by ; water and cut off from the rest of the town.

4 "Jacobus a Vitriaco gives the king of Jerusalem no more than 374 knights. Both the Franks and Moslems report superior numbers of the enemy, a difference which may be solved by counting or omitting the unwarlike Egyptians." *Decline and Fall,* LIX. Gibbon praises the masterly evolutions of Shirkuh throughout the campaign.

Asaduddin set out against them whereon they raised the siege[1] and he returned to Syria. A.H.562 A.D.1166-7.

In the year 564 the Franks marched into Egypt with a large army, captured Bilbays and laid siege to Cairo, but its governor set fire to it in fear of them and wrote to Nuruddin to solicite his aid, whereon Asaduddin arrived with his troops and the Franks abandoned Cairo on hearing of his approach,[2] and Asaduddin entered it. Al Aadhid sovereign of Egypt appointed him to the office of Wazir and bestowed upon him a robe of honor. Asaduddin did not long survive, dying after sixty-five days. Aadhid appointed his nephew Salahuddin in his place and entrusted him with administration of affairs and gave him the title of al Malik an Nasir and Salahuddin conducted his government in the ablest manner.

Among person accounts of al Mustanjid, ad Dahabi relates that from the time he fell ill,[3] in intense redness continued to appear in the sky and its reflection was observed upon the walls.

Of persons of note who died during his reign were ad Daylami author of the Musnadul Firdaus, al Imrani of the Shafiite school author of the Bayan ("*Elucidation of the secondary points of law*," in *ten volume*), Ibnul Bazri the Shafiite doctor of the people of al Jazirat *b. Omar,*[4] the Wazir b. Hubayrah, the Shaykh Abdulkadir al Jili, the Imam Abu Sai'd as Samaani, Abun Najib as Suhrawardi, Abul Hasan b. Hudayl the Qurãn reader and others.

---

1 A peace was concluded on the terms of a payment of money to be made to Shirkuh for the cost of the war, and that he in turn should surrender Alexandria to the Egyptians and evacuate Egypt with the Franks.

2 This expedition was led by Amaury king of Jerusalem in violation of the treaty above mentioned. "Amaury, says," Gibbon, retired with the shame and reproach that always adhere to unsuccessful injustice."

3 His perfect of the palace Adhududdin and the Emir Kaymaz concerted his death with his physician. He was ordered a hot bath and being carried into the room the doors were locked on him till he died.

4 A town three day's journey above Mosal.

A.H.566
A.D.1170.

AL MUSTADHI BI'AMRILLAH

Al Mustadhi biamrillah (*Seeking light from the command of God*) al Hasan Abu Muhammad son of al Mustanjid billah was born in the year 536. His mother was an Armenian slave concubine named Ghandhadha (*Dilicate*). He was acknowledged Caliph on the death of his father.

Ibnul Jauzi says that be issued a proclamation remitting the taxation and removing tyrannical exactions, and he displayed a justice and generosity, the like of which we never before witnessed in our lives. He distributed large sums of money among the Hashimites and the descendants of Ali and the learned, and upon colleges and on Ribats.[1] He was ever prodigal of wealth, holding it in no esteem ; forbearing, sedate and compassionate. When he assumed the Caliphate, he bestowed robes of honour upon the officals of state and others and the Master Tailor of the Stores relates that he distributed 1300 tunics of silk. His name was read in the khutbah, in the pulpits of Baghdad and the usual largesses were bestowed. He named Ruhbul Hadithi to the office of Kadhi and bestowed commands upon seventeen Mamluks.

The following is by Hays Bays[2] on him-

"O Imam of good guidance, thou art raised upon the summit of munificence

---

1 The Ribats says De Slane-(*Life of Nasr-us-ddaulat*) were fortified barracks along the frontiers. At an early period there were not less than 10,000 in Transoxiana alone. Travellers on arriving at a Ribat found every accommodation gratis. These establishments were supported by the government and their revenues were increased by private gifts. Military service in a Ribat was considered as an act of religion. For further particulars, reference is made to Ibn Haukal (extracts) in the Goegraphy of Abul Fida, pp. 235-487, of the Arabic Text.

2 Abul Fawaris Saada a celebrated poet and member of the tribe of Tamim. He Was a Shafiite doctor, but his profession of jurisprudence was mastered by his passion for litereature and poetry, and he was eminent for his knowledge of the various dialects of the desert Arabs. Seeing some people in a commotion, he asked what had caused the disturbance (*hays bays*) and he thus received the nickname. He died A.H. 574 (1179). Ibn Khall.

With wealth and silver and gold. A.H.566 A.D.1170.
Thou grantest lives and security of person and dost lavish provinces
Within the space of an hour of a day.
For what then shall praise be given thee, who verily
Hath exceeded the beneficence of seas and showers ;
Verily thou art a standing miracle,
Confounding intellects and imaginations.
The noble nature has been fashioned of power and liberality,
Of water and of fire !"

Ibnul Jauzi says, "al Mustadhi kept retired from the people at large and never rode save accompanied by his suite and none but Kaymaz[1] entered his presence. During his Caliphate the dynasty of the House of Ubayd passed away, and his name was read in the khutbah in Egypt and engraved on the coinage. On the arrival of the messenger of these good tidings, the markets were closed in Baghdad and triumphal cupolas were erected. I composed at the same time a work which I entitled the conquest of Egypt." These are the words of al Jauzi. Ad Dahabi states that during his reign, heresy declined in Baghdad and was subverted and the people lived in security, and great prosperity was enjoyed during his Caliphate. The khutbah was read for him in Yaman and Barkah and Tuzar[2] and Cairo as far Uswan (*Syene*) and kings submitted to him, and that in the year 567. The katib al Imad says that in 567 the Sultan Salahuddin b. Ayub demanded the full submission *of the*

---

1 The Emir Kutbuddin Kaymaz who shared with Adhududdin in the murder of al Mustanjid. Ibnul Athir says that they raised al Mustadhi to the Caliphate on the condition of his appointing Adhududdin his Wazir and Kaymaz the general of his troops. His tryrannies and exactions caused a revolt of the people instigated by the Caliph and he fled from the city while the populace plundered his palace. He died before reaching Mosal from the hardship he had to undergo in his flight. A.H. 570. Ibn Ath.

2 Tuzar is about ten parasangs from Neftah on the Shatt Kabir. North-western Africa.

A.H.567 *people* in the great mosque of old Cairo and that was by the
A.D.1171-2. establishment of the khutbah on the first Friday *of the month of Muharram*[1] for the House of Abbas. Thus heresy was destroyed and orthodoxy flourished and the khutbah was read for the House of Abbas on the second Friday in Cairo. This was followed by the death of al Aadhid on the 10th of Muharram. Salahudddin took possession of the palace with all the treasures[2] and valuables it contained, *which were so vast* that the sale of them over and above what Salahuddin had taken for himself, continued during ten years. Sultan Nuruddin dispatched Shihabuddin al Mudhahhar, son of the most learned Sharafuddin[3] b. Abi Usrun to Baghdad with the good news and ordered me to draw up a public announcement of it to be read in all the provinces of Islam. I accordingly indited a joyful proclamation beginning thus : "Praise be to God, the Exalter of Truth and its Revealer-the Destroyer of Falsehood and its Disabler." It contained also the following, "and there is not left in those provinces a pulpit but the Khutbah is appointed *to be read* therein for our lord the Imam al Mustadhi biamrillah, prince of the Faithful, and the mosques for the Friday prayers have been re-established and the temples of heresy destroyed"- and so the Katib goes on till he says : "Long have the past generations gone over them, and they have remained two hundred and eight years[4] harassed by the pretentious claim of vain dissemblers, filled with a crowd of devils; but the Lord gave us possession of those countries and established

---

1 Ibn Ath.

2 Among these, one curiosity, a drum, will provoke the incredulity or the envy of physicians. Its wonderful virtues are described in Reiske's Latin version of Abulfida.

3 He was a learned Shafiite doctor who taught publicly at Aleppo and Mosal. He was much esteemed by Nuruddin Mamud b. Zinki by whom he was appointed professor of several colleges and finally Kadhi of Damascus. Born at Mosal 492 (1099), died at Damascus 585 (1189). Ibn Khall.

4 The duration of the Ubaydite dynasty according to Ibn Ath. from the time of al Mahdi's first appearance at Sijilmasah in A.H. 296 (908-9) to the death of al Aadhid was about 272 years and a month. The text of the Kamil is here in error. The Upsala edition gives 299, for A.H. 296. Abulf has rightly 296. Of this period. 208 years represent the term of their rule in Egypt.

our authority in the land and placed in our power as we had hoped for, the extirpation of impiety and heresy and directed us unto one whom we have constituted our delegate in establishing the Abbaside authority in that place and bringing to destruction therein pretenders and heresiarchs." A.H.567 A.D.1171-2

There is a poem by al Imad on this in which are the following verses-

"Verily we have read the khutbah in Cairo for al Mustadhi,

The Vicegerent of the Chosen One, the Imam of the age

And by his victory we have brought down the arm of the Aider (*al Aadhid*)

And yet the Impotent who dwelt in the palace,.

And we have left the pretender seeking his own destruction

In ignominy under the grave stone and its confining.

In answer to the joyful tidings the Caliph sent robes of honor and presents to Nuruddin and Salahuddin, and standards and banners to the preachers of Cairo. He bestowed upon the Katib al Imad a robe of honor and a hundred dinars, upon which he wrote another poem in which was the following :

They have given victory in Egypt unto the summoner of the guides unto truth.

And taken revenge on the suspected son of the Jew.[1]

Ibnul Athir narrates that the occasion of the establishment of the khutbah for the Abbasides in Cairo was this, that when Salahuddin was firmly settled in power and the authority of al Aadhid had declined, Nuruddin wrote to him commanding him to establish it, but he excused himself for fear of an insurrection of the Egyptians, but Nuruddin would not listen to his words and sent to him insisting upon it. And it came to pass that al Aadhid fell sick whereon Salahuddin took counsel of the nobles, some of whom approved

1 Ubaydullah, see page 3.

A.H.567 while others among them were afraid. But it happened that a Persian
A.D.1171-2. known as al Amir al Aalim had just then arrived in Cairo and when he perceived their hesitation, he declared that he would be the first to begin it. When therefore the first Friday of Muharram came round, he mounted the pulpit before the preacher and offered up a prayer for al Mustadhi and no one showed any disapprobation. Wherefore when it was the second Friday, Salahuddin commanded the preachers to discontinue the khutbah for al Aadhid, and this was done without any opposition.[1] This occurred while al Aadhid was dangerously ill. He died on the 10th of Muharram.

In the year 569, Nuruddin sent presents and gifts to the Caliph, among them a striped wild ass, very savage and streaked as with rays and the people went forth to see the sight. And among them was a resident of the Attabi quarter of Baghdad of much pretension but thick-witted and without merit and some one called out, "If indeed we have been sent a wild ass streaked with rays (*attabi*), we possess an ass of the Attabi quarter."

In the same year hail stones fell in Iraq as big as oranges and destroyed houses and killed a great number of cattle, and the Tigris rose so high that Baghdad was flooded and the Friday prayers were held outside the walls. The Euphrates rose in the same way and villages and fields were laid waste and the people turned in supplication to the Lord. And it was extraordinary, that while this was the state of the flood, the fields adjacent to the Dujayl (*a branch of the Tigris*) were ruined by drought.

In this year died Sultan Nuruddin sovereign of Damascus, and his son al Malik as Salib Ismail being but al child, the Franks took to ravaging the coasts but they were conciliated by sums of money and a peace was concluded with them. During this year a faction among the Ubaydites and their partisans sought to establish and restore the pretensions of the family of al Aadhid, and some of Salahuddin's nobles approved their design, but Salahuddin being

1 Liberally-"and two goats did not fight for it with their horns."

informed of this, crucified them between the two palaces (*al Kasrayn*). A.H.527 A.D.1176.

In the year 572, Salahuddin ordered the building of the great wall surrounding the old town of Misr and Cairo and deputed the Emir Bahauddin Karakush to superintend its erection. Ibnul Athir says that its circumference was 29,300 Hashimi cubits. During the same he gave orders for the erection of the fort on the hill Mukattam,[1] the same that became afterwards the royal palace, but it was not finished until the reign of al Malik al Kamil nephew of Salahuddin, who was the first that resided in it. In the same year also, he built the mausoleum[2] of the Imam as Shafii.

In the year 574, a mighty wind swept over Baghdad at midnight and columns as of fire appeared in all quarters of the heavens, and the people prayed to God in exceeding supplication. In the year 575 died the Caliph al Mustadhi at the end of Shawwal having covenanted for the succession of his son Ahmad.[3]

Of distinguished persons who died during the reign of al Mustadhi were Ibnul Khashshab the grammarian, Abu Nizar al Hasan b. Safi the prince of grammarians (*Malikun Nuhat*), the Hafidh Abul Ala al Hamadani, Nasihuddin bud Dahhan the grammarian, the great Hafidh Abul Kasim b. Asakir of the Shafii school, al Hays Bays the poet, the Hafidh Abu Bakr b. Khayr and others.

AN NASIR LI DIN ILLAH

An Nasir li dinillah (*Defender of the religion of God*) Ahmad Abu Abbas the son of Mustadhi was born on Monday the 10th

1 This citadel was also enclosed within the rampart. Ibn Ath. Abulf.

2 This fact is not in accordance with Ibn Ath. and Abulf who state that he built a college for the Shafiite doctors *over* the burial place of the Shafiite Imam, at Karafah – the Pere la Chaise of Cairo.

3 The other authorities-Ibn Ath. Abulf, Ibn Khaldun, place his death in Dul Kaadah-the two former naming the 2nd day of the month (31st *March* 1180).

A.H.575 Rajab 553 His mother being a Turkish woman named Zumurrad
A.D.1180. (*Emerald*). He was acknowledged Caliph on the death of his father in the beginning of Dul Kaadah 575. A number of Traditionists among whom were Abul Husayn Abdul Hakk al Yusufi, Abul Hasan Ali Asakir al Bataihi and Shuhdah,[1] licensed him to declare traditions, and he granted licenses to others who used to relate traditions on his authority during his lifetime vying with each other therein, desiring vain-glory more than *correctness of* ascriptions.

Ad Dahabi says that on one ruled the Caliphate for a longer period than he, for he governed it forty-seven years, and the period of this life continued full of glory and splendour, *occupied* in the extirpation of enemies and the subjugation of princes. He found no oppression, nor did any rebel rise against him but he exterminated them, and no opponent but he overthrew him and whosoever thought to do him evil, the Lord confounded him with contumely. And with the prosperity of his undertakings, he was most vigilant in the good administration of his kingdom, nothing being concealed from him regarding his subjects, great or small. His spies kept him informed of both the public and private circumstances of monarchs, and he was a master of ingenious artifice and subtil cunning and device which none could fathom. He would bring about reconciliation between hostile princes without their perceiving *his intervention*, and sow discord between sovereigns in alliance, without their knowledge. When the envoy of the ruler of Mazandaran came to Baghdad, a letter reached him every morning *mentioning* what he had done the *preceding* night, and he used every effort at concealment, yet the latter regularly arrived. He made an assignation with a woman one night who introduced herself by a secret door. The letter reached him in the morning containing the

---

1 Shuhdah d of Abu Nasr Ahmad bil Faraj surnamed the "glory of women," and al Katibah (*the female scribe*). She ranked among the first scholars of the age and instructed a great number in traditions which she had received from the highest authorities. She died at Baghdad 574 (1178) and was interred outside the Abraz gate. He husband, whom she survived, was Abul Hasan Ali b. Muhammad b. Yahya ad Durayni, a man of rank and the favourite of the Caliph al Muktafi. Ibn Khall.

following. "Over ye was a coverlet upon which was a design of A.H.575
elephants." He was much astonished and quitted Baghdad not A.D.1180.
doubting but that the Caliph was acquainted with invisible things ; for the Imamiyah[1] believe that the Imam preserved inviolate from sin, knows what is in the pregnant womb and behind walls. And the ambassador of Khwarazm Shah once arrived with a secret message and a sealed letter, but he was told to return, as it was known what he had brought, and he returned, believing that they had a knowledge of the invisible. Ad Dahabi says that it was reported of an Nasir that he was ministered to by the genii. When (*Muhammad)* Khwarazm Shah had conquered Khurasan and Transxians and behaved with great arrogance and haughtiness, and had led great monarchs captive, and destroyed many peoples and abolished the khuthah for the House of Abbas throughout his dominions, and arrived at Hamadan on his march to Baghdad, a snow-storm continued to fall on them during twenty days, overtaking them out of its proper season. One of his confidants thereon suggested to him that this was *occasioned* by the anger of God for his march against the House of the Caliphs, and he heard *at the same time* that the Turkish tribes had gathered together against him and were eager to invade his dominions on account of his distance from them. This was the cause of his return and an Nasir was quit of his evil designs without a battle.[2]

An Nasir was one who when he furnished food, gave sufficient to satisfy, and when he struck, struck hard, and there were occasions when he gave as gives one who fears no poverty. And *once* there arrived a man with a parrot that could repeat, "Say God is one" (Qur. CXII), a present to the Caliph from India. In the morning it

---

1 "One of the exorbitant sects of the Sheeah who asserted that Ali was expressly appointed by Muhammad to be his successor." Lane, art ام I may add that they do not acknowledge the Imamate except in the posterity of Ali. For them a *visible* Imam no longer exists. See Sale's Prelim, Discourse.

2 This invasion of Muhammad Khwarazm Shah took place in 614 (1217). Weil states that an Nasir sent an embassy to Changiz Khan and sought his aid against Muhammad, p. 382, Vol. III. Ibn Athir alludes to the report and adds that any misdeed would pale beside the enormity of such a crime.

A.H.575 A.D.1180. was found dead and the man arose early in great consternation, when there arrived a footman (*from the Caliph*) asking for the parrot. The man wept and said that it had died in the night. The other replied, "verily we know that-bring the dead bird," and added, "How much didst thou think the Caliph would have given thee?" He answered, "Five hundred dinars." The other said, "Here are five hundred dinars ! Take them, for verily the Caliph hath sent them to thee, for he knew all about thee since thou didst set out from India."

When Sadr Jahan[1] set out for Baghdad with a number of jurisconsults, his people said to one of them, as he departed from his house in Samarkand mounted upon a fine mare, "if thou wouldst leave it with us, *it would be well* lest it be taken from thee at Baghdad." He replied "the Caliph himself could not take it from me." The Caliph, however, gave orders to a certain sharp fellow to set on him when he entered Baghdad and take it from him and escape in the crowd, which he did. The jurisonsult made a complaint but received no redress. When they returned from the pilgrimage, the Caliph bestowed a robe of honor upon Sadr Jahan and his suite and presented a robe of honor likewise upon the jurisconsult and his mare was presented to him bearing a golden saddle and a collar, and he was told that the Caliph had not taken his mare, but that a furnace-heater had done so, upon which he fell down in a swoon. The Caliph lavished munificent gifts[2] upon them.

Al Muwaffakuddin Abdul Latif[3] says that an Nasir filled all hearts with dread and terror ; and the people of India and Egypt feared him, as feared him the inhabitants of Baghdad. He gave new life to the majesty of the Caliphate which had perished at the death of al Muatasim and which expired again at his death. The very princes and nobles of Egypt and Syria, when the conversation

---

1 This title is usually given to the Kadhi al Kudhat or Chief Judge of any monarch. I cannot ascertain who is here referred to.

2 The Arabic must here he corrupt. The text is unintelligible. The MS. has مكراماتهم perhaps for بكراماتهم.

3 The author of the monograph on Egypt, translated by De Sacy.

turned on him in their private conferences, would lower their voices in fear and reverence. Once a merchant arrived in Baghdad with some gold-embroidered goods[1] from Damietta and he was questioned about them, but he denied having them. He was then given particulars about them, as tot heir number, colours and kinds, but he continued denying the more until he was told among other tokens *by which he was known,* was that he had revenged himself upon a Turkish slave of his and had taken him secretly to the sea coast at Damietta and had there slain and buried him. Of this no one had known. A.H.575 A.D.1180.

Ibnun Najjar[2] says that Sultans were abased before an Nasir, and those who had opposed him submitted to him. The proud and the rebellious were cast down before him, and tyrants were subdued by his sword ; his foes declined and his allies multiplied, and he overran many countries and conquered provinces as none of the Caliphs and sovereigns that preceded him had done, and his name was read in the khutbah in the provinces of Spain and in the cities of China. He was the sternest Caliph of the House of Abbas and the very mountains were rent in awe of him. He was of a good disposition, well-proportioned, endowed with mental and bodily excellence, fluent of speech and eloquent in expression. His rescripts were incisive and his words carried weight. His reign was a beauty spot in the face of the age and a pearl in the crown of glory. Ibn Wasil says that an Nasir was hardy, brave, of good judgment, and strong intellect, subtil and ingenious. He had spies in Iraq and the whole of the adjacent countires, who kept him informed of circumstances the most trifling, even to mentioning that a man in Baghdad had given a feast and had washed his hands before his

1 I read with the MS. مقانع The word قناع is in the singular and is therefore here inadmissible.

2 The Hafidh Abu Abdillah Muhammad surnamed Ibnun Najjar was born at Baghdad 578 A.H. (1183). He was a master of tradition and of the seven manners of reading the Qurãn. He spent 27 years in travelling, and noting down whatever information he could collect. He died in 643 (1245) at Baghdad. The best known of his works is the supplement in 16 Vols. To Abu Bakr al Baghdadi's History of Baghdad. De Slane, I.K.

A.H.575 A.D.1180. guests. This fact the spy reported to an Nasir who wrote in reply thereto, "bad manners in the host and officiousness in the news writer." He adds, "with all this, he was of vicious disposition towards his subjects, inclined to oppression and violence so that the people emigrated from their provinces and he seized their goods and property.

He would do things of a contradictory character. He was a Shiite, favouring the sect of the Imamites, opposing in this his ancestral *traditions,* so that one day Ibnul Jauzi was asked in his presence who was the best of men after the apostle of God. He replied, "the best of them after him was he whose daughter married the other (*or he who had married the daughter of the other*),[1] for he dared not distinctly mention Abu Bakr.

Ibnul Athir observes that an Nasir was of wicked disposition and that Iraq was ruined during his reign by the taxes he levied and his seizure of goods and property. He would do a things and then its contrary. He devoted himself to shooting with the cross-bow and in twirling pigeons.[2] Al Muwaffak Abdul Latif says that in the midst of his administrative duties he occupied himself with the relation of traditions, and he appointed licentiates with sanction to repeat them on his authority and to spread them abroad, settling allowances on them. He also indited permissive letters to princes and learned men *to the same effect,* and he made a compilation of seventy traditions, and on arriving at Aleppo caused it to be heard by the people. Ad Dahabi states that an Nasir licensed a number of the learned and they related traditions on his authority, among them being Ibn Sakkinah, Ibnul Akhdhar, Ibnul Damaghani and others.

---

1 The double meaning cannot be expressed in English by one phrase. This reply satisfied both parties, for as Ibn Khall says in his life of Ibnul Jauzi, the Sunnis maintained that he meant Abu Bakr whose daughter married Muhammad, while the Shiias insisted that 'Ali was intended because Fatima, Muhammad's daughter, was married to him.

2 Ibn Ath, does not mention the words- يعوى الحمام but speaks of his fondness for carrier pigeons المناسيب . The expression of Ibn Khaldun is اللعب بالحمام

Abul Mudhaffar grandson of Ibnul Jauzi and others relate that the eyesight of an Nasir began to grow weak towards the end of his life : others say that it went altogether, but none of his subjects were aware of this even to his Wazir and his own household, for he had a slave girl whom he had himself taught to write and she used to write a hand like his and indite the royal rescripts. Shamsuddin al Jauzi says that the water which an Nasir used to drink was brought on beasts of burden from a distance of seven parasangs above Baghdad. It was then boiled seven times, once each day, and afterwards kept in vessels for seven days more and then he would drink it : he died after having been given frequent soporifics to drink. He had been subjected to an operation and gravel was extracted from which he expired[1] on Sunday the last day of Ramadhan in the year 622 (*6th October* 1225). A.H.575 A.D.1180.

Among his pleasantries, *it is related* that a servant of his named Yumn (*Felicity*) wrote him a letter full of reproach whereon he penned the following –

"He who possesseth Yumn is fortunate,
He for whom a price has been paid, is of value,"[2]

When he assumed the Caliphate, he dispatched to Sultan Salahuddin a robe of honour and the investiture of his dignity and the Sultan wrote him a letter which ran as follows : Thy servant, praise be to God, reckoneth *for himself* priority of merit in Islam, for the House of Abbas was not so prospered by the early deeds of Abu Muslim, for he aided and then concealed, nor by the later services of Toghril Bek, for he defended but afterwards kept under restraint, whereas they servant hath made the death-rattle to be swallowed, the water of which the Lord hath stored up for inpouring within his sword. And he brought down the lying names *of pretenders to the Caliphate* riding aloft on the pulpits, and was

1 According to Ibn Ath, he died of dysentery.

2 I presume that I have misunderstood the sense, for I can make no pleasantly out of it.

A.H.575 A.D.1180. exalted by the assistance of Ibrahim and he demolished the concealed idols by his visible sword." Among events of his reign was a mandate which in 577 an Nasir[1] sent rebuking Sultan Salahuddin for adopting the title of al Malik an Nasir, knowing that the Caliph had chosen this name for himself.

In the year 580 the Caliph constituted the tomb of Musa al Kadhim[2] a sanctuary for those who took refuge therein, and many people fled to it and disturbances arose.

In the year 581 there was born at al Alth,[2] a child with a forehead a span and four fingers long and but one ear. During the same, news arrived that the khutbah was read for an Nasir in the chief towns of Mauritania. In the year 582 six of the planets were in conjunction in Libra and the astronomers announced a general devastation in all the provinces through a hurricane of wind. The people began to dig caves in the boundaries and to make them secure, closing their entrances against the wind ; and they carried thither water and provisions and took up their abode there in expectation of the night on which they had announced a hurricane *to take place,* like the hurricane *which destroyed the tribe* of Aad,[3] which was to be the night of the 9th Jumada II. Nothing, however, occurred therein, and not even a breeze blew, so that candles were lighted and the wind had not sufficient force to extinguish them. The poets commemorated this event. Among the verses written on it were the following by Abdul Ghanaim[4] Muhammad b-ul Muallim-

---

1 The text is in error. The words "al Malik" are not in the MS.

The son of Jaafar as Sadik and 5th in descent from Ali b. Abi Talib. Called al Kadhim or the Meek. He was one of the twelve Imams and famous for his holiness of life and his charity. He was born at Medina. A.H. 129 (746-7) and died at Baghdad in 183 or 186. His tomb is in the Shunizi cemetery on the west side of the river. Ibn Khall.

2 A village on the Tigris between Ukbara and Samarra.

3 See Sale's Prelim. Discourse, p. 5.

4 He was a native of Wasit and known generally by the appellation of Ibnul Muallim (*son of the preceptor*). He was born in 501 (1108) and died in 592 91196) at the village of Hurth ten parasangs from Wasit. (Cont...)

"Tell Abul Fadhl the words of one who confesseth : A.H.582
Jumada hath passed and Rajab hath come. A.D.1186.
Yet no hurricane hath happened as they announced,
Nor hath a comet appeared.
No, indeed-nor hath the sun been darkened, nor
Hath a cone appeared bearing on its point flaming fires.
One hath announced this who knoweth not
What will happen to himself, and this is strange.
Verily the falsehood of the astronomers hath become apparent,
And it every assertion, they make-how they lie !"

In the year 583, it came to pass that the first day of the year happened to be the first of the days of the week[1] and the first day of the solar year and the first according to the years of the Persians, and the sun and moon were in the first of the signs of the Zodiac (*Aries*)-and this was one of the most extraordinary coincidences.

During the same, many conquests were made. Sultan Salahuddin took many of the Syrian towns that had been in the hands of the Franks, the most important of which was Jerusalem, it having continued in the possession of the Franks ninety-one years. The Sultan effaced the memorials which the Franks had set up, and destroyed the churches they had introduced, and on the site of one of the churches he founded a college for the Shafiites-May the Lord reward him with blessings from Islam! But he did not destroy the church of the resurrection following the example of Omar who did not injure it when he took Jerusalem. Muhammad b. Asaad an Nassabah (*the genealogist*) says regarding this-

'Hast thou seen in a dream what I behold with my eyes
Jerusalem captured and the Franks routed.

(Cont. 618) His poetry is chiefly amatory and were considered so touching that they were sung by the Rifai dervishes at their concerts for the purpose of exciting the soul to mystic repture. Ibn Khall.

1 n Ath, says that it fell on a Saturday. He adds to the coincidences that the first day of the Christian year fell likewise at the same time.

A.H.583. A.D.1187.

And Kumamah swept of the *defilement*

By the removal of which it has been purified and by its own decline,

And their kings bound with thongs,[1]

And never before was one of their kings seen captive.

The aid of the Lord hath come and victory,

Which the apostle promised-therefore glorify God and ask for pardon.

O Joseph[2] *witness to the truth ! thou by conquering it*

Art its second Omar, the glory of the most pure Imam"

Among remarkable occurrences *is to be noted* that Ibn Barrajan[3] says in his Commentary on "Alif, Lam, Mim the Greeks have been overcome : (Qur. XXX) that Jerusalem will remain in the hands of the Greeks until the year 583 : they will then be overcome and it will be captured and become the house of Islam to the end of time" taken from a calculation of the verse-and so it came to pass.

Abu Shamah[4] observes that this prophecy of Ibn Barrajan is

---

1 Guy of Lusignan.

2 Saladin had the same names as the patriarch. Faruk (*the distinguisher between right and wrong*) was the surname of Omar.

3 The author of a commentary on the Qurãn which he explains after the mystic system of the Sufis. He died in the city of Morocco A.H. 531 (1141-2). Ibn Khall, (*art. Muhiuddin b-uz Zaki*) adds that from the time he met with the verse, and learnt Ibn Barrajan's account of it, he searched for the commentary and found the passage written marginally in a different hand from that of the text and is ignorant whether or no it be an interpolation. He also found a cabalistic calculation made from the words "a few years" in the verse of the Qurãn-which runs: "The Greeks have been overcome in the nearest part of the land, but after their defeat they shall overcome within a few years." See also Sale's Qurãn.

4 Abul Kasim Abdul Rahman, surnamed Shihabuddin and called Abu Shamah from a mole on his left temple. He was born at Damascus A.H. 599 (1202). He was a jurisconsult, a grammarian, traditionist and an historian. He has left two *abridgments* of the history of Damascus, one in 15, the other in 5 Vols. Besides the biographies of Nuruddin and Saladin, and several other works on theology and grammar. De Slane, I.K.

the one of the most remarkable that has occurred, for Ibn Barrajan A.H.592.
died some time before the event, and the precise date of his death A.D.1196.
is known.

In the year 589 died Sultan Salahuddin and the messenger *announcing the news* arrived in Baghdad with the Sultan's coat of mail, his charger and one dinar and thirty-six dirhams[1] which was all the property he left. Egypt fell to his son Imaduddin Othman al Malik al Aziz, Damascus to his son al Malik al Afdhal Nuruddin Ali, and Aleppo to his son al Malik al Dhahir Ghiyathuddin Ghazi.

In the year 590 died Sultan Toghril Bek Shah, son of the Arslan, son of Toghril Bek, son of Muhammad, son of Malak Shah, the last of the Slajukian sovereigns.

Ad Dahabi says that they were twenty and odd princes in number, the first being Toghril Bek, the one who restored al Kaim to Baghdad, and the duration of their sovereignty was one hundred and sixty years.

In the year 592 a dark storm blew at Mecca and swept over the whole country, and a reddish sand fell upon the people and a portion of the Rukn al Yamani (*the south-eastern portion of the Kaabah*) fell down. During the same[3] Khwarazm Shah fitted out an army, crossed the Oxus at the head of 50,000 men and sent to the Caliph demanding the Sultanate and the restoration of the Sultan's palace to its former state of *splendour, and threatening* that he himself would march to Baghdad, and that the Caliph would be subject to him as were the Saljukian princes. On this the Caliph demolished the Sultan's palace and sent back his envoy without a reply, after which the Lord sufficiently met his misdeeds as has already gone before.

In the year 593 a huge meteor fell and a terrible sound was heard at its fall, and houses and edifices were convulsed, and the

---

1 Ibn Ath. says forty, Ibn Khall on the authority of Ibn Shaddad, forty-seven,

2 This is inaccurate. The invasion of Khwarazm Shah occurred in 614 (1217).

A.H.592. A.D.1196. people called to the Lord for help and burst into public supplications, conceiving that it was one of the signs of the day of resurrection.

In the year 505 al Malik al Aziz died in Egypt, and his son al Mansur succeeded him, but al Malik al Aadil Sayfuddin Abu Bakr[1] the son of Ayub attacked and made himself master of it and was eventually succeeded by his son al Malik al Kamil.

In the year 596, the Nile delayed its rise in Egypt, thus causing it great damage, it not reaching thirteen cubits in height,[2] and there was a great dearth so that people eat carrion and men, and this living on human beings became notorious and public, and the strangest stories are told regarding it. They proceeded to such an extent that they dug open the graves and eat the corpses and the people of Egypt "dispersed with a complete dispersion." (Qur. XXXIV). Death from starvation increased so enormously that no one could walk in the streets without his foot or his glance falling upon the dead or the dying. The people of the village utterly perished, so that it a traveler passed through a village, he would not see a single soul[3] and would find all the houses open and the inhabitants dead. Indeed ad Dahabi recounts stories regarding this that make the flesh creep at hearing them. He says that the streets were strewn with dead bodies, and their flesh was the prey of carrion

---

1 This prince conspired with al Malik al Aziz whose name was Othman and wrested Damascus form al Malik al Afdhal whose name was Ali. The latter wrote to the Caliph a letter of complaint beginning. "My lord! Abu Bakr and his companion Othman have forcibly taken possession of the right of Ali. Behold the fortune of this name, how it experiences in our day what it met with in the past. The Caliph's witty reply may be found in Abulf, and his translator.

2 The fluctuations of the Nile's rise may be learnt from the 1st Chap. Book II, of Abdul Latif's Monograph of Egypt ; 18 cubits is the height it must reach to fully satisfy the requirements of the country. Any height less than 16 cubits must result in famine more or less severe according to the fall. The 2nd Chapter contains the horrible details of the picture but faintly sketched by as Suyuti. The Egyptian cubit is 22 inches and its measure together with the normal height of the Nile's rise, has remained unaltered since the days of Herodotus. Gib. C. XXVIII.

3 Literally, "one blowing fire into flame."

birds and wild beasts, and persons of good birth together with their children were sold for a few dirhams, and this state of things continued till the middle of the year 598. A.H.597. A.D.1200.

In the year 597 a great earthquake occurred in Egypt, Syria and Mesopotamia, and many houses and forts were destroyed and a village in the dependency of Busra[1] was swallowed up. At the close of Muharram in the year 599, the stars were in great commotion and sped like a flight of locusts and this continued till morning. The people were panic-stricken and cried out to the Most High, and the like of this was never seen save at the birth of the Apostle of God.

In the year 600 the Franks made a raid from Rosetta up the Nile against Fuwwah, and plundered and ravaged and returned. In 601 the Franks[2] took Constantinople and expelled the Byzantines in whose possession it had been before the rise of Islam and it remained under the Franks until the year 660. (25th *July*, 1261) when the Byzantines[3] again recovered it from them.

In the same year, a woman in Katufta[4] gave birth to child with two heads, two arms and four legs, but it did not live.

In the year 606 was the beginning of the Tartar ascendancy, and a narration of their history will presently follow.

In 615, the Franks captured the chain fort at Damietta. Abu Shamah says that this fort was the key of Egypt. It was a lofty tower in the middle of the Nile and opposite to it on the east side was Damietta and on the west the mainland of the Delta ; and on each side was a chain, one of them extending across the Nile to

---

1 There are two places of this name in Yakut. One is Syria near Damascus, the other a village near Baghdad close to Ukbara.

2 Under Dandolo.

3 In the reign of Michael Paleologus ; see for the whole of this period the 40th, 41st and 42nd chapters of Gibbon.

4 So the MS. Yakut gives the name and describes the locality-an extensive quarter on the western side of Baghdad. قطيعا As written in the text is not to be found in Yakut.

A.H.597. A.D.1200. Damietta and the other across the Nile to the mainland, obstructing the passage of ships from the ocean. In the year 616, the Franks captured Damietta (5th *November,* 1219) after several engagements and a prolonged investment and al Malik al Kamil (*Sovereign of Egypt*) was too weak to offer them any resistance. They introduced their innovations therein and converted the principal mosque into a church. Al Malik al Kamil then laid the foundations of a city at the branching of the two waters,[1] and named it Mansurah and strengthened it with ramparts and entered it with his army.

In this year the chief Kadhi Ruknuddin ad Dhahir entered into a correspondence with al Kamil, and al Malik, and al Malik al Muadhdham[2] *Isa* princes of Damascus had a personal ill-feeling against him, whereupon he sent him a parcel in which was a jacket and a halter and commanded him to wear it before the people in his judicial court. He dared not refuse, but after a short time, he rose and went to his house and kept to his room and died after a few months of rage, and cast forth a portion of his liver, and the people sorely grieved at this. It happened that al Malik at Muadhdham sent after this to as Sharafuddin b. Unayn[3] a present of wine and a

---

1 The Nile is joined to Lake Menzaleh by the canal of Ashmun which terminates at Mansurah.

2 Al Malik al Aadil during his lifetime partitioned his dominions among his sons. To al Malik al Kamil Muhammad he gave Egypt ; al Muadhadham had Damascus, Jerusalem, Tiberias, and other places ; part of Mesopotamia, Mayyafarikin, Khilat, &c. were given to al Malik al Ashraf, and the remainder among two other sons Shihabuddin Ghazi and Arslan Shah. These princes lived, says Ibn Ath., in great concord and were as if moved by one spirit, (p. 230) a statement difficult to reconcile with facts. See Ibn Ath., p. 274 and after – Weil, p. 448.-I do not feel assured that I have correctly apprehended the sense of this passage. Ad Dhahir can scarcely be another surname of Ruknuddin, yet I can give it no other sense.

3 "With him" says Ibn Khall, "closed the series of our great poets, his equal has never since appeared." His predilection for satire caused his expulsion from Damascus by Saladin, his poem "Scissors of reputations" having irritated the chief men at Damascus against whom it was directed. His travels extended to India and Transoxiana and he returned to Damascus when al Malik al Aadil took possession of it after Saladin's death, in 592 (1195) and he died there in A.H. 640 (1033).

striped garment, at a time when he affected an abstinent life, and said, "Praise God for this" Upon which he wrote in reply, saying, A.H.616. A.D.1219.

"O al Malik al Muadhdham the custom

That thou hast introduced shall continue for ages :

The princes after thee will follow thy way,

Giving robes of honor to Kadhis and presents to the devout."

In the year 618, praise be to God, Damietta was recovered from the Franks, and in 621 the School of Tradition al Kamiliyah, was founded at Cairo between the two palaces, and Abul Khattab[1] b. Dihyah was appointed professor. The Kaabah had up to this time been covered with white brocade since the days of al Mamun, but an Nasir covered it with green brocade and subsequently with black, and so it has continued up to this day.

Of persons of note who died during the reign of an Nasir were, the Hafidh Abu Tahir as Silafi, Abul Hasan b-ul Kassar the philologist, al Kamil Abul Barakat al Anbari, the Shaykh Ahmad bur Rifaai, Ibn Bashkual, Yunus, father of the Bani Yunus of the Shafiite school, Abu Bakr b. Tahir al Ahdab (*Humphacked*) the grammarian, Abul Fadhl father of ar Rafai, Ibn Malakun the grammarian, Abdul Hakk of Seville, author of the Ahkam (*Judgements*), Abu Zayd as Suhayil auther of the ar Raudh al Unuf (*Uuntrodden meadows*), the Hafidh Abu Musa al Madini, Ibn Barri the philologist, the Hafidh Abu Bakr al Harimi, as Sharaf b. Abi Usrun, Abul Kasim al Bukhari al Othmani,[2] author of the al Jami al Kabir (*the great Comprehender*) one of the most eminent of the hanafites, an Najm al Habushani known as Salah, Abul Kasim

---

1 He was a native of Valencia and surnamed Dun Nasabayn (*of the double pedigree*) being descended from Dihyah of the tribe of Kalb a companion of Muhammad on one side, and from al Husayn on the other. He was born in A.H. 544 (1150) and died at Cairo 633 (1235). The principal cities of Spain and of north Africa, as well Syria and Khurasan were visited by him for the sake of collecting traditions of which, he was considered a perfect master and attained to the dignity of a Hafidh. Ibn Khall.

2 Al Attabi. MS.

A.H.622. A.D.1225. b. Firrah as Shatibi author of the Kasidah,[1] Fakhruddin Abu Shujaa Muhammad b. Ali b. Shuayb bud Dahhan, doctor of the law of Inheritance, the first who made a table of Inheritance after the diagram of a pulpit[2] Burhan al Marghinani author of the Hidayah, of the Hanafite School, Kadhikhan author of the Fatawa (*decisions*) of the same school. Abdur Rahim b. Hajun, the devotee of Upper Egypt, Abul Walid b. Rashid author of the Philosophical Sciences, Abu Bakr b. Zuhr the physician, al Jamal b. Fadhlan of the Shafiite school, al Kadhi al Fadhil the master of Composition and epistolary style, Shihab at Tusi, Abul Faraj b-ul Jauzi, al Imad the Secretary, Ibn Adhimah the Qurãn reader, the Hafidh Abdul Ghani al Mukaddasi author of the Umdah (*Column*), ar Ruknuddin at Tausi author of the *Tarikatul* Khilaf (*System of Controversy*), Shamim al Hilli, Abu Darr al Khashini the grammarian, the Imam Fakhruddin ar Razi, Abul Saadat Ibnul Athir author of the Jamiul Usul *fiahadith ir Rasul (Combiner of the fundamentary Treatises on the Apostolic Traditions)* and the Nihayah fill Gharib (*The extreme or obscure terms in tradition*), al Imad b. Yunus author of the Sharh al Wajiz (*the Epitomized commentary*), as Sharaf[3] author of the Tanbih (*Admonition*), the Hafidh Abul Hasan b-ul Mufadhdhal, Abu Muhammad b. Hawtillah, and his brother Sulayman, the Hafidh Abdul Kadir ar Ruhawi, the devotee Abul Hasan bil Sabbagh Bikna, al Wajih bud Dahhan the grammarian, Takkiuddin b-ul Maktarih Abu Yumn al Kindi the grammarian, al Main al Hijiri author of the Kifayah (*Sufficiency*) of the Shafiite school, al Rukn al Amidi Author of the Tarikat bil Khilaf, Abul Baka al Ukbari author of the Iirab (*science of literal inflections*), Ibn Abi Usaybah the physician, Abdur Rahim b-us Samaani, Najmuddin al Kabari Ibn Abi Sayf al Yamani, Muwaffakuddin b. Kadamah al Hanbali, Fakhruddin b. Asakir and others.

---

1 On the Qurãn readings called Hirzul Amani wa Wajhul Tahani (*wishes accomplished and open congratulation*).

2 That is showing the family relations and their shares of inheritance by a diagram of steps, which would give it the appearance of a pulpit.

3 More correctly, author of the commentary on the Tanbih a work on jurisprudence by Abu Ishak as Shirazi. His more famous father, Kamaluddin Yunus died in the reign of al Mustansir, 17 years later.

AD DHAHIR BI'AMRILLAH

A.H.622.
A.D.1225.

Ad Dhahir bi amrillah (*Pre-eminent by the decree of God*) Abu Nasr Muhammad son of an Nasir li dinillah was born in the year 371. His father took the covenant for him as his heir and he succeeded to the Caliphate on his father's death, at the age of fifty-two. They said to him *on his accession*-"dost thou not rejoice?" He replied, "Verily the harvest is blighted." They said, "May God prosper thy days." He answered, "What can a man earn who opens his shop only late in the afternoon." He was beneficent towards his subject, reduced taxation, cheeked abuses and distributed large sums of money. (*Abu Shamah.*)

Ibnul Athir says in the Kamil, "When al Dhahir acceded to power, he displayed such justice and benevolence as to recall the administration of the two 'Omars, and it were said that none like unto him, governed the Caliphate since Omar b. Abdil Aziz, the speaker would say truly, for he restored an immense amount of property that had been unjustly taken, and goods confiscated in the time of his father and before it, and remitted all taxes in the towns and ordered a return to the former taxation throughout the whole of Iraq and the discontinuance of what his father had recently imposed ; all this being an amount beyond computation. As an instance of this, the town of Bakuba was originally assessed at ten thousand dinars, and when an Nasir became Caliph, he levied from it during the year, eighty thousand dinars, but ad Dhabir restored its original assessment on the appeal of the people. And when the old tax was again levied in the districts, a deputation obtained audience and represented that the greater number of the trees on their properties had withered and were ruined, whereupon he ordered that no tax should be levied except upon a sound (date) tree."[1] As an illustration of his justice, the Treasury scales exceeded just measure by half a kirat (*two grains*) in a mithkal (*twenty grains*) and they accepted payments according to this standard but issued

1 This quotation, is not exactly literal-portions of its are so, while the rest after the author's fashion, is an abridgment of the original, in his own style. The sense is however fairly given.

A.H.622. A.D.1225. them according to the scale of weights in use in the Provinces. Upon this a mandate was dispatched to the prime minister, beginning "Weo be unto those who give short measure" (Qur. LXXXIII) and it continued "we have heard such and such *reports:* let the Treasury scales be re-altered to what is customary in the mercantile transactions of the people." They wrote to him to the effect that a great disparity would result, which from the returns of the past year, they had calculated would amount to 35,000 dinars. He returned a reply, rejecting the suggestions of his correspondent and adding, "let it be discontinued though the disparity be 350,000 dinars." As another instance of his justice, the Superintendent of the finance registers returned from Wasit with more than 100,000 dinars obtained by oppression; he restored it all to the owners thereof. He released those who were in prison and sent ten thousand dinars to the Kadhi to pay it in satisfaction for those who were in distress,[1] and he distributed on the night of the festival of Sacrifice (10th *Dul Hijjah*) ten thousand dinars among the learned and the devout. It was said to him on one occasion that on one had over given scarce a portion of the sums that he had lavished, he replied, "I opened my shop late in the afternoon : suffer me then to do good,-for how much longer have I do live?" There were found in a room of his palace, thousands of letters all of which were sealed. He was asked why he did not open them, he answered, "I have no need of them ; they are all accusations *of informers.*" The whole of this in *taken* from Ibnul Athir.

Sibt b-ul Jauzi relates that once when he entered the Treasury, an attendant said to him, "This used to be full in the time of thy father." He replied, "the Treasury is not made to be kept full, but to be emptied and distributed for pious purposes, for verily to accumulate is the occupation of a trader." Ibn Wasil says that he displayed justice and diminished taxation and appeared much in public which his father rarely did. He died on the 13th Rajab,[2] 623 (10th *July,* 1226) ; his reign having been nine months and some

1 That is, for those who were imprisoned for debt. Ibn Ath. expresses the sense with greater clearness.

2 Ibnul Ath. 14.

days in duration. He was licensed by his father to recite traditions. A.H.623.
Abu Salih Nasr b. Abdir Razzak bil Shaykh Abdil Kadir al Jili recited A.D.1226.
them on his authority. An eclipse of the moon occurred twice in the year in which he died. Nasrullah bil Athir[1] arrived on an embassy from the governor of Mosal with a letter of condolence *to his successor* which began thus :

"Why should not day and night plead excuse when the calamity they have brought about is so great ?- and why should not the sun and moon be eclipsed when the third *luminary* has disappeared ?

"How desolate is the world, once so gladsome
And what solitude for those in it through one scene of death."

And he is our lord and master the Imam an Dhahir prince of the Faithful whose reign was a mercy unto both worlds.

AL MUSTANSIR BI'LLAH

Al Mustansir billah (*Seeking assistance in God*) Abu Jaafar Mansur the son of ad Dhahir bi amrillah was born in the month of Safar 588, his mother being a Turkish slave. According to Ibnun Najjar, he was acknowledged Caliph on the death of his father in Rajab 623. He dealt justly with his subjects and was equitable in his decisions and sought the society of men of wisdom and piety, and founded mosques and Ribats and colleges and hospitals. He set up the beacon of religion, extirpated the refractory, promulgated laws, restrained dissensions and brought his people under the most admirable regulations. He undertook religious wars with the utmost devotion and assembled armies for the defence of Islam, guarded the frontiers and captured many fortresses.

---

1 Better known as Dhiauddin Ibnul Athir-born in 558 (1163) died at Baghdad 637 91239-40). He entered the service of Saladin whose prime minister, he became. He ended his days as a writer of dispatches under Nasruddin Mahmud, governor of Mosal. Ibn Khall.

A.H.623. A.D.1226. Al Muwaffak Abdul Latif says, "When Abu Jaafar was acknowledged Caliph, he pursued an excellent course of conduct, re-established the ways of kindliness that had been effaced, set up the beacon of religion and the watch tower of Islam and won all hearts to the love of him, and all tongues to his praise, and the most captious found in him no reproach. His grandfather an Nasir courted his society and used to call him the Kadhi from his right judgment and intelligence, and repugnance to all vice that he met with." The Hafidh Zakiuddin Abdul Adhim al Mundiri[1] observes that all Mustansir was zealous in good works and earnest in the advancement of virtue of which many brilliant instances *are recorded* of him. He founded the Mustansiriyah college and settled good stipends on men of learning.

Ibn Wasil says that al Mustansir built on the eastern bank of the Tigris a college than which none more beautiful or more extensively endowed was ever constructed upon the face of the earth. He appointed four professors for the four orthodox doctrinal schools,[2] and built within it a hospital and provided a kitchen for the use of the jurisconsults and large cooling jars for cool drinking water and furnished their apartments with mats and carpets, olive oil, paper, ink and the like and over and above, a monthly stipend of a dinar for each jurist. Further he provided for them a Hammam, the like of which had never been done before. He enlisted a large army such as his father and grandfather had never organized before him, and he was withal of a lofty spirit, brave and of great intrepidity. The Tartars invaded his dominions, but his forces encountered them and the Tartars suffered a complete rout. He had a brother called al Khafaji of great courage who used to say that were he in supreme authority, he would cross the Oxus at the head of an army, wrest the provinces from the Tartars and root them out. When al Mustansir died, the Chief Secretary and High Steward were averse to the

---

1 A renowned Jurist and traditionist. He was born in Egypt in 581 (1185) and became Shaykh of the Kamiliyah School of Tradition founded at Cairo by al Malik al Kamil in 622. Ibn Khallikan was one of his pupils. He died in 656 (1258). De Slane, I.K.

2 Of Malik, as Shafii, Hanbal, and Abu Hanifah.

investiture of al Khafaji through fear of him, wherefore they set up the son of al Maustansir Abu Ahmad on account of his mildness of character and weakness of understanding, in order that the government might remain in their hands, "that God might accomplish the thing which was *decreed to be* done" (Qur. VIII) regarding the destruction of the Muslims during his reign and the Tartar domination-for we belong to God and unto Him do we return. A.H.623. A.D.1226.

Ad Dahabi says that the aggregate of the endowments of the Mustansiriyah college reached yearly over 70,000 mithkals (*dinars*). The building was begun in the year 625 and completed in 631. Books were sent to it to the number of one hundred and sixty camel-loads of valuable works. The complement of its jurists of the four doctrinal schools was 248. There were four lecturers, and a professor of tradition, of grammar, of medicine, and of the law of inheritance. It was further provided with bread, cooked flesh-meat, sweetmeats and fruit. The Caliph also placed thirty orphans on the foundation and endowed it to an extent that surpasses description. Ad Dahabi here enumerates the village and lands settled on it and adds that it was opened on *the first* Thursday of Rajab, the Kadhis, professors and nobles, and all the state officials being present, and it was a "day whereon men *were* assembled," (Qur. XI).

Among events in the reign of al Mustansir in 618, al Malik al Ashraf lord of Damascus ordered the building of a college of Traditions *called* al Ashrifiyah which was completed in the year 630.

In the year 632 al Mustansir gave orders for the coinage of silver dirhams to be used instead of chips of gold. The Wazir held an audience and summoned governors, merchants and money-changers : leather mats were spread out and the dirhams placed upon them and the Wazir said, "Our master, the prince of the Faithful hath prescribed your employment of these dirhams instead of gold chippings, out of kindness to you and to free you from illicit usurious traffic." Upon this they broke out in benedictions *upon him.* They were then circulated in Iraq and their currency fixed at ten for the dinar.

A.H.632. AD.1234. Al Muwaffak Abul Maali al Kasim b. Abil Hadid[1] said *with regard to this-*

"May we never lose thy excellent judgment among us.
Thou hast removed us far from unjust standards of measure.
Thou hast prescribed the use of silver so that we have become familiar with it
Which was never familiar to us before.
Not for hoarding *wealth* was thy prohibition against deviation[2]
But for a right course and for positive certitude."

In the year 635 the office of Kadhi at Damascus was held by Shamsuddin Ahmad al Juni. He was the first Kadhi who established stations for witnesses in the city, for before that time, the people had to attend the houses of witnesses to obtain their testimony. During the same, died the two brothers, the Sultans, al Ashraf prince of Damascus and two months after him al Kamil sovereign of Egypt. Kulamah[3] the son of al Kamil assumed the sovereignty of Egypt and was surnamed al Aadil, but he was subsequently deposed and his brother *al Malik* as Salih Ayyub Najmuddin usurped the government.

In the year 637 Shaykh Izzuddin[4] b. Abdis Sallam held the

1 He was a jurisconsult and a man of letters and ability ; born at al Madain in 590 and died at Baghdad in 656 (1258) soon after the taking of the city by the Tartars. He was the brother of Abu Hamid Izzuddin al Madaini who wrote a refutation of Dhiauddin Ibnul Athir's work called the Current Proverb. See life of this latter in Ibn Khall.

2 For the various meanings of عدل and صرف on the tradition لايقبل منه صرف و لاعدل See Lane, art.

3 His name was Sayfuddin Abu Bakr. I have nowhere met the name in the text.

4 He afterwards (638) repaired to Misr, fearing the revenge of al Malik as Salih, Ismail of Damascus whom he had reviled for surrendering two forts to the Franks on condition of their aiding him against his nephew as Salih Ayub of Egypt. The latter made him Kadhi of Misr which, says Aabul Fida, he reluctantly accepted. For an instance of his thaumaturgy, see reiske's note, p. 711.

office of public preacher at Damascus. He preached a discourse free from all heretical tendency. He abolished the use of the gilded standards and set up in their place black and white ones and only a single caller to prayer chanted before him. During the same Rasul ul Amin Nuruddin Omar b. Ali b. Rasulit Turkomani who had possessed himself of Yaman visited the Caliph to obtain the investiture of the Sultanate of Yaman after the death of al Malik al Masaud[1] son of al Malik al Kamil, and this sovereignty continued in his house till the year 865. A.H.637. A.D.1239.

In 639, *al Malik* as Salih sovereign of Egypt founded the college which is between the two palaces and the fort at Raudhah, but this fort was destroyed by his slaves in 651.

In the year 640, on Friday the 10th of Jumada II, (5th *December*, 1242) died al Mustansir. The poets composed elegies on him and among them Safiuddin Abdullah b. Jamil. As an instance of the virtues of al Mustansir, al Wajih al Kayrawani praised him in a poem in which he said-

> "Hadst thou been present on the day of Sakifah[2]
> Thou wouldst have been the foremost-the God-fearing Imam."

Whereupon some one in his presence exclaimed, "Thou hast

---

1 He had been sent to Yaman by his grandfather al Malik al Aadil I, in 611 (1225) and entered Mecca the same year where the Khutbah was read in his name. He retained his government under his father al Kamil's supremacy and died at Mecca in 626 (1229). For the fortunes of the Rasul dynasty in Yaman, consult Adulf, p. 524 Vol. 4 and 126, Vol. 5, Weil, 203. I am indebted to the courtesy and erudition of Mr. Stanley Lane Poole for the following note. "Rasul was an envoy of the Abbasi Caliph, who adopted the name of his office (Rasul) and was Governor of Mecca about 620. A.H. His son Nuruddin Omar b. Rasul is the founder of the dynasty of the Beni Rasul who governed Yemen from the death of its last Ayyubi ruler (al Malik al Masaud) to the subversion of the dynasty by the Beni Tahir in 853 A.H. the dynasty ruled at Zebid in the Tehamah and coins of two of the kings struck at Aden, are in the British Museum. There is a special history of the Rasuliyah at the India Office, by El Khazraji, and an account of them in Ibn-Ed. Deyba (B.M. MS.) and Johannsen's Historia Yamanae."

2 See page 53. note. 2.

A.H.640. erred for verily al Abbas the ancestor of the prince of the Faithful
A.D.1242. was then present, and none but Abu Bakr could have been the foremost." Al Mustansir assented to this speech and rewarded the speaker thereof with a robe of honor and commanded al Wajih to be banished who as ad Dahabi relates, departed for Egypt. Of persons of note who died during the reign of al Mustansir were the Imam Abul Kasim ar Rafii, al Jamal al Misri, Ibn Maghruz the grammarian, Yakut al Hamawi, as Sukaki author of the Miftah (*key*), the Hafidh Abul Hasan b-ul Kattan, Yahya b. Muti author of the grammatical treatise the Alifiyah (*consisting of 1000 verses*) al Muwaffak Abdul Latif al Baghdadi, the Hafidth Abu Bakr b. Nuktah, the Hafidh Izzudin Ali b-ul Athir, author of the History (*Kamil*), the Ansab,[1] and the Asadul Ghabah (*Lion of the forest*) Ibn Utbi the poet, as Sayf al Amidi, Ibn Fadhlan, Omar bil Faridh author of the Taiiyah[2] *fit Tasawwuf*, as Shihab as Suhrawardi author of the Awariful Maarif (*the divine cognitions is degrees of spiritual knowledge*) al Baha b. Shaddad, Abul Abbas al Aufi author of the Maulid an Nabawi (*the prophetical nativity*), the learned Abul Khattab b. Dihyah and his brother Abu Omar, the Hafidh Abur Rabiah b. Salim[3] author of the Iktifa *bi Maghazil Mustafa wal Khulafi al Thalathah (A sufficient account of the Military expeditions of the Chosen and the three Caliphs)*. Ibnul Shawa the poet, the Hafidh Zakiuddin al Barzali, al Jamal al Hasiri[4] the Hanafite Shaykh, as Shams al Juni, al Harrani, the Hafidh Abu Abdullah az Zaini, Abul Barakat b-ul Mustawfi, ad Dhiauddin bil Athir author of the Mathal al Sair (*the current Proverb*) Ibn Arabi author of the Fususul *Hikam (The Bezels of words of wisdom)*,

---

1 This was an abridgment in 3 Vols. Of Abu Saad as Samanis Ansab (*explanation of patronymics and other relative adjectives*). The Asadul Ghabah fi Maarifat is Sihabbah contains notices of 7500 of the companions, supplementing the omission of his predecessors and correcting their errors. Haji Khalifah.

2 This is a poem in the letter Ta on the doctrines of the Sufis. The text and MS are in error in writing the word تايه

3 Haji Khalifah states him to be the son of Musa.

4 So called from a quarter in Bukhara where mats (hasir) are made in which he must have resided. See Ibn Khall's life of al Amidi Ruknuddin : the MS. writes the word correctly. The printed text is in error.

Kamaluddin b. Yunus the commentator[1] on the Tanbih (*Admonition, of Abu Ishak as Shirazi*) and others. A.H.640. A.D.1242.

AL MUSTASIM BI'LLAH

Al Mustasim billah (*Seeking protection with God*) Abu Ahmad Abdullah son of Mustansir billah, last of the Caliphs of the two Iraqs was born in the year 609, his mother being a slave concubine called Hajir. He was acknowleged Caliph on the death of his father. Al Muwayyad[2] at Tusi granted him authority as a licentiate of traditions through Ibnun Najjar, and so likewise did Abu Ruh al Harawi and a number of others. Traditions were repeated on his authority and license by an Najm al Badarai, as Sharf ad Dimyati. Ad Dimyati has taken from his special narration forty traditions which I have seen in his handwriting. He was generous, mild of temper, of good disposition, and exemplary virtue. The Shayhh Kutbuddin says, that he was orthodox in religion, conforming to its precepts like his father and grandfather, but not their equal in vigilance, firmness of purpose and loftiness of soul. Al Mustansir had a brother known as al Khafaji of great bravery and valour, who used to say that if God would put him in possession of supreme power, he would cross the Oxus at the head of an army, wrest the country from the Tartars and exterminate them. But when al Mustansir died, the Chief Secretary and High Steward and the principal nobility did not approve the assumption of the government by al Khafaji for they feared him, wherefore they chose al Mustasim on account of his lenity and meekness, in order that the real power might rest with them. They accordingly set him in authority. Al

---

1 The Commentator was rather his son Sharafuddin who died in the reign of an Nasir. See note 3. p. 626.

2 this traditionist's family originally came from Tus, but he fixed his residence at Naysabur. He was considered the most authoritative traditionist of his time, and students flocked to him from all quarters. Ibn Khall himself was a licentiate of this master, born 524 91130) died 617 (1220). Ibn Khall.

A.H.640. A.D.1242. Mustasim placed his dependence upon his Wazir Muwayyaduddin al Alkami the heretic (*Shiite*) who ruined the country and played with the Caliphate as he willed. He carried on a secret correspondence with the Tartars, counseled with them and urged them to march into Iraq, to take possession of Baghdad and put an end to the Abbaside dynasty, in order that he might set up a Caliph of the posterity of Ali. Whatever information regarding them arrived, he concealed from the Caliph but kept the Tartars informed of the Caliph's movements until events happened as they subsequently did.

In the year 647 of his reign the Franks[1] took Damietta. The Sultan al Malik as Salih (*Ayyub*) was at the time ill, and he died on the night of the 15th of Shaaban. His wife Umm Khalil, called Shajarud Dur (*Spray of Pearl*) concealed his death and summoned his son Turan Shah al Malik al Muadhdham who arrived, but it was not long before he was assassinated, in Muharram of the year 648. His father's dependents assaulted and slew him an they raised up his father's wife Shajarud Durr and the Turks swore allegiance to her and to her chief minister Izzuddin Aybak the Turkoman. She began by bestowing robes of honor and rich presents upon the principal nobles and appointed Izzuddin to the Sultanate in Rabii II, and he received the title of al Muizz. Subsequently he withdrew from the dignity[2] and the troops swore allegiance of al Malik al Ashraf son of Salahuddin Yusuf bil Masaud bil Kamil, a boy of eight and Izzuddin remained as his guardian (*alabek*). They were both included in the khutbah and their names stamped upon the coinage.

In this year Damietta was recovered from the Franks. In the year 652 a fire appeared in the land of Aden and its sparks at night flew out towards the sea and a vast *column of* smoke arose from it by day. During the same, al Muizz set aside the nominal authority of al Malik al Asraf and assumed the Sultanate. In the year 654

---

1 Under St. Louis of France in the 6th Crusade. 1249.

2 It was thought expedient that an Ayyubite should, at least in name, hold the regal office.

appeared the fire in the prophetical city of Medina. Abu Shamah relates that he received letters from Medina with the following. "On Tuesday night, the 3rd Jumada II, a mighty rushing sound was heard followed by a great earthquake which continued at short intervals till the 5th of the month when a huge fire appeared in al Harrah[1] near Kuraydhah ; we saw it from our houses in Medina as if it were close upon as, and the there flowed from it rivers *of fire* towards Wadi Shata[2] like the rush of a flood. We ascended *our houses to* see it, when lo ! the hills ran with torrents of flame and they continued thus, and in the same way flames appeared like unto mountains from which sparks flew like a vast edifice so that the light of them could be seen throughout both Mecca and the desert. And all the people assembled at the holy tomb, praying for mercy and repentant, and this continued for more than a month. Ad Dahabi observes that the mention of this fire comes down in an uninterrupted tradition and it is this which the Chosen One predicted where he said, "the last day shall not be, until a fire riseth out of Hijaz which shall light up the necks of the camels in Busra;"[3] and verily more than one of those who were at Busra during *that* night have mentioned *this fire* and *that* the necks of the camel a were visible by its light. A.H.654. A.D.1256.

In the year 655, perished al Muizz Aybak Sultan of Egypt. He was murdered by his wife Shajarud Durr and they raised to the Sultanate in succession to him, his son al Malik al Mansur and during this the Tartars were spreading over the provinces, their enormities increasing and their flame kindling ; the Caliph and the people heedless of what was intended regarding them, and the Wazir al Alkami[4] seeking the destruction of the Abbaside dynasty and its transmission to the posperity of Ali and corresponding

---

1 The Banu Kuraydhah live near Khaybar and al Harrah is probably Harrat un Nar, which I adjacent to Khaybar.

2 This name is not given in Yakut and I am uncertain as to the correction of the text here. The MS. is manifestly corrupt. See a notice of this eruption in Burton's Mecca.

3 Near Harwan in Palestine.

4 Muayyaduddin b-ul Alkami. Abulf.

A.H.655. A.D.1257. secretly with the Tartars, while al Mustasim, absorbed in his pleasures had no knowledge of events nor interest in the public welfare. His father al Mustansir had largely increased his army and withal, had pacified the Tartars with gifts, made peace with and conciliated them, whereas al Mustasim when he came to power, being destitute of understanding and administrative ability, was counseled by his Wazir to disband the greater part of his troops, since his object would be attained by treating the Tartars with generosity and courtesy, and this he accordingly did. The Wazir subsequently entered into a correspondence with the Tartars, urged them to march upon the provinces and facilitated their purpose. He proposed himself as their governor o which they agreed and made preparations for their march upon Baghdad.

A brief notice of the Tartars.

Al Muwaffak Abdul Latif says in his account of the Tartars, that it is a narrative that absorbs all other narratives, a chronicle that supersedes all other chronicles, a history that causes all other histories to be forgotten, a misfortune that reduces to insignificance all other misfortunes, a calamity that involved the earth and filled it to its length and breadth. The language of this people is blended with that of India in the vicinity of which they dwell, and between them and Mecca is a *distance of* four months journey. As compared with the Turks, they have broader faces, are fuller in the chest, leaner in the flanks, have smaller eyes, ar tawny in colour, quick in movement both of body and mind. Accounts of other nations reach them, but no information respecting them penetrates to other countries, and it is scarcely possible that a spy can settle among them for a foreigner does not resemble them in appearance. When they purpose setting out in a certain direction, they conceal their design and execute it with sudden rapidity, so that the people of a city know nothing of them till they enter it, nor an army until they are in the midst of it : thus unto people the means of circumventing them are confounded and the ways of escape straitened. Their women fight as well as the men. Their principal weapons are arrows, and their food, any flesh-meat they can get, and there is no exception or quarter in their massacre, for they slay men women and children. Their aim was the destruction of the human race and the ruin of the world, not the desire of dominion or plunder. A.H.655. A.D.1257.

Another author observes that the country of the Tartars borders on the confines of China : that they dwell in deserts and are notorious for their malignity and perfidy. The occasion of their rise was as follows : The country of China is of vast extent, its circuit occupying a six months' journey. It is composed of six principalities and they have a sovereign chief who governs the whole six. He is the great Kan who resides at Tamghaj and is like the Caliph of the Muslims. The Sultan of one of these principalities was Dosh Khan who had married the paternal aunt of Jingiz Khan. After the death of her husband, Jingiz Khan went on a visit to her, and he was accompanied by Kashlu Khan and she informed them that the prince *her husband* had left no heir and suggested to her nephew that he should succeed him. Upon his Jingiz Khan assumed the government and was joined by the Moguls. He then dispatched presents to the great Kan, who foaming with rage ordered he tails of the horses that had been presented to him, to be cut off and that they should be driven away, and he put to death the envoys, because the Tartars had no previous title to possession, they being but nomad wanderers in China. When Jingiz Khan and his friend Kashlu Khan heard this, they vowed revenge, declared war against the Kan and a vast number of Tartars mustered round them. The Kan, aware of their power and malice, sent to conciliate them affecting at the same to warn and threaten them. This, however, availed nothing, whereon he marched to encounter them and they advanced to meet him. A great battle took place and they defeated the Kan and took possession of his dominions. Their excesses were prodigious and the country remained subject to Jingiz Khan and Kashlu Khan in common. They next marched against the country of Shakun on the confines of China and took possession of it Kashlu Khan soon after died and his son succeeded him, but Jingiz Khan held him of

A.H.655. no account and attacked and seized him and assumed sole authority.
A.D.1257. The Tartars submitted to him and acknowledged his away. They paid him divine honours and carried their devotion to the greatest extreme.

After this, their first irruption was in 606 from their own territories towards Farghanah and the Turkish dominions. Upon this Khawarazm Shah Muhammad b. Tukush lord of Khurasan-he, who had overthrown kings and conquered their territories and had marched against the Caliph (*an Nasir*) but unsuccessfully as has already gone before-ordered the inhabitants of Farghanah and Shash and Kasan and similar prosperous and flourishing towns, to quit them and to pass into Samarkand and other places. He then laid them all waste lest the Tartars should take possession of them as he knew he was unable to stand against them. The Tartars continued plundering and roving until the year 615 when Jingiz Khan sent an embassy and presents to Khawarazm Shah and the envoy spoke as follows : "The great Kan greets thee and says to thee that the magnitude of thy power and the lofty dominion to which thou hast attained and the extent of thy authority over the nations is not unknown to him, and that he considers an alliance with thee among necessary obligations and that thou art to him like the most honoured of his children-further, that it is not hidden from thee that he has conquered China and thou knowest his dominions, that they are rich in soldiers and horses and mines of gold and of silver and a sufficiency of other things ; if therefore thou seest fit to unite in friendship with him and to suffer the traders to proceed, in order that thou mayest learn the mutual interests of both countries, thou wilt act accordingly." And Khawarazm Shah answered him according to his desire and Jingiz Khan was glad, and things remained on this peaceful footing until traders arrived from his dominions. At that time the maternal uncle of Khawarazm Shah was in the government of Transoxiana with twenty thousand horsemen, and the coveted the goods of the traders and wrote to Khawarazm Shah, saying that these men had come in the disguise of traders, but that their design was no other than to spy, and he asked permission to act in their regard. Khawarazm Shah gave him sanction to keep a watch on them, whereupon he seized them and confiscated their property. Upon this the envoys of Jingiz Khan arrived before Khawarazm Shah, saying *on the part of their master,* "Verily thou didst give thy safe-conduct to the traders and hast played false, and perfidy is a base action and in a Muslim prince especially base; but if thou assertest that what thy uncle hath done, hath been done without thy permission, then deliver him up to us, otherwise thou wilt behold from me that which thou knowest of me in such a matter." The fear the seized upon Khawarazm Shah was such as to disturb his judgment, and he affected hardiness and ordered the envoys to be put to death and they were put to death. Alas ! for a deed which causing the blood of Muslims to be shed unavenged, drew from every side a torrent of blood. A.H.655. A.D.1257.

Then Jingiz Khan went forth against him and Khawarzm Shah crossed the Oxus to Nisabur and thence passed on to the castle of Hamadan in fear of the Tartars. But the enemy surrounded him and slew all that were with him and he escaped alone and betook himself to an island in the *Caspian Sea*. There he fell ill of a pleurisy and died alone and abandoned and *his corpse* was shrouded in the bedding[1] he had with him. This occurred in the year 617 and the Tartars took possession of the whole of the dominions of Khawarzm Shah.

Sibtul Jauzi says that the Tartars first appeared in Transoxiana in the year 615. They took Bukhara and Samarkand and slew the inhabitants and besieged Khawarzm Shah. After this they crossed the river (*Oxus*) but Khawarzm Shah had overthrown the princes of the cities of Khurasan, and the Tartars found none to oppose them. They therefore marched rapidly over the country slaying and taking prisoners and pressed onwards till they reached Hamadan and Kazwn in the same year.

Ibnul Athir says in his Kamil that the invasion of the Tartars was one of the greatest of calamities and the most terrible of

---

1 The MS. omits the word. فراش

A.H.655. visitations which fell upon the world in general and the Muslims in
A.D.1257. particular, the like of which *succeeding* ages have failed to bring forth; for if one were to say that the world, since God created it to the present time, was never so afflicted, one would speak truly, for history has nothing which approaches it. The utmost that historians have to mention is the treatment of Jerusalem and the children of Israel by Nabuchadnezzar, but what is Jerusalem compared with what these accursed wretched destroyed of the cities of Islam, and what are the children of Israel in comparison with those whom the Tartars slew ? This was a calamity of which the sparks flew far and wide and its misery was universal, flying over the earth like a cloud driven before the wind-for a horde issued forth from the confines of China and attacked the cities of Turkistan such as Kashghar and the territory of Shaghrak,[1] from thence of Bukhara and Samarkand which they captured, exterminating their inhabitants. Then a body of them pass on to Khursan, finishing by destroying, plundering, slaying and devastating it, and thence to Rai and Hamadan and to the borders of Iraq. Next they march to Adarbijan and its dependencies ravaging and laying them waste-all in less than the space of one year-an event the like of which have never been heard. From Adarbijan they passed to Darband Sharwan,[2] subjugated its territory and crossed over to Allah and al Lalkaz, slaughtering and making prisoners. Thence they marched to the plains of Kafjak[3] the people *whereof* were more numerous than the Turks and slew those who opposed them; the rest fled and the Tartars took possession of the country. Another band passed on to Ghazni and its dependencies and to Sijistan (*Drangiana*) and to Kirman (*Carmania*) and did there what those had done and indeed worse. Such as this has never before been heard of, for Alexander

1 This name is not in Yakut. He, however, gives Sagharj, (ساغرج) a place five parasangs from Samarkand.

2 This is a town in the vicinity of Darband built by Anushirwan from whom it takes the name. Allah and al Lalkaz are mentioned by Yakut as adjacent.

3 "The Dasht-i- Kipzac or plain of Kipzak," say Gibbon, "extends on either side of the Volga in a boundless space towards the Saik and Borysthenes and is supposed to contain the primitive name and nation of the Cossacks." For the rise and progress of the Tartars, see his LXIVth chapter.

who made himself master of the world did not do so with such rapidity, for he conquered it in about ten years and moreover he did not massacre and was content with submission. But these subjugated the greater part of the habitable globe, its fairest and most fertile regions, in about a year, and none remained in the provinces which they had not assaulted, save such as were tremblingly awaiting their coming. Moreover they were not dependent upon the transport of corn nor on supplies reaching them for they had with them their sheep and oxen and horses, the flesh of which they eat and nothing else. As for their horses, they dig up the ground with their hoofs and eat the roots of plants and know nothing of barley. As for their belief, they worship the sun at his rising and deem nothing unlawful. They eat the flesh of al animals and *even* of men ; they do not recognize marriage, for a woman in visited by more than one man. A.H.655. A.D.1257.

In the beginning of the year 656, the Tartars, 200,000 in number led by Hulaku, reached Baghdad : the army of the Caliph advanced to meet them but was defeated, and they entered the city on the 10th of Muharram. The Wazir-may god confound him-counselled al Mustasim to conciliate them, and said, "I will go forth to them myself to arrange *the terms* of peace :" and he set forth and secured from them the safety of his own person and returned to the Caliph, and said, "The monarch desires to marry his daughter to thy son the Emir Abu Bakr, and he will confirm thee in the office of Caliph as he has suffered the lord of ar Rum[1] to retain his sovereignty, and he seeketh nothing but thy submission to him as thy ancestors submitted to the Saljuk princes, and he will then depart with his

---

1 Sahib ur Rum. In Abulf, the expression is Sultan ur Rum, which Reiske translates Romanie domino-I understand the Sultan of Iconium to be here meant. This dynasty opposed some resistance to the Mogul arms. The Byzantine capital escaped the universal destruction though Hulaku threatened to march against it with 400,000 men, but he was diverted by the conquest of Baghdad and a long vicissitude of Syrian wars. See Gibbon, LXIVth Cap. Michael Paleologus was taken prisoner by the Tartars after the recovery of Constantinople by the Greeks, which the Oriental writers place in 655 (1257) and the European in 1261), and their general Noga married Maria his natural daughter and "guarded the dominions of his friend and father." Ibid.

A.H.656. army. Let then, my lord, consent to this, for verily thus will the
A.D.1258. blood of the Muslims be spared, and afterwards thou canst do what thou wilt, but it is advisable that thou go forth to him." Then the Caliph set out at the head of all the nobles and he was made to alight at a tent. The Wazir entered *the city* an summoned the jurists and principal men to witness the negotiation and they all came forth from Baghdad and their heads were struck off, and thus company after company came out and were decapitated until all the learned and the nobles, the chamberlains and principal men were put to death. Then a bridge was thrown across and the sword was let loose in Baghdad, and the massacre continued for about forty days till the number of the slain was more than a million souls and none escaped but those who hid themselves in wells and subterraneous canals. The Caliph was trampled to death. Ad Dahabi says, "I do not think that he was buried and there were slain with him a number of his children and uncles, and some were imprisoned, and it was a calamity such as had never befallen Islam." What the Wazir sought, however, was not fulfilled, for he tasted of ignominy and contempt from the Tartars and he did not long survive this event. The poets wrote elegies on Baghdad and its inhabitants and the words of Sibt at Taawidi[1] are applicable *to the Wazir*—-

"It perished and the people with it, and their mansions

Are desolate through the continuance of our lord the Wazir."

And another of them says :

"People of Islam, weep and mourn,

For grief of what hath befallen al Mustasim.

The ministerial authority before his time

Was in the hands of Ibnul Furat, and then passed to Ibnul Alkami.

---

1 Abul Fath Muhammad surnamed at Taawidi (*a writer of amulets).* He was born at Baghdad in 519 (1125) and died there in 584 (1188). He was a clerk in the fief office at Baghdad, and towards the close of his life became blind. His poetry which is much admired by Ibn Khall, he himself collected into a Diwan.

At the last khuthah preached at Baghdad the preacher opened it thus-"Praise be to God who hath overturned in death eminent lives and hath commanded the destruction of the people of the house. This-while the sword continues therein." A.H.656. A.D.1258.

There is a well-known poem by Takiuddin b. Ali Yusr on Baghdad and it as follows-

"*Harrowing* are the tales of Baghdad for him who weeps.
Why remainest thou when thy friends have departed ?
Approach not Baghdad, ye pilgrims
For in this guarded enclosure and abode there are no dwellers.
The crown of the Caliphate, the sojurn of spring, where are honoured
Its memorials-verily desolation hath effaced it.
In this abode there are marks of the wasting that hath come upon it,
And traces of tears upon its ruins.
O fire of my heart, *sprung* of the fire from the tumult of war
That flamed over her-a whirlwind hath swept over this dwelling place.
The cross hath been raised high over her pulpits
And he whom the belt[1] girdeth rules over her.
How many a chaste matron have the Turks foreibly made captive
Fenced by other veils than that *of modesty ?*
And how many moons *of beauty* were eclipsed in their full
From which to their fullness they shall never return ?
And how many a treasure hath become dispersed
Through plunder, which the infidels have captured ?

---

1 The "Zunnar" was a waist-belt worn by the Eastern Christians and the non-Muslim subjects, introduced by an ordinance of the Caliph al Mutawakkil (A.D. 859) to distinguish them from the Muslims.

A.H.656. A.D.1258.

And how many penalties were laid by the sword
On the necks *of men* through which their sins are put away?
Nay, I say that the captive was dishonoured by their dragging
Him to the shedding of *his* blood by the terribe foe."

And when Hulaku had completed the massacre of the Caliph and the inhabitants of Baghdad, and had appointed a governor over Iraq (and Ibnul Alkami had recommended them to set up a Caliph of the posterity of Ali, to which they would not consent and cast him aside, and he remained with them in the position of one of their slaves and died of grief-may God not have mercy upon him nor pardon him), he sent a letter to an Nasir,[1] lord of Damascus, as follows : "The Sultan al Malik an Nasir-may his life be prolonged-is aware that when we set out for Iraq and their forces opposed us, we slew them with the sword of God. Then the chiefs of the city and its notables came forth to us, but the issue of their speech was the cause of the destruction of lives meriting destruction. But as to the governor of the city, verily he came forth to serve us and entered under our obedience, and we asked him regarding certain things wherein he deceived us and deserved death, for his falsehood was manifest 'and they shall find that which they have wrought, present *before their eyes,"* (Qur. XVIII). Answer the lord of the earth and speak not of thy impregnable fortresses and thy valiant armies: and verily we have heard that a part of the army hath taken refuge with thee in flight and sought an asylum at thy threshold-

'Where is a place of refuge ? there is no asylum for the fugitive,
For ours are the two plains, the earth and the sea.'

Therefore on the instant of thy informing thyself of our letter,

1 Al Malik an Nasir Abul Mudhaffar Yusuf surnamed Salahuddin, son of al Malik al Aziz son of az Dhahir son of Saladin, born 627 (1230). He succeeded to Damascus and Syria on the death of his father but expelled by the Tartars, he lost his life at the hands of Hulaku in 1259. See, Abulf, p. 621. The full text of this letter which was written by the learned Nasiruddin and addressed to an Nasir and the princes of Syria will be found in Wassaf, P. 43. followed by their haughty and insulting reply.

make the summits of the Syrian fortresses *level with* the earth and A.H.656.
their length as their breadth, and peace *be to thee.*" Then he sent A.D.1258.
him a second letter saying, : "To al Malik as Nasir-now, verily, we have taken Baghdad and destroyed its kingdom and its monarch. He had indeed been avaricious of his wealth and undersirous *of the maintenance* of his troops *hoping* that his kingdom would continue in that manner, and verily his fame spread and his power increased until his moon was eclipsed at its full.

'When a thing reacheth its prime, its decline begins,

Expect decay when fullness is announced."

But we seek for increase during the march of ages. "Be not therefore as those who have forgotten God and whom he has caused to forget their own souls' (Qur. LIX), and show that is in thy mind, whether abstention from good offices or the furtherance of courtesy, and answer the summons of the lord of the earth, that thou mayest be secure from his wrath and enjoy his benefits, and be liberal with him of thy wealth and thy troops and delay not our messengers." Again he sent him a third letter, saying, "Now, we are the army of the Lord. By us He avengeth Himself of those who are insolent and vain, and who are rebellious and haughty and do not submit to the commands of God, and who if they are reprehended, become enraged, and if remonstrated with, continue *stubborn.* And, verily, we have overthrown cities and destroyed the inhabitants and have slain women and children. O ye who are left ! ye are about to attain to those who have passed away. O ye who ar heedless ! ye are being driven towards them-for we are the army of destruction, not the army of dominion. Our purpose is vengeance and our kingdom is beyond the desire *of men.* Our guest is not injured and our justice throughout our dominions is known far and wide, and where is there an asylum from our swords ?

'Where is there a place of refuge ? there is no asylum to the fugitive,

For ours are the two plains, the earth and the sea.

Lions are submissive to our power and have fallen

In my grasp, princes and Caliphs.'

A.H.656. A.D.1258. We are about to set forth against ye and it is for ye to flee and for us to pursue :

> 'Laila shall soon know what debt is to be paid
> And how importunate a creditor is her creditor.'

We have destroyed cities and made orphans of the children and extirpated the inhabitants, and have made them taste of affliction, and we have made their great ones little and their nobles captive. Ye think that ye can escape and be delivered from us, but ye shall shortly know to what ye are tending, and verily he is rendered excused who hath admonished."

Thus began the year 657 and the world without a Caliph. During this the Tartars descended upon Amida. The sovereign of Egypt *at this time* was al Mansur Ali bil Muizz, (*Aybak*) a boy, and his tutor was the Emir Sayfuddin Kotuz[1] al Muizzi a slave of his father, and the Sahib Kamaluddin al Adim[2] sent a messenger to them asking for aid against the Tartars. Upon this Kotuz assembled the nobles and principal men and there was present the Shaykh Izzuddin b. Abdi's Sallam who was celebrated for his oratory, and the Shaykh said ; "Since the enemy has overrun the provinces, it is incumbent upon the whole commonwealth to oppose them, and it is lawful to take from the people what they can afford of their substance on the condition that the public treasury be first exhausted, and that ye should sell what ye possess of girdles *of price* and furniture and content yourselves each of you, with horse and arms, so that ye and the commonalty be one an equal footing ; for to take the substance of the people and to leave wealth and, costly furniture in the hands of the army, can never be." A few days after this, Kotuz seized upon al Mansur, the son of his master, and said, "This is but a boy and the times are critical. It is necessary that a man of spirit

---

1 The text is in error in this name. The MS, is correct.

2 Omar b. Ahmad Chief Kadhi of Aleppo, born A.H. 588 (1192) and died at Cairo 660 (1261-2). He had been driven from Aleppo by the invasion of the Tartars. He wrote a biographical Dictionary mentioning the remarkable men who had been in the city. His life is given by De Sacy in the Biographic Universelle and by Freytag in his Selecta ex Historia Halebi. De Slane, I.K.

should arise to carry on the war against the infidels." Kotuz obtained the supreme authority and was surnamed al Mudhaffar. A.H.657. A.D.1259.

The year 658 now began, and the age still without a Caliph. During this the Tartars crossed the Euphrates and reached Aleppo and put it to the sword and then arrived at Damascus. In the month of Shaaban the Egyptians marched into Syria to oppose the Tartars, and al Mudhaffar sent on with his forces and his picked troops[1] Ruknuddin Baybars al Bandukdari. They and the Tartars met at Ain Jalut[2] and a battle took place on Friday the 15th Ramadhan. The Tartars were utterly routed and the Muslims were victorious, praise be to God.

The Tartars were slain with a great carnage and they fled precipitately and the people pursued them with eagerness, seizing and plundering them. A letter from al Mudhaffar with the *news of the* victory arrived at Damascus and the people were elate with joy. Shortly after, al Mudhaffar entered Damascus triumphant and victorious, and the people hailed him with great affection. Baybares pursued the Tartars to be territory of Aleppo and drove them from the provinces. The Sultan Kotuz had promised him *the government of* Aleppo, but afterwards retracted it which Baybare took to heart, and this was the cause of their estrangerment. The Sultan had intended to set out for Aleppo in order to sweep from the provinces all traces of the Tartars, but hearing that Baybars was alienated from him and was conspiring against him, he changed his mind and returned to Egypt. He had, however, resolved upon the overthrow of Baybars and he divulged it to one of his confidants and Baybars

---

1 I presume this to be the meaning of شاليش — which I have not met elsewhere and am ignorant of its derivation. The word جاليش occurs in the Maurad ul Latafat, p. 89 (*edition Cantab. Carlyle*), translated by Carlyle "milites," but he confesses (note 70), that it is conjecture. He adds, "In vita Saladini a Boheddino, scape occurrit verbum جاليش quod reddit Schultens per *Sagittaries.* The reading of the text is perhaps an error for جاليش though the MS. agrees. Were it not for the authority of Schultens, I should suspect Carlyle's reading, as his edition is extremely faulty.

2 A town below Nazareth in Palestine.

A.H.658. became acquainted with it. They set out for Egypt, each being on
A.D.1259. their guard against the other, till Baybars conspired with some of the nobles to slay al Mudhaffar, and they assassinated him on the way, on the 16th Dul Kaadah, and Baybars assumed the government and received the title of al Malik al Kabir. He entered Cairo and removed from the people the tyrannous exactions imposed upon them by al Mudhaffar. The Wazir Zaynul Millat waddin (*Glory of the faith and of religion*) Ibnuz Zubayr counseled him to change his title and said that no one who had borne it had prospered, for al Kahir the son of al Muatadhid had been so named, and he was subsequently deposed and blinded, and al Kahir the son of the governor of Mosal had been poisoned. The Sultan therefore put away this surname and took the title of al Malik al Dhahir. Then began the year 659, and the age as before without a Caliph until the month of Rajab when the Caliphate was re-established in Egypt and al Mustansir was acknowledged as we shall hereafter relate. The period during which the Caliphate was in abeyance was three years and a half.

Of persons of note who died during the reign of al Mustasim were the Hafidh Takiuddin as Sharifini, the Hafidh Abul Kasim b-ul Talisan,[1] Shamsul Aimmah al Kurdi one of the most eminent of the Hanafites, the Shaykh Takiuddin bus Salah, al Alamuddin as Sakhawi, the Hafidh Muhibbuddin b-un Najjar the historian of Baghdad, Muntakhabuddin the commentator of the Mufassal *fil Naho (Detailed exposition of the science of grammar by Zamakhshari*), Ibn Yaish the grammarian, Abul Hajjaj al Aksari the devotee, Abu Ali as Shalubini the grammarian, Ibnul Baytar author of the *Jami* Mufridatil *Adwiyat wal Adhdiyat (comprehending material medica and diet),* the learned Jamaluddin b-ul Hajib the Maliki Imam, Abul Hasanbul Dabbaj the grammarian, al Kifti author of the Memoir of Grammarians, Afdhaluddin al Khunji author of the Treatise on Logic, al Ardi author of (*hiatus in the MS.*) the Hafidh Yusuf b. Khalil, al Baha b. Bintul

1 More correctly I think Taylsan.

Hamiri, al Jamal b. Omrun[1] the grammarian, ar Ridha as Saghani author of the Ubabul *Zikhir* (*the Surging Billow*) and others *works*, al Kamal *uddin* Abdul Wahid az Zamlakani author of al Maani wal bayan wa Iijazul Qurãn (*significtions and exposition and the woudrous diction of the Qurãn*), as Shams al Khusru Shahi, al Majduddin b. Taymiyah, Yusuf Sibt Ibnil Jauzi author of the Miratuz Zaman (*mirror of the age*), Ibn Batish one of the most eminent of the Shafiites, and Najmuddin al Badarai, Ibn Abil Fadhl al Mursi (*Murcia*) author of the Commentary on the Qurãn and others. A.H.659. A.D.1261.

Of those who died during the abeyance of the Caliphate were az Zaki Abdul Adhim al Mundir, the Shaykh Abul Hasan, as Shadili the Shaykh of the Shadilites, Shalat the Qurãn reader, al Fasi the commentator of the Kasidat us Shatibiyah,[2] Saaduddin b-ul Uzza the poet, as Sarsari the poet, Ibnul Abbar the historian of Spain and others.

AL MUSTANSIR BI'LLAH AHMAD

Al Mustansir billah Ahmad Abul Kasim was the son of ad Dhahir bi amrillah Abu Nasr Muhammad b. un Nasir li dinillah. Shaykh Kutbuddin says that he wa kept in imprisonment in Baghdad, but when the Tartars captured it, he was released and fled and proceeded to the west of Iraq. When Baybars assumed, the Sultanate, he set out to visit him in the month of Rajab with ten of the Banu Muharish.[3] The Sultan went forth to meet him with the Kadhis and officers of State. He rode through Cairo and subsequently certified his family descent through the Chief Kadhi

---

1 His life is given by Ibn Khall, who makes him the son of Omar son of Abu Bakr-I have not before met the name in the text with which the MS. accords.

2 Kasidat us Shatibiyah. A poem on the Qurãn readings by Ibn Firruh as Shatibi (*native of Xativa*).

3 According to Makrizi they were the Banu Mihna and to Nuwairi the Banu Khafajah. Weil, Abbas Chal, in Eg. p. 24, Vol. I.

A.H.659. A.D.1261. Tajuddin b. Bintil Aazz and he was then acknowledged Caliph. The first who swore him allegiance was the Sultan ; next the Chief Kadhi Tajuddin, then the Shaykh Izzuddin b. Abdi's Sallam and lastly the nobles according to their degrees. This occurred on the 13th[1] Rajab, (12th May 1261) and his name was impressed on the coinage and read in the Khutbah, and he received the surnamed of his brother and the people rejoiced. He rode in procession on the Friday bearing the black mantle, to the mosque in the citadel. He then mounted the pulpit and preached a discourse in which he extolled the nobility of the House of Abbas, blessed the Caliph and the Muslims and prayed before the people. Next he proceeded to the ceremony of the bestowal on the Sultan of the robe of honor usually granted by the Caliph and the diploma of investiture. A pavilion was erected without the walls of Cairo and the Caliph and the Sultan rode to the pavilion on Monday, the 4th of Shaaban, and there were present the Kadhis, nobles and the prime minister. The Caliph with his own hand invested the Sultan with the dress of honor[2] and collar. A pulpit was created and Fakhruddin b. Lukman (*the Secretary of State*) ascended it and read the diploma of investiture. Then the Sultan rode in his robe of honor and entered by the Babun Nasr (*Gate of Succour*). Cairo was gaily adorned and the High Marshal rode bearing before him the diploma while the nobles proceeded on foot.

The Sultan then appointed for the Caliph an Atabek and Comptrollers of the Household, a High Steward, a Treasurer, a Chamberlain and a Secretary and settled upon him a revenue, and a body of slaves, a hundred horses, thirty mules and ten full-grown camels and the like. Ad Dahabi says that no one ever ruled the Caliphate after his nephew save this Caliph and al Muktafi. The prince of Aleppo the Amir Shamsuddin Akush[3] set up *another* Caliph and gave him the title of al Hakim biamrillah and the khutbah

---

1 9th Rajab. Weil.

2 This consisted of a black gold embroidered turban, a violet mantle, a gold chain for the neck and golden buckles for the feet. Weil, p. 25.

3 He came of the Turkish tribe of Burli to which Baybars also belonged. Reiske writes the name Barli, Quatremere Berki, see Weil, p. 17.

was read in his name which was also stamped on the coinage. A.H.660.
Subsequently the Caliph al Mustansir set out for Iraq accompanied A.D.1261-2.
by the Sultan who followed him till they arrived at Damascus.

The Sultan then furnished the Caliph and the three sons of the lord of Mosal[1] *for the expedition against Baghdad* and assigned him and them 1,000,000, dinars in gold and 66,000 dirhams. The Caliph then set out with the eastern princes, *al Malik as Salih Ismail* lord of Mosal, *al Malik al Mudhaffar Ali,* lord of Syria, and *al Malik al Mujahid* lord of Jazirat ibn. Omar. The Aleppo Caliph al Hakim also joined him and submitted to him and entered under his obedience. He then advanced and took Hadithah and Hit. Here the Tartar army[2] encountered him and a great number of Muslims were slain and the Caliph al Mustansir was missing. According to some he was slain, which was apparently the case; according to others he escaped and fled and lay concealed in the provinces. This occurred on the 3rd Muhurram 660 (28th *November,* 1261). His Caliphate lasted less than six months and he was succeeded a year later by al Hakim, the same who was declared Caliph at Aleppe in al Mustansir's lifetime.

AL HAKIM BI'AMRILLAH ABUL ABBAS

Al Hakim bi amrillah (*Ruling by the Command of God*) Abul Abbas Ahmad, son of Abu Ali al Hasan al Kubbi, son of Abu Bakr, son of the Caliph al Mustarshid, son of al Mustadhir billah, concealed himself at the time of the capture of Baghdad and escaped *the massacre.* He soon after left I accompanied by a retinue and sought

1 Badruddin Lulu called al Malik ar Rahim. He submitted to Hulaku after the taking of Baghdad. He died according to Abulf in 657. The names of his three sons are mentioned below. Ibn Khall, says (*Life of Arslan, Shah Nuruddin*) that he had been Mamluk of al Malik al Kahir son of Arslan Shah and was lieutenant-governor of Mosal and declared himself independent in 630 (*July* 1233).

2 Under Karabogha the Tartar governor of Baghdad.

A.H.660. A.D.1261-2. *the protection of* Husayn b. Falah Emir of the Banu Khafajah and remained with him for some time. He then proceeded with the Arabs to Damascus and resided for a time with the Emir[1] Isa b. Muhanna. *Al Malik* an Nasir lord of Damascus becoming informed of him, sent to invite him but the advance of the Tartars surprised him *and disconcerted his plans.* When, however, al Malik al Mudhaffar came to Damascus he sent the Emir Kilij al Baghdadi to summon him. He then joined him and swore allegiance to him and a number of the Arab chiefs set out to take service under him. With their aid he took Aanah, Hadithah, Hit and Anbar and engaged the Tartars and overthrew them. Subsequently Alauddin Taybars at that time lieutenant-governor of Damascus for[2] al Malik ad Dhahir *Baybars* wrote-inviting him, upon which he set out for Damascus in the month of Safar, and he sent him on to the Sultan, but al Mustansir billah having preceded him to Cairo by three days, he did not think it prudent to enter it for fear of being seized. He therefore returned to Aleppo, the prince of which and the nobles, among them Abdul Halim b. Taymiyah, swore allegiance to him and he gathered a considerable force and marched to Aanah. When al Mustansir returned, he met him at Aanah and al Hakim acknowledged his authority and submitted to him. But when al Mustansir was no more, after the battle mentioned in his biography, al Hakim set out for Rahbah and visited Isa b. Muhanna. At this time al Malik ad Dhahir Baybars wrote regarding him and summoned him and he went to Cairo with his son accompanied by a retinue. Al Malik ad Dhahir received him with all honor and they

---

1 The Emir of the Arabs under the Caliphs, according to De Slane, appears to have filled the same functions as the Ghassanide princes did under the Greeks of the Lower Empire and the princes of Hira under the Persians. They were phylarchs or comptrollers of the nomadic tribes. After the defeat of the Tartars at Ain Jalut, Kotuz appointed al Malik al Ashraf Musa to Emessa, Palmyrah and Rahabah, gave the government of Hamat, Barin and Maarah to al Malik al Mansur, and Salamiyah to the Emir of the Arabs Isa b. Muhanna. Abulf, p. 596, anno, 658. Weil, p. 17.

2 The text has و which is here certainly an error. The MS. omits the و and is not more intelligible. Read ل for و and the sense is as clear as the construction would be correct. In point of fact, Taybars held Damascus for Baybars. See Abulf, p. 632.

swore him allegiance as Caliph. His reign was long for his Caliphate extended over forty years. Al Malik ad Dhahir gave him as his residence the great Bastion in the Citadel and he preached frequently in the mosque of the Citadel. The Shaykh Kutbuddin says that on Thursday the 8th Muharram of the year 661 (22nd *November* 1262), the Sultan held a public audience and al Hakim biamrillah went on horseback to the Great Hall in the Citadel on the hill and sat with the Sultan, this being after the verification of his descent, and the Sultan received him and acknowledged his authority over the Faithful. Then he advanced to the Sultan and invested him with the administration of affairs, after which the people, according to their degrees did him homage. The next day being Friday, he preached a discourse in which he made mention of the religious war and the Imamate and represented what had occurred to the dishonor of the Caliphate and he proceeded thus,-But this Sultan al Malik ad Dhahir stood up in defence of the Imamate with but few adherents and scattered the hordes of the infidels after they had penetrated into the centre of the empire." The beginning of the discourse was, "Praise be to God who hath raised up a pillar and a defender for the House of Abbas." He then wrote to the provinces announcing his call.

A.H.660.
A.D.1261-

In this year and subsequently occurred successive arrivals of bodies of Tartars who had become Muslims, demanding asylum. They were given bread and a daily allowance and this was the beginning of the stay of their misdeeds.

In the year 662 was completed the Dhahiriyah College between the two palaces and the Chair of Shafiite theology was held by at Takiuddin b. Razin and the chair of Tradition by as Sharafuddin ad Dimiati. During the same, Egypt was convulsed by a great earthquake.

In the year 663 the Muslim Sultan of Spain, Abu Abdullah b-ul Ahmar was victorious over the Franks and recovered from their hands thirty-two towns, among them Seville and Murcia. During the same, conflagrations were frequent in divers parts of Cairo and wrappers were found upon the roofs of the houses containing

A.H.663. A.D.1264. fire and sulphur. In the same, was excavated the Canal of Ashmun,[1] the Sultan himself and the nobles working at it. In the same, died Hulaku the Tartar despot who was succeeded by his son Abagha. In this year the Sultan conferred the dignity of the Sultanate on his son al Malik as Said who was four years of age, and paraded him in state through the Citadel on the hill and bore the housings himself before his son, from the Babul Sirr (*the Secret Gate*) to the Bahus Silsilah (*the Chain Gate*) and then returned. While as Said rode to Cairo, the nobles walking before him. In this year also were re-appointed for the Egyptain territory, four Kadhis, one for each school of doctrine, and this was owing to the delay of the Kadhi Tajuddin b. Bintul Aazz in giving effect to the numerous decisions, so that affairs were at a stand still. To the care of the Shafiites was assigned the administration of the property of orphans and the department of the public treasury. Subsequently the same *reform* was carried out at Damascus. In the month of Ramadhan the Sultan placed a restraint upon the Caliph and forbade his intercourse with the people, as his followers were in the habit of entering the city and talking of affairs of State.

In the year 665, the Sultan commanded the erection of a mosque at Hasaniyah[2] which was completed in 667 and a Hanafite preacher was there installed.

In the year 674 the Sultan sent an army against Nubah and Dunkulah (*Dongola*) and was victorious. The king of Nubah was taken prisoner and sent to al Malik ad Dhahir and a tribute was laid on the people of Dunkulah, praise be to God. The first expedition against Nubah, says ad Dahabi, was in the year 31 A.H. when it was attacked by Abdullah b. Abi Sarh at the head of 5000 horsemen; he did not conquer it but concluded a peace and returned. It was again invaded in the time of Hisham but unsuccessfully and again in the reign of al Mansur. Tikn[3] az Zinki next invaded it ; then Kafur al Ikshidi : then Nasirud Daulah b. Hamdan, and finally Turan

1 Connecting Iake Menzaleh with the Nile at Damietta.

2 A town to the east of Mosal between it and Jazirat-ibn Omar.

3 I am doubtful about this pronunciation.

Shah brother of Sultan Salahuddin in 568, but it was never conquered until this year. Regarding this Ibn Abdiz Dhahir says : A.H.679. A.D.1280-

"This is a victory, the like of which I have not heard
Neither *from the testimony* of an eye-witness nor from
the depositions *of others.*"

In the year 676 died al Malik ad Dhahir at Damascus in the month of Muharram, and his son al Malik as Said Muhammad assumed the sovereignty at the age of eighteen. During the same at Taki b. Razin united the offices of Kadhi of Misr (*old Cairo*) and Cairo, and before this time, the judicial office of Misr was separate from that of Cairo.

In 678 al Malik as Sai'd was deposed and was sent to al Kark as Sultan of that place, but died the same year, and they placed in authority over Egypt his brother Badruddin Salamish who was seven years of age. He was surnamed al Malik al Aadil and the Emir Sayfuddin Kilawan was appointed his Atabek, and the coinage was struck with his name on one side and the name of his Atabek on the reverse, and both were prayed for in the khutbah. In the month of Rajab, Salamish was deposed without resistance and Kilawun usurped the government under the title of al Malik al Mansur.

In the year 679 on the day of Arafah (9th *Dul Hijjah*) large hail, stones fell in the Misr district and thunderbolts. In 680 the Tartar army reached Syria occasioning consternation. The Sultan marched out to engage them and a battle took place and great carnage ensued, but the victory remained with the Muslims-praise be to God.

In the year 688 the Sultan took Tripoli by the sword (26th *April*, 1289). It had been in the hands of the Christians from the year 503 up to this time, and had been first conquered in the reign of Muawiyah. At Tajuddin Ibnul Athir wrote a letter to the governor of Yaman announcing the good news in which he says :

"Of the Caliphs and sovereigns of those days, there was none but thought only of himself, absorbed in his festivals of pleasure,

A.H.693. A.D.1294. looking upon personal safety as a great good fortune, and who when mention of war was made before him, would ask only regarding the roads of flight. His desire was attained in his dignity, and he was content with the mint and the khutbah. Though their wealth were plundered and their dominions passed away, they troubled themselves not regarding what was wrested from them, and they were such as is described in the verse-

> 'If they fought, they were slain ; if they attacked, they were rounted ;
> If they waged war, they were despoiled ; if they contended for victory, they were overcome.
> Until the Lord brought forth one who defended His faith
> And abased infidelity and its demons."

Some say that the meaning of Tripoli in the Greek tongue is 'three forts united."

In the year 689 died Sultan Kilawun in the month of Dul Kaadah, and his son al Malik al Ashraf Salahuddin Khalil assumed the sovereignty. He made manifest the authority of the Caliph which had been of no account in his father's days, so much so, that his father had never solicited of him the investiture of the Sultanate. The Caliph then preached to the people on Friday and alluded in his discourse to his having appointed al Malik al Ashraf to the supreme authority in Islam. And when he had ended his discourse, the Chief Kadhi Badruddin b. Jamaah prayed before the people. The Caliph then preached a second time, proclaiming a religious war and spoke of Baghdad and urged its re-conquest.

In the year 691, the Sultan set out and invested Kalatur Rum.[1]

In 693, the Sultan was assassinated at Tarujah[2] (12th *Muharram*, 17th *December*, 1293) and his brother Muhammad

---

1 A strong fortress to the west of the Euphrates opposite Birah, between it and Sumaysat. It was taken after an investment of 33 days : the garrison consisting of Tartars and Armenians put to death, and the name of the fortress was changed to Kalatul Muslimim. Weil p. 184.

2 A village on the west bank of the Nile between Cairo and Alexandria.

b-ul Mansur was placed upon the throne and surnamed al Malik an Nasir, being at the time seven years of age ; but he was deposed in Muharram, 694 and Kethogha al Mansuri was proclaimed Sultan and he assumed the title of al Malik al Aadil (1st *December*, 1294). In this year Kazan b. Arghun b. Abagha b. Hulaku, the Tartar monarch embraced Islam, at which the people rejoiced and the Muslim faith spread among his troops. In 696 while the Sultan was at Damascus, Lajin[1] usurped the government and the nobles swore allegiance to him, not two of them opposing him, and he was surnamed al Malik al Mansur, and this in the month of Safar. The Caliph bestowed upon him the balck dress of honour and drew out his diploma of investiture and *Lajin* desptached al Aadil to Sarkhand as its governor. Lajin was assassinated in Jumada II, 698,[2] and al Malik an Nasir Muhammad bil Mansur Kilawun who had been banished to Kark was restored and invested with supreme authority by the Caliph. He transferred al Aadil to the government of Hamat where he remained till he died in 702. In the year 701 the Caliph al Hakim died on Thursday night, 18th of Jumada I, (18th *January* 1302). The afternoon prayer was read for him at the Horse Market under the Citadel, and his bier was attended by the principal officers of State, all of them on foot and he was buried near the tomb of as Sayyidah Nafisa.[3] He was the first of the Caliphs there interred,

A.H.693.
A.D.1294.

1 Husamuddin Lajin originally a Mamluk of Sultan al Malik al Mansur son of the first Mameluke Sultan Muizzuddin Aybak. He was purchased by Kilawun under whom he quickly rose to be governor of Syria. The vicissitude of these ephemeral reigns may be read in Weil's Gesch. des Abbas, Caliph in Eg.

2 According to Abulf, 11th Rabii II, (16th *January* 1299). So also Weil, on Makrizi's authority.

3 She was the daughter of al Hasan b. Zayd b. Hasan b. Ali Abi Talib. Her father was governor of Medina in the time of al Mansur, by whom he was imprisoned. Al Mahdi restored him to liberty and returned him the goods that had been confiscated from him. Nafisa was noted for her piety. When as Shafii died, his corpse was brought to her house, the site of which is now occupied by her mausoleum between old and New Cairo. The place was called the Derb us Sabaa, but the street fell into ruin and nothing remained in the time of Ibn Khall, save her funeral chapel and her tomb. Her husband was the son of Jaafar as Sadik. She died in 208, (824). Consult Ibn Khall and Abul Mahasin : annales.

A.H.701. A.D.1302. but it continued henceforward to be their place of burial. He had covenanted for the succession of the Caliphate to his son Abur Rabii Sulayman.

Of persons of note who died during the reign of al Hakim were: As Shaykh Izzuddin b. Abdis Sallam, al Alamuddin al Luraki, Abul Kasim al Kabbari the ascetic, az Zaynuddin Khalid an Nabulusi the Hafidh Abu Bakr b. Suddi, the Imam Abu Shamah, at Tajuddin b. Bintil Aazz, Abu Hasan b. Adhan, Majduddin b. Dakikul Iid,[1] Abul Hasan, b. Usfur the grammarian, al Kamaluddin Sallar al Irbili, Abdur Rahim b. Yunas author of the Tajiz *fi Mukhtazaril Wajiz, (Infestation, an epitome of the Wajiz, on the derivative doctrine of as Shafii),* al Kurtubi *Shamsuddin Mahmud* author of the Commentary on the Qurãn and the Tadkirat bi ahwalul Mauta wa Umurul Akhirat (*Note on the condition of the dead and what concerns the life to come),* the Shaykh Jamaluddin b. Malik, and his son Badruddin, an Nasir at Tusi chief of the philosophers, Khassah the Tartar at Tajuddin bis Subaai, treasurer of the Mustansiriyah College, al Burhan b. Jamaah an Najmuddin al Katibial Mantaki, the Shaykh Muhyiddin an Nawawi, as Sadruddin Sulayman the Hanafite Imam, at Tajuddin b. Muyassir the historian, al Kawashi the Commentator, at Takiuddin b. Razin, Ibn Khallakan author of the Wafaytul Aiyan (*deaths of eminent men*), Ibn Ayaz the grammarian, Abdul Halim b. Taymiyah, Ibn Juwan, Nasiruddin b. Munir, an Najm b-ul Barizi, al Burhan an Nasafi author of the compositions on Controversy and Rhetoric, ar Ridha as Shatibi the philologist, al Jamal as Sharishi,[2] an Nafisi, the Shaykh of the physicians, Abul Husayn bir Rabii the grammarian, al Ispahani *Shamsuddin Muhammad* the Commentator on the Mahsul *fi usulil Fikh (Summa on the principles of jurisprudence by Fakhruddin ar Razi*), al Afif at Tilmisani the poet imputed heterodox, at Taj b-ul Firkah, az Zaynuddin b. Murhil as Shams al Juni, al Izzal Faruki al Muhibb at Tabari, at Taki b. Bintul Aazz, ar Ridha al Kustantini, al Bahauddin b-un Nahhas the grammarian, Yakuq al Mustasimi, master of the Khatti Mansub[3] and others.

1 Reiske writes the name "Aid" but it is not easy to digest his pronunciation.

2 Not Sharbashi as in the text.

3 See page 2, note. 2.

AL MUSTAKFI BI'LLAH ABUR RABII

A.H.704.
A.D.1304.

Al Mustakfi billah Abur Rabii Sulayman son of al Hakim biamrillah was born about the middle of Muharram, 684. He occupied himself little *about affairs*. He succeeded to the Caliphate according o the covenant of his father in Jumada I, 701. His name was read in the Khutbah in the chief towns of Egypt and Syria and the welcome news thereof penetrated to all the dependencies and dominions of Islam. The Caliphs used to reside at Kabsh but the Sultan transferred them to the citadel and set apart a palace for them. In the year 702 the Tartars invaded Syria and the Sultan accompanied by the Caliph marched to engage them. They were victorious and made a great slaughter among the Tartars and the rest fled. During the same Egypt and Syria were convulsed by a great earthquake and many lost their lives in the destruction *caused by it.*

In the year 704 the Emir Baybars[1] al Jashangir al Mansuri, established stipends and lectures for the mosque of al Hakim and rebuilt it after its demolition by the earthquake, and he made the four Kadhis professors of jurisprudence. The lecturer on tradition was Saaduddin al Harithi, and on grammar Abu Hayyan.

In the year 708, the Sultan al Malik an Nasir Muhammad b. Kilawun set out with the intention of making the pilgrimage to Mecca.[2] He therefore left Cairo in the month of Ramadhan (24th) the venerable (7th *March* 1309) and a number of the nobles accompanied him to take leave of him whom he sent back. On passing Kark he turned aside towards it and a bridge was erected for him. As he reached the middle of it, it broke. Those who were in front of him escaped. His horse leaped with him and he was saved but those who wee behind to the number of fifty, fell, and four were killed. The greater number were *only bruised by their*

---

1 Comptoller of the Household to the Sultan and afterward raised to the throne under the title of al Malik al Mudhaffar.

2 This was but an excuse to escape from the control of his minister Sayfuddin Sallar and that of Baybars. Weil, p. 276, Abulf, 208.

A.H.704. A.D.1304. *fall* in the moat beneath. The Sultan remained at Kark. Subsequently he wrote a letter to the Egyptian provinces containing his abdication. This was verified by the Kadhis of Egypt and then dispatched to the Kadhis of Syria, and the Emir Ruknuddin Baybars al Jashangir was acknowledged Sultan on the 23rd Shawwal (5th *April* 1309) and surnamed al Malik al Mudhaffar. The Caliph invested him ad clothed him in the black mantle and circular turban, and the diploma of investiture was sent to Syria in a black satin bag and there published. It bore heading that it was from Sulayman, and, in the name of God the most Clement, the most Merciful.

In the month of Rajab 709 al Malik an Nasir returned, desirous of recovering his power. A number of the nobles favoured his undertaking and he entered Damascus in Shaabah and afterwards Cairo on the festival of al Fitr and went up into the citadel. Al Mudhaffar Baybars had already fled with some of his followers some days before his arrival, but he was subsequently captured and put to death in the same year. Al Ala al Widaai says regarding the return of an Nasir to power—

"Verily the fortune of al Malik an Nasir
Hath basked in the sunshine.
He hath returned to the throne,
As Solomon returned into his."

During this year the Wazir recommended that the non-Muslim subjects should return to the wearing of white turbans as they were subjected to a payment to the revenue of 700,000 dinars yearly, over and above the poll tax, but the Shaykh Takiuddin b. Taymiyah[1] rose up in strenuous opposition and it was rejected-praise be to

---

1 He persecuted the Christians with relentless hatred, perhaps in revenge for his own persecution by his co-religionists. Abulf, states that he was summoned from Damascus to Cairo in 705 and imprisoned for his unorthodox opinions in maintaining the corporeal form of the Godhead-a doctrine imputed to Ibn Hanbal. He was the author of a work entitled Masalat fil Kanais (*The question of the Churches*) in which he asserts the right of the Muslims to demolish all Christian Churches and that they were justified in closing them in Cairo. See D'Herb., p. 576.

God. During the same, the Tartar monarch Khuband,[1] spread heresy throughout his dominions and commanded the preachers to mention no one in the Khutbah but Ali b. Abi Talib and his two sons and the family of the Prophet, and this continued until his death in the year 716. His son Abu Sai'd succeeded him who reigned with justice and established the orthodox faith and the approval of *the rightful succession of the* two Shaykhs (*Abu Bakr and Omar*) followed by Othman and Ali in the Khutbah, and many discords were thus appeased, praise be to God. He was one of the best of the Tartar monarchs and the most praiseworthy in his conduct. He continued *to reign* till he died in the year 786, and after this there was no union in the nation and they were scattered far and wide. In the year 717 the Nile rose to a great height such as was before unheard of and many towns were submerged by it and a great number of people. In the year 724 the Nile rose similarly and remained covering the earth for three months and a half, and the damage caused by if was greater than its benefits. In the year 728 were repaired the roofs of the Holy mosque at Mecca, and the gates and such of the outer portion as is contiguous to the gate of the Banu Shaybah.[2] In 730 the Friday prayers were held in the hall of the Shafiites in the Salihiyah College between the two palaces and this was the first time they were held there. During the same the mosque begun by *the Emir* Kausun[3] outside the Zuwaylah Gate was completed and the khutbah preached therein in the presence of the Sultan and the nobles and the Chief Kadhi Jalaluddin al Kazwini preached the discourse on that day. Fakruddin b. Shukar was subsequently confirmed in the post.

A.H.709.
A.D.1309.

In the year 733 the Sultan prohibited shooting with bullets and *ordered* that the crossbows for it should not be sold, and forbade astrologers *to practice their profession.* During the same the Sultan caused to be made for the kaabah a door of ebony covered

---

1 Abulf, Kharbanda (خربندا).

2 Now called the Babus Salam. Burtom III, p. 178.

3 He married the daughter of Sultan an Nasir Muhammad and became prime minister and virtually the ruler of the kingdom under the nominal sovereignty of al Malik al Ashraf Alâuddin Kujuk.

A.H.733. A.D.1332. with silver plates the weight whereof was 35,300 *dirhams*[1] and a fraction. He had the old taken up and the Banu Shaybah took possession of it with its plates. It bore upon it the name of the governor of Yaman.

In the year 736, a misunderstanding occurred between the Caliph and the Sultan, and the later arrested the Caliph and imprisoned him in a tower and forbade him intercourse with the people. Subsequently he banished him to Kus[2] in the month of Dul Hijjah, him and his children and household and allowed them what was sufficient for their maintenance, they being about one hundred souls-for we belong to God and unto him do we return. Al Mustakfi remained at Kus till he died there in Shaaban in the year 740, (5th *February* 1340) and was there buried, being upwards of fifty years of age.

Ibn Hajral Askalani in his Durarul Kaminah[3] (*Hidden Pearls*) says that he was accomplished, and generous, wrote an extremely fine hand, was brave, skilled at polo and at shooting with bullets. He conversed with learned and literary men and was munificent to them and affected their society. During the whole of his reign, he was prayed for upon the pulpits in the khutbah, even during his incarceration and the period of his residence at Kus. There was considerable goodwill at first between him and the Sultan, for he used to accompany the Sultan to the fields and play at ball with him, and they were like brothers. The reason of the misunderstanding between them was that a plaint was taken to him in which was the handwriting of the Caliph to the effect that the Sultan should attend the session of the holy law,[4] at which the Sultan was angry and the

---

1 The weight is omitted in the Text and MS. it may possibly be ounces.

2 In Upper Egypt.

3 Durar ul Kaminah fi Aiyan il miat it Thaminah (*Hidden Pearls or Wrothies of the 8th Century*) a work alphabetically arranged in one large volume-which the author completed in 830 (1426). A compendium of it was written by As Suyuti and al Mubarrad – Ibn Hajr died in 852, (1448). Haj. Khall.

4 According to Weil the Sultan learnt that the Caliph was frequently visited by a Mamluk and a jurisconsult, and fearing a conspiracy he arrested the Caliph, imprisoned the Mamluk and beat the other to death.

affair come to this pass that he banished him to Kus and appointed for him a continuance of his favours greater than he had enjoyed at Cairo. A.H.733. A.D.1332.

Ibn Fadhillah in his biography from the Masalik ul Absar says that he was hold in action, and gentle in speech.

Of persons of note who died during the reign of al Mustakfi were the chief Kadhi Takiuddin b. Dakikul lid, the Shaykh Zaynuddin al Fariki the Shafiite Shaykh, and the head of the school of tradition over which he presided from the death of an Nawawi up to this time, Sadruddin b-ul Wakil presiding over it after him, as Sharf al Fazari, as Sadr b-uz Zarir bil Hasib, the Hafidh Sharfuddin ad Dimiati, ad Dhiya[1] at Tusi, Commentator on the Hawi al Saghir (*the Lesser Collector on the derivative principles of Shafiite jurisprudence by Kazwini*) as Shams as Saruji of the Hanafite School, Commentator of the Hidayah *fil* Furuu (*Guide to the derivative principle of Hanafite jurisprudence by Burhanuddin Ali al Marghinani*), the Imam Najmuddin bir Rifaah the Shafiite Imam of his time, the Hafidh Saaduddin al Harithi, al Fakhr an Nuri the Traditionist of Mecca, ar Rashid b-ul Muallim one of the most eminent of the Hanafites, as Sadr b-ul Wakil the Shafiite Shaykh, al Kamal b-ul Sharishi, at Taj at Tabrizi, al Fakhr b Bint. Abi Saad, as Shams b. Abil Izz the hanafite Shaykh, ar Ridha at Tabari the Imam of Mecca, as Safi Abut Thana, Mahmud al Urmawi, the Shaykh Nuruddin al Bakri, al Ala b-ul Attar the disciple of the Imam an Nawawi, as Shams al Ispahani author of the Commentary on the Qurãn and the Commentary on the Mukhtasar (*Epitome*) of Ibnul Hajib and the Commentary on the Tajridul *Kalam (Exposition of Metaphysics by Nasiruddin Abu Jaafar at Tusi,*) and the like, at Taki the goldsmith the Qurãn reader, the last of the Qurãn reading Shaykhs, as Shihab Mahmud the professor of the Art of Composition, al Jamal b. Mutahhar the Shiite Shaykh, al Kamal b. Kadhi, Shuhbah,

---

1 The word din must be understood after all these titles. Dhiyauddin, Light of religion. Shamsuddin, Sun of religion, &c.

A.H.740. A.D.1349. an Najm al Kumuli[1] author of the Jowahirul Bahr (*Pearls of the Sea an epitome of his Bakrul Muhit*), al Kamal b-ul Zamlakani the Shaykh Takiuddin b. Taymiyah, Ibn Jibarah the Shatibite Shaykh, an Najm al Balisi, Commentator on the Tanbih *fi Furuu us Shafiiyah (The Summons, on the derivative principles of Shafiite jurisprudence by Abu Ishak Ibrahim as Shirazi),* al Burhan al Fazari the Shafiite Shaykh, al Ala al Kunuwi Commentator on the Hawi *ul Saghir,* al Fakhr al Turkomani of the Hanafite School, Commentator of the Jami Kabir *of as Shaybani,* al Malik al Muwayyad lord of Hamat author of several works, among them the metrical version of the Hawi, the Shaykh Yakut al Arshi disciple of the Shaykh Abul Abbas al Mursi, al Burhan al Jabari, al Badr b. Jamaah, at Taj b. Fakahani, al Fath b. Sayyidin Nas, al Kutb al Halabi, az Zayn al Kinani the Kadhi Muhyiddin b. Fadhlillah, ar Rukn b-ul Kawai,[2] az Zayn b. Murhil, as Sharaf b-ul Barizi al Jalal al Kazwini and others.

AL WATHIK BI'LLAH IBRAHIM

Al Wathik billah Ibrahim was the son of the heir to the Caliphate al Mustamsik billah Abu Abdullah Muhammad son of al Hakim biamrillah Abu Abbas Ahmad. His grandfather al Hakim had covenanted for the succession for his son Muhammad and gave him the title of al Mustamsik billah, but be died during his lifetime, whereupon he took the covenant for al Mustamsik's son, this Ibrahim, believing him to be worthy of the Caliphate, but the *afterwards* discovered him to be unfit for it, through his pursuit of pleasure and his association with low company. He therefore turned from him and named his own son-that is, the son of al Hakim-al

1 Haj. Khall. Writes this word قملي -and pronounces it Kamali. The town Kumulah (قمولة) is in Upper Egypt to the west of the Nile. The text and MS. give the title of the work Jawahir *Wa'l* Babr which is inexact.

2 MS. كويع (Kawbah).

Mustakfi, the uncle of Ibrahim. It was Ibrahim who was the cause of the misunderstanding between the Caliph al Mustakfi and the Sultan after they had been like brothers, by his having carried to him a slanderous tale regarding him, after which happened what followed. A.H.740. A.D.1340.

Thus it came to pass that when al Mustakfi died at Kus, he named his own son Ahmad for the succession but the Sultan disregarded this and acknowledged[1] this Ibrahim who was surnamed al Wathik until when the Sultan was at the point of death he repented of what he had done, and deposed this Ibrahim, and acknowledged the heir Ahmad who received the surname of al Hakim. This took place on the 1st[2] of Muharram 742. Ibn Hajr says that the people petitioned the Sultan regarding Ibrahim and described his evil life, but he paid no heed to this and desisted not until the people acknowledged him. The populace nicknamed him al Mustata billah.[3]

Ibn Fadhlillah in the Masalik in the biographical notice of al Wathik says : "His grandfather named him for the succession, believing him to be virtuous and that he would respond loudly to him who called him to the Caliphate-but he grew up in dishonour, and inclined to nought, but the neglect of piety. He was led astray by sensualities, and did what he was not induced to do by his necessities. He associated with the mean and the base, His extravagance brought his reputation low-the evil of his conduct was disguised to him so that he thought it good-he was so blinded as to think praiseworthy what was wicked. Pigeon-flying and the

---

1 According to some authorities on the 6th, according to others the 14th Dul Kaadah. Weil, p. 406.

2 This must be the date of his assuming the surname, for the Sultan died 9 days earlier, *viz.*, the 21st Dul Hijjah, 741 which is given by as Suyuti as the date on which al Hakim was acknowledged. See his life, later.

3 "Begging of the Lord." He received this nickname on account of the small stipend granted him- Makrizi places the allowance of al Hakim biamrillah at 3550 dirhams a month and 19 Ardabbas of wheat and 10 of barley. Weil, p. 406.

A.H.740. A.D.1340. purchase of rams for butting, and fighting-cocks seduced him-and his emulation in *possession* fine-haired goats with long ears and the like of such things that degrade manliness and impair dignity[1] this *all led him* into evil dealings, and purchasing goods not worth their price, and renting houses the hire of which he could not defray, and scheming for money wherewith to fill his hands, and abominations wherewith to fill his mouth, and things forbidden of which he eat and caused his family to partake, so that he became a mark for contempt and a prey to men o his time. And when al Mustafi died at a time when the Sultan was in the height of his anger against him, and of his wrath which pressed upon him by reason of its excessive vehemence, he sent for this al Wathik the improvident, the witless, (save that he was not thereto compelled,- and he was one of those who had secretly defamed his uncle to the Sultan, and had fastened treacherous machinations round his brow like the binding of an amulet) and he presented himself before the Sultan and brought with him the covenant of his grandfather. The Sultan therefore undertook the covenant of allegiance to him notwithstanding its ambiguity and turned towards him the face of the Caliphate. And indeed the cancelling of this covenant and the annulling of this compact had already taken place. Then the Chief Kadhi Abu Omar b. Jamaah sought to turn the mind of the Sultan from introducing the name of al Wathik in the khutbah, but he would not do so. Au agreement at length was effected by omitting both claimants from the khutbah and being content therein with the name of the Sultan alone-so he went his way. Thus on the death of al Mustakfi the name of the Caliphate passed from the pulpits as if it had never risen over their summit, and the prayer for the Caliphs vacated the vaulted recesses of the mosques as if it had never

---

1 The MS has هدى for هذا of the printed edition, which is, I think, inadmissible in the sense of guiding to evil. The grammatical construction any way appears faulty.

reverberated at their gates or their flinty stones (Marwah[1]) It was as though he were the last of the Caliphs of the House of Abbas and its symbols upon him were as garments of mourning, and were sheathed those swords of steel. This state of things continued until the Sultan was near his end, and death had knocked at his rock (Safa[1]). Among his last injunctions was the restoration of authority to those to whom it belonged, and the carrying out of the covenant of al Mustakfi in favour of his son, and he said, "how hath the truth become manifest" (Qur. XII). And he was moved towards those who were remaining behind him and felt compassion, and Ibrahim was deposed[2] and grew lean-for verily he had fed as flock feed and covered his dishonour with the raiment of men of worth, till he grew fat and his body became swollen and he assumed the surname of al Wathik (*Firm in God),* and what was he to be the bearer of such a name, the fear of which had long penetrated into the hearts of men and the dread of it stretched to bursting, the places where the sides lie in sleep?[3] Go to ! The eagles are not counted as their painted effigies, nor is the gnat, however long its proboscis, like an elephant ; but verily the march of time brings to currency what is worthless and the cat by puffing itself out simulates the lion. Now verily he hath returned to the biting of his own hands and he who is despicable falls easily under contempt." This is the end of Ibn Fadhillah's words.

A.H.740.
A.D.1340.

---

1 Safa and Marwah are two small hills near Mecca, between which the Sai or Course of the Umrah or Lesser Pilgrimage is made. One of the gates of the Prophet's mosque is termed the Safa gate. The word signifies a rock or smooth stones. Marwah means a hard white flints. It is a small line in the lower slope of the Abu Kubays. Prayers are recited from these mounts by the pilgrims during the Sai; see Burton, p. 344-*et seq.*

2 I prefer taking this verb in the passive and would amend the pointing of the text.

3 امنت هيبته العيوب MS.

A.H.740.
A.D.1340.

AL HAKIM BI'AMRILLAH ABUL ABBAS

Al Hakim bi amrillah Abul Abbas Ahmad was the son of al Mustakfi. His father when he died at Kus covenanted for his succession to the Caliphate but al Malik an Nasir preferred to him his cousin Ibrahim on account of his personal feeling against al Mustakfi. Now the character of Ibrahim was depraved and the Chief Kadhi Izzuddin b, Jamaah exerted himself to the utmost to turn the Sultan from *appointing* him, but he would not yield. At length when he was at the point of death, he commended to the Emirs the restoration of the authority to the heir of al Mustakfi-his son Ahmad, therefore when al Mansur Abu Bakr the son of an Nasir assumed the supreme power, he convened an assembly on the 21st Dul Hijjah 741 (7th *June* 1341), and summoned the Caliph Ibrahim and their Ahmad and the Kadhis and said, "Who by law is entitled to the Caliphate ?" Ibn Jamaah replied, "Verily the Caliph al Mustakfi who died in the city of Kus bequeathed the Caliphate after him to his son Ahmad and had it attested by forty witnesses in the city or Kus, and this was proved before me after its confirmation before my deputy in the city of Kus." The Caliph therefore deposed Ibrahim, and swore allegiance to Ahmad and he was surnamed al Hakim biamrillah after the title of his grandfather.

Ibn Fadhillah says in his biography in the Masalik. "He was the Imam of our age and the white cloud of our land of Egypt. He arose in wrath against hi enemies and submerged *his well wishers* with the overflow of his munificence : through him affairs attained to their proper issue, and their intelligent apprehension was referred to him. He revived the usages of the Caliphate, and enjoined what was not in the power of any to disobey. He trod the ways of his ancestors that had been obliterated, and restored them by the glad aspects of his children, for verily they had been effaced. And he gathered together the sons of his father who had been long scattered; and he extended *his* assistance to them for fortune had been adverse, and he elevated his name upon the summits of the pulpits and verily a long time had elapsed and no such stars had arisen

except in his firmament, and no such mists and streaming raid had A.H.741.
gone forth save from his clouds. He was summoned after the death A.D.1341.
of the Sultan, and his authority and renown travelled abroad in universal allegiance and imperative submission. His father had appointed him by a prior covenant and committed its deposit unto men of trust. Subsequently al Malik al Mansur Abu Bakr the son of the *Late* Sultan succeeded to power, and residences were assigned to him under the authority of the monarch."

Ibn Fadhillah continues, "verily I drew up for him the form of the covenant of allegiance which was as follows :

"In the name of God the most merciful, 'Verily they who swear fealty unto thee, swear fealty unto God' (Qur. XLVIII) &c. as far as His word 'great'.[1] This is a covenant of acceptance and a covenant of benefit and a voluntary agreement to which the congregation of the faithful testify and testifies to it the Most Merciful-a covenant the conditions of which are obligatory on the necks of men,[2] and which circles in its fullness and the entirety of its import, deserts and seas covered with highways-a covenant by which way God improve the condition of the people, and through its means grant them prosperity, and thus mutual harmony be promoted and gladness pass through the land, till the stars of the constellations press thronging upon the multitudinous commingling of the Galaxy. A covenant fortunate and of happy augury, glorious, comprising within it security both in spiritual and temporal matters; a covenant jut and lawful, to be observed and guarded ; a covenant to which all desires vie in attaining, and all hearts strive to gain, and upon which the scattered nations are agreed. A covenant over which the clouds pour their plenteous rain and the full moon is resplendent.

---

1 "The rest of the verse is : 'The hand of God is over their hands. Whoever shall violate his oath, will violate it to the hurt of his own soul, but whoever shall perform that which he hath covenanted with God, He will surely give him a reward that is great."

2 This sentence is slightly modified from the following in the Qurãn XVII, كال انسان الزمنه طيره في عنقه The fate or actions of every man have we bound about his neck.

A.H.741. A.D.1341. A covenant consented to by the church and the concourse of the faithful, and to stretch their hands towards which the church hath assembled. They therefore who hear God and obey, have acknowledged its legality and every man had done his utmost towards its fulfillment. It hath obtained the consent of eyes and ears, and by its means Truth hath reached him who meriteth it, which the adversary hath acknowledged and *thus* dissension hath ceased. It is contained in 'a book distinctly written : those who approach near unto God are witnesses thereto.' (Qur. LXXXIII) and the most approximate *unto God* of the Imams accept it. Praise be to God who hath rightly guided us unto this, for we should not have been so directed, were it not that the Lord led us thereto on account of His mercy upon us and upon the people.

And praise be to God, there have agreed upon this covenant unto us and unto the House of Abbas, those who bind and loose, and the doctors of theological law in what relateth both unto matters of small and of great moment, the rulers in authority and governors, and those in places of dignity and power, the bearers of knowledge and of standards, the guardians of the sword and the pen, the chiefs of the sons of Abd Manaf, the low in dignity and the high, the chiefs of the Kuraysh, the rulers of the sons of Hashim and the stainless remnant of the House of Abbas, the chosen among the Imams and the commonalty. A covenant, the pavilions of which are seen in the two Sacred Cities and whose standards float over the two Straits.[1] Its blessings are known at Arafat and confessed at Mina, and acknowledged on the day[2] of the Great Pilgrimage. It is sough between the *Yamani* Corner[3] and Abraham's station *of*

---

1 Mazimayn." One between Mecca and Mina ; the other between Muzdalif and Mount Arafat.

2 When the day of Arafat (9th *Dul Hijjah*) falls on a Friday. See Burton, p. 226, III.

3 The Ruknul Yamani is the corner of the Kaabah facing south-where there is a stone called Mustajabud Dua "where prayer is granted" which pilgrims touch and ask pardon for their sins. The place of Abraham is a building south of the Kaabah said to contain the stone upon which Abraham stood when he built the Kaabah and which is believed to preserve the impression of his foot-but no pilgrim sees it as the frame holding it is (Cont.)

prayer and the *Black* Stone, and nought is desired through it save the glory of God. A covenant, the bond of which shall not be loosed not its obligation rejected, compulsory and absolute, continuous[1] and everlasting complete and universal, comprehensive and perfect, just and clear, ardours and yet rest giving. A.H.741. A.D.1341.

And there is none distinguished in science or judicial decision, nor one to whom men turn for bounty or the ordering of decrees, nor the Imam of a mosque nor a preacher, nor one of authority in judgment who is consulted and who answereth, nor those who fill the mosques, and none whom their vaulted recesses gather together; nor one who laboureth in the solution of a point and faileth or hitteth it, nor a narrator of tradition nor a discourser on the ancient and the modern, nor one known for piety and virtue, nor the horsemen of was and strife, nor one who killeth with an arrow, pierceth with a spear, or striketh with a sword, nor who moveth on foot, or flieth on wings, mixeth with the people of sitteth in retirement, nor a concourse great or small, nor one the hoisting of whose stardard riseth to Orion, nor whose contention in glory soareth above the stars of the Lesser Bear, nor the dweller in the desert or cultivated land, nor one who abideth, nor one who departeth, nor the first nor the last, nor who concealeth within, nor who divulgeth without, nor Arab nor barbarian, nor a pastor of camels or of sheep, nor one who is sedate, nor he who is hasty, nor the dweller in an abode in town or desert, nor the lord of columns, or of a wall, nor one who plungeth into stormy seas, deserts and barren wastes, nor one who betaketh himself frequently to the backs of steeds nor who letteth his skirt trail in the dust, nor one upon whom the sun of day shineth and the stars of night, nor whom the sky covereth and the earth beareth up, and none whose names in their diversities distinguish, and who are raised in station, one above, another but he hath put his truth in this covenant, and hath assented to it and is secure by reason thereof, for God hath been gracious to him and guided him unto it and hath

---

(Cont.672) always covered with red brocade. Burton's finances did not allow of his paying 5 dollars to enter the Makam Ibrahim and no European has ever entered it. See Vol. III, p. 177.

1 For دايبة read as in the MS دائبة.

A.H.741. acknowledged and attested it and cast down his eyes and dropped
A.D.1341. them abashed before it and extended his hands towards it in homage and his belief in submission, and acquiesced in it and approved it and gathered its commands upon himself and executed them, and entered under its obedience an acted according to its requirements. And justice hath been done among them in truth, and men say- Praise be to God, Lord of the genii and of mankind.

Now verily when the Lord made choice of His servant Sulayman Abur Rabii the Imam al Mustakfi billah prince of the Faithful, the Lord received him with honour and gave him in exchange for the Abode of Peace (*Baghdad*) the mansion of Salvation, and transferred him with cleansed hand from testifying to the orthodox religion, to the vision of perfect peace, where He made him near unto Him and confirmed him at His side and preferred him on account of what he had sent before him of his desired works and fruits, and chose for him a company to be nigh him, and placed him "with those unto when God hath been gracious of the prophets and the sincere, and the martyrs and the righteous; and these are the most excellent company" (Qur. IV). Great God for a day such as his! And were he to have no successor, "the earth would become too straight notwithstanding it is spacious" (Qur. IX). Every man shall be rewarded according to what he hath carned, and to every heart shall it be announced what it hath hoarded and gathered, for verily a flame hath been kindled, though it is within the ribs of the breast, and verily pulpit and throne will be in danger if there be not a virtuous successor to him, and of a truth, the governed and he who governs will be thrown into perplexity if thought doth not forecast the issue of affairs. And now there remaineth not of the family of Abbas, nor in the House of al Mustarshid, nor in any other of the pontifical Houses, of the remnants of their sires and grandsires, and not one whom the latter times hath brought forth, for they are barren and without progeny, and to whom the people of Muhammad may confide the bond of their designs and the secret of their purposes save one, and where is this one ? By Allah ! it is he who comprehendeth within himself the claims to the heritage of his stainless sires, the inheritance of his ancestors, and he is none other than one who hath wrapped about him the mantle of night and day, the heir of one who hath been borne to his Lord, the son of the Imam proceeding from his loins, one whom all agree to be in these days, the wonder of mankind, the Incomparable, and thus the great exemplar in creation : and verily he is excellent in dignity, since are looped upon him the garments of the East and the West, who hath the mastery of the empire between the rising and the setting sun, who ascendeth to the level of the sky of this sublime eminence, the sole remnant of Imams that have departed, a most excellent Caliph, in whom are centred the conditions of the Caliphate, conducting himself virtuously for the sake of God. while he is the heir of a House which shall retain the sovereignty till the day of doom, whose munificence puts the clouds to shame, whom his rival cannot withstand, nor his censurer deceive, who mounteth not the floor of a pulpit in the presence of the Sultan of his time, but he proclaimeth it to be by his order and riseth as there placed by him, who sitteth not upon the throne of the Caliphate but the Sultan knoweth that his Mustakfi[1] was not disappointed and his Hakim is not absent, the vicegerent of the Lord upon the earth and the successor of His apostle, his lieutenant and his descendant, the follower of his virtuous deeds and the heir to his knowledge, our lord and master, the servant of God and His friend, Abul Abbas the Imam al Hakin biamrillah prince of the Faithful, may God strengthen the faith by his abiding, and make of his sword a collar for *the necks of* the impious, and humble transgressors, beneath his standards, and grant him assistance until the Day of Requital, and by his warring for the faith throw prostrate upon their faces[2] the troops of the rebellious, and make the earth seek his protection from those who follow not religion, and cause to return through his justice the days of his ancestors the orthodox Caliphs and the rightly guided Imams, who judged with truth and by it were equitable, and acted in accordance with it,-and aid his allies, and ordain his power, and establish in all hearts the awe of his presence, and his majesty, A.H.741. A.D.1341.

1 These names of course include plays upon their meanings, which may be substituted for them.

2 Lit. "chins."

A.H.741. A.D.1341. and confirm him in life, and gather unto him his dominions. Wherefor when that prince passed to his Lord and beheld those who had gone before him, and was borne to the throne of Paradise from the chair of the Caliphate, and the age was without an Imam who might take up what remained of his *lustrous* day, and a Caliph who might overcome the increase of might by his splendours, and a successor of the Prophet like unto him and to his fathers, (for the world, after the death of his ancestor, the seal of the Prophets, needed no other Prophet to follow his footsteps, and he departed and left no successor, and nothing remained, since no text of the Qurãn was found apposite to such an emergency but the assembly of the Faithful, and upon it rested the election to the Caliphate after the Apostle of God without dispute),-the public welfare demanded the gathering of an assembly firmly knit together on every side, and the bond of a covenant testified to by God and the angels, and the people gathered to it and "that was a day whereon all men *were* assembled and a day whereon witness *was* borne," (Qur. XI).

But there was present *thereat* one that heeded not who should succeed to the Caliphate after him, and did not consider who covenanted with him and had stretched out his hand covetously for more beside it and had dissembled. But the people were unanimous in their voice it and had dissembled. But the people were unanimous it, and an oath was taken , strengthened by religious conviction and fortified by oaths, and compacts were made upon it and their faithful keeping proposed to all parties, so that every one present place the collar of this charge upon his neck, and laid his hand upon the holy book and swore by the Lord and perfected his assent.

And none discarded it or made a reservation regarding it nor hesitated ; and he who rejected it thoughtlessly, returned and renewed it. Verily every man who swore, purposed that the intention of his oath was the intention of one whom this allegiance bound, and the intention of one who pledged it his oath, and took upon himself the obligation of fidelity to it, by his responsibility and guarantee as is the custom in the oath of fealty, and to its reiterated conditions and commands and its binding asseverations, that he would render obedience to this Imam to whom obedience is obligatory and would not separate himself from the commonwealth, nor appeal from the council of the Faithful to *another* assembly,[1] and the like which are contained in the records of oaths in which are written the names of those who swear, set down in the writing of those who can write among them and the signatures of trustworthy witnesses for those who cannot write and who allow them to sign for them, according as they testify to it one for the other and the dwellers on earth and in heaven acting in concert therein. A covenant, the accomplishment of which hath been perfected by the will of God, and whose clouds are surcharged with abundant rain, and the people, cried, out, praise be to God who hath caused sorrow to depart from us, and hath given us good. And praise unto God who sufficeth His servant, and is abounding unto him who joineth His praise to His every gift. Again praise unto God for a blessing, the increase of which the prince of the Faithful desireth, and cautiously feareth, unless he combat the enemies of the Lord by its assistance, and by it discipline those who ascend the pulpits in his dominions throughout what interveneth between the divergence of their opposite extremes. We praise him and praise be to God and again praise unto God, a sentence which one wearieth not in repeating, and which doth not so descend that arrows can surpass the just directness of its course, and which cannot be discontinued save after observance of what compelleth the frequency of its repetitions, increase of dignity to those that love it, and the diminution of irreverence not of affection to what resembleth it. A.H.741. A.D.1341.

And we testify that there is no God but one, who hath no copartner, a confession of which the replenishing of its ink-flow resembles the blood drops of the martyrs, and the *dark* locks of youths and shining clouds contend for its favour, whose broidered

---

1 I am not sure that the reduplication of الجماعة is not a copyist's error, though the text and MS. are in accord. If it be so, the translation would run "nor quit the congregation."

A.H.741. letters are like unto that which the House of Abbas weareth of its
A.D.1341. symbols, the nights of their covering, and enemies of their mourning vesture. And we testify that Muhammad is His servant and His apostle, upon whom be the blessing of God, and upon the congregation of his family and those who succeed him of his posterity and who have gone before him of his ancestors. And may the Lord be well pleased with his companions and those that immediately followed them, and be merciful unto them till the Day of Requital.

Now since the Lord hath granted to the prince of the Faithful what had belonged to his grandsire, of the prophetical heritage, and bestowed upon him of the sovereignty of Solomon what is not meet for any one after him, and taught him the language of birds, in what is borne to him of remarkable events, by carrier pigeons, and subjected to him couriers upon the backs of steeds, as He subjected the wind to Solomon, and recompensed him through *Muhammad* the Seal of the Prophets, with what his father Sulayman acquired and possessed, and bestowed upon him a greatness which brought all creation under his obedience without contention, and appointed for him in the robes of the House of Abbas that which fulfilleth in him its sable symbols and its lordliness of ancestry, and scattereth of its swarthiness upon the shade of eyelashes what rendereth superfluous the dark profundity of the heart and the blackness of the eye, and extendeth his shadow over the earth and every part of the capital and the whole city of Baghdad, (he being one who worshippeth at night, and by day is like Asakari and in liberality like Jaafar the most munificent), he is therefore in perpetual supplication to the Lord for his grace, and in joy, forasmuch as he hath choked every enemy in his own spittle. And he hath begun this day of fealty with what is most important among the interests of Islam, and with such virtuous works as adorn mankind, and he maketh the fear of God his guide, and baseth his commands upon it, and followeth the holy law and abideth by it and maketh the people to abide thereby, and whoso will not receive his commands with voluntary obedience must submit to them by compulsion. And the prince of the Faithful hasteneth to set about what will pacify all minds, by which he may repeal the machinations of the devil who is verily in despair, and captivate the hearts of his subjects though he be independent of it, yet because he ruleth them. And the prince of the Faithful calleth God and his people to witness that he hath confirmed every holder of an office among the administrators of affairs, in his present position, that he may continue to repose under the protection of his shadow, according to the various classes of the rulers, and the courses of the provinces and marches, on land and sea, plain and mountainous country, east and west, far and near, gentle and simple, few and many little and great, lord and slave an governor, and the soldier before whom glanceth his glorious sword and his trusty spear, together with those whether ministers, judges or secretaries, or such as possess judgment in composition, and knowledge of accounts, and are conversant with affaris of postal service or collection of revenue, and such as are necessary and unnecessary, engaged in teaching, and in the colleges, in Ribats, cells and convents, those who have weighty engagements or whose attachments *to the world* are but slight, and all possessors of offices and holders of stipends, and such as have of the Lords bounty a determinate portion, and a claim whether unknown or recognized. And everthing shall remain in its present sate, so that he may ask the blessing of God, and it may be made clear to him what is before him for he who increaseth his worthiness, his merit is augmented. For the prince of the Faithful seeketh but the glory of God, and maketh no distinction of persons in the religion of the Lord, nor favoureth one right in preference to another, for partiality in *the administration of* justice is a deception towards the Muslims. Everything that hath continued up to the present, shall remain established according to the commands of God, as God hath taught him, and *his father* Sulayman hath instructed him. Nor shall the prince of the Faithful make in this nor in any portion of it, any alteration, in gratitude to God for His bountry, and thus shall be rewarded he who giveth thanks. Nor shall he distbub unto any one his watering place, and may God purify His clear bounty to him free from all defilement. And no expositor can affect to comment upon this save one who disowneth favours and is ungrateful, nor an objector find an evasion, for the prince of the Faithful seeketh

A.H.741.
A.D.1341.

A.H.741. A.D.1341. protection from God and let us fly to his reign for defence against all change. The prince of the Faithful, may the Lord exalt his power- hath commanded the preachers to proclaim the mention of him and that of the present Sultan, from the pulpits throughout the provinces, and that the coinage shall be stamped with the impress of their names and become freely current, and the robes of night and day he girdled with a prayer for them both, and that there shall be made manifest therewith that which shall illumine the face of the dirham and the dinar.

And verily the prince of the Faithful hath proclaimed in this full assembly what every preacher hath to announce and what will be repeated by all that are far and near, the purport of which is, that the Lord hath issued commands and prohibitions, and he is the Watcher *from whom nothing is hidden,* and the intelligent should apply their faculties to them, and the preachers deduce therefrom the courses of their precepts, and excellencies will be perfected by them, and the hidden *thoughts* of the holy in their retirements will be elicited through them, and those who hold discourse at night shall speak of them, and the camel driver and the mariner shall chant them, and their magic shall be sweet in the moonlit night and be inscribed upon the brow of the morn. The stony vallies of Mecca shall hear them in exhortation, and by their, vehement urging shall Kafah[1] be revived, and every father shall instruct his son therein, and every generous son shall question his father. And it is for you, O ye people on the part of the prince of the Faithful who hath furnished[2] you with an evident demonstration, and upon you is obligatory that by which he hath called you to the way of the Lord in wisdom and excellent admonition, and obediene to the prince of the Faithful is your duty, and were it not for the sake of the preservation of the people, the Lord would not have accepted the works of those *commandments*- nor restrained the waters by them, nor spread out the earth nor riveted the mountains thereof, nor

---

1 I cannot explain this name if it be a name. Yakut does not give it. The MS. appears to have Fanah which Yakut places in Nejd.

2 شد MS.

would voices have been unanimous upon one who is worthy-nor the Caliphate have advanced towards him trailing its robes. He hath therefore possessed himself of it to the exclusion of the *other* descendants of his father, and it hath been found meet for him alone, and he only is meet for it. A.H.741. A.D.1341.

And verily the prince of the Faithful hath sufficed you *against any occasion of* solicitation, through what the Lord hath opened unto you of the gates of provision and means of maintenance, and he hath rewarded you according to your merit and taught you commendable virtues, and maintained you in the benefits you possess, and hath not been niggardly through fear of expense. And you have now no claim left against the prince of the Faithful, but that he should cause to pass freely among you the book of God and the traditions of His apostle, and act according to what He hath sent, who hath gratuitously bestowed. May the Lord vouchsafe unto the prince of the Faithful a long reign, and augment *His mercies* upon those who have gone before and preserve the obligations of the pilgrimage and warring for the faith, and cause the people to slumber peacefully in their beds by reason of His all-comprehensive justice.

The prince of the Faithful will establish the pilgrimage every year according to the custom of his fathers, and his favour will include the dwellers in the Sacred Cities and the ministers of the holy house of God, and he will show the right path unto him who is astray, hoping that he will return to the state that was his in past times, and his swelling waters shall be poured forth upon those two temples, and he will send unto the third of them in Jerusalem, a streaming cloud, and by his justice he will set up the sepulchers of the Prophets-upon whom be peace-wherever they may be, and the greater number whereof are in Syria. And the Friday prayers and congregations, these shall continue with you according to their ancient traditions and right course, and in the reign of the prince of the Faithful, whose joineth him shall receive increase from what may be received of the provinces of the infidels and be delivered of them into his hands. As regardeth fighting for the faith, let the

A.H.741. warring of him suffice who is so appointed by the prince of the
A.D.1341. Faithful in his behalf, invested by him with authority over all that is beyond his throne. And the prince of the Faithful hath appointed in him-may the Lord cause his kingdom and sovereignty to endure-an eye that slumbereth not, and hath girded a sword, of which were the lightnings to sleep on any night, heedless of enemies, the dreams of these would unsheathe its image against them. The prince of the Faithful will presently arrange for the restoration of all that hath been captured by the enemy and indeed the order hath already gone forth for the continuance of hostitlities by land and sea against the prostrate foe. And he will not abstain from either slaying or making prisoners those whom he subdueth, nor will he free them from fetters and bonds, and he will not cease from sending against them by land his eagle steeds and by sea his raven *ships*, bearing each of them in its rider, a bird of prey. And he will guard his dominions from such as venture to disturb its confines or traverse its borders with their footsteps. And he will look to the welfare of the forts and fastnesses and the frontiers, and what is needful from them of implements of war, and the principal cities which are the stations of the troops and the lairs of the lions, and the nobles, the forces and legions, and their disposition on the right and the left and on the extended wings. And he will inspect their condition in review as to their horses closely compacted between heaven and earth, and their wealth of twisted mail, and swords covered with liquid gold as though they were beautiful maidens hidden from view, and cutting blades, and lances dyed by reason of being long bathed in blood, and arrows cleaving to the bows and leaving them yearning with the yearning of she camels[1] that have lost their young, and bows resounding with the clamour of the wrathful.

All this the prince of the Faithful desireth to cheer your hearts and to extend a lengthened train over your desires. Your lives and property and honor shall be preserved from exposure to danger,

---

1 The word مفارق should be more properly written مفاريق which is the true plural of مُفرق See Lane, art. فرق

save in what the holy law permitteth. And an increase of bounty shall be given to your in the measure of what is kept hidden by you or manifested. To proceed to particulars of affairs, verily ye know that he who separates himself from the prince of the Faithful excludes himself from remembrance such as this, and according to the difference of your degrees, you are all a charge *from God committed* to the prince of the Faithful, and all of you are equal in truth before him, and upon you rests the fulfillment of his precepts and showing obedience with a sincere heart. For verily every one of you hath entered under the protection of the prince of the Faithful and under his obedience, and the obligations of the oath of fealty are incumbent upon him and its conditions binding binding upon his neck. And each one of you will be known by his fulfillment of that which he hath learnt. "but whoever shall perform that which he covenanted with God, He will surely give him a reward that is great," (Qur. XLVIII). These are the words of the prince of the Faithful. A.H.741. A.D.1341.

The writer goes on to say, "He will so act in all this, that the issue of his deeds may merit praise, and on this condition the covenant is made with him and for it he covenanteth. And over and above this, as to injustice, the witness of it hath not been borne against him, now will it be borne. And the prince of the Faithful supplicateth the Lord for His mercy under every condition, and seeketh His protection against remissness, and He prayeth Him to help him to the attainment of the hopes that he desireth, and not to extend to him the cord of delay. And the prince of the Faithful will seal his words with the justice and benevolence that the Lord hath commended : and praise be to God that he is one of most to be commended[1] of his creatures, for the Lord hath bestowed upon him the kingdom of Sulayman. May the Lord permit him freely to enjoy what he hath bestowed, and give him to rule over the ends of the earth and after a long life, cause his posterity to succeed him. May his seat never cease ot be on the threshold of eminence, and

1 Ahmad "worthiest of praise" was one of the names of the Caliph.

A.H.741. A.D.1341. the splendour of majesty through him, be united to the supreme rule of the Caliphate, as though its Mansur had never died nor its Mahdi or its Rashid passed away."

Ibn Hajr says in his Durar that he was first surnamed al Mustansir and afterwards al Hakim. The Shaykh Zaynuddin al Iraqi states that the Caliph heard traditions form some of the later traditionists and that he himself related them. He died of the plague about the middle of the year 753. Among events of his days, Sultan al Mansur was deposed in the first year of his reign on account of the depravity of his life and his drinking of wine;-it was even said that he did not hold inviolate his father's wives. He was banished to Kus and there assassinated. This was a Chastisement from God for what his father had done to the Caliph, and such is the way of the Lord with those who set themselves to do evil unto one of the posterity of Abbas. He was succeeded by his brother al Malik al Ashraf Kujuk (21st *Safar-6th August,* 1341) who was deposed the same year and his brother Ahmad elected and surnamed an Nasir (3rd *Shaaban- 11th January,* 1342) and Shaykh Takiuddin as Subki Kadhi of Syria who had accompanied him, arranged the covenant of allegiance between him and the Caliph.

In the year 743 an Nasir Ahmad was deposed and his brother Ismail was raised to power and surnamed as Salih (*22nd Muharram,- 27th June* 1342). In 746 as Salih died (*4th Rabii II- 3rd August,* 1345), and the Caliph invested his brother Shaaban who was surnamed al Kamil. In 747 (*3rd Jumada II 20th September,* 1346) al Kamil was put to death and his brother Amir Haj[1] was elected and surnamed al Mudhaffar. In 748, al Mudhaffar was deposed and succeeded in power (14th *Ramadhan-18th December,* 1347) by his brother Hasan who was surnamed an Nasir.

---

1 Weil names him Zaynuddin Haji. He received the name of Haji or Haj (*pilgrim*) as he was born in 732 while his father Sultan Muhammad an Nasir was on the pilgrimage. Weil, p. 470.

In 749 occurred the universal plague[1] the like of which was never heard of. A.H.749. A.D.1348.

In the year 752 an Nasir Hasan was deposed and his brother Salih elected (28th *June, II-22nd August* 1351), and surnamed al Malik as Salih, who was the eighth who reigned of the descendants of an Nasir Muhammad b. Kilawun, and Shaykhu was made his Atabek. He was the first, an Ibn Fadhlillah adds in the supplement of the Masalik, who was named in Egypt the Great Emir.

Of personage of note who died during the reign of al Hakim were the Hafidh Abul Hajjaj al Mizi, at Taj Abdul Baki al Yamani, as Shams Abdul Hadi, Abu Hayyan, Ibnul Wardi, Ibnul Laban, Ibn Adhan, ad Dahabi, Ibn Fadhlillah, Ibn Kayyim al Jauziyah, al Fakhr al Misri the Shafiite Shaykh in Syria, at Taj al Marakashi and others.

AL MUATADHID BI'LLAH ABUL FATH

Al Muatadhid billah Abul Fath Abu Bakr the son of al Mustakfi was acknowledged Caliph after the death of his brother in the year 753 according to his covenant. He was virtuous and complaisant and a friend to men of letters. He died in Jumada, 1,763. Among the events of his reign occurred the deposition in 755 of al Malik as Salih (2nd *Shawwal,- 20th October,* 1254) and an Nasir Hasan was reinstated. In the year 756 orders were issued for the coining of new *copper* pieces of the size and weight of a dinar and four and twenty of these were made equivalent to a dirham. Before this the old copper pieces were a ratle and a half to the dirham, and from this may be known the value of the silver dirhams struck by Shaykhu and the Emir Surghitmish for the salaried officials of their colleges, for their dirhams signified two-thirds of a ratl in copper pieces.

1 This was the great plague or black death which spread over Europe in 1348 and desolated Florence. According to Arabic sources it took its rise in China in A.H. 742 and spread over Tartary ; thence to Constantinople, Asia Minor and Syria on one side, and Greece, Italy, Spain, France and the north of Europe on the other. In old and new Cairo in the months of Shaaban and Ramadhan 900,000 beings perished. In Aleppo the deaths were 500 a day and in Gaza 22,000 died in 33 days. For its further details, consult Weil, p. 479, from Makrizi, and Abul Mah.

A.H.753. A.D.1352. In the year 762 an Nasir Hasan was put to death and Muhammad the son of his brother al Mudhaffar was raised to the throne (9th *Jun. I – 17th March* 1361) and surnamed al Mansur.

Of persons of note who died in the reign of al Muatadhid were Shaykh Takiuddin as Subki, as Samin (*Shibahuddin Ahmad b. Yusuf al Halabi*) author of the Iirab (*treatise on inflexions in the Qurãn),* al Kawam al Itkami, al Baha b. Akil, as Salah al Alaii, al Jamal b. Hisham the Hafidh Maghlataii, Abu Imamah b-un Nakkash and others.

AL MUTAWAKKIL A'LA'LLAH ABU ABDULLAH

Al Mutawakkil alallah Muhammad the son of al Muatadhid, the father of the Caliphs of the present age, assumed the Caliphate by the covenant of his father, after his death in Jumada I, 763. His reign extended over forty-five years throughout the deposition and imprisonments that disturbed it, as we shall presently relate, and he left many children. It is said that he had one hundred children including those still-born, of whom many, male and female, died. Five among them held the Caliphate which is unprecedented, *viz,.* al Mustain al Abbas, al Muatadhid Dauud, al Mustakfi Sulayman, al Kaim Hamzah and al Mustanjid Yusuf. Of his children at the present time but one is left called Musa, much resembling Ibrahim the son of al Mustakfi, and of the posterity of Abbas now remaining, all are of the stock of this la Mutawakkil-may the Lord increase their number and give them increase of His aid. The following were among the events of his reign. In the year 764 al Mansur was deposed (14th *Shaaban*-29th *May* 1363). And Shaaban b. Husayn b. Nasir b. Kilawun succeeded to power and was surnamed al Ashraf.

In 773 the green badge on the turbans of the descendants of the Prophet was introduced by command of the Sultan that they might be thus distinguished and this was its first introduction. Abu

Abdullah b. Jabir[1] the blind grammarian, author of the commentary on the Alfiyah *of Ibn Malik,* known as al Aama wal Basir (*the blind and the discerning*) says regarding this- A.H.773. A.D.1371.

"They have given the descendants of the apostle a badge,
But a badge is a distinction for one who is unknown.
The light of prophecy is on their noble features,
The nobly born needeth no green decoration."

In this year began the irruption of the tyrant Tamarlang (*Tamarlane*) who devastated the provinces and destroyed the inhabitants and continued his depredations on the earth until he perished under the curse of God in the year 807.[2] And it has been said regarding him:

"The Tartars worked evil yet had they but witnessed
The deeds of Tamarlang how much more terrible !"
And his omen upon the people of greater ill boding !"

He was in his origin one of the children of the peasantry and bred to theft and highway robbery. Subsequently he joined the service of the Sultan's[3] master of the horse and was established in his place after his death, and he never ceased to rise until he attained to what he reached. A certain person was asked in what year occurred Tamarlang's irruption. He replied, "in the year of the Chastisement." (*Adab*), that is according to alphabetical enumeration 773.[4]

---

1 The text has Jabiz erroneously. Ibn Jabir died in 780 (1378). His commentary though a work of great merit, did not escape the criticism of as Suyuti whose indefatigable pen was employed in exposing its errors. See Haj, Khal.

2 The text has here a gross error, giving the year as 873. The MS. has a blank for the unit. Timur died according to Ibn Arab Shah on Wednesday the 17th Shaaban 807, (17th *February*, 1405). D'Herb, places his death on the 10th Shaaban.

3 Al Malik Husayn of Heart.

4 The beginning of his rise and power is fixed by most historians in 771 when he received from Sultan Surghatmish Chaghtai the succession to the satrapy of Samarkand and Tansoxiana, and as he died in 807, this would make his reign 36 years. He was born in 736. D'Herb.

A.H.779. In the year 775 the reading of al Bukhari was begun in the
A.D.1377. citadel during the month of Ramadhan in the presence of the Sultan, and the Hafidh Zaynuddin of Iraq was appointed reader, but later, Shihabul Uryani was associated with him on alternate days.

In the year 778 eggs became so dear at Damscus that a single one sold for three dirhams at the calculation of sixty *dirhams* to the dinar.[1]

In the year 778 al Ashraf Shaaban was put to death and his son Ali surnamed al Mansur succeeded to power (3rd *Dul Kaadah-14th March*), and *it happened* thus,. Al Ashraf was making the pilgrimage with the Caliph and the Kadhis and nobles, when the nobles conspired against him and he fled back to Cairo. The Caliph likewise returned and some others and they purposed to make the Caliph Sultan, but he declined. They therefore raised the son of al Ashraf to the throne and al Ashraf concealed himself, till they seized him in the month of Dul Kaadah.

In the same year the sunand moon were both eclipsed. The moon was under eclipsed on the 14th Shaaban, and the sun on the 28th of the same month.

In the year 779 on the 4th Rabii I, Inbak al Badri the war minister summoned Zakariya son of Ibrahim, son of al Mustamsik, son[2] of the Caliph al Hakim and bestowed on him a robe of honour and made him Caliph without *the formality of* the oath of allegiance and without the concurrence of the Faithful, and surnamed him al Mustasim billah. He further ordered al Mutawakkil to be banished to Kus for certain things[3] which he resented as having been done by him at the time of the assassination of al Ashraf. The Caliph set

1 The MS. has here a marginal note عشرون بيضه بدينار (20 eggs for a dinar).

2 The word بن is inadvertently omitted both in the MS. and Text, and in the latter ايبك is written by a misprint for اينبك

3 Inbak desired the Caliph to pronounce the deposition of the Sultan in whose place he sought to elect his own step on Ahmad. To justify this course he asserted that Ahmad's mother was with child by the Sultan Hasan an nasir before her second marriage with Yelboga al Chaski. The Caliph's refusal resulted in his deposal. Weil, p. 533.

out but returned the next day to his house and to the Caliphate on the 20th of the month, and al Mustasim was deposed, the duration of his Caliphate having been fifteen days. Al Mutawakkil was the sixth of the Caliphs residing in Egypt who were reinstated after some interruption of their Caliphate. This deposition therefore was in accordance with custom. A.H.779. A.D.1377.

In the year 782 a letter came from Aleppo stating that an Imam was reading public prayers when a person made sport of him during his praying, but he did not interrupt the prayers until he came to the end and when he pronounced the benediction, the face of the jester was turned into that of a hog and he fled to a forest in the neighbourhood. The people were in wonder at this affair and a deposition was taken of it.

In the month of Safar (23rd) 783 al Mansur died and his brother Haji son of al Ashraf succeeded him and was surnamed as Salih. In Ramadhan (19th) 784 (26th *November,* 1382) as Salih was deposed and Barkuk assumed the government and was surnamed ad Dhahir, and he was the first Sultan of the Cireassian race. In Rajab of 785, Barkuk arrested the Caliph, deposed him and imprisoned him in the fortress on the hill. Muhammad son of Ibrahim, son of al Mustamisk son of al Hakim was then acknowledge Caliph and surnamed al Wathik billah and he continued in the Caliphate till he died on Wednesday the 17th Shawwal, 788. The people then petitioned Barkuk to reinstate al Mutawakkil, but he refused and summoned the brother of Muhammad Zakariya, he who had been appointed for a short period-and swore fealty to him and he was surnamed al Mutasim[1] billah. He continued in office until the year 791. Barkuk then repented of what he had done to al Mutawakkil, and brought him out of confinement, restored him to the Caliphate and deposed Zakariya. Zakariya continued to dwell in his private residence till he died while under deposition; and al Mutawakkil remained Caliph till his death.

1 Weil says that according to the best MS. he was surnamed al Mutasim (*having recourse to God*) not all Mustasim, (p. 122, Vol. II). The MS. has this reading but the text, Mustasim, which is therefore incorrect.

A.H.791. A.D.1389. In the month of Jumada II, of the same year as Salih Haji was restored to the dignity of Sultan and his surname was changed to al Mansur. Barkuk was imprisoned at Kark.

In the month of Shaaban of this year the Muazzines after the summons to prayer, introduced the prayer and the salutation upon the Prophet, and this was the first time it was introduced. It was done at the instance of the Market inspected Najmuddin at Tumbudi. In the month of Safar 792 Barkuk was taken out of confinement and restored to power in which he continued till his death (14th) Shawwal 801, (19th *June*, 1399). He was succeeded (15th) by his son Faraj who was surnamed an Nasir and he remained in power till the 6th [1] Rabii I. 808 (1st *September,* 1405) when he was deposed from office and succeeded by his brother Abdul Aziz surnamed al Mansur. He was subsequently deposed on the 4th [2] Jumada II, of the same year and an Nasir Faraj reinstated. In this year died the Caliph al Mutawakkil on Tuesday night the 28th o Rajab, 808, (18th *January,* 1406)

Of persons of note who died during the reign of al Mutawakkil were as Shams b. Muflih the doctor of the Hanbalites, as Salah as Safadi, as Shihab b-un Nakib, al Muhibb the Commissary of the Forces, as Sharif Shihab b-un Nakib, al Muhibb the Commissary of the Forces, as Sharif al Husayni the Hafidh, al Kutb at Takhtani, the chief Kadhi Izzuddin b. Jamaah , at Taj bus Subki and his brother Shaykh Bahauddin, al Jamal al Asnawi, Ibnus Saigh al Hanafi, al Jamal b. Nubatah, al Afif al Yafii, al Jamal as Sharishi, as Sharaf b. Kadhiul Jabl, as Siraj al Hindi, Ibn Abi Hajalah, the Hafidh Takiuddin b. Rafi, the Hafidh Imaduddin b. Kathir al Unabi the grammarian, al Baha Abul Baka as Subki, as Shams b. Khatib Birud, al Imad al Husbani, al Badr b. Habib, ad Dhiya al Karami, as Shihab al Adrai, as Shaykh Akmaluddin, as Shaykh Saaduddin at Taftazani, al Badr az Zarkashi, as Siraj b. Malkan, as Siraj al Balkini, and the Hafidh Zaynuddin al Iraki.

---

1 According to Weil, the 25th.

2 8th, Weil.

AL WATHIK BI'LLAH OMAR

A.H.788.
A.D.1386.

Al Wathik billah Omar b. Ibrahim son of the heir al Mustamsik son of al Hakim, was acknowledged Caliph on the deposition of al Mutawakkil in the month of Rajab, 785, (*September,* 1383), and continued in the Caliphate till he died on Wednesday the 19th[1] Shawwal 788, (11th *November,* 1386)

AL MUTASIM BI'LLAH ZAKARIYA

Al Mutasim billah Zakariya. The son of Ibrahim the son of al Mustamsik was acknowledged Caliph on the death of his brother al Wathik. He was deposed in 791 (10th *Jumada I*-5th *June,* 1389) and remained at his residence in deposition until his death, and al Mutawakkil was restored as has been previously mentioned.

AL MUSTAIN BI'LLAH ABUL FADHL

Al Mustain billah Abul Fadhl al Abbas son of al Mutawakkil whose mother was a Turkish slave named Bai Khatun, was acknowledged Caliph according to his father's covenant in the month of Rajab, 808. The Sultan at the time was al Malik an Nasir Faraj.

When an Nasir set out to engage the Shaykh[2] in battle and was defeated and fled, the Caliph was acknowledged as Sultan in addition to the Caliphate. This book place on (25th) Muharram 815, (7th *May,* 1412). He did not, however, assent to this, save after

---

1 The date has already been given (*see page* 532) as the 17th The MS. and Text both have the discrepancy. Weil does not give the date and I am unable to determine which of the two is the correct one. According to the Calendric scales for verifying dates published by the Asiatic Society, the 19th of Shawwal 788 fell on a Tuesday.

2 Shaykh Mahmudi named by Faraj to the government of Damascus. He afterwards became Sultan under the title of al Malik al Muayyad.

A.H.815. A.D.1412. opposition and continueus protest and receiving the engagement of the Emirs on oath.[1] He then returned to Egypt accompanied by the Emire and occupied himself in appointing and removing *ministers.* The coinage was struck in his name but his title remained unaltered.

The Shaykhul Islam Ibn Hajr wrote his famous Poem on him which is as follows-

"The kingdom is on a sure foundation among us,
Through al Mustain the Just the Abbaside.
The dignity of the descendants of the uncle of Muhammad
Hath returned to its place after a long oblivion.
On the 2nd of the second Rabii the auspicious,
On Tuesday, rejoicings were made,
For the coming of the people's guide, their trusted one,
Preserved from defect, pure in his utterances.
The lord of a house round which men circle. Hath it been ever known.
That he who sough it, hath been turned back disappointed ?
A branch sprung from Hashim, in a garden
Of holy plantations and goodly shoots
Of the approved and selected of God,-the purchasers
Of praise, ornamented by and robed in it,
Among chiefs who have led calamities captive and purified
Themselves from contamination with the base.
Lions when present in fight, and when retired
In their social gatherings are as deer in their coverts.
And his star-like radiance amongst them
Is like the full moon that riseth in darkness.

1 He bound them in the event of his deposition from the Sultanate to maintain him as Caliph. Weil, p. 126.

And in his hand when attaching the sign *manual,* A.H.815. A.D.1412.
A pen the irradiates like the flash of a spark.
And in his countenance, for such as approach, are smiles
That are sought, and for the honour of al Abbas.
Then praise be to God who hath exalted His religion
After it had been in desolation,
By noble chiefs the pillars of greatness,
Between seekers of retaliation and the beneficent.
They rise with the burdens of noble qualities and ascend
To lofty dignities, the lordly, the steadfast.
They have left their enemies prostrate on the field of ruin.
And may God guard them from the temptations of the evil one.
And their Imam through his greatness precedeth them,
Like the precedence of the name of God upon a document.
And were not the ordering of the kingdom under his guidance,
The condition of men in the kingdom would not endure.
And how many a prince before him hath sought eminence,
Which, notwithstanding his exertions, cast him back in poverty.
Until he *alone* attained dignities, being meet for them,
Which have yielded to him after much refractoriness.
The hands of princes are submissive to him and are obedient
The fingers of the Meter of the Egyptain Nile.
For it is he who hath repelled evil from us,
In the world would evil abound were it not for him.
He hath effaced tyranny which embraced all princes
In every part and of all kinds.

A.H.815. A.D.1412.

By *the deposition of the recreant*[1] called, in opposition to his deeds,
The Defender, (*an Nasir* insecure of foundation.
How many gifts of God were his
Which were as though remote or in oblivion.
The mystery of evil never ceaseth to be within his sides
As fire, or his companionship with the sepulchers.
What wickedness hath he not done, the sins of which are upon him
Till the day of resurrection ? He shall have none to mourn *for him.*
He built its pillars in deceit, yet
In fraud were they built without foundation.
Every man is forgotten or remembered but once,
But he shall not be forgotten for evil.
The God of nations prolonged his days, so that
When they seized him, the bitterness of the cup *of death* did not pass him by.
And the Lord hath given us instead of him, a prince
Whose days are exalted beyond computation.
Mecca and the earth have heard the good tidings,
From the East unto the West, from Udayb[2] to Fez.
The signs of his glory none shall seek to disown
Among men, but the wicked fool.
The virtues of al Abbas have never been united
Save in his descendant, the Abbaside, king of men.
And the sway of al Mustain, shall renounce
Nor more in his kingdom, the thankless, the forgetful.
For after the sons of Umayya

---

1 The Sultan Faraj al Malik an Nasir.

2 Sweet waters belonging to the Banu Tamim, four miles from Kadisiyah, which is 15 parasangs from Kufah.

In past times, came the sons of Abbas. A.H.815. A.D.1412.
And he of the Scar[1] of the sons of Umayya came raising up
Justice, after the destroyer,[2] the base.
My prince, thy servant hath come to thee, hoping
For thy acceptance, let it not be accounted ill.
And were it not for awe *of thee,* his praises would be longer,
Wherefore hath he brought them in a balance.
May the God of mankind cause by glory to endure
Guarded in justice by the God of mankind.
And mayest thou live to hear praises from thy servant,
For were it not for thee he would endure sorrow.
A servant, pure in affection who chants as he drives his camel
And runs *from zeal* upon his eyes before his head.[3]
His praises of the posterity of the house of Muhammad
Are words of fragrant musk among men."

When al Mustain reached Egypt he took up his residence in the fort, and the Shaykh (*Mahmudi*) in the stables, and al Mustain consigned to his care the administration of the sovereignty throughout the land of Egypt and surnamed him Nidhamul Mulk. The nobles when they were released from duty at the palace, used to attend the Shaykh at the stables and their respects were next paid to him, and in his presence the business of administration was carried on. Then his Chancellor waited on al Mustain were the signature was attached to royal mandates and letters. It was then represented that the Caliph was not empowered to attach the sign manual *to a document* except after it had been shown to the

---

1 Omar b. Abdil Aziz.

2 Abdul Malik b. Marwan.

3 The words in this line have nearly all double meanings, being plays upon the Mecca pilgrimage.

A.H.815. A.D.1412. Shaykh. The Caliph was now in trepidation and his heart was straitened and his disquietude increased. Now when it was the month of Shaaban, the Shaykh demanded of the Caliph that he should resign the Sultanate into his hands according to custom. The Caliph assented on the condition that he might come down from the citadel into his own residence (1st *Shaaban,* 815-6th *November,* 1412) but to that the Shaykh would not consent, and usurped the Sultanate and assumed the title of al Muayyad, and he publicly proclaimed the deposition of al Mustain and acknowledged as Caliph his brother Dauud (16th *Dul Hijjah,* 816-7th *March,* 1414). Al Mustain was transferred from the palace to one of the houses of the citadel, and his people with him, and guards were appointed to prevent his access to the people. When this reached Nauruz, governor of Syria, he assembled the judges and the doctors and asked their judicial decision regarding what al Muayyad had done in deposing the Caliph and imprisoning him. They gave sentence that it was unlawful, and it was agreed to give battle to al Muayyad. The latter set out against Nauruz in the year 717 A.H. and dispatched al Mustain to Alexandria. He remained there imprisoned until the reign of Tatar[1] when he was released and permitted to proceed to Cairo, but he preferred to reside in Alexandria which *place* was agreeable to him and where he received considerable sums from the merchants and he continued to reside there until he died, in the cause of God,[2] of the plague in Jumada II, 813. *The following* were among the remarkable events of his reign. In the year 812, the Nile began its rise on the first day of *the month of* Masuri,[3] and

1 According to Weil, until the reign of Barsabai (825).

2 The term شهيد a martyr, is applied by the Prophet to such Muslims who die of colic, or who are drowned, or killed by a failing building, or die of pleurisy, or pestilence, and to a woman dying in pregnancy.

3 The Coptic month, answering to August, beginning on the 26th July. The rise of the Nile begins in the month of Abib or July and continues till September. At that period, Egypt, as its historian Abul Mahasin says, glitters like a white pearl. The following three months it appears like black musk, as the waters disappear. The next three months, it is like a rich emerald from the sprouting of the vegetation, and during the last three months from the ripening of the crops it is like molten gold. Abul Maha-Tom I, p. 32, The names of the Coptic months and the Syriah that correspond with them will be found here.

it reached a maximum of twenty-two cubbs.[1] A.H.815. A.D.1412.

In the year 814, Ghiyathuddin (*Mahmud Tughlak*) Aszam Shah b. Sikandar emperor of Hindustan sent to the Caliph for his investiture *of sovereignty* and sent him a large sum and a present to the Sultan.

Among the remarkable personages who died during his Caliphate *were* al Muwaffik an Nashiri the poet of Yaman, Nasrullah of Baghdad a doctor of the Hanbalites, Shamsul Muid the grammarian of Mecca, Shibabul Husbani, Shihabun Nashiri the jurisconsult of Yaman, Ibnul Haim author of the law of Inheritances and their computations Ibnul Afif, the poet of Yaman, and al Muhibb Ibn al Shahnah the Hanafi Jurisconsult, father of the Kadhi of the troops.

AL MUATADHID BI'LLAH ABUL FATH

Al Muatadhid billah Abul Fath Dauud b-ul Mutawakkil, whose mother was a Turkish slave named Kazal, was acknowledged Caliph on the death of his brother in the year 815[2] A.H. : the Sultan being al Muayyad who continued *such* till his death in Muharram 824.[3] His son Ahmad was then invested with the Sultanate and surnamed al Mudhaffar who appointed Tatar[4] his first minister. In the month of Shaaban (29th *August* '1421) Tatar arrested him, whereupon the Caliph invested Tatar with the Sultanate and he was surnamed

1 Abdul Latif in his account of Egypt gives 13 cubits as the minimum height requisite for the wants of Egypt, 19 cubits is rarely reached, and 20 is an excessive rise. Lib. II, Cap. I.

2 According to Weil, 16th Dul Hijjah, 816, 7th March, 1414.

3 8th Muharram, 823. 13th January, 1421, Weil.

4 A Circassian, educated in theology and jurisprudence by a slave dealer. He was purchased by the Sultan Barkuk for 12,000 dirhams, He was given his freedom by Sultan Faraj and thus gradually rose to power. See Weil, Gesch, Abb. Khal. Egypt, Vol. II, p. 161.

A.H.841. ad Dhahir. In Dul Hijjah (4th) of the same year Tatar died, and his
A.D.1438. son Muhammad was invested and surnamed as Salih who appointed Barsabai[1] his first minister. Subsequently Barsabai fell upon as Salih and deposed him, and the Caliph invested him with the Sultanate in (8th) Rabii II, 825 in which he contined till his death (16th) in Dul Hijjah, 841 (7th *June,* 1438), where on his son Yusuf received the investiture and the title of al Aziz who named as his first minister Jakmak; the latter then fell upon al Aziz and arrested him in Rabii I. (19th) 842 and the Caliph gave him investiture and he was surnamed ad Dhahir in whose reign the Caliph died.

Al Muatadhid was one of the first of the Caliphs in merit, acuteness and sagacity. He courted the society of men of letters and genius, and profited much by them and associated himself with them in their works. He was extremely liberal and munificent. He died on Sunday the 4th of Rabii I, 845 (22nd *July,* 1441), being according to Ibn Hajr, nearly seventy years of age, but his brother's daughter informed me that he lived 63 years.

The following are among the remarkable events of his reign.

In 816 Sadruddin bal Admi held the inspectorship of markets in addition to the office of Kadhi and he was the first who held the two together. In the year 819 Mankali Bugha assumed it and he was the first among the Turks in the world who held the post of inspector. In the same year a man appeared in Egypt who pretended that he ascended into heaven and had seen the Most High and spoken with him, and many of the common[2] people believed in him. A meeting was therefore convened regarding him, and he was asked to retract but he refused to retract : then the Maliki *jurisconsult* posted an order for his death on the testimony of two persons that he was of sane mind, but a number of doctors of

---

1 Also a slave originally of the Emir Dokmak governor of Malatya who made a present of him to Sultan Barkuk. All the Sultans since the last, with the exception of al Mustain had been Circassians. Weil writes the name, I think incorrectly, Bursbai. It is of Chaldaic origin signifying the son (*Bar*) of Sabai.

2 The text has عوالم the MS. عوام

medicine asserted that he was of unsound mind; he was therefore confined in the hospital. A.H.841. A.D.1438.

In the year 821 a buffalo at Bilbays gave birth to a young one with two heads and two necks and four forefeet, and the two connecting portions of the back and quarters in one, and two legs only, and the tail divided in two which was a wonder of creation. In the year 822 a great earthquake occurred at Arzankan[1] in which a number of people perished. During the same, was completed the Muayyadiyah College and Shams bal Mudiri was appointed head professor ; the Sultan attended his lectures and Ibrahim the son of the Sultan arranged the spreading of the Shaykh's praying carpet with his own hand. In the year 823 a camel was killed at Ghazzah and its flesh shone as shines a candle, and a piece of it was thrown to a dog but it would not eat it. In the year 824 the Nile continued at its full till the end *of the month* Hatur[2] and thus many of the sown fields were submerged. In the year 825 Fatimah daughter of the Kadhi Jalal uddin al Balkini gave birth to a child with two extra hands to his palms and horns on its head like the horns of a bull, but it died after a little while. During the same, Cairo was shaken by a slight earthquake, and also the Nile began its rise on the 28th of Abib.[3]

Among the remarkable personages who died during his reign were as Shihab b. Haji the jurisconsult of Syria, Burhan b. Rifaah the scholar, az Zayn Abu Bakr al Maraghi the jurisconsult of Medina and its professor of tradition, al Husam al Abiwardi, al Jamal b. Dhahirah Hafidh of Mecca, al Majd as Shirazi author of the Kamus, Khalaf an Nahriri one of the greatest of the Maliki doctors, as Shams b-ul Rabbani one of the greatest of the Hanafites, Abu Hurayrah b-un Nakkash, al Wanughi, Izzuddin b. Jamaah the preceptor, Ibnul Hisham al Ajami, as Salah al Akfashi,[4] as Shihab

---

1 Erzinjan, in Armenia.

2 November.

3 De Sacy writes this word ابيب Epiphi. See his L'Egypte. Abdul Latif.

4 The text has Afkashi which is incorrect. Akfahs is a town in Upper Egypt.

A.H.825. A.D.1422. al Ghazzi one of the doctors of the Shafiites, al Jalal al Balkini, al Burhan al Bijuri, al Wali al Iraki, as Shams bal Mudiri, as Sharaf al Rabbani, al Ala b-ul Mualla, Badr bud Damamini, at Taki al Hasini the commentator of Abu Shujaa, al Harawi, as Siraj reader of the Hidayah, an Najm b. Haji, al Badr al Bushtaki, as Shams al Barmawi, As Shams as Shatanufi, at Taki al Fasi, az Zayn al Kimani, an Nidham Yahya as Sirafi, Kara[1] Yakub ar Rumi, as Sharaf b. Muflih the Hanbalite, as Shams bal Kushayri, Ibn al Jazri, a teacher of reading of the Qurãn, Ibnul Khatib ad Dahashah, as Shihab al Abshiti, az Zayn at Tafihni, al Badr al Mukaddasi, as Sharaf b-ul Mukri the scholar of Yaman, author of the Unwan us Sharaf,[2] at Taki b. Hijjah the poet, al Jalal al Murshidi the grammarian of Mecca, al Humam as Shirazi the pupil of as Sharif, al Jamal b-ul Khayyat, the scholar of Yaman, al Busiri the traditionist, as Shihab b. al Muhammirah, al Ala al Bukhari, as Shams al Bisati, al Jamal al Kazruni, the scholar of Medina, al Muhibb al Baghdadi al Hanbali, as Shams b. Ammar and others.

AL MUSTAKFI BI'LLAH ABUR RABII

Al Mustakfi billah Abur Rabii Sulayman b-ul Mutawakkil assumed the Caliphate by the covenant of his brother *al Muatadhid*, who was his uterine brother. My father, may God have mercy upon him, drafted the original covenant which was in this form. "This is the dead whereby testifieth upon his noble person, which may God preserve, defend and protect and guard from afflictions, our lord and prince, in whom are centred dignities, princely, pure, stainless, pontifical, sublime, of the line of Abbas, the Prophetical, the God strengthened, the prince of the Faithful, the descendant of the Chief of the Apostle, and the heir of the orthodox Caliphs, al Muatadhid billah Abul Fath Dauud, may the

1 Not قرا as in the text.

2 Unwan us Sharaf al Wafi (*a little of ample nability*) a work on jurisprudence, grammar, history and prosody. Haji Khalifah has a short notice of this work.

Lord exalt the faith through him and prosper Islam and the Muslims by his long life,-that he hath made this covenant in favour of his uterine brother, the sublime seat *of dignity,* the learned doctor, the noble, the princely, high in rank and birth, of royal descent, my lord Abur Rabii Sulayman al Mustakfi billah, may God increase his dignity, for the sublime Caliphate and hath appointed him Caliph after him, and placed him as an Imam over the Muslims, according to covenant, legally, with full trust and approval, to counsel the faithful, and for the fulfillment of what is obligatory upon him for the due government of the affairs of those who believe in one God, and to follow the traditions of the orthodox Caliphs and rightly-guided Imams ; and this, because of what he knoweth of his faith, and goodness, and rectitude and sufficiency and fitness, and capability, forasmuch as he hath tested his condition, and become acquainted with his heart and verily he is one through whom one serveth God[1] for he is the most God-fearing[2] of any he hath seen and verily he knoweth of nothing that hath emanated from him which impaireth his claim there-unto : and verily were he to leave the State uncontrolled without committing it to the care of the above referred to, he would thereby bring trouble upon those who *have authority* to loose and bind in the choice of whom they should appoint to the Imamate and approve for that office : he hath, therefore, hastened to *the executive of* this covenant out of compassion to them and for the purpose of freeing them from this charge and that the supreme authority might fall to one worthy of it, because of his knowledge that this covenant is not in need of the approval of the whole of the people concerned in it : but it is incumbent upon him who heareth it and it is a charge upon him, that he should become acquainted with it and enjoin obedience to it at such time as it may be required, and summon the people to submit to it. Those, therefore, that have been present at it by his gracious permission, have ratified this respecting it, and previous to this, my lord al

A.H.845.
A.D.1441.

---

1 Compare the tradition of Ali مُحَبَّةُ العُلَمَاءِ دينُ يدانُ اللهُ بِهِ The love of the learned is a religion throught which God is served."

2 The MS. has اتقى الله a better reading than the text. اثقي ثفة

A.H.845. A.D.1441. Mustakfi Abur Rabii Sulayman who is mentioned in it-may God increase his dignity-hath writing his full acquiescence according to law, at his command."

He was one of the most virtuous of the Caliphs, pious, devout, religious, constant in worship and prayer and reading the Qurãn given to silence, shunning the society of men, of excellent disposition. His brother Al Muatadhid said to him "I have never known a serious fault in my brother Sulayman since he grew up :" and al Malik ad Dhahir had full confidence in him and recognized his worth. My father was his Imam and held a distinguished position *in his regard*, intimate with him and extremely honoured by him. As for us, we were brought up in his house and under his bounty, and his family are excellent in faith, devotion and virtues, and I do not think that there will be found on the face of the earth a Caliph, after the descendants of Omar b. Abdil Aziz, more virtuous than *those of* the house of this Caliph.

He died on Friday the close of Dul Hijjah[1] 854, being sixty-three years old : my father outlived him by forty days, and the Sultan attended the funeral to the grave and carried the bier in person.

Among the distinguished persons who died during his reign were at Taki al Makrizi, as Shaykh Ibadah, Ibn Kamil, the poet, al Wafai, al Kayani, and the Shaykhul Islam Ibn Hajr.

AL KAIM BI'AMRILLAH ABUL BAKA

Al Kaim bi amrillah Abul Baka. Hamzah b-ul Mutawakkil, was acknowledged Caliph in succession to his brother, who had not however, bequeathed it to him or to any other. He was hardy and intrepid, and restored somewhat of the pomp of the Caliphate, and he possessed a haughtiness of manner unlike his brothers. During his time, died al Malik al Dhahir Jakmak in the beginning of the year 857, and his son Othman was invested and surnamed al

1 Muharram 855. Weil.

Mansur, and he so continued for a month and a half. Then Inal[1] fell upon al Mansur and seized his person, whereupon the Caliph invested him in Rabii I (3rd -4th March 1453) and he was surnamed al Ashraf. Shortly after a rupture occurred between the Caliph and al Ashraf on account of a rising[2] of the troops against him, he therefore deposed him from the Caliphate in the month of Jumada II, 859 (*June* 1455) and sent him to Alexandria and there imprisoned him till his death in 863,[3] and he was buried near *the tomb* of the sister of al Mustain. What is strange regarding these uterine brothers, is that they were both deposed from the Caliphate, both imprisoned at Alexandria, and both there buried. A.H.859. A.D.1455.

My father and al Ala al Kalakshandi were the only ones of note who died during the reign of al Kaim.

AL MUSTANJID BI'LLAH, THE REIGNING CALIPH. ABUL MAHASIN

Al Mustanjid Billah Abul Mahasin Yusuf b-ul Mutawakkil succeeded to the Caliphate on the deposition of his brother, the Sultan at the time being al Ashraf Inal. The Sultan died in the year 865 (15th *Jumada I 26th February* 1461) and his son Ahmad was invested and surnamed al Muwayyad. Subsequently Khushkadam[4] set upon al Muwayyad and seized him and *the Caliph* invested him and he was surnamed ad Dhahir, and continued *in power* till his death in Rabii 872 (10th – 9th *October,* 1467), Balbai[5] was nest invested with office and surnamed ad Dhahir, but the army rebelled against him after two months and seized him, whereupon Timurbugha was raised to power and surnamed ad Dhahir, and

1 The text has ابال which is incorrect. The MS. has اينال and Weil's authority confirms it.

2 An outbreak of the Mamelukes on account of a sufficient number of camels of transport not being allowed them for the expedition to the Delta. Which was favoured by the Caliph, occasioned the repture.

3 17th Shawwal 862-28th August 1458. Weil.

4 He was first of the Mameluke Sultans, among whom he was the thirty-eighth, whose origin is known to be undoubtedly Greek.

5 Weil has Jelbai, but the MS. is in accordance with the text.

A.H.872. A.D.1468. they set upon him likewise after two months when the present Sultan Kaitbai was invested (6th *Rajab-31st January* 1468) and surnamed al Ashraf and his authority became established and his administration has attained a vigour and firmness equaled by no Sultan before him since the time of an Nasir Muhammad b. Kilawan, for the journeyed from Egypt to the Euphrates with a very slender escort of the troops, there not being among them a single one among his trusty commanders. As an instance of his excellent conduct, he never appointed a holder of a religious office, such as the judges and elders and professors except from the most worthy at the time, after long thought and deliberation, so that an office remained vacant for many months, and he never appointed a Kadhi or a Shaykh on any occasion, for a bribe. When Khushkadam first assumed power, Janim[1] governor of Syria advanced *to Egypt* under a private understanding between him and the troops regarding his assumption of the Sultanate when *news of* his approach reached ad Dhahir, he ordered the Caliph and the four Kadhis and the troops to mount to the citadel, and he sent to the governor of Syria insisting on his departure, who departed after making certain conditions.[2] The Kadhis and the troops returned to their quarters, but the Caliph remained a resident in the citadel, and the Sultan would not permit his return to his accustomed residence. He therefore remained there till he died on Saturday the 24th of Muharram, 884 (21st *April,* 1479) after suffering for about two years from paralysis. Prayers were read over him in the citadel, and he was then borne to the sepulcher of the Caliphs in the vicinity of the Nafisi shrine.[3] He had reached the age of ninety and perhaps passed it.

---

1 The text has inaccurately حاتم.

2 These were that the Sultan should support Janim against a religious faction of the Emirs at Damascus which the Sultan promised and performed, p. 293, Weil.

3 See note 3 p. 659.

A.H.885.
A.D.1480.

AL MUTAWAKKIL A'LA'LLAH ABUL IZZ

Al Mutawakkil alallah Abul Izz Abdul Aziz b Yakub bil Mutawakkil alallah was born in the year 819. His mother, whose name was Haj Malik, was the daughter of a soldier. His father never succeeded to the Caliphate. He grew up, reverenced, popular, beloved by gentle and simple, for his admirable qualities, and commendable virtues, and meekness and kind behaviour and geniality to every one, and for his manifold accomplishments. He also employed himself in acquiring knowledge and read with my father and others. His uncle al Mustakfi married him to his daughter, and he had by her, a virtuous, son, a Hashimite son among the descendants of Hashim. Now when the sickness of his uncle al Mustanjid had continued some time, he bequeathed the Caliphate to him, and when al Mustanjid died, he was sworn fealty to on Monday the 26th of Muharram (23rd *April*) in the presence of the Sultan and the judges and the nobles.

He first desired the title of al Mustain Billah; then he hesitated between al Mustain and al Mutawakkil, and al Mutawakkil was finally decided upon. He then rode from the citadel to his accustomed residence, preceded by the judges and administrative officials and nobles, and it was a "day upon which witness was borne" (Qur. XI). Then he returned at the end of the day to the citadel where al Mustanjid used to dwell.

In this year the Sultan al Malik al Ashraf journeyed to Hijaz to perform the pilgrimage, which was a function that had not been witnessed in a Sultan for more than one hundred years. He began by visiting Medina the noble, and spent there six thousand dinars ; he then proceeded to Mecca, and there spent five thousand dinars, and appointed for the college which he founded at Mecca, a Shaykh, and a Sufi, and he performed the pilgrimage and returned, and the city was decked out for some days in *honor* of his arrival.

A.H.886. A.D.1481. In the year 885[1], an army, at the head of which was the Chancellor Yeshbek, left Egypt for Iraq, and there encountered the troops of Yakub Shah b. Hasan[2] near Ruha ; the Egyptians were defeated and there were slain of them, those that were slain, and the rest were taken prisoners ; the Chancellor was captured and his head struck off. This occurred in the latter half of the month of Ramadhan.

It is a strange coincidence that a great rupture had taken place between him and the Hanafite Kadhi Shamsuddin al Amshati in Egypt, and each of them desired the fall of the other, and the beheading of the Chancellor on the banks of the Euphrates and the death of al Amshati in Egypt occurred on the same day.

In the year 886, the earth was convulsed on Sunday the 17th of Muharram late in the afternoon with a severe shock, and the earth and the mountains and the edifices rose and fell, and it continued for a short time and hen ceased, praise be to God for its ceasing. From this cause, a pinnacle of the Salihiyah College fell upon the chief Hanafite Kadhi Sharafuddin b. Abd, and he was Killed. "Verily we belong to God and verily to Him shall we return." In Rabii I of this year, a man arrived in Egypt from India called Khaki who asserted that his age was two hundred and fifty years. I went to see him and lo ! he was a robust man, his beard all black; reasonable conjecture would not admit that his age was seventy, far *less* anything beyond it, and he could bring not proof in support of what he asserted, and what I concluded *was* that he was a liar. As to what I heard from him *it was this :* he said that he had made the pilgrimage when he was eighteen years old : he then returned to

---

1 According to Weil. 887.

2 He was one of the sons of Usun Hasan, first ruler of Diarbekir and who subsequently extended his authority over a great part of Persia. He was of the dynasty of the White Sheep, defeated and slew Shah Jahan the chief of the Black Sheep, took Azarbijan and the western portion of Khurasan and measured swords even with Muhammad II. He sustained a crushing defeat at the hands of the Turkish Sultan in the spring of 1473, the victory being mainly due to the Turkish artillery. Weil tom. II. P. 340.

India and *there* heard of the advance of the Tartars on Baghdad to capture it; and then he traveled to Egypt in the reign of Sultan Hasan, before he had founded his college, but he never brought forward anything which *satisfactorily* explained his statement.

During the same year came the news of the death of Sultan Muhammad b. Othman, the lord of Asia Minor, and that his two sons disputed the sovereignty with each other. One[1] of them was victorious and established himself in the kingdom and the other set out for Egypt. The Sultan received him with great honor and entertained him. He afterwards proceeded from Syria to Hijaz, making the pilgrimage.

In the month of Shawwal letters arrived from Medina the noble, stating that on the night of the 13th of Ramadhan, a thunderbolt fell from heaven upon the city and set it on fire, and burnt the "roof of the holy mosque and all the treasures and books in it and nothing was left of it but the walls, and it was a terrible calamity.[2]

The Caliph died on Wednesday the last day of Muharram 903, (29th *September* 1497) and bequeathed the Caliphate to his son, Yakub and gave him the title of al Mustamisk billah. This is the conclusion of what has been obtainable for compilation in this history, and verily for the events *thereof,* I have relied on the history of ad Dahabi which ends with the year 700 : after that *date,* on the history of Ibn Kathir "which" ends with the year 738 : then on the Masalik and its supplement, to the year 773 ; then on the Inbaul Ghumr (*teaching of the unlearned*) of Ibn Hajr to the year 850 :

---

1 Bajazet II, who succeeded to the sovereignty in 1481, his ruler brother Mustafa having died. Jam, the third son, was twice defeated by Bajazet and forced to fly to the Sultan of Egypt for succour on the pretence of pilgrimage. Assisted by his new ally, he again tempted fortune, was again routed and took refuge with Pierro D'Aubusson, Grand Master of the Knights of Malta at Rhodes. Bajazet concluded a treaty with the latter, paying him an annual sum of 40,000 crowns of gold on condition of his safe custody of his brother. See D'Herbelot. Art. Gem.

2 Kaitbai, though of a fierce and brutal disposition, who had no hesitation in mangling and flaying the objects of his anger, burst into tears when he heard of this conflagration. See his character in Weil, Vol. II, p. 357.

but for other *matters* than these events, I perused the history of Baghdad by al Khatib in ten volumes, and the history of Damascus by Ibn Asakir in fifty-seven volumes, and the Awrak of as Suli in seven volumes, and the Tayyuriyat in three volumes, and the Hulyah of Abu Nuaym in nine volumes, and the Mujalasat of ad Dinawari, and the Kamil of al Mubarrad in two volumes, and the Amali of Thaalab in one volume and others. A former author has written a poem in the metre called Rajaz, containing the names of the Caliphs and *the dates of* their deaths up to the reign of al Muatamid, but I have composed a poem still better than it, and I think it advisable to conclude the book with it.

Note.

I have not thought it necessary to translate this rhythmical memorial technical which is a bald repetition of names and dates with here and there an incident recalling an even in the life of a Caliph. As a piece of doggerel by which to rocellect the succession of the Caliphs, it might be of some use to a Muhammadan student, but no English reader would care to learn by heart what an Index will readily supply him with, in a form which no poetry could render tolerable to the ear and which must be tedious in the most poetical of prose.

The Umayyad Dynasty in Spain.

The first of these *monarchs* was Abdur Rahman b. Muawiyah b. Hisham b. Abdil Malik b. Marwan. Allegiance was sworn to him as Caliph when he fled to Andalusia in the year 138 A.H. (755 A.D.) He was a man of learning and justice. He died in Rabii II, 170 (786). His son Hisham Abul Walid succeeded him and died in the month of Safar 180. (796). He was succeeded by his son al Hakam Abul Mudhaffar, surnamed al Murtadha who died in Dul Hijjah 206, (821). After him came his son Abdur Rahman, and he was the first of the Umayyads who exalted the monarchy, and clothed it with the splendor of the Caliphate. During his reign the wearing of embroidered garments was first introduced in Spain, and the coinage of dirhams, for no mint existed in it since it was conquered by the Arabs, and they used to employ the dirhams that were brought to them from the East. He resembled Walid b. Abdul Malik in his haughtiness, and al Mamun the Abbasside in his search for books on philosophy. He was the first who introduced *the study of* philosophy into Spain. He died in the year 239, (853). His son Muhammad succeeded him, and died in Safar 273 (886). His son al Mundir followed him, dying in Safar 275. Then arose his brother Abdullah, who was the most eminent of the Caliphs of Spain for his wisdom and virtue. He died in Rabii I 300 (912). He was succeeded by his grandson Abdur Rahman b. Muhammad, surnamed an Nasir and he was the first who assumed the Caliphate in Spain and the *title of* prince of the Faithful. This took place when the Abbasside power in the reign of al Muktadir was on the wane : those before his time calling themselves prince *(Amir)* only. He died in Ramadhan 350 (961). He was succeeded by his son al Hakam al Mustansir who died in Safar 366 (976). Then came his Hisham al Muayyad, who was deposed and imprisoned in 399 (1008-9). Next followed Muhammad b. Hisham b. Abdil Jabbar bin Nasir Abdur Rahman and he was surnamed al Mahdi, *continuing in power* sixteen months, when the son of his brother, Hisham b. Sulayman bin Nasir Abdur Rahman rebelled against him and was acknowledged Caliph and assumed the title of ar Rashid. His uncle, however, defeated and slew him, but the people conspired to depose his uncle who concealed himself, but was afterwards put to death. They then swore allegiance to the son of the brother of the murdered Hisham, Sulayman b-ul Hakam al Mustansir, who was surnamed al Mustain. Subseqnetly they rose up against him, and he was imprisoned in the year 406 (1015). Then Abdur Rahman b. Abdil Malik bin Nasir succeeded and was surnamed al Murtadha, but he was put to death at the close of the year. At this period the Umayyad power began to wane and the Allide family of Hasan arose, and an Nasir Ali[1] b Hamud assumed the sovereignty in Muharram of the year 407, (1016). He was slain in Dul Kaadah 408. Then followed his brother al Mamun al Kasim : he was deposed in the year 411. Next arose his nephew Yahya b-un Nasir Ali b. Hamud, who was surnamed al Mustaali and he was put to death after a year and seven months.

After this the Umayyad dynasty was restored and al Mustadhir Abdur Rahman b. Hisham b. Abdil Jabbar assumed the sovereignty: he was slain after fifty days, and Muhammad b. Abdir Rahman b. Ubaydillah bin Nasir Abdur Rahman rose to power, and was surnamed al Mustakfi. He was deposed after a year and four months. Then came Hisham b. Muhammad b. Abdil Malik bin Nasir Abdur Rahman, who was surnamed al Muatamid, (A.D. 1027). He continued in power for some time, but was afterwards deposed and imprisoned till he died in Safar of the Year[2] 400 and (*here a blank in the MS.)* –(428). At his death perished the Umayyad dynasty in Spain.

The impious dynasty of the House of Ubayd.

The first of them that arose in Africa was al Madhi Ubaydullah in the year 296 (908-9) : he died in 322. Then came his son al Kaim bi amrillah Muhammad : he died in the year 333 (944). Then arose his son Ismail we died in the year 341 (952). Next came his son al

---

1 The founder of the short-lived Hamudite dynasty. He was a descendant of Hasan son of Ali b. Abi Talib but his family had been settled in Africa for 200 years and had become "berherised," and he himself spoke Arabic extremely ill. Our author here is not quite in accordance with M. Dozy who makes Ali succeed directly after Sulayman, after having put him, his father and brother to death. To the reader who cares to follow the fortunes of the Caliphate in Spain, I recommend the perusal of M. Dozy's interesting volumes.

2 December 1036. With his death also closes the history of M. Dozy.

Muizzlidinillah Saad, who entered Cairo in the 362 and died in 365 (975-6). Then succeeded his son al Aziz Nizar,[1] who died in the year 382 (992), he was followed by his son al Hakim biamrillah Mansur who was slain in 411 (1020). Then came his son ad Dhahir li Izaziddin illah Ali : he died in 428 (1036). His son al Mustansir Maad succeeded him and he died in 487 (1094). He was thus Caliph for sixty years and four months. Ad Dahabi says that he knows of no Caliph or Sultan in Islam who reigned for this period. After him reigned his son al Mustaali billah Ahmad and he died in 495 (1101-2). After him was elected his son al Amir bi ahkamillah Mansur, a boy of five years of age and he was put to death in 524 (1130), leaving no children to succeed him. Next followed his cousin al Hafidh li din illah Abdul Majid b. Muhammad bil Mustansir, who died in 544 (1149). Then came his son ad Dhaur billah Ismail and he was assassinated in 549, and he was succeeded by his son al Faiz bi Nasrillah Isa, who died in 555 (1160). Then followed al Aadhid li dinillah Abdullah b. Yusuf bil Hafidh li dinillah, who was deposed in 567 (1171-2) and died the same year, when the Abbaside claim was set up in Egypt and the dynasty of the house of Ubayd became extinct. Ad Dahabi says "Thus there were fourteen violaters of covenants not successors[2] to the vicegerency."

The Dynasty of Tabataba,[3] descendants of Hasan and Ali.

Among them Abu Abdullah Muhammad b. Ibrahim Tabataba assumed the Caliphate in Jumada I, 199 A.H. (814) ; and about this period, there arose in Yaman, al Hadi Yahya b-ul Husayn bil Kasim

---

1 Se the MS. The printed text has Bazar which is an error ; see his life in Ibn Khall.

2 The MS. has مخالفا instead of مستخلفا

3 Ibrahim 6th in descent from Ali was surnamed Tabataba from his pronouncing the guttural K like a T. Calling for his waistcoat one day wishing to say Kaba, Kaba he said Taba, Taba, and was so nicknamed. According to Abul Mahasin it was in Jumada II, 199 the rebellion took place.

b. Tabataba for whom dominion over the Muslims was claimed : he died in Dul Hijjah 208 (823). His son Murtadha Muhammad succeeded him and died in 820 (932). Then came his brother an Nasir Ahmad who died in Safar 823. al Muntakhab[1] al Husayn his son followed and died 329 (940-1). Then his brother al Mukhtar al Kasim who was slain in Shawwal 344 (955). Then his brother al Hadi Muhammad : than ar Rashid al Abbas, and the dynasty became extinct.

THE TABARISTANI DYNASTY

Six persons governed in succession : three *of them*, the descendants of al Hasan, and three, from among the descendants of al Husayn. Hisham al Daaiilal Hakk al Hasan b. Zayd b. Muhammad b. Ismail bil Husayn b. Zayd il Jawwad bil Hasan bil Hasan,[2] b. Ali b. Abi Talib, in the year 250 (864) in Rai and Daylam. Then arose his brother al Kaim bil Hakk, Muhammad, who was slain in 288, (901). Then came his grand son al Mahdi al Hasan b. Zayd bil Kaim bil Hakk ; and after him[3] – (*the MS, is here a blank*).

Observation- Ibn Abi Hatim in his commentary, says, that he heard a tradition on the authority of Abdullah b. Amar bil Aas who said, "Since the world has been, a century has never closed, but a *great* event occurred at the close to it." I observe that at the end of the first century, of *the history of* this nation, there was the calamity of al Hajjaj,[4] and what shall make thee understand what al Hajjaj *was ?* In the second century, were the troubles of al Mamun and his wars with his brother, when the beautiful places of

1 Not Muntajab, as in the text.

2 Incorrectly الحسهن in the text.

3 For the Arabian dynsties consult the al Kamil of Ibnul Athir under the proper year.

4 See the life of Abdul Malik b. Marwan.

Baghdad were demolished and its people destroyed ; then his assassination *of his brother* : then the inquisition of the people concerning the creation of the Qurãn, and this was one of the greatest calamities on this nation, and the earliest, relative to a *distinct* call to heresy, for no Caliph before him ever invited *the people* to any thing approaching heresy. In the third century *occurred* the irruption of the Carmathians, and that will suffice for thee : then the revolution against al Muktadir, when he was deposed and Ibnul Muatazz acknowledged and al Muktadir restored next day, and the assassination of the Kadhi and a number of the learned, for a Kadhi had never been put to death before him in Islam. Then the disorganization of the empire and the predominance of the conquerors over the provinces which had continued up to this time. Among which also *is to be counted* the beginning of the sovereignty of the Ubaydites and enough for thee is their wickedness and infidelity and slaughter of the learned and the pious. In the fourth century was the calamitous *reign* of al Hakim biamri Iblis not biamrillahi,[1] and let what he hath done suffice thee. In the fifth century the Franks took Syria and Jerusalem. In the sixth century was the famine, the like of which had never been heard of since the time of Joseph and *then* it was that the Tartar ascendancy began. In the seventh century occurred the great Tartar disaster, the like of which was unheard of an which caused seas of Muslim blood to flow. In the eighth century was the irruption of Timurlang before the tremendous nature of which the Tartar misfortune was comparatively insignificant, and I implore of the Almighty that He will take us into His mercy before the occurrence of the calamity *to come* in the ninth century, through the glory of Muhammad, may God bless and preserve him, and his posterity and all his Companions. Amen.

1 The ruler by the command of the devil not by the command of God. See his deeds under "al Kadir billah."

LINE OF THE CALIPHS

Names	Date of Accession.	Deposal or Abdication.	Restoration.	Death.
Abu Bakr	12th Rabii, I, 11. 7th June (A.D.) 632	—	2/2	22nd Jumada, II, 13, 23rd August, 634.
Omar, ...	22nd Jumada, II, 13. 23rd August, 634.	—	10/3	26th Dul Hijjah, 23. 3rd November, 644.
Othman	29th Dul Hijjah, 23. 6th November, 644.	—	11/7	18th Dul Hijja, 35. 17th June, 656.
Ali	19th Dul Hijjah, 35. 18th June, 656	—	4/6	17th Ramadhan, 40. 21st January, 661.
Hasan	18th Ramadhan, 40. 22nd January, 661.	Rabii II or, Jumada I, A.H. 41.	—	—
		House of Umayyah		
Muawiyah-ibn Abi Sufyan	Rabii, 41. August, 661.	—	9	Rajab, 60. April, 680.
Yazid b. Muawiyah	Rajab, 60. April, 680	–	3	15th Rabii, I, 64. 11th November, 683.
Muawiyah b. Yazid	15th Rabii, I, 64. 11th November, 683.	—	—	About forty days after his accession.

Abdullah buz Zubayr, ..	Rabii II, 64. December, 683.	—	9	17th Jumada, I, 73. 3rd October, 692.
Abdul Malik b. Marwan	17th Jumada, I, 73. 3rd October, 692.	—	13	14th Shawwal, 86. 8th October, 705.
Al Walid b. Abdil Malik,	14th Shawwal, 86. 8th October, 705.	—	10	15th Jumada, II, 96. 23rd February, 715.
Sulayman b. Abdil Malik	15th Jumada, II, 96. 23rd February, 715.	—	2	10th Safar, 99. 22nd September, 717.
Omar b. Abdil Aziz	10th Safar, 99. 22nd September, 717.	—	3	20th or 25th Rajab, 101. 5th or 10th Feb. 720.
Yazid b. Abdil Malik	20th or 25th Rajab, 101. 5th or 10 Feb. 720.	—	4	26th Shaaban, 105. 28th January, 724.
Hisham b. Abdil Malik	26th Shaaban, 105. 28th January, 724.	—	19	6th Rabii, II, 125. 6th February, 743.
Al Walid b. Yazid b. Abdil Malik,	6th Rabii, II, 125. 6th February, 743	—	1	27th Jumada, II, 126. 16th April, 744.
Yazid an Nakis	27th Jumada II, 126. 16th April, 744.	—	—	7th Dul Hijjah 126. 19th September, 744.

LINE OF THE CALIPHS -- (Continued)

Names	Date of Accession.	Deposal or Abdication.	Restoration.	Death.
Ibrahim b. Abdil Malik	7th Dul Hijjah, 176. 19th September, 744.	14th Safar, 127. 25th November, 744.	---	---
Marwan al Himar	14th Safar, 127. 25th November, 744.	---	6	26th Dul Hijjah, 132. 5th August, 750.
		House of Abbas		
As Saffah	3rd Rabii, I, 132. 8th October, 750.	–	4	13th Dul Hijjah, 136. 9th June, 754.
Al Mansur	13th Dul Hijjah, 136. 9th June, 754.	---	21	6th Dul Hijjah, 158. 7th October, 775.
Al Mahdi	6th Dul Hijjah, 158. 7th October, 775.	---	10	22nd Muharram, 169. 4th August, 785.
Al Hadi,	22nd Muharram, 169. 4th August, 785.	---	1	16th Rabii I, 170. 15th September, 786.
Harun ar Rashid	16th Rabii, I, 170. 15th September, 786.	---	23	3rd Jumada, II, 193. 23rd March, 809.

Al Amin	3rd Jumada II, 193. 23rd March, 809.	—	4	24th or 25th Muharram, 198. 24th or 25th Sept, 813.
Al Mamun,	24th or 25th Muharram, 198. 24th or 25th Sept, 813.	—	20	18th Rajab, 218. 9th August, 833.
Al Muatasim,	18th Rajab, 218. 9th August, 833.	—	9	19th Rabii I, 227. 5th January, 842.
Al-Wathik billah	19th Rajab, 227. 5th January. 842.	—	5	24th Dul Hijjah, 232. 11th August, 847.
Al Mutawakkil alallah,	24th Dul Hijjah, 232. 11th August 847	—	14	5th Shawwal, 247. 10th December, 861.
Al Mustansir billah,	5th Shawwal, 247. 10th December, 861.	—	1	5th Rabii II, 248. 7th June, 862.
Al Mustain billah,	5th Rabii II, 248. 7th June, 862.	11th Dul Hijjah, 252. 4th January, 866.	4	—
Al Muatazz Billah	Dul Hijjah, 252, 4th January, 866.	Rajab or Shaaban, 255. July, 869.	3	—
Al Muhtadi billah,	29th Rajab, 255. 13th July, 869.	15th Rajab, 256, 18th June, 870.	1	—

LINE OF THE CALIPHS -- (Continued)

Names	Date of Accession.	Deposal or Abdication.	Restoration	Death.
Al Muatamid billah	15th Rajab, 256. A.H. 18th June, 870.	---	22	19th Rajab, 279. 14th October, 892.
Al Muatadhid billah,	Rajah, 279. October, 892.	---	10	22nd Rabii II, 289. 5th April, 902.
Al-Lauktafi billah	19th Rabii II, 289. 2nd April, 902.	---	5	12th Dul Kaadah, 295. 13th August, 907.
Al Muktadir billah	13th Dul Kaadah, 295. 14th August, 907.	---	25	27th Shawwal, 320. 31st October, 932.
Al Kahir billah	28th Shawwal, 320 1st November, 932.	6th Jumada I, 322 23rd April, 934.	2	---
Ar Radhi billah	6th Jumada I, 322. 23rd April, 934.	---	6	15th Rabii I, 329. 18th December, 940.
Al Mutakki lillah	15th Rabii I, 329. 18th December, 940.	20th Safar, 333. 12th October, 944.	4	–
Al Mustakfi billah,	20th Safar, 333. 12th October, 944.	22nd Jumada II, 334. 29th January, 949.	2	----

Al Mutii lillah,	22nd Jumada, 334.A.H 29th Januarym 949.	13th Dul Kaadah, 363. 5th August. 974.	28	—
Al Taii lillah,	13th Dul Kaadah, 363. 5th August, 974.	19th Shaaban, 381. 1st November, 991.	17	—
Al Kadir billah,	19th Shaaban 381. 1st November, 991.	—	40	11th Dul Hijjah, 422. 29th November, 1031.
Al Kaim biamrillah,	11th dul Hijjah, 422. 29th November, 1031.	—	44	13th Shaaban 467. 2nd April, 1075.
Al-Muktadi biamrillah	13th Shaaban, 467. 2nd April, 1075.	—	19	15th Muharram, 487. 4th February, 1094
Al Mustadhir billah,	15th Muharram, 487. 4th February, 1094	–	24	16th Rabii, II, 512. 6th August, 1118.
Al Mustarshid billah	16th Rabii II, 512. 6th August, 1118.	–	16	16th Dul Kaadah, 529. 27th August, 1134.
Ar Rashid billah	16th Dul Kaadah, 529 27th August, 1134.	16th Dul Kaadah, 530. 16th August, 1135.	—	—
Al Muktafi liamrillah	16th Dul Kaadah, 530. 16th August, 1135.	—	25	2nd Rabii, I, 555. 12th March, 1160.

LINE OF THE CALIPHS -- (Continued)

Names	Date of Accession.	Deposal or Abdication.	Restoration.	Death.
Al Mustanjid billah	2nd Rabii, I, 555,A.H. 12th March, 1160.	—	10	8th Rabii II, 566. 22nd December, 1170.
Al Mustadhi biamrillah	8th Rabii II, 566. 22nd December 1170.	—	10	2nd Dul Kaadah 575. 31st March, 1180.
An Nasir lidinllah	2nd Dul Kaadah, 575. 31st March, 1180.	—	45	30th Ramadhan, 622. 6th October, 1225.
Ad Dhahir biamrillah	30th Ramadhan, 622 6th October, 1225.	—	1	13th Rajab, 623. 10th July, 1226.
Al Mustansir billah	13th Rajab, 623. 10th July, 1226.	—	16	10th Jumada II, 640. 5th December, 1242.
Al Mustasim billah,	10th Jumada II, 640. 5th December, 1242.	—	16	14th Safar 656. 20th February, 1258.
Al Mustansir billah Ahmad,	13th Rajab, 659. 12th May, 1261.	—	—	3rd Muharram, 660. 28th November, 1261.
Al Hakim biamrillah Abul Abbas,	8th Muharram, 661. 22nd November, 1262.	—	40	18th Jumada I, 701. 18th January 1302.

Al Mustakfi billah Abur Rabii	Jumada I, 701. A.H. January, 1302.	---	38	5th Shaaban, 740. 5th February, 1340.
Al Wathik billah, Ibrahim,	6th Dul Kaadah, 740. 4th May, 1340.	21st Dul Hijjah, 741. 7th June, 1341.	1	---
Al Hakim biamrillah Abul Abbas,	21st Dul Hijjah, 741. 7th June, 1341.	---	11	Jumada II, 753. July-August, 1352.
Al Muatadhid billah Abul Fath,	Jumada II, 753, July-August, 1352.	---	9	Jumada I, 763. March, 1361.
Al Mutawakkil alallah Abdullah,	Jumada I, 763. March, 1361.	Rajab, 785. September, 1383.	22	---
Al Wathik billah Omar,	Rajab, 785. September, 1383.	---	3	19th Shawwal, 788. 12th November, 1386.
Al Muatasim billah Zakariya	19th Shawwal, 788. 12th November, 1386.	10th Jumada, I 791. 5th June, 1389.	3	---
Al Mutawakkil alallah Abdullah (2nd time)	---	---	10th Jumada 17 791 5th June, 1389	28th Rajab, 808. 18th January, 1406.

LINE OF THE CALIPHS -- (Continued)

Names	Date of Accession.	Deposal or Abdication.	Restoration.	Death.
Al Mustain billah Abul Fadhl	Rajab 808. January, 1406.	16th Dul Hijjah, 816. 7th March, 1414.	8	---
Al Muatadhid billah Abul Fath,	16th Dul Hijjah, 816. 7th March, 1414.	---	27	4th Rabii I, 845. 22nd July, 1441.
Al Mustakfi billah Abur Rabii	4th Rabii I, 845. 22nd July, 1441.	---	10	2nd Dul Hijjah, 845. 3rd February, 1451.
Al Kaim biamrillah Abul Baka,	Dul Hijjah, 854. February, 1451.	Jumada II, 859. Junem 1455.	4	---
Al Mustanjid billah Abul Mahasin,	Jumada II, 859. June, 1455.	24th Muharram, 884 21st April, 1479.	24	---
Al Mutawakkil alallah Abdul Izz	26th Muharram, 884. 23rd April, 1479.	--	---	31st Muharram, 903. 29th September.1497.

INDEX TO PROPER NAMES.

A.

Page

B

D

F

G

H

I

J

K

L

M